# Praise for *Xcode*

"I would recommend this book to an                                                lac.
It is an excellent resource; I plan to         INCLUDES CD

                                                                                 *lark*


"I've been doing Mac OS X development for seven years, so I was surprised at how much
new information I learned in this book. The details on building and the overview of
Instruments were invaluable."

*—Dan Wood*,
Karelia Software


"There isn't a better book on the market to understand Apple's powerful—yet-free integrated development environment, Xcode. Fritz Anderson stands among the most literate
programmers I know, simultaneously able to provide a high-level development narrative
while delving into the countless crucial details that make up modern development. I
recommend Xcode 3 Unleashed to both novices as an introduction and professionals as a
reference."

*—Jonathan 'Wolf' Rentzsch*
http://rentzsch.com


"Whether you are new to programming on Mac OS X or a seasoned veteran, Xcode 3
Unleashed has something for you. The book is full of examples and practical information.
I recommend this book for anyone doing serious development on Mac OS X 10.5."

*—Dave Dribin*

Fritz Anderson

# Xcode 3

## UNLEASHED

 | 800 East 96th Street, Indianapolis, Indiana 46240 USA

# Xcode 3 Unleashed

Copyright © 2009 by Pearson Education, Inc.

ISBN-13: 978-0-321-55263-1

ISBN-10: 0-321-55263-6

*Library of Congress Cataloging-in-Publication Data:*

Anderson, Fritz.
  Xcode 3 unleashed / Fritz Anderson. — 1st ed.
    p. cm.
  Includes bibliographical references and index.
  ISBN-13: 978-0-321-55263-1 (pbk. : alk. paper)
  ISBN-10: 0-321-55263-6 (pbk. : alk. paper)  1.  Operating systems (Computers)
2.  Macintosh (Computer)  I. Title.
  QA76.76.063A53155 2009
  005.4'32—dc22

                    2008017851

Printed in the United States on America

Third Printing: October 2009

## Trademarks

## Warning and Disclaimer

## Bulk Sales

Sams Publishing offers excellent discounts on this book when ordered in quantity for bulk purchases or special sales. For more information, please contact

**U.S. Corporate and Government Sales**
**1-800-382-3419**
corpsales@pearsontechgroup.com

For sales outside of the U.S., please contact

**International Sales**
international@pearsoned.com

---

## This Book Is Safari Enabled

The Safari® Enabled icon on the cover of your favorite technology book means the book is available through Safari Bookshelf. When you buy this book, you get free access to the online edition for 45 days.

Safari Bookshelf is an electronic reference library that lets you easily search thousands of technical books, find code samples, download chapters, and access technical information whenever and wherever you need it.

To gain 45-day Safari Enabled access to this book:

▶ Go to http://www.quepublishing.com/safarienabled.
▶ Complete the brief registration form.
▶ Enter the coupon code ARHL-WXMH-HFKV-DHHN-287M.

If you have difficulty registering on Safari Bookshelf or accessing the online edition, please email customer-service@safaribooksonline.com.

**Editor-in-Chief**
Karen Gettman

**Senior Acquisitions Editor**
Chuck Toporek

**Senior Development Editor**
Chris Zahn

**Managing Editor**
Kristy Hart

**Project Editor**
Jovana San Nicolas-Shirley

**Copy Editor**
Keith Cline

**Indexer**
Cheryl Lenser

**Proofreader**
Leslie Joseph

**Publishing Coordinator**
Romny French

**Multimedia Developer**
Dan Scherf

**Cover Designer**
Gary Adair

**Compositor**
Nonie Ratcliff

# Contents at a Glance

Introduction ........................................................... 1

**Part I**    **The Life Cycle of a Mac OS X Application**

  **1**    Kicking the Tires ........................................... 11

  **2**    Simple Workflow and Passive Debugging ............... 19

  **3**    Simple Active Debugging ................................. 29

  **4**    Compilation: The Basics .................................. 39

  **5**    Starting a Cocoa Application ............................ 47

  **6**    A Cocoa Application: Views .............................. 63

  **7**    A Cocoa Application: Controllers ....................... 75

  **8**    Version Control ............................................ 93

  **9**    Property Lists ............................................. 117

**10**    Libraries and Dependent Targets ...................... 141

**11**    File Packages and Bundles .............................. 153

**12**    Unit Testing .............................................. 167

**13**    Creating a Custom View ................................. 181

**14**    Dynamic Libraries and Frameworks ................... 203

**15**    Documentation in Xcode ................................ 221

**16**    Using the Data Modeling Tools ........................ 243

**17**    Cross-Development ....................................... 267

**18**    Spotlight (or, How to Build a Plug-in) ............... 281

**19**    Finishing Touches ....................................... 301

**Part II**    **Xcode Tasks**

**20**    Navigating an Xcode Project ........................... 331

**21**    Xcode for make Veterans ................................ 353

**22**    More About Debugging .................................. 373

**23**    Xcode and Speed ......................................... 395

**24**    A Legacy Project ......................................... 403

**25**    Shark and the CHUD Tools ............................. 421

**26**    Instruments .............................................. 437

**27**    Closing Snippets ......................................... 461

**Part III   Appendices**

**A**   Some Build Variables ............................................................ 475

**B**   Project and Target Templates ............................................. 485

**C**   Other Resources ................................................................ 501

Index ................................................................................. 507

# Table of Contents

**Introduction**                                                                  **1**

What's New in Xcode 3 ................................................................ 1

Obtaining Xcode ........................................................................ 3

Installing Xcode ........................................................................ 3

Uninstalling Xcode .................................................................... 7

Xcode 2.5 .............................................................................. 8


**Part I**   **The Life Cycle of a Mac OS X Application**

**1**   **Kicking the Tires**                                                       **11**

First Run .............................................................................. 11

Hello, World ......................................................................... 12

What Went Where ................................................................... 16

Summary .............................................................................. 18


**2**   **Simple Workflow and Passive Debugging**                                    **19**

Calculating a Linear Regression ................................................... 20

Plan of Action ....................................................................... 21

A Command-Line Tool ............................................................... 22

Build Errors .......................................................................... 23

Simple Debugging ................................................................... 27

Summary .............................................................................. 28


**3**   **Simple Active Debugging**                                                  **29**

The Next Step ........................................................................ 29

Active Debugging .................................................................... 30

Summary .............................................................................. 37


**4**   **Compilation: The Basics**                                                  **39**

Compiling ............................................................................. 39

Linking ................................................................................ 42

Dynamic Loading ..................................................................... 43

Legacy Technologies ................................................................. 45

   Prebinding ......................................................................... 45

   ZeroLink ........................................................................... 45

Summary .............................................................................. 46

**5    Starting a Cocoa Application                                          47**

Plan of Action ................................................................. 47
  Program Tasks ............................................................... 47
  Model-View-Controller ...................................................... 48
  The Model .................................................................. 48
  The Controller ............................................................. 51
  The Views .................................................................. 51
Starting a New Project ....................................................... 52
  Adding Linrg ............................................................... 52
Implementation: Model ........................................................ 54
  DataPoint Model Class ...................................................... 55
  Regression Model Class ..................................................... 58
  Model: Done ................................................................ 62
Summary ...................................................................... 62

**6    A Cocoa Application: Views                                            63**

Interface Builder ............................................................ 64
  Layout ..................................................................... 66
  Sizing ..................................................................... 69
  A Split View ............................................................... 72
Summary ...................................................................... 73

**7    A Cocoa Application: Controllers                                      75**

The Next Step ................................................................ 75
Adding a Controller .......................................................... 77
  NSObjectController: Document ............................................... 79
  NSObjectController: Model .................................................. 80
  NSArrayController: DataPoints .............................................. 82
Value Binding ................................................................ 82
Actions and Outlets .......................................................... 84
MyDocument ................................................................... 85
Application Properties ....................................................... 88
Building ..................................................................... 91
Summary ...................................................................... 92

**8    Version Control                                                       93**

Setting Up a Repository ...................................................... 95
Getting Ready for Subversion ................................................. 96
Telling Xcode About a Repository ............................................. 98
Controlling Linear ........................................................... 99
Getting a Controlled Linear ................................................. 103

Revising . . . . . . . . . . . . . . . . . . . . . . . . . . . . . . . . . . . . . . . . . . . . . . . . . . . 105
Rolling Back . . . . . . . . . . . . . . . . . . . . . . . . . . . . . . . . . . . . . . . . . . . . . . . 114
Tagging . . . . . . . . . . . . . . . . . . . . . . . . . . . . . . . . . . . . . . . . . . . . . . . . . . . 115
Summary . . . . . . . . . . . . . . . . . . . . . . . . . . . . . . . . . . . . . . . . . . . . . . . . . . . 116

**9    Property Lists                                                       117**

Data Types . . . . . . . . . . . . . . . . . . . . . . . . . . . . . . . . . . . . . . . . . . . . . . . . 117
Property List Files . . . . . . . . . . . . . . . . . . . . . . . . . . . . . . . . . . . . . . . . . . 118
    Writing a Property List . . . . . . . . . . . . . . . . . . . . . . . . . . . . . . . . . . 118
Examining Property Lists . . . . . . . . . . . . . . . . . . . . . . . . . . . . . . . . . . . . 127
    As Text . . . . . . . . . . . . . . . . . . . . . . . . . . . . . . . . . . . . . . . . . . . . . . . . . . 127
    Property List Editor . . . . . . . . . . . . . . . . . . . . . . . . . . . . . . . . . . . . . . 129
Other Formats . . . . . . . . . . . . . . . . . . . . . . . . . . . . . . . . . . . . . . . . . . . . . 132
    ASCII Property Lists . . . . . . . . . . . . . . . . . . . . . . . . . . . . . . . . . . . . . 132
    Binary Property Lists . . . . . . . . . . . . . . . . . . . . . . . . . . . . . . . . . . . . 133
Text Macros . . . . . . . . . . . . . . . . . . . . . . . . . . . . . . . . . . . . . . . . . . . . . . . 133
Summary . . . . . . . . . . . . . . . . . . . . . . . . . . . . . . . . . . . . . . . . . . . . . . . . . . . 139

**10   Libraries and Dependent Targets                                      141**

Adding a Target . . . . . . . . . . . . . . . . . . . . . . . . . . . . . . . . . . . . . . . . . . . 141
Library Design . . . . . . . . . . . . . . . . . . . . . . . . . . . . . . . . . . . . . . . . . . . . . 143
Modifying `Linear` . . . . . . . . . . . . . . . . . . . . . . . . . . . . . . . . . . . . . . . . . . 146
A Dependent Target . . . . . . . . . . . . . . . . . . . . . . . . . . . . . . . . . . . . . . . . 148
Examining the Library . . . . . . . . . . . . . . . . . . . . . . . . . . . . . . . . . . . . . . 149
Running the Library . . . . . . . . . . . . . . . . . . . . . . . . . . . . . . . . . . . . . . . . 152
Summary . . . . . . . . . . . . . . . . . . . . . . . . . . . . . . . . . . . . . . . . . . . . . . . . . . . 152

**11   File Packages and Bundles                                            153**

A Simple Package: RTFD . . . . . . . . . . . . . . . . . . . . . . . . . . . . . . . . . . . 154
Bundles . . . . . . . . . . . . . . . . . . . . . . . . . . . . . . . . . . . . . . . . . . . . . . . . . . . 156
Application Bundles . . . . . . . . . . . . . . . . . . . . . . . . . . . . . . . . . . . . . . . . 156
The `Info.plist` File . . . . . . . . . . . . . . . . . . . . . . . . . . . . . . . . . . . . . . . . 158
    Keys for All Bundles . . . . . . . . . . . . . . . . . . . . . . . . . . . . . . . . . . . . . 159
    Keys for Applications . . . . . . . . . . . . . . . . . . . . . . . . . . . . . . . . . . . . 160
    Keys for Plug-Ins . . . . . . . . . . . . . . . . . . . . . . . . . . . . . . . . . . . . . . . . 163
    Keys for Java . . . . . . . . . . . . . . . . . . . . . . . . . . . . . . . . . . . . . . . . . . . 163
    Keys for Preference Panes . . . . . . . . . . . . . . . . . . . . . . . . . . . . . . . 164
    Keys for Dashboard Widgets . . . . . . . . . . . . . . . . . . . . . . . . . . . . . 164
Summary . . . . . . . . . . . . . . . . . . . . . . . . . . . . . . . . . . . . . . . . . . . . . . . . . . . 165

**12    Unit Testing**       **167**

Adding a Unit Test Target ........................................................ 167
Refactoring ............................................................................. 171
Running the Tests ................................................................... 175
A Dependent Test ................................................................... 176
Crossing Architectures ........................................................... 179
Summary ................................................................................. 180

**13    Creating a Custom View**       **181**

Controller ............................................................................... 181
View ........................................................................................ 183
The Delegate Design Pattern .................................................. 187
The Custom View .................................................................... 189
Showing the Window .............................................................. 196
Testing .................................................................................... 196
Debugging a View ................................................................... 198
Summary ................................................................................. 201

**14    Dynamic Libraries and Frameworks**       **203**

Adding a Framework Target ..................................................... 204
    `Info.plist` ........................................................................ 204
    Assigning Files .................................................................. 205
Framework Structure ............................................................... 210
Using the Framework ............................................................... 211
Where Frameworks Go ............................................................ 214
    A Public Framework .......................................................... 216
    A Private Framework ......................................................... 217
Summary ................................................................................. 219

**15    Documentation in Xcode**       **221**

HeaderDoc .............................................................................. 221
User Scripts in Xcode ............................................................. 225
DocSets ................................................................................... 229
    Preparing the Workspace .................................................. 230
    The Least We Can Do ...................................................... 231
Shell Script Targets ................................................................ 233
Browsing ................................................................................. 235
API Documentation ................................................................. 238
Summary ................................................................................. 241

**16   Using the Data Modeling Tools**                                 **243**

Data Modeling ........................................................... 245
Revisiting the Model ................................................... 247
    DataPoint ........................................................... 248
    All DataPoints .................................................... 248
    Initializers ....................................................... 249
    Accessors .......................................................... 250
    Regression ......................................................... 251
    MyDocument ......................................................... 255
Interface Builder ...................................................... 256
Build and Run .......................................................... 258
Adding an Entity ....................................................... 259
    Adding to the Data Model .......................................... 259
    Human Interface ................................................... 260
    First Run ......................................................... 264
    One More Table .................................................... 265
Summary ................................................................ 266

**17   Cross-Development**                                             **267**

Cross-Development SDKs ................................................. 267
Weak Linking ........................................................... 271
NIB Compatibility ...................................................... 271
Universal Binaries ..................................................... 274
    Auditing Linear ................................................... 276
    Testing ........................................................... 276
Building for Different Operating Systems on Different Processors ....... 277
Project Compatibility .................................................. 279
Summary ................................................................ 279

**18   Spotlight (or, How to Build a Plug-in)**                        **281**

How Data Gets into Spotlight ........................................... 281
Uniform Type Identifiers ............................................... 284
The Spotlight Plug-In .................................................. 286
    The MetaLinear Project ............................................ 286
    MetaLinear Project Files .......................................... 287
    Packaging the Plug-In ............................................. 293
    Checking Our Work ................................................. 294
Core Data and Metadata ................................................. 294
The Proof of the Pudding ............................................... 297
Summary ................................................................ 299

**19   Finishing Touches                                301**

Trimming the Menus ................................................ 301

    Avoiding Singularity ........................................... 302

Localization ......................................................... 304

    `Credits.rtf` ................................................. 304

    `MainMenu.nib` ................................................ 305

    `MyDocument.nib` .............................................. 305

    `GraphWindow.xib` ............................................. 308

    `InfoPlist.strings` .......................................... 308

    Trying It Out ................................................. 310

    `Localizable.strings` ........................................ 311

Checking Memory Usage ............................................. 313

Instruments ......................................................... 315

    Leaked Blocks ................................................ 317

    Leaky Call Trees ............................................. 318

    The ObjectAlloc Instrument ................................... 319

    The Instruments Document ..................................... 321

    Human-Interface Logging ...................................... 321

The Release Build Configuration ................................... 323

Stripping the Product ............................................. 325

    Stripping the Symbol Table ................................... 326

    Stripping Dead Code .......................................... 327

Summary ............................................................. 328


**Part II   Xcode Tasks**


**20   Navigating an Xcode Project                      331**

Editor Panes ........................................................ 331

    Code Sense ................................................... 332

    Jumps ........................................................ 333

    The Navigation Bar ........................................... 334

    Code Focus ................................................... 335

    The Debugger Strip ........................................... 336

    Editor Modes ................................................. 337

Project Find Window ............................................... 338

The Favorites Bar ................................................. 339

Groups & Files List ............................................... 339

    The Project Group ............................................ 339

The Targets Group ................................................. 341

    The Executables Group ........................................ 343

    Smart Groups ................................................. 344

    Symbol Smart Group ........................................... 345

Class Browser Window . . . . . . . . . . . . . . . . . . . . . . . . . . . . . . . . . . . . . . . 345
Class Modeler . . . . . . . . . . . . . . . . . . . . . . . . . . . . . . . . . . . . . . . . . . . . . . . 346
Project Layout . . . . . . . . . . . . . . . . . . . . . . . . . . . . . . . . . . . . . . . . . . . . . . . 348
    Default Layout . . . . . . . . . . . . . . . . . . . . . . . . . . . . . . . . . . . . . . . . . 349
    All-in-One Layout . . . . . . . . . . . . . . . . . . . . . . . . . . . . . . . . . . . . . . . 350
    Condensed Layout . . . . . . . . . . . . . . . . . . . . . . . . . . . . . . . . . . . . . . . 351
Summary . . . . . . . . . . . . . . . . . . . . . . . . . . . . . . . . . . . . . . . . . . . . . . . . . . . . 352

**21  Xcode for `make` Veterans**                                           **353**
Xcode Build Variables . . . . . . . . . . . . . . . . . . . . . . . . . . . . . . . . . . . . . . . . 355
Custom Build Rules . . . . . . . . . . . . . . . . . . . . . . . . . . . . . . . . . . . . . . . . . . 356
Run Script Build Phase . . . . . . . . . . . . . . . . . . . . . . . . . . . . . . . . . . . . . . . 357
Under the Hood: A Simple Build . . . . . . . . . . . . . . . . . . . . . . . . . . . . . . . 359
    Copy Structural Files . . . . . . . . . . . . . . . . . . . . . . . . . . . . . . . . . . . 359
    Compile XIB . . . . . . . . . . . . . . . . . . . . . . . . . . . . . . . . . . . . . . . . . . . 360
    Run Script . . . . . . . . . . . . . . . . . . . . . . . . . . . . . . . . . . . . . . . . . . . . 360
    Copy Bundle Resources . . . . . . . . . . . . . . . . . . . . . . . . . . . . . . . . . 361
    Compile Sources . . . . . . . . . . . . . . . . . . . . . . . . . . . . . . . . . . . . . . . 361
    Linkage (First Architecture) . . . . . . . . . . . . . . . . . . . . . . . . . . . . . 363
    Compile Sources (Second Architecture) . . . . . . . . . . . . . . . . . . . 363
    Linkage (Second Architecture) . . . . . . . . . . . . . . . . . . . . . . . . . . 364
    Compile Data Models . . . . . . . . . . . . . . . . . . . . . . . . . . . . . . . . . . 364
    Create Universal Binary . . . . . . . . . . . . . . . . . . . . . . . . . . . . . . . . 365
    Finishing Touch . . . . . . . . . . . . . . . . . . . . . . . . . . . . . . . . . . . . . . . 365
The `xcodebuild` Tool . . . . . . . . . . . . . . . . . . . . . . . . . . . . . . . . . . . . . . . . 365
Settings Hierarchy . . . . . . . . . . . . . . . . . . . . . . . . . . . . . . . . . . . . . . . . . . . 366
Build Configurations . . . . . . . . . . . . . . . . . . . . . . . . . . . . . . . . . . . . . . . . . 368
Summary . . . . . . . . . . . . . . . . . . . . . . . . . . . . . . . . . . . . . . . . . . . . . . . . . . . . 371

**22  More About Debugging**                                               **373**
Debugging Techniques . . . . . . . . . . . . . . . . . . . . . . . . . . . . . . . . . . . . . . . 373
Printing Values . . . . . . . . . . . . . . . . . . . . . . . . . . . . . . . . . . . . . . . . . . . . . . 377
Custom Formatters . . . . . . . . . . . . . . . . . . . . . . . . . . . . . . . . . . . . . . . . . . 379
Breakpoint Commands . . . . . . . . . . . . . . . . . . . . . . . . . . . . . . . . . . . . . . . 381
Breakpoint Conditions . . . . . . . . . . . . . . . . . . . . . . . . . . . . . . . . . . . . . . . 383
Lazy Symbol Loading . . . . . . . . . . . . . . . . . . . . . . . . . . . . . . . . . . . . . . . . 384
Zombies . . . . . . . . . . . . . . . . . . . . . . . . . . . . . . . . . . . . . . . . . . . . . . . . . . . . 385
    Released-Pointer Aliasing . . . . . . . . . . . . . . . . . . . . . . . . . . . . . . . 386
    `NSZombieEnabled` . . . . . . . . . . . . . . . . . . . . . . . . . . . . . . . . . . . . . 388
The Mini Debugger, and the In-Editor Debugger . . . . . . . . . . . . . . . . . 389
Datatips . . . . . . . . . . . . . . . . . . . . . . . . . . . . . . . . . . . . . . . . . . . . . . . . . . . . 391
Summary . . . . . . . . . . . . . . . . . . . . . . . . . . . . . . . . . . . . . . . . . . . . . . . . . . . . 392
    Further Reading . . . . . . . . . . . . . . . . . . . . . . . . . . . . . . . . . . . . . . . 393

| 23 | **Xcode and Speed** | **395** |
|----|---------------------|---------|

Precompiled Headers ........................................................................ 395
Predictive Compilation ..................................................................... 396
Distributed Builds ............................................................................ 397
    All Distributed Builds ................................................................ 398
    Shared Workgroup Builds .......................................................... 398
    Dedicated Network Builds .......................................................... 399
Project Indexing .............................................................................. 399
Summary ......................................................................................... 401

| 24 | **A Legacy Project** | **403** |
|----|----------------------|---------|

Preparing the Project ....................................................................... 404
The Organizer .................................................................................. 405
    The Files List .............................................................................. 405
    The Organizer Toolbar ............................................................... 407
    Configure and Build .................................................................. 409
    Installing .................................................................................... 411
    Running ..................................................................................... 412
An External Build System Project ..................................................... 413
    Code Sense Is Here .................................................................... 416
    Running ..................................................................................... 417
    Debugging .................................................................................. 418
    The Limits of the External Build System ..................................... 418
Summary ......................................................................................... 419

| 25 | **Shark and the CHUD Tools** | **421** |
|----|------------------------------|---------|

Shark ............................................................................................... 421
    The Problem ............................................................................... 422
    Starting Shark ............................................................................ 422
    Analysis ...................................................................................... 423
    The Top-Down View ................................................................... 425
    Mining the Call Stack ................................................................. 425
    Measure, Then Optimize ............................................................ 428
    The Effect ................................................................................... 429
The Other Performance Tools ........................................................... 431
    BigTop ........................................................................................ 432
    Reggie SE ................................................................................... 432
    SpindownHD ............................................................................... 432
    Saturn ........................................................................................ 432
    MallocDebug ............................................................................... 433
    ObjectAlloc and Sampler ............................................................ 433
    Quartz Debug ............................................................................. 433

Spin Control ............................................................................. 435

Thread Viewer ......................................................................... 435

CHUD Remover ...................................................................... 436

Summary ..................................................................................... 436

**26   Instruments                                                                    437**

What Instruments Is ............................................................... 437

Running Instruments ............................................................. 438

The Trace Document Window ............................................. 439

The Toolbar ........................................................................ 439

The Track Pane .................................................................. 441

The Detail Pane ................................................................ 442

The Extended Detail Pane ............................................. 444

Controls .............................................................................. 445

The Library ............................................................................... 445

Running an Instrument ........................................................ 446

Instrument Configuration ............................................. 446

Recording ........................................................................... 447

Saving and Reopening ................................................... 449

The Instruments ..................................................................... 449

Core Data ........................................................................... 450

File System ......................................................................... 450

Garbage Collection ........................................................ 451

Graphics ............................................................................. 451

Input / Output .................................................................. 451

Master Track ..................................................................... 452

Memory ............................................................................... 452

System ................................................................................. 454

Threads/Locks .................................................................. 455

User Interface ................................................................... 455

Custom Instruments ............................................................. 456

The Templates ........................................................................ 458

Summary ..................................................................................... 459

**27   Closing Snippets                                                              461**

Miscellaneous Traps ............................................................. 461

Miscellaneous Tips ................................................................ 464

More Documentation ............................................................ 470

Documentation Set Updates ........................................ 470

Boolean Text Searches .................................................. 471

**Part III    Appendices**

**A    Some Build Variables                                    475**

Useful Build Variables ........................................... 476

  Environment ............................................. 477

  Build Targets ............................................ 478

  Source Locations ........................................ 479

  Destination Locations ................................... 479

  Bundle Locations ........................................ 480

  Compiler Settings ....................................... 481

  Search Paths ............................................ 482

  Deployment ............................................. 482

Source Trees ..................................................... 483

**B    Project and Target Templates                          485**

Project Templates ................................................ 485

  The Empty Project ...................................... 486

  Action .................................................. 486

  Application ............................................. 487

  Audio Units ............................................. 489

  Bundle .................................................. 489

  Command-Line Utility ................................... 490

  Dynamic Library ........................................ 490

  External Build System ................................... 491

  Framework .............................................. 491

  Java .................................................... 492

  Kernel Extension ....................................... 493

  Standard Apple Plug-Ins ................................ 493

  Static Library .......................................... 495

Target Templates ................................................. 495

  BSD .................................................... 496

  Carbon ................................................. 496

  Cocoa .................................................. 497

  Java .................................................... 498

  Kernel Extension ....................................... 498

  Ruby ................................................... 498

  Special Targets ......................................... 499

Legacy Targets ................................................... 499

  Cocoa .................................................. 500

  Java .................................................... 500

  Kernel Extension ....................................... 500

**C   Other Resources**                                                    **501**

Books . . . . . . . . . . . . . . . . . . . . . . . . . . . . . . . . . . . . . . . . . . . . . . . . . . . . 501
From the Xcode Documentation Window . . . . . . . . . . . . . . . . . . . 502
On the Net . . . . . . . . . . . . . . . . . . . . . . . . . . . . . . . . . . . . . . . . . . . . . 502
      Mailing Lists . . . . . . . . . . . . . . . . . . . . . . . . . . . . . . . . . . . . . . 502
      Usenet . . . . . . . . . . . . . . . . . . . . . . . . . . . . . . . . . . . . . . . . . . . 503
      Sites and Logs . . . . . . . . . . . . . . . . . . . . . . . . . . . . . . . . . . . . . 503
Face to Face . . . . . . . . . . . . . . . . . . . . . . . . . . . . . . . . . . . . . . . . . . . . 504
Text Editors . . . . . . . . . . . . . . . . . . . . . . . . . . . . . . . . . . . . . . . . . . . . 505
Tools . . . . . . . . . . . . . . . . . . . . . . . . . . . . . . . . . . . . . . . . . . . . . . . . . . . 505

**Index**                                                                  **507**

# Preface

Xcode is the central tool for developing software for Mac OS X. It was my privilege to help explain that tool in *Step into Xcode: Mac OS X Development*. Since then, Apple has released a new operating system, Leopard, and a new Xcode. Xcode 3 is the official development tool for Apple's iPhone. *Xcode 3 Unleashed* is a new edition for a new world.

I wrote *Xcode 3 Unleashed* for people who are new to Mac programming and to Xcode, but I've included plenty of material that will be new even to experienced developers. My approach is to lead you through a simple application project to give you a vocabulary for the workflow of Mac development, and how Xcode and the tools that accompany it fit in. After you have a solid grounding, we can move on to Part II, where the details and more advanced techniques can come out.

Part I is a practical introduction, showing how to use Xcode at every step, from building a command-line tool, to debugging, to building a human interface, to Core Data design and language localization. Companion tools such as Interface Builder and Instruments are essential to developing for the Mac, and I cover them.

Version control has become indispensable even to small, single-programmer projects. *Xcode 3 Unleashed* introduces you to source-code management early, and returns to it frequently.

Part II covers how to use Xcode to manage and navigate your code base, even if it comes from a large, open source UNIX project. It shows how Xcode's build system—the mechanism that decides how and when to turn your code into an application—works. I return to Instruments, the astonishing tool for timelining your programs' execution and use of resources, and introduce Apple's performance tools, led by the deep and powerful Shark statistical profiler.

## Version Covered

I started writing *Xcode 3 Unleashed* when Xcode 3.0 was in development. 3.0 was the version in general release when we went to press, although Apple had started a beta program for version 3.1, under nondisclosure. There are many improvements in 3.1, but none that significantly change this book's lessons.

Where I found bugs or feature gaps in Xcode 3.0, I noted them. If you're using a later version, you might find those bugs have been cleared. Apple's Xcode team continues to work hard on the developer tools.

# Typographic Conventions

*Xcode 3 Unleashed* uses a few conventions to make the material easier to read and understand.

---

**NOTE**

Notes are short comments on subjects that relate to the text, but aren't directly in the flow.

---

**WARNING**

Warnings raise points that might trip you up, commit you to a dead end, or even make you lose your work.

---

**Sidebars**

Sidebars are for extended discussions that supplement the main text.

---

- ▶ Monospaced type is used for programming constructs, filenames, and command-line output.

- ▶ Text that you type is shown in **monospace bold**.

- ▶ Human interface elements, such as menus and button labels, are shown **like this**.

- ▶ When new terms are introduced, they are set off *in italics*.

- ▶ And program listings are shown in the colors you would see in Xcode's editors.

The Mac keyboard provides four modifier keys, and Xcode uses them all liberally as shortcuts for menu commands. This book denotes them by their symbols as used in the menus themselves:

| | |
|---|---|
| Command | ⌘ |
| Shift | ⇧ |
| Control (Ctrl) | ˆ |
| Option (Alt) | ⌥ |

# About the Author

**Fritz Anderson** has been writing software, books, and articles for the Macintosh since 1984. He has worked for research and development firms, consulting practices, and freelance. He was admitted to the Indiana bar, but thought better of it. He now lives in Chicago, where he works for a large university.

# Dedication

*For Bess and Kate, of whom I stand in awe.*

# Acknowledgments

Books do not write themselves, and authors do not write them alone. I am grateful to all the people who helped me along in this process—none of whom, I should emphasize, are responsible for this book's defects.

This book was cleared and supported by my editor at Addison-Wesley, Chuck Toporek, who guided and encouraged me through a process that was much easier than I'd ever imagined. Romny French was a great help with the paperwork, and making sure a starving author got paid. And my development editor, Chris Zahn, got me over the hump. Jovana San Nicolas-Shirley guided me through the trials of copyediting.

I was never told the names of the hardworking Mac developers who reviewed early drafts of *Xcode 3 Unleashed*, but I am signally grateful to them. They alerted me to important nuances, and saved me many embarrassments. I repeat: The errors that remain in this book are mine alone.

Greg Doench edited, and Ann Sellers acquired, my first book, *Step into Xcode: Mac OS X Development*, of which this is the second edition. It was an adventure, and the foundation of many good things.

Here in Chicago, Jon Rentzsch and Dave Dribin offered helpful suggestions. This book is much better, and none the worse, for their help.

Selena and Chrissl continue to enlighten me.

# We Want to Hear from You!

As the reader of this book, *you* are our most important critic and commentator. We value your opinion and want to know what we're doing right, what we could do better, what areas you'd like to see us publish in, and any other words of wisdom you're willing to pass our way.

You can email or write me directly to let me know what you did or didn't like about this book—as well as what we can do to make our books better.

*Please note that I cannot help you with technical problems related to the topic of this book. We do have a User Services group, however, where I will forward specific technical questions related to the book.*

When you write, please be sure to include this book's title and author as well as your name, email address, and phone number. I will carefully review your comments and share them with the author and editors who worked on the book.

Email:     feedback@quepublishing.com

Mail:      Chuck Toporek
           Senior Acquisitions Editor
           Sams Publishing
           75 Arlington Street
           Suite 300
           Boston, MA 02116 USA

## Reader Services

Visit our website and register this book at informit.com/register for convenient access to any updates, downloads, or errata that might be available for this book.

# Introduction

**IN THIS INTRODUCTION**

▶ **What Xcode Is**

▶ **What's New in Xcode 3**

▶ **Obtaining Xcode**

▶ **Installing Xcode**

From the moment it first published Mac OS X, Apple, Inc., has made a complete suite of application development tools available to every user of the Macintosh. Since Mac OS X version 10.3, those tools have been led by Xcode, the integrated development environment Apple's own engineers use to develop system software and applications such as Safari, iTunes, Mail, and iChat. If you own a Mac, these same tools are in your hands today.

## What's New in Xcode 3

In October 2007, with the introduction of Mac OS X 10.5 (Leopard), Apple introduced version 3 of the Xcode developer tools suite. Among the changes were

▶ Extensive improvements to the Xcode integrated development environment (IDE), including

   ▶ Support for Objective-C 2.0, the first major revision to the language, with commands for converting existing code to the new language.

   ▶ Improved syntax coloring, now including distinctive colors for symbols like instance variables and method names.

   ▶ Code Focus, a ribbon beside the editor text that lets you see how blocks of code are organized, and allows you to fold long blocks down to the height of a single line.

   ▶ The projectwide **Find** command now works through the Spotlight text-searching engine, yielding better results faster.

▶ A debugger bar, offering simple debugging controls in any editor window.

▶ Datatips, allowing you to inspect the values of program variables during debugging, just by hovering the cursor over them in the code.

▶ A mini-debugger, injected into the programs you run, permitting debugging during mouse-down events and other "volatile" situations.

▶ Automatic access to the debugger whenever a program you run from Xcode crashes.

▶ Improved compile-time error reporting, interleaving compiler messages with the code they relate to.

▶ Automated refactoring, helping you rename classes, methods, and functions, shift methods from class to class, and even create new super classes, in an Objective-C project.

▶ Much improved support for source code management tools such as Subversion, CVS, and Perforce.

▶ Much improved support for using UNIX scripting languages to create and edit text.

▶ The Organizer, a window to hold references to frequently used files and projects.

▶ Among the command-line tools, the new xed tool enables you to open text files in Xcode, when a shell script or tool demands an interactive editor.

▶ A major upgrade to the documentation system, using RSS feeds for live updates, and permitting developers to add their own documentation to the system.

▶ A Research Assistant window that documents API symbols and build variables in real time, as they are selected.

▶ A completely revamped Interface Builder, with better tools for crafting nonvisual parts of the human interface, such as controller objects. Integration between IB and Xcode is even tighter than before.

▶ A new tool, Instruments, for profiling the resource usage (memory, I/O, graphics, threading) of a program, in real time, on a timeline so that you can see how each element of the performance picture relates to all the others.

Xcode 3 is a ground-up rebuild of the Mac OS X developer tools, and it has been well worth the wait.

# Obtaining Xcode

If you have an installation DVD for Mac OS X 10.5 or a new Mac on which Leopard has come installed, you already have Xcode. On the DVD, an installation package can be found in the `Xcode Tools` folder inside the `Optional Installs` folder. On new Macs, you'll find a disk image file for Xcode Tools in the `Additional Installations` folder at the root of your hard drive; double-click the disk image to mount it, and you'll find the installation packages inside.

However, Apple does not always coordinate the latest version of its developer tools with its Mac OS X distributions. Even if you have an installation package on your Mac, or on your distribution disk, it pays to check for a newer version at the Apple Developer Connection (ADC).

## Downloading Xcode

You must join ADC to download Xcode. Point your web browser to http://developer. apple.com/, and click the link that offers a membership (at the time of this writing, it was the **Sign Up** link at the top of the page). You will be offered a handful of options, some expensive. All you need is an Online membership—it's free. Fill out the forms offered to you; they will take contact information and ask you to consent to terms and conditions. There may be marketing questions and offers of mailings.

When you have completed the signup process, go to http://connect.apple.com. Fill in the username and password you chose. You will then be presented with a few options, among these being **Downloads**. This is what you want; click it.

Depending on your membership level, and how active Apple has been lately in releasing new software, you might not be able to find Xcode on this page. If you don't see it, click **Developer Tools** in the Downloads column at the right of the page. Scroll down to the first Xcode 3.x download you find (earlier releases may appear lower in the list, and versions of Xcode 2.5 may appear higher). It will be a disk image a bit over 1GB in size. This will comprise the full set of Xcode tools; there is no updater you can apply to a copy you may already have. Click to download.

# Installing Xcode

Now that you have the latest Xcode package, it's time to install it. Installation packages can be run straight from a DVD, a mounted disk image file, or your hard disk. There's no difference.

In the `Xcode Tools` folder, you will find three installation packages:

- ▶ `XcodeTools.mpkg`, which is the installation package for Xcode and the other tools needed for Mac OS X development.

- ▶ `Dashcode.mpkg` provides the Dashcode IDE for producing Dashboard widgets. Dashcode is also included in the standard install from `XcodeTools.mpkg`; this package is for those who are interested only in developing widgets.

▶ `WebObjects.mpkg` installs Apple's excellent WebObjects frameworks and tools, for developing sophisticated database-centered websites in Java. WebObjects is also available as an optional install from within the Xcode Tools Installer.

You will also find a folder named `Packages`, containing installation packages for components of the Xcode tools, like the CHUD performance-measuring suite, software development kits (SDKs) for X Window and earlier versions of Mac OS X, and version 3.3 of the `gcc` compiler suite (for PowerPC Macs only). All these are available as options (or within options) in the Xcode Tools Installer, but are here in case you omit them from the original installation and want to add them later.

If you've ever done an installation under Mac OS X, the Xcode tools install is familiar (see Figure I.1). Start by double-clicking the `XcodeTools.mpkg` installation package. A Welcome screen appears, at which you will press **Continue**. Next, the installer displays the license for Xcode and its related software; click **Continue**, and if you accede to the license, click **Agree** in the ensuing sheet.

FIGURE I.1    The Welcome panel for the Xcode Tools Installation package should be familiar to any experienced Mac user.

You are now at the Standard Install panel, but we will vary from the standard line. Click the **Customize** button to reveal the Custom Install panel. This panel (see Figure I.2) contains a table listing the components of the Xcode Tools installation. The single mandatory component is checked and grayed out; the optional components are active, and you can check or uncheck them to include or exclude them from the installation:

▶ **Developer Tools Essentials**. This is Xcode itself, and the graphical and command-line programs that complement it, plus SDKs for developing Mac OS X software for versions 10.4 and later. This is a mandatory component; it doesn't make sense to install the developer tools without installing Xcode and the tools needed for it to run.

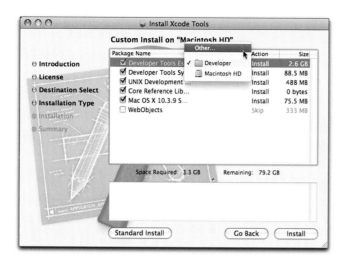

FIGURE I.2    The Custom Install panel for the Xcode Tools Installer. The top entry in the package list is for the core Xcode tools, and is not optional. In the Location column is a pop-up menu from which you can select where the developer tools are to go; the default is the Developer folder of your boot disk.

- ▶ **Developer Tools System Components**. These are the CHUD tools for investigating application performance, plus facilities for distributing application builds over more than one computer. You should install this package.

- ▶ **UNIX Development Support**. The "essentials" installation of Xcode installs components such as compilers and their support files in a usr subdirectory of the installation directory. If you will be doing command-line development—for instance, for building open source projects—you will want a set of development tools installed in the root /usr directory tree. This package installs copies of the command-line tools into /usr. You should install this package; examples in this book depend on it (see Chapter 24, "A Legacy Project").

- ▶ **Core Reference Library**. This package installs the panoply of introductions, references, technical notes, and sample code that document development on Mac OS X and the APIs you need to do it. Install this package.

- ▶ **Mac OS X 10.3.9 Support**. Installs the SDK and tools needed to produce software that targets Panther (Mac OS X 10.3). This includes version 3.3 of the gcc

> **NOTE**
>
> CHUD, gcc 3.3, and WebObjects are not flexible about where they are installed. They will be installed into /Developer no matter what location you choose for the Xcode tools.

> **NOTE**
>
> The gcc compiler suites installed with the Xcode tools are Apple-modified builds that take account of such Mac OS X features as frameworks and support for Objective-C 2.0. They are not the same as the gccs available under the same version numbers from the Free Software Foundation.

compiler suite, for PPC Macs only. This package is left out of the standard install, and whether you need it depends on whether you intend to build applications for 10.3 (see Chapter 17, "Cross-Development").

▶ **WebObjects**. This package installs the applications and files needed to develop web applications with Apple's WebObjects framework. You need not install this package.

Unlike earlier versions, Xcode 3 and 2.5 are flexible about where you install them. This is where you would make that choice. See the section "Another Install Location" for details.

> **NOTE**
>
> Earlier versions of Xcode offered to install reference material for the current Java development kits. These are still available through the Downloads section of ADC.

> **NOTE**
>
> With Xcode 3, Apple has dropped support for developing software aimed at Jaguar (Mac OS X 10.2). If you need to target 10.2, you must install Xcode 2.5 and use its 10.2.8 SDK. You cannot use Xcode 2.5 to build software using 10.5 technologies.

Now click the **Install** button. The standard authentication sheet will appear, into which you enter the name and password of an administrative user of your Mac.

The next panel contains a progress bar and a narrative of what is being installed. This process takes a number of minutes, at the end of which you are rewarded by a big green check mark. Close the installer; you are now ready to use Xcode.

## Another Install Location

Earlier versions of Xcode (earlier than 2.5) installed themselves only in the /Developer directory of the startup file system. Having one possible path to all the developer tools greatly simplified the task of locating them: If you needed the packagemaker tool, it was at /Developer/Tools/packagemaker, and that was that.

Things have changed since then. First, the Xcode package has grown larger and larger. The download package alone is 1.1GB in size, which expands to 3.3GB installed. It is reasonable to want to put Xcode onto another disk or partition. Second, it is now possible to install Xcode 2.5 (see the section "Xcode 2.5" that follows) in parallel with Xcode 3, and the two tool sets necessarily need two homes.

That is why, during your installation of Xcode, /Developer is still the default location, but you can choose another.

If you want another location, ignore the **Change Install Location** button on the Standard Install panel. The Installer application offers this button as a standard part of its workflow; if you press it, you will find that the boot volume is your only choice. If you find yourself at the Install-Location panel, click the **Go Back** button to back out.

The real choice comes in the Custom Install panel. In the Standard Install panel, click the **Customize** button to get to a list of components to install. The top line, **Developer Tools**

**Essentials**, has a pop-up menu for setting the location for installing the Xcode tools (see Figure I.2). The default location, /Developer, is shown initially.

Change the location by selecting **Other** from the pop-up. A standard open-file sheet will appear. Find the directory that you want to contain your Xcode directory. Use the **New Folder** button to create the Xcode directory there. Make sure that directory is selected, and then click **Choose**. The selected directory will contain the Applications, Documentation, and other directories that make up the Xcode tool set.

> **NOTE**
>
> Yes, you can put Xcode wherever you want, but accounting for that possibility in every reference to a component of the developer tools would make this book more tedious than it has to be. I'll just refer to the Xcode tools directory as /Developer, and trust you to make the transposition yourself.

You can continue the installation from there, as before.

# Uninstalling Xcode

All things come to an end, and there is no exception for Xcode. There are two reasons you might choose to remove Xcode from your hard drive. The first is that you just do not want it; you want the files gone, and the space reclaimed.

The second is that you want to install a later version of Xcode. When Apple comes out with new versions of Xcode, it does not distribute updaters. Only the full Xcode tools package will be available for download. Past experience has shown that a full upgrader is a bigger and more accident-prone undertaking than the Xcode team can sustain, especially when the alternative is to have Xcode users simply remove the earlier version and install the new version afresh.

The developer tools come in two parts. The most prominent is the /Developer directory itself, which contains all the graphical applications, documentation, and SDKs that make up the public face of Xcode. The other part is the tools embedded throughout the UNIX file system that make development possible. For instance, two versions of the gcc compiler are installed at /usr/bin; all the headers needed for development on the current system are in the huge /usr/include hierarchy. To properly uninstall the developer tools, these, too, have to be picked through and removed.

The first part of the uninstallation is easy: Find your Xcode tools directory, and drag it into the trash. That's 100,000-plus files gone.

Next, execute the tool /Library/Developer/Shared/uninstall-devtools from the command line. uninstall-devtools is a Perl script that walks through the saved installation receipts looking for every developer tools package going back to 2001. It deletes the files of every package it finds. Running uninstall-devtools will take a few minutes. At the end, you have a system fit for a fresh install.

This procedure is good enough if you mean to reinstall the developer tools. If you mean to go further, you also want to delete the directories /Library/Developer and

~/Library/Developer, and the preference files for the individual developer applications. The usual procedure spares these, because they contain customization files you may have created, which you would want to carry over to a new installation.

# Xcode 2.5

Many people have commitments to Xcode 2 that they can't get out of, even if they are running Leopard. Managers of a project nearing completion, with many developers, may be reluctant to revalidate their build processes for a new tool chain.

They might have NIBs that rely on palettes for Interface Builder 2, which are not usable in IB 3. Further, although Xcode and Interface Builder do provide "compatibility" modes, it is easy to produce files that earlier versions cannot open. Holding off on Xcode 3, at least for some projects, can be prudent.

That is why Apple released, in parallel with Xcode 3, Xcode 2.5. The Xcode 2.5 tools are strictly file compatible with those of the preceding version, Xcode 2.4. Unlike version 2.4, 2.5 can run on either Tiger (Mac OS X 10.4) or Leopard (10.5).

Like Xcode 3, Xcode 2.5 permits you to choose where to install its developer tools. As with the Xcode 3 installation, you are offered a **Customize** button for editing the components to be installed. The top component, representing the core developer tools, will have a pop-up enabling you to chose where to install Xcode 2.5. The default location is /Xcode2.5.

If you intend to develop specifically for Mac OS X 10.5, Xcode 2.5 is not for you; it does not support the Leopard SDK. For Leopard development, you have to use Xcode 3.

If you have Project Builder (.pbxproj) projects around, now is the time to convert them to Xcode projects, and 2.5 is the tool to do it. Xcode 3 has dropped the capability to import Project Builder projects.

Having two Xcodes on your system gives you two versions of Xcode-related command-line tools such as xcodebuild. If you opt (as I strongly recommend) to install tools in /usr/bin, it is a nice question which version of a tool is run when you execute it from the command line or a build script. The solution is this: The /usr/bin versions of these tools are in fact scripts that refer to the binary versions in the Xcode 3 or 2.5 install tree. You determine which version is used by running the xcode-select tool; man xcode-select for details.

# PART I

## The Life Cycle of a Mac OS X Application

## IN THIS PART

| | | |
|---|---|---|
| CHAPTER 1 | Kicking the Tires | 11 |
| CHAPTER 2 | Simple Workflow and Passive Debugging | 19 |
| CHAPTER 3 | Simple Active Debugging | 29 |
| CHAPTER 4 | Compilation: The Basics | 39 |
| CHAPTER 5 | Starting a Cocoa Application | 47 |
| CHAPTER 6 | A Cocoa Application: Views | 63 |
| CHAPTER 7 | A Cocoa Application: Controllers | 75 |
| CHAPTER 8 | Version Control | 93 |
| CHAPTER 9 | Property Lists | 117 |
| CHAPTER 10 | Libraries and Dependent Targets | 141 |
| CHAPTER 11 | File Packages and Bundles | 153 |
| CHAPTER 12 | Unit Testing | 167 |
| CHAPTER 13 | Creating a Custom View | 181 |
| CHAPTER 14 | Dynamic Libraries and Frameworks | 203 |
| CHAPTER 15 | Documentation in Xcode | 221 |
| CHAPTER 16 | Using the Data Modeling Tools | 243 |
| CHAPTER 17 | Cross-Development | 267 |
| CHAPTER 18 | Spotlight (or, How to Build a Plug-in) | 281 |
| CHAPTER 19 | Finishing Touches | 301 |

# CHAPTER 1

# Kicking the Tires

**IN THIS CHAPTER**

▶ Creating a Simple Xcode Project

▶ Running a Program

▶ The Files Xcode Creates

## First Run

Xcode is installed, and it's time to see what it looks like. Find Xcode in /Developer/Applications and double-click its icon to launch it. If you're running Xcode for the first time, the New User Assistant window, as shown in Figure 1.1, will display.

The default settings in this window are best for most purposes. Just click the **Next** button in each panel; in the last panel, click **Finish**. Every setting in the New User Assistant is accessible through Xcode's Preferences window, so you won't be committing to anything.

---

**FileVault and Xcode**

If you are using the Mac OS X FileVault feature to encrypt your home directory, the New User Assistant default settings will slow the performance of Xcode significantly. Compiling and linking an application requires a lot of successive reads and writes to files, and if FileVault is on, each read and write must pass through the encryption engine. Because compiler objects are unlikely to disclose significant secrets, this is wasted effort.

To avoid this problem, create new folders outside your home directory to hold intermediate and final build products. One possible location is in the /Users/Shared directory. In the second panel of the New User Assistant, select the radio buttons **Separate Location for Build Products** and **Separate Location for Intermediate Build Files**, and use the **Choose** buttons to designate the nonhome directories.

---

FIGURE 1.1    The New User Assistant. The dialog panels in this assistant capture your preferences the first time you run Xcode.

Xcode next presents you with a Welcome to Xcode window, a new addition to the documentation system (see Figure 1.2). The first tab, **Getting Started**, points you to resources for starting development with Xcode. The most interesting feature of the window is the second tab, **Xcode News**. This is a minireader for an RSS feed with the latest additions to the Apple Developer Connection (ADC) documentation set. Apple publishes new material for developers nearly every week, so this is a useful tool.

Not everybody needs all this information all the time. To prevent this window from popping up every time you start Xcode, check the box **Do Not Show This at Xcode Launch**, and close the window.

## Hello, World

We want to get Xcode to do something for us, however minimal. By tradition, this means building a terminal command that prints `Hello, World`! Select **New Project** from the **File** menu. Xcode presents the New Project Assistant, shown in Figure 1.3.

Xcode organizes your work around a *project*, a collection of files, tool settings, and *targets*. A target designates the project files used to build a particular product and the tool settings to apply. The most common kind of project, for building an application, has only one target—for building the application itself—but more complex projects may have several targets: for libraries, plug-ins, and unit tests.

> **NOTE**
>
> If you are coming to Xcode from CodeWarrior, the term *target* is used slightly differently. An Xcode target corresponds more closely to the CodeWarrior concept of a product. A CodeWarrior project typically has two targets—debug and final—for each product. Xcode has only one target—corresponding to the product—and any variant in building a target for debugging or release is a matter of *build configurations*.

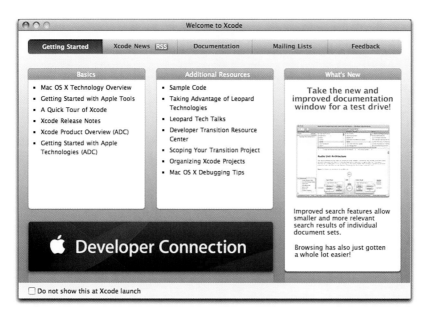

FIGURE 1.2　　The Welcome to Xcode window. The first tab, **Getting Started**, points you to resources for getting started with Mac OS X development. The second tab, **Xcode News**, brings you a regularly updated reference to the latest developer documentation.

FIGURE 1.3　　The New Project Assistant. Scroll down to **Standard Tool**, select it, and click **Next**.

Different target types require different tool settings and system libraries. Xcode eases the process of configuring a new project by offering you a choice of the most common target types for the first target in the project. We want to make a simple command-line utility that runs in the Mac OS X BSD UNIX subsystem. Scroll down the list to **Command Line Utility** and the subitem **Standard Tool** (see Figure 1.3), select that item, and click **Next**.

**NOTE**

The list of available project and target types is quite extensive. For a thorough review, see Appendix B, "Project and Target Templates."

The next panel—New Standard Tool Assistant (see Figure 1.4)—lets you name the project and place it on your disk hierarchy. For this exercise, type **HelloWorld** in the upper text field to name the project. The second field will echo what you type, designating ~/HelloWorld/ as the project directory. This means that the directory HelloWorld—which will be created if it isn't already there—will hold your *project file*, named HelloWorld.xcodeproj, and the other files needed to build your project's targets.

FIGURE 1.4    The New Standard Tool Assistant. To name a new project, type the name of the project. The assistant automatically names a new folder to enclose the project and its files.

Click the **Finish** button. Xcode creates the HelloWorld directory, copies some files into it, and opens the project window (see Figure 1.5). For a BSD command-line tool, the project starts with a main.c file for the tool's main() function, a HelloWorld.1 template file for the man page, and the HelloWorld product, shown in red in the list because Xcode can't find the file associated with it, which is natural enough, because we haven't built it yet.

These files are shown in the large *Detail list* on the right side of the project window. The contents of the detail list are controlled by the selection in the Groups & Files column. Selecting the first item under this heading selects the project, filling the detail list with every file included in the project. Below the project icon are folder icons representing subgroups of files; clicking a folder icon displays in the detail list only the files in that group.

FIGURE 1.5    The HelloWorld project window. Names of files, arranged in groups, appear in the Groups & Files column at left. The Detail list at right provides searchable details of whatever is selected in the Groups & Files column.

To the left of the project and folder icons are the familiar disclosure triangles. Clicking a disclosure triangle opens a container in a list. Expanding a file group folder shows the names of the individual files in the group.

If you've been exploring, click the project icon at the top of the Groups & Files column to restore the list of all files in the Detail list under File Name. Now double-click main.c. A window like the one in Figure 1.6 appears.

The placeholder for main() in the default main.c for a command-line tool is Hello,World. This simplifies our first run of Xcode considerably. First, let's be sure that when our program runs we will be able to see what it prints. Produce a console window by selecting **Console** from the **Run** menu (⇧⌘R). Xcode presents a window for standard text input and output.

At the top of the console window (and all the other windows) is a toolbar, one item of which is labeled **Build and Go**. Click that button. Several seconds may pass—the first build of a target is always longer—but you are soon rewarded with Hello, World! in the console window (see Figure 1.7). Success.

Quit Xcode (by pressing ⌘Q, or selecting **Quit Xcode** in the **Xcode** application menu). There's nothing to save, so the project and editor windows disappear immediately.

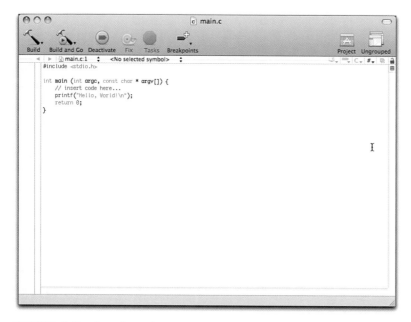

FIGURE 1.6    An editor window, showing the default `main.c` from the Xcode command-line tool template.

# What Went Where

Switch to the Finder and examine the `HelloWorld` folder in your home directory (see Figure 1.8). The `HelloWorld` directory is right where it was designated in the New Project Assistant and contains the files `HelloWorld.1` and `main.c` that came automatically with the new project. The blue `HelloWorld.xcodeproj` icon is the project document file; double-clicking it opens Xcode and shows the HelloWorld project as you left it.

The `build` directory contains a `Release` directory with the `HelloWorld` tool; and a folder named `HelloWorld.build`. This latter contains a dozen files or so, including the compiled object code from `main.c` and a number of files containing indexes to make it easier to navigate large projects and system libraries. You can ignore the `HelloWorld.build` directory; its use is strictly internal in Xcode.

The `HelloWorld` tool is a genuine UNIX executable, which you can demonstrate by using the command-line terminal. Open the Terminal application in the `Utilities` subfolder of the `Applications` folder. Dragging the `HelloWorld` tool file's icon from the Finder into the Terminal window has the effect of "typing" into the terminal the full path of what you dropped. Press the **Return** key. The tool runs, prints `Hello, World!`, and returns to the command-line prompt:

```
xcodeuser$ /Users/xcodeuser/HelloWorld/build/Release/HelloWorld
Hello, World!
xcodeuser$
```

At this point, we are done with the HelloWorld project. You can drag it and its files into the trash. Xcode will show no sign of having built or run HelloWorld.

FIGURE 1.7    The console window showing the output of `HelloWorld`.

FIGURE 1.8    The HelloWorld project in the Finder. Creating and building a command-line tool project in Xcode created a folder for the project, a project file, some template files, and a `build` directory containing the completed tool.

## Summary

In this chapter, we went through the very basics of running Xcode and using it to build and execute a simple program.

We ran Xcode and configured it for our use, then created a new project to build a command-line tool. We built and executed the tool, and verified that it can run from the command line.

We saw how Xcode creates and structures a project directory, and how to dispose of the project when we were done.

CHAPTER 2

# Simple Workflow and Passive Debugging

**IN THIS CHAPTER**

▷ Linear Regression: An Example Problem

▷ Creating a Command-Line Tool

▷ Dealing with Build Errors

▷ Simple Debugging

For most of this book, we work on applications that do *linear regression*, a simple but informative statistic. Suppose that you have a series of data pairs, such as the quarterly sales figures for a particular department, as shown in Table 2.1.

TABLE 2.1  Quarterly Sales Figures for a Hypothetical Company (millions of dollars)

| Quarter | Sales |
|---------|-------|
| 1 | 107.5 |
| 2 | 110.3 |
| 3 | 114.5 |
| 4 | 116.0 |
| 5 | 119.3 |
| 6 | 122.4 |

A *regression line* is the straight line that passes nearest all the data points (see Figure 2.1). The formula for such a line is $y = mx + b$, or the sales ($y$) for a given quarter ($x$) rise at a quarterly rate ($m$) from a base at "quarter zero" ($b$). We have the $x$ and $y$ values; we'd like to determine $m$ and $b$.

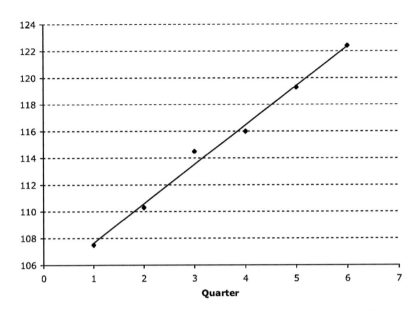

FIGURE 2.1    The sales figures from Table 2.1, plotted in a graph. The line drawn through the data points is the closest straight-line fit for the data.

# Calculating a Linear Regression

The formulas for linear regression are as follows:

$$m = \frac{n\sum\limits_{i=1}^{n} x_i y_i - \sum\limits_{i=1}^{n} x_i \sum\limits_{i=1}^{n} y_i}{n\sum\limits_{i=1}^{n} x_i^2 - \left(\sum\limits_{i=1}^{n} x_i\right)}$$

$$b = \frac{1}{n}\left(\sum\limits_{i=1}^{n} y_i - m\sum\limits_{i=1}^{n} x_i\right)$$

$$r = m\sqrt{\frac{n\sum\limits_{i=1}^{n} x_i^2 - \left(\sum\limits_{i=1}^{n} x_i\right)^2}{n\sum\limits_{i=1}^{n} y_i^2 - \left(\sum\limits_{i=1}^{n} y_i\right)^2}}$$

The value $r$ is the *correlation coefficient*, a figure showing how well the regression line models the data. A value of 0 means that the $x$ and $y$ values have no detectable relation to each other; ±1 indicates that the regression line fits the data perfectly.

Linear regression is used frequently in business and the physical and social sciences. When $x$ represents time, lines derived from regressions are trends from which past and future values can be estimated. When $x$ is volume of sales and $y$ is costs, you can claim $b$ as fixed cost and $m$ as marginal cost. Correlation coefficients, good and bad, form the quantitative heart of serious arguments about marketing preferences and social injustice.

The demands on a program for turning a series of $x$ and $y$ values into a slope, intercept, and correlation coefficient are not great: Keep a running total of $x$, $x^2$, $y$, $y^2$, and $xy$; keep note of the count ($n$); and run the formulas when all the data has been seen.

## Plan of Action

If you're an experienced programmer for UNIX operating systems, the solution to this problem comes almost by impulse: Write a command-line tool that reads data as pairs of floating-point numbers from standard input and writes $m$, $b$, and $r$ to standard output.

> **NOTE**
>
> Experienced C programmers will see more than one error in this code. The errors are intentional.

Here's the first draft of such a tool:

```c
#include <stdio.h>
#include <math.h>

int main (int argc, const char * argv[])
{
    int         nScanned;
    int         n;
    double      sumX, sumY;
    double      sumX2, sumY2;
    double      sumXY;

    n = 0;
    sumXY = sumY = sumX2 = sumY2 = sumXY = 0.0;

    do {
        double  x, y;
        int     nScanned = scanf("%lg %lg" x, y) ;
        if (nScanned == 2) {
            n++;
            sumX += x;
            sumX2 += x * x;
            sumY += y;
            sumY2 += y * y;
            sumXY += x * y;
        }
    } while (nScanned == 2);
    double      slope,  intercept;
    slope = (n * sumXY - sumX * sumY)
                / (n * sumX2 - sumX * sumX);
    intercept = (sumY - slope * sumX) / n;
```

```
double      correlation;
correlation = slope * sqrt((n * sumX2 - sumX * sumX)
                          / (n * sumY2 - sumY * sumY));
printf ("%g\t%g\t%g\n",    slope,    intercept,    correlation);
return    0;
}
```

# A Command-Line Tool

Let's put this plan into action. Start Xcode. As you did in the preceding chapter, select **Command Line Utility** from the list of project types, and name the new project. We'll be calling the new tool `Linrg`, so it's most convenient to give the same name to the project.

Once again, Xcode presents you with a project window set up for a BSD UNIX command-line utility. In Chapter 1, "Kicking the Tires," we double-clicked the listing for the `main.c` file to bring up an editor window for that file. This time, try clicking once on the **main.c** filename and then on the **Editor** button in the project window's toolbar. The contents of the file appear in the right half of the project window (see Figure 2.2). Selecting different filenames in the Groups & Files column or in the detail list displays the contents of those files in the editor area.

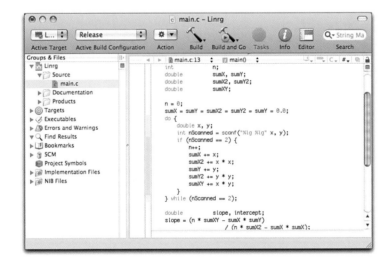

FIGURE 2.2    Editing the `Linrg` tool. Note that the small icon next to the filename `main.c` in the Groups & Files list and in the filename pop-up is darkened, indicating that the file has unsaved changes.

Whether you work in a separate editor window or in an editor in the project window is completely up to you. The two views are equivalent. The Detail list that formerly occupied the right half of the project window is still available. You can have it back by clicking the **Editor** toolbar icon again, or you can split the area between them by dragging the split bar that appears above the editor view or below the detail view. Xcode makes frequent use of completely closed split views, so be on the lookout for the telltale dimple in a thin bar at the edge of a view.

The content of `main.c` is, as before, the Hello, World program, which isn't nearly so useful to us this time. We substitute the source for our linear regression tool and click the **Build** button in the toolbar. If you hadn't saved the file before building, a dialog offers to do so before attempting the build; save the file. I've found that I always want to save changes before building; by visiting the Building panel of the Preferences window, you can set the **For Unsaved Files** pop-up to **Always Save**.

## Build Errors

All has not gone well. The Xcode icon in the dock now has a red badge with a 1 in it. The status bar at the bottom of the project window says `Build failed (2 errors)`. At the other end of the status bar is the word *Failed* and an error icon with the count of 2. (There was only one error in the program, but it was reported as two because of the double compilation done by the Release configuration. I'll show how to relieve this shortly.) Looking at the text of the program, we see a red bubble containing this message: `error: parse error before 'x'`. Sure enough, as we examine the line just above the bubble (see Figure 2.3), we find that we omitted the comma between the format string and the second parameter to the `scanf ()` call.

Searching for errors by hand will not scale well to builds that span many errors among dozens, or even hundreds, of files. Even Xcode's trick of placing red marks in the scrollbar to mark the position of errors in the current file helps only a little. Xcode provides a Build Results window for browsing error messages that arise in the course of

> **NOTE**
>
> If the message were a warning rather a build error, the bubble would be yellow.

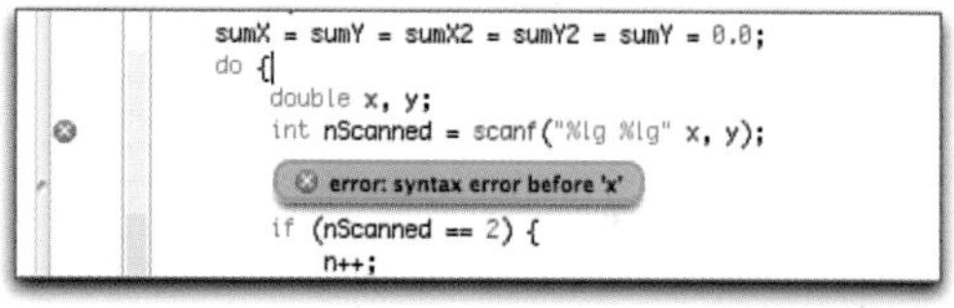

FIGURE 2.3    Error bubble after a line containing a syntax error, from the first attempt at building `Linrg`.

> **NOTE**
>
> Error bubbles are a great way to see error messages right next to the code that produces them, but when you come to edit your code, they are annoying and get in the way. You can hide a bubble by clicking its red or yellow badge in the left gutter. You can turn them off completely, or restrict them to errors only, with the **Show During Builds** pop-up in the Building pane of the Preferences window.

building a project. You can see this window at any time by clicking **Build Results** in the **Build** menu or by pressing ⇧⌘B. You can also open the Build Results window by clicking the error icons in the lower-right corner of any editor window.

Open the Build Results window now (see Figure 2.4). The top half is taken up with an abbreviated transcript of the build process, with the single error, error: parse error before 'x', highlighted in red. Click the highlighted line. The editor view in the bottom half of the window fills with main.c, centered on the line at which the error was detected.

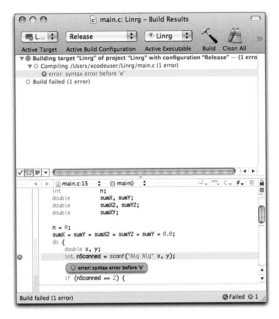

FIGURE 2.4    The Build Results window, showing an error in Linrg's main.c. Clicking the error line focuses the editor pane at the bottom on the line at which the error was detected. Any file in Xcode can have multiple editor panes open on it at one time.

It is common for Xcode to present editors for the same file in multiple windows. Source code may be displayed in the Build Results window, the project window, editor windows, the Debugger window, and even the source control window. In each case, the view is a full-featured, writable—to the extent that the target file is writable—editor on the file in question. You can make a change to a file wherever the file appears; Xcode knows that all the views are on the same file, so there is no danger that the views will get out of sync.

With this in mind, use the editor in the Build Results window to insert a comma after the format string, and click **Build** again. Now we are rewarded with the message Build succeeded.

Note the cluster of four icons at the lower left of the upper panel of the Build Results window. Clicking the icon that looks like a document with writing on it opens up the build transcript, which details the commands used to accomplish the last build and the messages returned by the tools. This transcript is worth looking at, first, for its value in showing how much goes on behind the scenes in response to a single command. Second, in the course of advanced tuning of the build process, this transcript is the only way to see what parameters are getting passed to the compilers, linkers, and other tools, and in what sequence. Third, although it is usually very good at picking out the informative error messages from what its tools print out, Xcode isn't perfect. Sometimes, looking at the transcript for the full message is the only way to make sense of an error.

We are just about ready to try Linrg out, but before we do, we have some setup to do. We want to change some settings to make sure that if anything goes wrong, we will have a clear indication of what has happened (see Figure 2.5).

1. Open the Preferences window (⌘**comma**).

2. Select the **Debugging** panel from the list of icons at the top of the window.

3. In the **On Start** pop-up menu, select **Show Console & Debugger**.

4. Under **Fonts and Colors**, select **Executable Standard Input** and click the **Set Font** button. Select the Bold variant of the Courier font.

5. Select **Executable Standard Output**, click the **Set Font** button, and select the Oblique variant of the Courier font.

6. Click the **OK** button in the Preferences window.

7. Bring the project window forward (⌘**0**), and from the pop-up menu labeled **Active Build Configuration**, select **Debug**.

FIGURE 2.5    The Debugging panel of the Xcode Preferences window. The fonts used for the standard input and output text, as displayed in the console window, have been changed to be distinctive. Xcode is set to display the Debugger window and the standard I/O and debugger console whenever a program is run.

Now we are set to run Linrg. From the **Build** menu, select the **Build & Debug** command (⌘Y). Xcode opens a Debugger window, and behind it a window named Linrg — Debugger Console. Bring the console window front; it's where we'll be typing the input for the Linrg tool, and where Linrg will display its output.

> **NOTE**
>
> This setup starts Linrg in a "debugging" mode. If you've been using CodeWarrior, you are used to the debugger's pausing before the first line of main(), waiting for your signal to proceed. Xcode sets no such automatic breakpoints; if you need to do setup tasks at the start of execution, you have to set an early breakpoint yourself.

The console will print out a message from the Free Software Foundation explaining the license terms of the gdb command-line debugger that underlies the Xcode graphical debugger. Read it once, heed it, and then feel free to ignore it.

For the first run, let's supply test data on the line $y = 2x$, adding a little bit of "noise" to make things more interesting. Type the following into the console window, and then press **Return**:

```
1.0   2.05
```

Once again, we have a problem (see Figure 2.6). The console prints out the message `Program received signal: "EXC_BAD_ACCESS"`, and the Debugger window, previously blank, fills with assembly language code. Mac OS X signals a bad access when a program tries to use memory in a way that isn't permitted, and a segmentation violation when a program tries to use memory that hasn't been allocated to its process. In a C program, this almost always means that a proper value has not been supplied for a pointer.

FIGURE 2.6    The first runnable build of Linrg crashes with a bad-access error.

# Simple Debugging

Although you might know what the problem with the Linrg tool is, let's prosecute this bug as though it were a mystery. It is time to start debugging.

Xcode's interactive debugger is a graphical interface for gdb, the GNU project's interactive command-line debugger. The command-line interface to gdb is still available—it shares the console window with the standard input and output text—but most debugging, especially the simple kind we will do now, can be done entirely through the Debugger window.

Click the Debugger window to bring it to the front. Beneath its toolbar, the Debugger window is divided into three parts: At the bottom is the editor pane we've become used to from other windows. At top left is a listing of the stack, showing the chain of function calls extending from our main() function up to the function that crashed—svfscanf_1. The top-right view is not yet of interest.

The stack listing has svfscanf_1 selected, and the editor is filled with assembly language code from that function. It doesn't give us much guidance, and probably wouldn't, without a lot of study and possibly a listing of the function in C. The same is true when we click scanf, although it at least has a recognizable name: We know we call it from within Linrg.

Whereas these first two functions' names appear in the listing in gray, main appears in black. The Xcode debugger displays in black all function names in the call stack for which it has access to source code. Selecting main rewards us with a listing of Linrg's main() function (see Figure 2.7). One line of the listing is highlighted, and a red arrow in the gutter points to it. This is the line in our program that set the crash in motion.

At this point, we can allow at least one scale to fall from our eyes: The scanf function requires *pointers* to the variables it fills from standard input, not the *values* of those variables. As we have found our error, there is nothing more for the crashed Linrg to tell us. Dispose

> **NOTE**
>
> When main is selected, the upper-right view fills with the names and values of variables used in that function. We examine these in detail in the next chapter.

> **NOTE**
>
> Even at this early stage, a prudent developer would consider putting the Linrg project under source-code management (SCM). SCM ensures that you can refer back to previous versions of your code, enabling you to understand the changes you made and reverse changes that turn out to have been a bad idea.
>
> SCM is indispensable insurance, but we put it off until Chapter 8, "Version Control," because it requires some setup that distracts from the flow of this book.

of its process by clicking the red **Stop** button in the Debugger window toolbar. Then edit the line

```
int     nScanned = scanf("%lg %lg", x, y);
```

to read

```
int     nScanned = scanf("%lg %lg", &x, &y);
```

Now this bug, at least, is killed.

FIGURE 2.7    The Debugger window after `Linrg` crashed. Selecting the first item in the stack listing at upper left that shows text in black (not gray) shows the line in the program that triggered the crash.

## Summary

In this chapter, we chose a problem to solve with a computer program and devised a strategy for solving that problem. We created a command-line tool that does standard input and output. We ran into a compilation error, saw how to get information on the error, and corrected it. We saw how the Xcode debugger can be used passively to provide an instrument for examining the state of a program when it has crashed and used the resulting insight to fix a bug.

CHAPTER 3

# Simple Active Debugging

**IN THIS CHAPTER**

▷ **Debugging Line by Line**

▷ **Breakpoints**

▷ **The Variable Pane**

▷ **Fixing a Running Program**

In Chapter 2, "Simple Workflow and Passive Debugging," we got the Linrg command-line tool to build without errors and used the Xcode debugger passively to track down and eliminate an early crashing bug. Let's run our tool again and see how it goes.

## The Next Step

Make sure that the project is built, and then select **Debug** from the **Run** menu. Select **Console** from the **Run** menu so that we can interact with Linrg. Type some data:

```
1.0  2.05
nan nan nan
```

Well, after we enter two numbers and press **Return**, Linrg does not crash. It just prints nan nan nan and quits. The status bar in the Debugger and Project windows says Debugging of 'Linrg' ended normally.

Something else is wrong. An illegal floating-point operation—such as dividing zero by zero, or square-rooting a negative number—took place somewhere in our calculations, resulting in a NaN (not a number), the special float value that signals an illegal operation. This need have happened only once; any arithmetic done with a NaN results in a NaN, so a single illegal operation early in the process could propagate the invalid-result marker through all the calculations that followed.

It makes sense that `Linrg` should report indeterminate results: Apparently, it tried to compute the regression line after reading only one point, which is not enough to determine a line. We suspect that this problem is therefore not in the computations, but in the early exit from the input loop.

The time-honored way to track down a bug like this is to put a `printf()` call after every calculation so that the problem code shows the state of the program at each significant step. If the right things are printed at the right time, you can see where the application went off the rails.

There is no need to instrument a step-by-step picture of `Linrg`'s state, however, because we have a computer to take care of that for us. The Xcode debugger will do everything we need.

# Active Debugging

In our previous encounter with the debugger, it took control over `Linrg` when a fatal error occurred. This time, we want the debugger to take control at a time of our choosing. By setting a breakpoint at a particular line in `Linrg`, we tell the debugger to halt execution of the application at that line, so that the contents of variables can be examined and execution resumed under our control.

The easiest way to set a breakpoint is to click in the broad gutter area at the left margin of the application source code in one of Xcode's editors. Select **main.c** in the Groups & Files list of the main Project window to bring that file into the editing area. Scroll down to the first line of the `main()` function if it isn't visible, and click in the gutter next to the line containing the statement `n = 0` (see Figure 3.1). On the screen, a long, dark-blue arrowhead appears in the gutter to show that a breakpoint is set there. You can remove the breakpoint by dragging the arrowhead to the side, out of the gutter; you can move the breakpoint by dragging it up or down the gutter.

Select **Build** and **Debug** (⌘Y) from the **Build** menu. As before, Xcode performs any tasks needed to bring the `Linrg` tool up-to-date, and starts running it. This

FIGURE 3.1    Clicking in the gutter at the left margin of an editor area to set a breakpoint at the adjacent line of code.

**NOTE**

Clicking the breakpoint turns it pale blue and deactivates it without removing it, which is useful when more complex behaviors are attached to breakpoints. Control-clicking the breakpoint—or right-clicking if you're using a two-button mouse—brings up a menu that allows you to remove, edit, or disable the breakpoint or to attach one of several useful breakpoint actions. Breakpoint actions are discussed in the "Breakpoint Commands" section of Chapter 22, "More About Debugging."

time, however, the Debugger window almost immediately shows that Linrg has halted at the breakpoint we set (see Figure 3.2).

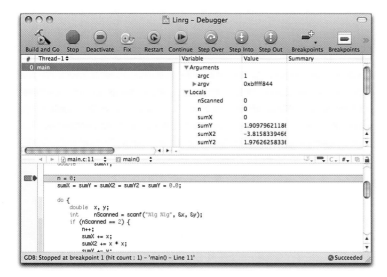

FIGURE 3.2    The Debugger window as Linrg stops for a breakpoint at the start of main(). The line at which execution paused is highlighted in the editor panel, and the current values of function arguments and local variables are in the upper-right Value panel.

Now we can take control. The top of the Debugger window consists of a toolbar (see Figure 3.3) that affords *precise* control over the execution of the program.

The buttons and their actions are as follows:

- **Build and Go**, available when the target application is not running, is a convenient way to return to debugging after editing application source in the Debugger window's editor pane.

- **Stop** halts the target application and ends debugging. When no program is running, this button label is **Go**, which relaunches the current target without rebuilding.

- **Activate/Deactivate** turns all the breakpoints in the program on or off. Effectively, this means you can switch between Run and Debug while the target program is running.

**Run, Debug, and Go**

Xcode offers three ways to run an application.

- **Debug** runs the application, and stops execution whenever a breakpoint is encountered.

- **Run** runs the application without stopping for breakpoints. If the application encounters a fatal error, the Debugger appears, with the code highlighted at the spot of the error.

- **Go** performs Run or Debug, depending on which you chose last. The **Build and Go** toolbar button in most Xcode windows builds the target, and then performs a "Go."

FIGURE 3.3    The toolbar of the Xcode Debugger window. The controls in the toolbar allow you to start and pause execution of the program being debugged or to step through the program line by line. Specialized commands enable you to step into functions and methods or to step out of the current function to its caller.

▶ **Fix** allows you to make some changes in programs while they are running under the Xcode debugger. This button compiles the file that is in the editor pane and attempts to patch the file into the running process.

▶ **Restart** halts the application being debugged and restarts it immediately under the debugger. This saves time over terminating the application and restarting both the debugger and the application.

▶ **Pause** (when the program is running) breaks execution of the target application wherever it happens to be.

▶ **Continue** (when the program is paused) lets the target application continue running uninterrupted to the end or until it encounters an active breakpoint or an error condition.

▶ **Step Over** lets the target application continue running until the next line in the function currently executing, stepping over any function calls. If the current line is the last line of the function, execution advances to the caller of the current function.

▶ **Step Into** lets the target application run until the next line, whether it is in the current function or in a function called in the current line. The debugger will step into function calls.

▶ **Step Out** lets the target application run until the current function returns.

▶ **Breakpoints** is a menu, allowing you to set options for the current breakpoint. These options include logging, beeping at, or speaking the breakpoint, instead of stopping. A quick click on **Breakpoints** adds or removes a breakpoint at the current line.

▶ **Breakpoints** (the second item of that name) makes the Breakpoints window appear. The Breakpoints window lists all the breakpoints set in the target program. You can add or delete breakpoints, set options on a breakpoint, or make stopping at a breakpoint conditional on some state in your program.

▶ **Console** opens the Console window, for standard I/O with your program, and also for issuing typed commands to the underlying gdb debugger.

Now we can step through `Linrg` one line at a time. To get a sense of this, scroll the variable display—at the upper right of the Debugger window—down so that the values of the `sumX` through `sumXY` variables are visible.

Click the **Step Over** button a couple of times. The highlight indicating the currently executing line moves down the display of `main.c` in the Debugger window's editor; as you pass the corresponding line, you see the values for `sumX`, `sumY`, and so on change to `0` (but see the Note on page 35). Whenever an entry in the variable display changes in value, the new value is shown in red.

But wait. We see `sumY`, `sumX2`, `sumY2`, and `sumXY` get set to `0`, but `sumX` still displays in black the junk value it had at the start. Did it get set? Will it? A quick examination of `main.c` in the editor pane shows that we don't initialize `sumX`. The line that should zero it out initializes `sumXY` twice instead.

Let's resolve to do something about that later. For now, we can force `sumX` into good order by double-clicking its value, typing **0**, and pressing **Return**. The Xcode debugger and `gdb`, on which it is based, enable you to set variable contents on-the-fly.

Another click of **Step Over** takes us to the following line:

```
int     nScanned = scanf("%lg %lg", &x, &y);
```

We click **Step Over** at this line and find that **Step Over** is disabled. What's happening? This line can't complete execution until the input of two floating-point numbers either succeeds or fails. Awaiting input, `scanf()` blocks. To supply some, click the Console window to activate, and enter the following:

**1.0  2.05**

Press **Return**. The application is no longer blocked waiting for input; `scanf()` returns, and the debugger can now honor our **Step Over** instruction by stopping at the next line.

Stepping slowly through the lines that follow, we see the progress of `Linrg` reflected in the changing values in the Variable pane:

▶ `nScanned` ← 2

▶ `n` ← 1

▶ `sumX` ← 1

▶ `sumX2` ← 1

▶ `sumY`← 2.04999... (floating-point math can't represent 2.05 exactly)

▶ `sumY2` ← 4.202499...

▶ `sumXY` ← 2.04999...

The next step takes us to the test for the `do...while` loop. Click **Step Over**; control goes not to the first line of the loop but to the first line after. The loop test failed.

Check the reason: Scroll to the top of the Variable pane to find nScanned. It isn't 2, so the loop test fails. It was 2 in the body of the loop; why isn't it now? Did it change? A review of the lines before the current one confirms that we didn't change it. There is no assignment and no possibility of pointer aliasing, all the way back to where nScanned is assigned.

Assigned—and *declared*—inside the loop. With a livelier eye, we now see two nScanned lines in the Variable pane, one of the lines labeled "out of scope." Sure enough, nScanned is declared inside the loop and separately as a local variable for the main() function. The outer variable, with its original garbage value, got tested in the loop condition; the loop-defined nScanned masked it from being updated.

How embarrassing. There's no point in continuing this run of Linrg, so click the **Stop** button.

Let's turn the declaration of nScanned at the beginning of the loop

```
int     nScanned = scanf("%lg %lg", &x, &y);
```

into a plain assignment:

```
nScanned = scanf("%lg %lg", &x, &y);
```

We can make the changes in the editor pane of the Debugger window. Click **Build and Go**. When the Debugger stops at the old breakpoint, click **Continue** and let the program run:

**1.0   2.05**

No crash; no early exit. Excellent.

Enter some more data to flesh out an approximate line of $y = 2x$:

**2.01   4**
**3   5.987**
**4   8.1**
**5   10.0**

Now what? Like many UNIX tools, Linrg is meant to read standard input until it runs out. One signals the end of input at a terminal by typing the end-of-file character, ^D. Typing ^D terminates the input stream in the Console window, too. Now scanf() returns -1 to signal end-of-stream, no further additions are made to the statistics, and the loop exits.

> **NOTE**
>
> The Console window won't catch the ^D unless it is pressed twice or entered on a separate line.

At last, Linrg responds with actual numbers:

**1.80163    0.618914    0.899816**

But something's wrong: $y = 1.8x + 0.62$ is an implausible result, given that our data never strayed more than 0.1 from $y = 2x$. And although a 0.90 correlation coefficient isn't bad, it doesn't reflect how close the data is to a straight line.

We have to step through Linrg again, line by line, looking for what went wrong. Make sure that the breakpoint at the beginning of main() is still set, and click the **Go** button in the Debugger window toolbar. (The last action to execute Linrg was **Debug**, so Go will once again activate the debugger.) We step through, watching the change in variables and deciding whether the changes make sense. Clicking **Step Over** once initializes n. Clicking the button again initializes the sum… variables (see Figure 3.4).

> ### NOTE
>
> You will probably get different results from this. In fact, Mac OS X 10.5 may initialize all of a program's memory to zero before it is run, making this bug completely invisible. Nonetheless, there is a real bug here, and for purposes of instruction, we'll prosecute it.

FIGURE 3.4     The sum… variables after the execution of line 12 in main.c of Linrg. On the screen, all the variables show 0, indicating that they have been changed to that value. Only sumX remains at its uninitialized value.

Oh, yes. Back when we were first stepping through Linrg, we meant to correct the failure to initialize sumX, and we haven't done that yet. We'll do so now. Don't click **Terminate**. Instead, edit the first sumXY in the line we just executed into sumX. Then click **Fix**; if you have not set builds to save files automatically, you should accept Xcode's offer to save your change to `main.c`. Almost immediately, the status bar in the Debugger window should indicate that the build succeeded and that the fix was incorporated into `Linrg`.

---

**Fixing Code in the Debugger**

You can't fix everything:

▶ You can't make a change that increases the number of local variables currently on the stack. Stack space has already been committed on the basis of the original, smaller demand, and Xcode has no good way of performing all the memory fixes that moving existing stack variables would require.

▶ For the same reason, you can't change the number of arguments a function on the stack takes.

▶ You can't change the name or return type of a function on the stack.

▶ You can't add an Objective-C class. New C++ classes are okay so long as they are not new specializations of template classes.

▶ You can't make a structural change to an Objective-C object: You can't add or remove methods or instance variables and expect the change to have effect on instances created before or after the change. The Objective-C runtime constructs its method-dispatch tables early in the life of an application, and the runtime is simply not designed for unloading and reloading class definitions.

Note also that if you fix a file that defines globals, they will be reinitialized.

Do a full-text search on "Modifying Running Code" in the Developer Tools Reference documentation set in the Xcode Documentation window for complete details.

---

Now drag the red arrowhead in the left margin of the Debugger window's editor up to line 11 (see Figure 3.5). This resets `Linrg`'s program counter so that line 11 will once again be the next line to be executed. Clicking **Step Over** executes the line, and we see by the Variable pane that `sumXY` is now initialized to 0.

Now click the **Continue** button, and enter the test data:

```
1.0  2.05
2.01  4
3  5.987
4  8.1
5  10.0
(^D)
2.00196    0.0175146    0.999871
```

We can believe $y = 2x + 0.018$, and a correlation as close to 1.0 as this makes no difference.

**FIGURE 3.5**    Dragging the red arrowhead in the margin of the editor pane of the Debugger window sets the next line to be executed. Here, we move the pointer to the line before our change that initializes sumX.

## Summary

In Chapter 2, we were led straight to a crashing bug when the debugger intervened at the crash. In this chapter, we used the Xcode debugger to take charge of how Linrg executes. We saw how to examine variables as they change value and how to change them directly from the Debugger window. We also saw how to fix minor bugs in a program without having to quit the program to edit, recompile, and relink. We even moved the program counter back so that our fix would be executed.

This chapter has completed our first pass through the life cycle—edit, compile, link, execute, and debug—of software development. In Chapter 4, "Compilation: The Basics," we step back and consider the elements of that life cycle.

CHAPTER 4

# Compilation: The Basics

**IN THIS CHAPTER**

▷ **What Happens in a Build**

▷ **The Task of Compilation**

▷ **Linkage and Symbols**

▷ **Dynamic Linkage**

Before continuing, let's review how computer programs get made. If you're coming to Xcode from long experience with GNU make or another development environment, this discussion will be very familiar to you.

Programmers use *source code* to specify what a program does; source code files contain a notation that, although technical and sometimes cryptic, is recognizably the product of a human, intended in part for humans to read and understand. Even the most precise human communication leaves to allusion and implication things that a computer has to have spelled out. When the Linrg tool refers to the local variable slope, for example, we cared only that the name slope should consistently refer to the result of a particular calculation; the central processor of a computer running Linrg, however, cares about the amount of memory allocated to slope, the format by which it is interpreted, how memory is reserved for the use of slope and later released, that the memory should be aligned on the proper address boundary, that no conflicting use be made of that memory, and finally, precisely how the address of slope is to be determined when data is to be stored or retrieved there. The same issues have to be resolved for each and every named thing in a program.

## Compiling

Fortunately, we have a computer to keep track of such things. A *compiler* is a program that takes source files and generates the corresponding streams of machine-level instructions. Consider the following lines from Linrg:

```c
int      nScanned;
do {
    double   x, y;
    nScanned = scanf("%lg %lg", &x, &y);
    if (nScanned == 2) {
        n++;
        sumX += x;
        sumX2 += x * x;
        sumY += y;
        sumY2 += y * y;
        sumXY += x * y;
    }
} while (nScanned == 2);
```

These 13 lines translate into 21 lines of *assembly code,* a notation in which each line is a separate instruction to the processor (a PowerPC in this case):

```
LC0:
    .ascii  "%lg %lg\0"  ; Reserve and initialize string constant
...
L2:                                            ; Top of loop
    addis   r3,r31,ha16(LC0-"L00000000001$pb")
    addi    r4,r1,80                           ; x is at r1 + 80
    addi    r5,r1,88                           ; y is at r1 + 88
    la      r3,lo16(LC0-"L00000000001$pb")(r3) ; point to format
    bl      L_scanf$stub                       ; call scanf ()
    cmpwi   cr7,r3,2                           ; Is result 2?
    bne-    cr7,L7                             ; No: jump to L7
    lfd     f0,80(r1)                          ; Yes: Fetch x.
    addi    r30,r30,1                          ; Add 1 to n
    lfd     f13,88(r1)                         ; Fetch y.
    fadd    f30,f30,f0                         ; sumX += x
    fmadd   f26,f0,f13,f26                     ; sumXY += x * y
    fmadd   f28,f0,f0,f28                      ; sumX2 += x * x
    fadd    f29,f29,f13                        ; sumY += y
    fmadd   f27,f13,f13,f27                    ; sumY2 += y * y
    b       L2                                 ; Loop back again
                                               ; Exit of loop
L7:
```

When imagining the tasks a compiler must perform in producing executable machine instructions from human-readable source, the first thing that comes to mind is the choice of machine

### NOTE

You don't have to understand this code deeply. The points to carry away are (1) source code becomes machine instructions; and (2) managing symbols is much of what a compiler does.

instructions: the translation of floating-point add operations into `fadd` add instructions or expressing the `while` loop in terms of `cmpwi`, `bne`, and `b`. Another important task is the management of *symbols*. Each C function and every variable has to be expressed in machine code in terms of regions of memory, with addresses and extents. A compiler has to keep strict account of every symbol, assigning an address—or at least a way of getting an address—for it and making sure that no two symbols get overlapping sections of memory.

In its analysis of `main()`, the compiler budgeted a certain amount of memory in RAM (random access memory) for local variables and assigned general-purpose register `r1` to keep track of that block. The 8-byte floating-point number x was assigned to the memory beginning 80 bytes into that block (80 + r1, or `80(r1)` in the assembler's address notation); y was assigned to the 8 bytes beginning at `88(r1)`. The compiler made sure not to use that memory for any other purpose.

The sums for the regression don't even get stored in memory but are computed in the processor's floating-point registers and used from there. Register `f30`, for instance, holds the value of the `sumX` variable. Once again, the compiler makes sure that each symbol gets associated with a particular piece of storage.

In an Xcode project, files that are to be compiled are found under the target to which they belong, in the Compile Sources build phase. Open the **Targets** group by clicking its disclosure triangle, and then open the application target's disclosure triangle when it appears. The build phases for that target will appear and can themselves be opened for inspection or editing. See Figure 4.1 for an example from the Linear application project we'll soon be building.

> **NOTE**
>
> Why don't the calculations in the compiled code from `Linrg` follow the order specified in the source code? For instance, the sum of products of x and y is calculated second in the compiled code, although the statement `sumXY += x * y` appeared last in `Linrg`'s read loop. The compiled code shown here was generated with optimization turned on, which among other things lets the compiler change the order of operations for efficiency, so long as the changes do not change the overall effect of the code. This reordering is why you generally shouldn't turn optimization on if you intend to observe execution in the debugger: Control will appear to jump discontinuously through the source statements, which is very confusing.

FIGURE 4.1    The build phases in the **Linear** target, with **Compile Sources** expanded to show the source files that go into the application. This listing is quite separate from the file listing in the upper part of the Groups & Files list. The upper listing determines whether the project contains a reference to a file, used or not; the file's presence in a build phase determines what Xcode will do with the file.

# Linking

The accounting task does not end there. Five lines after L2 comes the instruction:

```
bl    L_scanf$stub
```

This line is the translation of the call to the scanf() function. What sort of symbol is Lscanf$stub? This symbol refers to a short code segment produced behind the scenes by the compiler:

```
L_scanf$stub:
    .indirect_symbol    _scanf
    mflr    r0
    bcl     20,31,L2$_scanf
L2$_scanf:
    mflr    r11
    addis   r11, r11,ha16(L_scanf$lazy_ptr-L2$_scanf)
    mtlr    r0
    lwzu    r12, lo16(L_scanf$lazy_ptr-L2$_scanf)(r11)
    mtctr   r12
    bctr
.data
.lazy_symbol_pointer
L_scanf$lazy_ptr:
    .indirect_symbol _scanf
    .long dyld_stub_binding_helper
    .subsections_via_symbols
```

This code segment is a bit convoluted but amounts to loading the address stored at L_scanf$lazy_ptr and continuing execution at that address. The next question is this: What is stored at L_scanf$lazy_ptr? The code says that it is the address _scanf. And there the trail goes cold because the compiled code for main() does not assign any memory to a code block—or anything else—named _scanf.

And a good thing, too, because scanf() is a component of the standard C library. We don't want to define it ourselves: We want to use the code that comes in the library. But the compiler, which works with only one .c file at a time, doesn't have any way of referring directly to the starting address of scanf(). The compiler has to leave that address as a blank to be filled in later; therefore, in building a program, there has to be an additional step for filling in such blanks.

The product of the compiler, an *object file*, contains the machine code generated from a source file, along with directories detailing what symbols are defined in that file and what symbols still need definitions filled in. Under Xcode's gcc compiler, as with many others, C source files have the suffix .c; object files have the same name, with the .c removed and .o (for object) substituted. Libraries are single files that collect object files supplying useful definitions for commonly used symbols. In the simplest case, a library has a name beginning with lib and suffixed with .a.

The process of back-filling unresolved addresses in compiled code is called *linkage editing*, or simply *linking*. You present the linker with a set of object files and libraries, and, you hope, the linker finds among them a definition for every unresolved symbol your application uses. Every address that had been left blank for later will then be filled in. The result is an executable file containing all the code that gets used in the application (see Figure 4.2).

This process corresponds to the Link Binary with Libraries build phase in the application's target listing. This phase lists all the libraries and frameworks against which the application is to be linked.

# Dynamic Loading

In fact, it's one step more complicated than that. Standard routines, such as scanf(), will be used by many—possibly hundreds—of applications on a given system. Copying the machine code that implements scanf() into each application is a pointless waste of disk space. The solution is *dynamic loading*, referred to in the preceding assembly snippets by the abbreviation dyld: The application leaves the addresses of common library functions unresolved even in the final executable file, providing the partial executable code along with a dictionary of symbols to be resolved and the system libraries to find them in. The operating system then fetches the missing code and links it into the executable when the application runs.

Dynamic loading doesn't save only disk space but can also save RAM and execution time. Dynamic libraries—collections of object files set up for dynamic linking and having the prefix lib and the suffix .dylib—are loaded as read-only memory-mapped files. If two or more applications load the same dynamic library, the Mac OS X kernel will share the same in-RAM copy of the file between them. The second and subsequent users of a dynamic library therefore don't incur memory or load-time costs.

Also, dynamic libraries can be updated to fix bugs and improve performance. Installing a new version of a library will improve all the applications that use it, without any need to change the application code itself.

For these reasons, dynamic linkage is much preferred in Mac OS X's tool set over static linking (the merging of library components directly into the executable file). When you specify library names and search directories for linkage to an application, the linker will look for .dylib files for dynamic linkage first and will use static linkage with .a files only if there is no .dylib.

If dynamic libraries don't literally get linked with the application's executable code until runtime, why do they figure in the linkage phase of the build process at all? There are two reasons. First, the linker can verify that all the unresolved symbols in your application are defined somewhere and can issue an error

> **NOTE**
>
> Sometimes you prefer a static library, such as when you want a specific version, or can't rely on the dynamic version's being installed on your users' computers. To force the linker to use a static library, pass the library's full pathname in a -l option to the linker. This technique also works for libraries not named according to the lib*.a or lib*.dylib convention.

message if you specified a misspelled or absent function. Second, the linker-built tables in the dynamically linked code specify not only the symbols that need resolving but also what libraries the needed definitions are to be found in. With files specified, the dynamic loader does not have to search all the system's libraries for each symbol, and the application can specify private dynamic libraries that would not be in any general search path.

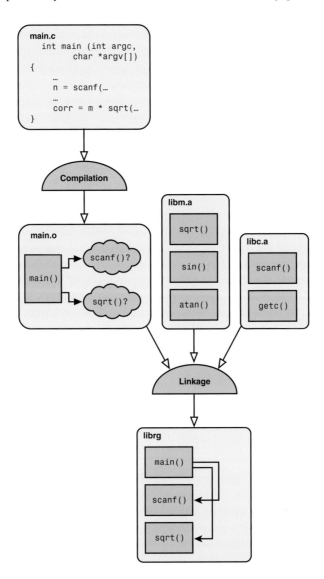

FIGURE 4.2    The greatly simplified process of building Linrg. Function main() in main.c refers to scanf() and sqrt(), but main.c provides no definitions; compiling main.c produces a main.o object file with unresolved references. Definitions are to be found in libc.a and libm.a. The linkage phase of building Linrg produces an executable file that contains both main() and the functions it refers to.

# Legacy Technologies

Up until Xcode 3.0, there were two other linkage options to consider: *prebinding* and *ZeroLink*.

## Prebinding

In Mac OS X before version 10.3.4, true dynamic loading—determining that a library is needed, staking out a stretch of RAM for it, and stitching together all the references to its contents—was not an efficient process. Assigning memory regions among the pieces of dynamically linked applications was slow enough to impose significant delays on the process of launching a Mac OS X application.

The solution to this problem was *prebinding*. A library is said to be prebound if it specifies an address at which it prefers to be loaded. The author of the library chooses an address that does not collide with any other prebound library, and the linker, when building the prebound .dylib, prefills any pointers in the library, on the assumption that the library will be loaded at its prebound address. A prebound application is built exclusively from prebound libraries and has almost all the address arithmetic necessary to load it already done.

By applying the Shark performance analysis tool to the dynamic loader, Apple engineers found ways to bind library addresses, at runtime, that are at least as fast as prebinding. As of Mac OS X version 10.3.4, prebinding of applications is no longer necessary.

## ZeroLink

You'll have gathered by now that the task of linking and loading a complex application is tedious and time-consuming. Indeed, with most development systems, the linker can add a significant delay between editing source code and running the results. This delay weighs particularly heavy in the edit-compile-link-run-debug work cycle most developers spend most of their days pursuing.

To answer this problem, Apple's Xcode engineers devised ZeroLink. When a program was built with ZeroLink, most linkage was skipped altogether: At runtime, only the barest core of the program was actually runnable; when unresolved symbols were found, ZeroLink would look for them among the program's object files, and only then load and link them. Because this would occur at runtime, when idle time is plentiful, and only for program features that were actually being exercised, ZeroLink could save a lot of time in the development cycle.

Three things transpired that took the bloom off the ZeroLink rose:

▶ Because ZeroLink skipped rigorous linkage altogether, programs never got checked for whether the symbols they used actually existed. Many programmers were confused when builds that went smoothly under ZeroLink failed without it.

▶ ZeroLink relied on finding a program's object files at runtime. It looked for them at specific paths in the developer's hard drive. Developers would often forget about this, and distribute ZeroLinked programs to others. Because they didn't have the separate object files, the programs wouldn't run. More confusion and embarrassment.

▶ Computers got faster, and in particular, Apple's linker got faster. ZeroLink no longer saves as much time as it had when it was introduced.

For these reasons, Xcode 3 no longer supports ZeroLink. A build setting for turning it on still exists, but the Xcode tools ignore it. It is preserved in case a project is shared with developers using Xcode 2.

## Summary

In this chapter, we reviewed the process of compiling and linking an application, with particular reference to Mac OS X. The big task in the entire process is the management of symbols. We covered dynamic loading, how prebinding was once a solution to problems with it, and how ZeroLink was used to shorten the development loop.

CHAPTER 5

# Starting a Cocoa Application

**IN THIS CHAPTER**

▷ **A Simple Graphical Application**

▷ **Model-View-Controller**

▷ **Adding Files to a Project**

In this chapter, we make the Linrg tool the heart of an application using the Mac OS X graphical human interface. Our framework for the application will be Cocoa, the application toolkit developed from NeXTStep and OpenStep; the language will be Objective-C.

## Plan of Action

### Program Tasks

We'll use Linrg unchanged for the computational part of the program. Our front-end program will therefore have the tasks of

- ▶ Storing a list of *x* and *y* data pairs

- ▶ Allowing the user to enter and edit the data-pair list

- ▶ Passing the data-pair list to Linrg

- ▶ Reading the results from Linrg and displaying them to the user

> **NOTE**
>
> Keeping Linrg as a separate executable is admittedly a strange decision: The code is so simple it would be easier to fold it into the main application. We're doing it this way to illustrate a few additional points about how Xcode builds applications.

## Model-View-Controller

Cocoa applications are built around the design pattern called Model-View-Controller (MVC). The pattern asserts that three kinds of things comprise an interactive program:

1. *Model objects* embody the data and logic of a particular problem domain. Models tend to be unique to each application.

2. *View objects* handle user interaction, presenting information and enabling the user to manipulate data or otherwise influence the behavior of the program. Views are usually drawn from a repertoire of standard elements, such as buttons, tables, scrollers, and text areas. Views tend to have no intelligence about any particular problem domain: A button can display itself and report button clicks without having to know what clicking would mean in your application.

3. *Controller objects* mediate between the pure logic of the model and the pure mechanics of the views. A controller object decides how model content will be displayed by the views and how user actions translate into model events.

> **NOTE**
>
> The MVC pattern is important to know, because many of Apple's developer tools are built on the assumption that you are using that pattern. If you aren't, you might find they don't support your efforts as well as they might, or that you are actually fighting them.

## The Model

It seems plain that the first task of our program—storing a list of data pairs—is the sort of task a model object performs. Similarly, the task of calculating the linear regression is purely a function of the data we present to the calculation and would be the same no matter how we managed the data points beforehand or presented the results afterward.

What we want, then, is a document containing a set of data points and the results of calculating a linear regression on them. This simple design is shown in Figure 5.1.

We will be working in Objective-C, which provides the easiest access to Cocoa. From the figure, it's natural to imagine the interface for a `DataPoint` object:

```
@interface  DataPoint : NSObject <NSCoding> {
    double      x;
    double      y;
}
- (id) init;
- (id) initWithX: (double) xValue Y: (double) yValue;

- (double)   x;
- (void)   setX: (double)  newValue;
- (double)   y;
- (void)   setY: (double)  newValue;
@end
```

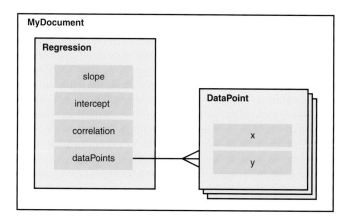

FIGURE 5.1    The minimal data model for a program that manages linear regressions. The document contains a list of data points and the results of the regression done on them. The regression refers to the list of data points.

This code segment declares DataPoint to be a subclass of the basic NSObject class, promises that DataPoint will be able to read and write itself in data streams according to the NSCoding protocol, and says that its data consists of two double-precision numbers: x and y. The code then declares a default initializer (init) and an initializer that sets the instance values (initWithX:Y:). After that comes accessors for reading and setting the x and y values. Simple.

The interface for the Regression class is mostly the same concept, applied to the four data members rather than two:

```
@interface  Regression : NSObject <NSCoding> {
    NSMutableArray *      dataPoints;
    double                slope;
    double                intercept;
    double                correlation;

    NSTask *              linrgTask;
}
- (id) init;

- (double) slope;
- (void) setSlope: (double) aSlope;

- (double) intercept;
- (void) setIntercept: (double) anIntercept;

- (double) correlation;
- (void) setCorrelation: (double) aCorrelation;
```

```
- (NSMutableArray *) dataPoints;
- (void) setDataPoints: (NSMutableArray *) aDataPoints;

- (BOOL) canCompute;
- (void) computeWithLinrg;
@end
```

Once again, we see the descent from NSObject, the promise of NSCoding, the four data members, and accessor methods for those members. We make dataPoints an NSMutableArray, which is a Cocoa class that keeps ordered lists of objects. There are two additional public methods:

1. The method canCompute returns YES—the Objective-C equivalent of true—only if at least two data points are available. This isn't a comprehensive test for whether the regression would be valid, but it's a start.

2. The method computeWithLinrg calculates the slope, intercept, and correlation coefficient.

One instance variable, linrgTask, didn't figure in our sketch model. This variable is an NSTask, an object used for running command-line tools from Cocoa applications. We'll be using an NSTask to run Linrg on our data points.

---

**Accessors**

For every property named *propertyName* of type *type* in a class, the key-value coding (KVC) protocol has us writing a pair of methods:

▶ (*type*) *propertyName*;

▶ (void) *setPropertyName*: (*type*) aValue;

The individual methods are not difficult to write—they are almost identical—but they are tedious. Can't we automate the task of generating property accessors?

We can. The solution is found in Xcode's **Script** menu—it appears in the menu bar as a scroll (  )—in the **Code** submenu. Select the four lines that declare Regression's instance variables, and select **Script > Code > Place Accessor Decls on Clipboard**. You can now paste declarations for setter and getter methods for each of the three instance variables into the header. Reselect the instance-variable declarations, and select **Place Accessor Defs on Clipboard** so that you can paste the complete methods into the implementation file.

If we were to use Objective-C 2.0, provided for Mac OS X 10.5 and later, we could take advantage of built-in accessors, which relieve the need to define accessor methods, and make shortcuts such as aDataPoint.x = 2.0 possible. However, we want Linear to be compatible with 10.4, so we can't use Objective-C 2.0 extensions.

## The Controller

The controller object we create will be an instance of `MyDocument`, a subclass of Cocoa's `NSDocument`. Xcode's template for a new Cocoa document-based application automatically includes skeleton code for a `MyDocument` class.

`NSDocument`s are automatically placed in the command-response chain of the application and bring with them the basics of loading and storing a document's contents in the file system. We can expect our documents to be told to load and store themselves, to compute the linear regression, and to add, edit, and remove data points. Therefore, we want to provide methods for loading and storing and computing. These tasks can be done through `Regression`, our top-level model object, so we conclude that `MyDocument` needs to add an instance variable only for a `Regression` object.

Strangely, we won't be providing any methods for managing the data points. More on this later.

```
@class    Regression;
@interface MyDocument : NSDocument
{
    Regression * model;
}
- (IBAction) compute: (id) sender;

@end
```

By the vagaries of the Objective-C language, it is not necessary to declare in the interface every method a class implements. One method we do need to declare is `compute:`, the method that triggers calculation of the regression. As a method that responds to commands from the application's human interface, `compute:` follows a strict signature—taking one anonymous object (type `id`), the sender of the command, and returning `IBAction`, which is `#defined` as `void` but serves to inform Interface Builder that this command may be issued to this class by the human interface.

## The Views

The view layer of our program is best specified by how we want it to look and behave. Figure 5.2 shows what we're aiming for.

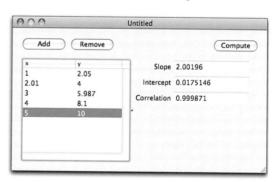

FIGURE 5.2     Planned layout of the main window of our linear-regression program. The **Add** and **Remove** buttons insert and delete points in the data set, which can be edited directly in the table at left. The **Compute** button passes the points to `Linrg` and causes the results to be displayed in the read-only fields below it.

# Starting a New Project

We start by selecting **New Project** from the **File** menu (or pressing ⇧⌘N). Once again, Xcode presents a choice of project templates; pick **Application > Cocoa Document-Based Application.** We'll name the project `Linear`.

Where will we put the new project? That depends on what we'll be doing with `Linrg`, which we intend to keep at the heart of Linear.

## Adding `Linrg`

We are going to embed the `Linrg` tool in our application. We want the build process for Linear to copy a completely built `Linrg` into the application bundle; if a completely built `Linrg` isn't available, we want one built. You can include the products of other projects in an Xcode project, with one restriction: The two projects have to put their products into the same directory; Xcode won't be able to track changes without it, even if a dependency is set up.

There are two ways to do this. One way is to double-click the project (top) icon in the Groups & Files list in each of the projects concerned and then in the **General** tab of the resulting Get Info panel, select **Place Build Products In > Custom Location.** Choose the same folder each time. That way, all projects will put their products in the same directory, satisfying the restriction.

The other way is to put both projects into the same directory. In that case, they will both use the same subdirectory, `build`, as their products directory. This also satisfies the restriction.

We'll go the second way: We will create Linear's project in the same directory as `Linrg`. In the project-naming panel, click the **Choose** button, and use the resulting open-file dialog to select the directory containing your Linrg project. Click **OK.** The path in the project-naming panel will now end in `/Linrg/Linear`, putting the new project in a subdirectory of `Linrg`, not the same directory. Delete `/Linear` from the path, and click **Finish.**

The skeleton of the Linear project, built from Xcode's template, now appears in a new project window. This skeleton consists of a `main.m` file, which you won't be editing, and a `MyDocument.m` file, which will host the principal controller code. The project is linked to the Cocoa framework, and other frameworks are included, but not linked, for ready reference. A `credits.rtf` file provides content for an automatically generated About box for the application. NIB files specify human-interface appearance and behavior.

We mean to include `Linrg`, so let's do that now. From the **Project** menu, select **Add to Project** (⌥⌘A). Find and select the `Linrg.xcodeproj` project document in the same directory as the Linear project, and click **Add.** Click **Add** again for the options sheet that appears next; we don't need to copy the file for local use, the default file-reference style and UTF-8 encoding are okay, and we have only one target it could apply to. An Xcode project icon labeled `Linrg.xcodeproj` can now be found under the **Linear** project icon.

We could also have added the `Linrg. xcodeproj` document by dragging it from the Finder into the Groups & Files list.

Having made the Linear project aware of the Linrg project, we now have to tell Xcode what to do with it—that we want `Linrg` built whenever Linear is built.

Opening the Targets group in the Groups & Files list reveals Linear, the only target this project has: Double-click the **Linear** application icon to open the Get Info window for the target. The first

tab of the window, **General**, includes a listing for **Direct Dependencies**. Click the + button below the list; in the sheet that emerges, select the **Linrg** product of `Linrg. xcodeproj` (see Figure 5.3). Then click **Add Target** and close the window. Now the process of building Linear will include a build, if necessary, of `Linrg`.

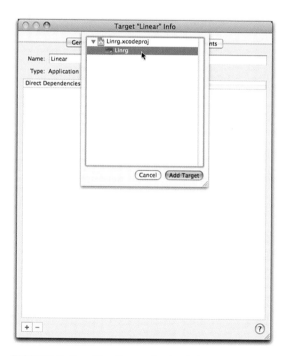

FIGURE 5.3　The **General** tab of the Target Info window for `Linear.app`, showing the sheet for adding a dependency. Only one Xcode project is inside the Linear project and there is only one product of that project. Selecting it and clicking **Add Target** ensures that `Linrg` will always be up-to-date when it is included among Linear's resources.

So far we have ensured that Linrg will be built. There is one more step in making Linrg a part of the Linear application: We want Xcode to move the newly-built Linrg into the Linear application package.

To do this, go back to the Linear target in the Targets group, and click the disclosure triangle next to the icon. This shows the steps that Xcode will take to produce the Linear application. You see that the first of these steps, building Linrg, is represented by a tool icon labeled "**Linrg (from Linrg.xcode-proj)**." But in addition to building Linrg, we want Xcode to copy it into Linear. Xcode does such copies in the second build phase, Copy Bundle Resources. Open the Copy Bundle Resources phase by clicking the disclosure triangle next to it. Inside the build phase are the application's NIB files, the Credits RTF file, and a file, InfoPList.strings, that specifies text to describe Linear in the Finder and elsewhere. We want to tell Xcode that Linrg belongs in this group.

We do this by finding Linrg in the Groups & Files list (click the disclosure triangle next to Linrg.xcodeproj) and dragging its icon into the Copy Bundle Resources phase (see Figure 5.4).

Now, whenever Linear is built, the Linrg tool will be made a part of the application.

> **NOTE**
>
> Mac OS X applications consist of a directory including the executable application file, plus the additional resource files it may need. See Chapter 11, "File Packages and Bundles," for details.

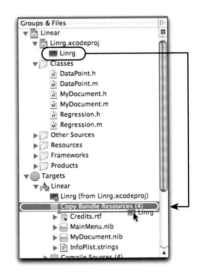

FIGURE 5.4    Telling Xcode that Linrg should be part of the Linear application by adding it to the Copy Bundle Resources build phase. Make sure that both Linrg (the one inside Linrg.xcodeproj, near the top of the Groups & Files list) and the Copy Bundle Resources build phase are visible (Targets > Linear > Copy Bundle Resources). Drag Linrg into the Copy Bundle Resources build phase.

# Implementation: Model

Now it's time to bring our design to reality. We start by creating source files for our model classes: DataPoint and Regression.

## DataPoint **Model Class**

Select **New** from the **File** menu or press ⌘**N**. Xcode will present you with a list of file templates, including the choice of creating a blank file. Following the example of Figure 5.5, choose **Objective-C Class** in the **Cocoa** category, and click **Next**.

FIGURE 5.5    The New File Assistant, showing the option of creating a pair of new files containing a template for a subclass of NSObject.

You are then asked to name your file and the class it defines; type **DataPoint**, leaving the .m suffix in the **Name** field (Objective-C implementation files use the .m suffix). Make sure to check the check box offering to create a corresponding interface (.h) file. Xcode now presents you with a new file, named DataPoint.h, containing the skeleton of DataPoint as a class derived from NSObject.

We already know the contents of DataPoint.h, having specified it in our design sketch. Fill it out, and then press ⌥⌘**up arrow**, which should make the counterpart—.c, .cpp, or .m file for .h, or vice versa—file for DataPoint.h visible. Here's the start of what should go in it—a reference to the interface file and the initialization and accessor methods:

```
#import "DataPoint.h"
@implementation DataPoint
// Default initializer. Sets x and y to 0.0.
 - (id) init
{
    return [self initWithX: 0.0 Y: 0.0];
}
// Designated initializer (all initializers lead to this one).
- (id) initWithX: (double) xValue Y: (double) yValue
{
```

```
    if (self = [super init]) {
        x = xValue;
        y = yValue;
    }
    return self;
}
#pragma mark Key-Value Coding
// Getters and setters for the x and y attributes.
- (double) x { return x; }
- (void) setX: (double) newValue { x = newValue; }

- (double) y { return y; }
- (void) setY: (double) newValue { y = newValue; }
```

Instances of DataPoint have two attributes, *x* and *y*, which in this simple case correspond directly to the instance variables of the same name. We provide getter and setter methods for each.

---

MyCompanyName

The comment header of this file, and of all files Xcode creates, includes a copyright notice in the name of \_\_MyCompanyName\_\_. How annoying.

You could edit the copyright notice whenever you generate it, or you could do a multifile search-and-replace when you've accumulated several. It's better, however, to have your name, or your company's, there in the first place.

Xcode does not provide a graphical preference for setting this string. The setting is, however, settable through defaults, the command-line tool for editing system and application preferences. Open the Terminal application and enter the following

```
    defaults write com.apple.xcode \
        PBXCustomTemplateMacroDefinitions \
        '{ ORGANIZATIONNAME = "Joan Smith"; }'
```

---

NOTE

In this book, we provide getter and setter methods—accessors—for every attribute of a class on which we use Cocoa's binding layer. The KVC protocol, which the binding layer uses to monitor and set object values, specifies that for every attribute named *name* of an object, there should be a getter of the same name and a setter with a selector of the form set*Name:* (note the capital letter after set). Strictly speaking, accessor methods aren't needed in the case of attributes that are implemented simply as instance variables; in practice, however, it's cleaner to have the accessor methods.

It is useful to put `#pragma mark` lines wherever they make sense in source files. The compiler ignores them, but the pop-up menu of function names immediately above the editor pane will show the mark text in boldface, making navigation much easier. You can group #pragmas in the menu by placing a `#pragma mark -`, which inserts a dividing line.

We continue with a couple of methods required to fulfill the class interface's promise that `DataPoint` follows the `NSCoding` protocol—encodeWithCoder: and initWithCoder:. These methods simply transfer the x and y instance variables to and from an NSCoder data stream:

```
#pragma mark NSCoding

- (void) encodeWithCoder: (NSCoder *) coder
{
    [coder encodeDouble: x forKey: @"x"];
    [coder encodeDouble: y forKey: @"y"];
}

- (id) initWithCoder: (NSCoder *) coder
{
    [self setX: [coder decodeDoubleForKey: @"x"]];
    [self setY: [coder decodeDoubleForKey: @"y"]];
    return self;
}

@end
```

---

**Objective-C**

This book focuses on the workflow of Mac OS X programming rather than on the specific techniques of a given language. A good tutorial and reference on Objective-C can be found in the ADC Reference Library; search for "Introduction to the Objective-C Programming Language." However, you'll be seeing a lot of Objective-C in this book, so a reading knowledge of the language might be helpful.

The first thing to know about Objective-C is that it is a proper superset of C. Any legal C program is legal Objective-C. Objective-C is only a small addition to C. It introduces only one new expression type, the *message invocation*. A message invocation is delimited by brackets, begins with an object pointer, and continues with the name of a message and the message's parameters. For example, `[foo retain]` sends the `retain` message to the object pointed to by `foo`. A more complex invocation might be as follows:

```
    NSSize    unitSize = { 1.0, 1.0 };
    unitSize = [myView convertSize: unitSize
                fromView: nil];
```

Here, an `NSSize` struct is sent, along with `nil`, in the message convertSize:fromView: to myView. The returned value, another `NSSize` struct, is assigned to unitSize. Parameters to messages are interspersed with the message name, which usually documents each parameter. The colons, indicating the need for a parameter, are a part of the message name; `aMessage` and `aMessage:` would be two different messages.

The variable at the beginning of a message invocation is an object pointer. There are no static or stack-based objects in Objective-C. Objective-C adds a type, `id`, for a generic pointer to an object (like a `void` `*` that can accept messages), or you can get some compile-time type checking by specifying an explicit type pointer, such as `NSView` `*` or `DataPoint` `*`.

Classes are objects and can have methods. Class methods are declared and defined with a leading +, whereas instance methods are declared and defined with a leading -. It's common to refer to methods by a plus or minus to indicate their domain, followed by the class and signature in brackets, such as `-[NSView convertSize:fromView:]` or `+[NSObject alloc]`.

Method invocation is not as tightly bound to types in Objective-C as member-function calls are in C++. The same message can be sent to objects in different classes even if they have no common ancestor; the only thing that matters is the message selector (its name). It is therefore common in Objective-C programs to establish *informal protocols*, groups of methods that objects can implement to participate in the workings of a package. Objective-C also has formal protocols, whereby the compiler ensures that the class adopting the protocol implements all protocol methods, and assures the runtime that member objects conform.

Our work would be a lot easier if we could use Objective-C 2.0, which provides garbage-collected memory management and high-performance collection iterators. However, Objective-C 2.0 features require a runtime library that ships only with Mac OS X 10.5 or later. We're targeting 10.4 so we can't take advantage of it.

Now that we've finished `DataPoint`, have a look at the Groups & Files list. Chances are that `DataPoint.h` and `DataPoint.m` appear at the top of the list, outside any of the groups below the project icon. It's helpful to keep project files organized as you go along; these files really should be inside the Classes group. To select both files, click one of them and Command-click on the other. Then drag the pair inside the Classes group (see Figure 5.6). This has no effect on the placement of these files on your disk, but allows you to manage the clutter in the file list.

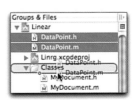

FIGURE 5.6  Dragging the `DataPoint` definition files into the Classes group. Command- or shift-click to select both files, and drag them so that an insertion bar appears below, and indented from, the Classes group folder.

## Regression **Model Class**

Now we can repeat the process for `Regression.m` and `Regression.h`. Create a new text file, make it for an Objective-C class, and include a header. Fill in `Regression.h` from the design, and then move on to `Regression.m`.

There isn't much new in the initialization and accessor methods of `Regression`, including the `NSCoding` methods; if you are stumped, you can find the full text of `Regression.m` in the CD-ROM directory for this chapter. What is new are the methods `canCompute` and `computeWithLinrg`:

```
+ (void) initialize
{
    // Let Key-Value Observing know that every time
    // dataPoints changes, canCompute may change.
    [self setKeys: [NSArray arrayWithObject: @"dataPoints"]
          triggerChangeNotificationsForDependentKey: @"canCompute"];
}

- (BOOL) canCompute
{
    return [dataPoints count] > 1;
}
```

Unlike `DataPoint`, `Regression` has a property, `canCompute`, that is not implemented as an instance variable and can't be directly set but must be computed by counting the number of points in the regression data. The `canCompute` method delivers the value of this property. Objects that monitor the state of `canCompute` will want to know when that state changes. Without a direct setter for the property, the change can't be detected directly, but in the `Regression` class-initialization method `initialize`, we use the class method `setKeys:triggerChangeNotificationsForDependentKey:` to tell the key-value observing system that any time the `dataPoints` property changes, `canCompute` may have changed, too.

The method `computeWithLinrg` passes data off to `Linrg` and makes our program ready to receive the results. This method is longer than the others we've seen, but the length owes more to tedium than to complexity:

```
- (void) computeWithLinrg
{
    if (! [self canCompute]) {
        // Regression not possible; zero out and give up.
        [self setSlope: 0.0];
        [self setIntercept: 0.0];
        [self setCorrelation: 0.0];
        return;
    }

    // With the Linrg tool...
    NSBundle *      myBundle = [NSBundle mainBundle];
    NSString *      linrgPath = [myBundle pathForResource: @"Linrg"
                                                   ofType: @""];
```

```objc
linrgTask = [[NSTask alloc] init];
[linrgTask setLaunchPath: linrgPath];

// ...hook into stdin...
NSPipe *        inputPipe = [[NSPipe    alloc] init];
NSFileHandle *  inputForData = [inputPipe
                                  fileHandleForWriting];
[linrgTask    setStandardInput: inputPipe];
[inputPipe    release];

//    ...hook into stdout...
NSPipe *            outputPipe = [[NSPipe alloc] init];
NSFileHandle *      outputForResults =
        [outputPipe fileHandleForReading];
[linrgTask setStandardOutput: outputPipe];
[outputPipe release];

// ...await   output   in   the   dataRead: method...
[[NSNotificationCenter defaultCenter]
    addObserver: self
        selector: @selector(dataRead:)
            name:
              NSFileHandleReadToEndOfFileCompletionNotification
          object: outputForResults];
[outputForResults readToEndOfFileInBackgroundAndNotify];

// ...and run Linrg.
[linrgTask launch];

// For each DataPoint...
NSEnumerator *      iter = [dataPoints objectEnumerator];
DataPoint *         curr;
while (curr = [iter nextObject]) {
  NSString *        currAsString;
  // ... format point as string...
  currAsString = [NSString stringWithFormat: @"%g %g\n",
                    [curr x], [curr y]];

  // ... reduce string to ASCII data...
  NSData *        currAsData = [currAsString
                                  dataUsingEncoding:
                                  NSASCIIStringEncoding];
  // ... put data into stdin...
  [inputForData writeData: currAsData];
}
```

```
    // ... then terminate stdin.
    [inputForData closeFile];
}
```

computeWithLinrg sets up Linrg as an external task and establishes pipes for communications with its standard input and output. The method runs Linrg and sends the data points, line by line, down the input pipe, until they run out. Then the method closes the pipe and returns. When it set up the output pipe, the method designated dataRead: as the method to handle the output:

```
- (void) dataRead: (NSNotification *) aNotice
{
    // When data arrives on stdout...
    NSDictionary *  info = [aNotice userInfo];
    NSData *        theData = [info objectForKey:
                            NSFileHandleNotificationDataItem];
    // ...convert the data to a string...
    NSString *      stringResult = [[NSString alloc]
                                initWithData: theData
                                encoding: NSASCIIStringEncoding];
    NSScanner *     scanner = [NSScanner
                                scannerWithString: stringResult];
    double          scratch;
    // ...and step through, collecting slope...
    [scanner scanDouble: &scratch];
    [self setSlope: scratch];

    // ... intercept...
    [scanner scanDouble: &scratch];
    [self setIntercept: scratch];

    // ...and correlation,
    [scanner scanDouble: &scratch];
    [self setCorrelation: scratch];
    [stringResult release];

    // Done with Linrg.
    [linrgTask release];
    linrgTask = nil;
}
```

Note the following two lines:

```
    NSBundle *      myBundle = [NSBundle mainBundle];
    NSString *      linrgPath = [myBundle pathForResource: @"Linrg"
                                        ofType: @""];
```

They reflect part of the structure of our application. The NSBundle class in Cocoa—and the CFBundle interfaces in Core Foundation—allow for programmatic access to structured directory trees, known as *bundles*. The application itself is a bundle, which can be accessed through the NSBundle object returned by [NSBundle mainBundle]. The method pathForResource:ofType: asks a bundle for the full POSIX-style pathname of a file within the bundle's Resources subdirectory, with the given name and extension.

This means that in the Finder, our program can appear as though it were a single file, Linear. In reality—and in command-line listings—the application would be a directory, Linear.app, containing a cluster of files needed for Linear to run, including, at Linear. app/Contents/Resources/Linrg, the Linrg command-line tool. See Chapter 11 for a detailed discussion.

## Model: Done

This finishes our model. Note how abstract the model classes are from the application we're trying to build: They don't do anything about displaying themselves, configuring editors, or responding to user input. The model classes just hold data and compute the regression statistics.

Nothing in our model classes would be out of place in an application that had no graphical interface. That's how we know that our model has been properly factored out of the rest of the application.

# Summary

In this chapter, we worked out a general design for a graphical program for doing linear regressions and analyzed it in light of the Model-View-Controller design pattern commonly used in Cocoa programming. We isolated the model tasks of managing the underlying data structures and produced Objective-C classes that did what we needed.

In terms of Xcode skills, we created a document-based Cocoa application and added classes to it, keeping the Groups & Files list organized along the way. We leveraged our work on the command-line tool Linrg by using the tool as the computational engine for the application and made the application depend on keeping Linrg up-to-date.

# CHAPTER 6

# A Cocoa Application: Views

**IN THIS CHAPTER**

▷ **Interface Builder**

▷ **Laying Out the Human Interface**

▷ **Making Rules for Sizing Views**

Now that the model is taken care of, we turn to the other end of the application: the views. Our design for the application relies on standard elements in the Mac OS X Aqua interface.

Interface Builder (IB) is the indispensable tool for laying out human interfaces for Mac OS X applications. It edits *NIB files*, which are archives of human-interface objects that your application reconstitutes when the files are loaded. All Cocoa applications have a main NIB file, which the Xcode application template names `MainMenu.nib`. This file contains at least the main menu bar for the application and may contain other application-wide windows and views.

An application can have more than one NIB, and a NIB can be loaded and its contents instantiated more than once. For instance, the Xcode template for a document-based Cocoa application includes a `MyDocument.nib` file. The file contains a trivial window for documents of the `MyDocument` class, and the template for the `MyDocument` class implementation specifies `MyDocument.nib` as the NIB to load when creating a new document.

Because our design calls for a window that displays the data points and regression statistics for each document, we want to edit the window in `MyDocument.nib` to match our design (which we laid out in Figure 5.2). In the Groups & Files list, click the triangle next to Resources to open that group. You should see `MyDocument.nib`, with the brass icon of a NIB file, in that group. Double-clicking this item launches Interface Builder and opens `MyDocument.nib` for editing.

# Interface Builder

The newly opened Interface Builder shows you four windows (see Figure 6.1). (Use **Hide Others** in the **Interface Builder** application menu to reduce the clutter.) The largest, named Window, contains a text element saying "Your document contents here" in the middle. Close this window.

FIGURE 6.1    Interface Builder on opening `MyDocument.nib`. The window that represents the NIB is at upper left; below it is the simple window, with some filler text, that comes in `MyDocument.nib` as provided in the template. To the right is the palette containing standard Aqua controls that can be dragged into windows, menu bars, or the NIB itself. In between is an inspector that enables you to set the properties of elements you add to the NIB.

The window at the upper left, MyDocument.nib, shows the NIB file as a file opened by Interface Builder (see Figure 6.2). It shows four icons. Three of them—**File's Owner**, **First Responder**, and **Application**—are placeholders for certain objects outside the NIB. Any other icons are for objects in the NIB—in this case, a window named **Window**.

Double-click the **Window** icon. The window we're building for the MyDocument class opens again.

> ## WARNING
>
> I have to be careful with my terminology here. At the upper-left corner of your screen is the window for the `MyDocument.nib` file. You opened that file with Interface Builder, you're editing the file, and you'll save it when you're done. Just below it is a window you're building for the use of the `MyDocument` class. In a sense, you're opening, editing, saving, and closing it, too, but the window is *inside* the `MyDocument.nib` file. I'll try to be as explicit as possible in distinguishing the NIB window from the prototype document window, but you might have to watch out for the distinction.

The window to the far right is a "Library" palette containing objects you can add to a NIB file (see Figure 6.3). We'll be using this window a lot.

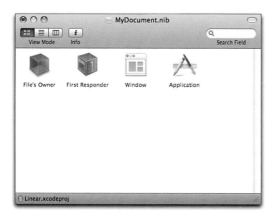

FIGURE 6.2    The window for the `MyDocument.nib` file contains icons for **File's Owner**, **First Responder**, and **Application**, which are placeholders for objects outside the NIB, along with an icon for every top-level object in the NIB. In this case, `MyDocument.nib` contains only a window, named **Window**.

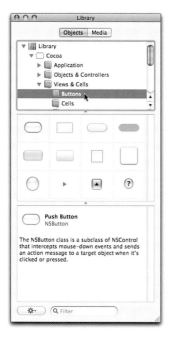

FIGURE 6.3    The Interface Builder Library palette. From this window, you can drag a wide variety of human-interface elements and other objects into your NIB. The top listing organizes the available objects into a hierarchical catalog. The middle array shows the objects that fit the current selection in the catalog, which can be further narrowed by typing search text into the field at the bottom of the palette. A description of the selected element appears just below the array.

In between is an "Inspector" palette. The contents of this window depend on what element of a window, or of the NIB itself, is currently selected. The Inspector displays properties of the selected object, such as title, appearance, and size, for you to edit.

## Layout

First, we will use Interface Builder as a pure layout tool for our human interface. We'll start by getting rid of that "Your document contents here" placard. Click it, and press the **Delete** key. It's gone.

> **NOTE**
>
> I've described these windows in terms of their position on the screen. Their exact relative positions will vary according to your previous use of Interface Builder: NIB files remember where their windows were last positioned, and Interface Builder itself preserves the positions of its palettes. You should identify the windows by their appearance, and not their relative positions.

Now let's add the buttons. We add human-interface elements to a window by dragging them from the Library palette into the window. The Library contains a lot of objects, so we have to narrow our choices down. There are two ways to do this. The first is to browse through the outline view at the top of the palette to find the element's category. In this case, we'd follow the path **Cocoa > Views & Cells > Buttons**. Or, we could type `button` into the search field at the bottom of the palette. Either way, the first object type to be found in the middle list is `NSButton`.

Drag the `NSButton` icon from the Library into the window we're building for `MyDocument` (see Figure 6.4). As you drag the button into the upper-left corner of the target window, blue lines appear at the window's margins. The Aqua human-interface guidelines specify certain margins between controls and within windows, and Interface Builder puts up guides to help you place your elements properly.

**Button** is not an especially informative title for a control. Our design calls for

FIGURE 6.4    Placing a button in Interface Builder. Drag the button from the Cocoa-Controls palette to the window being built. Lines will appear in the window when the button is placed properly according to the Aqua human-interface guidelines.

this button to be named **Add**. The easiest way to change the label is to double-click the button, making the text editable, and replace the title. Instead, we'll take this opportunity to have our first look at Interface Builder's Inspector. If the Inspector palette is not visible, make it so by selecting **Attributes Inspector** (⌘1) from the **Tools** menu. A utility window opens, offering a number of options for configuring the current selection—in this case, the button we just dragged in (see Figure 6.5). The field at the top of the Inspector is labeled **Title** and shows the current value, `Button`. Edit this to say `Add`, and press **Tab** or **Enter** to complete the edit. The button is now named **Add**.

Leave the Inspector window open. It will change to keep up with the currently selected element in the NIB, and we will need it later.

Repeat the button-dragging twice more, for the **Remove** and **Compute** buttons. Name the new buttons accordingly.

Next, we add the table of data to the window. Type **table** into the Library palette's search field to narrow its contents down to a table view. The icon for a Cocoa `NSTableView` object (embedded in an `NSScrollView`) should be the only element left in the array of available views. Drag this view into the window we're building. Lines will appear that allow you to place the table view a short distance below the buttons and just off the left edge of the window. Small blue knobs appear at the edges and corners of the view to let you resize it. Make the view wide enough to display two columns of numbers comfortably and tall enough to trigger a spacing guide line at the bottom of the window.

FIGURE 6.5    The Interface Builder Inspector, as a simple push button is selected. The default label for the button (**Button**) is replaced by **Add**.

What you've added to your document window is much more than just an `NSTableView`. Look at the main `MyDocument.nib` window, which should be at the upper left of your screen if you haven't moved it. There are three ways to organize your view of the NIB's contents, denoted by the segments of the **View Mode** control at the left of the NIB window's toolbar. Click the second segment, with horizontal lines on it, to select the outline view.

The NIB view changes to a hierarchical display of its contents. **File's Owner** and **First Responder** come first, followed by **Window**, which has a disclosure triangle next to it. The **Application** item comes last. Clicking the disclosure triangle next to **Window** shows that a Cocoa window contains one **NSView**, the content view, which, because it contains other views, also has a disclosure triangle. If we open the disclosure triangles next to **Content View > Scroll View > Table View**, we end up with something like Figure 6.6. What we last dragged into the window was in fact an `NSScrollView`, containing an `NSTableView`, which in turn contains two `NSTableColumns`.

FIGURE 6.6    The hierarchical view of the MyDocument NIB in progress. You reach this view by selecting the middle part of the **View Mode** control. It can sometimes be easier to select views in this list than in the window display.

Go back to the window we are building, and select the header of the first column of the table by double-clicking it. A text-field editor appears, allowing you to edit the header label for the column. Type **x**. In the second header, type **y**. Putting the cursor between the headers will enable you to drag the boundary between them, so you can resize the columns to equal size.

The last element we'll put in the window is an NSForm, a simple array of labeled text fields that we'll use for the results of the regression. Find the form element by typing **form** in the Library palette's search field; the item you want will look like a stack of text fields paired with text labels. Drag it into the right half of the window you're building, under the **Compute** button. As supplied, the form has two big defects: It's too narrow, and it shows only two items. The width problem is easy to solve: Drag the handles on the sides of the form until they hit the spacing guidelines.

Dragging the handles on the top and bottom, however, just gets you a taller form with two entries. (**Undo** is your friend here.) NSForm turns out to be a subclass of NSMatrix, a Cocoa class that manages an array of controls. You can add rows or columns to an NSMatrix in Interface Builder by dragging a resize handle *while holding the **Option** key down*. An option-drag downward on the bottom handle of the form gets us our third row.

Double-click the labels in the form until they become editable, and change them to **Slope:**, **Intercept:**, and **Correlation:**. These labels are too long to display fully in the form as it is laid out. If you resize the form, the labels and fields will be reapportioned so that the full text of the labels will be visible. Click away from the form to deselect it, and then click it to reveal the resizing handles. Drag one of the side handles to force the labels to resize. You can then resize the form so that it again conforms to the sizing guidelines.

## Sizing

At this point, the layout of the window is almost done. Why *almost*? Pull down the **File** menu and select **Simulate Interface** (or press ⌘R). Your window now "goes live" in an application called Cocoa Simulator. There's nothing behind your layout, but you can click the buttons and work the other controls.

Now try resizing the window. The contents of the window stay in place, neither resizing nor relocating to keep themselves usable (see Figure 6.7). This is not what we want. Quit the simulator by selecting **Quit Cocoa Simulator** in the application (**Cocoa Simulator**) menu (⌘Q). None of the changes you made during testing are permanent.

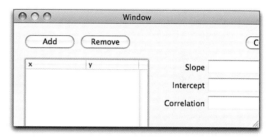

FIGURE 6.7    As supplied, Cocoa controls do not automatically size and position themselves in a window as the window resizes. You have to specify sizing and positioning behavior yourself.

Cocoa views can be set to resize or simply to stay put as their containers change size and shape. Click the **Add** button in the window we're constructing to select it. If the Inspector panel is not showing, select **Inspector** (or press ⇧⌘I) from the **Tools** menu. Select the third tab, labeled with a small ruler, at the top of the Inspector window, to display the Size inspector. (Note that you can bring the Inspector forward with the Size panel visible by pressing ⌘3.)

The Size panel is a stack of controls. At the top is a pop-up menu allowing you to select the standard size variants available to Cocoa controls. Below this is a Size & Position section, allowing you to set the exact placement of the selected view by typing in pixel values.

What interests us now is the Autosizing section (see Figure 6.8). At the left is a box with a smaller rectangle inside. This box controls how a view will resize and reposition itself when its enclosing view is resized. It contains a number of red lines, some solid (to show they are active), some dimmed and dashed (to show they are inactive). I call the lines inside the smaller rectangles *arrows*, and the T-ended outer lines *struts*. You can switch a line between active and inactive by clicking it.

When an outside strut is active, the view's position relative to that side of its container is kept constant. By default, the upper and left struts are active, anchoring the view relative to the upper-left corner of the enclosure. (If all struts are active and the view isn't resizable, lower and left win over upper and right.)

When an arrow is active, the view can resize itself in that direction. The exact resizing strategy depends on whether the struts permit the view to move. If both struts in a given direction (horizontal or vertical) are active, the view resizes so that its edges rigidly preserve their distances from the outer edge. If one or both struts in a given direction are inactive, the view preserves its proportionate size in the container.

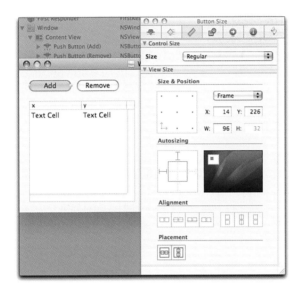

FIGURE 6.8    The Size Inspector for a view (the **Add** button) that should stay put, relative to the top left of its enclosing view. The inside arrows are both inactive, meaning that it never resizes. The outside struts below and to the right are inactive, meaning that those edges of the superview don't influence the view's placement.

The resizing strategy can be subtle, which is why Interface Builder presents a view that shows the current strategy in action. At the right of the Autosizing section is an animation that shows how the view's size and placement will vary when its enclosing view is resized. The enclosure is represented by a continually resizing white rectangle, and the view itself is represented by a red rectangle.

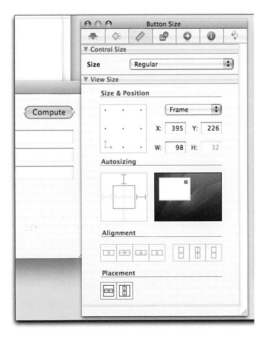

Reexamine the views in the window with an eye to how they should behave when the window resizes. The buttons should never resize and should stay where they are relative to the nearest corner—top left for **Add** and **Remove**, top right for **Compute**. Select each in turn, making Size Inspector for the **Add** and **Remove** buttons look like the one in Figure 6.8 and for the **Compute** button, as in Figure 6.9.

How do we want the form at the right of the window to behave? We certainly don't want it to shrink or stretch vertically with the window, but we wouldn't mind its

FIGURE 6.9    The **Compute** button should maintain its position relative to the top *right* of its enclosing view. The struts to the top and right are active.

growing if the window were to get wider. So the horizontal inner arrow should be active, to allow resizing in that direction, and the vertical arrow should be inactive, preventing resizing that way. We want it to keep its position near the right edge of the window, so the right outer strut should be active. We also want it to stay an inch or so below the title bar, so the top strut is also active. The bottom strut should be inactive, allowing the form to float free of that edge. The left strut also becomes inactive, indicating that the form will expand to take a share of the window rather than maintain a rigid margin from the left edge (see Figure 6.10).

The data table should be freest of all, widening with the window and also growing vertically to show more points if the window grows. Both internal arrows should be active. We anchor the view to the top left of the window by leaving those struts active; we also leave the bottom strut active. That way, when the window gets taller or shorter, the table will keep a constant distance of 20 pixels from the bottom of the window. The right strut is left inactive, so the table view will grow horizontally only to maintain its share of the horizontal space (see Figure 6.11).

FIGURE 6.10  The resizing specification for the form at the right side of the window. We don't want it to stretch vertically, so the inside vertical arrow is inactive. It would be nice if this view could take advantage of more room horizontally, so its horizontal arrow is active, allowing resizing in that direction. It is strictly bound to the top and the right side of the surrounding view. Being resizable horizontally and loosely bound to the left, this view resizes itself proportionately as the window resizes.

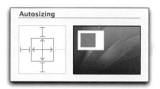

FIGURE 6.11  The resizing specification for the scroll view enclosing the data table. It resizes in both directions along with the window. It is strictly bound to the top, left, and bottom edges of its enclosing view, so it will resize to maintain its present distance from those edges; it is loosely bound to the right, so it will take only a proportionate share of growth in that direction.

**NOTE**

This raises the question of what to do with the size and placement of views while you are editing a window in Interface Builder. IB's default behavior is that resizing a view (or window) does not affect the size or placement of the views it contains. It is as though the subviews all have fixed size, and positioning fixed relative to the upper-left corner of the container. This is generally most convenient when you are first adding views to a new layout. The alternative is to select **Layout > Live Autoresizing**, whereby the views' size settings are active while you edit. This will serve well if, for instance, you are adding a view to an existing window, you have to resize the window to accommodate it, and you don't want to redo the other views' layout by hand.

Now press ⌘R to try out the window. Now resizing does not shove views out the window. You may want to experiment with other sizing options and see their effects. Remember, you can exit the interface test by selecting **Quit Cocoa Simulator** (⌘Q) from the application menu.

## A Split View

We've decided how much space to allocate between the table of data points and the form containing the output statistics, but maybe our decision shouldn't be the final one. The user might have other ideas. It would be better to put the two views inside a split view so that the user can drag the border between them back and forth.

Interface Builder provides both NSSplitViews and an NSScrollView in its Library palette, but there is an easier way to deploy them if you have already laid out the content views. To get a split view, select (Shift-click) the views you want to be in the split view—in this case, the scroll view containing the data table and the NSForm for the results. Then select the menu item **Layout > Embed Objects In > Split View** to wrap the views in a split view big enough to contain them and oriented so that the split comes between them (see Figure 6.12).

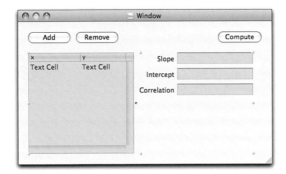

FIGURE 6.12    Adding a split view. Selecting two side-by-side views, and using the menu command **Layout > Embed Objects In > Split View** encloses the views in an NSSplitView, with the split bar between them.

Try out the new view by pressing ⌘R. The halves of the split view should resize as you drag the dimpled bar between them. The new split view comes with autosizing set to fix it to all edges (meaning it will ride up and down on the lower-left corner), and no resizing. Use the **Size** tab to activate the split view's internal (resizing) arrows so that it can resize with the window.

> **WARNING**
>
> When you save a NIB document package, Interface Builder does *not* necessarily preserve the
> `.svn` or CVS directories the package directory contains. These directories are vital to keeping
> the IB document in a version-control system (which I cover in detail in Chapter 8, "Version
> Control"). To make sure Interface Builder preserves such directories when you save the docu-
> ment, use the **Preserve Bundle Contents** check box in the standard save-file sheet. By
> default, this box is checked and your version-control information is saved. But IB preserves
> the setting on this box from NIB to NIB. If you ever uncheck it, *none of your future **Save** or
> **Save As** commands will preserve contents.* Conservative practice is to never to uncheck
> **Preserve Bundle Contents**.

# Summary

This chapter introduced Interface Builder, a tool no less important to Mac development
than Xcode itself. We used IB as a straightforward tool for laying out windows and views.
We saw how to set the many options for automatic sizing of embedded views and how
to use Interface Builder's own simulation engine to verify that our layout and sizing
choices work.

This does *not* end our work with Interface Builder. Because it is a constructor for networks
of Cocoa objects, Interface Builder has a big role to play as we move on to the controller
layer of our design.

# CHAPTER 7

# A Cocoa Application: Controllers

## IN THIS CHAPTER

▷ **Interface Builder Builds Controllers**

▷ **Assigning Classes in Interface Builder**

▷ **Connecting Data and Code in Interface Builder**

▷ **Setting Application Properties**

We've drawn and configured our views and are ready to work on the controller layer of our application. Surprisingly, we'll still be working with Interface Builder (IB) for much of this phase of development. Interface Builder is a powerful tool for storing Cocoa objects and specifying links between them.

## The Next Step

You have seen that IB keeps a placeholder for **File's Owner** in the NIB window. We're going to tell Interface Builder that the owner of this particular NIB will be an object of class MyDocument. From that, IB automatically determines what the structure of a MyDocument is. Additional objects do most of the work in managing the data in our application.

If MyDocument.nib is not already open, find it in the Resources group of the Linear project. Double-click MyDocument.nib to open it in Interface Builder.

Notice the bar at the bottom of the NIB window. It contains a green gem and the label Linear.xcodeproj. This indicates that Interface Builder is in communication with Xcode, and has recognized that the classes and objects named in the NIB correspond to the classes defined in the Linear project.

To see what this means, click the **File's Owner** icon in the NIB window, and issue the menu command **Tools > Identity Inspector** (⌘6). This shows in the top section of the inspector what class the NIB believes its owner to be—MyDocument (see Figure 7.1). The remaining sections show what attributes objects of that class have. The first section is labeled **Class Actions**, which has nothing to do with legal process. *Actions* are methods a class implements to respond to commands from the human interface. You remember that in Chapter 5, "Starting a Cocoa Application," we defined a method compute: in MyDocument.m, and declared it in MyDocument.h to have the type IBAction. That declaration signals Interface Builder that MyDocument has compute: as an action method, and sure enough, compute: is listed in the **Class Actions** section.

MyDocument.nib already knew that its owner is a MyDocument. The NIB was

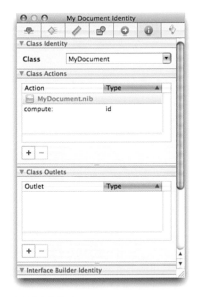

FIGURE 7.1    The Identity Inspector (⌘6) for the file's owner. In the **Class** combo box at the top, the owner object is designated to be of the class MyDocument. From this, and from structural information provided by Xcode, IB determines that the File's Owner object has one action method, compute:.

created from an Xcode template when we chose a document-based Cocoa application for the Linear project. The template included a MyDocument class, and a MyDocument.nib file that set the NIB owner's class to MyDocument. Knowing that, IB pulled in the class definition of MyDocument, and found the compute: method. We are free to designate a different class in the **Class** combo box (which would already list all the classes in the project), and its structure, also, would have been pulled in; but MyDocument is the correct class.

The link with the Linear project is permanent. If we were to make changes to MyDocument.h, the new structure would appear in the Identity Inspector, and in other IB displays, immediately.

We will now make the first link in our NIB file. While holding down the **Control** key, drag from the **File's Owner** icon to the **Window** icon. Release when the **Window** icon highlights or when the Window's window activates (see Figure 7.2). A heads-up display (HUD)

**NOTE**

If you are using a language (such as Python or Ruby) other than Objective-C that has a bridge to Cocoa, you have a little more work to do. Select **File's Owner**, and use the Identity Inspector to set the class name, and add outlets and actions by hand. In any language, to add an object of a custom class to a NIB, drag an NSObject into the NIB window (or an NSView into a window you're editing), select it, and use the Identity Inspector to set your custom class.

window pops up, displaying every *outlet* in MyDocument, including those in its superclasses. An outlet is an instance variable in one Cocoa object that points to another. We relate the two by having Cocoa fill in the pointers when the NIB is loaded in your program. Interface Builder is how you establish such connections.

The HUD window shows every possible outlet MyDocument has that will accept an NSWindow; in this case, the only such outlet is named window. Click **window** in the HUD list to make the connection.

What did we just do? The contents of a NIB file get instantiated when an object—an owner—decides to load that NIB. The loading process consists of unarchiving and initializing all the objects stored in the NIB and initializing all the references made between objects in the NIB, and between the owner and the object in the NIB. So, when MyDocument loads MyDocument.nib, the instance variable window in the MyDocument object will be set to point to the **Window** object loaded from the NIB.

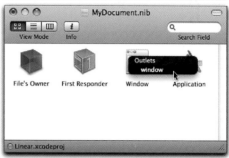

FIGURE 7.2    The result of Control-dragging from the **File's Owner** icon to the **Window** icon in the NIB window. While you drag (above), a blue line appears, extending from the **File's Owner** icon to your mouse pointer. When you release the mouse button over the **Window** icon (below), a HUD window appears, giving you a choice of the relations **Window** may have to **File's Owner**. In this case, click the only choice, **window**.

> **NOTE**
>
> As with the MyDocument class, MyDocument.nib already knew about the link between **Window** and the window outlet of **File's Owner**. The Cocoa document-based application template sets the NIB up so that the link is already there. This exercise merely demonstrates the principle.

# Adding a Controller

We are now going to add objects to MyDocument.nib that will serve as the controller layer for Linear. Select the Library palette, and type **controller** into the search field. The object array narrows down to objects derived from Cocoa's NSController class (see Figure 7.3).

**On Using an** NSObjectController

In this chapter, I devote a lot of trouble and attention to NSObjectController because managing controller objects is an important task in using Interface Builder. If I were teaching Cocoa from scratch, I wouldn't be doing that.

Cocoa bindings and the controller architecture are advanced topics; they look like magic if you aren't experienced in the underlying technology. Good, sound Cocoa programming for years used developer-built classes for the controller layer of applications. The custom class would be responsible for detecting changes in the model and view layers of the application, and for propagating those changes to the other end of the Model-Controller-View chain.

Writing your own controller layer is a much easier approach to understand, and if you are just learning Cocoa, it is one you should adopt before moving on to NSObjectController, NSArrayController, and their cousins. It is still a good, and sound, technique. See the extensive Cocoa tutorials, beginning with the Currency Converter project, to be found in Xcode's Documentation window.

Why, then, do I have you stringing bindings through Cocoa NSController objects? Two reasons. First, because this book is not a tutorial on fundamental Cocoa techniques, I chose a path that involves writing as little Objective-C code as possible. Second, this point in the book is a convenient place to cover Interface Builder's support for bindings.

These objects are represented as green bubbles, and plainly they aren't meant to represent anything that goes into a window. The icons represent instances of NSController subclasses, which can be used as building blocks for the controller layer of our application. Drag three of these subclasses—two of the bubbles containing a single blue cube (representing NSObjectControllers), and one containing the three blue cubes in a line (representing an NSArrayController)—into the main NIB window (the one with the icons, not the user interface window we built in the preceding chapter).

Make the Identity Inspector visible (⌘6), noting that the bottom section includes a text field labeled **Name**. We want to change the labels on the controller objects so that we can tell which is which. Select the first NSObjectController, and type **Document** into the **Name** field in the Inspector. Click the second controller and

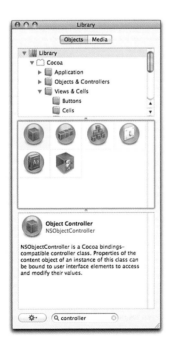

FIGURE 7.3    Classes displayed in the Library palette when **controller** is typed into the search field. The five classes represented by green bubbles are subclasses of NSController. You add instances of these classes by dragging the corresponding icon into the main NIB window. (The sixth class is for use in building Automator workflows, and just happens to have *controller* in its name.)

name it **Model**. Finally select the `NSArrayController` and name it **DataPoints**. These names will help us remember what kinds of data the `NSController` objects are managing.

## NSObjectController: **Document**

We will now weave the controller objects, our document, and our user interface elements into a mutually supporting web. Figure 7.4 maps the many steps to this process.

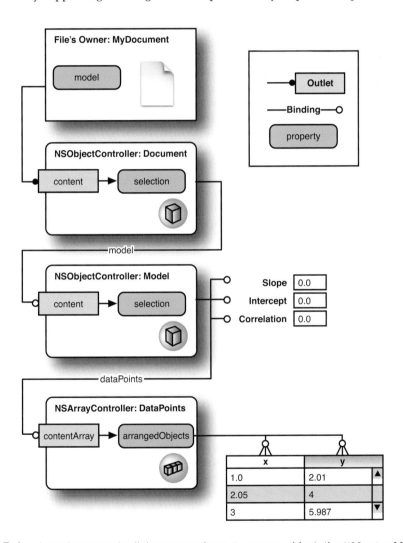

FIGURE 7.4    A road map to the links among the `MyDocument` object, the `NSController` objects, and the user interface objects in this chapter. The controller objects form a straight chain of references: (1) The **DataPoints** array controller gets (*binds*) its `contentArray` from the `dataPoints` property of the `selection` of the **Model** controller. (2) The **Model** controller gets (*binds*) its `content` from the `model` property of the `selection` of the **Document** controller. (3) The **Document** controller *links* to the `MyDocument` object itself to fill its content outlet.

First, we tell the document NSObjectController about the MyDocument instance it will be communicating with. The NSController's content outlet designates the object the controller is concerned with. This object is declared as an IBOutlet in the header for NSController, so Control-dragging can be used to establish a link between the **Document** NSObjectController's content pointer and the MyDocument that is the **File's Owner** of this NIB.

In short: Control-drag from the **Document** cube to **File's Owner** (see Figure 7.5). The resulting HUD will offer to connect the content outlet; accept this.

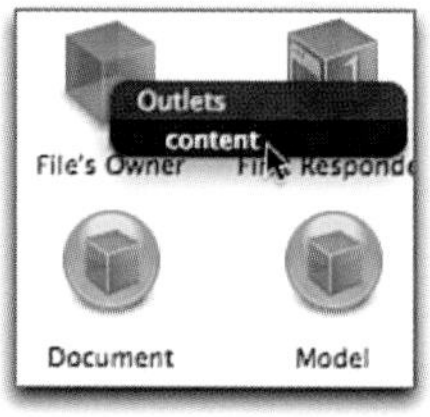

While we have the **Document** controller selected, press ⌘1 to bring up the Attributes Inspector. By default, NSController objects assume that they will be dealing with instances of NSMutableDictionary, but that isn't the case here. In the field labeled **Object Classname**, type **MyDocument**. Also, to tell Interface Builder that MyDocument has one property, model, of concern to IB, click the **Add** button at the bottom of the Inspector and edit the resulting new line in the list to read **model**.

FIGURE 7.5    Connecting the **Document** object controller to the **File's Owner**, which will be a MyDocument. Control-drag from the **Document** object controller to **File's Owner**, and confirm in the resulting HUD window that the owner should be linked to the controller's content outlet.

## NSObjectController: **Model**

As you might have guessed, this controller does whatever it does with the model property of MyDocument. Click the **Model** NSObjectController, and use the Attributes Inspector (⌘1) to specify that the name of the controlled class is Regression and that its attributes are **slope**, **intercept**, **correlation**, **canCompute**, and **dataPoints**. The Inspector should look like the left half of Figure 7.6.

> **NOTE**
>
> Adding attribute names to an NSController in Interface Builder is simply a convenience, building a list for you to pick from later. Adding or omitting items has no effect on the state or behavior of the final application.

How will the **Model** NSObjectController get at its Regression object? No object in the NIB represents the model member of the MyDocument object. Instead, the **Model** controller will ask the **Document** controller for the value of its content object's model property.

Press ⌘4 to bring up the Bindings Inspector. You want to bind the **Model** controller's content object to the model property of the **Document** controller's content. The Bindings

Inspector shows all the properties of the selected objects that can be bound to—can share values with—properties of other objects. The **Content Object** property is the second bindable property in the Bindings Inspector for an NSObjectController. Click the disclosure triangle next to the **contentObject** label to open the relevant subpanel.

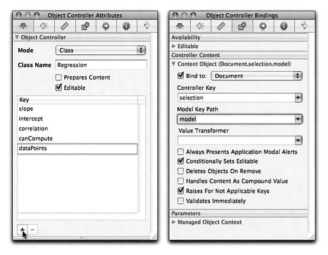

FIGURE 7.6    Setting up the second NSObjectController to manage Regression objects.

What object keeps track of the model object? It is the content object of our **Document** NSObjectController. Select **Document(NSObjectController)** from the **Bind To** pop-up. Now examine the choices that drop down from the **Controller Key** combo box. These are the **Document** NSObjectController properties that this relationship might observe. The only one you are interested in is **selection**; choose it.

> **NOTE**
>
> Bindings have this advantage over the linking of outlets: In short, when two objects are bound, each is notified of changes to the other. This makes it automatic to propagate changes between model objects and view objects. At the cost of some complexity in the basic concepts, this greatly simplifies the code needed to write Linear.

> **NOTE**
>
> In theory, a single NSController might shift focus among various objects as, for instance, the user clicks different objects to bring them forward for editing. The NSController would track such changes by changing its selection property to always point at the selected object. In practice, in our application, a given **Document** NSObjectController will always refer to only one Regression object, so the flexibility implied by "whatever the controller currently selects" is a little misleading.

Next, what facet of the current selection of the **Document** NSObjectController does the **Model** NSObjectController want to track? It wants to track the model property of the selected object. In the combo box labeled **Model Key Path**, select **model**. (**Model** is in the list because we told Interface Builder that the **Document** NSObjectController tracks objects that have a property named model.) The Bindings Inspector should now look like the right half of Figure 7.6.

## NSArrayController: **DataPoints**

Now it's time to set up the **DataPoints** NSArrayController. We want to make the **DataPoints** controller into something that knows about DataPoint objects. Select its icon, and bring up the Attributes Inspector (⌘1) on it. Enter **DataPoint** in the **Class Name** field, and add **x** and **y** to the key list (because every DataPoint object has those properties).

We want the controller to get DataPoint objects from MyDocument's model—we've already set up the **Model** NSObjectController to track model—and, specifically, get them from the model's dataPoints array.

Go to the Bindings Inspector (⌘4) and open the disclosure triangle labeled **Content Array**. This is where we point the **DataPoints** controller at the model's array of DataPoints. So, we do the following:

1. Select Model (NSObjectController) from the Bind To pop-up.

2. Select **selection** in the **Controller Key** combo box.

3. Select **dataPoints** in the **Model Key Path** combo box.

Now all three of the NSControllers we dragged into the NIB have been made "live." As long as a valid MyDocument exists as the owner of the NIB, the **Document** object will identify with it and make its model property bindable; the **Model** object will identify with the Regression model object and make its properties bindable, including the dataPoints array; and the **DataPoints** object will identify with the dataPoints array and make each DataPoint object within it bindable.

# Value Binding

All this binding is pointless if it does not move data. In the user interface window we've been building, click the **NSForm** object on the right; then click the top cell (**Slope:**). Press ⌘4 to bring up the Bindings Inspector (if it isn't already up), and note that the first available binding is **value**. Expand the item, and bind the value of this cell to **Model**, **selection**, and **slope** (see Figure 7.7). Turn off **Conditionally Sets Editable**, which would automatically make the form cell editable—there's not much sense in allowing user input of our results. While you're here, use the Attributes Inspector (⌘1) to uncheck the **Editable** property of this cell.

Repeat this process—select the cell, bind to a corresponding value of **Model** and **selection**, make uneditable—for the other two cells of the form. The effect of this, combined with our having made all the properties involved comply with the key-value observing (KVO) protocol, is that whenever the slope, intercept, or correlation values of a MyDocument change, the display in this window will reflect the change.

Now we wire up the data entry table, in the left half of the window. Click repeatedly the body of the first column of the table, until the column itself is selected (see Figure 7.8). Press ⌘4 to bring up the Bindings Inspector. Interface Builder is moderately smart: It knows that table columns should be bound to multiples of data, so the Inspector appears with the arrangedObjects of the **DataPoints** NSArrayController already selected. All you have to do is select the **x** property in the **Model Key Path** combo box.

> **NOTE**
>
> There is another way to select a specific object in Interface Builder without repeated clicking. If you click the second segment of the **View Mode** control in the NIB window's toolbar, IB displays the NIB's objects in an outline-formatted list. Click disclosure rectangles, beginning with the **Window** object, until the object you want is exposed, and select it. Double click a line item will highlight the corresponding object in the window being built.

Now select the second column and bind it to **DataPoints**, arrangedObjects, and y.

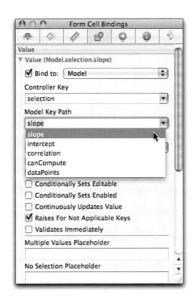

FIGURE 7.7    The Bindings Inspector, showing how to bind a cell of the results form to the slope of the model object.

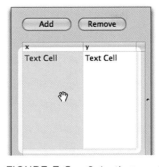

FIGURE 7.8    Selecting a column in an NSTableView. Click the table to select it, and then click the body of the column you want to select. In previous versions of Interface Builder, columns were selected by clicking the column header.

We have now ensured that the contents of the NSTableView will reflect the dataPoints of the current document and that any changes to the points will make their way back to the document. But all we've done is allow for display and editing of existing data. We have to do something about adding or computing new data.

> **NOTE**
>
> NSArrayController has a concept of an array *of arranged objects*, distinct from the content array that is its focus. The idea is that the content array may have constant membership and ordering, but the controller might sort it or filter subsets of it for presentation to the user. The current filtered-and-sorted subset of the content array constitutes the controller's arranged objects. When you want to operate on every user-visible member of an NSArrayController's array, you should ask for arrangedObjects.

## Actions and Outlets

It is time to hook up the buttons to the objects that will respond to them. Control-drag from the **Add** button to the **DataPoints** NSArrayController (see Figure 7.9). As you've come to expect, the connection HUD pops up. But this time, it doesn't show a list of fields, but rather a list of methods—you can tell, because they all end with colons—labeled **Received Actions**. Select the **Add:** action.

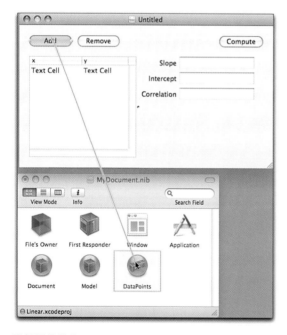

**FIGURE 7.9**   Linking a human-interface object to an object in the NIB window. Such links are established as any other link would be, except that the Control-drag begins in one window and ends in another. Because the drag originates in a control element, the resulting HUD will contain a list of action methods supported by the destination object.

What's going on here? As before, the Control-drag from the **Add** button to **DataPoints** makes Interface Builder propose a link from the one to the other. In the case of an

NSButton—or any other object derived from NSControl—IB does not offer to fill just any outlet in the button, but instead offers to fill a pointer named target *and* an action field. When an NSControl is triggered, it sends its designated action to its designated target. So what you see is a list of all the action messages that Interface Builder knows NSArrayController implements.

NSArrayController provides an add: message that takes care of allocating, initializing, and inserting a new instance of the proper type of object into the array it manages.

> **NOTE**
>
> Action methods always have the signature -(IBAction) action: (id) sender;. IBAction is #defined as void and has two purposes. The first is to document the purpose of the method to human readers. The second is to signal to the header parser in Interface Builder that this method is to be added to the list of action methods supported by this class. By convention, the sender parameter is whatever control sent the action message. If you send an action message yourself, be sure that your parameter responds to reasonable NSControl-like messages; otherwise, pass nil.

Control-drag from the **Remove** button to the **DataPoints** array controller, and select the **Remove:** action in the HUD window. Control-drag from the **Compute** button to the **File's Owner** icon. Interface Builder readily offers compute: as the action for this button, because Xcode told it about MyDocument.h, and IB saw that compute: was declared as an IBAction. Connect it.

One last thing: It's illegal to do a linear regression on only one data point. It makes no sense to speak of the one straight line that "fits" one point, and with a single point, all three statistics involve the ratio 0/0. In class Regression, we have a simple-minded check on this condition, called canCompute, which is YES if at least two elements are in dataPoints. (It's simpleminded because it does not handle the case in which the data set consists of the same point repeated.)

We'd like our human interface to reflect this constraint. Click the **Compute** button, and look at the available bindings (press ⌘4). An **enabled** binding is available; bind it to **Model, selection**, and **canCompute**.

Perhaps you remember that canCompute is a pure Objective-C method. No variable underlies it, and there is no way to set the property. That doesn't matter. As long as the canCompute property is accessible by a method of that name, you can bind to it.

This ends our work with Interface Builder. Make sure to save the NIB (press ⌘S), and return to Xcode.

# MyDocument

We have come far in our controller work without writing any code. We have yet to touch the MyDocument .m skeleton that Xcode provided when we created our project. Now we make our changes:

```
- (id)init
{
    self = [super init];
    if (self) {
        // Allocate and initialize our model
        model = [[Regression alloc] init];
        if (!model) {
            [self release];
            self = nil;
        }
    }
    return self;
}


- (void) dealloc
{
    [model release];
    [super dealloc];
}
```

The only changes to the original are that we create a model object when the document is created and release it when the document is destroyed. The template for MyDocument provides stubs of methods for loading and saving the contents of the document file. We fill them out:

```
// Turn the document contents into a single, savable lump.
- (NSData *)dataOfType:(NSString *)typeName error:(NSError **)outError
{
#pragma unused(typeName)
    // Produce the data lump:
    NSData * retval = [NSKeyedArchiver
                        archivedDataWithRootObject: model];
    // If the lump is nil, something went wrong.
    // Fill out the error object to explain what went wrong.
    if ( outError != NULL ) {
        // The sender wanted an error reported. If there
        // was a problem, fill in an NSError object.
        if (retval == nil) {
            // The error object should include an (unhelpful)
            // explanation of what happened.
            NSDictionary * userInfoDict = [NSDictionary
                        dictionaryWithObjectsAndKeys:
                    @"Internal error formatting data",
                            NSLocalizedDescriptionKey,
                @"Archiving of data failed. Probably a bug.",
```

```
                               NSLocalizedFailureReasonErrorKey,
                            @"There's nothing you can do.",
                         NSLocalizedRecoverySuggestionErrorKey,
                                                      nil];
       // Create the actual error object.
       *outError =
          [NSError errorWithDomain: LinearInternalErrorDomain
                             code: linErrCantFormatDocumentData
                          userInfo: userInfoDict];
    }
    else {
        // No problem. Don't supply an error object.
        *outError = nil;
    }
  }
  return retval;
}


// From the lump of data resulting from reading the document file,
// fill in the model.
- (BOOL)readFromData:(NSData *)data
            ofType:(NSString
             error:(NSError
{
#pragma unused(typeName)
    // Using the NSCoding rules we supplied in the classes,
    // extract the Regression and DataPoint objects from the lump.
    model = [NSKeyedUnarchiver unarchiveObjectWithData: data];
    [model retain];

    if (model) {
        // Nothing went wrong. Report success, and no error.
        if (outError != NULL)
            *outError = nil;
        return YES;
    }
    else {
        if (outError != NULL) {
            NSDictionary * userInfoDict = [NSDictionary
                dictionaryWithObjectsAndKeys:
                            @"Internal error decoding data",
                        NSLocalizedDescriptionKey,
                    @"Unarchiving of data failed. Probably a bug.",
                        NSLocalizedFailureReasonErrorKey,
                            @"There's nothing you can do.",
```

7

```
                        NSLocalizedRecoverySuggestionErrorKey,
                                              nil];
      *outError =
      [NSError errorWithDomain: LinearInternalErrorDomain
                     code: linErrCantDecodeDocumentData
                  userInfo: userInfoDict];
   }
   return NO;
  }
}
```

Here, we respond to the Cocoa framework's calls for us to load or save our data. Most of the work was done in the model object. All we have to do in the controller is specify the facilities—NSKeyedArchiver and NSKeyedUnarchiver—that do the transformation between objects and data stream. Also, we have to set up NSError objects for Cocoa to handle if the data conversions don't work.

This code adds some error-description constants to Linear. To accommodate these, add this to Regression.h:

```
extern NSString * const LinearInternalErrorDomain;
enum {
    linErrCantFormatDocumentData = 1000,
    linErrCantDecodeDocumentData
};
```

And add this after the #imports in Regression.m:

```
NSString * const LinearInternalErrorDomain =
                    @"org.manoverboard.Linear.ErrorDomain";
```

Finally, we add the command handler that glues the **Compute** button to the model:

```
- (IBAction) compute: (id) sender
{
#pragma  unused(sender)
    [model computeWithLinrg];
}
```

Once again, the model does most of the work.

# Application Properties

The programming is done, but we need to take care of two more chores. First, we have to associate our data files with our application. In the Groups & Files list in the Project window, open the Targets group, and double-click **Linear**, the only target in the group. A Get Info window for the target will open. Click the **Properties** tab (see Figure 7.10). This panel edits the `Info.plist` file of your application's package, which Launch Services uses to associate file types with your application. Some fields are already filled in with information from Xcode's template.

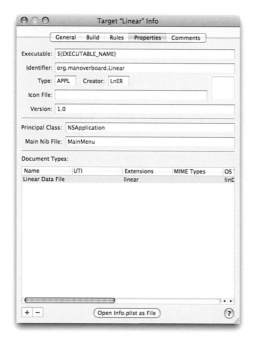

FIGURE 7.10     The Application Properties Info window. This window is used to set all the information that identifies the application and its documents to the Finder. This window is mainly an editor for the `Info.plist` file. Note that the table at the bottom—for information about document types—is much wider than the default size the panel allows.

▶ **Executable.** The name of the file containing the compiled and linked binary code for your application. The project template fills this setting with `$(EXECUTABLE_NAME)`, which will translate to the name of the application's executable binary file. Xcode makes the translation when it injects your `Info.plist` file into the application package. Xcode's build system derives the executable name from the final name of the application as set in the Target Info window's **Build** tab. Do *not* change this setting unless you have a specific reason to do so.

▶ **Identifier.** A string that uniquely identifies your application to the system. The convention is to use an inverted domain name followed by the name of the application. Xcode defaults this string to `com.yourcompany.ProjectName`. For Linear, set it to **org.manoverboard.Linear**.

▶ **Type and Creator.** Two four-character codes indicating the type of the file's contents and the application that created the file. Thus, the Macintosh, in 1984, could open a file with the correct application when you double-clicked its icon. Even though Mac OS X applications are no longer single files, the convention, dating from the beginning of the Mac OS, still holds that they have type and creator codes. The type of all applications is APPL. Leave this unchanged. The creator code to be set for this application and for all files created by it is, by default, ????. Change this to **LnER**.

▸ **Icon File**. We skip it for now because we don't have an icon yet.

▸ **Version**. 1.0.

▸ **Principal Class**. The main() function calls NSApplicationMain(), which in turn instantiates an application object, loads the main NIB, and runs the application. If you have a custom application class, you put its name here, and NSApplicationMain() uses that information in deciding what to run. Almost nobody needs a custom application class. Leave this as NSApplication.

▸ **Main NIB File**. The NIB file that contains at least the main menu bar and may contain other windows and views common to the whole application. As Xcode provides a MainMenu.nib file with a standard menu bar in it, you can leave this as MainMenu.

Next comes a table for all the documents that your application can create or at least read. As Xcode sets up the document-based application template to already have the MyDocument document class, the table has an entry for one document type. We can improve on the defaults:

> **NOTE**
>
> A surprising number of people want to know whether they can put the main menu bar in another NIB file. The answer is no.

▸ **Name**. A string used in the Finder to identify this file type. This string is also used as a parameter to the NSDocument methods for reading and writing document data. (The idea is that the same document class may handle more than one document type and would need the type name to know which was desired.) We can do better than DocumentType; substitute **Linear Data File**.

▸ **UTI and MIME Types**. Strings for accurately classifying the format and content of files. As Mac OS X becomes more and more sophisticated in how it handles file metadata, this information, particularly UTIs (uniform type identifiers), will gain importance. UTIs are used to distinguish file types for purposes of assigning Spotlight importers, which pull information out of data files for Spotlight to index. Specifying a UTI can be useful, but it imposes other requirements that would complicate this example. For now, leave it blank. In the case of MIME types, our application will be using a nonstandard file format that nobody else is expected to read; we can leave the MIME type blank.

▸ **Extensions**. The filename extension that will identify a file as being of this document type. We are not limited to three characters, and for most purposes, the extension will be hidden. Let's use **linear**—no dot. We could specify more than one, separated by spaces, if more than one extension is associated with this type, as with htm and html.

▶ **OS Types**. The type of codes that, together with this application's creator code, identify this document type. Again, there could be more than one, separated by spaces. Enter **linD**.

▶ **Class**. The class that handles the document type. When it gets a command to open or create a document, your application's NSDocumentController determines—from the type name the user specified or from the extension or OS type code of the existing file—the document class. Here is where you specify that class. We have only one NSDocument class—MyDocument—so we leave this unchanged.

▶ **Icon File**. Blank because we don't yet have a document icon for our data files. This would contain just the base name of a Mac OS X icon (.icns) file; that is, if the icon were in MyDocument.icns, you'd enter **MyDocument**.

▶ **Store Type**. This pop-up allows you to choose among the three file formats (plus an in-memory format) Core Data uses for storing documents. We aren't using Core Data (yet), so we can leave this as **binary**. After you become familiar with Core Data, you'll know which type is right for your purposes.

▶ **Role**. One of three roles an application can have with respect to a file: **Editor**, for reading and writing files of this type; **Viewer**, for only reading files of this type; or **None**, for merely defining an icon for a file a user can't separately open—for instance, for a configuration file. Our application both reads and writes this file type: **Editor**.

▶ **Package**. This button is checked if the document is saved not as a single file but as a structured directory tree. When Launch Services "notices" this entry in your application's Info.plist file, the document will appear in the Finder to be a single file. Our document is in fact a single file, so we leave this unchecked.

# Building

Our first iteration of Linear is complete. Try running it; run it under the debugger if you're cautious. Add lines to the data point table and fill them with data; note that the **Compute** button activates when the second point is added. Try removing a point. Click **Compute** and see whether the values displayed make sense. Close the document window and save it. Select **File > Open** to open it up again.

Linear behaves like a real application—albeit one that is short on such important features as automatic calculation, undo, and dirty-document detection.

**Introduction to Build Configurations**

Build configurations are covered in much more detail later in this book; for now, think of them as named groups of build-system settings that make a product more suitable for debugging or for release. Recall that in Section "Starting a New Project," of Chapter 5, we added Linrg as a dependency of the Linear target. Whenever something in Linrg changes, Linear sees to it that Linrg is recompiled and the fresh version imported.

But what settings are used to build Linrg in such circumstances? Are they the current compiler settings for Linear? The answer is no. Linrg will be built using the build configuration that has the same *name* as the active configuration of the project doing the building. If no matching name is found, Linrg will be built using its current configuration.

It is important to make sure that your configuration names are consistent across projects. Xcode templates take care of this, giving you debug and release configurations for every new project.

For now, select the **Debug** configuration from the **Active Build Configuration** pop-up in the project window's toolbar.

Build configurations, which are groups of build settings, are distinct from targets, which are groups of source files that build particular products.

## Summary

We continued our journey with Interface Builder in this chapter, into the controller layer of our design. We saw how Interface Builder adds to NIB files objects and relationships that go far beyond the simple scope of interface layout. We linked objects to outlets, and controls to targets with actions. We bound controllers to our document class and to each other and saw how to set up bindings that make human-interface elements automatically track values in our model. Finally, we used the Target Info window to set the properties of our application.

# CHAPTER 8

# Version Control

**IN THIS CHAPTER**

▸ **The Necessity of Version Control**

▸ **Putting a Project Under Version Control**

▸ **Xcode's Integrated Version Control Support**

▸ **Merging Versions**

▸ **Rolling Changes Back**

▸ **Creating Tags**

Linear and Linrg total just above 500 lines, plus the contents of the NIB files, but we have already invested a lot of time and trouble in them. So far, what we've done has simply been to create the source code and the structure of the human interface, but soon we will be moving on from *creation* to *change*. If you're like most programmers, you are conservative of the code you've written. An old method might no longer be required, but it may still embody a valuable understanding of the underlying problem. One solution might be just to keep all the obsolete code in your active source files, possibly commented-out or guarded by `#if 0` blocks. However, this bloats the file considerably and obscures the active core of the code. When the revisions get more than one layer deep, it can be difficult to track which blocked-out stretch of code goes with which.

A software configuration management (SCM, also known as version control) system is a database that keeps track of all the files in a project and enables you to register revisions of those files as they change. Version control frees you to make extensive changes, secure in the knowledge that all the previous versions of each file are still available if you need to roll your changes back.

You might have heard of SCM and concluded that it's only for large projects with many developers. It is true that SCM makes it much easier to manage large code bases (and to coordinate the efforts of large teams). But even if you work alone

- You will still make extensive changes to your source.

- You will still need to refer to previous versions.

▶ You will still need to revert to previous versions to dig yourself out of the holes you dug with those extensive changes.

▶ You will find it easier just to make changes cleanly, instead of trying to make sure you caught all the obsolete code in comments and `#if 0` blocks.

▶ You will likely need to work on more than one computer, each of which will contribute different changes to your code base.

As mentioned in Chapter 2, "Simple Workflow and Passive Debugging," if you are going to change your code, *ever*—if you save a file more than once—you probably ought to put it under version control.

Xcode 3 supports version control mediated by three SCM systems:

▶ CVS (Concurrent Versions System) has long been the standard for open source and enterprise version control in the UNIX/Linux world. CVS is open source software itself, and it has always shipped with the Xcode tools. Mac OS X 10.5 and Xcode 3.0 include version 1.12. The Darwin project, which makes most of the Mac OS X kernel available as open source, is built on CVS archives.

▶ Subversion is an open source SCM system with the design goal of being a better CVS. It is rapidly displacing CVS as the revision-control system of choice. Subversion embraces a variety of ways to access file repositories (including WebDAV and direct file access), semiautomatic merging of conflicting versions, support for deleting or renaming versioned files, and "atomic" check-ins. (If you try to check in a group of files and one fails to check in, none are checked in, thus heading off an inconsistency in the archive.) Subversion keeps a local copy of the last version of every file you check out, so you don't have to be in touch with the server to review or roll back any changes you make.

▶ Perforce is a commercial SCM system from Perforce Software. Its advantages are speed and scalability to very large file bases. Licenses for open source projects are free; for other terms, see the Web site (www.perforce.com).

Under Xcode 2, CVS was by a slight margin the better choice for SCM. More existing projects were controlled by CVS, Subversion and Perforce had to be installed separately, and Xcode's support for CVS was more reliable than for the other two. In addition, Apple provided a version of CVS that could "wrap" package directories—such as NIBs and Xcode project documents—so that the related files in them would always be kept, together, at the same revision level. (Apple no longer provides that version of CVS.)

Today, in Leopard, there is no contest: Unless you are constrained to use another SCM system, use Subversion. It is helpful, reliable, easy to understand, and easy to use, even on the command line. It comes installed with Mac OS X 10.5 itself—not just with the developer tools—and Xcode SCM support is modeled on the Subversion way of doing things.

This book was written on three different Macintoshes, kept in sync with a Subversion repository.

Perforce is a high-powered SCM system providing tools for central management of the code base. Its maker claims that it will perform well on code bases as large as hundreds of thousands of files while requiring little in the way of maintenance. Unlike the other two systems, which rely on the users to reconcile the changes they make to controlled files when they interact with the repository, Perforce enforces file consistency by permitting only one client at a time to check a file out as a writer. Perforce is free to try, but in early 2008 cost $800 per user for commercial development. Free licenses are available to open source projects.

# Setting Up a Repository

The heart of a revision-control system is its *repository*, the database that keeps the history of the files in a project. All version-control actions you take relate to a repository. We're going to set up a local repository intended for access only from the computer on which it resides. Networked repositories are beyond the scope of this book; consult the documents for your SCM system for instructions and tutorials if you're interested.

We will now create a repository for Linear. To do that, we need to use the command line. Open the Terminal application, found in /Applications/Utilities. To make the Linear repository easier to manage, and easier to share among users of the computer, we will place it in a Subversion directory in the Shared user's home directory: /Users/Shared/Subversion/Linear.

```
MyMac:~ xcodeuser$ mkdir -p /Users/Shared/Subversion/Linear
MyMac:~ xcodeuser$ cd /Users/Shared/Subversion/
```

Now use the Subversion repository-administration utility, svnadmin, to set up a repository in the new Linear directory. Then, make sure the repository will be readable, writeable, and listable for all users of this computer:

```
MyMac:Subversion xcodeuser$ svnadmin create Linear
MyMac:Subversion xcodeuser$ chmod -R a+rwX .
MyMac:Subversion xcodeuser$ ls -l Linear
total 16
-rw-rw-rw-   1 xcodeuser  wheel  229 Oct 25 14:56 README.txt
drwxrwxrwx   5 xcodeuser  wheel  170 Oct 25 14:56 conf
drwxrwxrwx   2 xcodeuser  wheel   68 Oct 25 14:56 dav
drwxrwxrwx  10 xcodeuser  wheel  340 Oct 25 14:56 db
-rw-rw-rw-   1 xcodeuser  wheel    2 Oct 25 14:56 format
drwxrwxrwx  11 xcodeuser  wheel  374 Oct 25 14:56 hooks
drwxrwxrwx   4 xcodeuser  wheel  136 Oct 25 14:56 locks
MyMac:Subversion xcodeuser$ cat Linear/README.txt
```

8

This is a Subversion repository; use the 'svnadmin' tool to examine it. Do not add, delete, or modify files here unless you know how to avoid corrupting the repository.

Visit subversion.tigris.org for more information.
MyMac:Subversion xcodeuser$

svnadmin creates a number of files and directories inside the repository, including a README.txt file that explains that the contents of the repository directory are, in short, not to be fooled with. From now on, we will use only Xcode (and the svn client tool) to make changes to the repository.

# Getting Ready for Subversion

We must now get our home directory ready for Subversion. Subversion keeps a configuration file (config) in a hidden directory (.subversion) of your home folder. This default configuration is not closely tailored to the needs of Mac OS X development. Let's fix that.

The first step is to get Subversion to create the .subversion configuration directory. Do this by running the Subversion client tool, svn, with a harmless command option—the command will fail because it won't be run from a Subversion-controlled directory, but it will create the .subversion directory, which is all we need now:

```
MyMac:~ xcodeuser$ svn status
svn: warning: '.' is not a working copy
MyMac:~ xcodeuser$
```

The default configuration file is now at .subversion/config in your home directory. You must edit it before we use Subversion with Xcode.

In Xcode, select **File > Open** (⌘O). When the open-file dialog appears, type the tilde (~) key. This opens a further sheet into which you can enter a directory path. From here, you can get inside the otherwise-invisible .subversion directory. Enter

```
~/.subversion
```

and press **Return**. You now see a list of files in the hidden directory. Select config, and press **Return** to open the file.

If you are familiar with the INI file format, you will recognize the structure of the config file: Phrases in square brackets divide the file into sections, and key-value pairs separated by equal signs provide the actual settings. Comment lines begin with the # character, and these constitute nearly all the file. They show examples of settings you might want to make.

> **NOTE**
>
> There are better editors for the config file than Xcode. Both TextMate and BBEdit will syntax-color the file, which makes the actual settings stand out in a file that is mostly comments. But, I assume that Xcode is what you have for a text editor.

We need to make only a few settings. The biggest one is for `global-ignores`. (Use Xcode's **Find** command, ⌘F, to locate the line.) Not everything in a project directory is suitable for recording in an SCM repository. You remember from Chapter 1, "Kicking the Tires," that building an Xcode project creates a `build` directory containing many files that represent the products of the build. None of those products need to be under version control, because your source code—everything sufficient to *generate* those products—will be under version control. If you want those products back, just build the project. So, when Subversion scans your project directory looking for files to check into the repository, you don't want the `build` directory to be included.

> **NOTE**
>
> The format for `global-ignores` specifications is the same "glob" wildcard notation you use for specifying files in a UNIX shell.

> **NOTE**
>
> You might not want to exclude `.pbxuser`, `.mode*`, and `.perspective*` files. These files reside inside Xcode project-file packages, and include user-specific settings for a project, such as window placements, custom executables, and breakpoint lists. If you have the same username on more than one machine, and want to preserve those settings on all of them, you might consider leaving those glob expressions out of the `global-ignores` list.

In the example Subversion provides, the `global-ignores` setting includes many file types you want to exclude—all types of intermediate-object files, the ubiquitous `.DS_Store` file—but doesn't go far enough. Delete the leading # character, to make the setting active, and append the following file types:

```
build *~.nib *.so *.pbxuser *.mode* *.perspective*
```

The other thing we need to do is to ensure that Subversion treats the files inside an `.xcodeproj` package as though they were text. In fact, they *are* text, and when Subversion knows a file contains text, it can do a better job of storing it in the repository, can report line-by-line changes, and when your local copy of the file conflicts with the latest version in the repository, Subversion is pretty good at merging the two.

> **NOTE**
>
> Apple's Xcode engineers have taken some pains to ensure that the files in an `.xcodeproj` package will be easy for Subversion's automatic merging to handle properly. For the rare instances in which you might have to edit those files by hand, to resolve conflicts, the files include comment lines that should make it easier to determine how to set the files to rights.

Subversion guesses (usually well enough) whether a file contains text. The type of a file is kept for it as a *property* in the repository. We want to make sure the file-type properties of files in an `.xcodeproj` package ensure they will be handled as text.

8

The first thing to do is to turn on *auto-properties*, which is the mechanism for making Subversion set particular properties for particular patterns of file names. Find the following line and uncomment it:

```
# enable-auto-props = yes
```

Then go to the end of the file, in the [auto-props] section, and append these lines:

```
*.mode* = svn:mime-type=text/X-xcode
*.pbxuser = svn:mime-type=text/X-xcode
*.perspective* = svn:mime-type=text/X-xcode
*.pbxproj = svn:mime-type=text/X-xcode
```

> **NOTE**
>
> It's possible Subversion will recognize that these files contain text without our having to say so. However, it isn't documented to do that, so conservative practice requires that we make it explicit.

With this, all the files (that I know of) in an .xcodeproj project document will be handled as text. Save config and close it.

## Telling Xcode About a Repository

Xcode must be made aware of a repository before it can take advantage of it. Every repository you'll use in Xcode must be registered in the SCM pane of the Preferences window. Select **Preferences** (⌘ **Comma**) from the **Xcode** menu. Select the **SCM** icon, well to the right in the list at the top of the window. Then select the **Repositories** tab (see Figure 8.1).

At the left of the Preferences window is a list (probably empty) of the repositories Xcode knows about. We want to add the Linear repository to the list. Press the + button at the bottom, and you will be presented with a sheet asking for a name for the new entry (type **Linear File Repository**), and its type (select **Subversion** from the pop-up menu). Click **OK** to proceed.

> **NOTE**
>
> Because the repository list is in Xcode global preferences, more than one Xcode project can make use of a repository. If you organize your SCM by having each of your projects in separate subdirectories of one repository, you need to identify the repository only once. Xcode makes it easy to add subdirectories to repositories, and to check files out from such subdirectories.

Now we enter the details of the repository in the text fields on the right of the window. When you start, Xcode shows a notification at the bottom, indicating the configuration is incomplete. As you proceed, the notification may be replaced by a red gem, indicating that Xcode cannot find a valid repository from the information entered so far.

You'll see that the **Name** field is already filled in. The next field is **URL**; Subversion identifies all repositories, even local file-based ones, by URL. The correct URL for our repository is file:///Users/Shared/Subversion/Linear. When you tab out of the **URL** field, the **Scheme** and **Path** fields are filled automatically. Had we filled in those fields, instead of the **URL** field, Xcode would have built the URL.

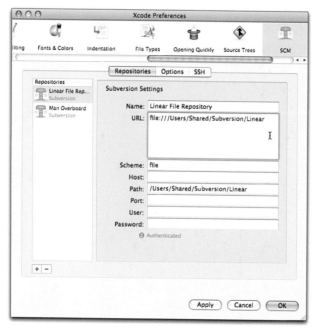

FIGURE 8.1     The SCM pane of the Preferences window, set up for the repository at /Users/ Shared/Subversion/Linear. Name the repository in the top text field, and give a URL for it in the second. Xcode fills the remaining fields automatically.

Now that the information has been filled in, and correctly identifies a Subversion repository, the gem turns green, and its label changes to **Authenticated**. Click the **OK** button to accept your work.

> **NOTE**
>
> The combinations of communications schemes, paths, and authentication methods are many. Our file-based repository is simple to deal with, but Xcode provides fields to construct more complex URLs.

## Controlling Linear

Now that Subversion is ready to receive an Xcode project folder, let's add Linear to the repository.

By convention, Subversion repositories contain three directories:

- ▶ trunk, which contains the initial files and directories of a project, and the revisions that derive from them.

- ▶ tags, which contains markers (to oversimplify) to identify particular stages of development—such as when you've finalized the file revisions that go into the 1.0 or 1.0.1 releases of your product.

▶ branches, which contains markers (again, to oversimplify) that represent lines of development that diverge from the main trunk. For instance, development of version 1.0.2 of a product might continue on the trunk, while the substantially different work on version 1.1 proceeds independently on a separate branch.

Using command-line Subversion (the svn tool), the way to add a project to a repository is to create an umbrella directory; add trunk, tags, and branches subdirectories; copy the contents of the Linrg project directory into trunk, and issue the svn import command to load the whole structure into the repository. (When files and directories are newly added to a repository, they are said to be *imported*. See the documentation for your SCM system for information about the relevant commands.)

We'll do it differently, using only the tools Xcode provides us. Select the menu command **SCM > Repositories**. The Repositories window (see Figure 8.2) appears.

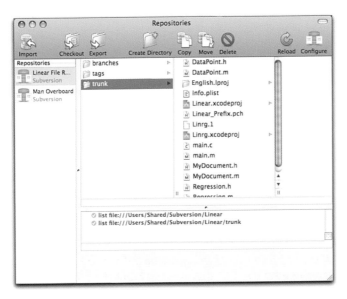

FIGURE 8.2    The Repositories window. All the repositories known to Xcode are listed at the left. When a repository is selected, the browser to the right is filled with all the directories and files the repository contains. Below the browser columns is a listing of the transactions the Repository window has had with the selected repository. Here, the local Linear repository has been loaded with the contents of the Linear project folder.

Rather than create a local directory tree to give the repository the contents we want, we can create the contents directly. Select the **Linear File Repository** from the list at the left. The browser, on the right, is empty, because the Linear repository has no contents. Click the **Create Directory** button in the toolbar (see Figure 8.3). A sheet appears asking you to name the new directory and provide a comment for the occasion. Enter **tags** and **The standard tags directory**, respectively. Then click the **Create Directory** button at the lower right of the sheet.

FIGURE 8.3    The toolbar of the Repositories window. The toolbar makes it possible to perform all but the most subtle operations on a repository without leaving Xcode

You're ahead of me if you want to click the **Create Directory** button again for the branches directory, but be careful! After the last step, the Repositories browser has selected the new tags directory. If you click **Create Directory** now, you will find that the new branches directory will appear inside tags. This is not what we want. The selection of tags turns out to be quite sticky. The only way to remove the selection, and ensure that the new directory will go in the root of the Linear repository, is to Command-click the tags item.

With no subdirectory of the Linear repository selected, you can now create a branches directory, name it, and enter a comment. Then click the **Create Directory** button.

The actual project directory—the Linrg folder, containing all the files and directories for Linrg and Linear—is trickier. Obviously, we can't create them out of nothing in the repository. We must import them into the repository.

Make sure, once again, that nothing within the repository is selected—Command-click to deselect—and then click the **Import** button at the left end of the toolbar. The Repositories window produces another sheet. This time, it's a variant on the standard open-file sheet seen throughout Mac OS X. Navigate to the Linrg folder—the project folder containing the files and directories that make up the Linrg and Linear projects. Select the Linrg folder, and fill the comment field at the bottom with something appropriate, such as "Initial check-in of the Linrg project directory." Then click the **Import** button at the lower right (see Figure 8.4).

Something is wrong, or at least not quite right: The browser for the Linear repository contains three directories: branches, tags, and... Linrg. Not trunk. If you click the Linrg directory, you see it contains everything we want in that directory, but the name is not what we want. We must correct that.

Select the Linrg directory in the Repositories browser, and click the **Move** button in the toolbar. Subversion, like UNIX, handles renaming as a "move" of the file. (The underlying command is svn mv.) Yet another sheet appears for the move operation. We want the Linrg directory in the repository to have a new name: trunk. Below the **Name** field is a browser for the repository, in which we can select the directory that is to receive the thing we are moving. We want to select the root of the repository, and once again, Xcode is stubborn about keeping the selection on a subdirectory.

> **NOTE**
>
> You'll notice that the build folder did not get added to the trunk directory of the repository. This is because build was one of the names we added to the global-ignores options in the **/.subversion** file.

Command-click to remove any highlighting, and then click the sheet's **Move** button (see Figure 8.5).

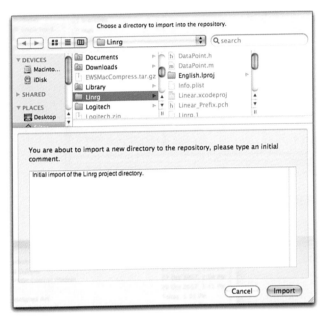

FIGURE 8.4    The sheet that appears when you click the **Import** button in the toolbar of the Repositories window. The upper part of the sheet is the familiar open-file browser. Select the folder containing the Linrg/Linear project files, enter a suitable comment, and click the sheet's **Import** button.

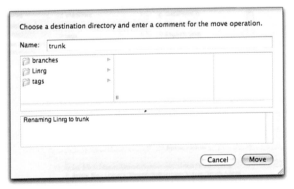

FIGURE 8.5    The Repositories window's **Move** function also serves to rename items in a repository. Type in the new name, and select the destination for the item to be moved. In this case, we want to "move" the file to the root of the repository (where it was already), so we must make sure none of the items at the root are selected.

The repository is now as we want it to be: Directories for branches, tags, and trunk, with trunk populated with the contents of our Linrg directory.

# Getting a Controlled Linear

Importing the Linrg directory into a repository does not mean that the local Linrg directory has the benefits of version control. A *working copy* of a project under SCM needs information associated with it that identifies the repository, designates what the last revisions of every file and directory are, and (in the case of Subversion) keeps a copy of every file in the condition it was in at the last time it was checked out from the repository. (Subversion keeps all this in a .svn directory within each directory of the working copy.)

So, we need to retrieve (check out) a working copy from the repository. On the command line, we do this using the svn checkout command, passing in a URL for the trunk subdirectory, plus the name of a directory to receive the checkout. However, Xcode provides a way to do this without resorting to the command line.

We already have the Repositories window open (**SCM > Repositories** if not). Designate the directory we want to check out by selecting trunk in the Repository browser. Click the toolbar's **Checkout** button. Xcode presents a standard save-file sheet. Use the sheet's browser to choose where the working-copy directory is to go, and then name the directory; let's call it **Linear**, to distinguish the working copy from the noncontrolled Linrg directory. Click the **Checkout** button of the sheet.

> **NOTE**
>
> If you want only the contents of the repository, without creating the .svn directories that make a working copy, use the **Export** button.

Subversion will create the Linear directory and swiftly transfer the contents of the repository's trunk directory into it. It will also create the .svn directories that turn a folder tree into a working copy.

As soon as the transfer is done, Xcode offers to open the Xcode project file (Linear. xcodeproj) it finds in the new working copy. Accept this by clicking the default button (or pressing **Return**).

As we use the version-controlled Linear project, we will want the SCM status of each file in the project displayed in the Groups & Files list. You can add columns to Groups & Files by right-clicking (Control-clicking) in the header of the list. This will pop up a menu showing all the additional columns the list might contain. (One might complain of a user interface design that hides features in contextual menus, but there's nothing to be done about it; Xcode simply has too many commands and options to put them all under the menu bar.) Select **SCM**, and the SCM column appears at the left of the list, headed by a cylinder (the traditional flow chart symbol for persistent storage).

Our work is still not entirely done. The header for the SCM column has an *X* through the cylinder symbol. Xcode has opened the project document from a working copy, but the project has not associated itself with a repository. (This is not as strange as it seems: When you checked the project document in, it had not associated itself with a repository. It comes out of the repository in the same condition.) We must still make the link by hand.

Double-click the project (top) icon in the Groups & Files list to open the Project Info window. If the **General** tab is not selected, click it. Select **Linear File Repository (Subversion)** in the **SCM Repository** pop-up at the bottom of the window. The $X$ in the SCM column header disappears. Because the working copy doesn't have any changes, and the repository has had no known changes since we checked Linear out, the SCM column is completely clear. This will change.

Click any file in the project (opening disclosure triangles as necessary), and then select **SCM > Get SCM Info** from the menu. An Info window appears for the file—in fact, it's the same window you get if you select the file and click the **Info** button in the toolbar, or press ⌘I—and select the **SCM** tab.

The window (see Figure 8.6) is dominated by a table and a text area. Each line of the table represents a revision—an instance of changing information in the repository—that affected the selected file. The table shows the revision number, author, date, and message for the change. When you select a line in the table, the text area fills with a more detailed summary of that revision. The buttons below the text area duplicate functions for managing your working copy of the file, and comparing it against previous revisions; these duplicate commands are available in the **SCM** menu.

FIGURE 8.6    The **SCM** tab of a file's Info window. The top of the window contains every Subversion revision that affected the selected file. Selecting one of these revisions fills the text area with a summary of the revision, including date, author, comment, and a list of all the files and directories changed in that revision.

**NOTE**

Every time you commit a revision to a repository, Subversion increments the revision number for the whole repository. In effect, a revision number represents the state of the whole project at any point in time. By contrast, CVS keeps a separate revision number for each file in a project. The files are coordinated in time by setting a tag, which keeps a list of files and revision numbers in effect when the tag was set.

# Revising

Let's have an exercise in managing changes through SCM. For the purpose of this exercise, I assume you have a second user account available to you on your Mac, and that Xcode has been run there, so all the first-run tasks are out of the way. I'll call your regular account UserA, and the account you'll use for the exercise UserB.

1. Switch to the other user account (UserB).

2. Open Xcode.

3. Using the SCM pane of the Preferences window, let Xcode know about the Linear repository, as we did in the earlier section "Telling Xcode About a Repository" (file:///Users/Shared/Subversion/Linear). For UserB's purposes, you can name the repository anything you like—it's a per-user convenience.

4. Select **SCM > Repositories** to open the Repositories window.

5. Select the Linear repository, and then the trunk directory.

6. Click the **Checkout** button, and place the new checkout directory in UserB's account. Naming the new folder **Linear** would be handy, but the name won't matter to Xcode or Subversion.

7. Click the **Checkout** button in the Checkout sheet.

8. Accept the offer to open Linear.xcodeproj.

9. In the **General** tab of the Project Info window, associate the project with the Linear repository.

10. Right- (Control-) click in the Groups & Files header to add the SCM column to it.

Now that we have a working copy of the Linear project set up and ready to edit, let's make a few changes.

At least in my copy of the project, I forgot to set the name of the copyright holder, leaving __MyCompanyName__ scattered throughout the project. We should relieve this embarrassing condition. Bring up the Project Find window (**Edit > Find > Find in Project**, or ⇧⌘F). See Figure 8.7.

Find-and-replace dialogs are surely familiar to you: Type **__MyCompanyName__** into the upper field, and **Frederic F. Anderson** (please) into the lower. Then click **Find**. Note that only when the search has completed will the **Replace** button be enabled; you must review the matches before you replace them.

The list in the middle of the window fills with all instances of __MyCompanyName__ found in the project. Most of these are in .m and .h files, but there is one surprise: InfoPlist.strings. We would likely have missed that in a file-by-file replacement. Now click the **Replace** button to change them all to Frederic F. Anderson (seriously, I *am* the copyright holder).

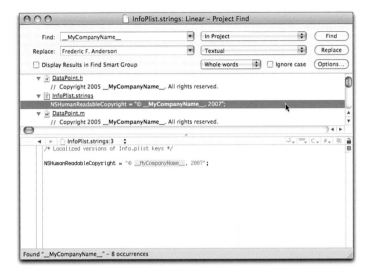

FIGURE 8.7    The Project Find window, filled out for replacing __MyCompanyName__ with something more accurate. The text to find is in the top field, and the text to replace it with is in the next lower. Clicking Find fills the list in the middle with the instances of the found text; clicking one of these fills the editor pane with the file in question. The Replace button is disabled until the search has been completed.

You've changed a number of files. Hold down the **Option** key and select **File > Save All** (or press ⌥⌘S). A dialog will appear listing all the files that have changed. Click the **Save All** button.

As soon as you do this, the letter *M* appears in the SCM column of the Groups & Files list next to every file that you saved. (If such files are in groups that are collapsed, the groups' icons have the M flag next to them.) This indicates that the Subversion status of those files is "modified"—your working copies are different from the files you checked out from the repository (see Figure 8.8).

**WARNING**

If you click one of the items in the "found" list, you'll discover that the replace operation will apply only to the selected instance of the found text. This is handy when you don't want to change every found instance: You can Command-click through the list to pick only the ones you want to replace. In this case, we want to replace all of them. Therefore, if you do have a line selected, **Edit > Select All** will focus the replacement on all of them.

Let's make a second change. Suppose UserB has decided to make it clear that the last few methods declared in DataPoint.h are there for the Key-Value Coding protocol. Open DataPoint.h, and add the following line just before the declaration for the method -[DataPoint x]:

```
// KVC Accessors
```

Save the file. Because `DataPoint.h` was already modified, there is no change in its M flag.

It's easy to remember the simple changes we have made to Linear's files, but suppose we had made more, and more subtle, changes. With `DataPoint.h` in the front window (or selected in the Groups & Files list), select **SCM > Compare With > Base**. This brings up a file-comparison window (new in Xcode 3—previously, file comparison was offloaded to the FileMerge application or BBEdit) showing the file as it was when we last checked it out, and the file as it exists after your edits (see Figure 8.9). The "old" file is on the left; your current working copy is on the right. (You can change the left-right ordering in the SCM panel of the Preferences window.)

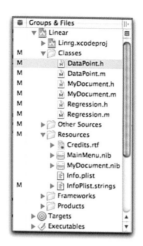

FIGURE 8.8     The Groups & Files list after files have been modified from what they were when checked out. Every modified file has an *M* next to it in the SCM column. Groups containing modified files are also flagged with an *M*, so you can find modifications even inside closed groups.

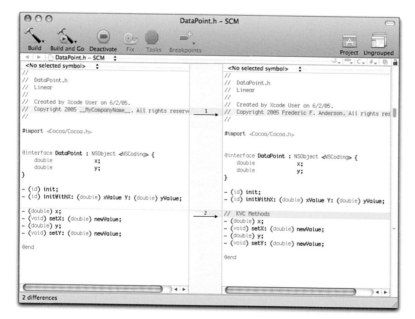

FIGURE 8.9     Xcode's file-comparison window. The "old" version of a file is shown in the left section of the editor; the version you are currently working on is in the right. The two views scroll together, and in the middle are markers indicating where the two versions differ. The differing lines are highlighted, and the highlights are visually linked.

> **WARNING**
>
> As of this writing, Xcode 3.0 will not save a file edited in the comparison window, nor propagate your changes to your working copy of the file. This is a bug, and it might be corrected by the time you read this. One workaround is to hold down the **Shift** and **Option** keys and select **File > Save a Copy As** (⌥⇧⌘S). You will be presented with a save-file sheet in which you can place and name the rightmost side of the comparison window so that it overwrites the original file. Another workaround is to select all the edited text, copy it, and paste it to replace the contents of the working-copy file. A third option is to select a different comparison application (such as FileMerge or BBEdit) in the **Options** tab of the SCM panel of the Preferences window.

Each region in which the two files differ is highlighted; the region on one side is linked to the corresponding region on the other by a continuation of the highlight through the gutter between them. There are several things you might do with a difference. The easiest is to do nothing at all, and let your working copy of the file stand as is. Or, you could edit the working copy in any way you want. Or, you can click the arrow in the gutter between the changed regions and select an option that edits your working copy to reflect the old version, the new version, neither, or both, one after the other. These are edits, like any other, and must be saved. Close the window when you have finished.

> **NOTE**
>
> You can jump quickly between differences in the comparison window by using the **up-arrow** and **down-arrow** keys. If you've shifted keyboard focus by clicking in one of the text views, click in the middle difference view to restore focus there, and the arrow keys will work again.

Leave the comment you added to DataPoint.h in place.

> **Base Versus Latest**
>
> Why compare against the "base" version rather than "latest," which is the option Xcode puts first and gives a Command key equivalent for?
>
> In this case, with the repository on the same machine and no one else having changed the repository (so far), there's no difference. "Latest" refers to the last revision *currently in the repository*. If someone has changed the file in the repository since you last checked it out or updated it, the last repository version is pulled in for the comparison. This is useful, but what if you are not in communication with the repository (it's on a network server, and you aren't on the net), or if you want to review only the changes you have made? The "base" version is *the last revision you checked out or updated*. Subversion keeps a snapshot of that version on your computer. There is no need to be in contact with the repository to make the comparison, and of course, any difference from the base version would only be due to your changes.

UserB has made all the changes he cares to make, and now wants to transfer them to the repository. Select **SCM > Commit Entire Project**. As with all operations that change a repository, you should provide a message that explains the change. A sheet appears for the purpose; type something like "Changed copyright holder; added KVC comment to DataPoint.h" and click **Commit**. The repository is now in sync with your working copy, and the M flags disappear from the Groups & Files list.

UserB is done. Now let's switch back to UserA. He has a working copy of the Linear project file open, and the Groups & Files list shows there isn't anything going on.

Now, if UserA were to select **SCM > Refresh Entire Project**, all the files UserB changed would be flagged with the letter *U* in the SCM column, indicating that there are updates available for each of them. If he's smart, UserA will then select **SCM > Update Entire Project** to pull all those changes into his working copy. But UserA isn't smart, or he doesn't refresh and update all the time, or he's simply out of communication with the repository. In any event, for the purposes of this exercise, he doesn't know an update is available.

> **NOTE**
>
> Suppose, on the other hand, you aren't satisfied with the changes you made since your last Subversion update. Perhaps you've done extensive work on an approach that didn't work out at all. If you haven't checked your changes in, there's a simple solution. Select **SCM > Discard Changes**, and you'll have the previous revision back. If you can't reach your networked repository, it doesn't matter; Subversion keeps your last update on your machine for just this purpose. The equivalent command on the command line is `svn revert`.

> **NOTE**
>
> It seems natural to think of any transfer of information from the repository to the working copy as being a *checkout*, but SCM systems use that term only for the initial creation of a controlled working copy on a client's computer. An *update*, making an existing working copy conform to changes that have occurred in the repository, is a separate concept, and gets a separate name.

Let's make a change to `DataPoint.h`. Like UserB, UserA thinks it is worthwhile to mark the Key-Value accessors as being special. But instead of inserting a comment before the x accessor, he inserts

```
#pragma mark Key-Value Coding
```

and then he saves `DataPoint.h`. As before, the M marker appears next to the file's name in the Groups & Files list. At this point, Xcode checks with the repository (if it can) and sees an update became available since UserA's last checkout. It flags `DataPoint.h` with a *U*. For the purposes of this exercise, UserA doesn't see the flag.

UserA thinks that "something attempted, something done" has earned a check-in of his changes, and he selects **SCM > Commit Entire Project**. He enters his message and clicks **Commit**.

The Linear project window comes to the front and a sheet indicates that the commit has failed. The repository keeps a linear progression of revisions, and Subversion refuses to check in a local version that does not reflect the changes to the repository that have gone before. (It actually is possible to continue simultaneous development on separate branches, but that's a later topic.) Now UserA has to deal with that update. He clicks **OK**, and then selects **SCM > Update Entire Project**.

The problem of `DataPoint.h` still hasn't gone away. Instead of a U flag, there is now a *C* next to the file's name, indicating that the working copy and the latest revision in the repository are in conflict. The two differ in ways that Subversion could not resolve automatically.

Note, by the way, that none of the other files UserB changed got flagged for a conflict. The change in copyright holders was straightforward. And if you examine those other files, you'll see that the change was made without fuss.

Open `DataPoint.h`. Note that even in this file, the change in the copyright holder got through. When it updates files, Subversion doesn't just substitute one file for the other. It *merges* the update's changes into the working copy. If the update changes a line that was not changed in the working copy, the change is made silently.

What you'll also find in DataPoint.h are *conflict markers*. Subversion presents, in a conflicted file, the questionable lines as they appear in your working copy, followed by the same region of the file as it appears in the latest revision in the repository. The two are separated by a line of equal signs. Your version is preceded by left arrowheads and `.mine`, and the repository's version is followed by right arrowheads and `.r`*N*, where *N* is the number of the latest revision in the repository:

```
- (id) initWithX: (double) xValue Y: (double) yValue;


<<<<<<< .mine
#pragma mark Key-Value Coding
=======
// KVC  Methods
>>>>>>> .r5
- (double) x;
- (void) setX: (double) newValue;
```

In this way, you have a choice between your changes and the changes made by UserB. In this case, remove the `.mine` line, and everything between the equal signs and the `.r`*N* line. UserA finds #pragmas much cooler than comments. Save the file.

# FileMerge

When it finds a file to be in conflict, Subversion creates four files. The file with the original name contains the conflict markers we just saw. There is a .mine file with exactly the contents of your working copy as of the update. There are also .rM and .rN files that contain the last revision you checked out, and the last revision in the repository. When you tell Subversion the conflict has been resolved, the extra files are removed.

These extra files provide enough information to give you a good visual impression of the contrast between the later revision (from the repository) and your working copy. Suppose you made your changes based on revision 5. The conflicting changes came from the repository at revision 11. If you could "subtract" revision 5 (.r5) from your revision (.mine), you'd have a list (call it A) of the changes you made. If you could "subtract" revision 5 (.r5) from revision 11 (.r11), you'd have a list (B) of the changes made by the other developer(s) since you last visited the repository. You want to match your changes (list A) against the other guy's changes (list B).

This is called a three-way merge, and the three files Subversion creates in a conflict are all you need to do one. Xcode's file-comparison window can't do a three-way merge (or, as this was written, *any* merges), but Apple's FileMerge application, installed at /Developer/ Applications/Utilities/FileMerge, can.

When it is first started, FileMerge presents a control panel set up for a simple two-file comparison (see Figure 8.10). You can specify a file by clicking the button on the left and using a standard open-file dialog, by typing the full path to the file in the text field, or by dragging the file's icon into the well at the right. In this case, we want to compare the two end revisions: the .r11 file (I prefer the revision that isn't mine on the left) and the .mine file (on the right).

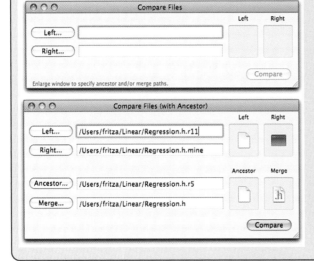

FIGURE 8.10    The control panel that is shown when you open FileMerge. At first, it offers a simple comparison of two files (top). If you resize the window so that it is taller (bottom), it provides spaces to specify a total of four files: The last is the file to receive the merged product. The next-to-last is the common ancestor of the revisions to compare. And the upper two are the revisions from which you will choose the changes.

Resize the window vertically, to disclose rows for two additional files. The **Ancestor** file is the common file from which the comparison files descended—the .r5 file. And the **Merge** file is the file that is to receive your choices, the one without any special extension.

When you click the **Compare** button, FileMerge displays the left, right, and merge files in a three-paned editor (see Figure 8.11). You can scroll up and down in the usual way. The arrows in the middle gutter show which alternative is currently in the merged product; by default, this is the version on the right. Select a difference and choose from the pop-up menu at the bottom right of the window to make a different choice.

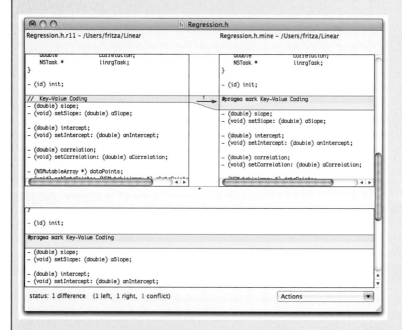

FIGURE 8.11     The FileMerge editor for a three-way merge. The branch files containing the differences between your version of the file and the last revision in the repository are at left and right, with differences highlighted in the gutter between them. The arrow in the gutter indicates which version will go into the merged product file (at bottom). Use the pop-up menu at the bottom right to select which version to use.

When you have finished, select **File > Save Merged File** (⌘**S**) to save the result. Go back to Xcode, mark the conflicted file as resolved, and commit your changes to the repository.

Apple hopes to do away with FileMerge in the near future, as soon as Xcode's own file-comparison facility catches up.

You have resolved the conflict, but Subversion doesn't know that. Select **SCM > Resolved** while DataPoint.h is selected or frontmost, to clear the conflict marker and remove the files auxiliary to the conflict.

The C flag is removed, *and is not replaced by an M*, despite the fact that the working DataPoint.h you have represents a modification from the latest version in the repository. This is a bug, and might have been resolved by the time you read this. For now, select **SCM > Refresh Entire Project** to force Xcode to review the status of all the files in the project. The M flag appears in the SCM column.

Repeat the commit process, and this time the commit goes through. You don't have to commit the entire project; it's often convenient to select **Commit Changes** from the **SCM** menu to check in just the changes to a single file.

It is instructive to select (or edit) DataPoint.h and do **SCM > Get SCM Info**. Look at the revision history at the top of the window (see Figure 8.12). You will see that the list marks each revision with the username of its author. Selecting a line puts the comment for that revision into the text area below the list.

Select the latest revision, and click the **Annotate** button. A new editor window appears, with content like this:

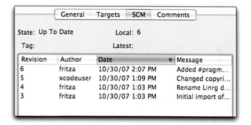

FIGURE 8.12     The revision list at the top of the **SCM** tab of the DataPoint.h Info window, showing the revisions we have put that file through. The table lists the author, date, and message for each revision.

```
3      fritza Tue 10/30/07 01:03 PM // Created by Xcode User...
5   xcodeuser Tue 10/30/07 01:09 PM // Copyright 2005 Frederic...
3      fritza Tue 10/30/07 01:03 PM //
```

That is, each line is labeled with the revision at which that particular line was checked in, who checked it in, and the time it happened. This corresponds to the blame (or praise, or annotate) command of the svn command-line tool.

**Why Are My Files Red?**

As soon as you divorce a project from the directory in which it was created, you may find that some of the filenames under the project group have turned red, indicating that Xcode can no longer find the file associated with that file reference. There are two causes.

First, the file may simply not be there. This would be the case for the file Linear.app in the Products group of the Groups & Files list. There is no build directory in the checked-out Linear project directory, and no built application inside it. Building Linear from the checked-out project will take care of that.

Second, the file may be there, but Xcode may have an absolute reference to it; that is, the file is specified by its full pathname on your hard drive. If the project is checked out or otherwise transferred to a machine that doesn't have access to the original file, the reference becomes vacant and is shown in red. You can resolve this problem by changing the absolute reference to a relative one, which is what it usually should have been in the first place.

Hold down the **Command** key and click all the red files under the project group to select them. Press ⌘I to open an Info window for all the selected references. Change the **Path Type** pop-up to **Relative to Enclosing Group** or **Relative to Project**. This will make Xcode search for the files relative to the directories associated with the groups the files are in or the project file, respectively.

In some cases, you might have to open an Info window on an individual file and use the **Choose** button to establish the path to the file.

The sheet presented when you add files to a project offers a choice of methods by which the project can refer to the added files. In general, it's wisest to avoid absolute paths for project-specific files.

# Rolling Back

One great advantage, I have said, of version control is that it can save you from disastrous changes to your source code. We've already seen how to do this before you've committed your changes—simply select **SCM > Discard Changes**. But we can do more.

Suppose you've repented of everything you've done with DataPoint.h. You can't revert (discard changes) because you've committed your own changes, and some changes were made by UserB. How do you deal with this?

Select DataPoint.h in the Groups & Files list. Select **SCM > Update To > Revision....** A sheet appears that is a mimic of the SCM Info window for that file. It is there so that you can select which version of the file you want to roll back to. Select the version that came before UserB's change of the copyright notice and insertion of the KVC comment. Click the **Update** button.

DataPoint.h is now flagged with a *U*, to reflect that the revision you now have does not reflect the latest revision in the repository. Open DataPoint.h, and see that your working copy of the file is indeed stripped of all the changes UserA and UserB made to it. If you want to, you can now proceed to edit and build with this version of the file. Before you can check your version in (*don't do this*), you have to update first, to reconcile your changes against the latest revision in the repository, but you're familiar with that process.

Rolling back wholesale to an earlier revision may be too drastic. We'd like to pick and choose among the changes that have been made. Select **SCM > Update To > Latest** (⇧⌘L) to abandon the rollback and return to the version with all the changes included.

The gentler solution is to compare your working file with a previous revision, and pick and choose among the changes. Select **SCM > Compare With > Revision**. The Xcode file-comparison

**NOTE**

My earlier caveat from the note in the "Revising" section applies here: Xcode 3.0 does not permit directly saving the merged working copy to disk. Later revisions may be able to do so. See the earlier note for a workaround.

window appears, highlighting every difference between that version of `DataPoints.h` and your working copy. You can select between each difference, and edit, as before. Save the result, and Subversion will note that your working copy is now modified and will need to be checked in.

# Tagging

As I noted before, each revision number in a Subversion repository represents the state of the project at the moment of each check-in. The repository is a series of snapshots of the project. On the command line, it is even possible to check out a version of the project as of a specific date.

However, when you want to refer to a specific revision—such as "the Linear project as of the end of Chapter 8"—it is not convenient to remember that that was revision 10 (or whatever). We want something that says "Chapter 8."

This is the rationale for the common SCM concept of *tags*. CVS has a distinct tag command to identify a slice of a project's revisions with a simple name. Subversion implements tags by *copying* a revision of the project to a new directory in the repository's tags directory.

> **NOTE**
>
> A "copy" sounds like a hideously expensive operation. Doesn't each tag multiply the size of the repository? No: Subversion "copies" repository directories by noting that the "copy" contains simply a particular revision of the original. The expense in terms of storage space, and processing time, is essentially nil.

FIGURE 8.13    The Repositories window after tagging the latest revision of Linear as Chapter-8. This was done by selecting the `trunk` directory (where all the changes had been checked in) and using the **Copy** button to create a `Chapter-8` subdirectory of the `tags` directory. This new directory will forever reflect the state of the project as of the time it was created.

Here is how to create a tag. Bring the Repositories window forward (**SCM > Repositories**). Make sure the Linear repository is selected and select the trunk directory—you should see the Linear files inside. Click the **Copy** button in the toolbar. A sheet will appear asking you to name the copy; call it **Chapter-8**. In the next part of the sheet, select the directory that will receive the copy—the tags directory. Then enter a message at the bottom, such as "Creating a tag for the Linear project as of the end of Chapter 8." Then click the **Copy** button.

From now on, if you want the Linear project as of the time you set the tag, just select the tags/Chapter-8 directory in the Repositories window, and check it out.

> **NOTE**
>
> Human nature being what it is, the repository might have moved on to additional revisions before you can mark a particular one with a tag. The svn copy command-line tool provides ways to designate particular revisions for the copy. See svn help copy and the Tags section of the Subversion book (*Version Control with Subversion*) available online at http://svnbook.red-bean.com/.

> **NOTE**
>
> After you have frozen a tag, you have some choices as to what you can do with it. From the Repositories window, you can check it out to a new directory (to create an on-disk working copy) or export it (to create a directory without SCM information). From the command line, you can use the svn switch command to change your working copy in-place to match the tagged version (all check-ins, however, will update the tag), or the svn merge command to alter your working copy to incorporate only some of the differences between it and the tagged version. See the Subversion book for details on these commands.

# Summary

This chapter has discussed what software-configuration management is and which SCM systems Xcode coordinates with. We went through the setup of a simple, local Subversion repository; and using Xcode's powerful support for SCM, we brought Linear under version control. We saw how to record changes in Linear in its repository, and how to reconcile versions of our files when changes come from more than one source.

We saw also how to roll back the changes we made, and how to designate a particular snapshot of our project with a named tag.

There is much more to Subversion than has been covered in this short chapter. The definitive source for reference and instruction on Subversion is the book *Version Control with Subversion* written by (some of) the authors of Subversion, and revised with each release of the tool. Find it at http://svnbook.red-bean.com/.

Once you know your way around Subversion, the command-line tool can steer you to the proper command forms and options. Use svn help and svn help *commandName* for pointers.

# CHAPTER 9

# Property Lists

**IN THIS CHAPTER**

▶ **Property Lists and their Importance**

▶ **Creating and Editing Property Lists**

▶ **Adding a Menu Command**

▶ **Text Macros**

Before continuing, we need to consider *property lists*. A property list is a simple, structured data format that is used throughout Mac OS X. Preference files, configuration files, the `Info.plist` files that specify bundle properties to the OS, and sometimes even application data files are all applications of the property list format. It's easy to use and powerful enough to serve as at least the first cut at most data storage problems and is the language of many OS services.

## Data Types

A property list consists of one item of data, expressed in one of seven data types. Five property list types are scalar (number, Boolean, string, date, and data), and two are compound (ordered list and dictionary). An ordered list can contain zero or more objects of any property list type. A dictionary contains zero or more pairs, consisting of a string and an object of a property list type.

A property list can express most collections of data quite easily. A single data point from our linear-regression application could be represented as a dictionary of two numbers with the keys $x$ and $y;$ a data set would be a list of such dictionaries.

Both Core Foundation and Cocoa provide reference-counted object types that correspond to the property list types (see Table 9.1). In fact, you can pass a Cocoa property list pointer to a Core Foundation routine for the corresponding type; you can also use a `CFTypeRef` for a property list type as though it were a pointer to the corresponding Cocoa object.

TABLE 9.1    Property List Types in Cocoa and Core Foundation

| Data Type | Cocoa | Core Foundation | Markup |
|---|---|---|---|
| Number | NSNumber | CFNumber | `<integer> <float>` |
| Boolean | NSBoolean | CFBoolean | `<true/> <false/>` |
| Text | NSString<br>NSMutableString | CFString<br>CFMutableString | `<string>` |
| Date | NSDate | CFDate | `<date>` |
| Binary data | NSData<br>NSMutableData | CFData C<br>CFMutableData | `<data>` |
| List | NSArray<br>NSMutableArray | CFArray<br>CFMutableArray | `<array>` |
| Associative | NSDictionary<br>NSMutableDictionary | CFDictionary<br>CFMutableDictionary | `<dict>`<br>`<key>...`<br>*plist type ...*<br>`</dict>` |

> **NOTE**
>
> The dictionary data type in Cocoa requires only that the keys in a dictionary be objects of an immutable, copyable type; Core Foundation dictionaries can be even more permissive. However, if you want to use a Cocoa or Core Foundation dictionary in a property list, all keys have to be strings.

# Property List Files

Let's investigate the property list file format by writing a plist file of our own. Both Cocoa and Core Foundation provide methods for converting their property list values directly to the plist format, so writing the file is a simple matter of extending our model to provide a property list type; our views, to include a user action to trigger the writing of the file; and our controller, to link the two.

## Writing a Property List

Let's break the Model-View-Controller design for property lists down by task.

### Model

Our first task is to add to Linear's data model the ability to express itself in property list types. We'll do this by adding categories to the Regression and DataPoint classes. *Categories* are an Objective-C mechanism for adding methods to a class—any class, even those supplied by Cocoa—without disturbing the core implementation of the class. (Realistically, there's no reason we shouldn't add our new methods directly to Regression and DataPoint. The original code is under our control, and nobody is relying on the old version.)

In Xcode, with the Linear project open, press ⌘N to bring up the New File Assistant. The variety of starter content Xcode offers for new files is extensive but doesn't cover category files. Select **Cocoa > Objective-C Class**, and type **Regression-PropertyList** as the base filename. Make sure that the box is checked for generating a header file.

Xcode now presents you with a skeleton class declaration for an NSObject subclass called Regression_PropertyList. Edit the declaration to look like this:

```
#import "Regression.h"
@interface Regression (PropertyList)
- (NSDictionary *) asPropertyList;
@end
```

We declare an interface for an additional category, named PropertyList, on an existing class (Regression) containing the single method -asPropertyList.

To save yourself the trouble of retyping it, copy the following line:

```
- (NSDictionary *) asPropertyList;
```

Press ⌥⌘**up arrow** (or click the small button at the top right of the editor view, labeled with two overlapping squares) to switch your view to the .m file. Once again, the template we're given has to be edited a bit, but it's close. Regression-PropertyList.m should look like this:

```
#import "Regression-PropertyList.h"
#import "DataPoint-PropertyList.h"

@implementation Regression (PropertyList)

- (NSDictionary *) asPropertyList
{
    // Make an array to hold the property-list version of
    // the data points.
    NSMutableArray *  pointArray = [NSMutableArray array] ;
    NSEnumerator *     iter = [dataPoints objectEnumerator];
    DataPoints *        curr;
    // For each data point, add its property-list version
    // to the pointArray.
    while (curr = [iter nextObject]) {
        [pointArray addObject: [curr asPropertyList]];
    }
    // Return a dictionary with the points
    // and the three statistics.
    return [NSDictionary dictionaryWithObjectsAndKeys:
            pointArray,
            @"points",
```

```
            [NSNumber numberWithDouble: [self slope]],
            @"slope",
            [NSNumber numberWithDouble: [self intercept]],
            @"intercept",
            [NSNumber numberWithDouble: [self correlation]],
            @"correlation",
            nil];
}
@end
```

> **NOTE**
>
> The time to get `Regression-PropertyList.m` (and `.h`, and all the other files we'll create as Linear goes forward) under version control is *now*, as we create them. You'll see the new files, in the Groups & Files list, are flagged with ?, meaning they are in the working copy's directory, but are unknown to SCM. Select those files, and then **SCM > Add to Repository**. The files are now flagged with *A*, meaning they will be added to the repository the next time you check the working copy in. The repository will not be changed until you commit those files. If you mark a file for adding, and decide you made a mistake, select it and choose **SCM > Discard Changes**; after you confirm the command, the file will once again be flagged with a ?. Note that because we've changed the project file by adding source files, the **Project** icon at the top of the Groups & Files list is now marked with an *M*.

In the first part of the `asPropertyList` method, we build up an `NSMutable-Array` containing the property list version of each data point. Then we build an `NSDictionary` with four keys—`points`, `slope`, `intercept`, and `correlation`—to identify the point list and the respective statistics. Note the use of `NSNumber` as the class embodying the simple number type for use in property lists.

You'll want to move the new files in the Groups & Files list into the Classes group.

The `DataPoint-PropertyList.h` header file uses the same principles:

> **NOTE**
>
> If you use the Groups & Files list to delete a file (not just to remove the project's reference to it), Xcode automatically removes it from the repository at the next check-in.

> **NOTE**
>
> Because all the objects created by the `asPropertyList` methods come from class convenience methods, not from methods with `new`, `alloc`, or `copy` in their names, we know that they are autoreleased, and we need not worry about releasing them ourselves.

```
#import "DataPoint.h"

@interface DataPoint (PropertyList)
- (NSDictionary *) asPropertyList;
@end
```

The same is true for the `DataPoint-PropertyList.m` implementation file:

```
#import "DataPoint-PropertyList.h"

@implementation DataPoint (PropertyList)
- (NSDictionary *) asPropertyList
{
    return [NSDictionary dictionaryWithObjectsAndKeys:
                [NSNumber numberWithDouble: x], @"abscissa",
                [NSNumber numberWithDouble: y], @"ordinate",
                nil];
}
@end
```

## View

Now that we have a way to get our model into property list form, we need a way to make use of it. The easiest way is to add a menu command that saves the active document as a property list. (The *right* way is to add `.plist` as a supported document type for the Linear application and to add support for it to the `dataOfType:error:` and `readFromData:ofType:error:` methods in `MyDocument`, but for instructional purposes, we'll do it the easy way.) Open the `MainMenu.nib` Interface Builder file (see Figure 9.1). The quickest way to do this is to click the Project (top) icon in the Groups & Files list, and then double-click `MainMenu.nib` as it appears in the detail list to the right.

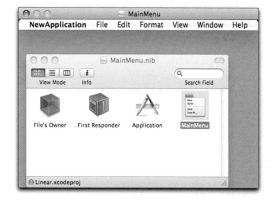

FIGURE 9.1     The `MainMenu.nib` file as it first opens. In a document-based application, the main menu NIB contains only the menu bar, represented by the small window at the top and the icon at the right of the NIB window. The other three icons are placeholders for objects outside the NIB.

`MainMenu.nib` contains only the application menu bar, which appears in a small window containing the menu titles as you would see them in the application's menu bar (see Figure 9.1). Clicking a title drops down a representation of that menu, identical except as hidden items are visible in the Interface Builder display (see Figure 9.2).

---

**Detail Searches**

The *className-categoryName* convention for naming category files can exploit the incremental search feature of the Project window's Detail view. For an example, fill the Detail view with all the files of the project by clicking the **Project** (top) icon in the Groups & Files list at the left. (If the Detail view isn't visible, click the **Editor** icon in the Project window's toolbar.) Now type **Regression** in the search field in the toolbar. The Detail view instantly narrows down to the four files that define the Regression class—Regression.m and .h and Regression-PropertyList.m and .h. If, instead, you type **Property,** the list narrows to Regression-PropertyList.m and .h and DataPoint-PropertyList.m and .h, the category files having to do with property lists. With the handful of classes in our application, this doesn't seem like much of a trick, but detail searches work as quickly on projects with hundreds of source files in dozens of group folders.

For another example, select the **Project Symbols** group toward the bottom of the Groups & Files list. The detail view fills with every method, class, and category defined in the project, as well as every property referenced in the project's NIB files. Typing **list** in the search field reduces the detail list to the definitions and implementations of the two PropertyList categories and the two asPropertyList methods.

---

We want to add a **Save as Plist...** item to the **File** menu. (We include an ellipsis after the label because we'll be presenting a save-file dialog that will allow the user to cancel.) Click the title of the **File** menu so that it drops down, as shown in Figure 9.2. In the Interface Builder Library palette, type **menu** into the search field, and drag the first rectangular icon (labeled **Item**) from the palette to the opened **File** menu, and drop it just below the **Save As...** item. (If you drop it somewhere else, it doesn't matter; if it bothers you, however, you can drag it from where you dropped it to where you wanted it to go.)

With the item in place, double-click the title (**Item**) and type **Save As PList…** as the new title. Press **Return** to end the edit.

Now we have a menu item. How do we make it do something? We know that

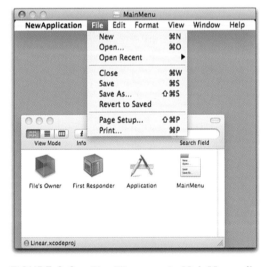

FIGURE 9.2    The **File** menu in **MainMenu.nib** expands when you click its title in the menu window. All items, including hidden ones, are visible in the menu as shown. Menu titles and key equivalents can be edited in place, and you can drag additional items into the menu from the Menus palette.

Cocoa objects that send user commands keep two pieces of information: the action (what is to be done) and the target (what is to do it).

The action is the name of an Objective-C method taking one parameter: It is an identifier ending with a colon. We haven't written the action method yet, but we can make up a name for it: saveAsPList:.

What about the target? To what Cocoa object will we assign the task of responding to saveAsPList:? *I don't know*, says a stubborn part of our subconscious, *anything that wants to, I guess*.

This turns out not to be a stupid answer in Cocoa. Cocoa keeps a continually updated *responder chain*, a series of potential responders to user actions. The chain begins at the "first responder," which may be the selected view in the front window, and then proceeds to the front window, the window's document, and finally to the application itself. You have probably noticed that the second icon in an Interface Builder NIB window represents the first responder. A user interface element can designate the first responder, whatever it may be at the time, as the target of its action, and Cocoa will shop the action up the responder chain until it finds an object that can handle it.

> **NOTE**
>
> The responder chain is a little more complicated than that. For more information, consult Apple's documentation for NSApplication, NSResponder, and the related programming topic articles.

If we try to Control-drag an action link from our new menu item to the **First Responder** icon, we will quickly be balked. Interface Builder will present a HUD for the link, asking us to designate the method selector for our desired action. The list it presents does not include **saveAsPList:**, because we just made that up. Before we make the link, we have to tell Interface Builder that **saveAsPList:** is a possible action.

Interface Builder enables you to do this by editing the properties of the **First Responder** object in the Inspector palette. Select the **First Responder** icon in the NIB window, and press ⌘6 to expose the Identity pane of the Inspector window. The Inspector shows the class of the first responder to be First Responder—another way of saying "whatever the class is of whatever the first responder happens to be at the moment." Under the class label is a list of actions a first responder might perform; an extensive list of "standard" methods is already there. We want to add one of our own.

Click the + (Add) button below the action list; the inspector adds a category for methods defined in MainMenu.nib. In the space for the name of the new action, type **saveAsPList:**. A helpful warning, in red, reminds us that the action method has to have a colon at the end—Cocoa considers saveAsPList and saveAsPList: to be valid, but completely different, method names. Then press the **Return** key to complete the entry. Interface Builder now knows that in this NIB, saveAsPList:, is one of the actions a first responder might perform (see Figure 9.3).

Arrange the NIB window and the menu bar window so that you can see both the new item and the **First Responder** icon. When everything is in place, hold down the **Control** key and drag from the new menu item to the **First Responder** icon. When the icon highlights, release the mouse button (see Figure 9.4).

Now a HUD window appears, listing every known method for the first responder. Move your cursor down to the downward-pointing arrowhead so that the list will scroll down to saveAsPList:. Click it, and the HUD disappears. You have now attached the **Save as Plist...** menu item to the saveAsPList: method of the first responder.

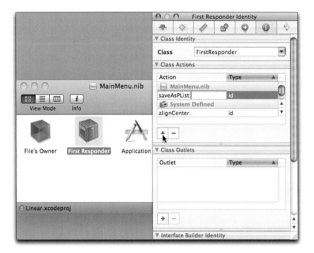

FIGURE 9.3    Editing the actions **First Responder** can respond to. Select the **First Responder** icon in the NIB window, and bring up the Identity Inspector (⌘**6**). Click the **Add** (**+**) button under the Action table, and type `saveAsPList:`, and press **Return** to end editing.

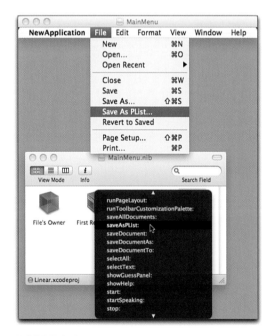

FIGURE 9.4    Linking a menu item to the **First Responder**. Control-drag from the new menu item to the **First Responder** icon. When the icon highlights, release the mouse button. A HUD window appears, offering a list of methods First Responder supports, including the `saveAsPList:` method we just added.

### Controller

When we pulled the name of the saveAsPList: method out of the air, we had no particular implementer in mind for it, but now we have to think about it.

- ▶ The implementer has to be on the responder chain; otherwise, it will never be offered saveAsPList: when it is shopped around.

- ▶ The implementer has to be associated with one, and only one, Regression set.

- ▶ The implementer should, preferably, be an existing class.

Fortunately, we have one such class: MyDocument. As a document class, it is on the responder chain. We've already made it the controller class associated with our Regression model. And, it exists.

We open MyDocument.m and add this line to the beginning:

```
#import "Regression-PropertyList.h"
```

We also add the following lines somewhere in the implementation section:

```
#pragma mark Saving Property Lists
- (IBAction) saveAsPList: (id) sender
{
    // The response to the Save As
    // PList... command
    NSSavePanel * savePanel = [NSSavePanel savePanel];
    // Take the shared save-file panel and set it to save only plists
    if ([savePanel respondsToSelector:
                        @selector(setAllowedFileTypes:)])
        [savePanel setAllowedFileTypes:
                        [NSArray arrayWithObject: @"plist"]];
        // Make a nice default name to present to the user
        NSString *              defaultName;
```

If you have Code Sense set to automatically suggest completions (set it **With Delay** in the Code Sense panel of the Preferences window), and you type a little slowly, you'll find that after you've entered, say, **#import "Regres**, Xcode will fill in sion.h". This looks useful, if incorrect. If Xcode is going to complete what we type, we want it to be the right header file. Press **Esc**; you are now presented with a choice of completions, including the correct one, Regression-PropertyList.h (see Figure 9.5). Arrow-key down to that item, if it isn't already selected, and then press **Return.** The correct header name fills in, and all you have to do is type the closing quote.

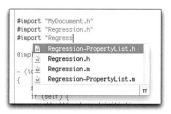

FIGURE 9.5    The word-completion pop-up list for an #include directive. Xcode pulls the names of files that might be included and offers them in a list. Use the arrow keys to make a selection, and then press **Return** to insert it. The π button in the lower-right corner shows that the list is shown in the order that Xcode judges most likely; toggling it to an **A** will set the list to alphabetic order.

6

```
        defaultName = [[self displayName]
                     stringByAppendingPathExtension: @"plist"];
        NSWindowController * controller1st;
        controller1st = [[self windowControllers] objectAtIndex: 0];

        // Present the save panel and designate
        // a method for receiving the result.
        [savePanel beginSheetForDirectory: NSHomeDirectory()
                                     file: defaultName
                            modalForWindow: [controller1st window]
                             modalDelegate: self
                             didEndSelector:
                  @selector(savePanelDidEnd:returnCode:contextInfo:)
                               contextInfo: NULL];
}

- (void) savePanelDidEnd: (NSSavePanel *) sheet
              returnCode: (int) returnCode
             contextInfo: (void *) contextInfo
{
    // The response to the Save-as-plist save panel
    if (returnCode == NSOKButton) {
        // The user OKed the save.
        // Get the property-list representation...
        NSDictionary * pList = [model asPropertyList];
        // ... and write it out
        [pList writeToFile: [sheet filename]
               atomically: YES];
    }
}
```

With all this hooked up and compiled, we run Linear and fill the data table with the old familiar not-quite $y = 2x$:

| | |
|------|--------|
| 1.0  | 2.05   |
| 2.01 | 4      |
| 3.   | 5.987  |
| 4    | 8.1    |
| 5    | 10.0   |

> **NOTE**
>
> Objective-C methods do not have to be declared in advance to be legal or usable by other objects.

We click the **Compute** button to update the statistics (2.00196, 0.0175146, and 0.999871, as before) and pull down the **File** menu to select our new **Save as PList...** command. A save-file sheet appears, most likely offering to save a file named Untitled in your home directory. You can change this if you like, but be sure that you put the file somewhere you can find it, because we will be inspecting its contents.

# Examining Property Lists

There are two ways to examine the contents of a property-list file. Most plist files are text, readable in any text editor; and all plist files are readable and editable in the structured Property List Editor application.

## As Text

When the save is done, we can quit Linear. Now go to the Finder and find the file you just saved. Drag its icon onto the **Xcode** icon in your dock. Xcode presents you with a text editor on the contents of the file, which looks something like this:

```
<?xml version="1.0" encoding="UTF-8"?>
<!DOCTYPE plist PUBLIC "-//Apple//DTD PLIST 1.0//EN"
          "http://www.apple.com/DTDs/PropertyList-1.0.dtd">
<plist version="1.0">
<dict>
    <key>correlation</key>
    <real>0.99987135988591502</real>
    <key>intercept</key>
    <real>0.017514563009515881</real>
    <key>points</key>
    <array>
        <dict>
            <key>abscissa</key>
            <real>5</real>
            <key>ordinate</key>
            <real>10</real>
        </dict>
        <dict>
            <key>abscissa</key>
            <real>4</real>
            <key>ordinate</key>
            <real>8.0999999999999996</real>
        </dict>
        <dict>
            <key>abscissa</key>
            <key>1</real>
            <key>ordinate</key>
            <real>2.0499999999999998</real>
        </dict>
        <dict>
            <key>abscissa</key>
            <real>3</real>
            <key>ordinate</key>
            <real>5.9870000000000001</real>
```

```
        </dict>
        <dict>
            <key>abscissa</key>
            <real>2.0 0 99999999999998</real>
            <key>ordinate</key>
            <real>4</real>
        </dict>
    </array>
    <key>slope</key>
    <real>2.0019605053266103</real>
</dict>
</plist>
```

You likely will be relieved to see that the property list file format is XML and that Cocoa's built-in writer for plist files indents them nicely. The top-level element is `<plist>`, which must contain one property list element—in this case, `<dict>`, for our `Regression` dictionary. A `<dict>` element's contents alternate between `<key>` string elements and property list value elements. One of the keys in the `Regression` dictionary, `points`, has an `<array>` value. An `<array>` may contain zero or more property list elements, of any type, but in this case, they are all `<dict>`s from our `DataPoint` objects.

The nice thing about XML is that it is standard: Correct XML will be accepted by any consumer of a document type definition, regardless of the source. A plist file generated by Cocoa will be treated the same as one generated by a text editor.

The difficult thing about XML is that it must be correct. If you forget to close an element or miss the strict alternation of `<key>` and property list elements in `<dict>` lists, you will get nothing out of Apple's parser. There are four ways to cope with this restriction.

First, you can always start your own plist files by editing a known good plist file. It's difficult to omit the processing instruction or the `<plist>` skeleton if they are already in the file.

Second, you can use the macro or glossary facilities of your text editor to create a document skeleton and wrap your entries in proper tags. Bare Bones Software's BBEdit comes with `.plist` clippings glossary for just this purpose. Xcode, surprisingly, does not include property list macros. We'll be fixing that later in this chapter.

Third, you can use the Property List Editor application, found among the Xcode tools at `/Developer/Applications/Utilities` (see Figure 9.6). The simplest use of Property List Editor is as a check on your text-edited file. Just attempt to open your file with Property List Editor. If the file doesn't open, something's wrong. If the error isn't obvious, find a way to cut about half the list to the clipboard, leaving what, you hope, will still be a legal property list. Try to open the file with Property List Editor again. If the file opens, the error is in the part on the clipboard; if not, it's in the part still in the file. In either case, paste the missing lines back into the file, and cut half the elements out of the half of the file in which you isolated the problem in the previous pass. Repeat this process, reducing your search by halves, until you arrive at a stretch of XML small enough to proofread.

Fourth, and maybe best, use the `plutil` tool. In the terminal, type **`plutil`** **`pathToPropertyList`**. You will then see `pathToPropertyList: ` OK, or a diagnostic message if all is not well. See `man plutil` for details.

> **NOTE**
>
> One of the most common errors is forgetting that the text portions of the property list XML are parsed character data, which means that < and & must be represented by &lt; and &amp;.

FIGURE 9.6    The Property List Editor application, found in the Utilities folder of the Developer Applications, presents the contents of property list files in a visual hierarchy that you may find easier to work with than the raw XML of the file itself. Trying to open a file with PLE is a good way to check whether the file contains a valid property list.

## Property List Editor

Of course, you could just use Property List Editor (PLE) to create your plist files in the first place. Select **New** in the **File** menu (or press ⌘N) to open a window on a new, empty list. Add a root element to the list by clicking the **New Root** button. A line labeled **Root** appears under PropertyList with **Dictionary** listed under Class. **Dictionary** appears as a pop-up menu; clicking in the Class cell shows the full range of choices of property list types.

The button at the upper left of the window is the **New...** button. Its meaning changes depending on what is selected in the list:

- ▶ When the property list is empty, the button is **New Root**. It puts one element in the file.

- ▶ When the selected line is an element inside a container—and is closed, if it is a container itself—the button is **New Sibling**. It adds one element to the same container as the selected element.

- ▶ When the selected line is an open container, the button is **New Child**. It adds one element to the selected container.

Because it is a container, a dictionary, the root element line can be opened. It is closed, so the rules say that the **New...** operation should be **New Sibling**, but there can't be more than one root element, so the **New Sibling** button is disabled. Open the root element, and click **New Child** three times. This creates three new key/value pairs, with the keys in the left column, the types of the values (string) in the middle, and the values themselves (empty) in the right. Name these key/value pairs `Ingredients`, `Material`, and `Method`; make the first two dictionaries and the third an array.

Open the Ingredients dictionary, and click **New Child**. Make the child's key `Eggs` and its type **Dictionary**. This dictionary, in turn, should have the key/string pairs `unit` > `count` and `quantity` > `3`. Take care to change the type of the quantity value to **Number** before setting it. Add more siblings to Eggs—or children to Ingredients—as shown in Table 9.2.

TABLE 9.2    The Remaining Ingredients in an Omelet

| Mushrooms | count | 2 |
|-----------|-------|---|
| Salt      | pinch | 1 |
| Butter    | ounce | 2 |

The Material dictionary should be simple key/string pairs, as shown in Table 9.3. The Method array should contain strings, as shown in Table 9.4.

TABLE 9.3    Materials for Making an Omelet

| | |
|---|---|
| Bowl | Small |
| Fork | Table fork or small whisk |
| Crêpe Pan | 10" nonstick |
| Spatula | Silicone, high-heat |
| Egg Slicer | Optional, for slicing mushrooms |

TABLE 9.4    Instructions for Making an Omelet

| |
|---|
| Heat pan to medium (butter foams but doesn't burn). |
| Warm eggs in water to room temperature. |
| Slice mushrooms. |
| Sauté in 1/4 of the butter until limp, set aside. |
| Break eggs into bowl, add salt. |
| Whisk eggs until color begins to change. |
| Coat pan with 1/2 the butter. |
| Pour eggs into pan, and tilt to spread uniformly. |
| When edges set, use spatula to separate from pan, then tilt liquid into gaps. |
| Leave undisturbed for 30 seconds. |
| Loosen from pan, and flip (using spatula to help) 1/3 over. |
| Top with mushrooms. |
| Slide onto plate, flipping remaining 1/3 over. |
| Spread remaining butter on top. |

If you followed along with this exercise (see Figure 9.7), you've probably been persuaded that the Property List Editor has its advantages and disadvantages. On the plus side, it always generates correct property lists, and no matter how complex your property list structure becomes, PLE makes it easy to navigate. On the minus side, PLE was never meant for creating large, repetitious lists. By the third ingredient, you were probably wishing you could duplicate the quantity/number-unit/string dictionary pattern. Instead, you were forced to use the keyboard, the **New...** button, and the **Class** pop-up. That PLE keeps dictionary keys in alphabetic order at all times is handy when you're browsing a property list, but it's a misfeature when you change a key and the line you are working on moves elsewhere on the screen.

FIGURE 9.7    Construction of the omelet property list.

# Other Formats

I mentioned in passing that text editors can display and edit only *most* property list files. There are two other formats a plist file may use. One is also text, the other is binary.

## ASCII Property Lists

Property lists came to Cocoa's architecture from its ancestor framework, OpenStep. In OpenStep, property lists were encoded in an ASCII format that Apple characterizes as a legacy technique, but is used often enough that you should be familiar with it. For instance, `defaults`, the command-line interface to the preferences system, and many of the internal Xcode configuration files, use the ASCII format.

ASCII property lists have only two primitive types: string and data (Table 9.5). Strings are surrounded by double-quote characters, which may be omitted if there is no space in the string. Number, date, and Boolean values must be stored as string representations. The convention for Boolean values is to use the strings YES and NO.

TABLE 9.5    Encoding for ASCII-Style Property Lists

| Type | Coding |
|------|--------|
| String | "Two or more words" *or* one Word |
| Data | <466f6f626172> |
| List | (Shirley, "Goodness and Mercy", 1066) |
| Associative Array | { key = value; "key 2" = < 332e3134313539 >; } |

Data elements are delimited by angle brackets and contain pairs of hexadecimal digits, representing the bytes in the data. Any spaces in the digit stream are ignored.

Arrays are surrounded by parentheses, and the elements are separated by commas. Dictionaries are surrounded by braces, and the elements are *followed by* semicolons, which means that the last element must be closed off with a semicolon.

The Property List Editor reads ASCII-format property lists and its **Save As...** dialog presents an option to save a property list in ASCII format.

## Binary Property Lists

In Mac OS X version 10.2, Apple introduced a binary property list format. In the binary format, plists are smaller than in XML or ASCII format and load more quickly. From Mac OS X version 10.4 onward, application preference files are written as binary property lists. Property lists can be converted between XML and binary format in place using the `plutil` command-line utility in the form

```
plutil -convert format pathToFile
```

where *format* is either `binary1`, for conversion to the binary format, or `xml1` for the XML format; and *pathToFile* is the path to the file to convert.

> **NOTE**
>
> Bare Bones Software's BBEdit text editor, beginning in version 8.6, automatically translates binary property-list files into XML for editing.

# Text Macros

Xcode 2.0 introduced text macros to its editor. A macro inserts previously prepared, commonly used text into the text being edited. Xcode may make simple substitutions as it inserts the macro, such as the current date, or the text that was selected when the macro command was issued.

Xcode comes with a set of macros for C, C++, HTML, Java, Objective-C, and the text-macro specification language itself. But, there is no set for XML property lists. We'll be adding one in this section.

To insert a macro while you're editing a file, choose the macro from its language submenu of the **Insert Text Macro** item of the **Edit** menu. Some macros that may have more than one useful variant, such as the if-else variant of the C family's if statement, will rotate through the variants if you invoke them repeatedly.

It's obvious that a command three menus deep is difficult to invoke once, let alone repeatedly. Apple's intention is that you should use the Key Bindings panel of the Preferences window to assign special key combinations to the macros you use most. Then, stepping through the variations of the if statement is as easy as repeatedly pressing, say, ⌃⌥⌘I.

Apple doesn't provide a way to extend or edit the macro sets except through writing your own macro-specification files. Xcode root specifications can be found in the resource directory of the Text-Macro plug-in in the Xcode application bundle. The installation process may create additional, systemwide specification files at /Developer/Library/ Xcode/Specifications/. Your own macro specifications would go into a Specifications subdirectory of an Xcode application-support directory. There are several places where the application-support directory might go. See the sidebar for all the possibilities.

---

### Where Xcode Support Files Go

The placement of support files such as macro specifications and project templates has become trickier in Xcode 3.0 than in 2.x. The files that come with Xcode can be found at /Developer/Library/Xcode. If you want to customize or add files, your custom work should go into the Application Support directory of the Library directory appropriate to how widely available you want the customization to be. See Table 9.6 for the details.

If you are running more than one version of Xcode—there is an Xcode 2.5 for those who must have 2.x compatibility on a Leopard machine—you can substitute Shared for 3.0 in the path, and the files in question will be available to all versions. Substituting 2.5 will make the customization available in Xcode 2.5 only.

TABLE 9.6    Summary of Available Locations for Xcode Support Files*

| File Path | Availability |
| --- | --- |
| /Developer/Library/Xcode | dau3 |
| /Network/Library/Application Support/Developer/3.0/Xcode | wau3 |
| /Network/Library/Application Support/Developer/Shared/Xcode | wauv |
| /Library/Application Support/Developer/3.0/Xcode | au3 |
| /Library/Application Support/Developer/Shared/Xcode | auv |
| ~/Library/Application Support/Developer/3.0/Xcode | u3 |
| ~/Library/Application Support/Developer/Shared/Xcode | uv |

*In addition to the locations listed in the preceding table, there is the /Network/Library directory, which would make its contents available to all users within a workgroup. Codes used in the Availability column: **d**-default; **w**-available to network workgroup; **a**-available to all users on the machine; **u**-available to the current user; **v**-applies to all versions; **3**-applies to version 3.x only.

Apple's release notes recommend examining the existing macro-specification files and developing your own from a copy of one that most nearly matches your needs. The nearest thing to an XML plist file is HTML, inside the Xcode application package at `Contents/PlugIns/TextMacros.xctxtmacro/Contents/Resources/HTML.xctxtmacro`, so let's start from that.

In examining `HTML.xctxtmacro`, the important thing is not to panic. First, it's just a property-list file, in the old, ASCII format. Second, it's merely a list of some fairly simple dictionaries, of three types: a header dictionary with the key `IsMenu` = `YES`, leaf dictionaries with `IsMenuItem` = `YES`, and category dictionaries with no menu characteristics at all. Every dictionary has an `Identifier`, with a dotted hierarchical name, such as `html`, `html.formatter`, or `html.formatter.bold`. The idea is that a menu item selects a leaf, and the leaf, together with its hierarchical ancestors, defines a `TextString` property that will be the text the macro inserts.

With that in mind, we can start with the root of the macro tree for property lists:

```
(
    Identifier = plist;
    Name = "Property List";
    IsMenu = YES;
    ComputerLanguages = ( plist ) ;
},
```

Next, we make a leaf macro for the skeleton of an XML property list file:

```
{
    Identifier = plist.skeleton;
    BasedOn = plist;
    TextString = "<?xml version=\"1.0\" encoding=\"UTF- 8\"?>\n
        <!DOCTYPE plist PUBLIC
        \"-//Apple Computer//DTD PLIST 1.0//EN\"\n
      \t\"http://www.apple.com/DTDs/PropertyList-1.0.dtd\">\n
        <plist version=\"1.0\">\n\t<#!text!#>\n </plist>" ;
    Name = "File Skeleton";
    IsMenuItem  =  YES;
},
```

Unfortunately, the string value of `TextString` had to be broken into several lines to fit on this page; to work properly, the string value must be in one line. Note that quotation marks in the string have to be escaped with backslashes and that newlines and tabs can be inserted with the familiar \n and \t sequences. The \t sequence does not mean a literal tab; instead, it means "tabbed one more level than the line the macro started at."

Now, we want the Boolean elements `<true />` and `<false />`. This suggests a simple application of a category node in the specification—the two tags are identical except for the names, so they can share some of the layout. We can define the `TextString` for both in the category, leaving the tag text to be specified by the leaf nodes:

```
{
    Identifier = plist.boolean;
    BasedOn = plist;
    TextString = "<$(Tag) />";
},
    {
        Identifier = plist.boolean.true;
        BasedOn = plist.boolean;
        Name = "True";
        IsMenuItem = YES;
        Tag = "true";
    },
    {
        Identifier = plist.boolean.false;
        BasedOn = plist.boolean;
        Name = "False";
        IsMenuItem = YES;
        Tag = "false";
    },
```

So, plist.boolean.false is a menu item (IsMenuItem = YES), with title **False** (Name = "False") and inserts <false /> (because TextString = "<$(Tag) />", plus Tag = "false", yields <false />).

Now we move on to the elements that contain character data:

```
{
    Identifier = plist.element;
    BasedOn = plist;
    TextString = "<$(Tag)><#!text!#></$(Tag)>";
},
    {
        Identifier = plist.element.string;
        BasedOn = plist.element;
        Name = "String";
        IsMenuItem = YES;
        Tag = "string";
    },
    {
        Identifier = plist.element.date;
        BasedOn = plist.element;
        Name = "Date";
        IsMenuItem = YES;
        Tag = "date";
    },
```

```
    {
        Identifier = plist.element.data;
        BasedOn = plist.element;
        Name = "Data";
        IsMenuItem = YES;
        Tag = "data";
    },
    {
        Identifier = plist.element.key;
        BasedOn = plist.element;
        Name = "Key";
        IsMenuItem = YES;
        Tag = "key";
    },
```

This time, the common TextString for these elements includes the string <#!text!#>.
This string is a placeholder for whatever text is selected when the macro was invoked. If,
for instance, the string

```
we shall prevail
```

was selected and the **String** macro was selected, the selection would be replaced with

```
<string>we shall prevail</string>
```

Just for fun, let's have a cycling tag:

```
    {
        Identifier = plist.element.number;
        BasedOn = plist.element;
        Name = "Integer";
        IsMenuItem = YES;
        Tag = "integer";
        CycleList = (
            plist. element.number,
            plist.element.number.real
        );
    },
        {
            Identifier = plist.element.number.real;
            BasedOn = plist.element.number;
            Name = "Real";
            IsMenuItem = YES;
            Tag = "real";
        },
```

These add two menu items, **Integer** and **Real**, which are like other `plist.element` nodes in inserting `<integer>` and `<real>` markup, respectively. We've added an element to `plist.element.number`, `CycleList`, which specifies that the first time the **Integer** command is invoked, it executes `plist.element.number`, but the next time, `plist.element.number.real`, and so on, alternately. So, if the current selection were:

1984

the **Integer** command would substitute

`<integer>1984</integer>`

the first time it is invoked, but

`<real>1984</real>`

the next time. Repeatedly issuing the same command would repeat the cycle.

We finish the specification with a category for the container classes:

```
{
    Identifier = plist.container;
    BasedOn = plist;
    TextString =
        "<$(Tag)>\n\t$(PreSel)<#!text!#>$(PostSel)\n</$(Tag)>";
    PreSel = "";
    PostSel = "";
},
    {
        Identifier = plist.container.array;
        BasedOn = plist.container;
        Name = "Array";
        Tag = "array";
        IsMenuItem = YES;
    },
    {
        Identifier = plist.container.dictionary;
        BasedOn = plist.container;
        Name = "Dictionary";
        Tag = "dict";
        IsMenuItem = YES;
        PreSel = "<key>";
        PostSel = "</key>\n\\t";
    }
)
```

So, the **Array** command makes the current selection the indented first item in `<array>` markup, and **Dictionary** makes it the indented first key in `<dict>` markup. Note how the

PreSel and PostSel variables, which are empty in the case of an array, carry the <key> tags and an extra line in the case of a dictionary.

Now all that remains is to install the specification. Save this file as plist.xctxtmacro in the Specifications folder of the folder Library/Application Support/Developer/3.0/Xcode in your home folder. Next, try to open the file with Property List Editor—remember it's simply an ASCII-format property list, and it should check out. If it doesn't, use the debugging strategy mentioned earlier in this chapter to track down the problem. *(Hint:* What bit me was \-escaping all the quotes in the TextString of the plist.skeleton node.)

> **NOTE**
>
> Apple-supplied text-macro packages, such as for C or HTML, include the feature of providing *completion prefixes*, which speed the use of macros considerably. If you were to type **ifelse**, and then **esc**, for instance, Xcode would offer you a list of completions that includes "If/Else Block." If you accept this, the prefix word will be replaced by the skeleton of the C if ... else block statement. Alas, completion prefixes rely on context provided by the Xcode Code Sense parser, which isn't available to third-party macro writers.

If Xcode is already running, you'll have to quit and restart it for it to see the new specification file. It should appear as **Property List** in the **Insert Text Macro** menu.

## Summary

This chapter introduced property lists, a ubiquitous data-storage format in Mac OS X. We've seen how to create them programmatically and how to use Property List Editor and text tools to manage them. We've even applied the ASCII property list format to create Xcode macros for XML property lists. By now, you should be pretty comfortable with the concept.

# CHAPTER 10

# Libraries and Dependent Targets

**IN THIS CHAPTER**

▷ **Adding a Target to a Project**

▷ **Assigning Files to Targets**

▷ **Including One Target in Another**

▷ **Examining Library Contents**

Doing all the statistical work within `Linrg` has been fun, but it's time to bring that tool into the application. In this chapter, we create a C library for linear regressions as an additional target for the Linear project. We'll see how to make one target in a project depend on another, so that we can ensure that our application target always has a current version of the library.

## Adding a Target

We want our project to produce an additional product: a static library. Each product in a project is the result of a target. In the **Project** menu, select **New Target...**. The New Target Assistant appears (see Figure 10.1), from which you should select **BSD > Static Library**. Name the target **Regression**, and let it be added to project Linear.

A couple of things happen in the Groups & Files list. Under Targets, a new item, Regression, appears, with an icon that looks like a toy building block. Above it, the Linear application target now has a small green badge with a check mark on it, indicating that it is the *active target*. All commands to build, run, or debug a project are sent to the active target.

Change the active target to **Regression**. The *active target* is the target in a project to which all build commands apply, and the default recipient of all new or added files. Use the menu command **Project > Set Active Target > Regression**, or just select **Regression** in the **Active Target** pop-up at the left end of the project window's toolbar. Note that the green check mark badge in the Targets list moves to Regression's icon.

FIGURE 10.1    The New Target Assistant window. Select **BSD > Static Library** for this example, a C library for linear regressions.

Also in Groups & Files, in the Products subgroup of the Project group, a new product, `libRegression.a`, has been added. (The name in the list is red because the file does not yet exist.) It is deeply ingrained in the GNU tool set that libraries have names with the prefix `lib`—the instruction to link this library to `Linear` will be `-lRegression`, and the linker will take that to mean `libRegression.a`. You *can* change the product name, but fighting the tools that way is inadvisable.

Press ⌘N to add a new text file to the project, a **C and C++ > C File**. The second panel of the New File Assistant takes on a new significance: Not only do we name the new file (**libRegression.c**) and opt for a matching header, but we also must assign the new file to a target in the current project. Even though **Regression** is the current target, **Linear** is checked, and **Regression** is unchecked. Turn that around so that **Regression** is checked and **Linear** unchecked, as in Figure 10.2.

FIGURE 10.2    In a multitarget project, the New File Assistant presents options on which target the newly created file is to be assigned.

# Library Design

Our specification is nothing special: Clients of our library should obtain an opaque pointer to the storage necessary to do a linear regression. The pointer is then presented to the library functions for any action related to that regression. The client should be able to add data points to the regression, and remove them. The regression should report on demand the regression statistics. To add interest, we'll add averages for *x* and *y* to the mix.

The public interface in `libRegression.h` follows naturally from the requirements:

```c
#ifndef LIBREGRESSION_H_
#define LIBREGRESSION_H_

void*       RGCreate(void);
void        RGRelease(void * aRegression);

void        RGAddPoint(void * aRegression,
                    double inX, double inY);
void        RGDeletePoint(void * aRegression,
                    double inX, double inY);

unsigned    RGCount(void * aRegression);

double      RGMeanX(void * aRegression);
double      RGMeanY(void * aRegression);

double      RGSlope(void * aRegression);
double      RGIntercept(void * aRegression);
double      RGCorrelation(void * aRegression);

#endif
```

In keeping with the plan to make the cookie returned by `RGCreate()` opaque to clients of the library, we define its inner structure in a private header, `libRPrivate.h`, which you can create with **File > New File**, choosing **C and C++ > Header File**:

```c
#ifndef LIBRPRIVATE_H_
#define LIBRPRIVATE_H_

typedef struct Sums {
    unsigned    count;
    double      sumX;
    double      sumY;
    double      sumXSquared;
    double      sumYSquared;
    double      sumXY;
```

```
    int             dirty;
    double          slope;
    double          intercept;
    double          correlation;
}   Sums, *SumsPtr;

#endif
```

We'll split the workings of the library into two C files: one for the regression functions, and the other for the distribution functions. Here is libRegression.c:

```c
#include "libRPrivate.h"
#include <stdlib.h>
#include <assert.h>
#include <math.h>

void *      RGCreate(void)
{
    SumsPtr     retval = calloc(1, sizeof(Sums));
    return retval;
}

void        RGRelease(void * aRegression)
{
    free(aRegression);
}

void        RGAddPoint(void * aRegression,
                       double inX,
                       double inY)
{
    SumsPtr     reg = (SumsPtr) aRegression;
    reg->count++;
    reg->sumX += inX;
    reg->sumY += inY;
    reg->sumXSquared += inX * inX;
    reg->sumYSquared += inY * inY;
    reg->sumXY += inX * inY;

    reg->dirty = 1;
}

void        RGDeletePoint(void * aRegression,
                          double inX,
                          double inY)
{
```

```
    SumsPtr    reg = (SumsPtr) aRegression;
    assert(reg->count > 0);

    reg->count—;
    reg->sumX -= inX;
    reg->sumY -= inY;
    reg->sumXSquared -= inX * inX;
    reg->sumYSquared -= inY * inY;
    reg->sumXY -= inX * inY;

    reg->dirty = 1;
}


static
void      CalculateRegression(SumsPtr aRegression)
{
    if (!aRegression->dirty ¦¦ aRegression->count < 2)
        return;

    aRegression->slope =
        (aRegression->count * aRegression->sumXY
        - aRegression->sumX * aRegression->sumY)
    /
        (aRegression->count * aRegression->sumXSquared
        - aRegression->sumX * aRegression->sumX);
    aRegression->intercept =
        (aRegression->sumY
        - aRegression->slope * aRegression->sumX)
    /
        aRegression->count;
    aRegression->correlation =
    aRegression->slope * sqrt(
                (aRegression->count * aRegression->sumXSquared
                - aRegression->sumX * aRegression->sumX)
                        /
                (aRegression->count * aRegression->sumYSquared
                - aRegression->sumY * aRegression->sumY)
                );
    aRegression->dirty = 0;
}
unsigned    RGCount(void * aRegression)
{ return ((SumsPtr)aRegression)->count; }

double      RGSlope(void * aRegression)
{
```

10

```
        CalculateRegression(((SumsPtr)aRegression)) ;
        return ((SumsPtr)aRegression)->slope;
}
double    RGIntercept(void * aRegression)
{
        CalculateRegression(((SumsPtr)aRegression)) ;
        return ((SumsPtr)aRegression)->intercept;
}
double    RGCorrelation(void * aRegression)
{
        CalculateRegression(((SumsPtr)aRegression));
        return ((SumsPtr)aRegression)->correlation;
}
```

And, finally, here is libRAverage.c (**New File, C and C++ > C File**, no header file):

```
#include "libRegression.h"
#include "libRPrivate.h"
#include <math.h>

double    RGMeanX(void * aRegression)
{
        return ((SumsPtr)aRegression)->sumX /
        ((SumsPtr)aRegression)->count;
}

double    RGMeanY(void * aRegression)
{
        return ((SumsPtr)aRegression)->sumY /
        ((SumsPtr)aRegression)->count;
}
```

> **NOTE**
>
> Now—or certainly after you test them—is the time to add the new files to your SCM reposi-tory (**SCM > Add to Repository**). Notice that the project icon itself, at the top of the Groups & Files list, is marked M, to reflect the addition of new files to the project.

# Modifying Linear

In the application Linear, Regression remains the model object responsible for maintain-ing the list of data points and farming it out for computation of the regression statistics. That computation had been done in the computeWithLinrg method, which we will now remove from Regression.h and .m, along with the dataRead: method. (Relax, it's still in SCM.) We will add a new method, computeFromLibrary. Declare the new method in Regression.h:

```
- (void) computeFromLibrary;
```

Put the method itself in Regression.m:

```
#pragma mark libRegression

#import "libRegression.h"

- (void) computeFromLibrary
{
    void *      reg = RGCreate();

    NSEnumerator *  iter = [dataPoints objectEnumerator];
    DataPoint *     curr;
    while (curr = [iter nextObject])
        RGAddPoint(reg, [curr x] , [curr y] ) ;

    if (RGCount(reg) > 1) {
        [self setSlope: RGSlope(reg)];
        [self setIntercept: RGIntercept(reg)];
        [self setCorrelation: RGCorrelation(reg)];
    }
    RGRelease(reg);
}
```

**NOTE**

Why use the set accessors instead of setting the instance variables directly? One way the Key-Value Observing protocol, on which the controller layer bindings are based, detects changes in observed properties is to intercept set accessors. When we use the accessors, we notify the NSForm in the document window that the values have changed, and the display updates automatically.

Make sure that MyDocument uses the correct method; modify the compute: action method as follows:

```
- (IBAction) compute: (id) sender
{
#pragma unused(sender)
    [model computeFromLibrary];
}
```

10

# A Dependent Target

Finally, make sure that whenever any part of the `libRegression` library changes, `Linear.app` will be rebuilt with the new library. The procedure for adding the dependency is broadly the same as when we added the dependency on `Linrg` in the "Adding `Linrg`" section of Chapter 5, "Starting a Cocoa Application."

Open the Targets group in the Groups & Files list in the project window, and double-click the Linear.app target. A Target Info window should appear. (It's easy to miss the target group and double-click the Linear application in the Products group under the project icon. If `Linear` started up when you double-clicked the item, you got the wrong one.)

In the **General** tab of the info window, press the + button, and select `libRegression` from the sheet listing possible dependencies. Now `libRegression` will be made up-to-date whenever `Linear` is built.

Now we have to make sure that `libRegression` is not only built but used. Make sure that Linear is the active target. Now select the project icon (the top icon) in the Groups & Files list. The Detail view, to the right, will fill with all the files contained in the project. The last column of the detail view contains check boxes. This column indicates whether the file on that line generates code that should be linked into the active target's final product. `AppKit.framework`, for instance, is not checked and should remain unchecked because it is included in the project simply for reference to the headers it contains.

Switch the active target back and forth a bit to see what files get included in which target. In some cases, the check box for a file disappears, as with the NIB files, which cannot be included in a library product. When you have finished, be sure to leave **Linear** as the active target.

Scroll down—or type in the search field in the toolbar—to find `libRegression.a`. Its box is unchecked, which is not what we want—we just changed the `Regression` class to use functions in that library. Check it. Doing so adds the library to the build sequence for `Linear`. See for yourself: If you open the disclosure triangles under the Linear target in the Targets group in the Groups & Files list, you will see a chain of build steps for `Linear` (see Figure 10.3).

Open the Link Binary with Libraries build phase; if **libRegression.a** was checked in the detail listing, this phase includes `libRegression.a`. As you check and uncheck **libRegression.a**—you may

FIGURE 10.3    The build chain for **Linear**, showing **Regression** at the head of the chain, and **libRegression.a** as part of the linkage step. Unchecking **libRegression.a** in the Detail listing removes it from this phase.

have to reselect the top project icon to get the check boxes back—the library appears and disappears in the link-library build phase.

We are done with Linrg and the project that generates it. Select Linrg.-xcodeproj in the Groups & Files list, and press **Delete**. A sheet will appear, to confirm that you want to remove it from the project. Accept the removal. This also removes the dependency in Linear and the placement of Linrg in Linear's Copy-Resources phase.

> **NOTE**
>
> It is also advisable to go to the Terminal and enter **svn rm Linrg.xcodeproj**. Then, future revisions in the Linear repository will not carry Linrg's project file, and future checkouts will not include it. Unlike in CVS, Subversion records changes in directories *and* in files, so changes in the Linear directory, like deletions and renames, will be reflected cleanly in the repository.

Now build. If you have a swift eye trained on the status bar at the bottom of the project window, you will see that even though libRegression.c is not a part of the active target, it nonetheless is compiled first, because it is needed to build libRegression.a, which we have specified as a prerequisite for our application.

While our attention is on the Groups & Files list, we should keep the list organized. Select libRegression.c and, using the **Shift** key, libRegression.h, libRPrivate.h, and libRAverage.c; then select the **Group** (⌥⌘G) command from the **File** menu, creating a new group folder, named New Folder, containing the files you selected. The name of the group is selected, so you can change it to something descriptive, such as **Regression Library**.

Groups, with tan folder icons, are solely a way to organize the Groups & Files list. They don't exist on disk and have no effect on the way your files are stored or built.

# Examining the Library

Two BSD tools you can run from the Terminal application are useful in examining libraries and verifying their contents. The first tool, nm, examines the symbol tables of object files—applications, .o objects, and .a and .dylib libraries. Each of these file types includes a *symbol table*, a dictionary of entities the file defines and of entities that were left undefined but needed by objects in the file.

Start up the Terminal application, and set the working directory to the Linear project directory. (The easiest way to do this is to type **cd_**—note the space after the **cd**—and then drag the folder containing the project file from the Finder into the Terminal window). Press **Return**. Type **nm build/Debug/libRegression.a**. The output should resemble this:

```
libRegression.a(libRegression.o):
0000022f t _CalculateRegression
00000041 T _RGAddPoint
000004e6 T _RGCorrelation
```

```
00000481 T _RGCount
00000000 T _RGCreate
00000108 T _RGDeletePoint
000004bd T _RGIntercept
00000028 T _RGRelease
00000494 T _RGSlope
         U ___assert_rtn
00000e80 s __func__.2981
         U _calloc
         U _free
```

> **NOTE**
>
> This assumes: (1) You have not changed your Build Products folder in either the Project Info (**General**) window nor in the Preferences window (Building). (2) You have been using the Debug build configuration (**Project > Set Active Build Configuration**).

```
libRegression.a(libRAverage.o):
00000000 T _RGMeanX
00000060 T _RGMeanY
```

This output shows libRegression.a to consist of two parts: libRegression.o and libRAverage.o. Both parts define various symbols in the text segment (the segment of an object file in which, by convention, Mach-O executable code is stored); for instance, _RGAddPoint begins 65 (hexadecimal 41) bytes into the text segment of libRegression.o. The lowercase t in _CalculateRegression's line reflects its status as a private symbol—CalculateRegression() was declared static.

Three symbols, including _calloc and _free, are marked U, for undefined. You would have to link in libraries defining these symbols for a project including libRegression.o to be satisfied.

The otool command gets into more detailed dissection of a library or object file. The various options for otool direct it to different parts of the archive or library file format. For instance, otool -av build/libRegression.a dumps the archive header in verbose (symbolic) format:

```
Archive  :  build/libRegression.a
-rw--r--r--501/501     220  Mon  Nov  5 10:19:15 2007   .__SYMDEF SORTED
-rw--r--r--501/501    6284  Mon  Nov  5 10:19:10 2007   libRegression.o
-rw--r--r--501/501    2244  Mon  Nov  5 10:19:10 2007   libRAverage.o
```

Using the -Sv switch dumps the .SYMDEF pseudofile from the archive:

```
Archive : build/libRegression.a
Table of contents from: libRegression.a(___.SYMDEF SORTED)
size of ranlib structures: 80 (number 10)
size of strings: 112
object          symbol name
libRegression.o _RGAddPoint
libRegression.o _RGCorrelation
libRegression.o _RGCount
```

```
libRegression.o  _RGCreate
libRegression.o  _RGDeletePoint
libRegression.o  _RGIntercept
libRAverage.o    _ RGMeanX
libRAverage.o    _ RGMeanY
libRegression.o  _RGRelease
libRegression.o  _RGSlope
```

The -t option displays the text segments of the archive as hex dumps; adding the -v verbosity option makes it a disassembly:

```
Archive : build/libRegression.a
build/libRegression.a(libRegression.o):
(__TEXT,__text) section
_RGCreate:
00000000 nop
…
00000006 pushl %ebp
00000007 movl %esp,%ebp
00000009 subl $0x28,%esp
0000000c movl $0x00000048,0x04(%esp)
00000014 movl $0x00000001,(%esp)
0000001b calll 0x00000eee
00000020 movl %eax,0xf4(%ebp)
00000023 movl 0xf4(%ebp),%eax
00000026 leave
00000027 ret
_RGRelease:
00000028 nop
…
0000002e pushl %ebp
0000002f movl %esp,%ebp
00000031 subl $0x18,%esp
00000034 movl 0x08(%ebp),%eax
00000037 movl %eax,(%esp)
0000003a calll 0x00000ee9
0000003f leave
00000040 ret
…
```

Both nm and otool offer much more than can be covered here. Be sure to run man nm and man otool for full documen-tation of what they make available to you.

> **NOTE**
>
> Intel is the native architecture on my Mac, and so the disassembly would be of the Intel code, even if libRegression.a were a universal binary. Use the -arch flag to direct otool to other (or all) processor types.

10

# Running the Library

The real proof of the new library, of course, is not in prodding it with command-line tools but in running it. So, issue the **Build and Debug** command (press ⌘Y, or use the toolbar), and see how it works.

Figure 10.4 shows the results of loading the old familiar data set and clicking the **Compute** button. We can see that there has been a change in that the statistics are now reported to twice as many digits' precision. In the previous version of Linear, all our data passed to and from the regression calculator through a printf() function, which limited the precision the calculator could receive or report. We should have fixed this bug in the previous version of Linrg. Now, however, the data for the statistical calculations are taken and reported as binary data, without reformatting or truncation.

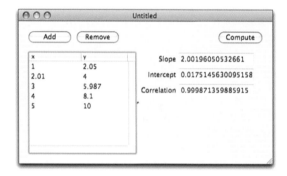

FIGURE 10.4    Linear, using the libRegression library. Because the data no longer passes through formatting steps on the way to and from the regression engine, we are given more digits of precision.

# Summary

In this chapter, you've seen how to gather functionality into a static library. We've made our project generate that library as an additional product and made sure that our main product, the Linear application, is always provided with an up-to-date version of the library. We've also touched on some tools for examining libraries and other object files to see, among other things, what objects they define and what objects they need other entities to define.

We've also done a little project management: We've seen how to allocate files in a project among its targets and how doing so affects a target's build order. We've also organized our files related to our new library into a separate file group.

# CHAPTER 11

# File Packages and Bundles

## IN THIS CHAPTER

▷ **Package Files**

▷ **Bundle Directories**

▷ **The** Info.plist **File**

Many of Xcode's products take the form of *packages*, directory trees that the Finder presents as single files. Let's pause to consider the problem of resources. Resources are the sorts of data that were historically handled by what is now the Carbon Resource Manager: strings, lookup tables, images, human-interface layouts, sounds, and the like. One of the innovations of the classic Macintosh software architecture was the separation of such constant or parameterized data from the executable code of applications.

Before Mac OS X, the customary vehicle for aggregating packets of data into a single file system entity was the *resource file*. Resource files kept their structured data in the *resource fork*, a data store that HFS, the Macintosh file system, associates with files in addition to the traditional unstructured data stream. The resource fork cataloged its contents by type, integer identifier, and name, and applications accessed resources by those keys through the Resource Manager.

The problem with the Resource Manager is that it does not scale well to sets of many, large, or changeable resources. The catalog written into each resource file was notoriously fragile, and any corruption resulted in the loss of every resource in the file. With the multiplicity of large resources—images, sounds, human-interface layouts, lookup tables—needed to support modern applications, the tasks involved in managing them become indistinguishable from the tasks of a file system. File systems are a solved problem; they do their work as efficiently and robustly as decades of experience can make them. Why not use the file system for storing and retrieving resources?

One reason to avoid shipping application resources as separate files is that an application that relies on them becomes a swarm of files and directories, all more or less critical to its correct working, and all exposed to relocation, deletion, and general abuse by the user. Meanwhile, the user, who simply wants one thing that does the application's work, is presented with a swarm of files and directories.

Mac OS X provides a way to have the flexibility of separating resources into their own files while steering clear of the swarming problem. The Finder can treat directories, called *packages*, as though they are single documents.

For many kinds of targets—applications especially—one of Xcode's most important tasks is to build package directories. To understand Xcode, you have to understand packages.

# A Simple Package: RTFD

A package can be as simple as a directory with a handful of files in it. The application that creates and reads the package determines how it is structured: what files are required, the names of the content files, what sort of subdirectory structure is used.

A common example of an application-defined package is the RTFD, or Rich Text File Directory. The Apple-supplied application TextEdit, in its standard Info.plist file, specifies the kinds of documents TextEdit can handle; among these is NSRTFDPboardType, which is listed as having suffix rtfd and is designated as a package file type. When it catalogs TextEdit, the Mac OS X Finder notes that directories with the .rtfd extension are supposed to be packages and so treats them as if they are single files, not ordinarily displaying the files within.

It is sometimes useful to look inside a package, however, and the Finder provides a way to do that. Control-clicking a package file produces a pop-up menu containing the command **Show Package Contents** (see Figure 11.1). Selecting that command opens a new window showing the contents of the package directory, which can be further navigated as in a normal Finder window (see Figure 11.2).

> **NOTE**
>
> The Cocoa application framework provides support for package-directory documents. NSDocument subclasses handle package reading and writing by overriding readFromFileWrapper:ofType:error: and fileWrapperOfType:error:. The NSFileWrapper class provides methods that assist in creating and managing complex file packages.

In the case of RTFD, the package directory contains one plain RTF file, TXT.rtf. The RTF file incorporates custom markup, such as the following:

```
{{\NeXTGraphic Pasted Graphic 1.tiff \width8840 \height3900
}}
```

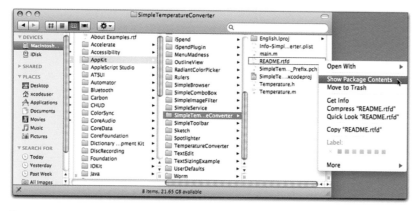

FIGURE 11.1    The **Show Package Contents** command is available in a pop-up contextual menu for any apparent file that is a package directory.

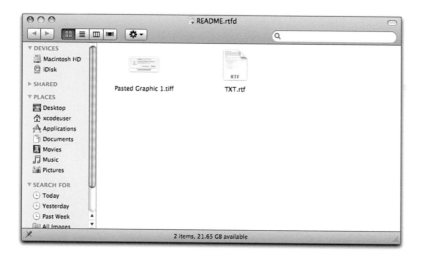

FIGURE 11.2    The contents of an RTFD package (in this case, a Read Me for one of the AppKit example projects). The contents are just a Rich Text Format (RTF) file with a standard name, plus a graphics file with a name referred to in custom tags in the RTF file.

Here, the markup refers to a graphics file—in this case, Pasted Graphic 1.tiff—that is also in the RTFD directory.

Having a name extension registered by a handling application as a file package is not the only way for a directory to be treated as a package. Directories are also treated as packages if they have the HFS "bundle" bit set, but this is not a useful variation.

# Bundles

A *bundle* is a particular kind of *structured* directory tree. Often, bundles are shipped as packages—the most familiar type of bundle, the application, is an example—but the concepts are separate. A directory can be a bundle without being a package, or a package without being a bundle, or both. Table 11.1 has examples.

TABLE 11.1   Examples of Directories That Are Bundles or Packages or Both

|  | Not Bundle | Bundle |
|---|---|---|
| **Not Package** | Other directories | Frameworks |
| **Package** | Complex documents | Applications |

There are two kinds of bundles: *versioned bundles*, which are used for frameworks; and *modern bundles*, which are used for applications and most other executable products. Versioned bundles are covered in Chapter 14, "Dynamic Libraries and Frameworks," where we build a framework.

At the minimum, a modern bundle encloses one directory, named `Contents`, which in turn contains all the directories and files comprising the bundle. The `Contents` directory contains an `Info.plist` file, which specifies how the bundle is to be displayed in the Finder and, depending on the type of the bundle, may provide configuration data for loading and running the bundle's contents. Beyond that, what the `Contents` folder contains depends on the type of the bundle.

# Application Bundles

Applications are the most common type of bundle (see Figure 11.3). An application directory has a name with the suffix `.app`. The `.app` directory is a file package; even though it is a directory, the Finder treats it as a single entity. This allows the author of the application to place auxiliary files for the application in a known place—inside the application bundle itself—with little fear that such files will be misplaced or deleted.

The `Contents` directory of an application bundle contains the following:

▶ `Info.plist`, an XML property list file that describes such application details as the principal class, the document types handled, and the application version. More on this file in the next section.

▶ `Resources`, a directory containing the application icon file, images, sounds, human interface layouts, and other parameterized content for the application. This directory may be further organized into subdirectories, according to your convenience. In addition, there may be localization subdirectories, which have the `.lproj` suffix. When an application seeks a resource, the Cocoa or Core Foundation bundle managers look first in the `.lproj` directory that corresponds to the current language and locale.

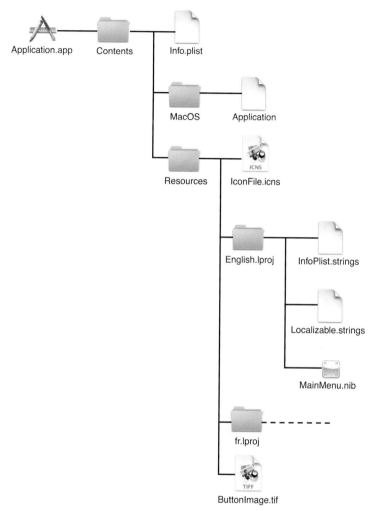

FIGURE 11.3    The structure of a typical application bundle. The executable file is at
`Contents/MacOS/Application`. The application's human interface for English-speaking users is
specified in `Contents/Resources/English.lproj/MainMenu.nib`; presumably, a French
version of `MainMenu.nib` is inside `Contents/Resources/fr.lproj`. The custom image for a
button, `ButtonImage.tif`, is common to all languages and therefore appears directly in the
`Resources` directory.

▶ `MacOS`, a directory containing the executable binary for the application, along with
any other executables used by the application. A bundle may be *fat*, containing
executable directories for all the supported target architectures, but for now, only
`MacOS` and `MacOSClassic` (for Mac OS 9) are supported. (This fat bundle is to be
distinguished from fat—or as Apple marketing prefers, universal—binaries, single

Mach-O executable files that include code compiled for more than one processor. An application that runs natively on 32- and 64-bit processors, Intel and PowerPC, would have a single executable file in the MacOS folder.)

▶ Frameworks, a directory of frameworks that are themselves versioned bundles, containing a dynamic library, resources needed by the library, and header files needed by users of the library. An application typically includes a framework because it links to the framework's library.

Individual resource files can be restricted to a target architecture by appending a hyphen and the architecture name to the resource's base name. This way, an application may ask for picture.tif, and the Core Foundation bundle manager will return picture-macos.tif or picture-macosclassic.tif, as appropriate.

# The Info.plist **File**

The Info.plist file, found in the Contents directory of any modern bundle, and in the Resources directory of frameworks, is the locus of much of the information Mac OS X needs to make sense of a bundle. This file provides icon and naming information to the Finder, flags and environment variables to Launch Services, and specifications for the basic structure of applications and plug-ins.

In almost every case, you can put together an Info.plist file by using the editor presented by the **Properties** tab of the Get Info box of an Xcode target. This enables you to set CFBundleExecutable, CFBundleIdentifier, CFBundle-PackageType, CFBundleSignature, CFBundleIconFile, CFBundleVersion, NSPrincipalClass, NSMainNibFile, and the CFBundleDocumentTypes array.

Some of these keys are localizable. A file named InfoPlist.strings should be in the .lproj directory for each localization of your application. Localizable keys can then be assigned per-locale values. For instance, InfoPlist.strings in the English.lproj directory might include the following pair:

```
CFBundleName = "Linear";
CFBundleDisplayName = "Linear";
```

The same file in the fr.lproj directory might include

```
CFBundleName = "Linéaire";
CFBundleDisplayName = "Linéaire";
```

For users whose language preferences place French above English, the **Linear** icon in the Finder will be labeled **Linéaire**. The name of the bundle directory, however, will still be Linear.app.

## Keys for All Bundles

The keys in this section apply to almost any kind of bundle, including applications.

▶ **Info**

  ▶ CFBundleGetInfoString, a string that supplements the version information
supplied by CFBundleShortVersionString and CFBundle-Version. Formerly,
this key was used for copyright strings, but that is now handled by
NSHumanReadableCopyright.

  ▶ CFBundleIconFile, the name of the .icns file, in the Resources directory,
containing the bundle's custom icon.

  ▶ CFBundleIdentifier, a unique identifier string for the bundle, in the form of a
Java-style reverse domain package name, such as com.apple.TextEdit. This
identifier is used, among other places, by the preferences system to identify
preference sets with the applications they relate to. Applications must specify
this key.

  ▶ CFBundleInfoDictionaryVersion, a compatibility-check version number for
the Info.plist format. Xcode injects this version number automatically when
it builds bundles. All Info.plist files should include this key.

  ▶ CFBundlePackageType, the four-character type code for the bundle. Applications are type APPL, frameworks are FMWK, plug-ins are BNDL or a code of your
choosing. See also CFBundleSignature. Applications must specify this key.

  ▶ CFBundleShortVersionString, a short string with the product version, such
as 10.5.2, of the bundle, suitable for display in an About box. See also
CFBundleGetInfoString. This key may be localized in InfoPlist.strings.
Applications must specify this key.

  ▶ CFBundleSignature, the four-character creator code associated with the
bundle. Applications must specify this key.

  ▶ CFBundleVersion, the build version of the bundle's executable, which may
identify versions within a release cycle, such as betas (2.1b3, for instance). This
may also be simply a single number, corresponding to a build number within
the life of the bundle. The build version is displayed in parentheses in the
About box. See also CFBundleShortVersion-String.

▶ **Localization**

  ▶ CFBundleDevelopmentRegion, the native human language of the bundle. If the
user's preferred language is not available as a localization, this is the language
that will be used.

▶ **Structure**

- ▶ `CFBundleExecutable`, the name of the executable file, which may be an application binary, a library, or plug-in code. It corresponds to the `EXECUTABLE_NAME` build setting; use `$(EXECUTABLE_NAME)` in the target's **Properties** tab to ensure this key is always properly set. A bundle that mismatches this entry with the actual name of the executable file will not run. Applications must specify this key.

- ▶ `CSResourcesFileMapped`, if `YES` or `<true/>`, Core Foundation memory-maps the bundle resources rather than reads the files into memory.

- ▶ `NSPrincipalClass`, the name of the bundle's main class. In a Cocoa application, this is normally `NSApplication`.

## Keys for Applications

These keys apply only to applications and cover launch configurations, help facilities, and information about the kinds of documents and URLs the application handles:

▶ **Documents and URLs**

- ▶ `CFBundleDocumentTypes`, an array of dictionaries specifying every document type associated with the application. Use the **Properties** panel of the application target's Get Info window to manage this array and its contents. See the section on "Application Properties" in Chapter 7, "A Cocoa Application: Controllers," for details.

- ▶ `CFBundleURLTypes`, an array of dictionaries defining URL schemes, such as `http:` or `ftp:`, for which the application is a handler. See Apple's documentation for details.

- ▶ `UTExportedTypeDeclarations`, an array of dictionaries that describe the types of documents your application can write, and which you want Launch Services to know about. The entries center on declaring a UTI and the chain of UTIs the principal UTI conforms to. This key is used by Spotlight to build its list of document types. It is ignored by Launch Services earlier than Mac OS X 10.5, where UTIs are superseding the declarations in `CFBundleDocumentTypes`. See Apple's documentation for the format of the dictionaries, and Chapter 18, "Spotlight (or, How to Build a Plug-in)."

- ▶ `UTImportedTypeDeclarations`, an array of dictionaries that describe the types of documents your application can *read*, and which you want Launch Services to know about. The entries are the same format as used in `UTExportedTypeDeclarations`. This key is new in Mac OS X 10.5.

▶ **Help**

- ▶ `CFAppleHelpAnchor`, the base name, without extension, of the initial help file for the application.

11

- ▶ CFBundleHelpBookFolder, the folder—in either the Resources subdirectory or a localization subdirectory—containing the application's help book.

- ▶ CFBundleHelpBookName, the name of the application's help book. This name should match the name set in a <meta> tag in the help book's root file.

- ▶ **Info**

  - ▶ CFBundleDisplayName, the name for the Finder to display for this bundle. The value in Info.plist should be identical to the name of the application bundle; localized names can then be put in InfoPlist.Strings files for various languages. The Finder will display the localized name *only* if the name of the application package in the file system matches the value of this key. That way, if the user renames your application, the name he intended, and not the localized name, will display. See also CFBundleName. Applications must specify this key.

  - ▶ CFBundleName, the short—16-character maximum—name for the application, to be shown in the About box and the **Application** menu. See also CFBundleDisplayName. This key may be localized in InfoPlist.strings. Applications must specify this key.

  - ▶ LSHasLocalizedDisplayName, the hint, if <true /> or nonzero, to the Finder that this application has localized versions of its display name (CFBundleDisplayName). Applications must specify this key.

  - ▶ NSHumanReadableCopyright, a copyright string suitable for display in an About box. This key may be localized in InfoPlist.strings. Applications must specify this key.

- ▶ **Launch behavior**

  - ▶ LSBackgroundOnly, indicating that, if its value is the string "1", the application will be run in the background only and will not be visible to the user.

  - ▶ LSEnvironment, a dictionary, the keys of which are environment variables and the values are their values, which are defined when Launch Services launches the application.

  - ▶ LSExecutableArchitectures, an array of strings (e.g., i386, ppc, ppc64, x86_64) indicating what architectures the application can run under. If you put ppc or ppc64 before i386 or x86_64, the application defaults to running under Rosetta on Intel systems. See also LSRequiresNativeExecution.

  - ▶ LSGetAppDiedEvents, indicating that, if YES or <true />, the application will get the kAEApplicationDied Apple event when any of its child processes terminate.

  - ▶ LSMinimumSystemVersion, a string in the form 10.x.x, specifying the earliest version of Mac OS X this application will run under. However, Mac OS X 10.1

ignored this key; 10.2, 10.4, and 10.5 honor this setting and display an alert explaining why the application could not be launched. On Mac OS X 10.3, the application would not be run, but the system did not explain why.

▶ LSMinimumSystemVersionByArchitecture, a dictionary. The possible keys are i386, ppc, ppc64, and x86_64. For each key, the value is a string containing the three-revision version number (e.g., 10.4.11) representing the minimum version of Mac OS X the application supports for that architecture. You can use this, for instance, to accept 10.3 for PowerPC execution, while requiring 10.4 for Intel.

▶ LSMultipleInstancesProhibited, indicating that, if <true />, only one copy of this application can be run at a time. Different users, for instance, cannot use the application simultaneously.

▶ LSPrefersCarbon and LSPrefersClassic, only one of which or LSRequiresCarbon or LSRequiresClassic may be assigned the string value "1". If set, the Finder's Get Info panel for this application will include the check box labeled **Open in the Classic Environment**, which is set (or not) by default, depending on which option is used.

▶ LSRequiresCarbon and LSRequiresClassic, which when one is set to string "1", restricts execution of this application to Carbon or the Classic environment, respectively.

Classic was never available on Intel machines, and with Leopard isn't even available on PowerPCs. The Classic keys are becoming obsolete.

▶ LSRequiresNativeExecution, if YES, the application will always run on the native processor architecture of the computer. Overrides the order of LSExecutableArchitectures. Use this to prevent your universal application from running under Rosetta.

▶ LSUIElement, if set to the string "1", identifies this application as an *agent application*, a background application that has no presence in the dock but that can present user interface elements, if necessary.

▶ LSUIPresentationMode, an integer between 0 and 4, representing progressively greater amounts of the system UI—dock and menu bar—to be hidden when the application is running. See Apple's documentation for details.

▶ LSVisibleInClassic, if set to the string "1", makes this background-only, or agent, application visible to the Classic Process Manager as a background-only application. Now that Classic is gone, this key is obsolete in Leopard and on Intel Macs.

▶ **Localization**

▶ CFBundleAllowMixedLocalizations, whether the localization system localizes strings and other resources on a bundle-by-bundle basis, instead of applying the localization used by the application to every case.

> ▶ CFBundleLocalizations, an array populated with codes for languages and regions in an application that handles localization programmatically rather than through localized resources.

▶ **Structure**

> > ▶ ATSApplicationFontsPath, a string. If your application contains fonts for its own use, it contains the path, relative to the application's Resources directory, to the directory containing the fonts.
>
> > ▶ NSAppleScriptEnabled, indicating that, if YES or `<true />`, this application is scriptable. Applications must specify this key.
>
> > ▶ NSMainNibFile, the base name of the application's main NIB file. Applications must specify this key.
>
> > ▶ NSServices, an array of dictionaries declaring the Mac OS X services this application performs, which will appear in the **Services** submenu of every application's application menu. The dictionaries specify the pasteboard input and output formats, the name of the service, and the name of the method that implements the service. See Apple's documentation for details.

## Keys for Plug-Ins

These tags provide information on how a plug-in bundle is to be accessed and configured.

> ▶ CFPlugInDynamicRegistration, indicating that, if YES (`<true />`), the plug-in in this bundle is to be registered dynamically.

> ▶ CFPlugInDynamicRegisterFunction, the name of the dynamic registration function for this plug-in, if it is not CFPlugInDynamicRegister.

> ▶ CFPlugInFactories, a dictionary used for static plug-in registration. See Apple's documentation on plug-in registration for more details.

> ▶ CFPlugInTypes, a dictionary identifying groups of entry points for plug-in registration. See Apple's documentation on plug-in registration for more details.

> ▶ CFPlugInUnloadFunction, the name of a function to call when the plug-in in this bundle is to be unloaded from memory.

## Keys for Java

Cocoa Java applications must request a Java virtual machine (VM) and specify class paths. These tags do that:

> ▶ NSJavaNeeded, indicating that, if YES or `<true />`, the Java VM will be started before loading the bundle. This is needed for Cocoa-Java applications but *not* for 100 percent pure Java.

▶ `NSJavaPath`, an array of paths to Java class files, either absolute or relative to `NSJavaRoot`. Xcode maintains this array automatically.

▶ `NSJavaRoot`, a string containing the path to the root of the Java class tree.

## Keys for Preference Panes

Panes for the System Preferences application specify the icons and labels used in the application's display window with these tags:

▶ `NSPrefPaneIconFile`, the name of the image file you provide in `Resources` as an icon for this preference pane in System Preferences. The picture should be 32 pixels by 32 pixels in size. Lacking this image, the bundle icon is used.

▶ `NSPrefPaneIconLabel`, the name of this preference pane, as shown beneath its icon in System Preferences. You can break the string into lines with the newline (the string "`\n`") sequence. Lacking this string, the `CFBundleName` is used.

## Keys for Dashboard Widgets

Dashboard widgets have their own set of keys, specifying their component files, security model, and basic layout. A widget `Info.plist` must also contain the keys `CFBundleIdentifier`, `CFBundleName`, and `CFBundleDisplayName` and should include other general-purpose keys, such as `CFBundleShortVersionString` or `CFBundleVersion`, as you see fit.

▶ **Layout**

    ▶ `CloseBoxInsetX` specifies how far right from the leftmost possible position to place the close box.

    ▶ `CloseBoxInsetY` specifies how far down from the uppermost possible position to place the close box.

    ▶ `Height`, the height, in pixels, of the widget.

    ▶ `Width`, the width, in pixels, of the widget.

▶ **Security**

    ▶ `AllowFullAccess`, indicating that, if `<true />`, the widget is given full access to the file system, network assets, command-line utilities, Java applets, and Web Kit facilities.

    ▶ `AllowInternetPlugins`, indicating that, if `<true />`, the widget is allowed to use Web Kit to access browser plug-ins.

    ▶ `AllowJava`, indicating that, if `<true />`, the widget is allowed to use Java applets.

▶ `AllowNetworkAccess`, indicating that, if `<true />`, the widget is allowed to use network or other non-file-based resources.

▶ `AllowSystem`, indicating that, if `<true />`, the widget is allowed to use command-line utilities.

▶ **Structure**

▶ `Font`, an array of strings naming fonts included in the widget bundle. Widget fonts are placed in the *root* of the bundle, not in a `Resources` directory.

▶ `MainHTML`, a required key: a path, relative to the bundle's root, to the main HTML (Hypertext Markup Language) file for the widget.

▶ `Plugin`, the name of a plug-in used by the widget.

# Summary

This chapter explored bundles and package directories, important concepts in Mac OS X development. Most Xcode product types are bundles. We reviewed the structure of simple packages and application bundles and examined the `Info.plist` file, which communicates a bundle's metadata to the operating system.

CHAPTER **12**

# Unit Testing

**IN THIS CHAPTER**

▸ **Creating a Unit Test Harness**

▸ **Testing an Application from Within**

▸ **Refactoring**

$A$ll of our development of Linrg and Linear so far has left out one essential consideration: *How do we know it works?*

Yes, we know generally what to expect, and we have used the Xcode debugger to verify that what the application does makes sense, but we don't have the time or the discipline to test for every possible error, every time. Nor to repeat those tests every time our code changes—which is the only way to be sure of catching bugs as soon as possible after we introduce them. This discipline of verifying that each little part of your application works is called *unit testing*. The meticulous search for errors is the sort of mind-numbing, repetitive, perfectionist task that computers were invented to do.

This is a well-enough understood problem that a solution has been devised in the form of testing frameworks. Such frameworks make it easy to take your code, more or less in the actual context in which you use it, present it with known inputs, and compare the results with what you expect. If everything is as expected, the test succeeds; otherwise, it fails. The framework provides a way to run all the tests, record the results, and issue a report on them.

## Adding a Unit Test Target

Unit tests are a separate sort of task from the main body of an application, and although they can work on the same code the application uses, they use the additional SenTestingKit framework, plus test code you write yourself. A separate executable with its own set of source files means a new target.

Select **Project > New Target...** to bring up the New Target assistant. From the list of targets, select **Cocoa > Unit Test Bundle**. Name the new target something like `Tests`, and make sure it goes into the Linear project. The new target is added to the Targets group in the Groups & Files list.

The Tests target produces a *bundle*, a structured directory containing executable code for another application to load and run (see Chapter 11, "File Packages and Bundles," for details). The target includes, at the end, a Run Script build phase that submits the bundle product to the `RunUnitTests` script in the `/Developer/Tools/` directory. This sets in motion the process of loading the test suite into the testing framework, running your tests, and reporting the outcome.

You must now specify which tests you want to conduct and how to conduct them. You do this by creating a subclass of `SenTestCase` for each series of tests you want to perform. A good rule of thumb, at least at the beginning, is to create a `SenTestCase` subclass for each class of your own that you want to test.

To create a test class, select **File > New File...** to bring up the New File Assistant. Choose **Objective-C Test Case Class** in the **Cocoa** group, click **Continue**, and give the file a descriptive name, such as **TestRegression.m** for a class that tests class `Regression`. Make sure to generate a header file, too, and attach the file to the Tests target only.

`TestRegression.h` is a skeleton. Fill it out like this:

```
#import <SenTestingKit/SenTestingKit.h>
@class Regression;
@interface TestRegression : SenTestCase {
    Regression * myRegression;
}
@end
```

Essentially, we inform the Objective-C compiler that there is such a class as `Regression`, and that our test class keeps an instance for the use of its tests.

A `SenTestCase` subclass groups a series of related tests. Each test consists of a series of actions that may be expected to have a particular result—returning an expected value, or throwing an exception. If the results are as expected, the test passes; otherwise, it fails. The `SenTestingKit` framework provides a number of macros that check results against expectations, and turns the outcome into a report that can go into a testing log.

> **NOTE**
>
> I can't list all the available macros here. You can find all their names in `SenTestingKit/SenTestCase.h`. All take an `NSString *` description as their last parameter, followed by additional parameters to satisfy `printf`-style format specifications in the description. For a shortcut, type one of the macro names into a file (Xcode may even offer to complete it for you), and Command-double-click it. You will be given a choice of two places where the macro is defined; the one in `SenTestCase.h` is the easier for reference, but `SenTestCase_Macros.h` includes documentation.

Before a test method is run, SenTestingKit runs the test class's -setUp method; it runs -tearDown afterward. You can use these to do initialization that every test will need. The tests themselves have only one requirement: They must be methods returning void, taking no parameters, and with selectors beginning with test. That's all. SenTestingKit will find them from there.

Here is what a *partial* test suite for the Regression class would look like:

```
#import "TestRegression.h"
#import "Regression.h"
#import "DataPoint.h"

@implementation TestRegression

-(void) setUp
{
    // Every test gets its own Regression object.
    myRegression = [[Regression alloc] init];
}
-(void) tearDown
{
    // Free the test's Regression object.
    [myRegression release];
}
-(void) testDataPointsExist
{
     STAssertNotNil([myRegression dataPoints],
            @"Regression should start with a dataPoints array");
}
-(void) testDataPointsEmpty
{
    NSMutableArray * points = [myRegression dataPoints];
    // STAssertEquals is very picky about matching data types.
    STAssertEquals((int) [points count], 0,
                   @"Regression's dataPoints array should "
                   @"start empty.");
}
-(void) testPerfectRegressionResults
{
    NSMutableArray * points = [myRegression dataPoints];
    DataPoint *        currPoint;

    // Set up a regression for the exact line y = 1 + 2x
    currPoint = [[(DataPoint *) [DataPoint alloc] initWithX: 1.0
                                                         Y: 3.0]
            autorelease];
```

```
    // Challenge it with an invalid data set.
    [points addObject: currPoint];
    STAssertFalse([myRegression canCompute],
                @"Regression shouldn't work on a single point");
    STAssertThrows([myRegression computeFromLibrary],
                @"Regression should throw an exception for "
                @"invalid data set.");

    currPoint = [[(DataPoint *) [DataPoint alloc] initWithX: 2.0
                                                          Y: 5.0]
                autorelease];
    [points addObject: currPoint];

    // Challenge it with the first valid data set
    STAssertTrue([myRegression canCompute],
                @"Regression should work on two points");
    STAssertNoThrow([myRegression computeFromLibrary],
                @"Regression should accept multiple points (1)");

    currPoint = [[(DataPoint *) [DataPoint alloc] initWithX: 2.5
                                                          Y: 6.0]
                autorelease];
    [points addObject: currPoint];
    currPoint = [[(DataPoint *) [DataPoint alloc] initWithX: 3.75
                                                          Y: 8.5]
                autorelease];
    [points addObject: currPoint];

    STAssertNoThrow([myRegression computeFromLibrary],
                    @"Regression should accept multiple points (2)");
    STAssertEqualsWithAccuracy([myRegression slope], 2.0, 1.0e-15,
                            @"Regression should yield slope of "
                            @"2 for a perfect line");
    STAssertEqualsWithAccuracy([myRegression intercept], 1.0, 1.0e-15,
                            @"Regression should yield intercept of "
                            @"1 for a perfect line");
    STAssertEqualsWithAccuracy([myRegression correlation], 1.0, 1.0e-15,
                            @"Regression should yield perfect "
                            @"correlation for a perfect line");
}
@end
```

As you can see, unit testing is an accumulation of maddening little things that you assume to be true of the basic units of an application. When those maddening little things turn out not to be true, your assumptions often block you from seeing the bugs.

Unit tests make sure that you can rely on the little things. Frequent tests tell you immediately when a change you make breaks your infrastructure.

There should be more tests, such as for regressions in which the data set is not perfect, and for the accuracy of the NSCoding and property-list methods. And, there should be more test classes, such as for class DataPoint. What I can show here is only an illustration.

# Refactoring

Why is -testPerfectRegressionResults littered with casts like (DataPoint *) [DataPoint alloc]? Try compiling TestRegression.m without, and see. For each instance of the method initWithX:Y:, there is a compiler warning that the class CIVector in the Core Image framework defines a method with the same selector. The compiler even says it will use the definition from CIVector.h, which means it will cast the parameters to CGFloat.

In this case, that's probably not too serious; but it might be, and we want to suppress those warnings anyway. Casting the results of [DataPoint alloc] to DataPoint * solves the problem.

But it's an ad hoc solution. The problem will come up, repeatedly, as long as we have a DataPoint class that collides with CIVector. The right solution is to rename -[DataPoint initWithX:Y:] and edit every use of it to conform.

Suppose we rename it to initWithAbscissa:ordinate:. It's ungainly, but not likely to cause collisions. There is a problem, however. The selector for this method consists of two words; this is not going to be a matter of a simple global search and replace. It will not be a matter of a global search and replace for each half of the selector—no other method in the Linear project uses initWithX: as part of its selector, and we *think* none uses Y:. But we might not be so lucky in the future. It will not even be a matter of a global search and replace for a regular expression. Remember we have to catch every case in which the selector is used, defined, or declared; we have to handle the case in which the selector is split between lines (possibly with comments); and we have to deal with the possibility that some other method uses initWithX:Y: as part of a signature with three or more parameters. Leave aside that we don't want to change the selector for instances of any class other than DataPoint.

We're stuck with searching for **initWithX**, and making each change by hand, aren't we?

No. Xcode 3 now offers a number of services under the name of *refactoring*. Refactoring refers to any of a number of actions that use an understanding of your code to make changes to it. Click in any instance of the initWithX:Y: selector, and issue the menu command **Edit > Refactor** (⇧⌘J). A refactoring window appears, offering to **Rename** initWithX:Y: to something else specified in a text field, which we fill in with **initWithAbscissa:ordinate:**. A text field immediately below alerts you to the fact that the change can't be made until the target selector has as many colons as the source. When you've entered the new selector, the button below the target field, labeled **Preview**, becomes active—Xcode does not allow you to proceed until you have seen and verified the changes.

Click **Preview.** The middle of the Refactoring window fills with a list of every file in which the change would be made, and how many changes would be made in each file. You can exempt a file by unchecking the box to the left of the file's name. Clicking a list item fills the bottom of the Refactoring window with a file-comparison view highlighting each proposed change (see Figure 12.1). As usual, you can click the arrow in the middle gutter to declare whether a particular change should go through.

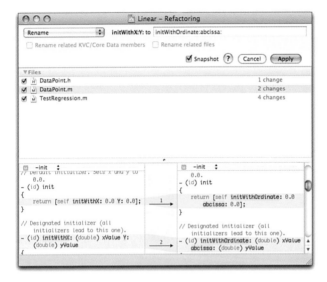

FIGURE 12.1    The Refactoring window, as you are ready to change the signature of a method. The operation, **Rename**, was selected by the pop-up menu at the upper left. The method's new signature is entered at upper right. Once previewed, the files to be changed are shown in the middle, and selecting one fills the comparison view so that you can pass on individual changes.

---

### Converting to Objective-C 2.0

The biggest refactoring service of all is the capability of Xcode to convert a Cocoa project to use Objective-C 2.0. I haven't covered this advance to the Objective-C language because it can be used only on Mac OS X 10.5 and later. The example Linear project has to be runnable on 10.4, and having a separate track for a new language isn't practical.

If you can stick to 10.5, ObjC 2.0 is well worth your time. Under the original language, memory management is a constant concern. It's easy to leak memory, and it's easy to release memory that is still in use. ObjC 2.0 is *garbage-collected*: Objects' memory is reclaimed when it is no longer in use, and not before. You don't have to do any tracking of your own.

Objective-C 2.0 also adds *properties* so that the getter and setter methods we've been using ([aRegression setSlope: 1.0]) can be replaced by the more-familiar and compact dot notation (aRegression.slope = 1.0).

It also adds *fast iteration*. By conventional methods, iterating through an NSArray by passing an index to `objectAtIndex:` or using an NSEnumerator incurs a large overhead at each pass. Under fast iteration

```
NSEnumerator *      iter = [dataPoints objectEnumerator];
DataPoint *         curr;
while (curr = [iter nextObject]) {
    [pointArray addObject: [curr asPropertyList]];
}
```

becomes

```
DataPoint *             curr;
for (curr in dataPoints) {
    [pointArray addObject: [curr asPropertyList]];
}
```

The `for...` in construct uses a back-door protocol by which NSArray allows fast, direct access to its contents for the loop.

Xcode 3 can port a project to Objective-C 2.0 by converting loops and property accesses. (Porting for garbage collection is something you'll have to do by hand.) Select **Edit > Convert to Objective-C 2.0**. Xcode will present a preview window that offers check boxes for **Modernize Loops** and **Use Properties**. Check the conversions you want, and click **Preview**. As with the other Refactoring window, you can review the changes, and if they suit, click **Apply**.

You've reviewed the changes, and you've set the ones you want to make. Xcode offers you an extra measure of safety: a *snapshot*. Snapshots are available to you at any time (**File > Make Snapshot** or **^⌘S**), but are especially offered to you when you refactor. A snapshot preserves the complete contents of the project's

> **WARNING**
>
> Be sure all your files are saved before you make a snapshot. Xcode won't save your files automatically before a snapshot is taken; so if your changes aren't on disk, they won't be in the snapshot.

"root directory." By default, this is the directory that contains your project file, but you can designate another by clicking the **Choose...** button at the top of the **General** tab of the Project Info window. After you have made a snapshot, you can revert to it at any time (**File > Snapshots**), discarding all the changes made since then (see Figure 12.2).

> **NOTE**
>
> The project root directory provides a starting point for many projectwide services, including searches, snapshots, refactoring, and SCM. You can designate a root directory for your project in the **General** tab of the Project Info window. The project root must be the directory that contains the project file or a directory that eventually contains the project file. A snapshot will preserve everything within the project root and its subdirectories.

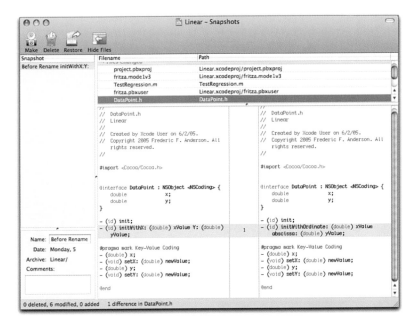

FIGURE 12.2    The Snapshot window, after you click the **Show Files** toolbar button. The list at the left shows every snapshot you have made; you may **Delete** these, **Restore** your project directory from them, rename them, or attach comments. Clicking a snapshot will produce (upper right) a list of files that have changed since you made that snapshot. Clicking one of them displays (lower right) a comparison between the two. The comparison is not editable.

Leave the **Snapshot** box in the Refactoring window checked. Click **Apply**. The snapshot itself will take several seconds, and then a progress window will briefly appear as the refactoring edits take place. Examine TestRegression.m and the other files that use or define DataPoint. initWithX:Y: is now initWithAbscissa:ordinate:.

> **NOTE**
>
> If we had chosen to refactor a symbol—a class name, an outlet, an action—that was used in a NIB, the symbol would be changed in the NIB, too; the objects and connections would not be orphaned because they would be changed by a mere substitution of text.

> **NOTE**
>
> It might strike you that snapshots are an alternative to version control. There are distinctions. Snapshots cannot permit reverting just one file, or rolling back just a few changes since a previous version. They are no use at all if you want to work with a project on different machines, or with more than one developer. They cannot reconcile changes made simultaneously by more than one developer. Snapshots are a valuable safety feature, but they are no substitute for SCM. *However:* Some organizations place restrictions on when its developers may check revisions into a repository, restrictions that may mean that significant intermediate changes to a project never get checked in. In that case, snapshots *do* serve as a useful, local supplement to regular SCM.

# Running the Tests

Our unit test for the `Regression` class is not quite ready. To exercise `Regression` and `DataPoint`, their code has to be linked into the test. Because `Regression` uses `libRegression.a`, that, too, must be linked in. Select the project icon at the top of the Groups & Files list, to fill the Detail view with all the files in the project. Make sure Tests is selected as the active target, so that the check boxes at the right of the list reflect whether the files are a part of that target. Check the boxes for the following:

- ▶ `DataPoint.m`

- ▶ `DataPoint-PropertyList.m`

- ▶ `Regression.m`

- ▶ `Regression-PropertyList.m`

- ▶ `libRegression.a`

> **NOTE**
>
> If the Detail list does not include these check boxes, right- (Control-) click in the header of the Detail list, and make sure that Target is checked.

Now build the Tests target. There is no need to run the target—in fact, there is nothing to run. The `SenTestingKit` framework is set up so that tests are run *at build time*, in a script in the target's last build phase. This has the advantage that failures in tests can be reported via error messages, which can be displayed in the test source just like any other error.

And errors we do have (see Figure 12.3). The Build Results window appears, with red-letter lines in the upper progress list. Clicking one of these brings you to the place where the error occurred. The last of these displays the part of `SenTestingKit`'s testing script where it was reported, and is of no interest. The other line, however, directs us to the `STAssertThrows` assertion in `test-PerfectRegressionResults`. Our test expected that `Regression` would raise a program exception when a client, in spite of the warning from the `canCompute` method, attempts to send `computeFromLibrary` with no adequate data to back it up.

Well, we knew this, but it does express something that `Regression` *should* do. It is a recommended use of unit tests, that you construct your test cases *before* you write any other code, so that the tests will enforce design requirements on your code. Let's comply with this requirement by changing `computeFromLibrary` as follows:

```
- (void) computeFromLibrary
{
    if (![self canCompute]) {
        NSException * exception =
            [NSException exceptionWithName: NSInvalidArgumentsException
                                    reason: @"A regression must have "
                                            @"at least two points "
                                            @"to be legal."
                                  userInfo: nil];
        @throw exception;
```

```
    }
    void * reg = RGCreate();

    NSEnumerator* iter = [dataPoints objectEnumerator];
    DataPoint * curr;
    while (curr = [iter nextObject])
        RGAddPoint(reg, [curr x], [curr y]);

    if (RGCount(reg) > 1) {
        [self setSlope: RGSlope(reg)];
        [self setIntercept: RGIntercept(reg)];
        [self setCorrelation: RGCorrelation(reg)];
    }
    RGRelease(reg);
}
```

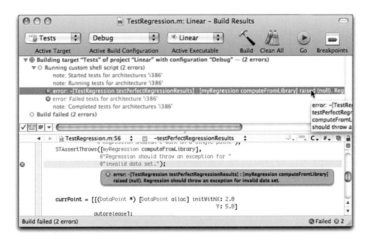

FIGURE 12.3    The Build Results window after a unit test has failed. As unit testing is done simply by appending the script that runs the tests to the process of building the test suite, the results of the build are just the results of the test. The failure appears as an error in the upper results pane. Selecting the error shows the offending assertion marked with a red bubble explaining the failure. Click the red badge in the gutter to hide the bubble.

Build again. After all the necessary compilation, Xcode is utterly silent. No errors, no Build Results window. That's what happens when your code passes all its tests.

## A Dependent Test

We can do better. SenTestingKit works well when the test is run as a standalone executable, but it can also *inject* a test into a running application. It can actually run your application, and apply your test suites from within. A test that works with your classes in the environment in which you intend to use them is much more reliable than one that works on them in isolation, in a test-only condition. Further, an injected test can work with the more complex structure of your program, using Cocoa, for instance, to create a new MyDocument instance, and then see what happens when MyDocument is told to create new DataPoints.

Because such tests require that the target program be fully built before testing can proceed, they are called *dependent tests*.

We'll be doing something less ambitious than a full-up exercise of the document framework. We will just restructure the Tests target so that it runs the TestRegression suite from within the Linear application. This is still a bit more complicated than our original, independent test.

First, if you are going to run a test inside Linear, it makes sense that the test can't proceed until Linear has been built correctly. Double-click the Tests target, select the **General** tab, and add the Linear application as a dependency of Tests.

Next, we have to change how Tests is built and run, because the requirements for it are out of the ordinary. This will be our first encounter with the **Build** tab of the Target Info window. (It will be far from our last.) If it isn't open already, double-click the Tests target, and select the **Build** tab in the window that appears (see Figure 12.4).

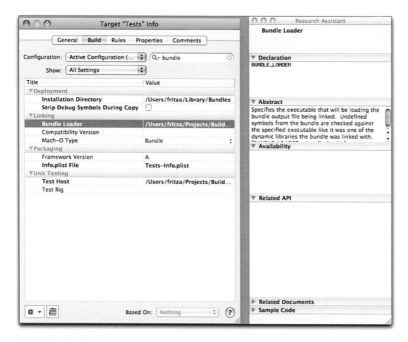

FIGURE 12.4    The **Build** tab of the Target Info window of Tests, next to the Research Assistant. By typing **bundle** into the search field, we restrict the build settings to only those that have that string in their titles, values, or descriptions. Clicking the stack-of-books button at the lower left of the **Build** tab reveals the Research Assistant, a ready reference for code and for build settings. Selecting a build setting puts a long description of the setting into the RA.

The table in the **Build** view contains many, many entries, and only two of them are of any interest to us. The options we want to change are related to Tests' product being a loadable bundle, so type **bundle** into the search field at the top. Also, we want any changes we make to affect all the build configurations Tests might use, so select **All Configurations** from the **Configuration** pop-up.

We have to tell Xcode that if a method, function, or variable is used, but not defined, in the test code, it should look to link it directly from Linear. We will be using Linear's code in-place, in the application. This entails giving the exact path to the Linear executable file. Double-click the right side of the line labeled **Bundle Loader,** and in the sheet that emerges, type the following:

```
$(BUILT_PRODUCTS_DIR)/Linear.app/Contents/MacOS/Linear
```

This is a full file system path to the actual executable code of Linear. The element $(BUILT_PRODUCTS_DIR) expands to whatever directory Xcode uses to receive the Linear application

> **NOTE**
>
> If this is a bit unclear to you, it might help to review Chapter 4, "Compilation: The Basics."

once it is built, in whatever directory the Linear project is in. Thus, the path will find the right file regardless of how you've moved or renamed Linear's directory, of whether you're using the Debug or Release configuration, or how Xcode organizes its build directories. Notice that the path continues, identifying the Linear executable file inside the Linear.app bundle.

We also need to tell Xcode that Linear will host Tests when Tests is run. The **Bundle Loader** setting was for linking; this setting tells Xcode how Tests is to be run. Double-click the right side of the **Test Host** line, and type $(**BUNDLE_ LOADER**). This means "whatever was in the **Bundle Loader** line." When you have finished editing, the right side of the **Test Host** line will fill with the full path to Linear's executable (/Users/

> **NOTE**
>
> If you Control-click in build setting table, you can toggle between **Show Definitions** and **Show Values**, alternating the right column between what you typed and what you meant. Similarly, **Show Setting Names** and **Show Setting Titles** toggle the labels between the descriptive title and the name of the build variable each line sets.

xcodeuser/=Linear...). In the build settings, Xcode expands all symbols so that you can see the effective value of what you have set. The actual value will still be $(BUNDLE_LOADER).

If Tests can link straight out of Linear, it follows that we don't need to link directly to Regression, DataPoints, or libRegression. Select the project icon in Groups & Files, make sure Tests is the current target, and uncheck all those files to remove them from Tests.

---

**The Research Assistant**

You are not expected to remember the effect of every setting in the build table, nor the symbol to use to refer to it. Apple provides a Research Assistant window to document build settings and other things. (See Chapter 15, "Documentation in Xcode," for details.)

To show the Research Assistant, click the button at the bottom of the **Build** tab that looks like a stack of books (📚). (It is also available through the **Help** menu.) As shown in the right half of Figure 12.4, the Research Assistant is divided into several sections. Most of these are for documenting API from Apple frameworks when such is selected in an editor view, but the upper two sections are relevant right now.

The top section, **Declaration**, shows the variable that carries the selected setting to the rest of the build system. This is how we knew that we could type `$(BUNDLE_LOADER)` as the value for **Test Host**, and get the same path as we entered into **Bundle Loader**.

The next section, **Abstract**, contains detailed documentation for the setting. (The abstract for **Bundle Loader** begins, "Specifies the executable that will be loading the bundle output file being linked.") The end of the abstract provides some additional information. It repeats the build-time variable for the setting (BUNDLE_LOADER), and it tells you that `-bundleloader` is the compiler flag that the setting influences.

---

Now you can build Tests, which will run your test suite. Because of the dependency chain, building Tests builds `Linear`, which in turn builds the Regression library. Once that is done, the `SenTestingKit` script launches `Linear`, runs all the tests, and closes it.

In this case, all we see is "Build succeeded"—`Regression` still passes all the tests in `TestRegression`. For a more interesting display, try changing one of the tests in `TestRegression` so that it fails—the test failure is reported as an error, and inline in `TestRegression.m`, just as before.

# Crossing Architectures

If you're building for more than one architecture, you'll want to be sure your tests catch errors, such as byte-order dependencies, that might arise from relying on the processor you develop on. If you're running an Intel Mac, there's a way to do this, using the Rosetta PowerPC emulator.

In the Tests target, the Run Script build phase consists of one command:

```
"$(SYSTEM_DEVELOPER_DIR)/Tools/RunUnitTests"
```

This command is responsible for actually running the test. The `RunUnitTests` tool examines the `ARCHS` build variable, and repeats the test for every architecture the variable lists—provided the machine you're running on supports that architecture. This means that if you are on an Intel Mac, you can run tests for `ppc` and `i386` at least, and `x86_64` if you have a 64-bit processor. The PowerPC test is available thanks to the Rosetta emulator. Rosetta can't emulate a 64-bit PowerPC, so an Intel Mac can build `ppc64` binaries, but can't test them. PowerPC Macs can't test Intel binaries at all.

Remember that in the Debug configuration ARCHS, which you set in the Target Info window's **Build** tab (the label is **Architectures**), is only the architecture you're running on. You won't get the multiple tests unless you change the setting or switch to the Release configuration.

## Summary

In this chapter, we introduced the practice of unit testing, and why it is useful—many would say essential—in the development process. We produced a test suite for a part of Linear and saw how it ran, then converted to a dependent test to make our tests run in the actual context of the running Linear application.

Along the way, we used Xcode's refactoring facility to relieve a name collision in Linear's code, and exercised the Snapshot service. We also made our first acquaintance with the build-settings panel.

# CHAPTER 13

# Creating a Custom View

**IN THIS CHAPTER**

▸ Adding a NIB to a Project

▸ Creating a Custom Class in
Interface Builder

▸ Generating Implementation
Files

▸ Connection HUDs

▸ Debugging Graphics

The three statistics—slope, intercept, and correlation—tell the whole story of a data set and its relation to the best line through it, but pictures are easier to understand. In this chapter, we add a window with a custom view that generates a simple graph of the regression line and the points in the data set. Along the way. we'll see how Interface Builder helps in placing and describing new view classes, and how we can use it to build complex relationships among views and controller objects.

## Controller

Let's start thinking about this new window by imagining how it should make its appearance. The user would issue a command, either by selecting a menu item or by clicking a button, for the window to appear. Commands are issued *to* objects in the Mac OS human interface; what would the target of the command be? Plainly, it should be the same MyDocument instance that manages the Regression model. The command would be that a graph window be opened on a particular regression line and data set.

We'll do this in the simplest possible way, amending MyDocument so that it is the owner of the new window and manager of our new custom view. This view will respond to commands to show the window. The interface for MyDocument then becomes

```
#import <Cocoa/Cocoa.h>

@class    Regression;
@class    LinearGraph;
```

```
@interface MyDocument : NSDocument
{
    Regression * model;
    IBOutlet LinearGraph * graphView;
    IBOutlet NSWindow *    graphWindow;
}
- (IBAction) compute: (id) sender;
- (IBAction) showGraphWindow: (id) sender;

@end
```

LinearGraph is a name we made up for a new subclass of NSView that displays graphs.
Both the new view (graphView) and its window (graphWindow) are declared as IBOutlets.
IBOutlet is #defined as an empty string so far as the Objective-C language is concerned;
the next time Xcode informs Interface Builder of the structure of MyDocument, it will identify graphView and graphWindow as potential outlets for connection to other objects.

Here is the code to add to MyDocument.m.
First, near the beginning (before the
@implementation line), insert the
following:

```
#import "LinearGraph.h"
```

Then, within the @implementation:

> **NOTE**
>
> If you're using Objective: C 2.0, Interface
> Builder will also pick up any property you
> define with the @property directive as a
> potential outlet. Further, for historical
> reasons, IB regards any instance variable
> defined with the id type as an outlet.

```
#pragma mark Graph Window
-(IBAction) showGraphWindow: (id) sender
{
    if (! graphWindow) {
        // If the graphWindow hasn't been loaded yet, load it.
        [NSBundle loadNibNamed: @"GraphWindow" owner: self];
    }
    // Make the graphWindow visible.
    [graphWindow makeKeyAndOrderFront: sender];
    // Make the graphView reload its data.
    [graphView refreshData];
}
```

You should also make the following
change to MyDocument's dealloc:

```
-(void) dealloc
{
    [model release];
    [graphWindow release];
    [super dealloc];
}
```

> **NOTE**
>
> Why release the graphWindow instance vari-
> able when we never retain it? In a NIB file,
> all top-level objects, such as windows, are
> instantiated with a retain count of 1. There is
> no need to retain it an additional time, and it
> is the responsibility of the file's owner to
> release it.

The Model-View-Controller (MVC) design pattern also leads us to believe that `MyDocument` should mediate the flow of data between the `Regression` model and the `LinearGraph` view. We can come back to that when we know more about `LinearGraph`'s requirements.

# View

In Cocoa, most drawing is done by subclasses of `NSView`, a class that maintains a position and size within an enclosing view and provides a coordinate space and drawing state for graphics inside its area. We could create our `LinearGraph` class files in Xcode—Xcode even provides a special new-file template for `NSView` subclasses. Instead, we will use Interface Builder to do at least the rough work.

Start Interface Builder and from the Choose a Template window, select **Window**. This sets up a new NIB with an empty `NSWindow` in it. Select the window, and use the Attributes Inspector (press ⌘1) to give it the title **Graph**. Also, uncheck **Behavior > Release When Closed**. We want this window to hang around, even when it is not visible, so that we can make it visible whenever we need it.

> **N O T E**
>
> Indeed, it is Apple's position that the best way to add a view class is to add the source files that define it to the Xcode project, and let Interface Builder pick it up automatically. We've already seen how IB does that with other classes; this time we'll start with Interface Builder.

Save the NIB file now. Name it **GraphWindow**, and place it in the `English.lproj` subdirectory of the Linear project directory.

Now is the time to attach the new NIB to the Linear project. Switch back to Xcode, and select **Project > Add to Project...** (⌥⌘A). Find `GraphWindow.nib` in the open-file sheet that appears, and click **Add**. Make sure `GraphWindow.nib` is associated with the Linear application target.

> **N O T E**
>
> Where `GraphWindow.nib` will appear in the Groups & Files list depends on what had been selected before. You'll want to drag it into the Resources group, just to keep it organized.

Switch back to Interface Builder, and you'll see that the status bar at the bottom of the main NIB window now includes a green gem and the label **Linear.xcodeproj**. This indicates that IB will draw class-structure information from the Linear project. Having a NIB file associated with a project early confers some advantages, as Interface Builder and Xcode are tightly integrated.

`GraphWindow.nib` will be loaded by `MyDocument`. Set the class of **File's Owner** to `MyDocument` by selecting it, invoking the Object Identity Inspector (⌘6), and filling the **Class** field with **MyDocument**. `MyDocument`'s actions and outlets fill into the inspector's lists.

13

Now we can make our first connection from the MyDocument instance into this NIB. Control-drag from **File's Owner** to the **Window** icon, and select the graphWindow outlet in the resulting HUD window.

Now we will fill the window with a LinearGraph. Navigate the Library palette (using **Tools > Library** (⇧⌘L) to make it visible, if needed) by traversing the hierarchy **Library > Cocoa > Views & Cells > Layout Views**. Among the objects in the middle array is a blue rectangle marked **Custom View**. Drag it into the Graph window so that a **Custom View** rectangle appears in it.

Resize the **Custom View** until it fills the window, and use the Size Inspector (press ⌘3) to make the view resizable in both axes and fixed to all edges.

As you can see from the Identity Inspector, a new custom view is given the class NSView. It might not have any special properties, but it has the size and position behaviors we need to lay it out. We want the view to have the class we mentioned in our changes to MyDocument.h—LinearGraph.

LinearGraph isn't defined in the Linear project yet, so Interface Builder doesn't know about it or its properties. Instead of defining it in Xcode, let's define it in Interface Builder. In the Identity Inspector, change the class of the custom view to **LinearGraph** by typing the name into the **Class** combo box at the top. (The view rectangle's label changes from **Custom View** to **LinearGraph**—Interface Builder labels a custom view with the name of the class that draws it.) The actions and outlets for the class disappear, but that doesn't matter; we'll provide our own.

LinearGraph has one feature that Interface Builder cares about: an outlet for its delegate. With the **LinearGraph** view still selected, return to the Identity Inspector (⌘6) to show the class attributes. Press the + button in the Class Outlets section, and in the resulting line in the outlets table name the outlet **delegate**. Leave the type as id. Now delegate will be included in HUDs and other displays of the outlets of a LinearGraph.

And now for something neat: Make sure the **LinearGraph** view is still selected. Select **File > Write Class Files…**. A save-file dialog appears (see Figure 13.1) offering to save the LinearGraph class as an **Objective-C** file (the other options are **Python** and **Ruby**, two other languages in which you can write Cocoa programs). Make sure the new files will be directed to the Linear project directory, and that the option to **Create '.h' File** is checked. Click **Save**.

Once again, go back to Xcode and select **Project > Add to Project** (⌥⌘A). This time select LinearGraph.m and .h. Make sure to assign them to the Linear target.

The LinearGraph files are bare skeletons, but they include all the attributes you specified in Interface Builder. Because we didn't specify any actions, the .m file is pretty sparse. LinearGraph.h looks like this:

```
#import <Cocoa/Cocoa.h>
@interface LinearGraph :
            /* Specify a superclass (eg: NSObject or NSView) */ {
    IBOutlet id delegate;
}

@end
```

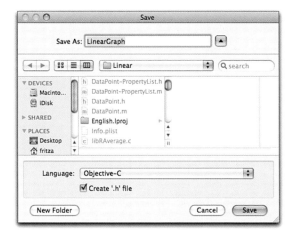

**FIGURE 13.1**    The save-file sheet that appears when you select **File > Write Class Files...**. The panel below the directory browser offers to write source files in **Objective-C** for implementing the class of the selected object. The **Language** pop-up offers **Ruby** and **Python** implementations, too. You will usually want to create a header file as well.

As the comment suggests, we type **NSView** after the colon in the `@interface` line.

One problem with the sparseness of `LinearView.m` is that it lacks the initialization (`initWithFrame:`) and drawing (`drawRect:`) methods that would be provided in the boilerplate code we'd have had if we selected **Objective-C NSView Subclass** in the New File assistant. Beyond what you see, Interface Builder doesn't generate code in the same sense that graphical interface tools for other frameworks do. It doesn't have to. NIB files are archives of the objects inside them, and loading a NIB consists simply of reconstituting the objects and their connections from the archive.

> **NOTE**
>
> An exception to the unarchiving rule is, ironically enough, the custom view. Most objects archived in a NIB are saved using the NSCoding protocol and are unarchived with NSCoding's `initWithCoder:` method. A custom view, however, may be an instance of a class whose implementation isn't linked into Interface Builder; if there's no implementation, there's no instance to archive. Custom views are therefore stored as specifications, and the NIB loader instantiates them with `initWithFrame:`. One may get the NSCoding behavior by writing an Interface Builder plug-in for the custom view class, but that's beyond the scope of this book.

When we return to Interface Builder, we notice in the Identity Inspector that the Class Outlets list for LinearGraph is now decorated with a bar that says **LinearGraph.h**. Now that Xcode's Code Sense index knows about LinearGraph and its definition, IB can look for that information in the header that defines it. If you press the arrow button at the right end of the **LinearGraph.h** bar, Xcode will come forward and display the header file.

Control-click the **LinearGraph** view in the Graph window. Interface Builder displays a HUD window listing all the outlets, actions, and bindings LinearGraph (or its super-classes) support (see Figure 13.2). It's a moderately long list, so it scrolls. If you click the button at the top right, a list pops up of each view that encloses the **LinearGraph** view. That way, you can work on the outlets, actions, and bindings of superviews without having to figure out how to click them.

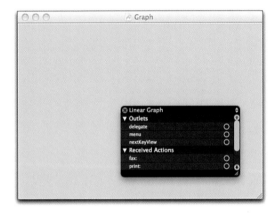

FIGURE 13.2    When you Control-click a view or icon in Interface Builder, you are presented with a HUD window listing all of that view's outlets, actions, and bindings. To see those properties of the view's superviews, click the double-arrowhead button at the top-right of the HUD.

This object-outlet HUD provides a new way to connect objects to outlets. We've already seen that if you Control-drag from the **LinearGraph** instance to **File's Owner**, you get a HUD of LinearGraph's outlets, and can connect **File's Owner** to the delegate outlet.

With the object-outlet HUD, there is a way to make the connection in a way that gives you better feedback on what you have done: When you are done, you can see the connection you have made. Notice the circles to the right of each line in the HUD (see Figure 13.3). Control-drag from delegate's circle to **File's Owner**. The connection is made, and to prove it, the delegate line now has an additional element, a lozenge labeled **File's Owner**. There is an X button in the lozenge; clicking it deletes the connection.

> **NOTE**
>
> You can readily replace connections by Control-dragging to establish the new ones, but the only way to empty an outlet is to Control-click the object that owns the outlet and click the outlet's **X** button.

FIGURE 13.3    (Left) The outlets HUD provides an additional way to make connections between objects. Control-dragging from the circle to the right of a connection name to another object establishes the desired connection. (Right) When a connection is made, the HUD for an object displays the target for the connection next to the connection name.

Now is the time to fill `MyDocument`'s `graphView` outlet. Control-drag a line from the **LinearGraph** view to **File's Owner** and select **graphView**.

# The Delegate Design Pattern

What is `LinearGraph` supposed to do? It should draw a set of points and a line. How, then, should it get that data? One strategy would be to decide that `LinearGraph` is merely an object that renders `Regression` objects. A `LinearGraph` should be given a reference to a `Regression`; whenever it needs data, the view can pull it straight from the model.

This approach is simple, but in a more complex project, marrying `LinearGraph` so closely to the `Regression` API means that every time `Regression` changes, `LinearGraph` probably has to change, too. In a very complex project, it might even be impossible to test `LinearGraph` without a fully developed and tested `Regression` to drive it!

Let's choose a slightly different strategy. We will have `LinearGraph` take data from a *delegate*, an object whose implementation—even whose class—we don't care about, so long as it responds to certain messages.

> **NOTE**
>
> Java programmers will recognize in this an analog to interfaces. Objective-C offers an even closer analog—*protocols*—for sets of methods a class guarantees it implements. In this case, we are just declaring an *informal protocol*—a set of methods with no compile-time guarantee. Whether a method is implemented can be checked at runtime.

We'll define our informal protocol as a category on NSObject. The effect will be that the Objective-C compiler will assume that any descendant of NSObject implements these methods, whether they do or not:

```
@interface NSObject (LinearGraphDelegate)
- (unsigned) countDataPoints;
- (void) dataPointAtIndex: (unsigned) index
                       x: (double *) outX
                       y: (double *) outY;
- (BOOL) definesLineOfSlope: (double *) outSlope
                 intercept: (double *) outIntercept;
@end
```

We can put this category declaration at the end of LinearGraph.h, so it will be seen in any .m file that deals with LinearGraph. To the declaration of the LinearGraph class itself, we add a pointer to the delegate object and the accessor methods:

```
@interface LinearGraph : NSView {
    IBOutlet id delegate;
}


- (void) refreshData;
- (id) delegate;
- (void) setDelegate: (id) newDelegate;
@end
```

The implementation, in LinearGraph.m, is a little more complicated than we've seen before:

```
- (void) refreshData
{
    // Force a redraw of the view, which means
    // a reload of the data.
    [self setNeedsDisplay: YES];
}

#pragma mark Delegate
- (id)  delegate { return delegate; }

static  BOOL NotImpl(id object, SEL aSelector)
{
    // Helper for setDelegate:
    // Detects whether a proposed delegate fails to
    // implement a method. Allow nil also.
    return (object != nil) &&
    ![object respondsToSelector: aSelector];
```

```
}

- (void) setDelegate: (id) newDelegate
{
    if (delegate != newDelegate) {
        // Check for compliance with (most of) the
        // informal protocol.
        if (NotImpl(newDelegate, @selector(countDataPoints)) ||
            NotImpl(newDelegate, @selector(dataPointAtIndex:x:y:))) {

            NSString * reason = [NSString stringWithFormat:
                        @"%@ doesn't implement needed methods",
                        newDelegate];
            NSException * exception = [NSException
                    exceptionWithName: NSInvalidArgumentException
                               reason: reason
                             userInfo: nil];
            @throw exception;
        }
        // Record the new delegate.
        delegate = newDelegate;
    }
}
```

Unlike the `setDataPoints:` accessor in `Regression`, the `setDelegate:` accessor does not attempt to retain or release the delegate object—by convention, delegates are not retained. In addition, `setDelegate:` uses a helper function to help test whether the object passed to `setDelegate:` implements two of the methods in the `LinearGraphDelegate` informal protocol; if the proposed delegate doesn't support them, an `NSException` is raised.

# The Custom View

Our graph will draw different colors for the axes, the regression line, and the data points. We could hard-code the colors into `LinearGraph`, but let's be a little fancier and configure them from a property list file. Although it can't encode an `NSColor` object directly, the property list format can capture red, green, and blue values for each color:

```xml
<?xml version="1.0" encoding="UTF-8"?>
<!DOCTYPE plist PUBLIC "-//Apple Computer//DTD PLIST 1.0//EN"
    "http://www.apple.com/DTDs/PropertyList-1.0.dtd">

<!--
    Select the following line and press ^R to validate this file:
    plutil ~/Linear/GraphColors.plist
```

```
    Unfortunately, you'll have to keep the path up-to-date.
-->

<plist version="1.0">
    <dict>
        <key>Axis</key>
        <!-- Light gray -->
        <dict>
            <key>r</key>
            <real>0.8</real>
            <key>g</key>
            <real>0.8</real>
            <key>b</key>
            <real>0.8</real>
        </dict>
        <key>Line</key>
        <!-- Black -->
        <dict>
            <key>r</key>
            <real>0</real>
            <key>g</key>
            <real>0</real>
            <key>b</key>
            <real>0</real>
        </dict>
        <key>Point</key>
        <!-- Medium green -->
        <dict>
            <key>r</key>
            <real>0.0</real>
            <key>g</key>
            <real>0.7</real>
            <key>b</key>
            <real>0.0</real>
        </dict>
    </dict>
</plist>
```

This file can be created by selecting **File > New File…** and choosing **Empty File in Project** or by editing a new plist in the Property List Editor. Either way, save the file as `GraphColors.plist`, making sure that it is explicitly included as part of the Linear project. To keep your

> **NOTE**
>
> As remarked in the comment at the beginning of `GraphColors.plist`, Xcode can execute a line in an editor window, in a UNIX shell, if you select somewhere in the line and press ^**R**. The result of the command will appear in the next line.

Groups & Files listing neat, you can drag `GraphColors.plist` so that it falls into the **Resources** group.

`GraphColors.plist` need be read only once, to initialize classwide instances of `NSColor`. The class method `initialize` is sent to a class before any member of that class is used and is the usual place to put classwide initializations:

```
#pragma mark Initialization
static NSColor *    sAxisColor = nil;
static NSColor *    sPointColor = nil;
static NSColor *    sLineColor = nil;


static NSColor *    ColorFromDict(NSDictionary *    dict)
{
    // Helper function for +initialize
    // Read a dictionary with r, g, b numbers into an
    // opaque NSColor.
    return [NSColor colorWithCalibratedRed:
                        [[dict objectForKey: @"r"] floatValue]
                                green:
                        [[dict objectForKey: @"g"] floatValue]
                                blue:
                        [[dict objectForKey: @"b"] floatValue]
                                alpha: 1.0];
}


+ (void) initialize
{
    if (! sAxisColor) {
        NSBundle *    mainBundle = [NSBundle mainBundle];
        // Find GraphColors.plist in the app's Resources:
        NSString * dictPath =
            [mainBundle pathForResource: @"GraphColors"
                                ofType: @"plist"];
        // Stop if we don't find it.
        NSAssert(dictPath, @"GraphColors.plist should exist.");

        // Read GraphColors.plist into a dictionary:
        NSDictionary *    colorDict =
                [NSDictionary dictionaryWithContentsOfFile: dictPath];
        // Stop if the plist doesn't parse into a dictionary.
        NSAssert (colorDict, @"GraphColors should be valid.");

        NSDictionary *    curr;

        // Read the Axis dictionary into sAxisColor
        curr = [colorDict objectForKey: @"Axis"];
```

13

```
    sAxisColor = [ColorFromDict(curr) retain];

    // Read the Point dictionary into sPointColor
    curr = [colorDict objectForKey: @"Point"];
    sPointColor = [ColorFromDict(curr) retain];

    // Read the Line dictionary into sLineColor
    curr = [colorDict objectForKey: @"Line"];
    sLineColor = [ColorFromDict(curr) retain];
    }
}
```

The two uses of the NSAssert() macro are cheap insurance. The first halts the program if dictPath is nil, which would happen if GraphColors.plist didn't make it into the application's Resources directory. This would mean that the application itself is malformed, and we can't proceed, so stopping is the right thing to do. Likewise, the second NSAssert() checks for a nil colorDict, which would happen if dictionaryWithContentsOfFile: could not parse GraphColors.plist as a property list containing a dictionary. Checking at this early moment is much easier than trying to figure out what went wrong from much later crashes or misbehaviors.

Now for the drawing. We are more or less on our own. From the NSView documentation, we know that all of a view's drawing takes place in a drawRect: method, taking the following form:

```
-(void) drawRect: (NSRect) rect
{
}
```

All we know is

- ▶ That rect is the portion of the view that needs redrawing
- ▶ What we can learn from the methods of NSView, and
- ▶ What we can demand from our delegate

Offhand, we can be sure that we want to erase the view—set the current color to white and fill the target rectangle with it—and do nothing else if the view has no delegate. So now we have this:

```
- (void) drawRect: (NSRect) rect
{
    [[NSColor whiteColor] set];
    NSRectFill(rect);

    if (delegate) {
    }
}
```

The question is, what happens inside the if(delegate) {} block? We should draw axes, a line, and some points. Where do we draw them? That is, if a point is at {x, y}, at what {u, v} in the view's coordinates do we plot it?

Fortunately, we can make this very simple by telling the view to have a coordinate space that matches the extent of our data set. For the moment, suppose that LinearGraph has a method, dataExtent, that reports a rectangle that encloses the data set. We'll get to it later. We can then enlarge the rectangle slightly—for an aesthetic margin—and use the NSView method setBounds: to make the data's coordinate system our own:

```objc
- (NSRect) dataExtent
{
    // A placeholder to satisfy the compiler
    return NSZeroRect;
}
- (void) drawRect: (NSRect) rect
{
    [[NSColor whiteColor] set];
    NSRectFill(rect);

    if (delegate) {
        // What rect encloses all the points?
        NSRect dataBounds = [self dataExtent];
        // Lower-left corner of the all-points rect
        NSPoint    origin = dataBounds.origin;
        float      margin;

        // Horizontal margin
        margin = dataBounds.size.width * 0.05;
        dataBounds.origin.x -= margin;
        dataBounds.size.width += 2.0 * margin;

        // Vertical margin
        margin = dataBounds.size.height * 0.05;
        dataBounds.origin.y -= margin;
        dataBounds.size.height += 2.0 * margin;

        // Make my coordinates == point coordinates
        [self setBounds: dataBounds];

        // Draw axes from the original minimum of dataBounds:
        [sAxisColor set];
        // vertical
        [NSBezierPath strokeLineFromPoint:
                    NSMakePoint(origin.x, NSMinY(dataBounds))
                        toPoint:
```

```
                    NSMakePoint(origin.x, NSMaxY(dataBounds))];

    // horizontal
    [NSBezierPath strokeLineFromPoint:
                    NSMakePoint(NSMinX(dataBounds), origin.y)
                              toPoint:
                    NSMakePoint(NSMaxX(dataBounds), origin.y)];

    // Draw regression line (if any):
    double    slope, intercept;
    if ([delegate definesLineOfSlope: &slope
                           intercept: &intercept]) {
        [sLineColor set];    // Use the line color
        // Y of regression line at the left.
        float y0 = intercept + slope * NSMinX(dataBounds);
        // Y of regression line at the right.
        float yN = intercept + slope * NSMaxX(dataBounds);
        // Draw the regression line across the view.
        [NSBezierPath strokeLineFromPoint:
                        NSMakePoint(NSMinX(dataBounds), y0)
                                  toPoint:
                        NSMakePoint(NSMaxX(dataBounds), yN)];
    }

    // Draw points:
    [sPointColor set]; // Use the point color
    unsigned    index, limit = [delegate countDataPoints];
    for (index = 0; index < limit; index++) {
        double x, y;
        [delegate dataPointAtIndex: index x: &x y: &y];
        //   Make a small rectangle around the point.
        NSRect pointRect = NSMakeRect(x - 2.0,
                                      y - 2.0,
                                      4.0, 4.0);
        //   Fill the small rectangle with the point color.
        NSRectFill(pointRect);
    }
  }
}
```

That should be it. We had put off the work of determining the smallest rectangle enclosing all the data points; let's do that now:

```
- (NSRect) dataExtent
{
    unsigned index, limit = [delegate countDataPoints];
```

```
    // Special case: No delegate or no points.
    // Return empty rect as a signal value.
    if (limit == 0)
        return NSZeroRect;

    double x, y;
    [delegate dataPointAtIndex: 0 x: &x y: &y];

    // Special case: One point. Return a tiny rect around it.
    if (limit == 1)
        return NSMakeRect(x -0.5, y -0.5,
                          1.0, 1.0);
NSRect     retval = NSMakeRect(x, y,
                              0.0, 0.0);

    for (index = 1; index < limit; index++) {
        [delegate dataPointAtIndex: index x: &x y: &y];
        NSPoint currPoint = NSMakePoint(x, y);
        if (!NSPointInRect(currPoint, retval)) {
            // If a point in the list is outside the known
            // limits, expand the limits to include it.

            if (currPoint.x < NSMinX(retval)) {
                retval.size.width += NSMinX(retval) -currPoint.x;
                retval.origin.x = currPoint.x;
            }
            if (currPoint.x > NSMaxX(retval))
                retval.size.width += currPoint.x -NSMaxX(retval);

            if (currPoint.y < NSMinY(retval)) {
                retval.size.height += NSMinY(retval)-currPoint.y;
                retval.origin.y = currPoint.y;
            }
            if (currPoint.y > NSMaxY(retval))
                retval.size.height += currPoint.y-NSMaxY(retval);
        }
    }
    return retval;
}
```

Because it has not been declared in the header file, this method should appear in LinearGraph.m before drawRect:. Undeclared methods in Objective-C are assumed to return id, and the compiler will complain if an NSRect struct is initialized from an undeclared method call. Placing the method definition before drawRect: declares the return type to be NSRect from that point forward.

## Showing the Window

We still have to do something about showing the Graph window. The simplest way is to add to the Regression window a button that makes the Graph window visible (see Figure 13.4). To open Interface Builder on the Regression window, double-click `MyDocument.nib`, in either the Finder or the Resources group in the Groups & Files list in the Xcode Project window.

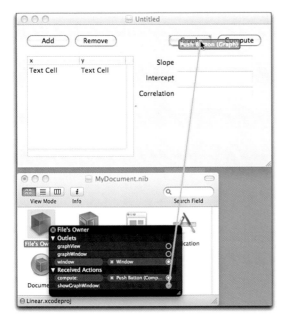

FIGURE 13.4    Having added the **Graph** button to the document window, direct its action to the `MyDocument` (**File's Owner**) by Control-clicking **File's Owner** and dragging from the `showGraphWindow:` action method to the button.

The `MyDocument` class has changed since the last time `MyDocument.nib` was saved, but Interface Builder knows about the changes, especially the new `showGraphWindow:` action method. Control-click the **File's Owner** icon in the NIB window to display the connections HUD, and drag from the `showGraphWindow:` circle to the **Graph** button.

Optionally, we might want to bind (⌘4) the **Graph** button's `enabled` attribute to the `canCompute` property mediated by the Model `NSObjectController`. There's little sense in trying to plot fewer than two points.

## Testing

It is time to see whether and how the new class works. Run `Linear`, and give it the old, familiar data set:

| 1.0 | 2.05 |
|-----|------|
| 2.01 | 4 |
| 3 | 5.987 |
| 4 | 8.1 |
| 5 | 10.0 |

When you're done, click the **Compute** button to make sure that the statistics are loaded into the model; if you haven't yet saved this frequently used data set in its own file, maybe you should. Remember to press **Return** or **Tab** after you enter the last of the data. A Mac OS X text field doesn't take a new value until you end editing by pressing one of those keys or otherwise take focus out of the field. Next, click the **Graph** button.

No graph window appears. Instead, in the Console window, we find a message much like this one:

```
2007-11-09 15:16:16.564 Linear[3866:813] <MyDocument: 0x15ba7110>
                                   doesn't implement needed methods
```

This is our NSAssert message in -[LinearGraph setDelegate:], triggered by the fact that we forgot to implement LinearGraph's delegate protocol. Had the assertion not been there, we'd have been presented with a blank window and fewer clues.

The setDelegate: method was called in the course of loading the GraphWindow.nib file. This is important to remember: When the NIB loader fills in outlets, it looks for setter methods and uses them. Many are the programmers who named an outlet temperature and had a completely unrelated method named setTemperature: and wondered why the outlet variable was never set. (The NIB loader called setTemperature: in the false confidence that it was setting the temperature outlet.)

We add #import "DataPoint.h" to the top of MyDocument.m, and the delegate glue to MyDocument:

```objc
#pragma mark LinearGraphDelegate
- (unsigned) countDataPoints
{
    return [[model dataPoints] count];
}


- (void) dataPointAtIndex: (unsigned) index
                       x: (double *) outX
                       y: (double *) outY
{
    DataPoint * item = [[model dataPoints] objectAtIndex: index];
    *outX = [item x];
    *outY = [item y];
}


- (BOOL) definesLineOfSlope: (double *) outSlope
```

```
                        intercept: (double *) outIntercept
{
    if ([model canCompute]) {
        [model computeFromLibrary];
        *outSlope = [model slope];
        *outIntercept = [model intercept];
        return YES;
    }
    else
        return NO;
}
```

Now we can run Linear and enter that data set again or, if we were provident, use **File > Open** to load it all at once:

| | |
|---|---|
| 1.0 | 2.05 |
| 2.01 | 4 |
| 3 | 5.987 |
| 4 | 8.1 |
| 5 | 10.0 |

Click **Compute** to update the model and **Graph** for the test. This time, a Graph window appears (see Figure 13.5). The contents are all right, in an abstract-expressionist sort of way, but on the whole, we must call them a disappointment. We have some debugging to do.

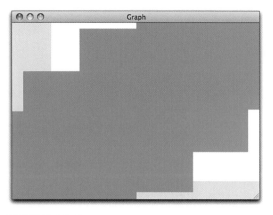

FIGURE 13.5    The first running example of LinearGraph is a disappointment.

# Debugging a View

The natural thing to do is to set a breakpoint at the beginning of drawRect: and follow the progress of drawing the LinearGraph view step by step. However, we find that this doesn't help. The first time drawRect: is executed, the Graph window is not even on the screen. Moving, hiding, and exposing the window do not trigger redraws. Resizing the window does trigger a redraw, but as you step through drawRect:, nothing appears in the window except the gray background of an empty window. The completed drawing appears, all at once, only when drawRect: is finished.

You have probably guessed what is happening: View drawing in Mac OS X is done in offscreen buffers and is transferred to the screen as a complete, painted pixel map. Intermediate stages are not available.

They can be made available. The NSGraphicsContext class embodies the graphical state of whatever medium your view is currently drawing into. By sending flushGraphics to the current NSGraphicsContext after every drawing operation, we can see what is happening as we step through drawRect:. Before the drawRect: method, we put the following:

```
#define FLUSH_GRAPHICS 1
#if FLUSH_GRAPHICS
    #define DEBUG_FLUSH [[NSGraphicsContext currentContext] \
                            flushGraphics];
#else
    #define DEBUG_FLUSH
#endif
```

And after every drawing operation, we add  DEBUG_FLUSH:

```
        .
        .
        .


            [NSBezierPath strokeLineFromPoint:
                        NSMakePoint(NSMinX(dataBounds), y0)
                            toPoint:
                        NSMakePoint(NSMaxX(dataBounds), yN)];
            DEBUG_FLUSH
        }
            // Draw points:
        [sPointColor set];          // Use the point color
        unsigned index, limit = [delegate countDataPoints];
        for (index = 0; index < limit; index++) {
            double    x, y;
            [delegate dataPointAtIndex: index x: &x y: &y];
            // Make a small rectangle around the point.
            NSRect pointRect = NSMakeRect(x - 2.0,
                                    y - 2.0,
                                    4.0, 4.0);
            // Fill the small rectangle with the point color.
            NSRectFill(pointRect);
            DEBUG_FLUSH
        }
```

Running this version, with FLUSH_GRAPHICS set to 1, we find that we still can't watch the first pass through the drawing code—it's to a window that isn't on screen yet. But allowing the window to display, and then a slight move of the resize box, forces a redraw, and stepping through drawRect:—past the drawing of the axes and the line to the drawing of the first point—leaves us with a partially drawn view that looks like Figure 13.6.

That rectangle in the lower-left corner on the screen is supposed to be four-by-four units in size. It is very large. But wait: We redefined the units of measurement for this view when we called setBounds: with a rectangle made loosely around the data points. Looking at the variable summary, we see that dataBounds has an origin at {0.8,1.6525} and a size of {4.4, 8.745}. So, a rectangle "four units wide" would turn out to be most of the width of our view! This would explain why all the lines are so thick.

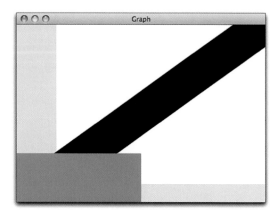

FIGURE 13.6    Using -[NSGraphicsContext flushGraphics] to get step-by-step access to our drawing gets us a clearer picture of what's wrong.

What we'd like to know is how big, in graph units, *one pixel* is. Fortunately, NSWindow is always sized in terms of pixels, and NSView provides a way of converting sizes—and points and rectangles—to and from the coordinate systems of other views and the window. Passing a size of {1,1} to convertSize:fromView:, with nil (the window) as the source view, yields the size, in the graph's coordinates, of a rectangle 1 pixel by 1 pixel. We can then set the default width for all line drawing and express, in terms of that size, the rectangles for the data points:

```
[self setBounds: dataBounds];
NSSize unitSize = {1.0, 1.0};
// Convert the windows one-pixel size
// to this views coordinate dimensions.
unitSize = [self convertSize: unitSize fromView: nil];
[NSBezierPath setDefaultLineWidth: MIN(unitSize.height,
                                       unitSize.width)];
    .
    .
    .

for (index = 0; index < limit; index++) {
    double    x, y;
    [delegate dataPointAtIndex: index x: &x y: &y];
    // Make a small rectangle around the point.
    NSRect pointRect = NSMakeRect(
                          x - 2.0 * unitSize.width,
                          y - 2.0 * unitSize.height,
                          4.0 *unitSize.width,
                          4.0 *unitSize.height);
    // Fill the small rectangle with the point color.
    NSRectFill(pointRect);
```

Make this change and **Stop** Linear, if you haven't already quit it. Re-#define `FLUSH_GRAPHICS` to be 0, and build and debug Linear one more time. It feels like turning the crank: Load the data set, make sure the regression has been computed, and click **Graph** (see Figure 13.7).

This time, it works. You can move the window, close it, and reopen it. Resize it, and the graph resizes so that it always fills the window, assuming you set the sizing struts properly when you laid out the Graph window in Interface Builder. It uses the colors specified in the configuration file.

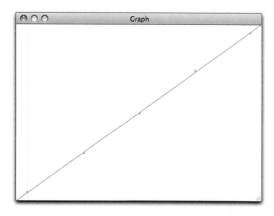

FIGURE 13.7    The Graph window, containing the `LinearGraph` view, working as designed.

## Summary

In this chapter, we took an `NSView` subclass from idea to reality. We used Interface Builder to create the initial shell for the class and to hook it up to its controller, `MyDocument`, leaving virtually no initialization work to be done in code.

We saw how to configure class options from a property list file embedded in the application. We fleshed out the skeleton Interface Builder gave us into a working graphing class. We saw how to use `NSGraphicsContext` to debug the drawing of `NSView` subclasses.

`LinearGraph` is far, far from being a first-rate graphing class. At the very least, it should label its axes to give some context for what you're seeing. There should be options for colors and for the shapes of points. There should be a way to specify the range the axes span, instead of simply blowing the graph up to the region of the data set. But it's a start, and it adds a little life to what was a text-bound application.

# CHAPTER 14

# Dynamic Libraries and Frameworks

**IN THIS CHAPTER**

▸ **Frameworks and Dynamic Libraries**

▸ **The Structure of Frameworks**

▸ **Grouping Files**

▸ **Public and Private Frameworks**

▸ **Installing Frameworks**

Let's do some more with our statistics package. We already have a static library that accumulates sums toward a linear regression. This library has some limitations, however:

▸ The statistics are limited. For instance, because the library doesn't keep individual data points, we can't calculate standard deviations.

▸ The header file is a separate entity from the library. By the standard means of distributing libraries and headers, users of our library will have to separate the header and the library into different directories, such as /usr/local/lib and /usr/local/include, and specify the additional directories at build time, an accident-prone process. One file or the other can get lost, be deleted, or miss a revision to a new version.

▸ The problems of the associated header file are multiplied if the library has other kinds of associated files, such as configuration or image files. If we want to add features that could take advantage of such files, our library will become much more fragile.

The first limitation can be overcome by an enhancement to the existing design for our static library, adding to the library some means to access our data through either copying or a callback. The other limitations are inherent to a conventional library and are remedied by switching from a conventional library to *a framework*.

A framework is a bundle—a structured directory tree—containing a dynamic library, headers, and resources. When a framework is passed to the gcc that ships with Xcode, using the -framework option, gcc correctly searches the framework's subdirectories for the library and headers. Both Cocoa's NSBundle class and Core Foundation's CFBundle afford easy access to files inside frameworks.

# Adding a Framework Target

We start with the Linear project and add a framework target by selecting from the **Project** menu **New Target** and picking **Cocoa > Framework** from the list of target templates. Name the new target **Statistics**.

## Info.plist

As soon as you create the framework, Xcode presents you with its Target Info window, showing the **Properties** tab. Properties tabs edit the more commonly used properties of Info.plist files. Frameworks contain an Info.plist file in the Resources directory for each version. (Most bundles put Info.plist in the root Contents directory, but frameworks can encompass more than one version of themselves, each of which must supply its own information.) The source for the file appears in the Groups & Files list as Statistics-Info.plist to distinguish it from the Info.plist for Linear.app.

This is the same properties display you see for an application, including document information, which doesn't apply to frameworks. The interesting fields are as follows:

▶ **Executable** (CFBundleExecutable), the name of the principal library file in the framework. You generally don't need to change this; it is initially set to $(EXECUTABLE_NAME), which will ensure that the library name set in the **Build** settings carries over to the Info.plist file (as it must).

▶ **Identifier** (CFBundleIdentifier), a reverse domain-style string that will uniquely identify the framework. Xcode's template defaults this as com.yourcompany. Statistics for this target. We'll use **org.manoverboard.Linear.Statistics**.

▶ **Type** (CFBundlePackageType), the HFS file type for the bundle; this is always FMWK for a framework.

▶ **Creator** (CFBundleSignature), a four-character code to serve as the HFS creator code for the framework bundle. You can leave this as ????; in our case, it makes sense to use LnER, the code for Linear.app.

▶ **Version** (CFBundleVersion), the marketing version number for the framework. Xcode starts you at 1.0. This version number is distinct from the compatibility versions, such as A, B, C, that may be built into the framework as it evolves.

The remaining parts of the panel aren't used with frameworks. There are, however, additional keys that may be used in Info.plist for a framework:

- ▶ NSHumanReadableCopyright, a copyright string for the framework

- ▶ CFBundleGetInfoString, an additional string to be displayed in the Finder's Get Info window

- ▶ CFBundleGetInfoHTML, the same as CFBundleGetInfoString but formatted in HTML

## Assigning Files

This new target could be the home of all our consumers of lists of points, so let's move LinearGraph out of the application and into the framework. Select the **Project** (top) icon in the Groups & Files list to make the target-membership check boxes visible in the detail view. Make Linear the active target, using the pop-up in the toolbar or the submenu in the **Project** menu, and uncheck LinearGraph.m and GraphColors.plist. Switch the active target to **Statistics**, and add the implementation and header files for LinearGraph and GraphColors.plist to the target.

Why does LinearGraph.h have a check box for the Statistics target and not for the Linear target? Header files are *used* in the making of an application, but they don't ship as a *part* of it. Frameworks, however, usually contain header files to afford access to the framework for its users.

We'll be using Cocoa in this framework, so make sure that Cocoa.framework is checked in the Statistics listing. Don't remove Cocoa.framework from Linear.

> **NOTE**
>
> This can also be done by selecting the file you want to switch, and opening the **Targets** tab of the File Info window (**File > Get Info**, ⌘I, or just click the **Info** button in the project window's toolbar). There you will find a list of targets, with a check box next to each. Even better you could select all the files you want to switch, **Get Info** on them, and make your settings on all of them at once.

For our statistical consumer of points, we define a new Objective-C class, PointStat:

```objc
#import <Cocoa/Cocoa.h>

@interface PointStat : NSObject {
    unsigned        count;
    double          sumX;
    double          sumY;
    double          sumXSquared;
    double          sumYSquared;

    double          slope;

    double          sumSqFromMeanX;
    double          sumSqFromMeanY;
```

```objc
    BOOL            dirty;
    id              delegate;
}

- (id) init;
- (void) refreshData;
- (double) meanX;
- (double) meanY;
- (double) stdDeviationX;
- (double) stdDeviationY;

- (BOOL) regressionValid;
- (double) slope;
- (double) intercept;
- (double) correlation;

- (id) delegate;
- (void) setDelegate: (id) newDelegate;

@end
```

As with `LinearGraph`, `PointStat` does not define any storage for the individual data pairs it deals with. Instead, like `LinearGraph`, it relies on a delegate to store the points and report their number and content. In fact, `PointStat` will use the informal `LinearGraphDelegate` protocol for access to the data set.

`PointStat.m` implements what the header promises. No statistic is calculated until the client asks for one. A private method, `collectStatistics`, is then called, and the `dirty` flag is cleared to indicate that the sums don't have to be recalculated. When it changes its data set, the delegate is supposed to inform its `PointStat` by sending it `refreshData`, which does nothing more than set the `dirty` flag, forcing a recalculation the next time a statistic is asked for:

```objc
#import "PointStat.h"
#import "LinearGraph.h"
#import <math.h>

@implementation PointStat
- (id) init
{
    dirty = YES;
    return self;
}

- (void) dealloc
{
```

```
    [super dealloc];
}

- (void) refreshData
{
    dirty = YES;
}

- (BOOL) collectStatistics
{
    if (! delegate || ! dirty)
        return NO;
    count = [delegate countDataPoints];
    if (count <= 1)
        return NO;

    sumX = sumY = sumXSquared = sumYSquared = sumXY = 0.0;

    double x, y;
    unsigned index;

    for (index = 0; index < count; index++) {
        [delegate dataPointAtIndex: index x: &x y: &y];
        sumX += x; sumXSquared += x * x;
        sumY += y;
        sumYSquared += y * y;
        sumXY += x * y;
    }
    sumSqFromMeanX = sumSqFromMeanY = 0.0;
    if (count > 0) {
        double    meanX = sumX / count;
        double    meanY = sumY / count;
        for (index = 0; index < count; index++) {
            [delegate dataPointAtIndex: index x: &x y: &y];
            double    term = x - meanX;
            sumSqFromMeanX  += term * term;
            term = y - meanY;
            sumSqFromMeanY  += term * term;
        }
    }
    if (count > 0) {
        slope = (count * sumXY - sumX * sumY)
        /
        (count * sumXSquared - sumX * sumX);
    }
    dirty = NO;
```

```
    return YES;
}
#pragma mark Accessors
- (double) meanX
{
    [self collectStatistics];
    return sumX / count;
}

- (double) meanY
{
    [self collectStatistics];
    return sumY / count;
}

- (double) stdDeviationX
{
    [self collectStatistics];
    return sqrt(sumSqFromMeanX) / count;
}

- (double) stdDeviationY
{
    [self collectStatistics];
    return sqrt(sumSqFromMeanY) / count;
}

- (BOOL) regressionValid
{
    return delegate && [delegate countDataPoints] > 1;
}

- (double) slope
{
    [self collectStatistics];
    return slope;
}

- (double) intercept
{
    [self collectStatistics];
    return (sumY -slope * sumX) / count;
}

- (double) correlation
```

```
{
    [self collectStatistics];
    return slope * sqrt((count * sumXSquared - sumX * sumX)
                        /
                        (count * sumYSquared - sumY * sumY)
                        );
}
#pragma mark Delegate
- (id) delegate { return delegate; }

static BOOL NotImpl(id object, SEL aSelector)
{
    // Helper for setDelegate:
    // Detects whether a proposed delegate fails to
    // implement a method. Allow nil also.
    return (object != nil) &&
                     ![object respondsToSelector: aSelector];
}


- (void) setDelegate: (id) newDelegate
{
    if (delegate != newDelegate) {
        // Check for compliance with (most of) the
        // informal protocol.
        if (NotImpl(newDelegate, @selector(countDataPoints)) ||
            NotImpl(newDelegate, @selector(dataPointAtIndex:x:y:))) {

            NSString * reason = [NSString stringWithFormat:
                                 @"%@ doesn't implement needed methods",
                                 newDelegate];
            NSException * exception =
                    [NSException exceptionWithName:
                                       NSInvalidArgumentException
                                     reason: reason
                                   userInfo: nil];
            @throw exception;
        }
        // Record the new delegate.
        delegate = newDelegate;
    }
}
@end
```

PointStat's delegate and setDelegate: methods are exactly the same as for LinearGraph.

Other edits are needed to complete the transition. We've removed `GraphColors.plist` from the main bundle and put it into our framework, so `LinearGraph`'s `initialize` class method has to be amended:

```
if (! sAxisColor) {
    NSBundle *    mainBundle =
                       [NSBundle bundleForClass: self];

    // Find GraphColors.plist in the frameworks's Resources:
    NSString *    dictPath =
               [mainBundle pathForResource: @"GraphColors"
                                    ofType: @"plist"];
```

We now have six files (including `Statistics-Info.plist` and `GraphColors.plist`) that belong exclusively to the Statistics framework. They deserve a group of their own: Select all of them, and issue **Project > Group** (⌥⌘G). Name it **Statistics Framework**, or whatever pleases you—file groups in the Groups & Files list have no effect on the build or the actual files.

One last thing: In the Groups & Files list, open the **Targets** group, and select **Statistics**. The Detail listing now shows every file included in the Statistics target, including the headers. The second column, Role, shows a pop-up menu for the headers, offering a choice of **Public**, **Private**, and **Project**.

▶ A public framework header is built in to the product framework's `Headers` directory and is intended for the use of clients of the framework.

▶ A private framework header is built into the framework's `Private Headers` directory. It is not intended that general users of the framework #include such headers, but they might be needed by developers with privileged access to framework code.

▶ Project headers are used solely for building the framework and are not intended for distribution in the framework bundle.

Make sure that both `LinearGraph.h` and `PointStat.h` are set to **Public**.

## Framework Structure

Now issue the **Build** command to compile the `Statistics` library and marshal its framework directory. If you switch to the Finder and look in the `build` directory of your project folder, you will find `Statistics.framework`, a directory with a structure like that shown in Figure 14.1.

If you chose a different location for build products in the **Build** tab of the Preferences window, or in the **General** tab of the Project Info window, finding `Statistics.framework` is a little more complicated. In the Groups & Files list, the last group before the Targets group is labeled Products. Open this, and Control-click (or right-click) `Statistics.framework`. From the contextual menu, select **Reveal in Finder**.

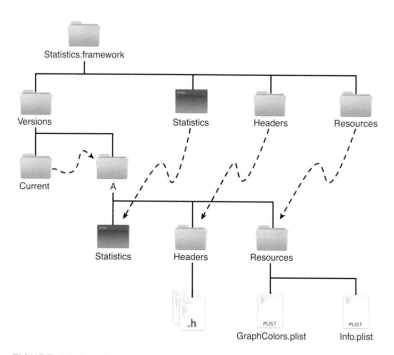

FIGURE 14.1    The layout of `Statistics.framework`. The top-level directory contains a `Versions` directory and links to the current versions of the `Statistics` library and the `Headers` and `Resources` directories. The `Versions` directory in turn contains all versions of the framework contents—only version A, in this case—and a link indicating which version is current. The A directory contains the library and its associated headers and resources. The `Headers` directory contains all project headers that were marked **Public** in the Detail listing of the `Statistics` target.

## Using the Framework

Now let's switch Linear over to using the `Statistics` framework.

First, we have to figure out how to fit `PointStat` into our document model. `MyDocument` already implements the `LinearGraphDelegate` informal protocol, and the scope of the data that `PointStat` asks for and keeps is the same as the scope of the document. It follows that we should add a `PointStat` to the `MyDocument` data members:

```
@class      Regression;
@class      LinearGraph;
@class      PointStat;

@interface MyDocument : NSDocument
{
    Regression *    model;
    PointStat  *    statEngine;
```

Make sure that it gets initialized and released:

```
#import <Statistics/PointStat.h>
@implementation MyDocument
- (id)init
{
    self = [super init];
    if (self) {
        // Allocate and initialize our model
        model = [[Regression alloc] init];
        statEngine = [[PointStat alloc] init];
        if (!model || !statEngine) {
            [self release];
            self = nil;
        }
        [statEngine setDelegate: self];
    }
    return self;
}


- (void) dealloc
{
    [statEngine release];
    [model release];
    [graphWindow release];
    [super dealloc];
}
```

Finally, incorporate it into the `compute:` action method:

```
- (IBAction) compute: (id) sender
{
#pragma unused(sender)
    [statEngine refreshData];
    [model setSlope: [statEngine slope]];
    [model setIntercept: [statEngine intercept]];
    [model setCorrelation: [statEngine correlation]];
}
```

Note that headers inside frameworks are always #imported or #included with a path prefix of the framework name. gcc will have been told of the framework name in a command-line option and will identify an #include in this form as being from that framework.

> **NOTE**
>
> A smarter design would observe model's dataPoints array, send refreshData to statEngine whenever it or any member changed, and update slope, intercept, and correlation accordingly. This would eliminate the **Compute** button and make Linear a more satisfactory interactive application. We're keeping it simple here.

Next, we have to switch Linear from depending on `libRegression.a` to `Statistics.framework`:

- ▶ Make sure the Linear application target is active, by selecting it in the **Active Target** pop-up in the project window's toolbar, or from the **Project > Set Active Target** menu.

- ▶ Select the project icon at the top of the Groups & Files list. The detail list will fill with all the files, libraries, and products in the project.

- ▶ The check boxes at the right of the detail list indicate what files are members of the active target. Uncheck `libRegression.a`, and check `Statistics.framework`.

- ▶ We also want to change the build dependency, so `Statistics.framework`, and not `libRegression.a`, is built before Linear. Open the Linear target's Target Info window, and show the **General** tab. Use the - button to remove the Regression target, and the + button to add Statistics.

**14**

Because `libRegression.a` is gone from the project, the `computeFromLibrary` method in class `Regression` is now obsolete. Remove the method's declaration from `Regression.h`, and its implementation from `Regression.m`. Also remove the `#import` of `libRegression.h`.

Set a breakpoint at the beginning of `collectStatistics` in `PointStat.m`, by clicking in the gutter next to the first line. If the debugger stops execution at that breakpoint when we test this latest revision of `Linear`, we'll know that it is using the dynamic library `Statistics` package, not our earlier code.

Making sure that Linear is the current target, select **Build and Debug** from the **Build** menu. Linear should build cleanly and launch under the supervision of the Xcode debugger. Enter a data set and click **Compute**. Sure enough, the debugger breaks execution at the beginning of `collectStatistics`. It will break there a couple of times more as the slope, intercept, and correlation are retrieved, but the `dirty` variable guards you from making the full computation every time.

Note that there was no difficulty in setting a breakpoint in `collectStatistics`, even though it was a method defined in a dynamic library that was not the product of the active target. The debugger underlying Xcode, `gdb`, is pretty smart about such things.

---

**System Frameworks**

The other main provider of frameworks for your application is, of, course, Apple itself. Apple-provided frameworks are found at `/System/Library/Frameworks`. The ones most used, `Cocoa.framework` and `Carbon.framework`, are included as needed in the new-project templates Xcode provides.

When you add a framework (or any other library) to a project, always make sure you add the file or directory *directly from where your current system keeps it*. That is, from `/System/Library/Frameworks`, `/usr/lib`, or the like, and not from an SDK directory in the developer-tools tree. Using the in-system files will guarantee your application will find them when it is run, and if an SDK version is needed for building, Xcode will find that version automatically.

Many of Apple's frameworks are *umbrella frameworks* containing additional library and header packages that themselves are frameworks. For instance, `Quartz.framework`, the graphical library, contains a `Frameworks` directory that includes `PDFKit.framework` (for rendering and editing PDFs) and `QuartzComposer.framework`. This subdivision is for Apple's convenience in engineering and for yours in finding headers, but don't rely on it by trying to import a subframework of an umbrella framework.

If a framework is part of an umbrella framework, it may rely on sister frameworks' also being linked in order to work properly. Apple does not document such dependencies. Further, Apple reserves the right to refactor its umbrella frameworks, so linking against a subframework is not guaranteed to be stable.

The rule is not to link against any system framework that doesn't appear directly in `/System/Library/Frameworks`. In the few cases in which a top-level framework is also included in an umbrella—such as `Foundation.framework` within Cocoa—the subframework will be available both ways.

The common practice, when writing C-family programs, is to #include or #import header files by providing direct or relative paths to the individual files. When writing for a Carbon dialog, for instance, it is tempting to begin a source file with #include <Carbon/Dialogs.h>; that, or something like it, was what you did in Mac OS 9. Don't do this for Mac OS X. Instead, include the whole header set for any umbrella framework you use: #include <Carbon/Carbon.h>. Computers are much faster than they were when they ran Mac OS 9, and the build-time penalty is very small, especially when you precompile the #includes into the prefix header for your target. Including umbrella headers is the only way to be sure the header you want is found; it's the only way that works.

The Xcode tools do not support the creation of umbrella frameworks. Apparently, they require some hand tuning that Xcode does not automate.

# Where Frameworks Go

There are two issues in deciding where to put a framework:

- ▶ First: Where will gcc look for the framework, at build time, so that it can find its headers and check linkage against its dynamic library?

- ▶ Second: When an application uses the framework, at runtime, where will the Mac OS X dynamic linker look for the framework, so that it can load the framework's dynamic library and actually link it into the application?

Question one—how does Xcode tell gcc where to find frameworks—is the easier one to answer.

You tell Xcode to use a particular framework at all by adding it to a target. Xcode then adds `-framework frameworkName` to the build flags for gcc's compilation and linkage. gcc will then be able to find the framework's headers and dynamic library as long as the framework is in a standard location (`Library/Frameworks` in the user, local, network, or system domains).

If the added framework is *not* in a standard location, Xcode adds the framework's location to gcc's search path using the `-F` switch. You can add further pathnames to the search path by editing the **Framework Search Path** setting in the **Build** tab of the Target Info window—but you usually won't need to.

So the short answer to getting Xcode to find a framework (and tell gcc about it) is this: Add the framework, and Xcode will find it.

> **NOTE**
>
> Actually, for something like a gcc search path, which is apt to be useful to all the targets in a project, you'd probably want to edit the setting in the Project Info window. Settings made there affect how all targets are built, whereas settings in a Target Info window affect only that target (and override the equivalent settings at the Project level).

Question two is harder, and requires a bit of background.

The core of a framework is a dynamic library—something you encountered in the "Dynamic Loading" section of Chapter 4, "Compilation: The Basics." The Mac OS X dynamic linker has a search path of directories it successively tries when looking for a dynamic library (essentially `Library/Frameworks` in the user, local, network, and system domains). It is not wise to rely on that search, however. First, it is bad citizenship, because every library that forces a repeated search whenever it is loaded adds to the time it takes to launch applications. Second, it is bad security, because you don't know whether some other framework of the same name has come ahead of you in the search path.

For speed and security, each time an application is built against a dynamic library, the application records the one location where it should find the correct library. That implies the framework's installed location should be known at build time. And that, in turn, implies that dynamic libraries must build their expected installation paths into themselves.

So the not-so-short answer to the second question—where is a framework found at runtime—is this: hopefully, at the place you baked into the framework when you first built it.

> **NOTE**
>
> Wait a minute, you say. When we test-ran Linear, and used the Statistics framework, the framework wasn't in `Library/Frameworks` anywhere, and we didn't set a special location. How was `Statistics.framework` found? Xcode sets environment variables so that regardless of anything else, the program you are developing will look for frameworks and dynamic libraries, first of all, in the same directory as the program itself. While you are running your application out of Xcode, you don't have to worry about installation paths. Once you run it outside of Xcode, the need for an installation path comes back.

**14**

Which gives rise to the third question: How do you bake the installation location into the framework?

The relevant setting is **Installation Directory**. Use the **Build** panel of the Get Info window for the framework target. Find **Statistics** under the **Targets** group in the Groups & Files list, and double-click it for the Target Info window; then select the **Build** tab. You find that scores of settings can influence the build of `Statistics.framework`. Fortunately, Xcode provides ways to sort through the mass of options.

> **WARNING**
>
> We *must* use the Target Info window for this setting, and not the Project Info window. We are specifying an installation path for the Statistics framework, and for that target *only*.

I happen to know that Xcode classes the installation directory as a "Deployment" option, so we can scan down the list, looking for the section marked with a gray bar labeled **Deployment**. (The sections are arranged alphabetically, and can be collapsed with the disclosure triangles at the left.) **Installation Directory** is to be found a few lines below the section bar. A quicker way, that doesn't depend on guessing the category, is to type **installa** in the search field near the top of the window. **Installation Directory** is one of the two lines remaining.

## A Public Framework

Suppose we mean to make `Statistics.framework` available to any user or application that cares to use it. It would be a *public framework*, and that is the easiest kind to specify. In the **Configuration** pop-up, select **All Configurations**—you want to affect the content of the framework regardless of whether it is built for debugging or release. Double-click the **Installation Directory** line, to produce a sheet for editing the setting (see Figure 14.2). You'll notice that the default setting from when the Statistics target was added is `$(HOME)/Library/Frameworks`, which means that for all time, users of `Statistics.framework` will look for it in *your* home directory. You surely do not want this.

Perhaps we want to install `Statistics.framework` in `/Users/Shared/Frameworks`. Type that path into the sheet, click **OK**, and it is done.

There is little reason to go to the trouble of installing *a public* framework anywhere but in the global `/Library/Frameworks` directory. Even though that's on the dynamic loader's default search path, remember speed and security, and specify it. You have to get it out of your home directory anyway.

> **NOTE**
>
> The issues of making build settings at the Target or Project level, and of applying them to one or more build configurations, can be subtle, and I cover them in detail in Chapter 21, "Xcode for `make` Veterans." For now, know that the Debug configuration packages a group of settings that produce a product that is quick to build and easy to debug; and the Release configuration produces a product that runs faster, smaller, and on more than one architecture.

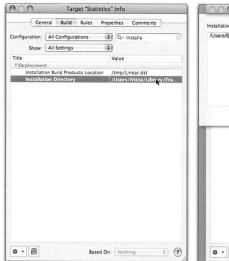

FIGURE 14.2    (Left) Specifying that `Statistics.framework` should be sought at runtime in `/Users/Shared/Frameworks`. Note that typing **installa** in the search field at the top of the window narrowed the multitude of settings in the window enough to make the installation setting visible. **Installation Directory** is shown in boldface, indicating that the setting has been changed from the value effective at the Project level. (Right) Double-clicking the entry drops a sheet for editing the setting. Because **All Configurations** has been selected, any value we enter will be set for the Debug and Release configurations simultaneously.

Truth be told, you'll rarely publish a framework for the general use of all comers on the computer. It's mostly an option for developers of suites of programs (Apple and OmniGroup come to mind) that will share a significant library of code and resources. Most frameworks will be private, installed inside an application's bundle. That's the next section.

## A Private Framework

Suppose that our goals for `Statistics.framework` have changed, and we no longer want to make it available to all comers. We just want to use it in our own application, Linear. We can install the framework *inside* the application bundle.

The first task is to set the dynamic-loader information so that when Linear runs, the loader will look in the right place for `Statistics.framework`. As Linear could be installed anywhere, an absolute path is not possible, but a special path notation is available for just this purpose. Open the Target Info for Statistics and select the **Build Tab**, find the **Installation Directory** line again, and set it to

```
@executable_path/../Frameworks
```

This says, "Application, look for a sister directory in the application bundle, named Frameworks."

You should also check the **Skip Install** setting in the **Build** tab of the Target Info window for the Statistics target. A full, final build of an Xcode project attempts to place all the products in their intended installation locations. We, however, have just specified a Statistics.framework installation path that is relative, and makes no sense at the time it is being built and installed. Checking **Skip Install** avoids the confusion by keeping Statistics.framework in the build directory.

> **NOTE**
>
> Beginning in Mac OS X 10.4, bundles that are not the principal executables of a process—plug-ins, for instance—can refer to load paths within the plug-in's own bundle. A framework installed in a plug-in bundle, for instance, can have @loader_path/../ Frameworks as its installation directory.

Now that the framework advertises its destination properly, we have to make sure that it gets there. We will add a build phase to the Linear application target that copies Statistics.framework into the application bundle. Make sure Linear is the active target (for instance by selecting it in the **Active Target** pop-up), and select **Project > New Build Phase > New Copy Files Build Phase**. A Phase Info window will appear (see Figure 14.3); in the **Destination** pop-up, select **Frameworks**.

We've now specified that *something* will be copied to Linear.app's Frameworks subfolder whenever Linear is built. What? Obviously, Statistics. framework. Under the Targets group, use the disclosure triangles to open first the Linear target and then the **Copy Files** build phase. Drag **Statistics.framework** from the Products group above into the **Copy Files** phase. This specifies what gets copied to the Frameworks subfolder in the build process (see Figure 14.4).

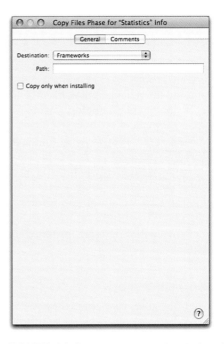

FIGURE 14.3    The Phase Info window that appears when you select **Project > New Build Phase > New Copy Files Build Phase**. In the case of adding a framework to an application bundle, we need only choose **Frameworks** in the **Destination** pop-up, leaving the other elements untouched.

Build the Linear target one more time; when that is done, Control-click the completed application, in the `build` subdirectory of the project directory, in the Finder, and select **Show Package Contents**. Open the `Contents` folder and then the `Frameworks` folder inside, and you should see `Statistics.framework`.

You should also run the `Linear` application to verify that it works with the embedded framework.

Here, in days gone by, we would set our framework up for prebinding (see Chapter 4). Prebinding became obsolete back at Mac OS X 10.3.4, and so we no longer need to consider it.

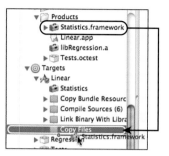

FIGURE 14.4    Putting `Statistics. framework` into a **Copy Files** phase in the build of Linear. We had previously added the phase with a command from the **Project** menu and specified that the target for the phase was the output package's `Frameworks` directory. Now we have dragged `Statistics.framework` from the Products category down to the **Copy Files** phase to specify that it is to be copied.

**14**

> **NOTE**
>
> If you look in the `Resources` folder, it's possible you will find, to your surprise, that `Linrg` and `GraphColors.plist` are still there. *Still there* is the operative phrase—when Xcode builds an application package, it builds it in-place, in the existing package directory. Files that were copied in during previous builds will stay there, even if the build phases that copied them in are long gone from the project. Clean the project (select **Clean** from the **Build** pop-up button in the project window's toolbar) to wipe out the old application package and its contents, and then build again. The product then will contain only the things the project currently builds.

# Summary

Frameworks are an essential part of the Mac OS X developer's repertoire. We reviewed the structure of the framework bundle and how to access framework contents. We built a framework and solved the problem of where to put it: first by placing it in a standard directory and then by embedding it in an application bundle. We mastered the Copy Files build phase, and examined Linear's internal structure to verify that our private framework is in place.

# CHAPTER 15

# Documentation in Xcode

**IN THIS CHAPTER**

▶ **Generating Documentation Automatically**

▶ **Customizing HeaderDoc**

▶ **Shell Script Targets**

▶ **Extending the Documentation Window**

▶ **Adding to the Research Assistant**

The users of the finished executable are not the only consumers of a software project. Sooner or later, other developers will have to work with our source code, and they deserve our pity no less than end users. Even the simplest application develops its own API, and it us up to us, who created it, to document it.

Along the way, we'll be exploring Xcode's own documentation system: how to use it, and how to extend it.

## HeaderDoc

The easiest tool for producing useful documentation from source code is HeaderDoc. As the name implies, HeaderDoc generates API documentation from the declarations in your header files, as you tag them with special block comments. HeaderDoc takes account of any comment that has an exclamation point immediately after the opening (`/*!`). The text of the comment documents the entity that follows it: Put `/*! This is my class */` before the `@interface` line of your class declaration, and you have documented the class (although not informatively).

> **NOTE**
>
> If you need more power, with images that graph inheritance relationships and call trees, and output in HTML, PDF, and LaTeX, you might care to investigate Doxygen, http://www.doxygen.org/. It's a great package (it will generate Xcode 3 docsets automatically), but is more than this chapter needs.

HeaderDoc comes in the form of two command-line tools, `headerdoc2html` and gatherheaderdoc. At the simplest

```
$ headerdoc2html -o hdoc *.h
```

scans all the .h files in a directory for HeaderDoc markup, and fills the hdoc directory with web pages for the headers that have such markup. Executing

```
$ gatherheaderdoc hdoc
```

adds a master table of contents page to hdoc that ties the header-based sites together.

Even these simple additions to `PointStat.h` will produce useful and attractive documentation (see Figure 15.1):

```
/*!    The PointStat class, which pulls x, y data from
       a delegate to derive statistics from them. */
@interface PointStat : NSObject {
    /*!    The number of points pulled into the statistics. */
    unsigned count;
    double sumX;
.
.
.
- (double) correlation;
/*!    The delegate object, from which the x, y data are pulled. */
-(id) delegate;
/*!    Set the delagate object. It must conform to
       the LinearGraphDelegate informal protocol. */
- (void) setDelegate: (id) newDelegate;
```

But we can do better than the basics. Like its cousin JavaDoc, HeaderDoc supports tags in its comments that enhance the documentation it generates. These include tags for short, summary descriptions; parameters; and return values.

The difference in the two methods can make a big difference in the resulting documentation (see Figure 15.2):

```
/*!    The arithmetic mean of all the x values. */
-(double) meanX;
...
/*!
    @abstract    The standard deviation of all the x values.
    @discussion  This method calculates the population standard
                 deviation from the x values pulled from the delegate.
    @result      double, the value of the standard deviation
*/
- (double) stdDeviationX;
```

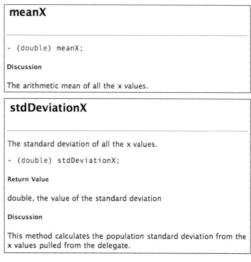

FIGURE 15.1    Even simple HeaderDoc comments, placed before an @interface declaration, an instance variable, and a couple of method declarations, will produce useful documentation, tailored to the context.

FIGURE 15.2    Prefixing a method declaration with a simple HeaderDoc comment will result in simple documentation for the method (top). Providing more information, such as an abstract and a description of the return value fleshes the documentation out (bottom).

In the sample code for this chapter, I've added to PointStat.h and LinearGraph.h a full complement of comments, documenting the Statistics framework. Also, I added Statistics.hdoc, to document the framework itself:

```
/*!
    @framework    Statistics
    @abstract     Simple framework for calculating and plotting
                  bivariate statistics
    @discussion
    Statistics.framework provides a PointStat class for
    collecting data points and calculating mean, standard
    deviation, correlation, and regression line.
    It also provides an NSView subclass, LinearGraph, that
    scatter-plots x, y data points, along with a line (presumably
    a regression line) among them. A property list file in the
    framework sets the colors used in the plot.
*/
```

To see the results of these efforts, point `headerdoc2html` at the headers and the `.hdoc` file, pass the contents of the product directory to `gatherheaderdoc`, and display the table of contents page:

```
$ headerdoc2html -o hdoc *.h *.hdoc && \
> gatherheaderdoc hdoc && \
> open hdoc/masterTOC.html
.
. progress output
.
$
```

When you examine the table of contents generated by `gatherheaderdoc`, you notice that the tool has put a smart-aleck title and copyright notice on the page. Not only are both vaguely insulting, the copyright notice is legally useless.

For most purposes of `headerdoc2html`, the default layout and style is adequate, and other things, such as copyright, can be taken care of with tags in your HeaderDoc markup. `gatherheaderdoc` is another matter: To correct the copyright notice, we have to make our own copies of the HeaderDoc's configuration file and the template HTML file used by `gatherheaderdoc`.

The configuration file can be in a couple of places. The systemwide one is at `/Library/Preferences/com.apple.headerDoc2HTML.config`. (Note the uppercase *D* and HTML.) You can put a per-user file at the `~/Library` directory of your home directory. Neither is suitable for us—what if we had projects with different copyright requirements? So, we take up the third possible location: a file named `headerDoc2HTML.config`, in the directory in which `headerdoc2html` is run.

To repair the TOC file, do this in the terminal to make your own copy of the preference file and the TOC template, and open them in Xcode:

```
$ cd ~/Linear # or wherever the Linear project is
$ cp \
>     /Library/Preferences/com.apple.headerDoc2HTML.config \
>     headerDoc2HTML.config
$ cp \
>     /Library/Preferences/com.apple.headerdoc.exampletocteplate.html \
>     TOCTemplate.html
$ # Note the absence of an m in the source file's template.
$ xed headerDoc2HTML.config TOCTemplate.html
$
```

In `headerDoc2HTML.config`, edit the `TOCTemplateFile` entry so that it refers to your copy of the table of contents template:

`TOCTemplateFile => TOCTemplate.html`

> **NOTE**
>
> xed is a command-line tool that accepts a path to one or more files, and opens them for editing in Xcode. See more by typing **man xed** on the command line.

And, in `TOCTemplate.html`, find the copyright notice near the end of the file, and change it into something usable. Also, you noticed that the function list in the middle of the page is a bit crowded. This is determined by the `$$functionlist` directive in the template file. Edit it like this—I'm splitting the line in the interest of space:

```
$$functionlist cols=3 order=down atts=border="0" cellpadding="1"
              cellspacing="0" width="640"@@
```

Finally, fix the title by changing it to the following:

```
<title>$$title@@</title>
```

Save both files. Now when you execute

```
$ headerdoc2html -o hdoc *.h *.hdoc && \
>     gatherheaderdoc hdoc && \
>   open hdoc/masterTOC.html
.
. progress output
.
$
```

you find you have a title and a copyright notice you can live with, and a more-readable function reference.

# User Scripts in Xcode

HeaderDoc comments are simple to write, but they can be tedious. What @ tags apply to what sorts of entities? Have you forgotten any? And couldn't you derive a lot of documentation content from the declaration it applies to?

The Xcode team thought of these things, and have provided *user scripts* for these purposes. The **Script** menu in Xcode appears in the menu bar between the **Window** and **Help** menus, and is labeled with a black 🐚 icon rather than a word. In it, you will find a list of submenus, organizing commands for things such as accessor functions (which we saw in Chapter 5, "Starting a Cocoa Application") and, it happens, HeaderDoc comments.

At the end of the 🐚 menu is **Edit User Scripts**, which we will come to shortly.

The **HeaderDoc** scripted commands are straightforward, with names like **Insert @header template** and **Insert @method template**. For the ones that apply to specific declarations, you need only select the declaration

```
@interface PointStat : NSObject {
```

and then select the appropriate script command, and a partially filled HeaderDoc comment will be inserted in front of the declaration:

```
/*!
    @class          PointStat
    @superclass     NSObject  {
    @abstract       <#(brief description)#>
    @discussion     <#(comprehensive description)#>
*/
@interface PointStat : NSObject {
```

The supplied scripts are not perfect. As you see, the `@class` parser doesn't strip the brace after the superclass, and the `@method` parser doesn't work at all unless the selected method declaration conforms to Apple's white space–phobic coding standard. Further, although the `@method` template properly suppresses the `@result` tag when the method returns `void`, it still offers the tag in the case of `IBAction`s, which are a mere `#define` away from being `void`:

```
/*!
    @method         doSomething:
    @abstract       <#(brief description)#>
    @discussion     <#(comprehensive description)#>
    @param          <#sender (description)#>
    @result         <#(description)#>
*/
- (IBAction) doSomething:(id)sender;
```

The so-called "top-level" tags, such as `@class` and `@method`, were prominent in versions of HeaderDoc before the current Version 8. HeaderDoc can now infer what type of documentation is being specified from the context of the comment. Top-level tags influence the output in only a few cases; look up HeaderDoc in the Xcode Documentation window to learn what these are. However, it still makes sense to provide separate scripts for the different entities. It's hard for short scripts to make the same contextual inferences that the full HeaderDoc tools make. And, when you select the type of comment you want, a script can give you the specialty tags that apply to that type.

Let's fix just that flaw. Select 🐷 > **Edit User Scripts**. The Edit User Scripts window appears (see Figure 15.3). At its heart, this window is an editor for the **Script** menu. The list at the left contains a list of items you recognize as the categories in the **Script** menu itself. Clicking the disclosure triangles reveals the scripts that are the submenu items. Select one of these, and you see that the large text-editing area to the right fills with the text of the selected script.

This script editor is not inconsiderable. It is syntax-colored, and accepts most common scripting languages (including sh, Perl, Ruby, and Python, to be selected via the standard "shebang" (#!) line at the top). The script works as an ordinary UNIX filter tool. For its standard input (selectable in the top pop-up button), it can have the whole content of the front window, the selected text, or nothing. Standard output (the pop-up just below the editor) can be ignored; made to replace the selection or the whole document; inserted after the selection or at the end of the document; or displayed as HTML, an alert, or a new document. These options suggest a wealth of uses to which a user script can be put.

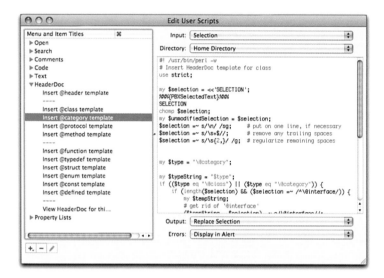

FIGURE 15.3   The Edit User window. The scripting system is organized around an editor, to the left, for the Xcode **Script** menu. Using the **+** pop-up menu, you can add existing scripts and Automator workflows, as well as create new scripts to be edited in the large, syntax-colored text area to the right. The pop-ups above and below the text area determine where the script's input will come from, what its working directory will be, where the output will go, and how errors are to be handled.

%%%{PBX}%%% **Text**

This flexible scripting facility is new to Xcode 3. In earlier versions, Xcode would match scripts to their environment by providing variables that would be textually inserted into a script before executing it. To preserve compatibility with scripts written for this system, Xcode still performs these substitutions. The @method commenting script we'll be editing is an example. In that script, you will find the lines

```
my $selection = <<'SELECTION';
%%%{PBXSelectedText}%%%
SELECTION
```

where whatever was substituted for %%%{PBXSelectedText}%%% is put into a "here" string and loaded into a global variable. PBXSelectedText is the placeholder into which the contents of the front window's selection are substituted. Other substitution markers include the following:

▶ PBXAllText, the entire contents of the front window.

▶ PBXTextLength, the number of characters in the front window.

> ▶ PBXFilePath, the pathname of the front window's file.
>
> ▶ PBXSelectionStart, the index of the start of the selection, counted into the contents of the front window.
>
> ▶ PBXSelectionEnd, the index of the end of the selection, counted into the contents of the front window.
>
> ▶ PBXSelectionLength, the number of characters in the selection.
>
> ▶ PBXSelection, when inserted into the output, marks the place where the insertion point is to be located in the output text. If it is used twice, the selection will extend between the two markers.
>
> There were several other markers that specified the name of the script's entry in the **Script** menu, the links to standard input and output, and other housekeeping attributes. These are not likely to come up in scripts you will see in Xcode 3.

In the menu-editor view, select **HeaderDoc > Insert @method Template**. The script we want to modify appears at right in the editor area. As provided, the Edit User Scripts window is narrow enough that most lines in the script will be wrapped. Adjust the window until most of the line wrapping is relieved.

**NOTE**

For safety's sake, before editing the script, click in it, copy its contents, and paste them into a new file. The script editor applies its changes "live"; and although you have the usual undo/redo facility, there is no concept of saving or reverting to a saved version.

Look for the line

```
if ((defined($return)) && ($return ne 'void')) {$returnsAValue=1;};
```

and change it to

```
if ((defined($return)) &&
    ($return ne 'void') &&
    ($return ne 'IBAction'))
    {
        $returnsAValue=1;
    };
```

The edited script takes effect immediately. If we select our dummy IBAction declaration and select **Script > HeaderDoc > Insert @method Template**, the template no longer includes a @result tag:

```
/*!
    @method        doSomething:
    @abstract      <#(brief description)#>
    @discussion    <#(comprehensive description)#>
    @param         <#sender (description)#>
*/
- (IBAction) doSomething:(id)sender;
```

Where do user scripts come from, and where do they go? When you first run Xcode, all the user scripts are drawn from a property list file at /Developer/Library/Xcode/ XCUserScripts.plist (assuming you accepted the default placement of the developer tools at /Developer). As soon as you make changes, the whole file, as edited, is copied to ~/Library/Application Support/Developer/-3.0/Xcode/XCUserScripts.plist. Placement of Xcode resources was discussed in detail in the "Text Macros" section of Chapter 9, "Property Lists."

Scripts you write in the script-editor view are included verbatim in the property-list file. You can include separate script files in the **Script** menu, too—select **Add Script File** from the + pop-up menu in the Edit User Scripts window, and select the script file in the open-file sheet that appears. Double-clicking the added script's line item will allow you to give it a descriptive name without renaming the file. Clicking the editing (pencil) button under the script list will open the script file in an editor window.

The scripting property list will record the external file as an absolute file system path; so if you move or rename the script file, the menu item will no longer work.

# DocSets

So far, we have produced a set of documentation that we can open with a web browser and read from there. The potential for our documentation subproject goes beyond that. In the Apple-supplied documentation sets, you can use the Documentation window to do a full-text search of all the provided documentation, and search APIs for classes, methods, functions, and constants. When you Option-double-click on a documented API symbol, the window opens and displays its documentation. And, when you select a documented API symbol (or even click in it), the Research Assistant window shows brief documentation for the symbol.

We can display our documentation with the Xcode documentation system, and take advantage of all the features it affords.

To integrate documentation into Xcode, we must organize it into a *documentation set* (docset). A docset is a bundle (see Chapter 11, "File Packages and Bundles"), which means it is a structured directory tree with a Contents directory, an Info.plist file, and a Resources/Documents directory containing the documentation tree, as shown in Figure 15.4.

The docset bundle must have four files in addition to the HeaderDoc-generated documentation tree:

- ▶ Info.plist, which should be familiar to you by now

- ▶ docSet.dsidx and docSet.skidx, providing indexes for full-text searching

- ▶ Nodes.xml, which describes the structure of your documentation to the indexer

- ▶ A fifth file, Tokens.xml, is needed if you want to index API.

FIGURE 15.4    The structure of a documentation set. It is a bundle, and therefore has a prescribed structure organized by an Info.plist file. Its name is made unique by being in reverse-domain format. The documentation tree we generated with HeaderDoc is placed in Contents/Resources/Documents. The additional files in Contents/Resources are required by the documentation system.

## Preparing the Workspace

Before we go further, we should set aside a directory for our documentation and its supporting files. We'll call the new directory Docs, and keep it in the Linear project directory. The straightforward way to do this would simply be to open the Linear folder in the Finder and use **File > New Folder** to create the directory. This causes a problem, however, when it comes time to check the contents of Docs into SCM. Docs won't be under control, and so neither can its contents be. Any files we add to the directory will not be marked with ? flags because they have no status with respect to our repository.

There are two solutions, both requiring the command line. The first is to use the Finder to create the directory anyway, and then enter svn add Docs. The other is to have Subversion create the directory itself: svn mkdir Docs. Either way, the new directory will be set up to control files within it, and will be checked in at the next commit.

Begin the new organization of our documentation task by moving headerDoc2HTML.config, TOCTemplate.html, and Statistics.hdoc into Docs. If those files aren't under SCM, that's a simple matter of dragging them into the folder. If they are under SCM, then again you'll have to use the svn command-line tool so that Subversion can ensure that they will still be tracked in the repository:

```
$ svn move headerDoc2HTML.config Docs
$ svn move TOCTemplate.html Docs
$ svn move Statistics.hdoc Docs
$
```

We also need the skeleton of the docset bundle to be in place. It must be given a unique name, in reverse-domain format,

> **WARNING**
>
> Don't use SCM commands to create these directories. The docset bundle is a *product*, to be generated from files under version control, and products don't belong under SCM.

ending in `.docset`. It must contain `Contents/Resources/Documents`. The rest can be generated automatically. The easiest way to do this, again, is from the command line; the following command assumes that the current working directory is `Linear/Docs`:

```
$ mkdir -p org.manoverboard.Statistics.docset/\
> Contents/Resources
$
```

I omit the trailing `Documents` directory, because we'll be getting that from the `hdoc` directory we've already built.

## The Least We Can Do

Now we have new files to create to make our HeaderDoc documentation available in the Xcode documentation system. Create these within the new `Docs` directory.

For minimal support in Xcode, the requirements are not stringent. `Info.plist` need have only three keys; call the file in `Docs` **Documents-Info.plist** so that you can distinguish it from the other `Info.plist` files Linear manages—we'll be copying it into the docset bundle, and can set the name of the copy then:

```xml
<?xml version="1.0" encoding="UTF-8"?>
<!DOCTYPE plist PUBLIC "-//Apple//DTD PLIST 1.0//EN"
                    "http://www.apple.com/DTDs/PropertyList-1.0.dtd">
<plist version="1.0">
<dict>
    <key>CFBundleIdentifier</key>
    <string>org.manoverboard.Statistics.docset</string>
    <key>CFBundleName</key>
    <string>Statistics Framework</string>
    <key>DocSetFeedName</key>
    <string>Man Overboard</string>
</dict>
</plist>
```

Notice that the `CFBundleIdentifier` is the same as the name of the docset. This isn't required, but they both have the same needs for uniqueness and description, so why not? The minimal `Nodes.xml` file, providing a name and root for our documentation, is as follows:

```xml
<?xml version="1.0" encoding="UTF-8"?>
<DocSetNodes version="1.0">
    <TOC>
        <Node type="folder">
            <Name>Statistics Framework</Name>
```

```
            <Path>index.html</Path>
        </Node>
    </TOC>
</DocSetNodes>
```

Now is the time to populate the docset bundle. We could run HeaderDoc to fill the
Documents directory, but we already have a full documentation tree in Linear/hdoc. Move
hdoc into the docset's Resources directory, and rename it **Documents**. Then copy the
working copies of our support files into the appropriate places in the bundle. Again, I
assume your current working directory is Linear/Docs:

```
$ cp -f Documents-Info.plist org.manoverboard.Statistics.docset/\
> Contents/Info.plist
$ cp -f Nodes.xml org.manoverboard.Statistics.docset/Contents/Resources/
$
```

The index files must be there for Xcode to recognize the docset; as a bonus, they allow
us to use the Documentation window's search field to do full-text searches on the documents. The indexes are built by the docsetutil command. Invoke docsetutil as follows:

```
$ /Developer/usr/bin/docsetutil index \
> org.manoverboard.Statistics.docset
Indexing Statistics Framework (1 nodes)
1: masterTOC.html
Linking up related token references
Sorting tokens
$
```

The developer-tools installation does not
copy docsetutil into /usr/bin, so you
have to invoke it directly from its location within /Developer. Indexing
proceeds automatically from there;
docsetutil crawls through the links in
your documentation tree, producing a
full-text index for the use of the documentation system.

> **NOTE**
>
> The files Nodes.xml and Tokens.xml (which
> we get to later) aren't used in an installed
> docset. They do no harm, however, and so
> we won't remove them at this early stage.

Your custom documentation must go into the Library subdirectory of your home directory, or in the systemwide /Library directory, at Library/Developer/Shared/
Documentation/DocSets. Create that chain of directories if it doesn't already exist. Copy
the docset into …/DocSets.

Xcode won't see a new docset until it is restarted. Quit Xcode and open it up again. Then
select **Help > Documentation.** You should see "Man Overboard" (from Info.plist's
DocSetFeedName) in the left column as a new provider of documentation, and below it

"Statistics Framework" as a documentation set. Select the docset, and see our documentation displayed (see Figure 15.5).

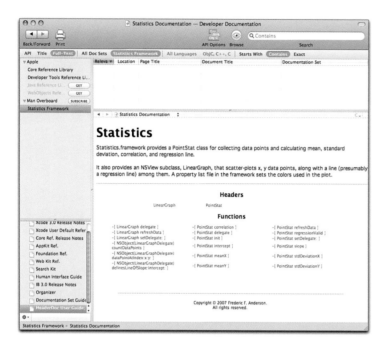

FIGURE 15.5    Generating a docset is tedious, but when it is done, you are rewarded with your organization listed alongside Apple as a documentation-set provider, and your docset shown beneath it.

# Shell Script Targets

Generating a documentation set from the command line is tedious. Xcode provides a build model for automating such processes. Select **Project > New Target...**, and in the ensuing New Target assistant, choose **Special Targets > Shell Script Target**, and name the new target `Docset`. Make sure the new **Docset** target is active.

A Shell Script target consists of one or more Run Script build phases. Each Run Script phase executes a script for the UNIX shell or another scripting language. Find the Docset target in the Targets group, and open its disclosure triangle to reveal the single Run Script build phase. Double-clicking the Run Script phase brings up a Phase Info window with the **General** tab selected; in this case, this includes a text area for entering the script (see Figure 15.6).

FIGURE 15.6    The Phase Info window for a Run Script build phase. The topmost field is for selecting the interpreter for the script; this is /bin/sh by default, but might be another, such as /usr/bin/ruby. The large text area in the middle receives your script. Below are lists for input and output files; if these are filled, Xcode will use them to determine whether the script needs to be run.

To match the four phases of building the Statistics docset, we will use four Run Script build phases. Fill the large scripting area of the Phase Info window with the following:

```
cd Docs
PACKAGEPATH=org.manoverboard.Statistics.docset/Contents/Resources/Documents
mkdir -p $PACKAGEPATH
headerdoc2html -o $PACKAGEPATH ../.h *.hdoc
gatherheaderdoc $PACKAGEPATH
exit 0
```

What we'll be doing is to create the whole docset bundle in-place in the Documents directory. The mkdir -p command ensures that the correctly named package will contain a Documents directory, which will receive the output of headerdoc2html. The script ends with exit 0; if a script exits with a nonzero status, the Xcode build process halts with an error.

It is possible to restrict Run Script build phases to run only when input files (like the headers we're documenting) are newer than outputs (like masterTOC.html deep in the docset). With a brief process like our docset build, such dependency checking wouldn't save much time. But see Chapter 21, "Xcode for make Veterans," for a detailed discussion.

Close the Phase Info window and create another phase. Select **Project > New Build Phase > New Run Script Build Phase**. (This command will be grayed out if the original Run Script phase is still selected. Select the Docset target and the command will be available.) Fill this phase with

```
cd Docs
PACKAGEPATH=org.manoverboard.Statistics.docset/Contents

cp -f Documents-Info.plist $PACKAGEPATH/Info.plist
cp -f Nodes.xml $PACKAGEPATH/Resources/

exit 0
```

Then two more Run Script phases. First, for indexing

```
cd Docs
/Developer/usr/bin/docsetutil \
    index \
    org.manoverboard.Statistics.docset/
rm org.manoverboard.Statistics.docset/Contents/Resources/Nodes.xml
```

and then for installation

```
cd Docs
mkdir -p ~/Library/Developer/Shared/Documentation/DocSets
# or /Library/Developer/Shared/Documentation/DocSets
cp -R org.manoverboard.Statistics.docset \
    ~/Library/Developer/Shared/Documentation/DocSets/
# or ~/Library/Developer/Shared/Documentation/DocSets/
```

Try this target out. If there is a org.manoverboard.Statistics.docset directory in Docs, remove it; if the Documentation window is open, close it; and click **Build** in the project window's toolbar (or ⌘**B**). In a few seconds, a new documentation set will be built and installed into your Library directory.

# Browsing

The Documentation window, by default, shows a list at the top for the results of documentation searches. There is an alternate view, a hierarchical browser, that enables you to drill down through a docset, from section to subject to document. You can switch between the views by clicking the **Browse** button in the Documentation window's toolbar.

Our Statistics docset doesn't make use of this feature because we have defined only the root level of the hierarchy in Nodes.xml. Let's add a browsable hierarchy of our own.

The `Nodes.xml` file serves to define this hierarchy for the documentation system. The principal structure is `<TOC>` (table of contents), which contains a `<Node>`. Each `<Node>` may contain the following:

▶ A `<Name>`, the name to be shown for the node in the browser

▶ A `<Path>`, the location of the corresponding file in the docset, relative to `Contents/Resources/Documents`

▶ Optionally, a `<File>` name, which is a path to the corresponding file, relative to that specified in `<Path>`

▶ `<Subnodes>`, a list of nodes contained within the current `<Node>`

We'll specify a simple two-level hierarchy, going from the header pages to the pages for the classes and the category:

```
<?xml version="1.0" encoding="UTF-8"?>
<DocSetNodes version="1.0">
  <TOC>
    <Node type="folder">
      <Name>Statistics Framework</Name>
      <Path>masterTOC.html</Path>
      <Subnodes>
        <Node id="1" type="folder">
          <Name>PointStat.h</Name>
          <Path>PointStat</Path>
          <File>index.html</File>
          <Subnodes>
            <Node id="3" type="folder">
              <Name>PointStat</Name>
              <Path>PointStat/Classes/PointStat_</Path>
              <File>index.html</File>
            </Node>    <!-- id 3 -->
          </Subnodes>
        </Node>        <!-- id 1 -->
        <Node id="2" type="folder">
          <Name>LinearGraph.h</Name>
          <Path>LinearGraph</Path>
          <File>index.html</File>
          <Subnodes>
            <Node id="4" type="folder">
              <Name>LinearGraphDelegate</Name>
              <!-- The next line is split for line-width purposes
                   Rejoin these two lines to make them correct: -->
              <Path>LinearGraph/Categories/
                        NSObject_LinearGraphDelegate_</Path>
              <File>index.html</File>
```

```
        </Node>    <!-- id 4 -->
        <Node id="5" type="folder">
          <Name>LinearGraph</Name>
          <Path>LinearGraph/Classes/LinearGraph_</Path>
          <File>index.html</File>
        </Node>    <!-- id 5 -->
      </Subnodes>
    </Node>        <!-- id 2 -->
  </Subnodes>
</Node>            <!-- root -->
</TOC>
</DocSetNodes>
```

> **NOTE**
>
> All the nodes in this hierarchy are marked `type="folder"`. You should mark a node as a folder node when its `<Path>` designates a directory containing many HTML files to be indexed. However, a folder node is also a destination in the docset's table of contents; when the node is selected in the Documentation window's browser, something has to be displayed. The `<File>` component designates which file among the folder's contents is to be that "landing page." If the node is to be just a single page, you designate it with `type="file"` (or just omit the `type` attribute). There are also bundle (localized) and web-based nodes, but I won't cover them.

Build the Docset target again, and then quit and restart Xcode so that it notices the change in the Statistics docset. Click the **Browse** button in the toolbar of the Documentation window so that the browser appears. The browser now shows our documentation in the hierarchy we specified (see Figure 15.7).

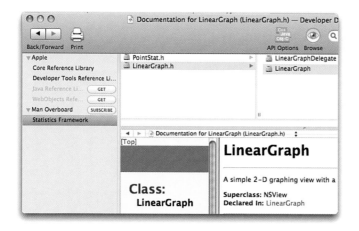

FIGURE 15.7    The Statistics docset made browsable. The **Browse** button in the Documentation window toggles between a listing of search results and a hierarchical browser of a documentation set. By adding structure to `Nodes.xml`, we can produce a guide that allows the user to drill down to class documentation directly.

# API Documentation

We can do still better. When you
Option-double-click on a symbol (such
as a class or method name) for which
Apple has provided documentation, the
Documentation window comes forward
and displays the reference material for
that symbol. We can get the same
service from our own docset if we
provide a `Tokens.xml` file that indexes
our symbols into our documentation
pages.

`Tokens.xml` consists of a list of files that
document our API, and within those
files, `<Token>`s that identify the API
elements we want to provide option
references for.

> **N O T E**
>
> This greatly oversimplifies the things you can
> do in a `Tokens.xml` file. In the Documen-
> tation window, select the **Developer Tools
> Reference** docset and do a full-text search
> for "Supporting API Lookup in Documentation
> Sets" for the full scoop. Be sure to use the
> docset, and not the *Xcode User Guide* avail-
> able through the **Help** menu. The *User Guide*
> contains only the basic instructions on how
> to use Xcode, which is a small fraction of the
> docset's information on all the developer
> tools.

Here's what `Tokens.xml` would look like, taking only two of the methods defined in
`PointStat`:

```xml
<?xml version="1.0" encoding="UTF-8"?>
<Tokens version="1.0">
    <File path="PointStat/Classes/PointStat_/Methods/Methods.html">
        <Token>
            <TokenIdentifier>
            //apple_ref/occ/instm/PointStat/delegate
            </TokenIdentifier>
            <Abstract>Returns the delegate object used as a
                data source. </Abstract>
            <Declaration>-(id) delegate;</Declaration>
            <DeclaredIn>
                <!--Split for width; merge these three lines. -->
                <HeaderPath>
                    Statistics.framework/Headers/PointStat.h
                </HeaderPath>
                <FrameworkName>Statistics</FrameworkName>
            </DeclaredIn>
            <Anchor>//apple_ref/occ/instm/PointStat/delegate</Anchor>
            <RelatedTokens>
                <TokenIdentifier>
                    //apple_ref/occ/instm/PointStat/setDelegate:
                </TokenIdentifier>
            </RelatedTokens>
        </Token>
        <Token>
```

```
<TokenIdentifier>
//apple_ref/occ/instm/PointStat/setDelegate:
</TokenIdentifier>
<Abstract>Set the data-source delegate.</Abstract>
<Declaration>
    - (void) setDelegate: (id) aDelegate;
</Declaration>
<DeclaredIn>
    <!--Split for width; merge these three lines. -->
    <HeaderPath>
        Statistics.framework/Headers/PointStat.h
    </HeaderPath>
    <FrameworkName>Statistics</FrameworkName>
</DeclaredIn>
<Anchor>//apple_ref/occ/instm/PointStat/setDelegate:</Anchor>
<RelatedTokens>
    <TokenIdentifier>
        //apple_ref/occ/instm/PointStat/delegate
    </TokenIdentifier>
</RelatedTokens>
    </Token>
  </File>
</Tokens>
```

The Tokens.xml file included in the
sample code will flesh out the token set.
Each <Token> includes the following:

▶ <TokenIdentifier>, an apple_ref
   string that identifies the symbol by
   language, type, defining class, and
   symbol name. There is a rule to
   constructing these strings, but
   HeaderDoc does the work for you.
   You can find the apple_ref string
   for a symbol in the generated
   HTML file where that symbol is
   documented.

▶ <Anchor> the name of the <a> tag
   that marks the place in the HTML
   file where the symbol is documented. In the case of methods,
   this takes the form of the method
   selector; look in the generated
   HTML to be sure.

> ## NOTE
>
> You will find that if you try to examine a
> HeaderDoc-generated HTML file, you won't
> be able to see the source—Xcode obsti-
> nately renders it as a documentation page.
> Xcode does this with any HTML file it deems
> to be documentation; one of its criteria is
> whether there is a <META> tag identifying
> HeaderDoc as the generator of the file. If you
> have another text editor, like BBEdit or
> TextMate, use them for this task. The only
> solution available within Xcode is this: Add
> the Docs directory to the project (⌥⌘A and
> select the directory), making sure to select
> **Create Folder References for Any Added
> Folders** in the resulting add-file sheet. This
> option will be explained in Chapter 20,
> "Navigating an Xcode Project." The effect will
> be to add to the Linear project a live group
> containing whatever is in the Docs directory.
> Drill down the Docs hierarchy to the HTML
> file you want to examine. Control- (or right-)
> click it, and select **Open As > Source Code
> File**. Then you'll have the page source.

15

▶ <Abstract>, <Declaration>, <DeclaredIn>, and <RelatedTokens>, which provide information for the Research Assistant. These are optional.

We need to modify the second and third Run Script build phases of the Docset target to take account of Tokens.xml. It has to be present in the Contents/Resources directory during indexing, and should be absent when the docset is ready to install:

```
cd Docs
PACKAGEPATH=org.manoverboard.Statistics.docset/Contents
cp -f Documents-Info.plist $PACKAGEPATH/Inf o .plist
cp -f Nodes.xml $PACKAGEPATH/Resources/
cp -f Tokens.xml $PACKAGEPATH/Resources/
exit 0
```

And in the indexing phase

```
cd Docs
/Developer/usr/bin/docsetutil \
index \
org.manoverboard.Statistics.docset/
rm org.manoverboard.Statistics.docset/Contents/Resources/Nodes.xml
rm org.manoverboard.Statistics.docset/Contents/Resources/Tokens.xml
```

Save, build, and restart Xcode. Open the Documentation window, and do an **API** search in **All Doc Sets** for API containing **defines**. The listing of search results quickly narrows down to definesLineOfSlope:intercept: from the Statistics framework. Clicking the item brings up the documentation for that method.

Select the Statistics Framework docset in the Documentation window. Open the Linear project, and its file LinearGraph.m. Find the use of definesLineOfSlope:intercept:, hold down the Option key, and double-click on either word of the selector. Again, the documentation for that method appears in the Documentation window.

Our work in providing the text of method declarations (<Declaration>), abstracts (<Abstract>), and references to other methods related to each token (<RelatedTokens>) has also paid off. Open any .m file in the Linear project that uses the Statistics framework. Select any call to the delegate or setDelegate: methods, and then open the Research Assistant palette (**Help > Show Research Assistant**). The Research

> **NOTE**
>
> It appears that Option-double-clicking will not always find API documentation if the docset that contains it is not selected. Apple docsets do not have this trouble.

> **NOTE**
>
> For Research Assistant to work, Code Sense must be active. (See the Code Sense pane of the Preferences window.) To select the proper API, Research Assistant needs the class context that Code Sense provides.

Assistant shows the declaration of the method, our brief abstract, and a reference to the other method (see Figure 15.8).

FIGURE 15.8    The Research Assistant window, showing the brief documentation we created in `Tokens.xml` for `delegate`. The top pane includes links to the more-detailed documentation available in the Documentation window, and to the declaration of `delegate`. The other panes are for the declaration prototype, our description of the method, and a link to `setDelegate:`, which we designated as a related method. The panes shown closed here may be filled in by supplying additional information in `Tokens.xml`.

> **NOTE**
>
> If you use the `Tokens.xml` file provided in the sample code, you'll find that although the `LinearGraphDelegate` methods are browsable in the Documentation window, you can't get any help on them from Research Assistant. This is because any object derived from `NSObject` can implement those methods, and there is not enough Code Sense context to select the proper documentation.

## Summary

In this chapter, we explored how to produce documentation for a framework, from simple web-browsable content to a documentation set that can be browsed or searched by text or API in the Documentation window. We saw how to add our API to the Research Assistant, to provide instant reference as developers write software using our framework.

Along the way, we also learned how to use the many resources the Xcode documentation supplies.

# CHAPTER 16

# Using the Data Modeling Tools

## IN THIS CHAPTER

▷ Branching in Version Control

▷ Designing a Data Model

▷ Un-coding for Core Data

▷ Adding to a Data Model

▷ Core Data's Prebuilt Human Interface

Mac OS X 10.4 (Tiger) introduced Core Data, an object-persistence framework that can front for a binary file, a flat XML file, or an SQLite database. Core Data automates most tasks in storing, retrieving, and managing complex data models. In this chapter, we make `Linear` a Core Data–based application.

---

### Version Control: Branching

We have come to a divergence in our project. For the Core Data version, we have begun work on a separate "product" from the Linear we've produced so far. We want the option of developing the base version from where it is now, but we also want the Core Data version to develop and progress on its own.

SCM systems provide for such divergent, independent lines of development by supporting *branching*. In Subversion, this is done by copying the `trunk` of the repository into the `branches` directory, and then switching the working copy so that it "points" to the new branch. With the repository URL switched, all future check-ins will be against the branch, and not the main line on the trunk.

Creating the branch is easy. Bring up the Repositories window (**SCM > Repositories**), select the Linear repository in the left column, and then the `trunk` directory in the browser on the right. Click the **Copy** button in the toolbar. This sets up a copy of the trunk. In the resulting sheet, select the `branches` directory, and name the copy **CoreData** by typing it into the text field at the top. Make sure to provide a comment describing the purpose of the branch (see Figure 16.1).

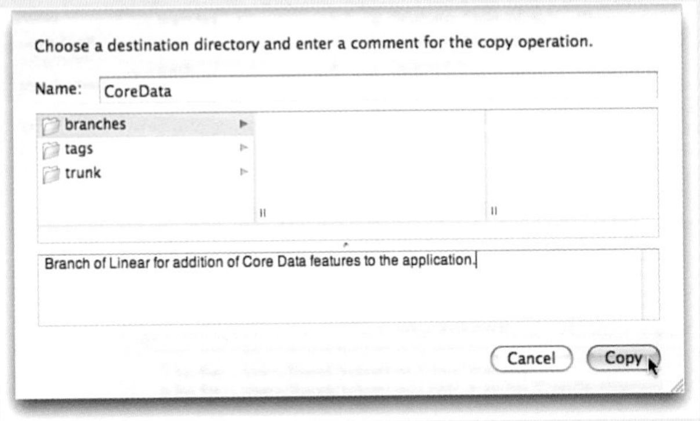

FIGURE 16.1    The sheet for specifying the destination for copying within a repository. The operation started in the Repositories window, by selecting the `trunk` directory in the Linear repository and clicking **Copy** in the toolbar. This sheet appeared; we name the copy (**CoreData**) and select the `branches` directory to hold it. We type in a descriptive comment for the log, and click **Copy**.

The second step, pointing the working copy at the branch, has to be done on the command line. The change is accomplished with the command `svn switch`. Because this is an operation involving the contents of a repository, we must supply a URL. We just named the branch CoreData, and it's in the `branches` directory. So:

```
$ cd ~/Linear        # Be sure we're in the Linear directory
$ svn info           # What URL is the working       copy using?
Path: .
URL: file:///Users/Shared/Subversion/Linear/trunk
Repository Root: file:///Users/Shared/Subversion/Linear

.
. more information
.

$ svn switch \
> file:///Users/Shared/Subversion/Linear/branches/CoreData
At revision 44.
$ svn info            # What URL now?
Path: .
URL: file:///Users/Shared/Subversion/Linear/branches/CoreData
Repository Root: file:///Users/Shared/Subversion/Linear

.
. more information
.
$
```

Now, whatever changes we check in from our working copy will be made against the CoreData branch, leaving the trunk untouched.

If we want to return to the original line of development, we can switch back to the old URL in the repository:

```
$ svn switch \
> file:///Users/Shared/Subversion/Linear/trunk
```

Subversion will take care of adding, removing, and updating files as needed to bring the working copy back to where it was when you made the branch.

# Data Modeling

So far, we've been working with data to which we had some thread of reference. DataPoints contained x and y components and were themselves indexed components of a Regression object that was kept by the MyDocument instance.

By contrast, Core Data works like a database, keeping a "soup" of objects—instances of NSManagedObject or classes descended from it—that exist independent of any reference to them, retrievable by evaluating a fetch request. All objects that are simultaneously accessible share an NSManagedObjectContext, which fronts for all the mechanisms that handle the storage, retrieval, and life cycle of the objects. The structure of an NSManagedObject— its attributes, relationships, default values—is specified by an NSEntityDescription. Entities, and the relationships among them, are specified in an NSManagedObjectModel.

An NSManagedObjectModel, the blueprint for the object store, is specified in a managed-object model (.mom) file. The file, read at runtime to initialize the object store, is produced by compiling an Xcode data model (.xcdatamodel) file.

Our first concrete step will be to produce a data model file. Choose the **New File...** command from the **File** menu; in the New File Assistant, scroll down to select **Design > Data Model**. Click **Next**. Name the data model file **Linear.xcdatamodel**, make sure it is assigned only to the Linear target, and click **Next**.

Xcode can derive much of a data design from existing source code. The Assistant presents a window for just that purpose (see Figure 16.2). At the left is a truncated view of the Groups & Files list, from which you can select the files or groups that contain your model objects. In the case illustrated, the DataPoint and Regression objects, along with others, were defined in the Classes group. Selecting Classes filled the next list, **Available Classes**, with the names of the classes defined in that group. From this, we can select only our model classes and use the **Add** button to transfer them to the **Selected Classes** list. When the list on the right contains DataPoint and Regression, click the **Finish** button. We are rewarded with a simple diagram (see Figure 16.3) that is not so very far from the data model we originally sketched (see Figure 5.1).

16

FIGURE 16.2    The New Data Model File Assistant. The list at left shows all the groups and files in the current project. Selecting a group (**Classes**) in this list fills the next list (Available Classes) with the names of all the classes defined in that group. You can then select classes to add to the Selected Classes list at right. Click **Finish** when done.

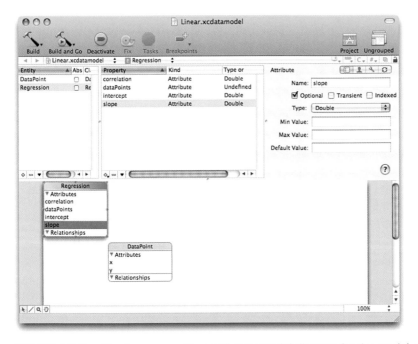

FIGURE 16.3    The "reverse-engineered" data model diagram for the model classes of Linear. The process for generating a new data model file reads the headers for the classes and detects the instance variables as attributes of the respective data entities. Slope, intercept, and correlation are correctly typed as Double.

Above the graphical model in Figure 16.3, are tables for browsing and editing the model. At the left, we see that the model contains two *entities*, or kinds of storable objects: `Regression` and `DataPoint`. `Regression` is selected, so the middle table shows all its attributes: `slope`, `intercept`, `dataPoints`, and `correlation`. In this table, `slope` is selected, and we see at the right that it is set up in the model as optional—it may have no value at all— of type Double, and without minimum, maximum, or default values.

The model as set up automatically is not quite satisfactory. All the attributes are set to be optional, but by the logic of our application it makes no sense for any of them to have no value. We might grumble as we resigned ourselves to clicking on each attribute in the two entities and clicked each **Optional** check box. We might grumble a little less if we noticed that by Control-clicking in the header of the middle table, we get a contextual menu that can add the **Optional** check box to that table, saving us a step.

But there is something even better. In the left table, a sensible thing to do is Shift-click on both `Regression` and `DataPoint`. The middle table fills with the properties of *both* entity types. Now select all the items in the middle table (see Figure 16.4). The Attribute editor on the right fills with all the options common to all the attributes. It has the **Optional** box checked. Uncheck it. This really does clear the optional property in all the selected attributes.

FIGURE 16.4    If more than one attribute is selected in the middle table, any edits you make with the Attribute editor on the right are applied to each selected attribute.

Now unselect dataPoints by Command-clicking it. It's the only attribute listed that is not a Double. Set a default value of 0 for all the `double`-valued attributes in the two entity types.

> **NOTE**
>
> At some point, click **Linear.xcdatamodel** in the Groups & Files list, and select **SCM > Add to Repository.**

# Revisiting the Model

Now that we have a new way of putting it into practice, it might be time to rethink our data design. Certainly, the implementation of the design has to change to suit the way Core Data works, but what about the design itself? Should the *shape* of the design change in light of what Core Data needs and what it makes possible?

One thing stands out. Our design says that a `MyDocument` has one `Regression`, which has an array of `DataPoints`. Both the `Regression` and the `DataPoints` are stored when the `MyDocument` is stored. But is the *has-a* relationship between `Regression` and `DataPoint` really necessary? It connects all the `DataPoints` in the document to all the `Regressions` (one) in the document. Core Data's fetch requests give us a way to summon up all instances of an entity type in a context, so the relationship adds no information. There's nothing special about being a DataPoint in the Regression's dataPoints array.

In the data model, select the dataPoints attribute of Regression in either the diagram or the middle table. It's no longer useful, so press the **Delete** key.

## DataPoint

Now we can rework DataPoint to reflect what Core Data will do for it. DataPoint has been an NSObject, implementing the NSCoding protocol. Now, because we want Core Data to manage DataPoint, it must be a subclass of NSManagedObject instead. This is no loss, because NSManagedObject is a subclass of NSObject.

We've also promised ourselves that we can replace Regression's list of all the DataPoints in the document with one obtained from Core Data. Let's add a method that produces such a list, and another that counts all the DataPoints in the document. Also, you see that we've removed the instance variables, x and y. Our managed-object model already specifies that a DataPoint has two double-valued attributes of those names; that is enough for NSManagedObject to provide storage and persistence for them automatically:

```
@interface DataPoint : NSManagedObject {
}
+ (NSArray *) allDataPointsInContext:
                        (NSManagedObjectContext *) context;
+ (unsigned) countDataPointsInContext:
                        (NSManagedObjectContext *) context;
```

The +es at the beginning of the method declarations mean that allDataPointsInContext: and countDataPointsInContext: are class methods, to be sent to the DataPoint class itself, not to an instance of DataPoint. You must pass these methods an instance of NSManagedObjectContext to identify the "soup" of objects from which you want to draw or count the DataPoints. A MyDocument object would specify the document's own context, whereas a Regression or another DataPoint would specify the context it came from.

## **All** DataPoints

The first thing we'd add to DataPoints.m is an implementation of allDataPointsInContext:. This consists of the most basic type of fetch request, one that specifies only an entity type—in this case, type **DataPoint**, which yields every object of that type in the context. The method constructs the request, executes it, and returns the result. countDataPointsInContext: works the same way, only using a Core Data method that counts the DataPoints without loading them all into memory:

```
// Return an array containing every DataPoint in the context
+ (NSArray *) allDataPointsInContext:
                        (NSManagedObjectContext *) context
{
```

```
    NSError *               error;
    NSArray *               retval;
    NSFetchRequest *        request = [[NSFetchRequest alloc] init];

    [request setEntity:
        [NSEntityDescription entityForName: @"DataPoint"
                      inManagedObjectContext: context]];
    retval = [context executeFetchRequest: request
                                    error: &error];
    return retval;
}

// Return the number of DataPoints in the context.
+ (unsigned) countDataPointsInContext:
                            (NSManagedObjectContext *) context
{
    NSError *               error;
    unsigned                retval;
    NSFetchRequest *        request = [[NSFetchRequest alloc] init];

    [request setEntity:
        [NSEntityDescription entityForName: @"DataPoint"
                      inManagedObjectContext: context]];
    retval = [context countForFetchRequest: request
                                     error: &error];
    [request release];
    return retval;
}
```

## Initializers

We look further into DataPoint.m and see that the init method is no longer needed. It initializes the instance variables to 0. We no longer have instance variables, and we have the managed-object model initialize the equivalent storage to 0 automatically.

What about initWithAbscissa:ordinate:, which covered arbitrary initialization? We could put together a substitute initializer, one that called through to NSManagedObject's designated initializer, but first let's check whether this initializer is in fact used. Select **Find > Find in Project** (⌘⇧F) to search for **initWithAbscissa:**. Type the search string in, and select **In Project**—you aren't interested in finding the string in framework headers— **Textual**—you don't need a regular-expression search, and you need more than the definition—**Whole Words**, and don't **Ignore Case**. Click **Find**.

The list below the search-criterion pane fills with matches: the declaration and definition of initWithAbscissa:ordinate:—and its uses in TestRegression.m. The method is used. We'll have to bring it up-to-date with NSManagedObject, having the initializer call the superclass's designated initializer, initWithEntity:insertIntoManagedObjectContext:.

This will entail passing the managed-object context into the initializer (the entity description can be obtained with just the entity name `DataPoint`), and altering the unit tests to obtain an MOC to pass to the `DataPoint` initializer. We ought to do this, but for the sake of keeping this book brief and on-point, we won't.

We grit our teeth and decide that `initWithAbscissa:ordinate:` isn't currently used in the application itself, but ought to be revived at some later date. Delete the method's definition, and leave the declaration as a comment, to remind ourselves that we ought to do something about it.

## Accessors

We now confront the accessor methods: `x`, `setX:`, `y`, *and* `setY:`. Obviously, our simple methods that front for instance variables are obsolete. Core Data guarantees that the key-value coding methods will always work for object attributes; so if we want to access the `x` attribute of `aPoint`, we might write the following:

```
double        pi = 3.1415926;
// setter:
[aPoint setValue: [NSNumber numberWithDouble: pi]
        forKey: @"x"];
// getter:
pi = [[aPoint valueForKey: @"x"] doubleValue];
```

But this is awkward for us, at least in the getter case, because we make such extensive use of the x and y accessors in calculations. As we analyze the `DataPoint` code, we see we can't easily live without x and y, but `setX:` and `setY:` are expendable.

The pattern for accessing attributes in a managed object is to first reserve the attribute by sending the object `willAccessValueForKey:`, then fetch the attribute by using

> **NOTE**
>
> Using the `@property` feature of Objective-C 2.0 would make this much simpler, but we're keeping away from that version of the language to keep the door open for compatibility with pre-10.5 versions of Mac OS X. Do a title search for *The Objective-C 2.0 Programming Language* in the Core Reference Library documentation set for more details.

`primitiveValueForKey:`, and, finally, relinquish the attribute by sending the object `didAccessValueForKey:`. The method `primitiveValueForKey:` just moves the data from the data store without additional housekeeping; Core Data assumes you have taken responsibility for that:

```
#pragma mark Key-Value Coding
// Getters for the x and y attributes.

- (double) x
{
```

```
    [self willAccessValueForKey: @"x"];
    NSNumber *  xAsObject = [self primitiveValueForKey: @"x"];
    [self didAccessValueForKey: @"x"];
    return [xAsObject doubleValue];
}

- (double) y
{
    [self willAccessValueForKey: @"y"];
    NSNumber *  yAsObject = [self primitiveValueForKey: @"y"];
    [self didAccessValueForKey: @"y"];
    return [yAsObject doubleValue];
}
```

Delete setX: and setY:. We called them directly only in our NSCoding methods. Core
Data takes care of key/value access to the setters automatically. Also, because Core Data
handles storage and retrieval, delete encodeWithCoder: and initWithCoder:.

We also rewrite the asPropertyList method in DataPoint-PropertyList.m to access the
x and y values of the DataPoint through the accessors rather than through the no-longer-
existing instance variables:

```
- (NSDictionary *) asPropertyList
{
    return [NSDictionary dictionaryWithObjectsAndKeys:
        [NSNumber numberWithDouble: [self x]], @"abscissa",
        [NSNumber numberWithDouble: [self y]], @"ordinate",
        nil];
}
```

## Regression

In Regression.h, once again, we must change the superclass from NSObject <NSCoding>
to NSManagedObject and remove all the instance variables. True to our theory that it is no
longer Regression's business to track DataPoints, remove the declarations of the accessor
methods for dataPoints. We'll keep the rest of the accessors, however, because we use
them elsewhere in our code.

Turning to Regression.m, examine the init method. It initializes the statistics variables to
0—our managed-object model does that anyway—and allocates the dataPoints array,
which is obsolete. The init method does nothing we need, and dealloc serves only to
release dataPoints. Delete init; dealloc will have new uses. The NSCoding methods,
initWithCoder: and encodeWithCoder:, are no longer needed. Delete them, as well as the
dataPoints accessor methods: dataPoints, setDataPoints:, and countOfDataPoints.

Replace canCompute. Previously, it counted the dataPoints array and returned YES if it
had more than one member. Now it can ask the DataPoint class to count all the
DataPoints itself:

```
- (unsigned) countDataPoints
{
    return [DataPoint countDataPointsInContext:
                             [self managedObjectContext]];
}
```

The accessors for `slope`, `intercept`, and `correlation` can no longer use simple instance variables. We'll have to use primitive accessors guarded with notifiers. Fortunately, you can save a lot of trouble in writing explicit accessors by selecting the attributes of interest in the data model diagram, Control- (or right-) clicking, and selecting **Copy Method Implementations to Clipboard**. None of the methods this command generates are mandatory—Core Data will perform the basic services for your data without them—but they can be useful. In this case, we need setters and getters but not the validation methods.

Here are the generated getter and setter for `slope`; the other two pairs are substantially identical:

```
- (double)slope
{
    NSNumber * tmpValue;

    [self willAccessValueForKey:@"slope"];
    tmpValue = [self primitiveValueForKey:@"slope"];
    [self didAccessValueForKey:@"slope"];

    return (tmpValue!=nil) ? [tmpValue doubleValue] : 0.0;
}

- (void)setSlope:(double)value
{
    [self willChangeValueForKey:@"slope"];
    [self setPrimitiveValue:[NSNumber numberWithDouble: value]
                     forKey:@"slope"];
    [self didChangeValueForKey:@"slope"];
}
```

The `asPropertyList` method, in `Regression-PropertyList.m`, needs only one change:

> **NOTE**
>
> I've slightly altered the implementation of `slope`, `setSlope:`, and the other accessors so they still accept and return doubles.

```
- (NSDictionary *) asPropertyList
{
    // Make an array to hold the property-list version of
    // the data points.
    NSMutableArray * pointArray = [NSMutableArray array];
    NSArray *        dataPoints = [DataPoint
```

```
            allDataPointsInContext: [self managedObjectContext]];
    NSEnumerator * iter = [dataPoints objectEnumerator];
    .
    .
    .
```

Now, we redefined our data points set from "the array of DataPoints held by the model Regression," to "all the DataPoints in the current soup." By the same token, we are redefining our model object as "the only Regression object in the soup." This singleton definition has to be implemented by reference to the data store. We can define a new Regression class method that returns the one-and-only Regression object in an NSManagedObjectContext, or creates one if there isn't one yet:

```
+ (Regression *) sharedRegressionInContext:
                        (NSManagedObjectContext *) aContext
{
    NSError *          error;
    NSArray *          allRegressions;
    NSFetchRequest *   request = [[NSFetchRequest alloc] init];
    Regression *       retval = nil;
    // Ask for all the Regressions, hoping there's only one
    [request setEntity:
            [NSEntityDescription entityForName: @"Regression"
                        inManagedObjectContext: aContext]];
    allRegressions = [aContext executeFetchRequest: request
                                             error: &error];
    [request release];
    // Squawk if there is more than one
    NSAssert([allRegressions count] <= 1,
          @"Should never be > 1 Regression object");
    if ([allRegressions count] < 1) {
        // If there are none, make one
        retval = [NSEntityDescription
                    insertNewObjectForEntityForName: @"Regression"
                             inManagedObjectContext: aContext];

        // This isn't a user action; don't allow it to be undone
        [aContext processPendingChanges];
        [[aContext undoManager] removeAllActions];
    }
    else    // If only one, return it.
        retval = [allRegressions objectAtIndex: 0];

    return retval;
}
```

16

Add the declaration

```
+ (Regression *) sharedRegressionInContext:
                      (NSManagedObjectContext *) aContext;
```

to `Regression.h` so the singleton can be found by other classes.

One last thing in `Regression.m` is the `initialize` class method. It tells the key-value observing mechanism to signal a change in the `canCompute` key whenever there is a change to `dataPoints`. There is no longer a `dataPoints`; how to replace this functionality? Core Data provides a notification whenever a managed-object context changes. We can make sure that every `Regression` object will get this notice and signal a possible change in `canCompute` when the count of `DataPoints` may have changed. The designated initializer method for `NSManagedObject`, `Regression`'s new superclass, is `initWithEntity:insertIntoManagedObjectContext:`. We can provide an override for that method to register each new `Regression` for the notification. We make sure that `dealloc` (revived for this purpose) ends the registration:

```
- (id) initWithEntity: (NSEntityDescription *) entity
   insertIntoManagedObjectContext: (NSManagedObjectContext *) context
{
    self = [super initWithEntity: entity
                       insertIntoManagedObjectContext: context];
    if (self) {[[NSNotificationCenter defaultCenter]
                      addObserver: self
                         selector: @selector(storeChanged:)
                             name:
                  NSManagedObjectContextObjectsDidChangeNotification
                           object: context];
        }
        return self;
}


- (void) dealloc
{
    [[NSNotificationCenter defaultCenter] removeObserver: self
    [super dealloc];
}

- (void) storeChanged: (NSNotification *) notice
{
    NSSet *            inserted = [[notice userInfo]
                                objectForKey: NSInsertedObjectsKey];
    NSSet *            deleted = [[notice userInfo]
                                objectForKey: NSDeletedObjectsKey];

    if ([inserted count] > 0 || [deleted count] > 0) {
        [self willChangeValueForKey: @"canCompute"];
```

```
        [self didChangeValueForKey: @"canCompute"];
    }
}
```

The initializer registers `storeChanged:` as the message to send when the managed-object context changes. This message checks for object insertions or deletions and forces the key-value observing mechanism to register any change in the `canCompute` property.

## MyDocument

In `MyDocument.h`, change the base class of `MyDocument` from `NSDocument` to `NSPersistentDocument`. This Core Data–supporting `NSDocument` subclass adds many automatic behaviors, including reading and writing the document file and maintaining the in-memory object-model store.

Reading and writing the file are now done by `NSPersistentDocument`, so `dataOfType:error:` and `readFromData:ofType:error:`, in `MyDocument.m`, are obsolete. Delete them both.

We have to do something about the `model` instance variable. We want the `model` variable to reflect a `Regression` object loaded from a `.linear` file when opening an existing document, and we want it to be a fresh `Regression` object when creating a new document. It has to point to a proper model after any saved model is loaded but before any data is displayed.

Fortunately, `NSDocument` provides a method that gets called at just the right moment. Cocoa sends a new or freshly opened document `windowControllerDidLoadNib:` after data arrives and the contents of the document's NIB have been loaded and hooked up, but before anything is displayed. The template for a document-based Cocoa application supplies the skeleton for this method in `MyDocument`. We can use our `sharedRegressionInContext:` method to find an existing `Regression` if it is there or create one if there isn't one. We then use `setValue:forKey:` to set our own `model` instance variable. The use of `setValue:forKey:` is one way of making the change visible to the key-value-observing mechanism on which our user interface bindings depend:

```
- (void)windowControllerDidLoadNib:(NSWindowController *) aController
{
    [super windowControllerDidLoadNib:aController];

    Regression *       myModel =
                     [Regression sharedRegressionInContext:
                         [self managedObjectContext]];
    [self setValue: myModel forKey: @"model"];
}
```

Remove the allocation and initialization of `model` from `MyDocument`'s init method—and remove `! model` from the `if` statement that tests whether internal initialization succeeded; `model` won't be initialized until later. Keep the release of `model` in the `dealloc` method—the `setValue:forKey:` has the effect of retaining the shared `Regression` instance for the document.

Two of `MyDocument`'s methods implementing the `LinearGraphDelegate` informal protocol drew from the `Regression` model object for a list of all `DataPoints`. `Regression` no longer knows about `DataPoints`. We change the methods so that they pull the lists from the data store:

```
#pragma mark LinearGraphDelegate

- (unsigned) countDataPoints
{
    return [DataPoint countDataPointsInContext:
                               [self managedObjectContext]];
}


-(void) dataPointAtIndex: (unsigned) index
                       x: (double *) outX
                       y: (double *) outY
{
    NSArray *   allPoints = [DataPoint allDataPointsInContext:
                                   [self managedObjectContext]];
    DataPoint * item = [allPoints objectAtIndex: index];
    *outX = [item x];
    *outY = [item y];
}
```

Core Data stores objects in one of three formats. Binary format is a fast, compact, serialized format that is not indexed. XML format is bulkier and slower but is readable by humans and other applications without much trouble. It is not indexed. SQL format is best for large collections of objects and for rapid searches. Double-click the **Linear** target icon to open its Get Info window, select its **Properties** tab, and in the Document Types list, switch **Store Type** from **Binary** to **XML**. Just for fun.

# Interface Builder

Our use of the Cocoa Controller-layer classes will remain much the same. But there is a slight modification to make now that we are pulling our point list "out of the soup" and not from a list linked to the `MyDocument` through a `Regression`.

Open `MyDocument.nib` in Interface Builder (double-clicking it in the Groups & Files list, in the Resources group, will do). `MyDocument` hasn't changed substantially, but `DataPoint` and `Regression` are practically new, and we have to restructure the `NSController` objects that control them.

In the NIB window for `MyDocument.nib`, select the **DataPoints** `NSArrayController:`. In the Attributes Inspector (⌘1), change the **Mode** of the controller from **Class** to **Entity**, and set the **Entity Name** to `DataPoint`. Also, make sure that the **Prepares Content** box is checked. Setting this ensures that the controller will perform the initial query to load the content set and will subscribe to notifications of changes in the managed-object context to keep the content current.

In Bindings (⌘4), unbind the content array by opening the Content Array item and unchecking the **Bind** box. Bind the `managedObjectContext` property to **File's Owner / managedObjectContext** to ensure that the **DataPoints** controller will be working from the same data store as the `MyDocument` that owns this document window. The combination of specifying the `DataPoint` entity type, specifying the `MyDocument` managed-object context, and not making any further fetch specification in the first Attribute pane is exactly analogous to the fetch done in the `allDataPointsInContext:` class method of `DataPoint`.

The other two controllers remain the same. The **ModelController** `NSObjectController` provides access to the `slope`, `intercept`, and `correlation` properties of the model `Regression` object, just as it did before it became a Core Data–managed object.

The `NSTableView` is bound to the **DataPoints** controller just the same as before, but there is a trick to using numeric values in the user interface with Core Data. Core Data wants numeric values to come as instances of `NSNumber` and nothing else. However, the contents of cells in an `NSTableColumn` are provided as `NSStrings` *unless* an `NSFormatter` intervenes to translate the string value to another object type. We need to add `NSNumberFormatters` to the columns of our point table.

Obtain an `NSNumberFormatter` (in the Library palette, search for **Formatter**). Drag the formatter onto the sample text in the x column; the text will highlight, and a heads-up label will appear, saying "Text Field Cell (Text Cell)"; release the mouse button. If the drag works, the sample text will change to a number. Repeat with the y column.

We can adjust the text formatter to our needs. After a formatter has been installed, click the sample text repeatedly—slowly—until the sample text is highlighted, and a badge appears below the right end (see Figure 16.5). The badge represents the `NSNumberFormatter` we just dropped on the cell.

Selecting the badge, and opening the Attributes Inspector (⌘1) presents options for adjusting the behavior of the formatter (see Figure 16.6). The panel will offer a variety of prepared number formats, which you can use as is or as a

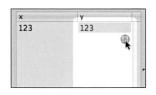

FIGURE 16.5    Clicking repeatedly on the sample text in a table column will drill down to the column's text-editing cell. When the cell is selected, a badge appears below it to represent the `NSFormatter` attached to the cell. Clicking on it will allow you to use the Attributes Inspector (⌘**1**) to set its properties.

basis for custom formats of your own. Select **Decimal** from the **Style** pop-up; the defaults for that setting will do, except for **Grouping Separator**, which inserts commas every three digits. We don't want those; uncheck the box.

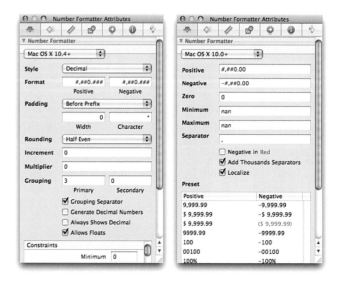

FIGURE 16.6    Configuring an `NSNumberFormatter` for the cell of an `NSTableColumn`, using the Attributes Inspector for the formatter. The **Style** pop-up provides a repertoire of formatting options that suffice for most purposes; the remaining controls allow you to customize the format in more detail. The Constraints list at the bottom permits you to set maximum and minimum values for the cell, among other options. *(Right)* The `NSFormatter` classes underwent a substantial revision at Mac OS X 10.4; the pre-10.4 compatibility options are available when you select **Mac OS X 10.0+** from the pop-up menu at the top.

# Build and Run

Build Linear and run it. It should behave more or less as before. You won't be able to reload any previously saved `.linear` files, because we've specified an XML file format for this new version of Linear, and earlier versions used a binary format produced by `NSKeyedArchiver`, and even if we chose a binary Core Data format, it would not coincide. In general, Core Data data files are not compatible across any changes to the object schema.

Save a `.linear` file in the new format, and drag its icon from the Finder onto the Xcode icon in the dock. Xcode will open it in a text editor, and you can verify that the file is, in fact, XML, and in a pretty easily understood format:

> **NOTE**
>
> There are solutions to this problem. Do a title search for *Versioning and Data Migration* in the Core Reference Library documentation set for more information.

```
<?xml version="1.0"?>
<!DOCTYPE database SYSTEM "file:///System/Library/DTDs/CoreData.dtd">

<database>
    <databaseInfo>
```

```
.
. database-description metadata
.

        </databaseInfo>
        <object type="REGRESSION" id="z102">
            <attribute name="correlation" type="double">1</attribute>
            <attribute name="intercept" type="double">0.114761904761906</attribute>
            <attribute name="slope" type="double">1.895238095238095</attribute>
        </object>
        <object type="DATAPOINT" id="z103">
            <attribute name="x" type="double">1</attribute>
            <attribute name="y" type="double">2.01</attribute>
        </object>
        <object type="DATAPOINT" id="z104">
            <attribute name="x" type="double">2.05</attribute>
            <attribute name="y" type="double">4</attribute>
        </object>
</database>
```

# Adding an Entity

Let's do one more thing just to see what Core Data and its associated programming tools can do. Suppose that our `DataPoint` data came from various sources and that it is important to keep track of which points come from which sources. We could imagine a `DataSource` entity, with the properties `title`, `author`, and `date`. Let's add it.

## Adding to the Data Model

In Xcode, bring up `LinearData.xcdatamodel`, and click the + button in the entity list at the top left of the data model browser. This creates a new entity, named `Entity`, which we rename `DataSource`. (Double-click the name in either the entity list or the title bar of the new entity in the diagram.) We will not be subclassing `NSManagedObject` for the `DataSource` entity but instead will be adding an entirely new data type—with zero code.

With `DataSource` selected in the entities list, select **Add Attribute** three times from the + drop-down menu (at the lower-left of the property list). Rename the new attributes, respectively, **title**, **author**, and **date**. Hold down the Command key and select `title` and `author`; in the editor pane at the right, give them the **String** type. Select the `title` attribute, and uncheck the **Optional** property. Select the `date` attribute and make it of type **Date**.

What's new about `DataSource` is that it does have a restrictive relationship with other entities—only certain `DataPoints` are associated with a given `DataSource`. We have to define the relationship between `DataSource` and `DataPoint`. One way to do this is

to select **Add Relationship** from the +
drop-down menu; another is to select
the line-drawing tool at the bottom of
the data model diagram and drag from
the DataSource block to the DataPoint
block (see Figure 16.7).

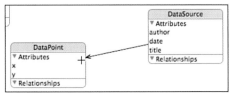

Select the new relationship—the data
modeler calls it newRelationship—in
the center browser pane, and edit the
properties of the relationship. Rename
newRelationship to **reportedData**. Make
it a to-many relationship—a single
DataSource can report more than one
DataPoint. The arrowhead of the relationship line from DataSource to
DataPoint is doubled to reflect the
multiplicity. Change the **Delete Rule** to
**Cascade**. (Deleting a source will delete
all the associated data points.)

We'll also add an inverse relationship,
from DataPoint to DataSource. Draw a
line from the DataPoint block to
DataSource, or add a relationship to the
middle browser while **DataPoint** is
selected in the left browser. Name the
relationship **source**; let it not be
optional; and set its **Inverse** to
**reportedData**. The lines between the
DataSource and DataPoint entity blocks
will change to one line, with a single
arrowhead going into DataSource, and a
double arrowhead going into DataPoint.

The inverse relationship for the
DataSource-to-DataPoint relationship,
going the other way, is set automatically.

**FIGURE 16.7**    Creating a new relationship in
the data model. *Above:* By choosing the line-
drawing tool at the bottom edge of the data
model diagram and dragging from DataSource
to DataPoint, we create a new relationship
between the two entity types. Initially, the relationship is named newRelationship. *(Below)*
The attributes of the new relationship can then
be edited, giving it a name, making it a to-many
relationship, and specifying that deleting the
source object also deletes the DataPoints it
points to (**Cascade**).

> **NOTE**
>
> Remember to select the arrow tool at the
> lower-left corner of the diagram before
> selecting the relationship line or moving the
> entities around.

## Human Interface

Now that we have an additional data type to manage, we need some way to input and
examine it. Open MyDocument.nib in Interface Builder. Make the prototype document
window roughly double its original height. Place it on the screen so it can be visible at
the same time as your data model window.

Bring your data model window, in Xcode, forward. Make sure that the large empty space in the document window in Interface Builder is visible. Hold down the Option key and drag the DataSource block from the data model diagram to the empty space in the prototype document window.

Switch to Interface Builder, which is now seeking your attention for a dialog window. IB asks what sort of user interface you want to create for data source objects. Select **Master/Detail View** from the pop-up menu, and check the **Search Field**, **Detail Fields**, and **Add/Remove** boxes. A rough diagram of what the resulting human interface will look like is shown on the right side of the window. Click the **Next** button.

In the next page, IB lets you select which attributes of DataSource to include among the detail fields that will appear below the master list of DataSources. Leave them all checked.

Click **Finish**, and IB presents a full master-detail editor for DataSources. The shape and position of the box will probably be unsuitable; resize the other elements in the window to make more room, move the box, and resize it until it all fits (see Figure 16.8).

> **WARNING**
>
> Be sure that **Layout > Live Autoresizing** in IB is not selected; otherwise, resizing the window will not open up any space.

> **NOTE**
>
> The autoresizing of the split view at the top of the window will have to be changed so that it is anchored to the top and sides, and of constant height. This view will be hard to select; click exactly on the splitter, or click anywhere inside it, and use ^⌘↑ to ascend the view hierarchy until resizing handles appear around it.

> **NOTE**
>
> Resizing the DataSource box may be a bit tricky, too, because it contains an NSView that organizes the box's content. That view won't (and shouldn't) have resizing handles, but clicking inside the box will almost always select the content view and not the box. The label on the box is part of the NSBox alone. Click that. Or, click anywhere inside the box and use ^⌘↑ until resizing handles appear around the box.

**16**

The link from Xcode to Interface Builder has done all the necessary work for making this human interface work. It has even added an NSArrayController for all the DataSources in the document's managed-object context.

> **WARNING**
>
> All the contents of the generated interface are set to resize as you would expect. However, as this was written (Xcode 3.0), they will not resize along with the enclosing box in Interface Builder, even with **Layout > Live Autoresizing** selected. A fix is expected in a later version.

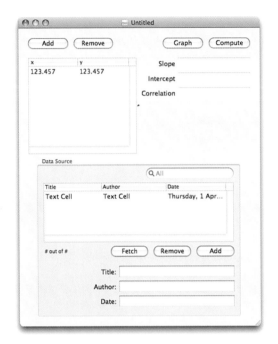

FIGURE 16.8    The automatically generated UI for DataSource. Option-dragging the DataSource block from the data model window in Xcode to a window being built in Interface Builder produces your choice of human-interface styles for that entity type, including single-instance views, and simple lists. The master/detail variant is shown in the bottom half of this window.

There's another way to do the same thing. Search for **Core Data** in the Library palette. The object you'll find is labeled Core Data Entity. When you drag this into a window you're constructing, IB will present a browser (see Figure 16.9), giving you access to all the data models available in projects currently open in Xcode. Select an entity from a model, click **Next**, and again, you are given the options for the style and content of the human interface you want to create. We could easily generate almost the whole Linear document interface with just three drags.

> **NOTE**
>
> Feel free to experiment with the New Core Data Interface Assistant. With each attempt, just delete the UI elements added in the last round, and Option-drag the DataSource entity from the diagram again. You will find that you'll accumulate an extra NSArrayController in the NIB window for each drag, so delete them all and make one last drag to produce an human interface linked properly to your final controller.

The **Fetch** button in the generated interface is used to fill the data-source array controller with the results of a custom fetch request, which you can set in the Attributes Inspector for the controller, or programmatically. We are interested only in listing all the DataSources, and don't use this feature. We can delete the **Fetch** button.

FIGURE 16.9    The entity browser that appears when you drag a Core Data Entity object from the Library palette to a window under construction. Interface Builder searches all open Xcode projects for data models, and presents them and the entities they contain. Selecting one of these, clicking the **Next** button, and choosing some options, automatically generates a human interface for the selected entity.

What can't be done automatically is expanding the interface for DataPoints so that we can set the DataSource of each point. We need an extra column in the DataPoint table to make the setting. Because we will have to widen the table to accommodate the new column, widen the window and drag the splitter to make the DataPoint table wide enough to accommodate a third column. The **Live Autoresizing** option is helpful for this.

Select the table—this will probably involve clicking in the list once, to select the enclosing NSScrollView, and again to select the NSTableView. In the Attributes Inspector (⌘1), change the number of columns from two to three. You will probably have to drag the column boundary, after selecting the table header, to make the third column visible.

We will fill the new third column with a pop-up list, from which the user can choose the title of a data source. Search the Library palette for **popup**; the icon with the simple border will be for an NSPopupButtonCell. Drag it onto the third column of the table (the column will highlight) and drop it there. The sample content of the third column will now bear the double arrowheads of a pop-up menu.

To link the column to the controller layer, click in the third column, below the sample cell, to select the column; you might have to click more than once to go down the hierarchy of views. When the column is highlighted and the Inspector shows that an NSTableColumn is selected, name the column **Source** in the Attributes Inspector (⌘1), and then edit the column's bindings (⌘4). Make the following bindings:

▶ **content**. The things being chosen should be bound from the **Data Source Array Controller > arrangedObjects**. That's what Interface Builder sets it up to be; so, all you have to do is check the **Bind** box.

- ▶ **contentValues.** The way the choices are displayed in the list. Again, this is taken from **Data Source Array Controller > arrangedObjects > Title**.

- ▶ **selectedObject.** The choice made for this DataPoint. Bind it to the **DataPoints Controller > arrangedObjects > Source**.

## First Run

Build and run the Linear target. Try opening an old .linear file from a previous Core Data run, if you saved any. No luck. We've changed the structure of the Linear data store, and the old contents just don't fit.

Instead, we'll create a new file by filling in the untitled document Linear presents when it opens. Start by adding data sources, such as those in Table 16.1. Click the **Add** button under the data source table, and fill in the data, either in the form below the buttons or directly into the table. When you're finished, the search field is fully functional.

TABLE 16.1    Sources for Budget Trend Lines

| Title | Author | Date |
|---|---|---|
| Economic Report of the President | OMB [Bush 43] | 15-Jan-2004 |
| Predictions | The Great Wizzardo | 22-Oct-1545 |

Then add DataPoints to the top table as before, using Table 16.2 as a guide. The third column is filled with pop-ups containing the titles of the source documents. Selecting a source assigns a point to the source.

TABLE 16.2    Data for Budget Trend Lines

| x | y | Source |
|---|---|---|
| 2004 | 472.5 | Economic Report of the President |
| 2005 | 490.0 | Economic Report of the President |
| 2006 | 525.3 | Economic Report of the President |
| 2007 | 530.9 | Economic Report of the President |
| 2008 | 529.0 | Predictions |
| 2009 | 538.0 | Predictions |

You can graph and regress this data as you could before. Try selecting the Predictions of The Great Wizzardo in the data source table and clicking **Remove** below that table. Because the deletion rule for the DataSource-to-DataPoint relationship is **Cascade**, deleting the source also deletes the associated points.

> **NOTE**
>
> You will probably find that the format for the date in the table and the form are unwieldy, providing time, day of week, and long month names. The cells for the date column and the form both have NSDateFormatters attached to them. Select these, and use the Attributes Inspector (⌘**1**) to adjust the format to something more practical.

Selecting **Edit > Undo** (⌘Z) restores Wizzardo's place in the public debate. Again: You needed only Interface Builder to do all this.

## One More Table

When examining DataSources, it would be convenient to see what data comes from each source. Looking at the list of all DataPoints and attending only to the items from one source would get unwieldy with a large data set. We'd like another NSTableView, one that displays just the DataPoints belonging to the selected DataSource.

This is solely a job for Interface Builder. Enlarge the prototype document window enough to accommodate a two-column table next to the automatically generated interface for DataSources (see Figure 16.10). Drop an NSTableView into the space from the Library palette, and adjust it to a reasonable size.

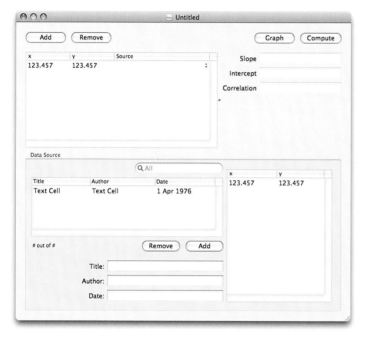

FIGURE 16.10    The last iteration of Linear's human interface in Interface Builder. This time, we add an NSTableView next to the automatically generated browser for DataSources. We create an NSArrayController linked to the reportedData relationship of the selection of the Data Source NSArrayController, and bind the x and y values of its arrangedObjects to the columns of the table.

We will need something that gives the table access to the reportedData relationship of the selected DataSource. We already have an NSArrayController named Data Source Array Controller that monitors the whole "soup" of DataSources, and one of the keys NSArrayController affords is selection—the selected DataSource. Because we're interested in more than one thing, all we need is an `NSArrayController` that sources from controller **Data Source**, key **selection**, and path **reportedData**.

From the Library palette, drag an `NSArrayController` into the MyDocument.nib window. In the Identity Inspector (⌘6), set the name of the controller to something like **Points for Source**. In the Attributes Inspector (⌘1), make sure that the new controller's content type is the *entity* DataPoint and that **Prepares Content** is set. In the Bindings Inspector (⌘4), bind **Content Set**—because the contents of a relationship form an unordered set, not an array—to **Data Source Array Controller > Selection > reportedData.**

> **NOTE**
>
> That the result of a Core Data fetch is unordered has an effect on Linear—the DataPoints' table will no longer be in the order we created them. The solution is outside the scope of this book. We'll just have to get along by clicking table headers to sort the contents.

Don't forget to bind the **Points for Source** controller's **Managed Object Context** to **File's Owner's managedObjectContext.**

Drop `NSNumberFormatters` onto the cells of each column of the table, and label the columns **x** and **y**, respectively. Bind the **Value** of the first column of the table to **Points for Source > arrangedObjects > x**, and the second to **Points for Source > arrangedObjects > y.**

Save the NIB file; then build and run Linear. Reload a multiple-source document, or create one. Now selecting a row in the Data Source table will fill the table to the right with the data points provided by the selected `DataSource`.

# Summary

In this chapter, we used Xcode's data-modeling tool to reverse-engineer Linear's data model, and produced a managed-object model (`.mom`) to drive a Core Data–based version of Linear. We saw how to use the modeling tools to set attribute properties, such as default values and whether a property is optional.

We saw how Interface Builder supports Core Data development by allowing us to set up objects based on simple queries to the managed-object context. We used IB to add major features to the Linear application, without writing additional code.

# CHAPTER 17
# Cross-Development

**IN THIS CHAPTER**

▷ **Targeting Other OS Versions**

▷ **Targeting Other Architectures**

▷ **Using Other Versions of Xcode**

Linear is working pretty well for us now, so it is time to throw a wrench into the works. Let's decide that we want to serve a wider audience and make a version of Linear that is compatible with Mac OS X version 10.4.

Apple has anticipated such needs. Up to now, we've been compiling and linking against headers and libraries that "came with the system"—the libraries we ended up using were the same as the ones used in running the computer we compiled on, and the headers reflected those libraries. An Xcode project can be directed away from a machine's base development environment to use libraries and headers from earlier releases of Mac OS X.

## Cross-Development SDKs

Apple provides a cross-development software development kit (SDK) for the current version of Mac OS X and the last release of the previous two major versions. The easiest way to choose an SDK is through a projectwide option. Double-click the project (top) icon in the Groups & Files list (or select **Project > Edit Project Settings**), and select the **General** tab of the Get Info window. From the pop-up menu labeled **Cross-Develop Using Target SDK**, select **Mac OS X 10.4 (Universal)**.

A sheet will appear, warning you that big things may happen to the project, as its build environment will change. We know this; we seek it. Click **Change**.

We also need to change a *target* setting, one that specifies, for runtime, rather than for building, the earliest version of Mac OS X we mean to support. Double-click the **Linear** target, and select the **Build** tab in the Get Info window. Select **All Configurations** in the

> **NOTE**
>
> At the time this was written, the pop-up menu for the deployment target showed up empty when it was set to the default. Click the pop-up to see what the setting is.

**Configuration** pop-up, because there should be no difference between the debugging and release versions. In the search field, type `Deployment`, and look for the setting **Mac OS X Deployment Target**, a pop-up menu that defaults to **Compiler Default** (which means whatever system you're building on); select **Mac OS X 10.4** instead. This line of the **Build** table becomes bold, to show that the setting represents a change from the default.

The Linear product includes the Statistics framework, so you'll have to make the same change in the **Build** tab of its Target Info, too.

Let's see how extensive the changes were in switching to the 10.4 SDK. Clean out all the previous build products by issuing a **Clean All** from the **Build** pop-up button in the Project window toolbar or selecting **Build > Clean All Targets**. Now build.

> **NOTE**
>
> We use **Clean All Targets** because we mean to force a rebuild of every part of the Linear project. Ordinarily, a simple **Clean** should suffice—Xcode should be able to figure out what targets would be affected if the current target were stripped of its build products. However, the Xcode dependency checks aren't always perfect, and it is sometimes a good idea to do a **Clean All Targets** to get the project back into a consistent state.

Already, we see signs of trouble. The build yields no errors, but there is a warning:

```
warning: 'NSManagedObjectContext' may not respond to
                            '-countForFetchRequest:error:'
    (Messages without a matching method signature will  be   assumed to
    return 'id' and  accept '...' as arguments.)
warning: assignment makes integer from pointer without a cast
```

This is a serious warning. Because of the dynamic nature of Objective-C, the compiler has to give the benefit of the doubt when it finds a method signature used that it hasn't seen before, but the most common source of the "may not respond" warning is that the method in question does not exist, and calling it will result in an error at runtime.

Both warnings apply to the same line in `DataPoint.m`, in the method `+[DataPoint countDataPointsInContext:]`:

```
    retval  =  [context  countForFetchRequest: request
                                    error: &error];
```

We can see the reason for the "makes integer from pointer" warning. We assign the result of `countForFetchRequest:error:` to `retval`, which is an unsigned integer. The compiler assumes the unknown method returns the pointer type `id`, so it flags the discrepancy.

What's going on here? Let's look at the declaration for the method **countForFetchRequest:** of `NSManagedObjectContext`. The easiest way would seem to be to Command-double-click on the selector where we use it in `DataPoint.m`. But that doesn't work. `countForFetchRequest:error:` isn't defined in the Linear project any more.

Investigate further by opening the Project Find window (⇧⌘F), entering `countForFetchRequest` in the **Find** field, and selecting **In Frameworks** from the scope-of-search pop-up between the **Find** field and the **Find** button. The search does find the declaration:

```
#if MAC_OS_X_VERSION_MAX_ALLOWED >= MAC_OS_X_VERSION_10_5
// returns the number of objects a fetch request would have returned
    if it had been passed to -executeFetchRequest:error:. If an
    error occurred during the processing of the request, this method
    will return NSNotFound.
- (NSUInteger) countForFetchRequest: (NSFetchRequest *)request
                             error: (NSError **)error;
#endif /* MAC_OS_X_VERSION_MAX_ALLOWED >= MAC_OS_X_VERSION_10_5 */
```

The declaration is guarded by an `#ifdef` that prevents its being read when `MAC_OS_X_VERSION_MAX_ALLOWED` is less than the equivalent of Mac OS X 10.5. The method was added in Leopard, and isn't available now that we're building against the SDK as it existed in 10.4.

This is a problem. We *like* `countForFetchRequest:error:`. It counts the `DataPoints` in our document without having to load them all into memory. However, under 10.4, you can't count managed objects without fetching them all and counting the results. What to do?

Because Objective-C is a dynamic language, you can determine whether an object implements a method, and use the method only if it exists. Rewrite `countDataPointsInContext:` to take advantage of this:

```
// Return the number of DataPoints in the context.
+    (unsigned) countDataPointsInContext:
                          (NSManagedObjectContext *) context
{
    NSError * error;
    unsigned retval;
    if ([context respondsToSelector:
                 @selector(countForFetchRequest:error:)]) {
        // Count the DataPoints directly if we can
        NSFetchRequest * request = [[NSFetchRequest alloc] init];
```

17

```
            [request setEntity: [NSEntityDescription entityForName: @"DataPoint"
                                        inManagedObjectContext: context]];

            retval = [context countForFetchRequest: request
                                        error: &error];
            [request release];
            }
    else {
        // Fetch all DataPoints and count the results if we must.
        retval = [[self allDataPointsInContext: context] count];
    }
    return retval;
}
```

Now try building Linear again. The warning is still there—we'll take care of that presently—but we know we've guarded against the possible runtime error the warning alerted us to. Run Linear, open the most recently saved document from it, and click the **Compute** button to force Linear to count the DataPoints. Linear runs correctly on both Leopard and Tiger.

What about those warnings? In practice, when you are targeting software at an earlier version of Mac OS X, you should set *only* the **Mac OS X Deployment Target** setting. This represents the *minimum* version of the operating system your software will support.

When you are using features from a later version of Mac OS X—even if, as here, you have to use them only conditionally—select the SDK for that later version. This is the *maximum* version of the operating system from which you will draw OS features. Linear uses countForFetchRequest:error:, a 10.5-and-up feature. Go to the Project Info window, **General** tab, and select the 10.5 SDK.

With the 10.5 SDK selected, the warning about countForFetchRequest:error: will no longer appear; that SDK defines the method. The reason we dropped back to the 10.4 SDK was that when we switched to an API set that didn't support 10.5 features, the compiler told us exactly what those features were.

> **NOTE**
>
> The (low) deployment and (high) SDK versions are translated for the compiler into MAC_OS_X_VERSION_MIN_REQUIRED and MAC_OS_X_VERSION_MAX_ALLOWED, respectively. As we saw, these macros are used in #if directives to guard API declarations, version by version.

> **NOTE**
>
> If you add public libraries or frameworks to your project, you'll find you apparently have some choices: The files as they appear in your root file system (/System/Library, /usr/lib, etc.); or the files in the equivalent places in an SDK. *Always* add the libraries and frameworks from the root file system. Xcode will take care of referring the linkage and header inclusions to the proper SDK.

# Weak Linking

What does the gap between the deployment target and the SDK do? It makes the SDK's symbols known to the compiler and the linker, but makes the functions defined in the SDK, but not implemented in the low-end deployment OS, *weak linked*. Normally, when an SDK function is linked in, the linker fills in all uses of the function with the function's address. If the function isn't there, the linker (or dynamic loader) raises an error, and the application can't proceed.

Weak linking adds some forgiveness to the loading process. If the function doesn't exist, the loader doesn't fail; instead, it sets all pointers to the function to 0 (NULL). At runtime, your code can check for whether the weak-linked function exists (is non-NULL) before calling it. Otherwise, you can execute a workaround, as we did for counting DataPoints, or just do without.

Any function (or class) that is defined in the current SDK but isn't implemented in the minimum target OS will be weak linked. If you're running under that earlier OS, there's no harm in the symbol being present in your code, so long as you don't use it. You determine whether to use it by testing it against NULL:

```
if (DebugPrintTracedEvents != NULL) {
    DebugPrintTracedEvents();
}
else {
    // A workaround, if any...
}
Class aClass = NSClassFromString(@"NSAlert");
if (aClass != NULL) {
    // Okay to use class NSAlert
}
```

Weak linking is a slightly different issue from the method-implementation technique demonstrated in the preceding section. Whether an Objective-C object responds to a method selector is something that the object itself can determine. Weak-linked symbols must be examined directly to see whether they are NULL.

# NIB Compatibility

The Xcode IDE is not the only editor responsible for Linear. We spent nearly as much time in Interface Builder as we did in Xcode. It is as easy to accidentally introduce dependencies on 10.5 in a NIB as it is to do so in code. How do we track these down?

Interface Builder makes this easy. Open MyDocument.nib in Interface Builder, and find the **Info** button in the toolbar of the NIB window. Clicking it will present the NIB Info window; or select **Window > Document Info** (see Figure 17.1). This window provides some basic information about the NIB—the Xcode project it is associated with and the directory that encloses it, and the versions of the underlying software.

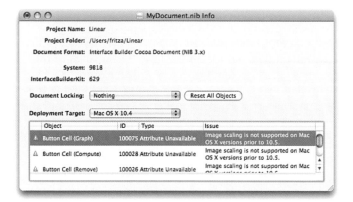

FIGURE 17.1    The NIB Info window in Interface Builder. The top section of the window identifies the Xcode project from which IB draws class information for NIB objects. Below that is a
pop-up button for protecting NIB contents from accidental alterations. The remainder of the
window displays the objects in the NIB that are incompatible with a given version of Mac OS X.

The next part of the NIB Info window allows you to "lock" the file against accidental
changes. When you edit a NIB for localization to another language, you want to change
things such as the size and text of human-interface elements, but not affect things such
as bindings and control actions that are part of the operation of the HI. The locking
options allow you to restrict locking to only the properties that are inherent, and
shouldn't be localized (or vice versa).

The Identity Inspector (⌘6, scroll to the bottom) for individual Interface Builder objects
permits you to lock just those objects. These locks override the NIB-wide setting. Locking
a view propagates the lock to its subviews, unless they override the lock themselves.
To clear all of these individual locks, click the **Reset All Objects** button in the NIB Info
window.

The rest of the window provides the compatibility information we're looking for. Select
the **Deployment Target**, the *lowest* version of Mac OS X your application will run on,
and the table at the bottom of the window will list every instance of incompatibilities
between the NIB and what that version can support.

Selecting **Mac OS X 10.4** from the **Deployment Target** pop-up fills the table with four
warnings, one for each of the buttons we put at the top of the document window. Each
says, "Image scaling is not supported in Mac OS X versions prior to 10.5." It seems when
you drag an NSButtton from the Library palette into a window, the imageScaling property of the button is set to **Proportionally Down**. But imageScaling is new with Leopard,
so if you're relying on that setting, the window won't comply with it on Tiger. This is
presented as a warning, rather than an error, because having the setting won't have any
adverse effect when you load the NIB in Tiger (other than that the setting is ignored).

Double-clicking an entry in the table displays, and selects, the object for which the
warning or error was reported.

We don't care about problems in button image scaling because we don't have images in our buttons. The warnings are easily cleared. Select all the problem buttons—**Add**, **Remove**, **Graph**, and **Compute**— and bring up the Attributes Inspector (⌘**1**). Find the **Scaling** pop-up and change it from **Proportionally Down** to **None**. The warnings instantly disappear from the NIB Info window.

Now, what if we want compatibility back to Mac OS X 10.3? Select that version from the **Deployment Target** pop-up. This yields a plethora of warnings and errors, almost all of them having to do with our use of Core Data, which isn't available before 10.4. Many of these are outright errors, such as "The binding "managedObjectContext" is not supported on Mac OS X versions prior to 10.4." Because of the errors, loading this NIB on 10.3 or earlier will fail.

> **NOTE**
>
> Cross-compilation for Mac OS X 10.2 isn't supported. The SDK is no longer supplied with the Xcode tools, and the 10.2.8 SDK from earlier versions of Xcode are not compatible with Xcode 3. You can still *target* 10.2 by setting the **Deployment Target**.

---

## NIB File Formats

Interface Builder 3.0 can store NIBs in one of three formats, which you can select in the save-file sheet from **File > Save As**:

- ▶ **Interface Builder 2.x**. The NIB will take the form of a package of three files: `classes.nib`, `info.nib`, and `keyedobjects.nib`. The last of these contains all the information Cocoa needs to reconstitute objects for use in an application. The other two files contain information about the class hierarchy and other settings that made it possible to edit the NIB in IB 2.0; removing them produces a NIB package that is usable, but not editable (unless you deselect "Flatten compiled XIB files" in your target's build settings). This form of NIB can be used on any version of Mac OS X, and edited by IB 2 or 3.

- ▶ **Interface Builder 3.x**. This is also a package, and is the format IB 3 uses for developing NIBs. It also contains `keyedobjects.nib` for the actual object archive, and `designable.nib` for information particular to presenting the NIB for editing. The NIB package is usable on any version of Mac OS X that supports the objects it contains, and it is editable only with IB 3.

- ▶ **XIB**. A XIB file is not usable in an application. Instead, it is an XML file that serves as source to a XIB-to-NIB compiler run when Xcode builds your application. The product is a flat (nonpackage) NIB file, equivalent to the `keyedobjects.nib` file in a package-style NIB. This flat NIB is usable on any version of Mac OS X that supports the objects you put in it. Because compilation ignores the editing information in the XIB, the NIB product is not editable in Interface Builder.

Apple's documentation refers to XIBs as "human readable," but don't treat them as human writable. They are subtle and quick to corruption. Interface Builder is the editor for XIB files,

17

and you can make indirect changes (such as for localization) through the `ibtool` command-line tool.

Putting XIB files under version control is problematic. They are XML files, but contain structures and binary data that might confuse the diff'ing tools SCM systems use. Merging XIBs changed by different developers may or may not work. Consider designating them as binary files in your SCM tool's configuration, and using your SCM system's locking facility to inhibit simultaneous editing. Unfortunately, Xcode's SCM support doesn't cover file locking.

# Universal Binaries

Intel processors were introduced to the Mac while Mac OS X 10.4 was the current operating system. At the time, under Xcode 2.1, producing software that ran on both PowerPC and Intel processors was a big deal, and required that the developer ask for it specifically.

Apple introduced the concept of a *universal binary*, a single file implementing the same software for more than one architecture, to address the problem of delivering applications for both processors in a single package. Apple's promotion of universal binaries encompassed only PowerPC and 32-bit Intel at first,

> **NOTE**
>
> The first architecture added to universal binaries was the 64-bit (G5) PowerPC. But the big push for building universal applications came with the introduction of Intel Macs.

but the scheme now encompasses 64-bit versions of those architectures, too; a single Mac OS X binary file may contain as many as four compiled versions.

Under Xcode 2.1, up to Xcode 3, PPC/Intel binaries were momentous in the development process. You had to ask for a universal build by checking both the PowerPC and Intel boxes in a target's Architectures setting. Today, the process is much simpler: The Debug configuration builds for whatever architecture Xcode is running on (using the `NATIVE_ARCH` build variable), and the Release configuration is set to 32-bit PowerPC and Intel. If you double-click the **Architectures** label in the Target Info's **Build** tab, the choices you are offered are not PPC and Intel, but 32 bit and 64 (see Figure 17.2).

Clicking in the setting itself allows you to type directly the architectures you want to support; see the **Valid Architectures** setting for the available choices. This is the only way to choose or exclude either PowerPC or Intel builds.

> **NOTE**
>
> If your 64-bit application links to anything but `libSystem` (the default library), it has to use the Mac OS X 10.5 SDK. No other libraries were 64-bit compatible before then. Your own libraries, too, must be built for 64 bits for your application to work.

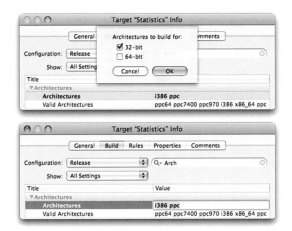

FIGURE 17.2    Choosing which processor architectures to build for. *(Top)* If you double-click the **Architectures** setting (except on the setting text) in the Target Info window, you will be offered a choice of 32- and 64-bit architectures, for both Intel and PowerPC. *(Bottom)* Clicking in the text of the setting (**i386 ppc**) allows you to edit the choices directly, so you can set any of the processor types listed in the **Valid Architectures** setting immediately below. There is a third option, **$(NATIVE_ARCH)**, which will select whatever architecture Xcode is currently running on.

Even though building for both Intel and PowerPC architectures is the default, it still amounts to cross-development. The PowerPC is "big-endian" (integers are stored in memory with the most-significant byte first), whereas Intel is "little-endian" (integers are stored with the least-significant byte first).

Additional points of peril include the following:

▶ Assembly

▶ Altivec (Velocity Engine) or MMX instructions

> **NOTE**
>
> Some developers have been tripped up by the Debug configuration's use of only the native architecture for its builds—they build (for instance) on Intel, send the result to a colleague with a PowerPC, and immediately hear that the application won't launch. Because Apple had so many complaints from bewildered developers, they chose for Xcode 3.0 to make Release the default configuration even for new projects at the first, debugging stage of development! The real solution is this: If you're going to release a product to someone, use the Release configuration.

▶ Binary numerics in a context that might be shared with other devices, such as a network, low-level file system structures, or Macintoshes of other architectures

▶ UTF-16 or UTF-32 encoding for Unicode text, without the use of a byte-order marker (BOM)

▶ Arrays of char in unions to examine the contents of other data types

▶ Bitfield struct or union members in cross-platform data

17

▶ bool, which is 32 bits in gcc on the PowerPC but 8 bits on Intel (and in CodeWarrior)

Writing code that relies on processor-specific features can be hard to avoid. Code that obviously uses one architecture or the other can easily be guarded with preprocessor symbols built in to gcc:

> **NOTE**
>
> Of course, you'd write such code in C, and switch to assembly only if actual measurement in Shark proved that code was a hot spot.

```
    // Built-in symbols begin and end with two underscores
#if __ppc__
    // Altivec or PPC assembly here
#end
#if __i386__
    // MMX/SSE2 or Pentium assembly here
#end
```

## Auditing Linear

When we examine Linear for Intel-porting issues, we find nothing much. There is no reliance on machine code or processor features. Linear does a lot of numeric computation internally, but internal use is not an issue. Similarly, passing numbers to and from the human interface is not an issue: Although reading and displaying numeric strings involve an external interface, it's to a string format, not a binary format. The Macintosh frameworks themselves are of the same endianness as the machine they run on, so they're of the same endianness as our numerics; no byte-swapping issue there.

What about our storage formats? If we include the early version of Linear that used NSCoding, we have three. Core Data saves properties as text for XML files, and byte-swaps the other formats as needed. The plist format has no byte-swapping issues because the numbers are translated into XML character data; it's not a binary format.

That leaves the reading and writing of .linear document files under NSCoding. We used NSKeyedArchiver and NSKeyedUnarchiver to reduce our data to the file format. Apple ensures that anything that passes through the Cocoa archivers is byte-order safe. An old-style .linear file written on any Mac would be readable on any other.

> **NOTE**
>
> Search in the Documentation window for the *Cross-Development Programming Guide* to learn all the subtleties of developing for more than one architecture.

## Testing

If you release software for the two major architectures, you have to test on both. If you develop on an Intel Mac, you can get a rough idea of how well an application handles

PowerPC by executing it under the Rosetta PowerPC emulator. This is most easily done through the **Project > Set Active Architecture** menu. Select **ppc** to debug your product under Rosetta.

This solution is not perfect. First, Rosetta isn't perfect; if your application uses Objective-C 2.0 garbage collection, for instance, it won't work under Rosetta, even on 10.5. To be really sure, copy your project folder to a PowerPC Mac (that's what server-based version control is for), and debug there.

# Building for Different Operating Systems on Different Processors

Compiling the same software for different architectures gave rise to this question: What if the requirements for the two architectures are different? Mac OS X 10.4 was relatively new when Intel Macs were introduced. The market demanded that developers make their applications compatible with 10.3—even though that OS supported only PowerPC—*and* with Intel processors—even though those processors had to run at least 10.4.

This makes it necessary to do the other kind of cross-compilation, using two different software development kits for simultaneous builds of the same software. Let's work through an example. Suppose we decide to package the Statistics framework for other developers, and want to make it compatible, for PowerPCs, back to Mac OS X 10.3.9. Xcode enables you to set different build settings in a target for each architecture you build.

But, you will say, the SDK for the whole Linear project was chosen in the **General** tab of the Project Info window. How can we set the SDK for just one target?

It turns out that the **Cross-Develop Using Target SDK** pop-up is a front for a build setting in the Project Info window—select the **Build** tab for the project and type **SDK** into the search field to see it. Any projectwide build setting can be overridden for a target by a corresponding setting in the Target Info window.

Close the Project Info window (if it's open), and double-click Statistics in the **Targets** group to open the Target Info window. Select the **Build** tab, and **All Configurations** from the **Configuration** pop-up. We want to add a variant on the **Base SDK Path** setting just for PowerPC.

> **NOTE**
>
> Didn't I just say that setting an earlier-than-current SDK is just a temporary measure to catch potential incompatibilities? In that case, it was. However, in the case of the Statistics framework, we don't just want 10.4 and 10.5 APIs to be weak linked; we don't want those APIs *at all*. The 10.3 SDK is what we really, finally want to compile and link against. Because we must use a later SDK for Intel builds (the libraries would be PPC only), we don't change the SDK on that side.

Find **Base SDK Path** and select it—it should reflect the project-set 10.5 SDK. Go to the Action menu (the button with a ✿ icon at the lower-left of the window), and select **Add Per-Architecture Setting For > PowerPC** (see Figure 17.3).

17

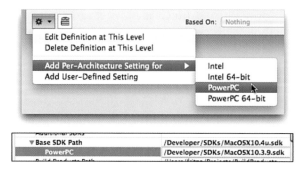

FIGURE 17.3    Adding and setting a processor-specific build setting. *(Top)* Do this by selecting the desired architecture from the **Add Per-Architecture Setting For** submenu of the Action (⚙) menu at the lower-left corner of a Target or Project Info window. *(Bottom)* The selected setting becomes a hierarchical item, with the general setting next to the label, and processor-specific values shown under a disclosure triangle. Click the value and edit it.

The **Base SDK Path** item acquires a disclosure triangle, and a setting for the added architecture is shown below. Edit the latter so that it reads $(DEVELOPER_ SDK_DIR)/MacOSX10.3.9.sdk.

Switch the active target to Statistics, and click **Build** (or **Build > Build**, or ⌘B). The build proceeds without errors, but if you're on an Intel machine, you'd expect that—Debug builds have been built for Intel all along, and that architecture still uses the 10.5 SDK. Switch the active build configuration to **Release** for the real test.

The Release configuration specifies multiple target architectures (32-bit Intel and PowerPC by default). If you watch the progress of the build, in brief in the status bars at the bottom of most windows, or in detail in the Build Results window (⇧⌘B), you'll see that the compiler runs twice as many times as under the Debug configuration. There is nothing magical about building universal binaries; compilation is a separate process for each architecture, and has to be repeated for each architecture on each file.

> **NOTE**
>
> Why $(DEVELOPER_SDK_DIR), when the setting is displayed as /Developer/SDKs/ MacOSX10.3.9.sdk (or something like it)? Remember that with Xcode 2.5/3, the location of Xcode and its supporting files can vary. The solution for this problem (and for possible future reorganizations of the developer-tools directory) is to provide build settings for paths to major components of the Xcode tools. DEVELOPER_SDK_DIR is among these. When you aren't editing such a setting, Xcode displays it with the variable expanded, so you can see whether the path makes sense.

> **NOTE**
>
> How did I know that MacOSX10.3.9.sdk was a proper name for an SDK? There's no way to do it from within Xcode. You have to examine /Developer/SDKs in the Finder to see what's installed.

Once again, the build is clean, except for this: "Warning: Deployment target 10.5 for architecture 'ppc' and variant 'normal' is greater than the maximum value for the Mac OS X 10.3.9 SDK." Remember the rule: The SDK specifies the *maximum* features your code *uses*, and the deployment target specifies the *minimum* operating system your code *needs*. We didn't change the target architecture for the Statistics framework, and the two values got crossed. This is all the enforcement you'll see of that requirement.

Open the **Build** tab of the Target Info window for Statistics, find **Mac OS X Deployment Target**, and set it to **Mac OS X 10.3**. Better yet (indeed, the correct way), add a per-architecture setting to **Mac OS X Deployment Target** for PowerPC, and set *that* to **Mac OS X 10.3**. Now the Statistics build comes through without errors or warnings. If you switch the active target to Linear, it too builds cleanly.

Being a careful developer, you will of course test the Statistics package on 10.3.

# Project Compatibility

It's not strictly a cross-development issue, but Xcode 3 accommodates the need to share projects among developers using different versions of Xcode.

Xcode 3 project files can be used with Xcode 2.4.1, the last release exclusively for Mac OS X 10.4, and Xcode 2.5; just set the **Project Format** in the **General** tab of the Project Info window to **Xcode 2.4-Compatible**. This will constrain the features you can use with the project in Xcode 3; Xcode will display a warning flag in the Project Info window if switching the compatibility version causes compatibility problems. Click **Show Conflicts** for the details. In the case of Linear, you can't use per-architecture build settings.

Changing the project format pop-up won't make any changes to your project. The only immediate effect is to display compatibility warnings.

If you open a 2.4/2.5 project in Xcode 3, it will remain 2.4 compatible. Of course, setting 2.4 compatibility won't make Xcode 3 features available in the earlier versions, and the 10.5 SDK can't be used on Mac OS X 10.4. You can't build Leopard applications on Tiger.

# Summary

In this chapter, we've seen how to change the fundamental development environment for an Xcode project to ensure that its products will be compatible with a particular version of Mac OS X. We looked at how combining an early deployment-target build setting with a current software development kit allows you to make applications that take advantage of Mac OS X features as they may be available on the target machines.

We also examined how to prepare an application designed on any Macintosh for distribution as a universal binary, runnable on both Intel and PowerPC processors. We covered a brief checklist for auditing your applications, especially for byte-order problems, which are the most common source of incompatibility. We went through the steps in building a universal version of Linear and experimented with techniques for mixing a 10.5 Intel release with a PowerPC binary designed for earlier versions of Mac OS X.

# CHAPTER 18

# Spotlight (or, How to Build a Plug-in)

**IN THIS CHAPTER**

▶ Creating an OS Plug-In Project

▶ Setting Uniform Type Identifiers

▶ Building a Plug-In into an Application

Before our excursion into Core Data, there was not much worth sharing about Linear's data files. You may remember that when we laid out the data file type, I skipped the uniform type indicator (UTI) declaration, because it wasn't worth complicating Linear as example code.

The expansion of Linear's data files to encompass data sources has changed this. Think only of the query "every file sourced from the Economic Report of the President," and you can see that Linear data files are now a natural for indexing in the Spotlight metadata system.

## How Data Gets into Spotlight

Metadata is information that isn't necessarily *in* a file but is *about* the file. All file systems maintain modest amounts of metadata, such as file ownership, creation and modification dates, access privileges, and the like. With Mac OS X 10.4, Apple added to the Macintosh file system a metadata database that can hold large amounts of almost arbitrary metadata in any category a developer chooses.

The `mdls` command-line tool shows what metadata is associated with any file or package. Here is what came back when I typed `mdls Final\Outline.oo3/` to examine the OmniOutliner 3 file package that contains my initial notes for this book:

```
com_omnigroup_OmniOutliner_CellCount         = 0
com_omnigroup_OmniOutliner_CheckedItemCount  = 20
com_omnigroup_OmniOutliner_ColumnCount       = 2
```

```
com_omnigroup_OmniOutliner_ColumnTitles          = (
    Topic
)
com_omnigroup_OmniOutliner_IndeterminateItemCount = 2
com_omnigroup_OmniOutliner_ItemCount             = 346
com_omnigroup_OmniOutliner_MaxItemDepth          = 5
com_omnigroup_OmniOutliner_NamedStyleCount       = 3
com_omnigroup_OmniOutliner_NamedStyles           = (
    Highlight,
    Citation,
    Emphasis
)
com_omnigroup_OmniOutliner_UncheckedItemCount    = 324
kMDItemAlternateNames                            = (
    "Final Outline.oo3"
)
kMDItemContentCreationDate       = 2007-10-25 18:29:36 -0500
kMDItemContentModificationDate   = 2007-12-18 20:24:43 -0600
kMDItemContentType     = "com.omnigroup.omnioutliner.oo3-package"
kMDItemContentTypeTree                           = (
    "com.omnigroup.omnioutliner.oo3-package",
    "public.composite-content",
    "public.content",
    "com.apple.package",
    "public.directory",
    "public.item"
)
kMDItemDisplayName                       = "Final Outline"
kMDItemFSContentChangeDate       = 2007-12-18 20:24:43 -0600
kMDItemFSCreationDate            = 2007-10-25 18:29:36 -0500
kMDItemFSCreatorCode                       = ""
kMDItemFSFinderFlags                       = 16
kMDItemFSHasCustomIcon                     = 0
kMDItemFSInvisible                         = 0
kMDItemFSIsExtensionHidden                 = 1
kMDItemFSIsStationery                      = 0
kMDItemFSLabel                             = 0
kMDItemFSName                        = "Final Outline.oo3"
kMDItemFSNodeCount                         = 1
kMDItemFSOwnerGroupID                      = 501
kMDItemFSOwnerUserID                       = 501
kMDItemFSSize                          = (null)
kMDItemFSTypeCode                          = ""
kMDItemKind                          = "OmniOutliner 3"
```

```
kMDItemLastUsedDate                          = 2007-12-18 20:24:45 -0600
kMDItemTitle                                 = " "
kMDItemUsedDates                             = (
    2007-12-18 00:00:00 -0600
)
```

The metadata listing is a roster of tag/value pairs. We can recognize many of these, such as kMDItemFSCreationDate, as carryovers of common file system metadata. The operating system will keep this information current itself. More interesting are the tags that begin with com_omnigroup_OmniOutliner_, at the beginning of the listing. From these, we can see that it's an outline with 346 items: 20 checked, 324 unchecked, 2 indeterminate. There are two columns, and the outline goes as much as five levels deep. You could get this information by opening the file and doing the counts yourself, but with the metadata and its keys published from OmniOutliner 3, any application, such as the Finder's Get Info window (see Figure 18.1), can say something useful about an OmniOutliner file without having to open the file and understand its format.

The final thing to attend to in the metadata listing are the tags kMDItemContentType and kMDItemContentTypeTree. The content type identifies the UTI associated with this document. In this case, the identifier is in reverse domain name style— com.omnigroup.omnioutliner.oo3-package—for a private document type. The type tree identifies other, published UTIs that also describe OO3 outline documents:

▶ public.item, because anything is an item; the root UTI

▶ public.directory and com.apple.package, because it's not a single file but a directory and is handled by the Mac OS X Finder as a single-document package

▶ public.content, because the document contains its information rather than refers to it or serves as a flag

▶ public.composite-content, because an outline document may mix text, images, and media

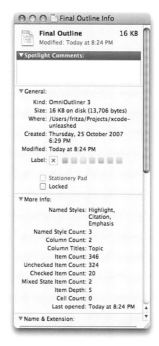

FIGURE 18.1    The Finder's Get Info window for an OmniOutliner 3 document. Because the Omni Group has provided a Spotlight plug-in for OO3 files and published the meanings of its custom metadata tags, applications like the Finder can show useful information about the content of OO3 files without having to understand the file format.

This is live, actionable information for you. If you have the suffix oo3, you can obtain the UTI associated with that suffix and determine that it's a package document type:

```
CFStringRef    uti;
uti = UTTypeCreatePreferredIdentifierForTag(
                            kUTTagClassFilenameExtension,
                            CFSTR("oo3"), NULL);


Boolean        isPackage;
isPackage = UTTypeConformsTo(uti, CFSTR("com.apple.package"));
```

The UTI is the key by which Spotlight selects the plug-in for a file. A Spotlight importer is a piece of code that understands how to extract metadata from a particular type of file and enter it into the Spotlight database. The task of making a Spotlight-friendly application, then, consists of properly setting up UTIs for the application's documents and providing an importer for the metadata.

## Uniform Type Identifiers

Obtaining a UTI for Linear data files is easy—we make it up: `org.manoverboard.linear.regression` for regression data from Linear. UTIs must not contain uppercase letters.

Add the UTI to the document type declaration in the `Info.plist`. This is most easily done by opening the Target Info window—double-click the Linear icon under Targets— and selecting the **Properties** tab. `Linear Data File` should be the only entry in the document type list. Type **org.manoverboard.linear.regression** into the second column, for the UTI.

This takes care of associating the UTI with Linear data files, but does not fully declare the UTI to the system. To do this, you must edit the text of Linear's `Info.plist` file directly. At the bottom of the Target Info window, click the button **Open Info.plist as File**. Add an array to the `Info.plist` with the key `UTExportedTypeDeclarations`:

```
<?xml version="1.0" encoding="UTF-8"?>
<!DOCTYPE plist PUBLIC "-//Apple//DTD PLIST 1.0//EN"
          "http://www.apple.com/DTDs/PropertyList-1.0.dtd">
<plist version="1.0">
<dict>
.
. previously existing content
.
    <key>UTExportedTypeDeclarations</key>
    <array>
        <dict>
            <key>UTTypeIdentifier</key>
            <string>org.manoverboard.linear.regression</string>
            <key>UTTypeReferenceURL</key>
```

```
            <string>http://www.manoverboard.org/</string>
            <key>UTTypeDescription</key>
            <string>Linear Data File/</string>
            <key>UTTypeConformsTo</key>
            <array>
                <string>public.data</string>
                <string>public.content</string>
                <string>public.item</string>
            </array>
            <key>UTTypeTagSpecification</key>
        </dict>
                <key>com.apple.ostype</key>
                <string>linD</string>
                <key>public.filename-extension</key>
                <array>
                    <string>linear</string>
                </array>
            </dict>
        </dict>
    </array>
</dict>
</plist>
```

The `UTExportedTypeDeclarations` array contains one dictionary for each type declared. Here, we declare only one, `org.manoverboard.linear.regression`. We give a URL for further information about the type and resolve to provide such information some day. The `UTTypeDescription` is a human-readable name for the type. For type conformance, we search in the Documentation window for the title "Uniform Type Identifiers Overview," and look at the system-declared UTIs; the header `UTCoreTypes.h` also contains essential details.

A `.linear` file is necessarily a `public.item` and definitely a `public.content`; it's not clear whether a Core Data store qualifies as the "simple" byte stream envisioned for `public.data`, but we'll take it for contrast to packaged documents.

The `UTTypeTagSpecification` dictionary tells the system how to identify a file as an `org.manoverboard.linear.regression`. We provide the old-style Mac OS creator code `linD` and the `linear` suffix.

> **NOTE**
>
> In fact, we could do more. We're using the XML format for Core Data storage, making the file eligible for classification as `public.text` and `public.xml`. If those types were listed and no importer for `org.manoverboard.linear.regression` were available, Spotlight would run an XML or text importer whenever a Linear data file is saved. (Spotlight runs only one importer—the one for the most specific type—for each file.) This time through, we'll reserve our option to change the format by not publishing the fact that we're currently using XML.

**18**

With this much done, build `Linear`, and if you have not done so already, run it so that you can save a Linear data file. Switch over to the Terminal application, point it at the directory in which you saved the data file, and tell the Spotlight importer to analyze that file, with the debugging level set to 1:

```
$ cd ~
$ mdimport -d1 savedFile.linear
2007-12-18 21:03:16.896 mdimport[17597:10b] Imported
    '/Users/xcodeuser/savedFile.linear' of type
    'org.manoverboard.linear.regression' with no plug-in.
$
```

The response from `mdimport` should show that the saved file was correctly identified as being of the type `org.manoverboard.linear.regression` but that no Spotlight plug-in was defined for the type. That means the `UTExportedTypeDeclarations` we added to `Info.plist` was seen and incorporated into the type system. If instead it tells you that the type was a long hashed string beginning with `dyn.`, the `regression` UTI is not yet known, and the system generated a "dynamic" UTI for the nonce. Recheck your `Info.plist` file. Make sure that it parses (use `plutil`) and includes everything we covered.

# The Spotlight Plug-In

Xcode provides a project template for Spotlight plug-ins that takes care of a world of detail you do not want to deal with. As a Core Foundation plug-in, it must supply a universally unique identification (UUID) string identifying the metadata plug-in API with which it complies. It must supply, in three places, a second UUID to uniquely identify itself. It must do certain setup and teardown chores and take care of reference counting from its host application. All this is necessary, but none of it has anything directly to do with passing metadata from a file to Spotlight. The template generates files that do all the housekeeping automatically. Use the template.

Using the template, however, commits us to putting the plug-in in its own project. We might prefer to have the plug-in share its project with the main application, but there is no target template for Spotlight plug-ins. Further, we find that if we try to put the plug-in project in the same directory as Linear, Xcode offers to overwrite various of the main application's files. We'll have to give the plug-in its own directory.

## The MetaLinear Project

Let's do it. Create a new project, choosing the template **Standard Apple Plug-Ins > Spotlight Plug-In**. Name the project **MetaLinear**, and put it in a directory of its own. To make SCM easier, put that directory inside the Linear project directory—if the Linear directory is in your home folder, the **Project Directory** field should read `~Linear/MetaLinear/`.

With the `MetaLinear` directory in place, and populated, it is time to get it under version control. Xcode's SCM support does not extend to operations on directories, such as the project-file package, the `English.lproj` directory for localized resources, or indeed the `MetaLinear` directory itself. If you want to add a directory to a working copy, you must do it from the command line:

```
$ cd ~/Linear/
$ # What is the Subversion status of the Linear directory?
$ svn status
?       MetaLinear
$ # ... plus other uncontrolled, modified, or added files.
$ # MetaLinear is not known to Subversion. Add it:
$ svn add MetaLinear/
A           MetaLinear
A           MetaLinear/English.lproj
A (bin)     MetaLinear/English.lproj/InfoPlist.strings
A (bin)     MetaLinear/English.lproj/schema.strings
A           MetaLinear/GetMetadataForFile.c
A           MetaLinear/Info.plist
A           MetaLinear/main.c
A           MetaLinear/MetaLinear.xcodeproj
A (bin)     MetaLinear/MetaLinear.xcodeproj/project.pbxproj
A           MetaLinear/schema.xml
$
```

Return to the MetaLinear project in Xcode, and take the usual steps to make the project aware of SCM:

1. In the **General** tab of the Project Info window, set **SCM Repository** to the Linear repository.

2. Control- (right-) click in the header of the Groups & Files list and select **SCM** to display SCM status.

3. Select **SCM > Refresh Entire Project** to update the display of the version-control flags. For all the files in the project, these should be A, showing they've been marked for addition to the Subversion repository, but not yet checked in.

4. Use **SCM > Commit Entire Project...**, and supply an appropriate comment, to secure the new files in the repository.

## MetaLinear Project Files

The project comes populated with all the files it will ever need:

▶ `Info.plist` and `InfoPlist.strings` are old friends.

▶ `schema.xml` describes any metadata keys, beyond the Apple-defined ones, that we define for our documents.

- ▸ schema.strings provides plain-text equivalents for the custom metadata keys, for presentation to the user.

- ▸ GetMetadataForFile.c contains the single function we will write to transfer the metadata to Spotlight.

- ▸ main.c takes care of all the housekeeping details for the plug-in.

### Info.plist

If you haven't written your UTExportedTypeDeclarations UTI in Linear's Info.plist already, the plug-in's Info.plist provides a commented-out form for one, with a comment recommending that you put the declaration in your application's Info.plist. If we were building a standalone Spotlight plug-in, we'd duplicate the UTExportedTypeDeclarations here; but MetaLinear will ship only in the Linear application, so it isn't necessary.

Under CFBundleDocumentTypes, we see a placeholder, SUPPORTED_UTI_TYPE, for our **UTI**, org.manoverboard.linear. regression; make that substitution. For the CFBundleIdentifier, replace the com.apple placeholder with something that distinguishes this bundle from all others, even from the application bundle; I used org.manoverboard. linear.importer. The rest you can leave alone.

> **NOTE**
>
> You'll see ${EXECUTABLE_NAME} and ${PRODUCT_NAME} placeholders in Info.plist, too. When MetaLinear is built, Xcode will substitute the actual values of these build variables. Using the build variables ensures these critical values will be set properly even if you change them.

### schema.xml

We are supposed to declare custom metadata keys, if any, in schema.xml, which gives rise to this question: What metadata are we going to export? Values for *x* and *y* in data tables are numerous and usually undistinctive, making them a poor choice for identifying documents. Characteristics of data sources are a better bet. Let's settle on the authors of the sources, the titles of the sources, and the number of sources.

> **NOTE**
>
> The Spotlight Plug-in template supplied with Xcode 3.0 assigns the file type text.plist to the Info.plist file. This type refers to NeXT-style property lists, so syntax coloring and the Code Focus ribbon won't show up correctly. Select Info.plist in the Groups & Files list and **File > Get Info** (⌘I). In the **General** tab, set **File Type** to text.plist.xml.

Wherever possible, we should use existing metadata keys. Proliferating keys would overwhelm users with a huge list of search categories, and would make search terms so restrictive they'd be useless except for finding Linear documents. So we search for the title "Spotlight Metadata Attributes Reference" in the Documentation window, and look for the closest match to what we want to publish.

For the authors of data sources, kMDItemAuthors would be a poor choice, because that plainly is meant for authorship of the file itself. kMDItemContributors, for "entities responsible for making contributions to the content," looks to be closest. For source titles, kMDItemWhereFroms is a stretch, but fits.

There is nothing close to a count-of-sources attribute. For this, we'll have to define a custom key, which by convention uses reverse-domain name formatting for uniqueness: org_manoverboard_Linear_SourceCount. Dots are not acceptable in metadata keys; use underscores for separators. Now that we know what we want, we can turn to schema.xml. We need only declare our unique key; the standard metadata keys will take care of themselves.

The schema.xml provided by the project template includes helpful instructions in the form of XML comments, which you should eventually delete. We must declare our custom key three times:

1. Take the <attributes> section out of the comment. The <attribute> tag declares a new attribute key to the system. For the com_Foo_YourAttrName name placeholder, substitute org_manoverboard_Linear_SourceCount.

2. Change the multivalued attribute to "false"—our key identifies a single value, not an array of them.

3. type="CFNumber" is what we need; our key identifies an integer value.

4. In <types>, for the one UTI MetaLinear will handle, change the name attribute to org. manoverboard.linear.regression.

> **NOTE**
>
> The allowed types for <attribute>s are CFString, CFNumber, CFBoolean, CFDate, and CFArray.

5. In the <allattrs> group, declare org_manoverboard_Linear_ SourceCount as among "all of the attributes [a Linear file] normally has."

6. In <displayattrs>, declare that org_manoverboard_Linear_SourceCount, kMDItemContributors, and kMDItemWhereFroms are to be displayed in Finder Get Info windows.

The final schema.xml file should look like this (the <schema> tag is truncated for space):

```
<?xml version="1.0" encoding="UTF-8"?>

<schema version="1.0" ...>
    <attributes>
        <attribute name="org_manoverboard_Linear_SourceCount"
                            multivalued="false" type="CFNumber"/>
    </attributes>
```

```
<types>
    <type name="org.manoverboard.linear.regression">
        <allattrs>
            kMDItemContributors
            kMDItemWhereFroms
            org_manoverboard_Linear_SourceCount
        </allattrs>
        <displayattrs>
            org_manoverboard_Linear_SourceCount
        </displayattrs>
    </type>
</types>
</schema>
```

When you have edited the `schema.xml` file and saved it, open the Terminal application, set the working directory to the MetaLinear project directory, and test the schema with the mdcheckschema command:

```
$ cd ~/Linear/Metalinear
$ mdcheckschema schema.xml
schema.xml : successfully parsed.
$
```

**schema.strings**

The `schema.strings` file governs how a custom metadata key is presented in the human interface—in the label in the Get Info window or the explanation in the list of searchable attributes. For each custom key, the short name is assigned in the form *key* = "short name";. The brief documentation is assigned in the form *key*.Description = "brief documentation";.

`schema.strings`, rewrapped to fit this page, should be:

```
org_manoverboard_Linear_SourceCount = "Source count";
org_manoverboard_Linear_SourceCount.Description =
        "How many sources are cited in the document";
```

**GetMetadataForFile.c**

There remains nothing to write but the plug-in itself. The project template provides us with this shell of the import function (wrapped):

```
Boolean GetMetadataForFile(void* thisInterface,
            CFMutableDictionaryRef attributes,
            CFStringRef contentTypeUTI,
            CFStringRef pathToFile)
{
```

```
/* Pull any available metadata from the file at the specified path */
/* Return the attribute keys and attribute values in the dict */
/* Return TRUE if successful, FALSE if there was no data provided */

#warning To complete your importer please implement the function
    GetMetadataForFile in GetMetadataForFile.c
return FALSE;
}
```

We will be summarizing a Core Data–generated file and adding the summary to the `attributes` dictionary passed into the function. To do this with Core Data, we have to add the Cocoa framework to the project, add our object model, and initialize an `NSManagedObjectModel` with that. From there, we must get an `NSPersistentStoreCoordinator`, create an `NSManagedObjectContext`, and point it at the `NSPersistentStoreCoordinator`.

This is beginning to look a little heavyweight. Spotlight plug-ins are not supposed to be heavyweight; they are run in the background, in stolen cycles. They are supposed to be quick and undemanding of memory. Initializing the whole Core Data stack for two short string lists and a number seems like overkill.

Anticipating just this quandary, Apple has provided API for Core Data applications to embed metadata in Core Data files. The originating application, which has the Core Data stack open anyway, does the extraction, and all the plug-in has to do is pick up the metadata and pass it on.

> **WARNING**
>
> At least as of Xcode 3.0 The Spotlight Plug-in project template does not copy `schema.xml` and `schema.strings` into the plug-in's Resources directory. If you let this stand, your custom attribute will not appear anywhere in the Spotlight system, and the "Contributors" attribute will not be displayed for Linear's data files. Fix this by dragging these files, in the Groups & Files list, into the Copy Bundle Resources build phase of the MetaLinear target.

So, we need Core Data and Objective-C, but not as much of them. Add the Cocoa framework to the project (**Project > Add to Project**, and find `Cocoa.framework` in `/System/Library/Frameworks`, *not* in an SDK). To switch the plug-in source file to Objective-C, Option-click **GetMetadataForFile.c** in the Groups & Files list (making the name editable) and change its suffix from `c` to `m`.

As soon as you press **Return** to finalize the name change, Xcode presents a sheet warning that the file is under SCM, and that if you rename it, Xcode will automatically rename it in the repository. This is exactly what we want to happen, so accept the renaming.

If you look at the Subversion status of the MetaLinear directory, from the command line, you'll see the following:

18

```
$ cd ~/Linear/MetaLinear
$ svn st
A +    GetMetadataForFile.m
D      GetMetadataForFile.c
M      MetaLinear.xcodeproj/project.pbxproj
$
```

This reflects the correct renaming of a file in the working copy: Under Subversion, formally, the original file is deleted (D); the same file, under the new name, is added (A), but carries over the revision history of the original (+). And, of course, the project file changed (M) when one of its source files was renamed. The equivalent Subversion command would have been svn rename GetMetadataForFile.c GetMetadataForFile.m.

The finished GetMetadataForFile.m becomes

```
#include <CoreFoundation/CoreFoundation.h>
#include <CoreServices/CoreServices.h>
#import <Cocoa/Cocoa.h>

Boolean GetMetadataForFile(void* thisInterface,
                           CFMutableDictionaryRef attributes,
                           CFStringRef contentTypeUTI,
                           CFStringRef pathToFile)
{
    // Turn the path into a URL
    NSURL * url = [NSURL fileURLWithPath:
                                 (NSString *) pathToFile];
    // Get the prepared metadata from the file
    NSDictionary * metadata = [NSPersistentStoreCoordinator
                        metadataForPersistentStoreWithURL: url
                                                    error: NULL];
    if (metadata) {
      // If there was metadata, add it to the set Spotlight gave us.
      [(NSMutableDictionary *) attributes
                        addEntriesFromDictionary: metadata];
        return YES;
    }
    else
        return NO;
}
```

The plug-in is now complete. Build it to make sure that everything is correct. If we were shipping the plug-in as a standalone product, we'd now install it in /Library/Spotlight, and we'd also uncomment the UTI declaration in its Info.plist. With an importer for the Linear data file UTI in the well-known place, even users without Linear would be able to search for Linear documents by source and see in Finder Info windows the number and titles of the sources (see Figure 18.2).

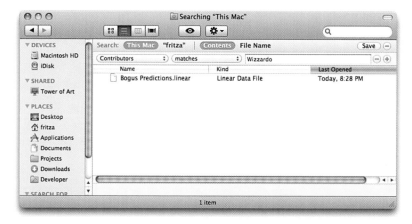

FIGURE 18.2    A Finder search window, showing a search for documents having "Wizzardo" in their **Contributors** property.

## Packaging the Plug-In

Our plug-in is not to be a standalone product; it will be packaged as part of the Linear application. We should modify the build process for the application to make sure that the plug-in is included in the proper place.

Add the MetaLinear project to the Linear project. There is no need to add it to any target; we just need to be able to refer to it and its product, the plug-in, in the next couple of steps.

The plug-in is part of the Linear product: Importers are typically delivered inside application packages in the Contents/Library/Spotlight directory. The plug-in, therefore, should be a dependency of Linear. This can work only if the two projects share a build directory. In the Groups & Files list of the MetaLinear project, double-click the top project directory; in the **General** panel, select **Place Build Products In: Custom Location**, and click the **Choose…** button. Navigate to Linear's build directory, and select it.

> **NOTE**
>
> If you chose a customized location for build products when you first ran Xcode, or set one up in the Building pane of the Preferences window, there is no need to match the build locations in Project Info windows; they're already matched.

A Copy Files build phase completes the packaging. With the Linear application the selected target, select **Project > New Build Phase > New Copy Files Build Phase**. For the new build phase, set the destination path to Contents/Library/Spotlight in the **Wrapper** destination. The build phase knows *where* to copy; now to tell it *what*. Find the plug-in project in the Linear project's Groups & Files list, and open the disclosure triangle next to it to make MetaLinear.mdimporter visible. Drag the plug-in icon to the new Copy Files build phase.

## Checking Our Work

We don't yet have a .linear data file ready for importing, but at this point, we can see whether the metadata system can find and identify the MetaLinear plug-in. This will be a good check on our work. You can get a listing of all the plug-ins Spotlight knows about by passing the -L flag to the mdimport tool:

```
$ mdimport -L
2008-01-03 17:04:37.430 mdimport[6863:10b] Paths: id(501) (
    "/System/Library/Spotlight/Audio.mdimporter",
    "/System/Library/Spotlight/Chat.mdimporter" ,




    "/Users/xcodeuser/Projects/BuildProducts/Debug/Linear.app/
            Contents/Library/Spotlight/MetaLinear.mdimporter",




    "/System/Library/Spotlight/iPhoto.mdimporter",
    "/System/Library/Spotlight/SystemPrefs.mdimporter",
)
$
```

(The output is wrapped to fit this page.)

We find MetaLinear.mdimporter, nestled in the contents of the Linear application, among the other plug-ins registered with Spotlight. If MetaLinear does not show up for you, first try running Linear. If that does not fix it, verify that the schema.xml and Info.plist files are correct. Also, be certain that MetaLinear installs at Contents/Library/Spotlight in the Linear.app bundle; it's easy to treat it as a simple resource and load it into Contents/Resources instead.

# Core Data and Metadata

Core Data's ability to attach metadata to a file in an easily accessed packet made the writing of the plug-in very simple but shifted the responsibility for generating the metadata to Linear itself. The code shown here for attaching metadata to a Core Data persistent-store file is derived from the code provided in Apple's tutorial on NSPersistentDocuments.

In the life of an NSPersistentDocument, there are two moments at which metadata should be patched: when the persistent store—the file—is created, and when the persistent store is saved. The bottlenecks are at the end of configurePersistentStoreCoordinatorForURL: ofType:error: and at the beginning of writeToURL:ofType:forSaveOperation: originalContentsURL:error:. In the first case, Apple seems to recommend checking the persistent store to see whether one's metadata has already been added. It isn't clear why this is so, but the code here follows suit.

Both cases lead to our own method, setMetaDataForStoreAtURL:, which searches the doument's Core Data store and uses the NSPersistentStoreCoordinator method setMetaData:forPersistentStore: to pack the metadata away in the file:

```objc
#pragma mark Metadata
- (NSArray *) fetchUniqueColumn: (NSString *) columnName
                       ofEntity: (NSString *) entityName
{
    // Given a named property for a named entity, return an
    // array of the unique values for that property among all
    // instances of the entity in this document.
    // Get all instances of the entity.
    NSManagedObjectContext * moc = [self managedObjectContext];
    NSFetchRequest *         fetch = [[NSFetchRequest alloc] init];
    [fetch setEntity: [NSEntityDescription entityForName: entityName
                                  inManagedObjectContext: moc]];
    NSError *        anError;
    NSArray *        objects = [moc executeFetchRequest: fetch
                                                  error: &anError];
    [fetch release];
    // Return nil if there are none; otherwise pick out the values.
    if (objects) {
        // Extract the values for the column name
        NSArray *    values = [objects valueForKey: columnName];
        // Put them into a set, to ensure the values are unique
        NSSet *        valueSet = [NSSet setWithArray: values];
        // Convert the set back into an array
        NSArray *    valueArray = [valueSet allObjects];
        return valueArray;
    }
    else
        return nil;
}


- (BOOL) setMetadataForStoreAtURL: (NSURL *) aUrl
{
    // New to MyDocument.
    // Upon writing or creating a Linear document, compile the
    // document's metadata and add it to the store.
```

```objc
    NSManagedObjectContext *         moc =
                                     [self managedObjectContext];
    NSPersistentStoreCoordinator *  psc =
                                     [moc persistentStoreCoordinator];
    id                               store =
                                     [psc persistentStoreForURL: aUrl];
    if (store) {
        // Start with existing metadata.
        NSMutableDictionary *    metadata =
            [[psc metadataForPersistentStore: store] mutableCopy];
        // Get author list and save as contributors.
        NSArray *                dataList;
        dataList = [self fetchUniqueColumn: @"author"
                                 ofEntity: @"DataSource"];
        if (dataList)
            [metadata setObject: dataList
                        forKey: (NSString *) kMDItemContributors];
        // Get title list and save as where-froms.
        dataList = [self fetchUniqueColumn: @"title"
                                 ofEntity: @"DataSource"];
        if (dataList)
            [metadata setObject: dataList
                        forKey: (NSString *) kMDItemWhereFroms];
        // Set Linear as the creator of the document.
        [metadata setObject: @"Linear"
                    forKey: (NSString *) kMDItemCreator];
        // Count the titles and save as source count.
        [metadata setObject: [NSNumber numberWithInt:
                                      [dataList count]]
                    forKey:
                        @"org_manoverboard_Linear_SourceCount"];
        // Set the file's metadata to the updated dictionary.
        [psc setMetadata: metadata forPersistentStore: store];
        return YES;
    }
    return NO;
}


- (BOOL) configurePersistentStoreCoordinatorForURL: (NSURL *) aURL
                                     ofType: (NSString *) aType
                                     error: (NSError **) anError
{
    // Override of an NSPersistentDocument method.
    // New persistent store. First do default setup.
    BOOL    retval =
    [super configurePersistentStoreCoordinatorForURL: aURL
```

```
                                        ofType: aType
                                         error: anError];
       if (retval) {
           // Verify that our metadata (e.g. source count) is not
           // already present, and then add our data to store.
           NSManagedObjectContext *        moc =
                                        [self managedObjectContext];
           NSPersistentStoreCoordinator *  psc =
                               [moc persistentStoreCoordinator];
           id              store = [psc persistentStoreForURL: aURL];
           NSDictionary * prevMetadata =
                          [psc metadataForPersistentStore: store];
           if (! [prevMetadata valueForKey:
                          @"org_manoverboard_Linear_SourceCount"])
               retval = [self setMetadataForStoreAtURL: aURL];
       }
       return retval;
    }


    - (BOOL) writeToURL: (NSURL *) destURL
                ofType: (NSString *) fileType
       forSaveOperation: (NSSaveOperationType) saveOperation
    originalContentsURL: (NSURL *) originalURL
                  error: (NSError **) anError
    {
        // Override of an NSPersistentDocument method.
        // Existing persistent store. Update the store's metadata.
        if ([self fileURL])
            [self setMetadataForStoreAtURL: [self fileURL]];

        // Continue with the default behavior.
        return [super writeToURL: destURL
                          ofType: fileType
                 forSaveOperation: saveOperation
              originalContentsURL: originalURL
                           error: anError];
    }
```

# The Proof of the Pudding

We already know that Spotlight can find the MetaLinear plug-in. The next step is to run
Linear, with its new metadata-exporting code. At the very least, you should put breakpoints at the two bottleneck methods to assure yourself that you understand what they
are doing and that the correct values are being added to the metadata dictionary. You
should also generate a file or two to be entered in the Spotlight database.

It's trickier to watch the import in progress. Metadata importing is in the hands of a
system daemon, running in the background on its own schedule. What you can do is use
the mdimport tool to force an application of the indexing mechanism to a file. The -d flag
governs how much debugging output the tool produces. Point your Terminal application
session at the directory in which you saved the metadata-enabled files, and run mdimport
(results wrapped and truncated for space):

```
$ cd
$ mdimport -d 2 Bogus Projections.linear
(Info) Import: Import '/Users/fritza/Bogus Projections.linear'
    type 'org.manoverboard.linear.regression' using
        '/Users/fritza/Projects/BuildProducts/Debug/Linear.app/
            Contents/Library/Spotlight/MetaLinear.mdimporter'
2008-01-03 19:20:36.213 mdimport[7261:10b]
    Imported '/Users/fritza/Bogus Projections.linear'
    of type ' org.manoverboard.linear.regression'
    with plug-in/Users/fritza/Projects/BuildProducts/Debug/inear.app/
                Contents/Library/Spotlight/MetaLinear.mdimporter.
2008-01-03 19:20:36.216 mdimport[7261:10b] Attributes:
    NSPersistenceFrameworkVersion = 0;

.
. various other metadata
.

    kMDItemContentType = "org.manoverboard.linear.regression";
    kMDItemContentTypeTree =   (
        "org.manoverboard.linear.regression",
        "public.data",
        "public.item",
        "public.content"
    );
    kMDItemContributors =   (
        "The Great Wizzardo",
        "OMB [Bush 43]"
    );
    kMDItemCreator = Linear;
    kMDItemDisplayName =
        "" = "Bogus Projections.linear";
    ;
    kMDItemKind =
        "" = "Linear Data File";
    ;
    kMDItemWhereFroms =   (
        Predictions,
        "Economic Report of the President"
```

```
    );
    "org_manoverboard_Linear_SourceCount" = 2;
$
```

At debug level 2, we learn the following.

▶ The system identifies `Bogus_Projections.linear` with the UTI
   `org.manoverboard.linear.regression`, as we intend. This comes from `Linear`'s
   `Info.plist`.

▶ Before the plug-in is run, the file starts with a handful of attributes, derived from
   the file and type systems.

▶ The system identifies the UTI `org.manoverboard.linear.regression` with
   `MetaLinear.mdimporter`. If it didn't, we'd know that something was wrong with
   `MetaLinear`'s `Info.plist`.

▶ Running our plug-in did add all the metadata attributes and values we expected. If it
   hadn't, we'd be in for a tricky bit of debugging.

Because of the environment in which it runs, debugging a Spotlight plug-in is a matter of
carefully auditing the source files and placing statements that will print status messages to
the system console.

The real proof of the MetaLinear plug-in is whether the attributes it extracts from Linear
documents shows up in Spotlight and the Finder. For the first, open the Spotlight menu
and type **Predictions** (or some other source title or author you know is in one of your
Linear documents), and Press **Return**.
The matching Linear files should appear
in the results list.

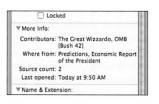

The other test is to select in the Finder a
Linear document that has sources, and
then **File > Get Info**. If the More Info
section of the Info window is collapsed,
click the disclosure triangle to open it
up. The More Info section should
include Contributors and Where From
(see Figure 18.3).

FIGURE 18.3    The More Info section of the
Get Info window for a Linear document. Thanks
to the MetaLinear Spotlight plug-in, the Finder
displays the metadata we attached to the
document.

# Summary

This chapter took us through the building of a project that was separate from, but coordinate to, our main project. We reviewed how to add the product of such a project as a
dependent target of our main project and saw how to route the plug-in to its proper place
in the application package. With considerable help from Apple's project template, we saw
what was involved in writing a standard `CFBundle` plug-in. We also added Spotlight visibility to our application, which is a good thing in itself.

CHAPTER 19

# Finishing Touches

## IN THIS CHAPTER

▶ Localized Resources

▶ Pitfalls of SCM and Localizations

▶ MallocDebug

▶ Introduction to Instruments

▶ Building for Release

▶ Stripping a Binary

We've taken Linear a long way, starting with a simple command-line tool, adding a graphical human interface, reorganizing it into libraries, and bringing it into the world of Core Data. We've put it under version control, tested its components, documented its code, and augmented it with a system plug-in. We're nearly done.

But not quite. There are a few rough spots in the human interface, the binary code is not optimized for speed and size, and there are still a couple of bugs to look for. And there might be some issues to address to bring Linear to a global market.

This chapter covers these "just one more" issues.

## Trimming the Menus

When we created the Linear project, the MainMenu.nib we got was generic for a document-based application. Most of the contents of the menu bar in that NIB do apply to Linear, but a few items will never be used, and a handful still refer to "NewApplication." Now that we've settled on a final feature set, we can edit the menu bar to reflect what Linear does.

Double-click **MainMenu.nib** in either the Groups & Files list or the Finder. When the file opens, double-click the **MainMenu** icon in the NIB window to make sure that the prototype menu bar is visible.

> ▶ The **Application** menu is named **NewApplication** in the NIB. If you've been observant, you've seen that when Linear is running, this menu is named **Linear**. That's because Cocoa substitutes the localized

CFBundleName from an application's Info.plist as the title of the application menu. So even though it doesn't change anything, double-click the menu title and change it to **Linear.**

Three items in the application menu use the dummy name **NewApplication**: **About**, **Hide**, and **Quit**. (All three are handled automatically by NSApplication, by the way.) Edit each so that **NewApplication** becomes **Linear**. We don't have a Preferences panel, so delete the **Preferences** item and one of the gray-line separator items to either side of it.

▶ In the **File** menu, NSApplication, NSDocument, and NSPersistentDocument handle almost every item. Alas, Linear doesn't print. Delete the last three items (**Print**, **Page Setup**, and the separator above them).

▶ In the **Edit** menu, to the extent that we use text fields, we support **Cut**, **Copy**, **Paste**, **Delete**, and **Select All**. Switching to Core Data gave us **Undo/Redo** support. Linear doesn't support finding, spelling, substituting, or speaking text, however, so once again, delete the last five items (counting the separator) in this menu.

This turns out to be a little tricky: A menu item that has a submenu can't be deleted if its menu is visible. Clicking once on the item selects it and displays the submenu. Clicking again closes the submenu. Now you can press **Delete** to delete the item.

▶ We don't need the **Format** or **View** menus. Click them once (the menu drops down), then again (the menu collapses). When the menu is collapsed, you can delete it.

▶ The **Window** menu is managed, and filled, automatically by Cocoa. No changes are needed.

▶ The **Help** menu can be deleted, because we don't have a help system (which is a shame).

Save MainMenu.nib and quit Interface Builder.

## Avoiding Singularity

Linear does not check for having all data points the same. Having all-identical data points amounts to having only one, and a single point does not define a line. A well-behaved program should prevent this from happening and give notice of the condition rather than permit an undefined computation, which results in dividing zero by zero.

MyDocument has an abstraction for getting at all the points in the document and access to a window to which to attach an alert sheet. It is the obvious place to put a check for a singular data set. We'd add a method, pointsAllTheSame, to detect the problem condition and change the compute: action method so that it puts up the alert sheet if the condition is detected:

```objc
- (BOOL) pointsAllTheSame
{
    double       x, y, x0, y0;
    unsigned     count = [self countDataPoints], i;

    if (count <= 1)
        return YES;

    [self dataPointAtIndex: 0 x: &x0 y: &y0];
    for    i = 1; i < count; i++) {
        [self dataPointAtIndex: i x: &x y: &y];
        if (x != x0 || y != y0)
            return NO;
    }
    return YES;
}

- (IBAction) compute: (id) sender
{
#pragma unused(sender)
    if ([self pointsAllTheSame]) {
        NSAlert * alert = [[NSAlert alloc] init];
        [alert setMessageText: @"No distinct points"];
        [alert setInformativeText: @"There must be at least two "
                                   @"distinct data points for a "
                                   @"regression to be possible."];
        [alert addButtonWithTitle: @"OK"];
        [alert beginSheetModalForWindow: [self windowForSheet]
                      modalDelegate: nil
                      didEndSelector: NULL
                          contextInfo: NULL];
        [alert autorelease];
    }
    else {
        [statEngine refreshData];
        [model setSlope: [statEngine slope]];
        [model setIntercept: [statEngine intercept]];
        [model setCorrelation: [statEngine correlation]];
    }
}
```

Now run Linear and enter a data set consisting of two or more points, all identical. Because there are at least two points, the **Compute** button activates, but pressing it brings up the alert sheet, as shown in Figure 19.1.

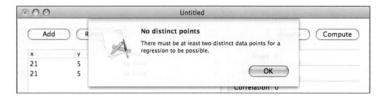

FIGURE 19.1    The no-distinct-points alert as it appears in `Linear`. The string set in the `NSAlert` instance method `setMessageText:` appears in boldface on the top line of the alert, and the rest of the text is supplied by the string passed to `setInformativeText:`.

# Localization

We're pretty satisfied with `Linear`, but having it available in French would really make it perfect. Users of Mac OS X specify what languages they understand by setting a list of available languages in order of preference in the **Language** tab of the International panel of the System Preferences application. When a user's list sets French at a higher priority than English, we'd like `Linear` to present menus, alerts, and labels in the French language.

When they search for application resources, the `NSBundle` and `CFBundle` facilities first search the subdirectories of the application bundle's Resources directory, in the order of the user's preferences for language. Language subdirectories are given such names as `English.lproj`, `fr.lproj`, or `en_GB.lproj`; plain-text language names are now deprecated, and it's preferred that you use ISO-standard language abbreviations, optionally suffixed with a code to identify a regional variant.

If we look in the Finder, we see that an `English.lproj` directory is associated with `Linear` and contains `Credits.rtf`, `InfoPlist.strings`, `MainMenu.nib`, and `MyDocument.nib`, as well as Interface Builder's backup copies of NIBs.

Reviewing those files in Xcode's Groups & Files list, under the **Resources** group, we see that every file that appears in the `English.lproj` directory has a disclosure triangle next to it. Opening the disclosure triangle reveals the localized versions—in every case so far, English.

## Credits.rtf

We haven't looked at `Credits.rtf` before. If a file by that name is available in `Resources` or a localized subdirectory, its contents will be displayed in a scrollable view in the application's About box. The file is filled with silly credits that are obviously intended to be replaced. We will not replace them but instead make them French.

Control-click the **Credits.rtf** line of the Groups & Files list and select **Get Info** from the menu that pops up. (Or, select the line and click the **Info** button in the toolbar, or press ⌘I.) The window is punctiliously titled as being for *localized group* `Credits.rtf`. The **General** tab contains a list of localizations, with only one item, **English**. Click the **Add Localization** button. A sheet will slide down, asking for a name for the localization, and the combo box for the name will include **French** in its choices, but enter **fr** instead. Click **Add**, and **fr** now appears in the list.

Go to the Finder and see what happened: A new directory, fr.lproj, has been added to the Linear project directory and includes a Credits.rtf file. Returning to Xcode and opening the disclosure triangle next to **Credits.rtf**, we see that the group now contains both **English** and **fr** and that both versions seem to be identical. The credits file for French should become

- **Les ingénieurs**. Certains gens

- **Conception d'interface humaine**. D'autres gens

- **Test**. On espére que ce n'est pas personne

- **Documentation**. N'importe qui

- **Nous remercions particuliérement**. Maman

## MainMenu.nib

Select what we now know is the localized group for MainMenu.nib, and open the Info window for it. Click **Add Localization**, and enter **fr**. Once again, the English version of MainMenu.nib is copied into fr.lproj, and both versions appear under the **MainMenu.nib** group in Groups & Files.

To open it in Interface Builder, double-click the **fr** localization of **MainMenu.nib**. The goal is to translate every menu title and item into French. At this point, we have to decide what name Linear should have in French. We'll go with Linéaire. We proceed to edit the menus, using the terms found in Table 19.1.

## MyDocument.nib

Using the same technique as before, make a fr-localized copy of MyDocument.nib, and open that copy with Interface Builder. Use the glossary in Table 19.2 to translate the items. The buttons and the form, you will notice, are made a little bit wider by the changes in the text; you'll have to adjust their placement to bring them back into Aqua standards. Localization can often make NIB elements much larger than they were in English, which is why there isn't any good way to automate the translation of NIBs.

TABLE 19.1   French Equivalents for Linear's Menus

| Linear | Linéaire |
| --- | --- |
| About Linear | À propos de Linéaire |
| Services | Services |
| Hide Linear | Masquer Linéaire |
| Hide Others | Masquer les autres |
| Show All | Tout afficher |
| Quit Linear | Quitter Linéaire |

**19**

TABLE 19.1     Continued

| File | Fichier |
|------|---------|
| **File** | **Fichier** |
| New | Nouveau |
| Open... | Ouvrir... |
| Open Recent | Ouvrir récent |
| Clear Menu | Effacer le menu |
| Close | Fermer |
| Save | Enregistrer |
| Save As... | Enregistrer sous... |
| Save As PList... | Enregistrer sous format plist... |
| Revert to Saved | Revenir à la version enregistrée |
| **Edit** | **Edition** |
| Undo | Annuler |
| Redo | Rétablir |
| Cut | Couper |
| Copy | Copier |
| Paste | Coller |
| Delete | Supprimer |
| Select All | Tout sélectionner |
| **Window** | **Fenetre** |
| Minimize | Masquer |
| Zoom | Réduire/agrandir |
| Bring All to Front | Mettre tous au premier plan |

TABLE 19.2     French Equivalents for Linear's Document Display

| # outof # | # de # |
|-----------|--------|
| Add | Ajouter |
| All | Tous |
| Author | Auteur |
| Compute | Calculer |
| Correlation | Corrélation |
| Data Source | Source des données |
| Date | Date |
| Fetch | Chercher |
| Graph | Tracer |
| Intercept | Interception |
| Remove | Enlever |
| Slope | Pente |
| Source | Source |
| Title | Titre |
| Untitled | Sans titre |
| Window | Fenêtre |

One thing that might catch you in the translation of the NIB: The label text below and to the left of the Data Source table contains the dummy string "# out of #," but that isn't how the label will be filled when Linear runs. If you look at the bindings for the label (⌘4), you will see that the label is bound to two

values—the count of the selection and the count of all `DataSources`—formatted by the string `%{value1}@ out of %{value2}@`. It is here that you'll have to translate *out of* into *de*.

Another trap lies in the `NSSearchField` in the upper-right corner of the Data Source (Source des données) box. It has placeholder text to be translated in its General (⌘1) settings and a pop-up menu that describes what fields it filters on. The internal names of these fields don't change, of course, but the names displayed in the menu should be translated. Inspect the bindings (⌘4) for the field, and translate the display name for each of the predicate bindings.

Save and close `MyDocument.nib`.

---

**SCM and Localizations**

Adding a localization `.lproj` directory to the `Linear` project directory exposes an SCM problem that Xcode doesn't handle very well. As I mentioned before, Xcode does not cover the case in which a new directory ought to be brought under version control.

If you examine the Groups & Files list (with the SCM column added), you'll see that the `fr` localizations don't have any SCM flags at all. This is misleading. Normally, this means that a file is current with the repository, but in this case, it means that it has no SCM status because it is not part of the working copy.

The solution is not as easy as adding the `fr.lproj` directory from the command line: `MainMenu.nib`, in the localization directory, is a package directory, and it was copied into `fr.lproj` when we added the localization. Along with the NIB information, Xcode copied the `.svn` directory inside the NIB, containing all the links to the *English* `MainMenu.nib` in the repository. This can only lead to confusion and data loss.

The only thing to do is to use the command line to remove any `.svn` directories (from `fr.lproj` *only*), and then check `fr.lproj` in:

```
$ find fr.lproj -name .svn -exec rm -rf \{\} \;
find: fr.lproj/MainMenu.nib/.svn: No such file or directory
find: fr.lproj/MyDocument.nib/.svn: No such file or directory
$ # The warning messages are to be expected.
$ svn add fr.lproj
A        fr.lproj
A        fr.lproj/Credits.rtf
...
$
```

Upon returning to Xcode, select **SCM > Refresh Entire Project**, and the correct A flags will appear in the Groups & Files list. Because `fr.lproj` is now under control, any *flat* localized files you add will be flagged with a ?, so you can add them to the repository from within Xcode.

However, if you add a localization—for German, for instance—you must repeat this procedure. The new `.lproj` won't automatically be added to the repository.

Further, any time you add a localization *of a package* file (most commonly a NIB), you must repeat this procedure (for that NIB directory *only*). Remember, the copy for localization is made completely, including an inappropriate `.svn` or CVS for the NIB.

## GraphWindow.xib

`GraphWindow.xib`, the next item in the Resources group, doesn't have any localized variants. Left as it is, it would be copied directly into the application bundle's `Resources` directory, and that one file would be used regardless of the user's locale. Do we need to localize it? Yes: It has a title, Graph, or Trace in French, so add the fr localization, and open it.

Select the window, and in its Attributes Inspector (⌘1), change the title from Graph to Trace. Save and close the XIB.

## InfoPlist.strings

The next item in the Resources group is **Info.plist**, but it is unique in that there is only one per bundle. If you want to localize strings in an `Info.plist`, you do so by editing the `InfoPlist.strings` file in the appropriate `.lproj` directory. So what we want to do is localize and extend the `InfoPlist.strings` file. Select it and add a **fr** localization. Select the **fr**-localized variant in the Groups & Files list.

Because a `.strings` file is a text file, the contents appear in the editor portion of the project window, if you have it open. You can edit the file directly in Xcode. The file consists of a list of *key* = *value* pairs, where the keys are in the `Info.plist` file, and the values are localized string values for those keys. Only certain keys are localizable; check the section "The `Info.plist` File" in Chapter 11, "File Packages and Bundles," or Apple's documentation, for which keys are localizable.

We now have an additional challenge. Adding a French localization gives us a second name—Linéaire—for our application. It wouldn't do to have the name "Linear" appear under `Linear`'s icon in the Finder. The Finder has a mechanism for displaying an application's localized name, even when the application's package directory—`Linear.app`— remains the same.

This involves adding the key `CFBundleDisplayName` to the application's `Info.plist`. The `Info.plist` file does not include this key, and the Target Info window does not set it, because Apple does not recommend including it in nonlocalized bundles.

Our task is to add the key, with a default value, to the `Info.plist` file itself, and then provide localizations in the respective `.strings` files.

This is all very easy. Edit `Info.plist` to include `CFBundleDisplayName`:

```
<key>CFBundleName</key>
<string>$(PRODUCT_NAME)</string>
<key>CFBundleDisplayName</key>
<string>$(PRODUCT_NAME)</string>
<key>CFBundlePackageType</key>
<string>APPL</string>
```

Notice that instead of a simple, literal default, like **Linear**, we provide a variable `$(PRODUCT_NAME)`. When Xcode installs the `Info.plist` in the application bundle, it will substitute such build variables with their values. That way, if we change Linear's name (in the **Build** tab in the Target Info window), all the related values will follow suit.

Next, we override those settings in the localized `.strings` files. Yes, that means the default name is obscured in every case we provide for, but `CFBundleDisplayName` and `CFBundleName` have to be present in `Info.plist`, and have to have a value. Both values have to be localized because `CFBundleName` controls the name of the application menu.

Here's the English version of `InfoPlist.strings`, which I've already edited for purposes of illustration:

```
/* Localized versions of Info.plist keys -English */

CFBundleDisplayName = "Linear";
CFBundleName = "Linear";
NSHumanReadableCopyright = " © Myself, 2008. All rights reserved.";
```

And here's the translation:

```
/* Localized versions of Info.plist keys -French */

CFBundleDisplayName = "Linéaire";
CFBundleName = "Linéaire";
NSHumanReadableCopyright = © Moi, 2008. Tous droits réservés.";
```

See the discussion of `CFBundleDisplayName` and other localizable keys in the "The `Info.plist` File" section of Chapter 11.

> **NOTE**
>
> In `.strings` files accented characters pose no problem, because they are supposed to be encoded in UTF-16 Unicode. By contrast, program source code is not guaranteed to be correct if it strays from 7-bit ASCII.

## Trying It Out

The obvious way to test all this localization is to shuffle your language preferences in the System Preferences application, launch Linear, and see whether it has become Linéaire. This would, however, also make any other application you launch use its French localization until you switch the preference back. This is inconvenient unless, of course, you prefer to work in French.

A command-line option is available to change your language preference only for the application being launched. To the command that launches the application, just append the flag -AppleLanguages and the value: in this case, (fr).

To accomplish this within Xcode, open the Executables group in the Groups & Files list, and double-click **Linear**. Select the **Arguments** tab. Add two items to the upper list of arguments. Make the first -**AppleLanguages** and the second \(**fr**\). (The parentheses have to be guarded with backslashes to protect them from being interpreted by the shell during handling.) See Figure 19.2.

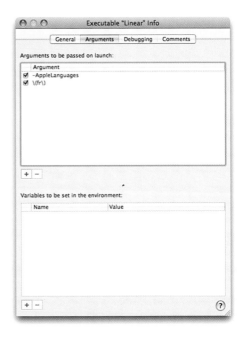

FIGURE 19.2    Passing an **AppleLanguages** preference list specially to Linear. Open the Info window for the Linear executable, and select the **Parameters** tab. Click the + button twice to add two parameters, and make the first -**AppleLanguages** and the second \(**fr**\). (The parentheses must be escaped.)

**NOTE**

The Linear application is represented in three places in the Groups & Files list. The first is the Linear target in the Targets group, which is where you order and populate the build phases, and make the settings that control how Linear is built. The second is the Executables group, in which you designate which application is to be launched when you run or debug a target—this is important when you are building application plug-ins because the thing to be launched is the host application, not the plug-in itself. It's also where, as here, you need to pass arguments and set the environment for your product. The third is the Products group, which lets you use a contextual menu for commands that treat your products as files—renaming them, adding them to SCM repositories, or revealing them in the Finder.

We are rewarded by an application that presents its human interface in the French language, as in Figure 19.3. There is, however, one problem: If we give Linear a data set containing two or more identical points, the alert sheet we see is still in English.

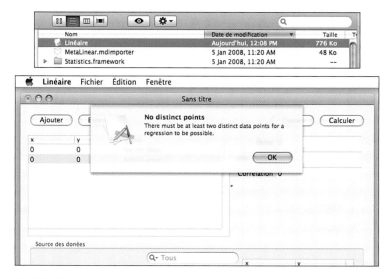

FIGURE 19.3    Linear (mostly) working in French. (Top) Setting CFBundleDisplayName causes the Finder to display the localized name Linéaire when the system language preference favors French. (Bottom) The menus, document window, and About box of Linear all display in French—but the distinct-points alert, whose text was set literally in the application code, is still in English.

## Localizable.strings

A bundle, including an application bundle, can have .strings files of its own. In Cocoa, the NSBundle method localizedStringForKey:value:table: returns the string, from the named .strings table, for the best current locale for a given key. The value: parameter is a default in case no value is found in a .strings file.

Most commonly, the localizedStringForKey:value:table: method is wrapped in one of a family of macros. These macros have two advantages. First, they provide convenient defaults for the bundle—the application main bundle—and the table file (Localizable.strings). Second, the genstrings command-line utility can scan source code for these macros and generate .strings files automatically.

The simplest of these is NSLocalizedString, which takes a key string to identify the string and a comment string to clarify, in a comment in the .strings file, the purpose of the string. We can edit compute: to use NSLocalizedString:

```
if ([self pointsAllTheSame]) {
    NSAlert * alert = [[NSAlert alloc] init];
    [alert setMessageText:
            NSLocalizedString(@"No distinct points",
```

19

```
                                        @"Alert message for singularity")
        ];
        [alert setInformativeText:
                // Note that the first three lines are one string
                NSLocalizedString(@"There must be at least two "
                                  @"distinct data points for a "
                                  @"regression to be possible.",
                                  @"Alert detail for singularity")
        ];
        [alert addButtonWithTitle:
                NSLocalizedString(@"OK",
                                  @"Singularity alert dismissal")
        ];
        [alert beginSheetModalForWindow: [self windowForSheet]
                            modalDelegate: nil
                          didEndSelector: NULL
                             contextInfo: NULL];
        [alert autorelease];
    }
```

We can then fire up the Terminal application, point the command line at the Linear project directory, and have genstrings produce a Localizable.strings file, working from MyDocument.m:

```
$ cd ~/Linear
$ genstrings MyDocument.m
```

Listing the Linear directory shows that a Localizable.strings file is now there. Go back to Xcode, and select **Project > Add to Project...** (⌥⌘A). Browse for the new Localizable.strings file, and add it to the project.

Be careful! The added-file sheet that appears next will offer to interpret the text encoding of the new file as UTF-8, an 8-bit encoding. *This is not what you want.* Remember that .strings files are encoded as 16-bit Unicode. Select **UTF-16** from the encoding pop-up before accepting the file. Take the straight UTF-16; the "endian" UTF-16 encodings should be used only for data read by an application that explicitly requires a specific byte order.

If by accident you accepted the file in an 8- or 7-bit encoding, Xcode will show most of its contents as characters interspersed with gray inverted question marks, signifying the null bytes that lead UTF-16 characters coinciding with the ASCII character set. All is not lost. Select the problem file in the Groups & Files list, open the Info window on it, and select **Unicode (UTF-16)** from the **File Encoding** pop-up. An alert will ask whether you mean to convert the file to UTF-16 or to reinterpret it as UTF-16. Choose **Reinterpret**, and you're back in business.

For the sake of neatness, move `Localizable.strings` to the Resources group in Groups & Files. Open a File Info window for `Localizable.strings`. Because the `genstrings` tool put the file into the `Linear` project directory, and not into `English.lproj`, Xcode does not recognize it as a localizable resource; there will be no localizations list in the **General** tab. Instead, there will be a button at the bottom, **Make File Localizable**.

Click that button, and examine the **General** tab again. `Localizable.strings` has been moved into `English.lproj`, and the localizations list is now displayed. Add the **fr** localization to copy the file into the `fr.lproj` directory, ready to receive our translations (line-broken here in the interest of space):

> **NOTE**
>
> Apple makes AppleGlot glossaries for much of its software available at http://developer.apple.com/intl/localization/download/. These glossaries provide a base of precedents you can draw on in translating resources into the more common languages.

```
/* Alert message for singularity */
"No distinct points" = "Les points ne sont pas distincts";

/* Singularity alert dismissal */
"OK" = "OK";
/* Yes, the standard French localization of "OK" is "OK." */

/* Alert detail for singularity */
"There must be at least two distinct data points
for a regression to be possible." = "Il doit y avoir au moins
deux points distincts pour qu'une régression soit possible.";
```

Save both localizations, and add them to the SCM repository.

# Checking Memory Usage

We are confident about our discipline in handling Cocoa memory, but the fact remains that without garbage collection (which is unavailable before Mac OS X 10.5), handling Cocoa memory—or the reference-counted objects of Core Foundation—is a discipline. You have to take care to do it right. To see whether we slipped, let's run Linear under the supervision of the MallocDebug application. Select **Run > Start with Performance Tool > MallocDebug** to launch MallocDebug and direct it at `Linear`.

When MallocDebug opens, it displays a window showing the path to the application and its command-line parameters; if the parameters are still `-AppleLanguages \(fr\)`, maybe you want to blank that field out. Click

> **WARNING**
>
> Make sure you build (**Build > Build**, ⌘**B**) Linear before letting MallocDebug launch it. Xcode will not bring Linear up-to-date automatically.

**Launch**. A standard authorization dialog will appear, requiring you to permit MallocDebug to hook into Linear.

Now exercise Linear just enough that it does some allocations and releases. Create a couple of data sources and a few points. Allocate the points among the sources. Click **Compute**. Click **Graph**. Close the Graph window and the document window, and don't bother to save. Don't quit: MallocDebug drops its statistics when the target application quits!

We've now taken Linear through a cycle that should have created all the structures associated with a document and then released them: a full life cycle of a document. MallocDebug, meanwhile, has been recording every allocation of memory and the complete call stack at the time of the allocation. Switch over to MallocDebug; from the second pop-up, select **Leaks**. MallocDebug then examines every malloc-allocated block in the application heap and makes note of every block that appears not to have any references. In a garbage-collected memory-management system, these blocks would be released.

Use the first pop-up to switch the stack-trace display to **Inverted** (see Figure 19.4). The inverted display lists in the first column of the browser the routines that made those allocations. Each column subsequent to an entry represents the caller of that allocation routine. The actual allocators tend to be buried deeply in the system libraries, so you may have to trace several columns to the right before you can find a routine whose name you would recognize.

FIGURE 19.4    Leak analysis of Linear. MallocDebug launched Linear and recorded every allocation and release of memory blocks in the course of creating, filling, and closing a document. By selecting **Leaks** and the **Inverted** tree view, it's easy to find where Linear allocates blocks that end up not being referenced.

In my run of MallocDebug, there are two routines (designated by hexadecimal addresses) that allocated a total 2.4KB, and 128 bytes, respectively, that did not get released. Tracing the 2.4K right, we come through +[NSObject alloc] to a method name that has a C source file icon next to it: +[DataPoint allDataPointsInContext:]. Above that, the trail splits into methods in MyDocument and Regression that call into allDataPointsInContext:.

The list below the method browser shows that the leak occurred many times, in 52-byte increments. You can double-click any of the lines to inspect a hex/ASCII dump of a leaked block. In this case, the dumps don't tell us much.

+[DataPoint allDataPointsInContext:] is under our control, so let's see what is happening there. Double-click its entry in the browser, and an Xcode editor window on DataPoint.m will appear, with the method highlighted.

```
+ (NSArray *) allDataPointsInContext: (NSManagedObjectContext *) context
{
    NSError *          error;
    NSArray *          retval;
    NSFetchRequest *   request = [[NSFetchRequest alloc] init];

    [request setEntity:
        [NSEntityDescription entityForName: @"DataPoint"
                    inManagedObjectContext: context]];
    retval = [context executeFetchRequest: request
                                    error: &error];
    return retval;
}
```

Note that we allocate an NSFetchRequest and never release it. It outlives its usefulness after it is sent in the executeFetchRequest:error: message. Adding [request release] between that message and the return statement fixes the leak.

What about the 128-byte leak, which seems to have occurred in 8 allocations of 16 bytes? Examining the allocated blocks suggests nothing. Tracing up the stack shows a long journey through low-level libraries and Cocoa methods, which begin to be recognizable at the function name NSBeginAlertSheet. It doesn't hit our code until the main() function. The intervening layers make a lot of references to closing a window. We infer that it has to do with the sheet that asks whether to save the document we created, that it's a leak in Cocoa, and that there isn't anything we can do about it.

# Instruments

There is another approach to the problem of leaking memory: We can watch Linear execute with the tools provided by the Instruments application (new with Xcode 3.0). Instruments allows you to apply any of a number of tools (themselves called "instruments") to a running application. The list of available instruments is long, and will be

covered in Chapter 26, "Instruments."
For the moment, we're interested in the
ones covering memory usage.

The lower part of the **Run** > **Start with
Performance Tool** menu is devoted to
running Instruments with specialized
suites of instruments. If you corrected
the NSFetchRequest leak in the preceding section, comment the fix out, build
Linear, and start it through
Instruments, using the **Leaks** suite.

Instruments opens, and runs Linear
immediately. The top half of an
Instruments document window shows a
timeline that expands to the right as
Linear executes. The display takes the
form of a stack of *traces*—graphs—one
for each instrument in the document.
Below, Instruments shows details of
the data collected by the selected
instrument.

When execution starts, the graph for the
top instrument, ObjectAlloc, increases

> **NOTE**
>
> We've previously seen that the **Go** command
> in the **Run** menu and under the **Build and Go**
> toolbar button runs the target application by
> the same method (run or debug) as was last
> used. If your last launch was through **Start
> with Performance Tool**, that, too, is retained
> as the method **Go** will use.

> **WARNING**
>
> To do its work, Instruments needs privileged
> access to install needed software and to get
> access to the inner workings of target appli-
> cations. It will present a security dialog to
> get an administrator's password. This dialog
> may come *after* Linear has been launched,
> so that Instruments will run its traces
> without the ability to use some of its instru-
> ments. If this happens, use the **Stop** button
> to stop the trace, quit Instruments, and try
> again.

steadily, reflecting the allocation of memory for the data structures of a new document.
The lower instrument, Leaks, periodically displays the total of bytes Linear has leaked.

The steadily building traces in the Instruments document may exert some pressure on
you, but take your time! Repeat the test cycle: Fill in some sources, add some data points
and assign sources to them, compute a regression and display a graph, and then close the
document, declining the offer to save the document. This time, you can quit Linear;
Instruments preserves its data when its target application quits.

Now you can examine the Instruments document (see Figure 19.5). The amount of detail
available is almost overwhelming, but take the window piece by piece. The top view in
the window is devoted to the traces for the instruments included in the Instruments
document. The ObjectAlloc graph displays the total number of bytes in use in Linear's
heap. In the figure, you can see a blip in memory usage as the unsaved-document sheet
appears, and then disappears. The Leaks graph displays the total amount of memory
taken up by leaked objects. By the default settings for that instrument, Instruments scans
for unreferenced objects every 30 seconds, so leaks will show up in periodic, sudden
jumps.

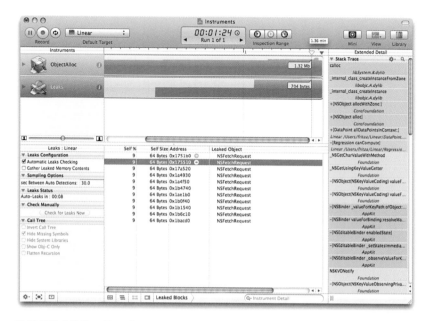

FIGURE 19.5    Running Linear under Instruments and selecting the Leaks instrument produces an incredibly rich analysis of how Linear uses memory. The Detail view has been made visible using the window pane icon in the control bar at the bottom. Selecting a leaked block and opening the Extended Detail view (using the button depicting a window with a sidebar) displays a stack trace of the block's allocation, color coded by the library from which each call was made. The block's item in the Detail view indicates that the leaked object was an NSFetchRequest.

## Leaked Blocks

In the lower half of the window is the Detail view. (It should have opened automatically when Linear started running, as shown in the figure; if it isn't open, click the **View** button in the toolbar, and select **Detail** from the resulting pop-up menu.) This is where the details appear of whatever data the selected instrument captures. Select the track for the Leaks instrument.

The Detail list shows each leaked block. In our brief run, all the blocks are NSFetchRequests, as we expected from our run of MallocDebug. But even here, Instruments gives us a bonus: It identifies the type (NSFetchRequest) of the object that was leaked. Click one of these blocks, and open the Extended Detail view by clicking the button below the list that looks like a square with a sidebar, or by selecting **Extended Detail** from the **View** pop-up menu.

The Extended Detail pane appears at the
left with a color-coded stack trace for
the allocation of the selected block. Each
color represents a different library—
AppKit, CoreFoundation, the modules
that make up Linear—from which each
succeeding call was made. It is easy to
find +[DataPoint allDataPointsIn
Context:] in the list; double-clicking it
gives you an Xcode editor that highlights, not just the whole body of the
method, but the exact line at which the
offending call was made.

> **NOTE**
>
> Instruments can identify methods and line
> numbers because under the Debug configu-
> ration, that information is included in the
> Linear executable. If we switched to the
> Release configuration, debugging information
> would be stripped out, and the identification
> of methods and lines would not be possible.

## Leaky Call Trees

The Leaks instrument allows you to approach a leak problem from the perspective of
leaky allocation calls, instead of block by block, just as with MallocDebug. Switch to the
call-tree view by pressing the button below the Detail view that looks like indented lines
of text.

The call-tree view starts with a single line that says the start routine (or the functions it
calls) accounts for 100% of the leaks in the program. It has a disclosure triangle to expand
an outline of leaky calls below start. Repeatedly expanding these will eventually lead to
two lines that say 81.8% of the leaks come through a method of NSUndoManager and
18.1% from a method of NSApplication. And so on, until you drill down to an allocation
primitive on each line of leaky calls. Your problem call is somewhere within each of
those lines.

Selecting any line will fill the Extended Detail view with the "heaviest stack trace," reflecting the most-leaky line of execution from that level.

This does well enough for our simple leak in one location, but in a more realistic case, the
top-down outline is not convenient. For one thing, you have to plow through layer after
layer of system-supplied routines that don't tell you anything about your code.

The Leaks tool affords a solution, in the Options panel at the left end of the Details view.
Under the Call Tree section, check **Hide System Libraries**. Now the call tree omits the
calls you have no control over, and contains only the calls your own code made. Option-
click the disclosure triangle on the top (start) line to open the whole outline, which is
now much abbreviated (see Figure 19.6).

We can complete the match to our run of MallocDebug by checking **Invert Call Tree** in
the Options pane. Now the outline is rooted at allDataPointsInContext: (which is what
we wanted to know), and its branches trace out every call to that method that resulted in
its leaking.

| Leaks : Linear | Total % | # Leaks | Bytes | Library | Symbol Name |
|---|---|---|---|---|---|
| ▼ Leaks Configuration | 100 | 11 | 704 bytes | Linear | ▼ start |
| ☑ Automatic Leaks Checking | 100 | 11 | 704 bytes | Linear | ▼ _start |
| ☐ Gather Leaked Memory Contents | 100 | 11 | 704 bytes | Linear | ▼ main |
| ▼ Sampling Options | 81.8 | 9 | 576 bytes | Linear | ▼ -[Regression storeChanged:] |
| sec Between Auto Detections:  30.0 | 81.8 | 9 | 576 bytes | Linear | ▼ -[Regression canCompute] |
| ▼ Leaks Status | 81.8 | 9 | 576 bytes | Linear | +[DataPoint allDataPointsInContex |
| Auto-Leaks in : 00:08 | 18.1 | 2 | 128 bytes | Linear | ▼ -[MyDocument windowControllerDidL |
| ▼ Check Manually | 18.1 | 2 | 128 bytes | Linear | ▼ -[Regression canCompute] |
|   Check for Leaks Now | 18.1 | 2 | 128 bytes | Linear | +[DataPoint allDataPointsInContex |
| ▼ Call Tree |  |  |  |  |  |
| ☐ Invert Call Tree |  |  |  |  |  |
| ☑ Hide Missing Symbols |  |  |  |  |  |
| ☑ Hide System Libraries |  |  |  |  |  |
| ☐ Show Obj-C Only |  |  |  |  |  |
| ☐ Flatten Recursion |  |  |  |  |  |

FIGURE 19.6   The Leaks Detail list, showing the call tree for leaky routines in Linear. The options at left control how the list is displayed: Here we have checked **Hide System Libraries** to restrict an otherwise long and complex list to only the calls we have some control over.

## The ObjectAlloc Instrument

The standard Leaks suite includes another instrument, ObjectAlloc, that we can examine briefly. As I mentioned, the trace for this instrument follows the total number of bytes currently allocated in Linear: As Linear allocates memory, the graph goes up; as it deallocates it, the graph goes down.

When you select the ObjectAlloc instrument, you find the Detail view fills with a list of every class (or CoreFoundation type) of object that Linear created in the course of its run. In each class, ObjectAlloc provides statistics for all the blocks that were ever allocated (Overall), and for all the blocks that remained alive at the end of the trace (Net). The statistics are the count of such objects, and the total number of bytes those objects took up. Each line has a bar next to it, showing the overall (pastel) and net (solid) number of such objects that were allocated. The bars are yellow or red if there were considerably more allocations than currently survive—a sign that you may have allowed a lot of temporary objects to accumulate without cleaning them out promptly.

> **NOTE**
>
> You'll generally find, in small applications like Linear, that the ObjectAlloc trace goes up much more than it goes down. The Cocoa framework creates many data structures early in the run of an application; they persist until the application quits. As the application, or the document data set, gets larger, the transient, document-based memory allocations come to dominate Cocoa's overhead.

The **Inspection Range** tool in the toolbar enables you to examine these statistics over a specific span of time, not just for the whole life of the target application. Click the time scale at the top of the instrument traces to move the trace "head" to that time—you can drag the head to place it more exactly. Designate the start of your time span by clicking the start-time (left) part of the **Inspection Range** control. Set the ending time by moving the head, and clicking the end-time (right) part of the control. The statistics in the Detail view now reflect the totals and changes just in that time period (see Figure 19.7). You can clear the span (effectively making it cover the whole trace) with the center segment of the control.

| Graph | Category | Net Bytes | # Net | Overall Bytes | # Overall | # |
|---|---|---|---|---|---|---|
| ☑ | * All Allocations * | 1315072 | 13485 | 18645216 | 163545 | +++ |
| ☐ | AXUIElement | 0 | 0 | 2816 | 88 | |
| ☐ | CFAllocator | 2112 | 22 | 2112 | 22 | |
| ☐ | CFArray | 18224 | 471 | 371840 | 10158 | |
| ☐ | CFArray (store-de... | 18416 | 258 | 652544 | 6352 | |
| ☐ | CFAttributedString | 144 | 9 | 144 | 9 | |
| ☐ | CFBag | 1280 | 20 | 1280 | 20 | |
| ☐ | CFBag (key-store) | 1344 | 21 | 36144 | 50 | |
| ☐ | CFBag (value-store) | 1344 | 21 | 36144 | 50 | |
| ☐ | CFBundle | 800 | 10 | 960 | 12 | |
| ☐ | CFCharacterSet | 384 | 12 | 13216 | 413 | |
| ☐ | CFData | 24848 | 79 | 316368 | 1115 | |
| ☐ | CFData (store) | 0 | 0 | 1216 | 154 | |
| ☐ | CFDate | 80 | 5 | 1952 | 122 | |
| ☐ | CFDateFormatter | 0 | 0 | 528 | 11 | |
| ☐ | CFDictionary | 62672 | 946 | 264544 | 4070 | |
| ☐ | CFDictionary (key-store) | 52768 | 881 | 1077760 | 5664 | |
| ☐ | CFDictionary (value-st... | 52768 | 881 | 1077760 | 5664 | |
| ☐ | CFKeyedArchiverUID | 0 | 0 | 432 | 27 | |
| ☐ | CFLocale | 1056 | 33 | 1056 | 33 | |
| ☐ | CFMachPort | 1152 | 18 | 1152 | 18 | |

| ⊞ | ≡ | ⋮⋮ | ▢ | Object Summary ⟩ | Q· Category |

FIGURE 19.7    The Detail list for the ObjectAlloc instrument. Each line represents a class of object allocated during the run of Linear. The counts and byte totals for all allocations, and surviving objects, of the given class are given, along with a histogram comparing the number of each class of object that were allocated and remained. The search field below the list can narrow the list to desired classes; it is a token field, so you can enter more than one class name (or fragment of a name) and list classes that match all, or any, criteria.

The top line, "* All Allocations *," sums the statistics for all the classes. It has a check box next to it, indicating its net byte total is what is being graphed. You can uncheck this, and check individual classes, to trace the usage for just those classes.

If you mouse over a classname, you will see a "more info" (arrow) button next to the name. Click it to display the history of the creation of each block of that class. The Extended Detail pane will display the stack trace for the allocation call. A "breadcrumb" list at the bottom of the Detail view allows you to navigate back to the overall list.

ObjectAlloc, too, has a call-tree view (press the indented-text button at the bottom of the Detail view). The lines in the Detail view still represent classes of allocations, but they now include disclosure triangles breaking out the stack traces of the allocations for that class of object. As with Leaks, these trees are rooted at the start symbols for the threads of your application, and can be inverted and pared down to only your own calls.

A third view, called the diagram view, brought up by the button with four rectangles on it, lists every allocated block in the order in which they were allocated. This list can be usefully pared by selecting the **Created & Still Living** radio button in the Options pane—an option available with all the ObjectAlloc detail views.

**NOTE**

A third tool for tracing and analyzing allocation and deallocation events is to be found in Shark. I'll be skipping it because MallocDebug is simpler to use, and Instruments a solution that is easier than Shark's, and more comprehensive.

## The Instruments Document

Click **Record**, on the left side of the Instruments toolbar, launches the target application (Linear) for another run. The graphs are cleared out, and Instruments starts recording from zero. The data from the previous runs is not lost. Under the elapsed-time counter in the middle of the toolbar, you see **Run 2 of 2** between two arrowheads. When Instruments is not recording, you can switch back and forth among your runs using the arrowheads.

Saving the Instruments document saves the document's configuration, as well as the datasets that underlie the run of each recording session. Saving involves a lot of processing of the data sets, so be prepared for a pause of half a minute or so while the save is in progress.

After you've accumulated runs in an Instruments document, a disclosure triangle appears to the left of each instrument track. Opening it displays the traces for that instrument in *all* the runs in the document. You can also review previous runs in a sort of "Cover Flow" format, using **View > Run Browser**. This view shows the traces of each run in a side-by-side flowing series of billboards; you can scroll through them to find the one you want, and select (or delete) it.

## Human-Interface Logging

It's easy to see how the events in a trace relate to the use of a program in the simple in-and-out runs we've been doing under Instruments. As runs get longer, and our tests grow more complex, we could lose track: Did that memory blip occur before the save sheet? Did the end of the blip coincide with the closing of the sheet, or the closing of the window?

Instruments provides instruments that allow you to mark your trace with the human-interface events that occur as the test goes on. Open the library of instruments by clicking the **Library** button in the toolbar, or by selecting **Window > Library** (⌘L). The Library window is a simple list of the available instruments, with an icon and short description for each.

Find the User Interface instrument (it may help to shorten the list by selecting **Master Tracks** from the filter pop-up at the top of the window), and drag it into the upper, Trace portion of the Instruments document.

Click **Record** to launch Linear again and start recording it. Because Instruments has to inject itself into the Cocoa event-dispatch code, Instruments will ask you to enter an administrator's password before it can proceed.

Run your quick test again. Linear may become a little choppy, as Instruments intercepts each human-interface event.

> **WARNING**
>
> In version 1.0, as available when I wrote this, Instruments seemed unable to cope with a User Interface recording that included clicks in a pop-up in a table view. For this run of Linear, *do not* set sources for your data points.

**19**

When you have quit, the new run shows a thumbnail in the User Interface trace at each event: keys pressed and released, mouse buttons up and down (see Figure 19.8). Each thumbnail captures the part of the screen the mouse was over, and at the top left, it shows a small icon designating the event. The Detail view shows each event in a table: a thumbnail of the screen surrounding the mouse pointer, the type of event that was recorded, the key (if any) that was involved (green-edged thumbnails in the trace view), and the title of the control (if any) that was involved (blue-edged thumbnails for these and other mouse events). System events get yellow-edged thumbnails.

> **NOTE**
>
> Replaying a User Interface trace relies on the "accessibility" features of Mac OS X to feed the events to the application. Make sure **Enable Access for Assistive Devices** is checked in the Universal Access panel of System Preferences.

> **NOTE**
>
> If you want to record a new UI track instead of replaying the existing one, click on the **i** button in the track label to open an inspector for the track (see Figure 19.9). Change the **Action** pop-up from **Drive** to **Capture**.

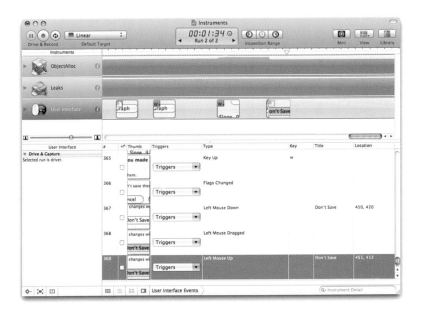

FIGURE 19.8    The Instruments document with a User Interface trace included. Everything you did in the course of an Instruments-controlled run of Linear is captured as a thumbnail in the User Interface track. The corresponding line in the Detail view gives details on the event. Note that the **Record** button at the left end of the toolbar has been renamed **Drive & Record**.

Notice that the label under the **Record** button now says **Drive & Record**. Clicking it would relaunch Linear, as before, but *replays the same HI events* we produced when we first ran the instrument. You can try this: click **Drive & Record**, and stand back. The mouse movements and keystrokes you recorded are repeated.

Imagine one use for this: You have instrumented a bug in your code—a leak of memory or file descriptors, for instance—and are trying out various solutions. Having a precise human-interface playback means you can trigger the same bug, repeatedly, to exactly the same effect. Alternating the runs with building your attempts to fix the bug will provide, run by run, a record of your progress.

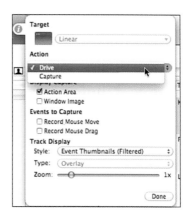

FIGURE 19.9     The inspector for the User Interface instrument, which appears when you click the **i** information button in the label of the User Interface track. After you have recorded a User Interface trace, Instruments sets up the next run to feed the target application with a repeat of the recorded HI events. To record a new User Interface trace, instead of playing back the previous one, select **Capture** in the **Action** pop-up.

# The Release Build Configuration

So far, we have been working with Linear/Linéaire versions that were expressly built with our convenience as developers in mind. The application is built with no optimizations that would confuse the flow of control in a debugger and slow the progress of builds. The build products contain cross-references between addresses in the binary and lines of code, so the debugger can find and display the currently executing line in the source. No attempt is made to analyze the code for unused routines that could be excluded from the product. We don't build for processor architectures we aren't running on, so Linear won't even run on some machines!

This can't go on. We have to get Linear into releasable shape, which means changing all the developer-friendly build settings to settings that befit a finished product. Xcode makes such wholesale changes easy by collecting each set of options into *build configurations*.

For the gcc compilers and linker and for the Xcode packaging system, each configuration encompasses settings that are useful for a particular variant of a product build. The project templates provide two configurations for each target: Debug and Release. The Debug configuration contains the development-friendly settings we are used to; the Release configuration provides values for these settings that are more appropriate for a released product.

We've worked with build settings before: Examine the settings for the `Linear` application by selecting the Linear target under the **Targets** group in the Groups & Files list, and double-clicking it; then select the **Build** tab. The pop-up menu at the top of the panel gives you a choice of what set of build settings to display and edit: One for each configuration set; one for whichever set is current; and an **All Configurations** item, which allows you to edit settings and apply them to both the Debug and Release configurations. The pop-up also contains an option to create a new configuration set of your own (see Figure 19.10).

The build configuration list you see in the target Info window shows all the settings that apply to that target. The items that are shown in plain type are settings that are inherited from the project or default values for those settings. Items in boldface are settings that have been customized, for this target, in the currently displayed configuration. Narrow the list down to just the settings made for this target, in the Debug configuration, by selecting **Settings Defined at This Level** from the **Show** pop-up.

For string-valued settings, the empty string is a valid customization. This would be displayed as a boldface label next to an empty column on the right side. If you want the default value for such a setting, not just a blank value, select the item, and press **Delete** so that the item reverts to plain type.

Switch the display from the **Debug** configuration to **Release** to see the

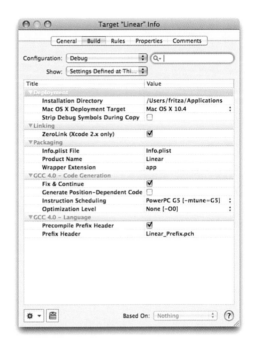

FIGURE 19.10    The Debug configuration as shown in the Info window for the Linear target. By selecting **Show > Settings Defined at This Level**, we can see exactly which settings this configuration overrides. Here, among other things, the application is set to **ZeroLink** (though Xcode 3 ignores this setting), to maintain (not strip) debugging information, to enable **Fix & Continue** patching from the debugger, and to eschew any attempt to optimize the generated code.

> **NOTE**
>
> "Default value" is not strictly accurate. The unset (nonbold) settings are those that have been set *at a higher level* in the project hierarchy. Those unset values for the target may have been set in the project file, and inherited from there. This is explored fully in Chapter 21, "Xcode for `make` Veterans."

difference: ZeroLink (a setting kept only for the benefit of those building in Xcode 2.x) is removed from the build, and debugging symbols are shifted out to an external dSYM file.

Optimization disappears from the list; the value from the project level is used, which is -Os, for small, fast code.

Select **Release** in the **Active Build Configuration** menu in the project window's toolbar, and build Linear. Changing the configuration directs the build process to a different subdirectory of the project's build directory, so targets will be built for the Release configuration independently of whether they had been up-to-date for the Debug configuration: The two products exist in parallel. The result will be that a complete, self-contained version of Linear appears in the build/Release directory.

# Stripping the Product

One last thing we can do for our application is to strip extraneous material from its executable file. Left to themselves, Xcode and the gcc tool chain will leave two kinds of additional code and data in an executable:

▶ gcc includes in the executable file a *symbol table*—a comprehensive list relating function and data names to their addresses. This is useful when the binary is being linked, or for applications and plug-ins to find objects within each other. It is also how tools like Instruments and the Apple crash reporter can annotate stack traces with the actual names of the routines in the call chain.

▶ If you use static libraries, or are in the habit of providing data structures in your application code with more operations than the application particularly demands, you will have *dead code*—functions and data that are never actually used.

Neither is necessary to the actual functioning of your code, and although it is reasonable to leave them in, you can remove them as your application is built. This is called *stripping*. It is controlled by the **Build** tab of the Target Info panel. As you review the options for stripping, be sure to set the **Configuration** pop-up to **Release**. Stripping is a time-consuming process, and the result would hinder our efforts at debugging. Stripping is therefore unsuited to the Debug configuration.

For any stripping to take place—symbol table or dead code—we must first check **Deployment Postprocessing**.

> ### NOTE
>
> The ownership, permissions, and "installation" actions are a bit more complicated than that. They have an additional enabling setting, **Deployment Location**, which defaults to off; further, **Install Owner** and **Install Group** default to your owner and group. All of these defaults make it easier to overwrite the product, should that be necessary; otherwise you'd jump through hoops enabling write permission on an entire application tree that belonged to root/wheel. The best solution is to do such builds using xcodebuild install on the command line, with privileges elevated by sudo.

Deployment postprocessing is a kind of master setting that enables the final steps in readying an Xcode product for release. In addition to enabling stripping, it sets the owner, group, and permissions of the product's files and directories, and "installs" the product in a designated directory.

19

## Stripping the Symbol Table

Stripping symbols from a product's binary file is controlled by four options:

- ▶ **Strip Linked Product** authorizes Xcode to strip symbol tables from the build product.

- ▶ **Strip Style** controls how much of the embedded symbol tables will be stripped. By default, for applications, all entries in all tables are removed, but you may elect to strip fewer, removing only symbols local to each module; or fewer still, removing only symbols used for debugging.

  The default for dynamic libraries is **Debugging Symbols**. Code that uses dynamic libraries specifies the routines in them by name only. The dynamic loader uses the embedded symbol tables to convert those names into memory addresses.

- ▶ **Use Separate Strip** will perform symbol-table stripping through the strip tool, instead of through the gcc linker. This would be useful if the linker did not strip the product as you expected, or if you wanted finer control of the process through the **Additional Strip Flags** setting. (man strip for details.)

- ▶ **Strip Debug Symbols During Copy**. Because stripping is ordinarily a link-time process, building an umbrella product like an application has no effect on whether nonapplication binaries, such as dynamic libraries or plug-ins, are stripped. Setting this option applies the strip tool to such files as they are copied into the application package.

> **NOTE**
>
> Symbol tables are not the same as the more-extensive debugging information, in the STABS or DWARF format, that may be incorporated into the executable code or kept in a separate file. This information relates memory and processor registers to variable declarations, and associates machine instructions with individual lines in your source code. Debugging data can be quite large, and the Release build configuration provides (for the superior default DWARF format) that it be kept in a separate .dSYM file package.

Although it need not be as voluminous as full debugging tables, symbol-table data can take up a significant portion of an executable. We can dig into Linear.app using **Show Package Contents** from the Finder's contextual menu, to find the executable file at Contents/MacOS/Linear. In my unstripped build, the Linear executable is 78,140 bytes (out of a total application size of 785,909).

When Linear is rebuilt (we'd have to do a **Build > Clean All** first, because Xcode doesn't treat settings changes as requiring a rebuild), with **Deployment**

> **NOTE**
>
> If your executable is about half this size, make sure you're using the Release build, and are set up to build at least the i386 and ppc architectures.

**Postprocessing** and **Strip Linked Product** set, the `Linear` executable comes in at 63.652 bytes—a saving of 19%.

---

**NOTE**

Why is Linear so very large? In my build of the application, `MainMenu.nib` and `MyDocument.nib` include `designable.nib`, the file that provides Interface Builder with additional information for building an editing interface for those NIBs. These are quite large compared to the other components of the application, and are unnecessary for its functioning. It might be a good idea to add a Run Script build phase to remove those files (only in the built product!) as a last step. `GraphWindow.nib`, by contrast, was compiled from a XIB file, and takes only 4K.

---

## Stripping Dead Code

In the process of writing `Linear`, we saw that it is easy to write more functions for a data type, for completeness, than are used. Most libraries include many functions that may be useful to all applications, but it is rare that all are useful to any one application.

The static linker ordinarily does nothing special with unused code. If an object file— either alone or inside a library archive—is presented to the linking process and any symbol from the file is used, the whole contents of that file get added to the product. This will seem wasteful to CodeWarrior veterans, who are used to a linker that goes function by function, not file by file, but this is conservative practice under gcc. The object-file format used by the gcc tool chain can't guarantee absolutely correct linkage at less than the file level.

However, it is possible for `ld` to identify sections of code that never get used, assuming no assembly tricks are involved. The linker can slice object files into functions and remove the ones that aren't needed. In a large program that makes use of many static libraries, this can result in significant reductions in the size of the executable. To do this, the linker needs the help of debugging symbols—full debugging symbols, not just symbol tables—to identify entities that may be strippable.

Here are the settings that control dead-code stripping; make sure you set these in the Release configuration only:

▶ **Dead Code Stripping** is the setting that tells Xcode to perform the strip.

▶ **Level of Debug Symbols** has to be set to **All Symbols**. This provides the debugging-information support the linker needs.

▶ **Don't Dead-Strip Inits and Terms** determines whether initialization and termination functions for dynamic libraries are removed. These functions are called by the dynamic loader itself, and not by application or library code, so they will look as though nothing calls them. If you are building a dynamic library, you should set this option.

19

If we try dead-code stripping on Linear, we find it makes no difference at all. The Linear binary file does not shrink by a single byte. There are two reasons for this.

First, Linear makes no use of statically linked libraries. Every library it uses, including the Statistics framework, is dynamically linked; so even if parts of those libraries go unused, they are not under the control of the process of producing the Linear executable file.

Second, Linear was written in Objective-C. In Objective-C, methods are found dynamically, at runtime. There is no way, in principle, to determine whether a method gets used or not, so there can't be any dead code.

## Summary

This chapter began with some cleanup in the NIB file, followed by an improvement to our controller algorithm that incidentally added some English-language text to our application. We took stock of the places where human-readable text was to be found in Linear and found ways to provide alternative text for French localization. We checked our memory usage and fixed a leak. We learned how to strip both dead code and embedded symbol tables, for little total gain in this application in which resources dominate the size of the executable.

# PART II

## Xcode Tasks

## IN THIS PART

| CHAPTER 20 | Navigating an Xcode Project | 331 |
| CHAPTER 21 | Xcode for make Veterans | 353 |
| CHAPTER 22 | More About Debugging | 373 |
| CHAPTER 23 | Xcode and Speed | 395 |
| CHAPTER 24 | A Legacy Project | 403 |
| CHAPTER 25 | Shark and the CHUD Tools | 421 |
| CHAPTER 26 | Instruments | 437 |
| CHAPTER 27 | Closing Snippets | 461 |

# Navigating an Xcode Project

IN THIS CHAPTER

▷ The Code Sense Project Index

▷ Project Find Options

▷ The Groups & Files List

▷ Navigating Class Trees

▷ Project Window Layouts

Part I of this book showed the use of Xcode in building a small project. We covered many features of the development environment, but the necessities of the task kept us from attaining much depth on any feature. In Part II, we look at Xcode's features in greater detail.

So far, we've been picking up Xcode's features in passing. For instance, we have been using the Groups & Files list, and the Project Find window casually, taking the obvious features we needed for simple tasks, while leaving the rest alone. In this chapter, we step back from the workflow to go deeper into the structure of the editors, the project window, and the various tools that help in getting around in a project.

## Editor Panes

In Xcode, practically everything that can move on the screen has an editing pane attached to it. This includes the project window. If you click the **Editor** button in the toolbar, Xcode will replace the Detail listing with a text editor for the contents of whatever single text file is selected in the Groups & Files list. The draggable split bar across the top edge of the editor (or below the Detail list— look for the tiny dimple that identifies the splitter) allows you to share the rightmost side of the project window between the Detail list and the editor.

The editor pane in the Debugger window allows you to not merely see but also change the code you're executing. The one in the SCM Results window (again, look for the splitter) lets you review versions and diffs. There are even windows that are only for editing text, with nothing in them but an editor pane.

The editor pane has a few features that we'd miss if we didn't stop to look at them. So let's do a quick review.

## Code Sense

Code Sense is Apple's name for the Xcode facilities that take advantage of indexing your project and its frameworks. Code Sense includes code completion, Command-double-clicking to jump to the definition of a symbol, class browsing, class modeling, and the Project Symbols smart group. It is the facility that provides class-structure information to Interface Builder.

After you turn it on (in the Code Sense panel of the Preferences window), code completion will be with you continually as you edit your code. When you type an identifier, Xcode will, after a brief pause, offer to complete what you've typed by showing the rest of the symbol in gray after the cursor. Pressing **Tab** accepts the completion; pressing **Esc** brings up a scrollable list of all known completions; and continued typing proceeds as normal. See Figure 20.1 for details.

Code Sense services rely on creating an index for a project the first time it is opened and updating the index whenever a file in the project is saved. This indexing is done on a background thread, and in most cases does not impose a noticeable performance cost on Xcode. You can see what background tasks Xcode is performing by selecting **Window > Activity Viewer**. If you find that Xcode is not responsive enough and you can live without the Code Sense services, you can try turning indexing off, by selecting the second panel (Code Sense) in the Preferences window and unchecking **Indexing: Enable for All Projects**.

The Code Sense panel also controls how code completion behaves. You can turn off the signaling of available completions, or you can have Xcode suggest completions automatically after a short delay. You can also decide whether you want code completion to include placeholders for function and method arguments.

> **NOTE**
>
> Some code completions do not rely on Code Sense. Words you add to a file will be offered as completions even before you save the file.

If Code Sense services seem to be misbehaving, you can rebuild its index by opening the Project Info window (double-click the top, project icon in the Groups & Files list) and clicking the button **Rebuild Code Sense Index** in the **General** tab.

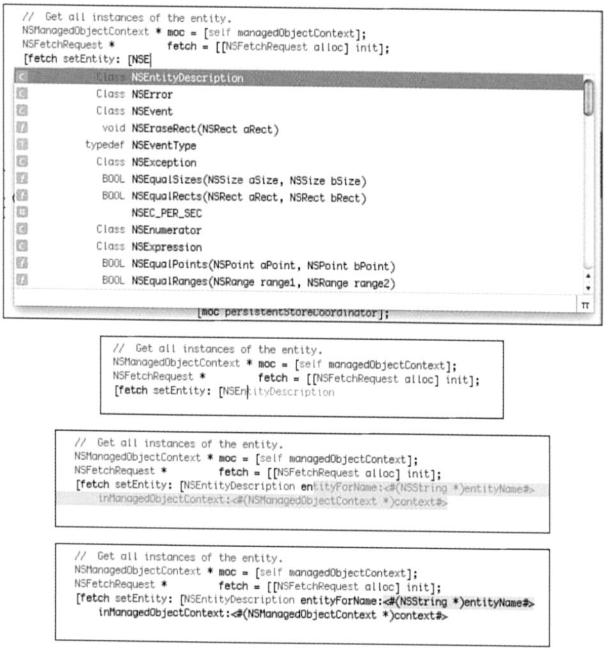

FIGURE 20.1   Progressing through a line with code completion. *(First)* Typing **NSE** in the context of a method accepting an NSEntityDescription parameter, and pressing **Esc**, brings up a scrolling list of symbols Xcode knows about that begin that way. The $\pi$ button at the lower right shows that the list is sorted to favor the "most likely" completions; switching it to **A** sorts the list alphabetically. *(Second)* Instead of pressing **Tab** to accept a choice, press **Esc** again to dismiss the list, and press **N**. Xcode offers to complete NSEntityDescription by displaying the rest of the symbol in gray. *(Third)* Press **Tab** to accept the completion and begin the method name with en; Xcode offers a completion for a long method selector, with placeholders for the parameters. *(Fourth)* Pressing **Tab** again selects the first placeholder; pressing ^/ will select the next.

## Jumps

When the Code Sense index of a project is complete, you can jump to the definition of any symbol in the project or its included frameworks by holding down the Command key and double-clicking the symbol. Multiple matches are possible: The same method may be defined in more than one class. In that case, a pop-up appears, showing the possible matches, with badges indicating the type—method/member function, instance variable, #defined constant, and so on—and the context of each symbol (see Figure 20.2). If there are more matches than will comfortably fit in a pop-up menu, a **Find More** item appears at the bottom of the menu, displaying the remaining choices in the Project Find window.

```
- (id) initWithCoder: (NSCoder *) coder
{
    [self setX: [coder decodeDoubleForKey: @"x"]];
    [self setY: [coder decodeDoubleF  ☐ -[NSCoder(NSExtendedCoder) decodeDoubleForKey:]
    return self;                      ☐ -[NSKeyedUnarchiver decodeDoubleForKey:]
}
```

FIGURE 20.2    The result of Command-double-clicking decodeDoubleForKey:. Two classes define that method, so a pop-up menu appears, offering a choice of which definition to visit.

This feature could be very helpful if we were writing methods to comply with a formal or informal protocol. We could type the name of the protocol (such as LinearGraphDelegate) and Command-double-click. The @interface definition of the protocol would appear in a new window, and we could then copy the method declarations for our own code, and return to the original window to paste it in.

As we learned in Chapter 15, "Documentation in Xcode," Option-double-clicking a symbol or a partial symbol opens the Documentation window and displays an API search for the symbol from the active docsets.

> **NOTE**
>
> If you have set the rightmost button in the editor window's toolbar to **Grouped**, Command-double-clicking will display the definition in the same window you started from. Press ⌥⌘← to return to the previous file.

## The Navigation Bar

At the top of each editor pane is a series of pop-ups and buttons for navigating in and among files. The editor pane carries with it the concept of a navigation history, much like the history of a web browser. You can go back and forth through this history or jump between documents in it.

The first three controls in the navigation bar are for traversing the pane's history. The first two buttons are arrowheads representing a jump to the previous or next file in the browsing sequence; you can hold the mouse button down on these to see a pop-up of files in the respective directions. ⌥⌘← and ⌥⌘→ are equivalent to these buttons. The third button is a pop-up menu of the full history of the pane, sorted alphabetically. Options at the bottom of the menu allow you to limit the history list to the last 10, 20, or 40 files.

Next to the history pop-up is a pop-up for landmarks in the file. The pop-up allows you to jump to class, method, and function declarations; #defines and typedefs; function definitions; markers set by #pragma mark; and comments beginning with TODO: or FIXME: (the colons are important). This menu is also active when displaying a class or a data model; the menu is filled with the names of the classes or entities in the diagram. If you hold down the Option key when clicking, the pop-up will be sorted alphabetically.

The remaining buttons stick to the right end of the navigation bar (see Figure 20.3). The first is the bookmark menu, which lists all the bookmarks in the currently displayed file. Set a bookmark by pressing ⌘D (or selecting **Edit > Add to Bookmarks**) and typing the name for the new bookmark. Bookmarks are stored in the .pbxuser-suffixed file inside the project .xcodeproj package and aren't shared between users.

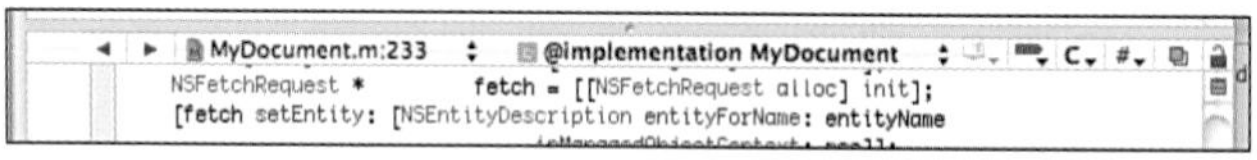

FIGURE 20.3     The navigation bar of an editor pane.

The breakpoint menu lists all the breakpoints set in the currently displayed source file.

The class menu (**C**) shows all the superclasses, subclasses, and categories of the class currently being edited. Select one to be taken to its definition. This feature relies on Code Sense's being active.

Next comes the header menu. This menu lists every header included, directly or indirectly, in the current source file. If the current file is a header, the menu also lists every implementation file that includes it, directly or indirectly. Choosing an item in the menu focuses the editor on that file.

The counterpart button looks like a stack of two squares. It is almost universal that for every implementation source file (.m, mm, .c, or .cp) in a C-family programming language, there is a header file of the same base name. Xcode calls such header-implementation file pairs "counterparts" and allows you to switch between them by clicking this button or by pressing ⌥⌘↑. See the section "Editor Modes" for one more variant on this service.

Last in line is the lock button. If you do not have write access to the displayed file, this button shows a locked padlock. On files to which you do have write access, you can click this button to prevent changes to the file; it will set the `locked` attribute in the HFS file system, so the condition persists and affects other applications.

Below the lock button is the pane splitter, a button showing a gray window with a horizontal line across it. Clicking this button divides the editor pane into two independent editors, one above the other, on the same file. Each half has a splitter button and below it a button showing a gray window with no line across it. This button closes the pane it is attached to.

If you hold down the Option key while clicking the split button, the split will be vertical rather than horizontal. All further splits are in the same orientation as the first.

## Code Focus

Xcode 3 adds a new feature to the gutter when you edit a source file, the Code Focus ribbon (see Figure 20.4). Any more-than-trivial source code encompasses many block scopes, such as for function bodies or the alternatives in `if` statements. These blocks could be nested several layers deep, and may be too long for the beginning and end to be visible in one window. It may be unclear which block delimiters match with which others. Often, you'd like to be able to ignore the details of a block and concentrate on the higher-level structure.

The Code Focus ribbon helps you visualize nested scopes and get them out of your way as needed. You can use it passively for visualization. It sits next to your code, and indicates nesting by displaying a darker gray with each deeper nesting level. Code next to one shade of gray is all at the same level.

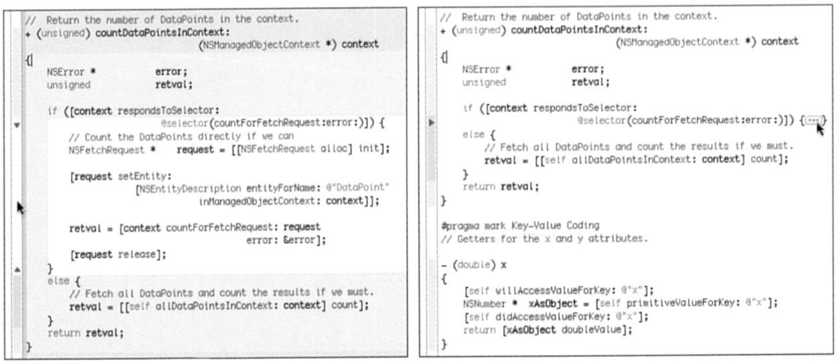

**FIGURE 20.4    The Code Focus ribbon. *(Left)* The ribbon is darker the more deeply the code next to it is nested. Moving the mouse into the ribbon highlights the scope next to the ribbon. *(Right)* Clicking the ribbon collapses that scope. A disclosure triangle appears in the ribbon, and the elided text is represented by a yellow ellipsis button (see the mouse pointer).**

The ribbon shows nesting even more clearly when you move the cursor into it. Pointing next to a line of code highlights the block to which it belongs; shallower nesting levels are shaded with darker grays.

Finally, Code Focus allows you to collapse a nesting scope entirely. Click the ribbon and the corresponding code is replaced by a yellow marker with an ellipsis (…) in it. Double-clicking the marker expands the collapsed block, or you can click the disclosure triangle that now appears in the ribbon.

Code Focus relies on a parser, which makes it smarter than the folding facilities of some other text editors: It does not rely on block delimiters having matching indentation levels, and it works with scripting languages and XML.

> **NOTE**
>
> If you edit an XML .plist file, you may find that Code Focus isn't available. The problem is that when Xcode encounters a .plist file, it may not know whether it's an XML file or a NeXT-style property list. Tell it by opening the **General** tab of the file's Info window and selecting **text.plist.xml** in the **File Type** pop-up.

## The Debugger Strip

Another bar appears in editor panes when your product is running under the debugger: the debugger strip. The bar appears beneath the navigation bar when a target is run under the debugger.

The debugger strip compresses all the controls of the debugger into a space only a few pixels high (see Figure 20.5). In the middle are the control buttons for turning all breakpoints on and off, pausing or running the application, stepping through the code line by line, stepping down into a function being called in the current line, or stepping out into the function that called this one. Additional buttons reveal the Debugger and Console windows.

At the left of the strip is a pop-up menu enabling you to switch focus to any thread in the application being debugged. At the right, a pop-up for selecting any function in the current call chain, similarly to clicking in the stack-trace list at the upper left of the Debugger window.

FIGURE 20.5    The in-editor debugger bar, providing in miniature the controls for debugging an application.

We haven't had much exposure to the debugger strip because we've been using the separate Debugger window for debugging Linear. The reason for this is that although the bar, plus datatips, provide all the necessary tools for debugging *in theory*, in practice they are not as clear to use as the Debugger. The bar shows all the call chain in the rightmost pop-up, but it does not show you the chain, and your position in it, at a glance. Similarly, while you can hover the cursor over variable names in your source to view their variables in datatips, you can't watch the values change as you step through, and you can't browse instance variables that aren't referenced in the current method.

## Editor Modes

Different people have different styles of working with their development environments, and Xcode tries to accommodate as many of the common choices as possible.

One such preference is the number of editor windows the IDE opens for you. Some developers are used to working with a separate window for each source file, building up a stack of windows, much like having each file on a sheet of paper. Other developers find a multiplicity of windows cluttered and obstructive and instead want the editor window to know about all the files they are interested in and to be able to present each in the same view, as needed.

You can choose between these behaviors with the **Grouped/Ungrouped** button in the toolbar of separate editing windows (see Figure 20.6). If the icon for the button shows a single window (**Grouped**), additional files will open in the same editor window. If the icon shows a stack of windows (**Ungrouped**), additional files will open in their own windows.

FIGURE 20.6    The **Grouped/Ungrouped** button in the toolbar of editor windows determines whether additional files will open in the same window (left) or each in its own (right).

In the case of ungrouped windows, there is an additional variant: Xcode allows you to switch quickly between implementation (m, .c, or .cp, for instance) files and the associated header (.h) files. In the default Xcode key mappings, this is done with ⌥⌘↑. A strict rule of a new window for every file would have such counterpart files appear in separate windows, but even developers who prefer many editor windows may make an exception in this case: It's very common to edit an implementation file in one half of a split editor and its header in the other. For this case, open the General pane in the Preferences window and Select **Counterparts Always Load in Same Editor** if you want headers and implementation files to alternate in the same editor window, even though you generally want many editor windows.

# Project Find Window

The Project Find window, which we have seen before, allows you to search for a string or a symbol in either your project or the frameworks it includes. This window consists of three panes. The bottom pane, as usual, is an editor pane. The middle pane contains the results of any searches you do. Each file containing a match for the search string is displayed with a disclosure triangle next to it; when the triangle is open, each match is shown in context. Selecting a match displays it in the editor pane. The top pane of the Project Find window allows you to specify the search you want to perform (see Figure 20.7).

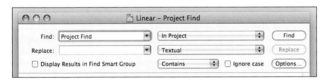

FIGURE 20.7    The Project Find window controls.

The **Find** and **Replace** combo boxes are straightforward. Type the text you want to search for and, optionally, replace it with. The drop-down feature of the combo box enables you to browse recent find and replace strings. Selecting an old find string recalls the results of that search (which may be obsolete).

There are three pop-up menus next to the text-entry boxes. The top menu allows you to specify what files to search: files already open; files selected in the Groups & Files list; files included in the project, its frameworks, or both; or files in all open projects. By clicking the **Options** button, you can edit or add to these choices. You can define a set extending to open documents or open projects; to selected files in a project, all files in a project, or all files in all open projects; files in projects or frameworks; files with names matching one of a list of regular expressions; or files in a list of files and folders.

> **WARNING**
>
> You can edit the default search scopes in the top pop-up menu just as if they were your own. It is easy to click the **Options** button, make changes, and discover you've changed one of the standard scopes beyond recognition. If you want to edit a search scope, make sure you click the **Add** button first, so that you can edit and test a scratch copy.

The second pop-up determines whether the search is:

▶ Textual—the search string is searched for literally.

▶ Regular-expression-based—the search string is interpreted as a pattern to be matched.

▶ For a definition—the search string is applied to definitions and declarations of classes, functions, types, and methods.

▶ By symbol—detecting only declarations and method names that include the search string.

The third pop-up specifies whether the search is for a simple match (**Contains**) or for a string that extends to a word boundary at either or both ends (**Starts With, Whole Words, Ends With**). You can make the search non-case-sensitive (**Ignore Case**).

Finally, you can click **Display Results in Find Smart Group**. This check box is misnamed; after all, every search you do will add the search to the Find Results group in the Groups & Files list, and selecting the search will recall the results of that search (which, again, may be obsolete). Checking this box will put the results of the search in the project's Detail view, where you can narrow the results list further by use of the search field in the toolbar. For instance, you can search for `volume` in your project and then use the search field in the toolbar to narrow the list to lines that also contain the string `max`.

# The Favorites Bar

The Groups & Files list is a simple device for accessing files in a hierarchy of folders (groups). However, the list can encompass thousands of files in hundreds of groups. These might go many layers deep, and it isn't always convenient to dig through the list to find a much-used file, or to leave a deep tree open just for access to an active group. The favorites bar is the solution to this problem.

Add the favorites bar to your project window by selecting **View > Layout > Show Favorites Bar**. A gradient bar will appear in the project window, just below the toolbar. You can drag almost anything you want into the favorites bar. If the item is a file, clicking it will display it in the Detail view and, if it's visible, the associated editor. If it's a group, holding the mouse button down will drop down a menu of all the items in that group.

The possibilities don't end with items from the Groups & Files list. Anything displayable in an Xcode editor window can go into the favorites bar. For instance, if you often refer to a page in the developer documentation, you can drag the icon from its title bar into the favorites bar.

# Groups & Files List

The Groups & Files list at the left of the project window is at the root of all the work you do in Xcode. All access to project files and build settings starts in this list. A close look shows that it is more than a hierarchical file list.

## The Project Group

The first "group" in the Groups & Files list is the Project group. Every file in your project appears somewhere in this group. I didn't say that the Project group includes every file that goes into building your product—although it does. The Project group also includes anything, anywhere, that you might want to search, copy, or otherwise refer to. It's *target membership* that identifies the files that are ingredients for a product.

An example: Cocoa applications link to Cocoa, an umbrella framework that includes the AppKit, Foundation, and Core Data frameworks, but doesn't give ready access to the headers of those frameworks. So the Cocoa-application project template includes separate references to AppKit, Foundation, and Core Data, *without* linking to them. That gets them included when the project is indexed and searched. But of the four, only Cocoa has its target-member box checked.

Within the Project group, you can have subgroups, identified by their disclosure triangles and their little yellow folder icons. You are free to use or ignore subgroups, as you prefer. Subgroups have nothing to do with disk organization or with how any of your targets are built. Subgroups are there for you to organize your files however you like.

For instance, most project templates have a Resources subgroup inside them and contain files that will end up in the product bundle's Resources directory.

Moving a file out of the Resources subgroup doesn't change anything; the file will still be copied into the product's Resources directory. By the same token, moving a file into the Resources subgroup does nothing to your product; if you want it in your product's Resources directory, make sure that it shows up in the Copy Resources build phase of the product's target in the Targets group.

In two instances, the structure of a subgroup *does* represent something in the outside world. Both involve adding a directory rather than a file to the project. Suppose that we were to add a Linear option that would offer the user a choice of graphics to be drawn at each point of its graph view. We might have the Linear's Resources directory include a subdirectory containing an image file for each available graphic.

We get busy with our favorite art program and soon have a directory of a dozen .png files. We drag the folder from the Finder into the Groups & Files list or use **Project > Add to Project...** and select the directory. We are presented with the familiar add-to-project sheet, as shown in Figure 20.8. Look at the radio buttons in the middle. If you make the first choice, a new subgroup, with the same name as the directory and containing the same files, will be added to the project. Any subdirectories become subgroups of the new subgroup, and so on. These are still simple groups, however. You can move the listed groups and files in the Groups & Files list as if you'd added them one by one. So that is the first exception: You can add a directory to your project, and Xcode will start the added files off in your on-disk organization scheme.

The second choice, **Create Folder References for Any Added Folders**, does something quite different. First, the new folder icon in the list will be blue, not yellow. Second, Xcode will track the contents of that directory as they change. As you remove and add files in your repertoire of point markers, Xcode will automatically build your application with the correct set of files. Xcode adds the whole folder, with whatever its contents might from time to time be, to the Copy Bundle Resources build phase.

Those are the two ways that Xcode's Groups & Files list gets influenced by the file system world. Groups & Files can influence the file system in three ways.

- ▶ If you add a file or a folder to your project, the check box at the top of the add-to-project sheet offers **Copy Items into Destination Group's Folder (If Needed)**. This normally means that when you borrow a source file from one project directory, you can decide whether to copy it into the other or to use it in place.

- ▶ You can rename any file or group in the project group by Option-clicking it, or slowly clicking the name twice. That will make the name editable. Editing the name renames the file. If your project is under SCM, Xcode will also issue the SCM commands necessary to rename the file in the repository.

FIGURE 20.8     The add-to-project sheet, showing the option to add folders as live references to file directories. This would ensure that every build of the targets selected in the list at bottom is given an up-to-date set of files.

- ▶ Deleting a file from the Groups & Files list could mean one of two things: You want to have the file out of the list, but do you also want to have it out of the file system? Xcode presents you with the option to delete only Xcode's reference or to delete the file itself, too.

## The Targets Group

Next under the Project group is the Targets group. Inside this group is an entry for each target in the project. Selecting a target fills the Detail view with every file included in that target. Double-clicking the target reveals an Info window for that target, which has the following tabs:

- ▶ **General** lets you name the target and designate other objects in the project—other targets or targets in included project files—that this target depends on. Such dependencies will be brought up-to-date before the target is built.

- ▶ **Build** is the repository for all the switches and environment variables that control the building of the target.

- ▶ **Rules** instructs the build system which tool to use for each type of source file. You can add a source file type by clicking the + button and specifying a suffix for the type and a compiler or script to do the processing. You will rarely need to use this tab.

20

▶ **Properties** provides a convenient user interface for editing the Info.plist of the target's product. Projects with more than one bundle target will have more than one Info.plist, in files distinguished by different prefixes; this panel will always edit the correct one. It's almost inevitable that you will need to edit an Info.plist file directly; the **Properties** tab includes an **Open Info.plist as File** button that will take you to the right file.

▶ **Comments** allows you to enter comments for your benefit or for others. The Detail list can be made to show comments, and you can then search on the comment column.

Clicking the disclosure triangle next to each target reveals the build phases that Xcode goes through to produce the target's product. Build phases, in turn, can be opened to reveal exactly which files participate in each phase. One way to add a file to a target is to drag its icon into the desired build phase of a target.

You can add a build phase to a target with one of the commands at **Project > New Build Phase** or by Control- (right-) clicking the target and selecting **Add > New Build Phase** in the contextual menu. The possible build phases are as follows:

▶ Copy Files, if you need to fill custom locations in your product bundle with custom contents. Use a Copy Files phase for each item to copy. The most common use for this phase is to place embedded frameworks in the Frameworks directory of application bundles. There can be as many Copy Files phases as there are files or directories to copy.

▶ Run Script, to put arbitrary UNIX shell scripts anywhere in the build process. You can specify input and output files for the phase so that the build system can do dependency analysis on the inputs and products. You might use script phases for running testing frameworks, custom preprocessors, or documentation generators. There can be as many Run Script phases as you need.

▶ Copy Headers, to move all library headers marked "public" or "private" to Headers or PrivateHeaders, in a framework target, or to /usr/local/include, in a static library target.

▶ Copy Bundle Resources, the phase into which most noncode members of a target will fall. All the files in the Copy Bundle Resources phase are copied into the product's Resources directory. This phase is automatically a part of Cocoa and Carbon application targets.

▶ Compile Sources, the phase that analyzes the dependencies of source and object files and compiles any sources that are—or that include files that are—newer than their objects. This phase is part of most targets.

▶ Compile AppleScripts, to compile AppleScripts in an AppleScript Studio application, yielding .scpt files in Resources/Scripts. Note that this phase does not *execute* AppleScripts; the Shell Script phase is the only way to insert custom behaviors in the build process.

- Link Binary With Libraries, a phase in any target that produces an executable. This phase contains any libraries and frameworks that are part of the target.

- Build Java Resources, for putting the files in the phase into the product .jar file for Java applications.

- Build ResourceManager Resources, for using the Rez resource compiler to compile .r files and copy .rsrc files into an application resource file.

## The Executables Group

The Executables group contains references to every application or tool that you may run or debug while working on your project. The executable products of the project's targets are automatically added to this group; typically, that's all you'll need. However, you may add other executables with the command **Project > New Custom Executable....** We'd do this, for instance, if a project built plug-ins to be hosted by a third-party application; we could set up the host application as a custom executable. With the custom executable set as the active executable for your project, running or debugging the plug-in is just a matter of issuing the **Run** or **Debug** commands.

Double-clicking an executable's icon will bring up an Info window with the following tabs:

- **General** allows you to designate the location of the executable, whether to use debug or profile variants of dynamic libraries (see the section on "Debugging Techniques" in Chapter 22, "More About Debugging"), how standard I/O is to be handled for runs, and what the initial working directory for the executable will be. It's important to remember that executables are guaranteed a particular working directory under Mac OS X only when run from the command line.

- **Arguments** lets you edit one list that supplies command-line arguments to the executable, and another list that specifies key/value pairs for environment variables. Once added to a list, any element can be made active or inactive by clicking the check box next to it.

- **Debugging** allows you to specify the debugger to be used on the executable. This panel is valuable if you want to switch to gdb to debug Objective-C code used in an AppleScript application, for instance. A pop-up controls how standard I/O is handled for debugging sessions. The panel also sets up remote debugging, specifies whether to run the executable immediately on starting the debugger, and whether to treat Carbon Debugger() and DebugStr() calls as debugger breaks.

  A check box, **Auto-Attach Debugger on Crash**, is important when you are executing your product by the **Run** command, instead of **Debug**. Ordinarily, if the product crashes, it simply goes away, just as it would if you were running it from the command line or the Finder. When this option is set, crashing will open the debugger at the site of the crash.

Xcode provides an editable list for where gdb (and therefore the Debugger window) will search for the product's source files. This becomes an issue when your project refers to source files from outside the project directory.

▸ **Comments** allows you to add any comments you want.

## Smart Groups

The Project group has a limitation. Any given file can appear in the list only once. This means that you must pick your classifications carefully; for example, you can put your AirFlowView.m file in a Views group or an Aerodynamics group, but not both.

Smart groups are a way for files to belong to additional groups, based on patterns in their names. For instance, AirFlowView.m could be tucked away in a manual Aerodynamics group but also be found in a Views smart group that includes all files matching the wildcard pattern *View*. Any new files with View in their names would automatically be added to the Views group.

For another instance, suppose that you've been sticking to the pattern of using hyphens only in the names of files that define Objective-C categories. You could then have a smart group that automatically includes header and implementation files for all your categories. Select **Project > New Smart Group > Simple Regular Expression Smart Group** to create a smart group and open an Info window for configuring it (see Figure 20.9).

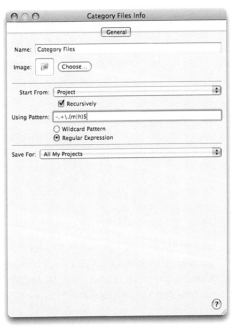

All we need to do is give the group a name (**Categories**) and a regular expression ('`-.+\.(m¦h)$`') for files ending with .m or .h and containing a hyphen, and close the window. The new smart group will appear at the end of the Groups & Files list.

Had we wanted a group that covered only, say, project resources, we could do this, because the configuration panel allows us to restrict the search to groups within the Groups & Files list. If it is very specialized and applicable to only one project, the smart group can be restricted to the current project; alternatively, it can be made available to all projects.

FIGURE 20.9    Creating a regular-expression smart group. This Info window appears when you issue the command **Project > New Smart Group > Simple Regular Expression Smart Group**. You can name the new group, substitute your own icon for it, root its search anywhere in the Groups & Files hierarchy, and have it match file names either by regular expression or by "glob" wildcard patterns. Smart groups can be project-specific or available to all projects.

Smart groups appear last in the Groups & Files list, which makes them less accessible than they might otherwise be. You can drag a smart group higher in the list. Or, if you have the favorites bar active, you can drag a smart group into it, where the smart group will serve as a drop-down menu of its members.

## Symbol Smart Group

The Project Symbols smart group is another feature that relies on the Code Sense index. This group is found near the bottom of the Groups & Files list, with a blue cube for an icon. Clicking it fills the Detail view with a listing of every symbol—function, method, instance variable, constant, and so on—in your project, including NIB and data model files. Symbols that have definitions (in implementation files) separate from declarations (in header files) will be listed twice. The list can be sorted by identifier, type, or location. Clicking a list item takes you to the definition or declaration that item represents. The list is searchable on any column, using the search field in the toolbar.

Control-clicking (or right-clicking) a Project Symbols item raises a contextual menu:

▶ **Reveal in Class Browser** opens the Class Browser window, with the class list expanded to select the relevant class. If the symbol is a member of the class, it is selected in the member list.

▶ **Find Symbol Name in Project** performs a textual **Project Find**, with the name of the selected symbol as the target. This will yield at least every reference to the symbol in your project.

▶ **Copy Declaration for Method/Function** puts the name and parameters for the function or method, as it might appear in a header, on the clipboard.

▶ **Copy Invocation for Method/Function** puts a use of the function or method on the clipboard. The parameters, including any object to which the method might be sent, are marked with placeholder strings.

The Groups & Files list is configurable; Control- (or right-) clicking in the list brings up a contextual menu that includes a **Preferences** submenu, allowing you to include or exclude any groups in the list. For instance, the Breakpoints list is not included, but you can add it to the Groups & Files list by checking it in the **Preferences** submenu.

Control- (or right-) clicking in the *header* of the Groups & Files list brings up a contextual menu allowing you to add or remove columns in the list. We have already made use of this feature to add an SCM status column.

# Class Browser Window

By selecting **Project > Class Browser**, you can open a window for browsing the headers for classes in frameworks, and for your own classes. The Class Browser window is anchored by a list of classes at the left side. Selecting a class from the class list fills the member list at top right with a list of all methods and instance variables; selecting one of these displays the selected item in the editor pane below.

20

If a method is declared in an interface, selecting it in the member list will always take you to the interface declaration. If it is not declared in the interface, selecting it will take you to the definition in the implementation file.

The anchor list of classes on the left is filtered according to the **Option Set** pop-up in the Class Browser window's toolbar. The standard option sets determine whether the class listing is flat, or hierarchical by inheritance; and whether the listing is of all classes or restricted to classes defined in the current project.

By clicking the **Configure Options** button, you can change these options or add option sets of your own. For instance, it is often easy to miss class features that are implemented by a superclass and not by the class itself. One of the options available is to include all inherited members in the member listing for a class.

Classes and methods from Apple-supplied frameworks, and for which there is online documentation, are marked with a small blue book icon. Clicking the icon will present the rele-

> **WARNING**
>
> As with the Project Find options editor, it is easy to change the settings for one of the option sets provided with Xcode, and there is no **Revert** or **Cancel** button. Click the **Add** button if you're experimenting.

vant documentation in the Class Browser window's editor space. The browser also displays documentation icons for items in your own docsets, but as of Xcode 3.0 this did not always happen.

# Class Modeler

When building the data model editor for Core Data, the Xcode team took care to make the graphical modeling framework as general as possible. The first added application is the class modeler tool. The easiest way to see a class model is to select some files in the Groups & Files list of the Project window and select the menu command **Design > Class Model > Quick Model**. The modeling tool uses the Code Sense database to produce an annotated diagram similar to the data model diagram from Chapter 16, "Using the Data Modeling Tools." See Figure 20.10.

As with the data model diagram, the class model diagram is supplemented by three panels at the top, displaying all the classes in the diagram, all the members—both properties and operations—of the selected classes, and a display of the properties of the selected members. Unlike the data model diagram, the class model diagram does not allow you to edit your class model by using the diagram or browser views.

Models may be *static* or *tracking*. A static model is a snapshot of the classes when they were presented for modeling; it documents particular classes at a particular moment. A tracking model observes the groups you designate when you select groups and files to include in the model; as files enter and leave the included groups, the classes they define enter and leave the model, too.

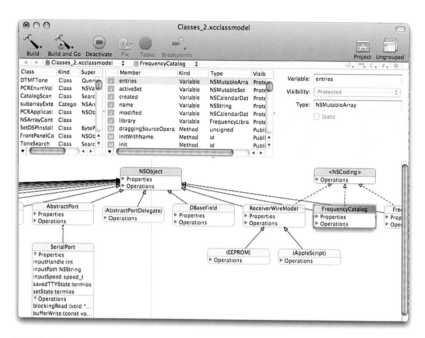

FIGURE 20.10    A part of a class model diagram, showing NSObject and some of the classes in a large project that derive directly from it. Classes are shown in boxes with blue title bars, categories with green, and protocols with red. Entities outside the immediate scope of the classes that were presented to the model, such as NSObject and NSCoding here, are shown with slightly darker title bars. Disclosure triangles control the visibility of class properties and operations; class SerialPort has both open in this view. Because class hierarchies, especially in Objective-C, tend to be broad and shallow, these diagrams often turn out to be one page tall and many wide.

A tracking model is available only through the **File > New File...** (⌘N) command. Select **Design > Class Model** from the New File Assistant, and you will be presented with a sheet that allows you to pick groups and files from your project (see Figure 20.11). The sheet will also allow you to choose a static or a tracking model. Remember that a tracking model must include at least one group, or folder, icon. This model will be added to your project as a file with the .xcclassmodel extension.

The class model tool uses the Code Sense project-indexing facility as the source of its information. If you've turned Code Sense off or if the index isn't yet fully built, class model diagrams won't be available.

If the class model seems to be missing classes from a framework—perhaps you're using the Address Book framework and it doesn't show up in the model—be sure that the root header for the framework is #included somewhere in your source or headers. In our example, the following line should appear somewhere *in addition to* your prefix header:

```
#import <AddressBook/AddressBook.h>
```

20

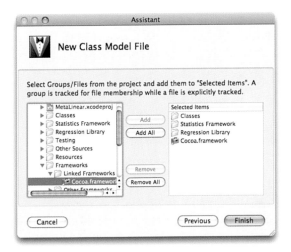

FIGURE 20.11    The New Class Model Assistant, which is the last stage of adding a class model file to a project through the **File > New File...** command. The list at the left shows all the files and groups in the project; select from these and use the buttons in the middle to add the classes they define to the model.

Graphics from the modeling view can be exported to other programs. Select the objects you want to export, hold down the Option key, and drag your selection into the Finder, where it will become a picture clipping, or to the working area of your favorite graphics program.

## Project Layout

Xcode is a tool for a diverse corps of developers, each with his or her own habits in managing the work of development, and using the full range of available screen sizes. Some developers like the orderly feel of a development environment that keeps all tasks in a single window; others are happiest when separate objects get separate representations on screen. There is every gradation between.

Xcode reflects Apple's effort to accommodate as many development styles as possible.

▶ The default layout provides separate windows for each kind of task but showcases the Groups & Files and Detail displays as the center of the project.

▶ An all-in-one format consolidates every operation into a single window.

▶ A condensed format sacrifices the Detail view in favor of something more familiar to CodeWarrior veterans.

The format can be changed only when no project window is open. Set the format in Preferences (**Xcode > Preferences**, or ⌘ **Comma**), in the General (first) pane. Make your choice in the pop-up provided.

# Default Layout

Your Xcode projects will have the default layout unless you decide otherwise. The Project window is anchored by the Groups & Files list on the left, which lists first all the files associated with the project, then all the project's targets, then all the associated executables, and then various automatically generated file groups. At the right of the window is a Detail view, the contents of which are determined by the current selection in the Groups & Files list.

Clicking the **Editor** icon in the toolbar switches the right side of the window between all-editor and the Detail view, possibly shared with the editor.

### Build Results

This window, which **Build > Build Results** brings forward, is divided into a browser pane at top and an editor below. The browser consists of a list of the warnings and errors encountered in the course of building a target. Clicking an error or a warning will focus the editor on the place in your source code where the error was detected. At the bottom of the list are three buttons and one drop-down menu:

▶ The first button controls whether the list includes all the steps in the build, or only the ones that generated warnings or errors.

▶ The second controls whether warnings are shown in the list.

▶ The third opens and closes a third pane in the window, between the browser and the editor, containing a transcript of the actual commands used to accomplish the build, and the messages the underlying tools displayed in response.

▶ The menu determines, for this project only, whether the Build Results window will appear automatically and, if so, on what conditions; maybe you want to see it only if there are errors, for instance. The same settings, for *all* projects, can be made in the Building section of the Preferences window.

The detailed build transcript can be a useful tool. If you aren't sure which flags are being passed to the compilers, or if Xcode's interpretation of an error message isn't clear, refer to the transcript. The Build Results window is also useful in that it contains pop-up menus allowing you to set **Active Target**, **Active Build Configuration**, and **Active Executable**.

### Console

The Console window (**Run > Console**) allows you to choose the active target, configuration, and executable, and to build and run the active executable. While the executable is running, this window displays its standard output, and receives its standard input.

If the executable is running under the debugger, the window also channels standard I/O for gdb. With four roles to play, the Console window can be confusing to read. By setting the font for each role, in the **Fonts and Colors** section of the Debugging pane of the Preferences window, you can make the distinctions clear.

The contents of the Run Log accumulate until they are cleared, either by the **Run > Clear Console** command (which is visible only when you hold the Control and Option keys down) or by clicking the **Clear Log** button in the Console's toolbar.

The default size of the Console window runs the **Clear Log** button off the right end of the toolbar. Use the pop-up at the end of the toolbar, or simply widen the window.

### SCM Results

Selecting **SCM > SCM Results** (⇧⌘V) displays the SCM Results window. The window lists all the files in the project for which the SCM status is other than current. Selecting an editable item in the list, such as a source file, puts the contents of that file in the window's editor pane, which may be hidden; look for the dimple of the view splitter at the bottom of the window.

At the bottom left of the listing is a button with a representation of lines of text in it. Clicking this button switches the display to a log of Xcode's interactions with your chosen SCM system.

Next to that button is a pop-up menu that controls what is shown in the upper list. By default, this is **Flat**, in which all the noncurrent files are listed one by one. Switching to **Interesting** shows the file hierarchy to which the noncurrent files belong. **All** lists all the files in the project, current or not.

## All-in-One Layout

This layout does away with the great variety of specialist windows put up by the default layout. Instead, everything is done in the Project window, which has pages for two phases in the project life cycle: editing and debugging (see Figure 20.12).

### Editing

The Editing page has four tabs: **Detail**, **Project Find**, **SCM Results**, and **Build**.

Selecting **Detail** gets you much the same window you have in the default layout. The only difference is that what were specialty windows in the default layout replace the Detail view in the all in one. Pressing ⌘⇧F, for instance, does not bring up a separate Project Find window; instead, it switches the Project window to the **Project Find** tab. Pressing ⇧⌘B switches to the **Build** tab instead of showing the Build Results window.

### Debugging

In the all-in-one layout, the Console is an additional pane at the bottom of the Debugger page. This cuts down on the precious vertical space available for other uses in the Debugger window but does relieve the common problem of losing the console in the stack of Xcode windows. That is the only difference from the separate Debugger window in the default layout.

The debugger strip appears in the editor pane, if you switch back to the Editing page while debugging.

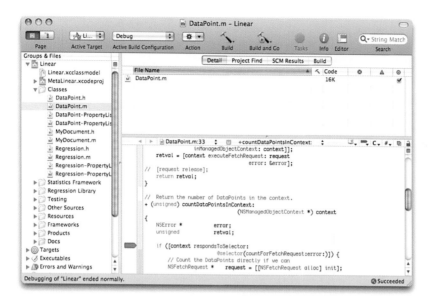

FIGURE 20.12    Unlike the default layout, the all-in-one project layout has a **Page** selector in the upper-left corner for switching between editing and debugging functions, as well as tabs over the rightmost portion of the window for selecting services within a page.

## Condensed Layout

The condensed layout (see Figure 20.13) pares the Project window down to a subset of the Groups & Files list, a format familiar to Code Warrior users. Which subset of Groups & Files is shown is controlled by three tabs at the top of the view: **Files**, **Targets**, and **Other**.

The **Files** tab is simply the first portion of the full Groups & Files list, the one dealing with the file system entities that are included in the project. Double-clicking an entry in the list brings up an editor window for that file.

The switch to the condensed layout leaves us with some settings that don't work well without the full Project window. Without the Detail view, there is no way to control what source files belong to a target. We can customize the

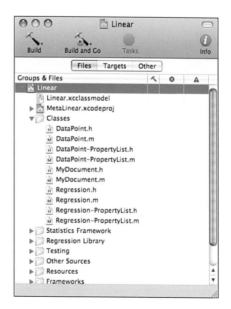

FIGURE 20.13    The condensed layout does away with the Detail and editor portion of the Project window to provide an experience similar to the Code Warrior IDE.

Groups & Files view to make up for the loss. Control-click in the Groups & Files header and select the **Target Membership** item. This adds a column of check boxes to the list, enabling you to include or exclude files in the active target.

The **Targets** tab includes the Targets and Executables groups. The ability to open the build phases of a target and edit the files that go into them is analogous to the linkage view of a Code Warrior project.

The **Other** tab covers all the automated groups—Errors and Warnings, Find Results, Bookmarks, SCM, Project Symbols, and the smart groups.

If you left the Xcode defaults unchanged, the major notice you will have of errors and warnings after a build will be the status bar at the bottom of the Project window, plus the columns for error and warning counts for each (visible) file. By default, Xcode does not display a window listing errors after a build. You can summon the Build Results window by clicking one of the build-status icons in the status bar or by double-clicking the Errors and Warnings group icon.

Or, you can have the Build Results window open automatically. The Building (third) panel of the Preferences window allows you to set the conditions on which the Build Results window will open and close. For instance, if you want visible feedback when you start a build, change **Open During Builds** from **Never** to **Always**. If you don't want the window cluttering up your screen if it contains no news, you can change **Close After Builds** from **Never** to **On Success**.

If you do a **Project Find**, using the condensed layout, and check **Display Results in Find Smart Group**, Xcode will open an additional project window just to show a Detail list. Double-clicking an existing find smart group opens the **Project Find** with the results of that search.

Project Symbols is a dead loss in the condensed layout, relying as it does on the Detail view; there is no Detail view in the condensed layout. Double-clicking Project Symbols opens a new Class Browser window, which is not the same thing at all. The Details window gets the intended functionality back for you, at the expense of opening what is effectively another project window.

You can select **View > Detail** to punt from the Condensed format entirely. The command makes a window appear that is essentially the Default-format project window, but without the option of an editor pane. Project Symbols works in this window.

## Summary

In this nuts-and-bolts chapter, we toured every visible feature in the main windows of Xcode. We covered the Project window, in all three layouts, and the Groups & Files list, which is at the heart of the Xcode workflow. We saw how editor windows work. We looked at the specialty windows: Project Find, Class Browser, and Class Modeler.

# CHAPTER 21

# Xcode for make Veterans

**IN THIS CHAPTER**

▶ **The Xcode Build System**

▶ **Controlling Build Parameters**

▶ **Customizing the Build System**

▶ **Building from the Command Line**

▶ **Build Configurations**

This chapter is for experienced UNIX programmers who are accustomed to controlling application builds with a dependency manager, such as GNU make. It's also useful to any user of Xcode who wants a better grasp of how Xcode builds projects.

As an integrated development environment, Xcode is at first glance far removed from the tools you are used to. But Xcode is not a tightly integrated tool set. The editor, the build system, and some convenience services run as part of Xcode's process; but for preprocessing, compilation, and linkage, Xcode is a front end for gcc and other command-line tools. You may feel that your builds have been sealed away from you in a black box; in this chapter, I hope to open the box for you a little.

A makefile is organized around a hierarchy of goals. Some goals, such as the frequently used clean or install targets, are abstract, but most are files. Associated with each goal is a list of other goals that are antecedents—dependencies—of that goal and a script for turning the antecedents into something that satisfies the goal. Most commonly, the antecedents are input files for the tools that the script runs to produce a target file. The genius of make comes from the rule that if any target is more recently modified than all its antecedents, it is presumed to embody their current state, and it is not necessary to run the script to produce it again. The combination of a tree of dependencies and this pruning rule makes make a powerful and efficient tool for automating such tasks as building software products.

The organizing unit of a makefile is the target-dependency-action group. But in the case of application development, this group is often stereotyped to the extent that you don't even have to specify it; make provides a default rule that looks like this:

```
%.o     :    %.c
    $(CC) -c $(CPPFLAGS) $(CFLAGS) -o $@ $<
```

So, all the programmer needs to do is list all the constituent .o files in the project, and the built-in rule will produce the .o files as needed. Often, the task of maintaining a makefile becomes less one of maintaining dependencies than of keeping lists.

In the same way, Xcode makes dependency analysis a matter of list keeping by taking advantage of the fact that almost all projects are targeted at specific kinds of executable products, such as applications, libraries, tools, or plug-ins. Knowing how the build process ends, Xcode can do the right thing with the files that go into the project.

A file in the Xcode Groups & Files list is a member of three distinct lists:

▶ By being in the Groups & Files list, the file is part of the *project*. This has nothing to do with whether it has any effect on any product of the project. It might, for instance, be a document you're keeping handy for reference or some notes you're taking.

▶ A file may belong to zero or more *targets* in the project. A file is included in a target's file list because it is a part of that target's product, whether as a source file or as a resource to be copied literally into the product. When a file is added to a project, Xcode asks you which targets in the project should include the file. You can select what files belong to a target through check boxes in the detail view or, optionally, in the Groups & Files list. You can select what targets a file belongs to with the **Targets** tab of the file's Info window.

▶ What role a file plays in a target depends on what *phase* of the target the file belongs to. When a file is added to a target, Xcode assigns it to a build phase, based on the type of the file. Files with gcc-compilable suffixes get assigned to the Compile Sources phase, libraries, to the Link Binary with Libraries phase, Rez source and .rsrc files to the Build Resource Manager Resources phase, and so on (see Figure 21.1). Files that don't fit anywhere else are put in the Copy Bundle Resources phase, for incorporation into the product's Resources directory.

> **NOTE**
>
> A target is completely identified with the set of files that comprise it. There is no concept of including or excluding files from a single target on the basis of its being built with a Release or Debug configuration. If you need disjoint sets of files, make a separate target for each set; a file can belong to more than one target.

When you create a target, either in the process of creating an Xcode project or by adding a target to an existing project, you specify what type of product you want to produce, and you can't change that type except by making another target. The target type forms one anchor—the endpoint—in the Xcode build system's dependency analysis. It tells the build system what the product's desired structure—single file or package—is and how to link the executable.

The other anchor of the build system is the set of build-phase members for the target. The Compile Sources build phase, along with the sources you add to it, yield object files, which are the inputs to the executable-linkage phase implicit in your choice of target type. The various file-copying phases and the files you supply for them yield the copy commands needed to populate the auxiliary structure of an application.

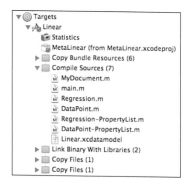

FIGURE 21.1     Build phases in a modest project. You gain access to build phases by opening the disclosure triangle next to the Targets group in the Groups & Files list and then opening the triangle for the target of interest. Each phase, in turn, contains the files that belong to it. Files can be added to a phase by dragging; removed, by selecting them and pressing **Delete**.

## Xcode Build Variables

The action for the default make rule for .c files parameterizes almost the entire action. The command for the C compiler and the set of flags to pass are left to the makefile variables CC, CPPFLAGS, and CFLAGS. You set these flags at the head of the file to suitable values, and all the compilations in your build comply.

Xcode relies similarly on variables to organize build options but at a much finer granularity. There is one variable for each of the most common settings. For instance, the variable GCC_ENABLE_CPP_RTTI controls whether gcc's -fno-rtti will be added to suppress generation of runtime type information. This variable is set by a check box in the **Build** tab of the Get Info window for the target.

In the Groups & Files list of any Xcode project, find the Targets group, and click the disclosure triangle next to it to open the group and reveal the contents. Double-click one of the targets inside. This should reveal the Get Info window for the target, as shown in Figure 21.2. Click the **Build** tab if it isn't already selected.

The list you see is a front end for most of the build variables Xcode maintains for this target. To understand these it helps to select **Help > Research Assistant**; this opens the Research Assistant floating window. As you select a setting, the RA window fills with text describing what that item does. In brackets, at the end of the description, are the name of the build variable the item controls and what gcc option, if any, it affects. Labels, descriptions, and values are searchable. The list in Figure 21.2 was narrowed down to five entries by typing **runtime** into the search field at the top of the window.

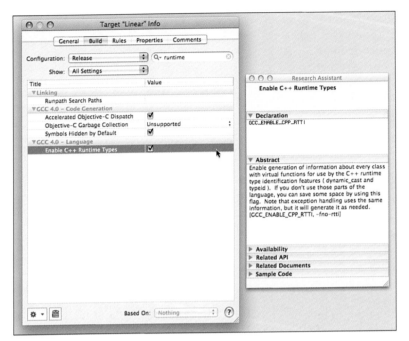

FIGURE 21.2    Finding a specific gcc option in a target's settings. Open the Targets group in the Groups & Files list, and double-click a target to open the Info window. The **Build** tab lists most of the settings for which Xcode maintains build variables. The search field at the top of the window will narrow the list down by the description, build variable, or gcc flag the option controls. The Research Assistant (*right*), available from the **Help** menu, documents each setting as you select it.

## Custom Build Rules

The Xcode build system can be extended to new file types and processing tools. The default rules in the build system match file extensions to product types and process any source files that are newer than the products. You can add a custom rule that instructs the build system to look for files whose names match a pattern and apply a shell command to such files (see Figure 21.3).

Create a rule by double-clicking a target icon in the Groups & Files list, selecting the **Rules** tab, and clicking the + button. At the top of the list, a "slot" will be added that has two pop-up menus

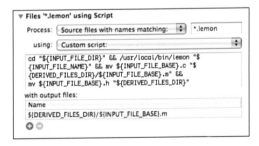

FIGURE 21.3    A custom build rule. This rule captures all target files that have the suffix .lemon; passes them to the lemon parser generator; and if that step succeeds, moves the product files to the project's derived-sources subdirectory. The rule specifies the form of the output file's path so that the build system knows whether, and when, to trigger the rule.

completing the sentence "Process... using...." For a custom rule, you select **Source Files with Names Matching** and **Custom Script**. Doing so opens a text field for the matching pattern, into which you will type the matching pattern—a glob pattern, such as `*.lemon`—and a second field for the single shell script line to process the matched file. Don't worry about the size of this field; it will grow vertically as you type. Remember also that you can chain shell commands with the `&&` operator.

You may use any build variable you like in the shell command. In addition, some variables are specific to custom rule invocations:

▶ `INPUT_FILE_PATH`, the full path to the source file
  (`/Users/xcodeuser/MyProject/grammar.lemon`)

▶ `INPUT_FILE_DIR`, the directory containing the source file
  (`/Users/xcodeuser/MyProject`)

▶ `INPUT_FILE_NAME`, the name of the source file (`grammar.lemon`)

▶ `INPUT_FILE_BASE`, the base, unsuffixed, name of the source file (`grammar`)

> **NOTE**
>
> In this example, adding a `.lemon` file to the project won't do what you'd hope. The build rule recognizes the file as a source file, but Xcode doesn't. Simply adding the file will put it into a Copy Bundle Resources build phase. You'll have to drag the file from the copy phase to the Compile Sources phase. After that, with the product file in the derived-sources directory, the product file will be compiled automatically.

Apple recommends that intermediate files, such as the source files output by parser generators, be put into the directory named in the `DERIVED_FILE_DIR` variable.

# Run Script Build Phase

You can add arbitrary script actions to a build by adding a Run Script build phase. Select **Project > New Build Phase > New Shell Script Build Phase**, and you will be presented with an editor into which you can type commands in the scripting language of your choice (see Figure 21.4).

A Run Script phase can have specific files as inputs and outputs. If these files are present, they are taken into account by the Xcode build system; if all the outputs are newer than all the inputs, the phase is skipped. If outputs are unspecified, the phase is always executed. The sequence in which a Run Script phase is executed is determined by the availability of its inputs and the need for its outputs, *not* by its place among the phases of the target.

When a Run Script build phase is executed, the script is copied to a temporary directory, and a series of `setenv` commands copy build variables into the environment. The script is then run, with your permissions, with the project directory current, with the input files passed in as parameters.

FIGURE 21.4    The Run Script build phase window. You can specify any interpreter you could use in an executable script file. By adding files to the input and output files lists, you can have the Xcode build system run the script only when its products are out-of-date.

There are two caveats about build variables and Run Script phases:

► **You can't change them.** They are passed to your script by doing a `setenv` for each variable before the script is invoked. When the script finishes, those environment variables, along with any changes you might have made to them, go out of scope.

► **You don't get all the build variables.** Apple's documentation suggests that variables that set options specific to a single tool, such as the variables that begin with GCC, are not supposed to be exported to the Run Script environment. However, some GCC variables *are* exported. The rule seems to be that if it has been changed from the default by the current build configuration, it will be exported. The thing to do is to examine your build transcripts to see if a variable is set, and if you use it, provide a suitable default if the current run does not define it.

> **NOTE**
>
> You can see the environment variables passed to your script by checking **Show Environment Variables in Build Log** in the phase's Info window. This takes up a lot of space in the build transcript, so you'll probably want to uncheck the option once you're satisfied with the script.

# Under the Hood: A Simple Build

The Xcode build system—to repeat—is just a front end for `gcc` and other command-line tools. Xcode dependency analysis identifies which tasks need doing and issues high-level commands to accomplish those tasks. The high-level commands, in turn, map to shell commands, the execution of which Xcode monitors for warnings and errors.

The Build Results window, accessible through the **Build** > **Build Results**, shows the progress of a build and a table of the results. By clicking the third icon to the bottom left of the results list (it looks line a stack of lines), you can open an additional panel in the Build Results window; this panel contains a transcript of the build commands and the literal console output from the tools Xcode invokes.

In this section, we sample the build transcript of a Core Data–using program as it is built from a clean start for both PowerPC and Intel architectures. The transcript will be heavily edited for space and readability; the line breaks (\) and ellipses (…) don't appear in the original. The project directory is designated /Pro96, even though the actual commands would encompass the full path to the directory.

This section was prepared by selecting the text in the build transcript and copying it to the clipboard. If you need to debug a stage in a build, depress the first two buttons at the bottom left of the build-results pane (to give a full listing of each step), select the step that concerns you, and copy it. The corresponding build command and its results will be placed on the clipboard.

```
Building target Pro96 of project Pro96
    with configuration Release
```

This build uses the Release configuration rather than the Debug configuration. The Debug configuration for this target does not take the extra time to build for both architectures, and I want to show a universal build.

## Copy Structural Files

The first thing that happens in a clean build is that `Info.plist` and `PkgInfo`, two files you may not have directly edited but that must be present in any application package, are copied from intermediate storage to their places in the application package. This step doesn't correspond to any build phase in the target but is performed when needed.

Here, we see the operation for `Info.plist`. Xcode makes sure the application's `Contents` directory exists, and then uses an internal `info-plist-utility` tool to process the `Info.plist` from the project directory into the final `Info.plist` and `PkgInfo` files in the application package:

```
Processing /Users/fritza/Projects/BuildProducts/Release/Pro96.app/\
    Contents/Info.plist Info.plist
        mkdir /Users/fritza/Projects/BuildProducts/Release/Pro96.app/Contents
        cd ~/Pro96
    <com.apple.tools.info-plist-utility> \
```

```
    /Users/fritza/Projects/Pro96/Info.plist \
     -genpkginfo    /Users/fritza/Projects/BuildProducts/Release/\
  Pro96.app/Contents/PkgInfo -expandbuildsettings \
     -o /Users/fritza/Projects/BuildProducts/Release/Pro96.app/\
        Contents/Info.plist
```

The build transcript shows the high-level commands flush left, with the commands that implement them indented in the lines that follow.

## Compile XIB

XIB files are single XML files that describe the content and editing state of NIB files, which are archives of objects (mostly human-interface elements) to be reconstituted when an application runs. XIBs must be compiled into NIBs before the application can use them. The high-level CompileXIB command maps to a cd and an invocation of the ibtool compiler:

```
CompileXlB ~/Pro96/English.lproj/MainMenu.xib
    cd ~/Pro96
    /Developer/usr/bin/ibtool --errors --warnings --notices \
    --output-format human-readable-text --compile \
    .../Pro96.app/Contents/Resources/English.lproj/MainMenu.nib \
    ~/Pro96/English.lproj/MainMenu.xib
```

## Run Script

The build phases for this application apply some scripts right at the beginning. Xcode copies the script from the build phase into a temporary file, cds to the project directory, sets up the environment, and executes the temporary script:

```
PhaseScriptExecution \
    /Users/fritza/Projects/BuildProducts/Pro96.build/Release/\
    Pro96.build/Script-1F605E030A08BC65 0 0 0F5DEA.sh
        cd ~/Pro96
        setenv ACTION build
        setenv ALWAYS_SEARCH_USER_PATHS YES
        setenv APPLE_INTERNAL_DEVELOPER_DIR /AppleInternal/Developer
  .
  .
  .

        setenv XCODE_VERSION_MAJOR 0300
        setenv YACC /Developer/usr/bin/yacc
/bin/sh -c /Users/fritza/Projects/BuildProducts/Pro96.build/Release/\
    Pro96.build/Script-1F605E030A08BC65000F5DEA.sh
```

## Copy Bundle Resources

The next series of high-level commands, CpResource, are issued in response to your explicit request, once for each file or directory in the Copy Bundle Resources phase. In this example, the file cb.plist gets copied into the application's Resources directory:

```
CpResource \
   .../BuildProducts/Release/Pro96.app/Contents/Resources/cb.plist \
   cb.plist
     mkdir .../BuildProducts/Release/Pro96.app/Contents/Resources
     cd ~/Pro96
     /Developer/Library/.../pbxcp -exclude .DS_Store -exclude CVS \
       -exclude .svn -strip-debug-symbols-resolve-src-symlinks \
       ~/Pro96/cb.plist \
       .../BuildProducts/Release/Pro96.app/Contents/Resources
```

Project Builder-X cp, or pbxcp, is a private variant of the cp tool, offering options the regular command does not, such as the ability to exclude SCM directories from copy operations, and strip debugging symbol tables (which isn't an issue with a property-list file, but would be if the resource being copied were an executable).

## Compile Sources

The build system then turns to producing executable binaries (C/C++/Objective-C). The first task is to produce a precompiled header for each architecture on which the binary is to be runnable. The process of building a universal binary is mostly the same as building standalone binaries for each architecture separately and then combining them into a "fat" binary file. Because we'll be compiling once for each of two architectures, we need two precompiled headers.

Precompiled headers are kept in a subdirectory of /Library/Caches. The high-level command ProcessPCH specifies what precompiled header file to create, from what prefix (.pch) file, using what dialect, for which architecture, and which parser. The command maps to a cd to the project directory, and an invocation of gcc:

```
ProcessPCH /Library/Caches/.../Pro96Prefix .pch.gch \
     Pro96_Prefix.pch normal ppc objective-c \
     com.apple.compilers.gcc.4_0
         cd ~/Pro96
     /Developer/usr/bin/gcc-4.0 -x objective-c-header -arch ppc -pipe \
         -Wno-trigraphs -fasm-blocks -Os -mdynamic-no-pic -Wreturn-type \
         -Wunused-variable -fmessage-length=0 -mtune=G5 \
         -fvisibility=hidden -mmacosx-version-min=10.4 \
         -I.../Pro96.build/Pro96.hmap \
         -F.../BuildProducts/Release \
         -I.../BuildProducts/Release/include \
         -I.../Pro96.build/DerivedSources \
```

```
            -isysroot /Developer/SDKs/MacOSX10.4u.sdk \
            -c ~/Pro96/Pro96_Prefix.pch \
            -o /Library/Caches/.../Pro96Prefix.pch.gch

ProcessPCH /Library/Caches/.../Pro96_Prefix.pch.gch \
    Pro96_Prefix.pch normal i386 objective-c \
    com.apple.compilers.gcc.4_0
        cd ~/Pro96
        /Developer/usr/bin/gcc-4.0 -x objective-c-header -arch i386 -pipe \
        -Wno-trigraphs -fasm-blocks -Os -mdynamic-no-pic -Wreturn-type \
        -Wunused-variable -fmessage-length=0 -mtune=G5 \
        -fvisibility=hidden -mmacosx-version-min=10.4 \
        -I.../Pro96.build/Pro96.hmap \
        -F.../BuildProducts/Release \
        -I.../BuildProducts/Release/include \
        -I.../Pro96.build/DerivedSources \
        -isysroot /Developer/SDKs/MacOSX10.4u.sdk \
        -c ~/Pro96/Pro96_Prefix.pch \
        -o /Library/Caches/.../Pro96_Prefix.pch.gch
```

When the precompilation is done, the Xcode build system runs through every C-family source file in the Compile Sources build phase and compiles them for the first architecture:

> **NOTE**
>
> Paring down these commands for readability leaves the impression that the .pch.gch products are one and the same file. In fact, they go into directories with different hashed names.

```
CompileC .../BuildProducts/.../ppc/MyDocument-8FE91DC2.o \
    ~/Pro96/MyDocument.m normal ppc objective-c \
    com.apple.compilers.gcc.4_0
        cd ~/Pro96
        /Developer/usr/bin/gcc-4.0 -x objective-c -arch ppc -pipe \
        -Wno-trigraphs -fasm-blocks -Os -mdynamic-no-pic -Wreturn-type \
        -Wunused-variable -fmessage-length=0 -mtune=G5 \
        -fvisibility=hidden -mmacosx-version-min=10.4 \
        -I.../Pro96.build/Pro96.hmap \
        -F.../BuildProducts/Release \
        -I.../BuildProducts/Release/include \
        -I.../Pro96.build/DerivedSources \
        -isysroot /Developer/SDKs/MacOSX10.4u.sdk \
        -include /Library/Caches/.../Pro96_Prefix.pch \
        -DTONE_SEARCH_STRING=@"S?" -c ~/Pro96/MyDocument.m \
        -o .../Objects-normal/ppc/MyDocument-8FE91DC2.o

MyDocument.m: In function '-[MyDocument setWeather]':
MyDocument.m:59: warning: local declaration of 'origin'
                                hides instance variable
```

The high-level `CompileC` command divides into a `mkdir` for the intermediate-product directory for the current architecture, a `cd` to make sure that the project directory is current, a `setenv` to designate the target version of Mac OS X, and finally, the invocation of gcc.

I chose as a representative sample a file that produced a warning. Xcode reads error and warning text directly from gcc's standard error stream and interprets it. In the build transcript, the standard error text is shown in a slanted font; the text of warnings and errors is collected and put into the list in the Build Results window, and into the error bubbles displayed in the source code.

Xcode is good at parsing gcc error messages, but not every message passes intelligibly through to the IDE. If you're ever in doubt as to what an Xcode error message means, looking at the build transcript for gcc's exact output might clear things up. Clicking the message in the upper log panel focuses the transcript on it.

## Linkage (First Architecture)

The `Ld` high-level command links the compiled objects with the libraries and frameworks designated in the Link Binary with Libraries build phase:

```
Ld .../Objects-normal/ppc/Pro96 normal ppc
    cd ~/Pro96
    /Developer/usr/bin/gcc-4.0 -o .../Objects-normal/ppc/Pro96 \
    -L.../BuildProducts/Release -F.../BuildProducts/Release \
    -filelist .../Objects-normal/ppc/Pro96.LinkFileList \
    -framework Cocoa -framework IOKit -arch ppc -mmacosx-version-min=10.4 \
    -isysroot /Developer/SDKs/MacOSX10.4u.sdk
```

In this case, the `-framework` option is used to link the Cocoa and IOKit frameworks. The object files aren't listed to the gcc invocation but are drawn via a `-filelist` option from a file Xcode generates in the intermediate-products directory.

## Compile Sources (Second Architecture)

Because this target is destined for both PowerPC and Intel architectures, the compilation and linkage phases have to be done all over again, the only differences being the `-arch i386` option passed to gcc and the use of an `i386` intermediate-products directory:

> **NOTE**
>
> If you're building 64-bit variations, the codes for the respective architectures are `x86_64` and `ppc64`.

```
CompileC .../BuildProducts/.../i386/MyDocument-8FE91DC2.o \
    ~/Pro96/MyDocument.m normal i386 objective-c \
    com.apple.compilers.gcc.4_0
        cd ~/Pro96
        /Developer/usr/bin/gcc-4.0 -x objective-c -arch i386 -pipe \
```

```
       -Wno-trigraphs -fasm-blocks -Os -mdynamic-no-pic -Wreturn-type \
       -Wunused-variable -fmessage-length=0 -mtune=G5 \
       -fvisibility=hidden -mmacosx-version-min=10.4 \
       -I.../Pro96.build/Pro96.hmap \
       -F.../BuildProducts/Release \
       -I.../BuildProducts/Release/include \
       -I.../Pro96.build/DerivedSources \
       -isysroot /Developer/SDKs/MacOSX10.4u.sdk \
       -include /Library/Caches/.../Pro96_Prefix.pch \
       -DTONE_SEARCH_STRING=@"S?" -c ~/Pro96/MyDocument.m \
       -o .../Objects-normal/i386/MyDocument-8FE91DC2.o
```

```
MyDocument.m: In function '-[MyDocument setWeather]':
MyDocument.m:59: warning: local declaration of 'origin'
                                    hides instance variable
```

## Linkage (Second Architecture)

The linking phase, too, is repeated for the Intel architecture:

```
Ld .../Objects-normal/ppc/Pro96 normal i386
    cd ~/Pro96
    /Developer/usr/bin/gcc-4.0 -o .../Objects-normal/i386/Pro96 \
    -L.../BuildProducts/Release -F.../BuildProducts/Release \
    -filelist .../Objects-normal/i386/Pro96.LinkFileList \
    -framework Cocoa -framework IOKit -arch i386 -mmacosx-version-min=10.4 \
    -isysroot /Developer/SDKs/MacOSX10.4u.sdk
```

## Compile Data Models

This application makes use of a Core Data managed-object model drawn from a
.xcdatamodel data model created in Xcode. Xcode data models are not directly usable
by Core Data but must be compiled into .mom managed-object model files.

This is done by the momc compiler embedded in Xcode's data-modeling plug-in. The
compiler processes the data model and deposits the resulting .mom in the application's
Resources directory.

The Xcode IDE lists .xcdatamodel files in the Compile Sources build phase:

```
DataModelCompile \
    .../Pro96.app/Contents/Resources/MyDocument.mom \
    ~/Pro96/MyDocument.xcdatamodel
        cd ~/Pro96
        /Developer/Library/.../momc -XD_MOMC_TARGET_VERSION=10.4 \
        ~/Pro96/MyDocument.xcdatamodel \
        .../Pro96.app/Contents/Resources/MyDocument.mom
```

## Create Universal Binary

In the respective intermediate-products directories, the two linkage phases produced separate binary files, for Intel and PowerPC. The delivery format for binaries compatible with both architectures is a single file containing both versions of the binary. This is known as a *universal binary*. The high-level command CreateUniversalBinary uses the lipo tool to assemble the binary in its final form and position in the application bundle:

```
CreateUniversalBinary \
    .../Pro96.app/Contents/MacOS/Pro96 \
    normal "ppc i386"
        mkdir .../Pro96.app/Contents/MacOS
        cd ~/Pro96
        /usr/bin/lipo -create .../Objects-normal/ppc/Pro96 \
            .../Objects-normal/i386/Pro96 \
            -output ... /Pro96.app/Contents/MacOS/Pro96
```

## Finishing Touch

Finally, the application package directory is touched to make its modification date match the end of the build process, which is what, intuitively, it ought to be:

```
Touch .../Pro96.app
    cd .../Pro96
    /usr/bin/touch -c .../Pro96.app
```

# The xcodebuild **Tool**

Sometimes there is no substitute for a command-line tool. The UNIX command line presents a well-understood interface for scripting and controlling complex tools. Apple has provided a command-line interface to the Xcode build system through the xcodebuild tool.

Using xcodebuild is simple. Set the working directory to the directory containing a .xcodeproj project package, and invoke xcodebuild, specifying the project, target, configuration, and any build settings you want to set. If only one .xcodeproj package is in the directory, all these options can be defaulted by simply entering the following

```
$ xcodebuild
```

That command will build the first target in the current configuration, of the only .xcodeproj package in the working directory. Apple's intention is that xcodebuild have the same role in a nightly build or routine-release script that make would have.

In building a target, specify one of four actions for xcodebuild:

▶ **build**, the default, to build the specified target out of SRCROOT into SYMROOT. This is the same as the **Build** command in the Xcode application.

▶ **clean**, to remove from SYMROOT the product and any intermediate files. This is the same as the **Clean** command in the Xcode application.

▶ **install**, to build the specified target and install it at INSTALL_DIR (usually DSTROOT). The Installation Preprocessing build variable is set. There is no direct equivalent to this action in Xcode, because there is no good way to elevate the Xcode's privileges for setting ownership, permissions, and destination directory.

▶ **installsrc**, to copy the project directory to SRCROOT. In earlier versions of Project Builder, Xcode's ancestor, this action restricted itself to the project file package and the source files listed in it, but it now seems to do nothing a Finder copy or command-line cp wouldn't do.

If more than one .xcodeproj package is in the current directory, you must specify which one you are interested in, with the option -project, followed by the name of the project. Not specifying a target is the same as passing the name of the first target in the -target option; other target options are -activetarget and -alltargets.

> **NOTE**
>
> Settings such as SRCROOT can be set for a run of xcodebuild by including assignment pairs (*SETTING=value*) among the parameters.

It's a little different with configurations. The absence of a specification selects the default configuration, as selected in the pop-up menu at the bottom of the **Configurations** tab of the Project Info window; -activeconfiguration uses, as you would imagine, the active configuration for the selected project; and -configuration followed by a configuration name selects that configuration.

# Settings Hierarchy

Build settings in Xcode can be set at any of four—or, in the case of xcodebuild, five—layers in a hierarchy. A setting may be made in

▶ A BSD environment variable

▶ A default, set for the Xcode application

▶ A configuration at the project level, if that configuration is active

▶ A configuration at the target level, if that configuration is active

▶ A command-line parameter, if xcodebuild is doing the build

Settings in each layer override the
settings from the ones below it, as
shown in Figure 21.5.

**21**

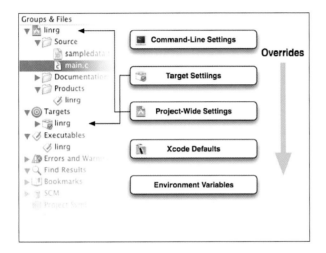

FIGURE 21.5    The hierarchy of build settings in Xcode and xcodebuild. A setting may be
made at one or more of these layers, but the topmost setting in the hierarchy controls. Settings
in higher layers may refer to settings from lower layers by the variable reference $(VALUE). The
top layer, command-line settings, is present only in an xcodebuild invocation.

For example, consider the build variables ZERO_LINK and GCC_PREPROCESSOR_DEFINITIONS_
NOT_USED_IN_PRECOMPS. By default, ZERO_LINK is 0, and GCC_PREPROCESSOR_DEFINITIONS_
NOT_USED_IN_PRECOMPS is empty. In Figure 21.6, ZERO_LINK defaults to NO in Xcode, and
the Release configuration doesn't change that at either the project or the target levels. But
the project setting for the Debug configuration sets ZERO_LINK to YES, and that is the
value used when the Debug configuration is active. GCC_PREPROCESSOR_DEFINITIONS_
NOT_USED_IN_PRECOMPS is empty so far as Xcode is concerned, and at the project level, the
policy is to set DEBUG_LEVEL to 2 for Debug builds and to 0 for Release builds. But for this
target only, the developer decides to set DEBUG_LEVEL to 1 for Release builds.

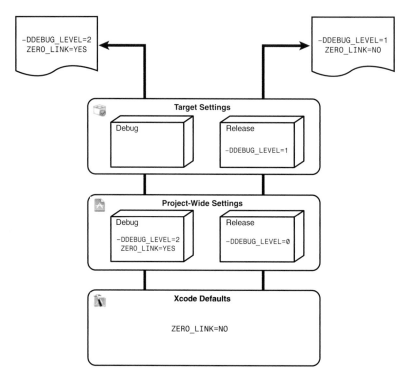

FIGURE 21.6    The build-settings hierarchy in action.

As a result, when the Debug configuration is selected, `ZERO_LINK` will be set to `YES`, and `GCC_PREPROCESSOR_DEFINITIONS_NOT_USED_IN_PRECOMPS` will be `DEBUG_LEVEL=2`. When the Release configuration is selected, `ZERO_LINK` will be `NO`, and `GCC_PREPROCESSOR_DEFINITIONS_NOT_USED_IN_PRECOMPS` will be `DEBUG_LEVEL=1`.

# Build Configurations

In a software development project, you typically don't want to use the same build settings for your day-to-day development as for releases of the product. In a development build, you'll want #define symbols that unmask debugging code, and compiler switches that suppress optimization and generate debugging symbols, but these settings would hurt performance and product size in a release build.

In a makefile, you take care of this need by drawing your compiler and linker flags from variables and setting the variables according to the intended use of the build. CFLAGS, for instance, might include -g -O0 for a working build and -Os for release.

In Xcode, you can organize groups of build-variable settings by purpose, using the build configuration feature. When a new Xcode project is created, it contains two configurations: Debug, for quick turnaround and easy debugging; and Release, for optimal size and performance. Release is set as the default configuration.

You can review the configurations in a project by double-clicking the project icon at the top of the Groups & Files list (or selecting **Project > Edit Project Settings**) and selecting the **Configurations** tab (see Figure 21.7).

When you edit the settings for a configuration using the **Build** tab of the Project Info window, you are setting a policy for all the targets in your project. For instance, you might want **Fix & Continue** to be on for the Debug configuration and off for Release. You want this to be the case for everything (all the targets) you build with this project, so you double-click the project icon at the top of the Groups & Files list to open the Project Info window and select the **Build** tab. With the **Configuration** pop-up at the top of the window showing **Debug**, you check **Fix & Continue**; you switch the pop-up to the **Release** configuration, and make sure that **Fix & Continue** is unchecked.

Note that the **Fix & Continue** item label turns to boldface when you set it. When a window contributes a setting to a configuration, the setting's label is shown in boldface. This is an important point: An item may be blank or unchecked, but its label will be in boldface. This does not mean "no setting!" It

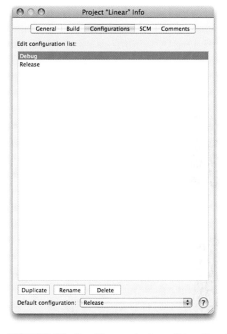

FIGURE 21.7    The project configuration list, showing the standard configurations—Debug and Release—in an Xcode project. You can add configurations of your own by selecting a configuration you want to start from and clicking the **Duplicate** button. You can also delete or rename the selected configuration. The default configuration, selected with the pop-up menu at the bottom of the window, is the configuration xcodebuild uses for builds for which you do not specify a configuration.

means that this window affirmatively makes the setting blank or NO. To change a setting to "no setting," select the setting's line, and press the **Delete** key. The line will lose its boldfacing, and the value shown will be the default, or inherited, value.

Not every build setting need be left to projectwide policy; some may be set per target. The obvious cases are such things as the names of the targets' products, but it might be that you intend to use -O3 optimization, for instance, rather than -Os, for a library target. Open the Targets group in the Groups & Files list, and locate the target of interest. Double-click it, and an Info window will appear; it, too, will have a **Build** tab for you to alter build settings.

The **Build** panel of the target Info window is the place where you can see what settings will apply to that target in the selected configuration. Settings you make in the target window override the values inherited from the project level and below, but what you see in the target window is the final word.

At both the project and the target levels, you can select from the **Configuration** pop-up menu which configuration your settings apply to. You can apply your settings to all configurations by selecting **All Configurations** in the pop-up.

---

### Xcode Configuration Files

Project and target **Build** tabs are convenient, but they are not documents. All the settings that go into a build are there. You can search for them. You can browse for them. What you can't do is *read* them, or share them as a common policy across your organization's projects. If you had a published policy, you'd still have to pick through the **Build** tab and adjust each setting.

Xcode configuration (`.xcconfig`) files are the solution. At the bottom of the **Build** tab is a pop-up labeled **Based On**. This menu contains one item for each file in the project that has the `.xcconfig` extension. Selecting one draws settings from the configuration file, and you can make changes from there.

A configuration file is just a text file filled with key-value pairs:

```
VERSION_INFO_SUFFIX =
VERSIONING_SYSTEM =
VERSION_INFO_BUILDER = $(USER)
MOMC_NO_WARNINGS = NO
MOMC_NO_INVERSE_RELATIONSHIP_WARNINGS = NO
GCC_FAST_OBJC_DISPATCH = YES
GCC_AUTO_VECTORIZATION = NO
GCC_OBJC_CALL_CXX_CDTORS = NO
```

The keys are the build-setting variable names you can find in the Research Assistant notes on the **Build** tab entries, or in the list you'll get in the Documentation window if you search for `"build setting reference"` (include the quotes).

You don't have to work from a list. Start a configuration file by selecting **File > New File** and choosing **Xcode > Configuration Settings File...** in the New File Assistant. The assistant takes care of providing the right extension and adding the file to the project; be sure *not* to add the new file to any target—Xcode will try to compile it, and fail, or copy it into your application.

Open a Target or Project Info window that comes closest to the settings you want. Select a setting line, and drag (or copy + paste) it into the configuration file. The line is converted to text as a key-value pair. You can select all of the lines (**Edit > Select All**) and drag or copy them *en masse*. Save the file, select it in the pop-up on the **Build** tab, and you're done.

You can have a separate configuration file for each combination of Project/ Target levels, and build configurations (Debug, Release, and so forth). Changes you make in a **Build** tab that is based on a configuration file override the settings in the file.

> ### NOTE
>
> Dragging or copying settings when you've selected **All Configurations** in the **Configuration** pop-up is problematic: Xcode will refuse, because it won't know how to handle "<multiple values>" entries. Pick a configuration.

# Summary

This chapter covered Xcode as a build system like make that is a front end for command-line tools that consume source files to replace out-of-date product files. We saw how to customize the build process by adding build rules and inserting shell-script build phases. We also discussed how build configurations can apply packages of build-time environment variables to a project.

21

# CHAPTER 22

# More About Debugging

**IN THIS CHAPTER**

▶ **Debugging Tips**

▶ **Customizing the Variable Display**

▶ **Augmenting Breakpoints**

▶ **Debugging Memory Errors**

▶ **The In-Editor and Mini Debuggers**

We've done a fair amount of debugging with Linear in Part I of this book, but one simple application can't demonstrate every tip and technique. This chapter expands on the topic of debugging, offering some tips, and demonstrates some additional tools, including how to tackle the knotty problem of debugging memory errors.

## Debugging Techniques

We've been using the Debugger window since Chapter 2, "Simple Workflow and Passive Debugging." Here are a few points that haven't been covered yet:

▶ The stack-trace and variable-list views of the Debugger window are at the top of the window. For many screens, vertical screen real estate is more valuable than horizontal. **Run > Debugger Display > Vertical Layout** will make those panes appear at the left side of the window, allowing you to see more of the editor view.

▶ The Breakpoints window, available through **Run > Show > Breakpoints** (⌥⌘B) or the **Breakpoints** toolbar button, does more than display the breakpoints you set in the margins of your code. You can also set symbolic breakpoints in your code or in Apple-supplied libraries. The last item in the list of breakpoints shows a blue cube next to the label "Double-Click for Symbol." Double-clicking the line makes it editable. Here you can type in the name of any method or function at which you want to break.

For instance, it is often useful to set a breakpoint at **objc_exception_throw**. This sets a gdb "future break" (fb) so that the Debugger will get control whenever a Cocoa routine issues a diagnostic message. The prompt stoppage gives you a better chance at finding the problem.

> **NOTE**
>
> In Mac OS X 10.4 and earlier, you had to back up obj_cexception_throw with a breakpoint at -[NSException raise]. (You'd type exactly that into a new symbolic breakpoint line.) This is no longer necessary because obj_cexception_throw now catches both NSExceptions and exceptions raised with the @throw construct.

▶ The Console window allows you to type commands directly into the gdb session that underlies the Xcode Debugger. It accumulates output from those commands, as well as serving to read and write your application's standard I/O. This output accumulates indefinitely. If you want to clear it out, click the **Clear Log** button in the Console window's tool bar. (Or **Run > Clear Console**—you have to hold down **Control** and **Option** to see it.) By default, the Console is too narrow to show the **Clear Log** button; widen the window to make it visible, or use the pop-up at the right end of the toolbar to use it. If you always want the Console to be cleared when you start a new session, check **Automatically Clear Log** in the **General** (first) pane of the Preferences window.

▶ Many of the system frameworks for Mac OS X have "debug" variants, which check the validity of arguments, log events, and test assertions for internal consistency. This is important because it is easy to pass illegal arguments to system routines and not know it, because the production frameworks let the errors pass without comment. The first you'll know of it will be a crash some time later. The debug frameworks raise exceptions and log the errors as soon as they happen.

For instance, the Carbon framework contains the dynamic libraries Carbon (for regular use) and Carbon_debug (for the extra checks). The dynamic loader has a simple rule for adding a suffix to the name of any library that gets loaded; just set the environment

> **NOTE**
>
> Many of the messages and breaks you will encounter will be strictly routine; be prepared to ignore a few breaks and continue from them.

variable DYLD_IMAGE_SUFFIX to the desired suffix. You can do this easily from within Xcode by opening the Executables group in the Groups & Files list and double-clicking the desired executable to open its Info window (or by selecting **Project > Edit Active Executable**). In the **General** tab of the Info window is a pop-up labeled **Use...Suffix When Loading Frameworks**. Select **No**, **Debug**, or **Profile** from the pop-up menu. Apple releases debug and profile variants of system libraries through the ADC downloads program; these change with each minor release of Mac OS X, so be sure to keep current.

▶ The Debugger variables view does not, by default, include any global variables, because an application may have many of them, and probably only a handful are of interest at any given moment. Double-clicking the **Globals** label or selecting **Run > Show > Global Variables** opens the Globals Browser. The left column of the browser lists every library comprising the application; your application will be listed as one of these libraries, so look for its name.

Selecting a library lists in the table at right every global variable the library exports; Xcode must extract the global symbols from the library, so allow it a few seconds to bring the list up. If the list is long, you can use the search field to narrow it down. Check the box next to a global's name to include it in the Variables panel. Globals are always legal in the Debugger's Expressions window (**Run > Show > Expressions**). See Figure 22.1.

▶ In addition to breakpoints, the Xcode Debugger exposes gdb's ability to set *watchpoints*. A watchpoint is like a breakpoint, but interrupts execution not when execution arrives at a particular place in the code but when the value of a variable changes. It often happens that a bug shows up as an inexplicable value in a variable, but you can't divine where in a complex or long execution it gets trashed. A watchpoint is the answer.

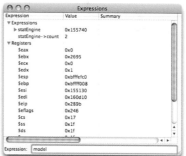

FIGURE 22.1     The Xcode Debugger's Globals Browser *(top)* and Expressions window *(bottom)*.

To set a watchpoint, stop the program in the Debugger at a point where the variable of concern is in scope. Select the variable in the Variables pane of the Debugger and select **Run > Variables View > Watch Variable**. A magnifying glass icon appears next to watched variables. Continue the program. The watchpoint interrupts execution if the value of the variable changes.

On Intel Macs, gdb can take advantage of up to four watch-address registers in the processor. If you go beyond four watchpoints, or use any at all on the PowerPC, the target application slows down appreciably.

▶ Have you deleted a file from your project (and the file system)? If you had set break-points in that file, they will stick around in Xcode's breakpoint list, and the Debugger will complain that it can't find those files. Select the orphans in the Breakpoints window and press the **Delete** key to remove them.

▶ You may find some breakpoints in the Breakpoints window that you can't delete. The Breakpoints window lists all the breakpoints that are *associated* with the current project. If the current project includes another, the Breakpoints window will list breakpoints set in the included project, but only that included project can manage those breakpoints.

▶ If you use key-value observing (KVO) and don't override the `description` method of your observed classes, you'll find your observed objects described not as, for instance, <MyObject... but as <NSKVONotifying_MyObject.... The KVO mechanism substitutes an ad hoc class when objects are observed. To see a list of which objects are observing an object, use the gdb command po[*myObject* observationInfo].

▶ Suppose that you want to debug an application that doesn't run well in the Xcode environment—the classic example is a Terminal application that uses the ncurses library, which the Console window can't respond to. The trick is to launch the application in an environment it works well in and then attach the Xcode Debugger to it. Open the **Executables** group in the Groups & Files list, select the application, open an Info window, and in the **Debugging** tab, uncheck **Start Executable After Starting Debugger**. When you're ready to debug, start the Debugger, and then launch the target application in its friendly environment. In the Debugger's gdb console, type **attach** *applicationName*, and your debugging session is under way.

▶ Unchecking the **Start Executable After Starting Debugger** option for an applica-tion allows you to start the Debugger, and then perform debugging tasks, such as setting breakpoints, before clicking **Restart** to actually start the application. This is similar to how the CodeWarrior Debugger worked.

▶ The list at the left of the Breakpoints window is just another incarnation of the Groups & Files list but with only the **Breakpoints** group included. One Groups & Files command that may prove useful is **Project > Group**, which encloses the break-points you select in a subgroup of the **Breakpoints** list. Once you have a group of breakpoints, you can use a contextual menu (Control- or right-click the group) to enable or disable the whole group.

▶ gcc can generate debugging information in two formats, DWARF and STABS. DWARF is the default under Xcode 3, but older projects may still be set to generate STABS tables. DWARF is by far the superior choice. It is more stable and more detailed. DWARF will allow access to some local variables that STABS simply loses track of. STABS could not distinguish among instantiations of C++ templates, so a breakpoint set in the template's source would break only in one of the instantiations.

The lesson here is this: Unless you have a very unusual and compelling reason to do otherwise, set Debug Information Format to **DWARF** (for the Debug configuration) or **DWARF with dSYM** (for Release). The setting is in the **Build** tab of the Project or Target Info window; typing `dwarf` in the search field will narrow the list down.

If you must compile with gcc 3.3, DWARF is not an option for you.

▶ If you share your code across development environments, such as Windows or the pre-10 Mac OSes, you may find that the Debugger's current-line highlight is off by a line or two. Check the file to make sure the line-ending conventions have not been mixed—such as some lines ending with \n (the Mac OS X convention), and others \r\n (the Windows convention). Xcode can handle files using any line-ending style, but it can't handle a file that mixes line endings. Use the **General** pane of the file's Info window (for multiple files) or **View > Text** to correct the current file.

▶ The Xcode/gdb combination is extremely complex, and doesn't always behave as it should. When you encounter bugs, be sure to report them to Apple at http://bugreport.apple.com/ (free ADC registration required). You must include a gdb log in your report. Get one by selecting **GDB Log** in the Debugging panel of the Preferences window and reproducing your problem. You can edit the path the log is written to. Examining the log may even point you to a workaround.

▶ gcc has an option to optimize *tail recursion*—the case where a function does nothing at its end other than calling another function. A naive approach to such functions is to leave the caller's data on the stack, but that data, in such cases, will never be used. The optimization is to clean the calling function's data and address out of the stack, and make it as though the called function were called by the calling function's caller.

Very clever, but it means that tail-recursive functions will not appear in stack traces. The displayed call stack will jump from the current function to the top, non-tail-recursive, caller. If you see strange calling chains such as this, set the Optimization Level setting (in the Target Info window's **Build** tab) to **None [-O0]**, which is what it should be in the Debug configuration.

# Printing Values

The Variables pane of the Xcode Debugger is a nice presentation of program data, but it is limited by the table format it uses. Cocoa and Core Foundation container objects, for instance, are represented by their addresses in hexadecimal and a notation of how many objects they contain. Often, you want to know *what* they contain. The easiest way to do this is to Control-click the variable in the table and select **Print Description to Console**. For Cocoa objects, this will write the result of the debugDescription method to standard error; for others, it writes to standard error the result of passing the value to CFShow().

The standard error stream is echoed to the Console. Early in this book, I had you go into the Preferences window's Debugging panel, and set **On Start: Show Console & Debugger**, so finding the Console window hasn't been an issue. If you've changed that setting, you can make the Console visible by pressing the **Console** button in either the Debugger window's toolbar, or in the Debugger Strip. The default size of the Debugger window hides the **Console** button; widen the window to see it.

The gdb console gives you unlimited flexibility in accessing values in your application. You can print Cocoa objects with the print-object (po) command. Core Foundation and CF-compliant Carbon objects can be examined by calling CFShow() from the console, the results of which will appear in the application's standard output:

```
(gdb) po item
<DataPoint: 0x167c80> (entity: DataPoint; id: 0x1994f0 <x-core...
    source = nil;
    x =  20 05;
    y =  1330;
})
Current language:  auto; currently objective-c
(gdb) call (void) CFShow(allPoints)
<CFArray 0x13ea40 [0xa00ab1a0]>{type = immutable,  count  = 2,...
    0 :  <DataPoint: 0x167c80> (entity: DataPoint; id: 0x1994f0...
    source = nil;
    x = 2005; y = 1330;
})
    1 :  <DataPoint: 0x1afa80> (entity: DataPoint; id: 0x1ad740...
    source = nil;
    x = 2006;
    y = 1455;
})
)}
(gdb)
```

The call to CFShow() is an example of how gdb can execute, for its own use, code linked into an application.

You can examine any address with the gdb x command, which takes the form x/*format address*, where *format* is a repeat count (1 if omitted), a format, and a size code (see Table 22.1). For instance, you can disassemble the next 20 machine instructions with the command x/20i $pc, where $pc denotes the CPU's program counter.

The print command, which may be abbreviated as p, enables you to print the result of any expression. The expression's syntax is that of the language in which the current file is written. You can use any variable in the current scope. You may specify most formats— using the format letter only, not the count or size parameter—by appending /*format* to the print command. You cannot print in formats s or i.

TABLE 22.1    gdb Format Codes for x and print

| Format | |
| --- | --- |
| a | address |
| c | character |
| d | decimal |
| f | float |
| i | instruction |
| o | octal |
| s | string |
| t | binary |
| u | unsigned decimal |
| x | hexadecimal |
| **Size** | |
| b | 1 (byte) |
| h | 2 (halfword) |
| w | 4 (word) |
| g | 8 (giant) |

# Custom Formatters

Some data types do not give up their secrets casually. Take as an example the DataPoint managed-object type from Chapter 16, "Using the Data Modeling Tools." The earlier version of DataPoint had x and y instance variables that could readily be inspected, but when we changed DataPoint to a subclass of NSManagedObject, we eliminated the instance variables and made DataPoint into a black box.

Consider the method dataPointAtIndex:x:y:, in MyDocument.m:

```
- (void) dataPointAtIndex: (unsigned) index
                        x: (double *) outX
                        y: (double *) outY
{
    NSArray *    allPoints = [DataPoint allDataPointsInContext:
                                        [self managedObjectContext]];
    DataPoint * item = [allPoints objectAtIndex: index];
    *outX =   [item  x];
    *outY =   [item  y];
}
```

Suppose we are stopped at a breakpoint at the beginning of the function's fourth line. We have a new value for item and would like to know what it is. We have a choice of methods:

- ▶ We could try opening the disclosure triangle next to item's name in the Variable list. This yields us almost nothing, because the instance variables for an NSManagedObject reflect the task of storing and retrieving data, not the data itself.

- ▶ We could use gdb's print-object command: po item. This is simple and produces in the Debugger log a message that deals mostly with access particulars of the DataPoint *and* its DataSource reference, but does include the x and y values of the point.

- ▶ We could Control-click item's line in the Variable view and select **Print Description to Console** from the resulting pop-up menu. This is equivalent to typing **po item**.

- ▶ We could step over the next two lines and enter first **print *outX** and then **print *outY**, to see what the x and y values were. This certainly solves the problem in this case, but in the general sense, it's cheating: We won't always have convenient direct assignments of exactly the values we want to monitor. This method, and the two print-object methods, share another disadvantage, in that they don't make the x and y values continually accessible. You have to do something special to make them visible.

Data formatters were added to the Xcode Variables panel for exactly the purpose of providing continual, at-a-glance summaries of complex data structures. With the application stopped at a breakpoint at line 4 of dataPointAtIndex:x:y:, find item in the Variables panel. Double-click in the Summary column, and enter this:

```
(x = {[$VAR x]} y = {[$VAR y]})
```

When you press **Return** to end editing, the expression you entered is replaced with a string like (x = 1.0 y = 2.01). A data formatter consists of literal text in which are embedded expressions and references to values within data structures. In this case, the formatter pattern contains two expressions, set off with braces. $VAR takes the value of the variable itself, and in the first part of the formatter, we send the message [$VAR x].

The formatter we use for DataPoint calls methods of DataPoint. In fact, x and y, relying as they do on Core Data calls, are fairly complex operations. Be aware that you can use application code in your Debugger data formatters. The good side of this is that you are free to do whatever you need to see what your data is. The bad side is that you make the Debugger subject to the good behavior of the code you are debugging. If the data formatter calls application code that crashes, the least that will happen is that you'll be notified of an exception triggered inside gdb, and the variables display will be degraded.

> **NOTE**
>
> Determined debuggers and testers may introduce to their code functions and methods that exist solely to be called from the Debugger console, to produce formatted output or reset objects to known states. Ambitious debuggers might even devise application browser windows to be opened from Debugger console commands.

This problem becomes acute if the variable being examined hasn't been initialized yet. The uninitialized variable might contain values that trigger exceptions in the data formatter. To avoid this, you may have to declare and initialize the problem variable earlier; avoid single-stepping through code where the problem variable is uninitialized; or select **Run > Variables View > Enable Data Formatters** to uncheck that menu item.

A data formatter "sticks" to its data type, not to the instance or data it was created for. By setting a data formatter for one DataPoint, we have set the Summary data column for the Xcode Debugger wherever it finds a pointer to a DataPoint. As the value of the DataPoint changes, the numbers (and only the numbers) in the summary are highlighted in red.

> **NOTE**
>
> If DataPoint still kept its x and y values in instance variables, there would have been no need to resort to expression substitutions. Members of structured data types can be referenced by path in custom-format strings by setting them off with %s, as in (x = %x% y = %y%). Such % substitutions can be followed with a colon and n, v, t, or s, to indicate that the substituted text should be what would appear in the Name, Value, Type, or Summary column if that element were displayed on its own line in the Variables display.

> **NOTE**
>
> You can add to the variable view a column that identifies the type of each variable, by selecting **Run > Variables View > Show Types**.

# Breakpoint Commands

Sometimes, you need a breakpoint for information rather than as a place to stop execution. Suppose, for instance, that we were interested in what happens when the managed-object context changes. A method, storeChanged:, in Regression is called whenever a change is made to the context:

```
- (void) storeChanged: (NSNotification *) notice
{
    NSSet *    inserted = [[notice userInfo]
                            objectForKey: NSInsertedObjectsKey];
    NSSet *    deleted = [[notice userInfo]
                            objectForKey: NSDeletedObjectsKey];

    if ([inserted count] > 0 || [deleted count] > 0) {
        [self willChangeValueForKey: @"canCompute"];
        [self didChangeValueForKey: @"canCompute"];
    }
}
```

22

We'd like to see what gets inserted and deleted at each change notification, but we aren't interested in anything else. We can use the Debugger's Breakpoints window to associate a series of commands with a breakpoint. Set a breakpoint at the `if` statement in `storeChanged:`, by which time `inserted` and `deleted` are set. Open the Breakpoints window, either from the button in the Debugger toolbar or via **Run > Show > Breakpoints**.

> **NOTE**
>
> You see that there are two buttons in the toolbar named **Breakpoints**. The first is a pop-up menu allowing you to set specialized breakpoints at the selected line of code. The second is a button that reveals the Breakpoints window.

The Breakpoints window lists all the breakpoints set in the current project, and in all the projects it references. It is easy to find the one set in `storeChanged:`. Just open the disclosure triangle at the left end of its line in the table. A bubble appears, with a + button for you to add an action to the breakpoint.

You will add three actions:

> ▶ A log action, which will print some text into the gdb log. Fill the text with **Breakpoint '%B' hit with insert/delete:**, and select the **Log** radio button. You have a choice of having the log text written or spoken.
>
> ▶ A Debugger command, printing the object value of the `inserted` symbol:
>
> **po inserted**
>
> There is no need to check the **Log** box, because the result of the command itself is printed to the gdb transcript.
>
> ▶ Another Debugger command to print `deleted`:
>
> **po deleted**

On the original, top line of the listing for this breakpoint, at the rightmost end, is a check box, under a column header with an arrowhead symbol in it. Checking this box will tell gdb not to stop at this breakpoint but to continue program execution after all commands are executed. We want to continue, so check the box (see Figure 22.2).

Now, as you use Linear, this sort of message appears in the gdb console, without otherwise interrupting the flow of the program:

```
Breakpoint '-storeChanged: - Line 81' hit with insert/delete:
{(
    <DataPoint: 0x1ba450> (entity: DataPoint; id: 0x1bdc20 ... {
    source = nil;
    x = 0;
    y = 0;
})
```

```
)}
Cannot access memory at address 0x0
Breakpoint '-storeChanged: - Line 81' hit with insert/delete:
Cannot access memory at address 0x0
Cannot access memory at address 0x0
```

FIGURE 22.2    The Breakpoints list, with the breakpoint in -[Regression storeChanged:] expanded to show its actions. Clicking the + button at the right edge of the action list adds an action. The first action prints a label for the breakpoint occurrence, and the next two are gdb commands that output the objects inserted and deleted. The top line of the breakpoint listing shows the condition of the breakpoint—it fires only if inserted or deleted is not nil—and a check box to indicate that gdb is to continue after all the breakpoint actions have been done.

The first pair reflects the addition of a newly initialized DataPoint to the managed-object context (with no deletions); the second, a change in an attribute of the data (no insertions or deletions).

An especially good application of command-and-continue breakpoints is in debugging handlers for continuous human-interface operations, such as drag and drop. You can have the Debugger print out status information without stopping a drag in the middle.

You can remove breakpoint actions by pressing the - button on the action or by deleting the associated breakpoint.

# Breakpoint Conditions

The breakpoint commands we set in the preceding section were convenient, but you'll find that the breakpoint triggers every time a change is made to the managed-object context—four times for each DataPoint (three properties plus creation) and four times for each `DataSource` (three properties plus creation). After a while, we may decide that these breakpoint commands are generating too much noise from events in which there are no changes in context membership.

One solution might be to move the breakpoint to the line after the `if` test, but there is another. We can have `gdb` make a test of its own.

As before, we find the breakpoint in the list in the Breakpoints window. We are looking for the same breakpoint at `-[Regression storeChanged:]`, at the `if` statement, and we want it to fire only when either `inserted` or `deleted` is not nil: **inserted ¦¦ deleted**. Type this expression into the last text column of the breakpoint's line in the table.

The first thing `gdb` will do when execution arrives at the `if` statement in `storeChanged:` will be to evaluate the condition. If it is `true`, the breakpoint actions are executed as before; otherwise, the program continues silently.

Of course, conditions work with breakpoints that have no associated commands, too. You can remove the condition from a breakpoint by clearing the cell in the Condition column.

# Lazy Symbol Loading

As you start debugging your application, you may look at the Breakpoints window and find a couple of breakpoints for which the **Enabled** check box is neither checked nor unchecked but has a minus sign (–) in it. In the editor window, the breakpoint arrows are not blue while the program is running, but orange.

This indicates that `gdb` understands you mean these breakpoints to be active but has yet to determine an address for the corresponding machine code. The reason for this is that `gdb` is set to load debugging symbols "lazily," waiting to resolve symbols that occur in not-yet-loaded object files until those files are loaded. The alternative is to examine every dynamic library as `gdb` starts up, which takes a significant amount of time in a large application.

Unfortunately, this means that in some cases, symbols, such as breakpoint addresses, are not resolved when they are needed—that is, in time to break on entry to a function. If you find that a breakpoint you set is getting missed, particularly if it's in a plug-in or other shared library, you should tell `gdb` to load the relevant symbols earlier.

While the application is running under the Debugger, open the Shared Libraries window (see Figure 22.3) by selecting **Run > Show > Shared Libraries**. The table will show the name of every loadable module associated with the application, the address of that module, and how the symbols defined in that module are exported to `gdb`, both at startup (Starting Level) and now that the application has run a while (Current Level).

The symbol levels are settable as pop-up menu items, offering choices of **Default**, **None**, **External**, and **All**. If a breakpoint is getting missed, locate the module in which the problem code occurs—you can use the search field to narrow the list down—and set the Starting Level for that module to **All**. Doing so ensures that all the debugging information for that module will be loaded as soon as gdb starts debugging the application. To load all the symbols for a module for just the current session, select **All** in the Current Level column.

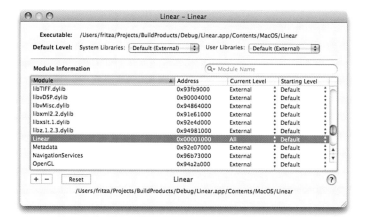

FIGURE 22.3     The Shared Libraries window from the Xcode Debugger. All the loadable modules associated with the application being debugged are listed in this window, along with the initial and current levels of importation of symbols from those modules to gdb.

The two pop-ups at the top of the window determine what the Default setting means; this can be set separately for user and system libraries. Initially, the Default policy is **External**, meaning that only the symbols published by a module as external are loaded when gdb starts. With all libraries initially set to Default, setting these pop-ups effectively sets symbol loading for the entire project.

Another approach to problems with lazy symbol loading is just to turn the feature off. In the Preferences window, in the Debugging pane, you can uncheck **Load Symbols Lazily**. The performance penalty, for smaller projects, should not be great.

# Zombies

The project Garden in the CD-ROM directory for this chapter contains a simple program for managing a simple garden. The program maintains a list of Gardens, each of which contains one prize Lily. You can plant new Lilys in a Garden, but that replaces any existing prize Lily. A Lily has a string to describe its variety, and knows whether it has been gilded. Lily and Garden both implement the standard description method, which provides a string describing the recipient of the message.

The Garden project defines in its NIB a window that contains a one-column table, in which we will list the prize Lily of each Garden. There is a button to add a new garden to the collection; the button makes sure that each garden gets a different variety of Lily so that we can tell them apart. There is a button that will gild the lily in the first garden. And, a button marked **Vandalize** sends the prize Lily object in the first garden a release message. As prize Lilys are held by only one reference—their respective Gardens—this will have the effect of returning the first Lily's memory to free storage.

## Released-Pointer Aliasing

Build Garden and run it under the Debugger. Click the **Add Garden** button twice. The action method for that button does a reloadData on the table, so in the table, we immediately see the following:

```
A Lily, calla, not gilded
A Lily, white, not gilded
```

Now click the **Vandalize** button. Here is the action method for that button:

```
-(IBAction) vandalize: (id) sender
{
    Garden *        garden = [allGardens objectAtIndex: 0];
    [[garden prizeLily] release];
    [self addGarden: sender];
}
```

The vandalize: method adds a new Garden to our list, but before that it arbitrarily releases the first Garden's prize Lily. This is a bug. The Garden at index 0 of allGardens still maintains a pointer to what it thinks is a Lily, but that pointer has been invalidated. The application is walking dead.

But it is still walking. You can move the window around. You can even try clicking **Add Garden** again. In some cases, depending on things you can't control, the list of Gardens changes to what you see in Figure 22.4. In this state, the application won't crash as long as you stay away from the **Vandalize** button, but will simply display not the prize Lily of the first Garden but the description of the new Garden.

What happened? When vandalize: released the prizeLily object of the first member of allGardens, the storage for that Lily, and the address associated

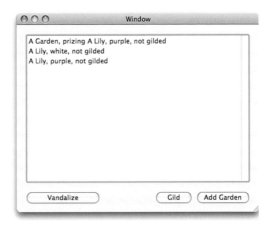

FIGURE 22.4    A memory-management bug that shows up as a behavioral error in a simple application. Pressing **Add Garden** twice added two lines of Lilys from the added Gardens to the list. **Vandalize** released the first of these Lilys and created a new Garden at the same address as the old Lily. An attempt to describe the released Lily, to fill the first line of the table, instead describes the new Garden (which supplanted that Lily).

with it, were returned to free storage. That address became available for use by new objects. Sure enough, when vandalize: allocated a new Garden, the same address was used for the new object.

The first Garden, in the meantime, has no clue that its prizeLily object has been deallocated and its storage given to something else. So far as it knows, prizeLily still points to an instance of Lily. When it comes time to supply content for the first line of the table, description gets sent to prizeLily of the first Garden. It happens that Garden also implements description, so the description of the replacement object, the third garden, appears in the table.

What happens if you try to send a message that Garden doesn't implement? The **Gild** button triggers this action handler:

```
- (IBAction) gildFirstLily: (id) sender
{
    Garden *        garden = [allGardens objectAtIndex: 0];
    [[garden  prizeLily] gild];
    [gardenTable reloadData];
}
```

If you click the Gild button, nothing happens. But if you look in the Console, you'll see the following message:

```
2008-01-24 15:18:15.188 Garden[30579:10b] *** -[Garden gild]:
                    unrecognized selector sent to instance 0x1769802
```

This message would not be mysterious to you because you know what's going on: gildFirstLily: sends gild to an object that turns out to be a Garden, and Gardens don't implement gild. Usually, however, your bugs are not so deliberate. The first sign of trouble may be that nothing happens, and a message like this shows up in the standard error stream, where you might not notice it till much later. When you see a selector-not-recognized message, especially for a strange class, suspect an over-released object.

I said that when you clicked **Vandalize**, the strange behavior we've been discussing *might* happen. What else might happen? Usually, what happens is that the application halts, and standard error contains the message "Program received signal EXC_BAD_ACCESS." If you are running the application under the Debugger, you will see that execution stopped somewhere in the runtime library function objc_msgSend. The crash in objc_msgSend is another strong indicator of an over-released object.

But crashes and error messages are good news. It's the first mode of failure—no crash, just subtly incorrect behavior—that's scary. What we badly need is a way to turn the subtle run-on bugs into identifiable bugs.

## NSZombieEnabled

Fortunately, there is such a way. Cocoa provides a mechanism that does not free released storage for reuse. Instead, the freed object is replaced by a *zombie* object that knows what kind of object was originally stored there. A zombie traps any message sent to it, and raises an `NSException`, which you can use to break into the Debugger. This facility is controlled by a switch called `NSZombieEnabled`. The switch is accessible by #importing Foundation/ `NSDebug.h` into `main.m` and setting `NSZombieEnabled = YES` before anything else.

`NSZombieEnabled` is also accessible as an environment variable. Open the Executables group in the Groups & Files list, select the Garden application, and open the Info window. Select the **Arguments** tab, and click the + button under the lower list of environment variables. Set the name of the new environment variable to **NSZombieEnabled** and its value to **YES** (see Figure 22.5).

Either way, when we repeat the experiment of vandalizing a `Garden`, the Debugger intervenes with the following message:

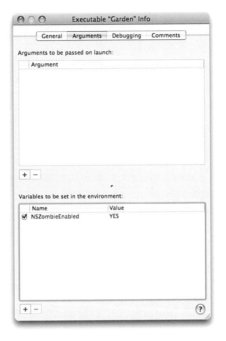

FIGURE 22.5    The **Arguments** tab of an Executable Info window. The upper list is for command-line arguments to be passed to the application, the lower for name/value pairs of environment variables. Use the attached **+** button to add to a list; select an item and press the **-** button to delete an item. You don't have to delete an item to stop using it: Only items that are checked are used.

```
2008-01-25 11:15:58.557 Garden[32025:10b] *** -[Lily description]:
                 message sent to deallocated instance 0x1db820
```

This time, there's no ambiguity. The zombie object reports the message it was sent and what kind of object (`Lily`) was over-released. It doesn't matter what method is called—the zombie class, which replaces the dealloc'ed object in memory, squawks at any method call.

The stack trace shows the method `tableView:objectValueForTableColumn:` as the deepest locus in the chain for Garden's source. The offending line is

```
return [[garden prizeLily] description];
```

`description` is a valid method for Garden, but not for a zombie (nothing is).

In Mac OS X 10.4 and earlier, NSZombieEnabled didn't work with Core Foundation objects (CFTypes). This was a big problem, because the fundamental types in Cocoa's Foundation framework (NSString most prominent among them) are implemented through their Core Foundation equivalents; this is

> **NOTE**
>
> This still leaves the problem of debugging memory allocations made with malloc. That's beyond the scope of this book, but see the man page for malloc for some useful environment variables.

known as *toll-free bridging*. The solution was to set the CFZombieLevel environment variable to a numeric value that controls how CFType memory may be scribbled and prevented from being recycled. (5 is the value generally regarded as closest to NSZombieEnabled.)

The situation is much better in Mac OS X 10.5. Now, CFTypes can become zombies if NSZombieEnabled is set. If NSZombieEnabled is set, CFZombieLevel is ignored.

## The Mini Debugger, and the In-Editor Debugger

Xcode 3 introduces a floating window, the Mini Debugger, that gives you access to debugging commands in your target application, without the need to switch back and forth between the application and Xcode. You can control breakpoints, break into the Debugger, and step through your application's code, all without incurring the changes of state that come when you deactivate and reactivate the target by switching in and out.

To obtain the Mini Debugger, open the Debugging panel of the Preferences window, and select **Open Mini Debugger** from the **On Start** pop-up. This does mean Xcode will no longer open the Debugger and Console windows when you launch a target, but when the Mini Debugger is active, it will have buttons for getting to those windows.

When you launch your target application to debug it, a HUD window appears in front of all other windows, containing the minimal set of controls that mark the Mini Debugger in its "inactive" state (see Figure 22.6).

There are four buttons:

▶ **Stop** forces the target application to quit.

▶ **Pause** breaks the target's execution wherever it happens to be. In the routine case, this might be

FIGURE 22.6   The Mini Debugger, in its inactive state, running in front of Linear. The buttons in the window halt (force quit) the target application; pause it for debugging; bring Xcode's project window forward; and activate/deactivate breakpoints.

anywhere, with little reference to your own code; in the case of an infinite loop, however, the offending code would be in the call stack.

▶ **Project** switches to Xcode and brings the target's project window to the front. This has the side effect of closing the Mini Debugger, abandoning the MD debugging style in favor of an Xcode-centered one. You can get the MD back by selecting **Run > Mini Debugger**, or ⌃⌘home (which on a laptop Mac is **fn-⌃⌘←**).

▶ **Breakpoints Active/Inactive** controls whether breakpoints will pause the execution of the application. The breakpoint arrow in the button is black when breakpoints are inactive, and blue when they are active.

When the target application is paused, either by pressing **Pause** or by hitting a breakpoint, the Mini Debugger expands into the active state (see Figure 22.7). In the active state, the Mini Debugger looks much like an editor pane as shown while your target application is running; it displays the current line in

> **NOTE**
>
> You'd be tempted, now that you have less need to see Xcode, to do a **Hide Others** to get it out of sight. The problem with this is that hiding Xcode also hides the Mini Debugger.

the current source file, and the debugger strip appears across the top of the window. You can't, however, edit the text in the active MD window.

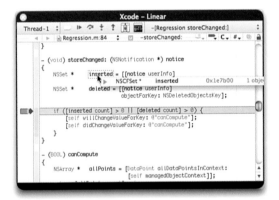

FIGURE 22.7    The Mini Debugger in its active state, as Linear breaks in `storeChanged:`. Except for the ability actually to edit text, this is an Xcode text-editing pane, with a debugger strip and a navigation bar at the top, and a breakpoint gutter and code focus ribbon at the left. Datatips are available in this window as they would be in Xcode.

The navigation bar is familiar from Chapter 20, "Navigating an Xcode Project." As for the debugger strip

▶ The first control in the strip is the **Thread** pop-up. Your application may span more than one thread of execution, and the Debugger has no way to determine which of them you are interested in. This pop-up enables you to switch among them, and browse in the stack trace (the last pop-up) to find which one you want.

- ▸ **Breakpoints Active/Inactive** toggles between permitting and not permitting breakpoints to interrupt the target. When breakpoints are active, the arrow in this button is white; when inactive, the arrow is black.

- ▸ **Continue** (right arrowhead) resumes running the target once it is paused.

- ▸ **Step Over** (arrow arcing over a dot) advances the target program line-by line, executing each.

- ▸ **Step In** (arrow down to dot) causes the Debugger to follow the execution of the target into a function or method called on the current line.

- ▸ **Step Out** (arrow up from dot) executes the target until the current line is in the caller of the current function.

- ▸ **Debugger** (window with spray can) reveals the Debugger window in Xcode— although it does not activate Xcode.

- ▸ **Console** (black window with gdb written in it) reveals the Console window in Xcode. Again, it does not bring Xcode to the front.

- ▸ The **Stack Trace** pop-up shows all the function calls leading to the execution of the current line. You can browse the pop-up to see the current line in each calling function, and to examine the data in those functions.

The ability to activate and deactivate breakpoints is more valuable in the Mini Debugger than in the main Xcode Debugger. If you are searching for a bug that is triggered only after a long sequence of human-interface operations, you can leave breakpoints off until just before you do the one thing that triggers your bug. Not having breakpoints trigger during your lead-up saves you a lot of back and forth with Xcode, and makes for fewer factors in masking the bug.

# Datatips

Datatips are a valuable supplement in debugging with a text-editing pane. Datatips reduce the need for the Debugger window's variables list by showing the value of a variable in a yellow floating window when you hover the mouse pointer over it (see Figure 22.8).

The datatip shows the same information as would be shown in the variables list. If you move the cursor over the double-headed arrow in the datatip, you will be presented with a pop-up menu for selecting what information is shown. The pop-up also offers to print an object's description string to the Console, view it in a separate Expressions window, or show it in a raw-memory browser. You can also jump the editor window to the object's definition or display its documentation in the Documentation window.

Notice in Figure 22.8 (top) that the summary formatter we set earlier for DataPoint is used in the datatip as well as in the Debugger's variables list.

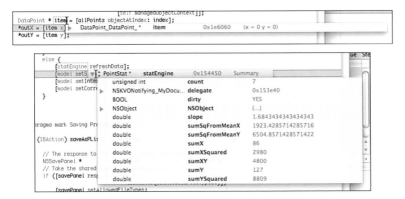

FIGURE 22.8     When you are debugging an application, either in an Xcode text editor or the Mini Debugger, datatips will appear whenever you hover the cursor pointer over a variable. *(Top)* Just hovering the cursor will show the value of the object. *(Bottom)* Moving the cursor (without clicking) into the datatip's disclosure triangle will show an additional datatip covering object members.

Objects and `structs`, of course, don't give up all their secrets in one line. At the left end of their datatips is a disclosure triangle. Don't click it! Simply hovering over the triangle will show another, larger datatip with a line for each member of the object.

> **NOTE**
>
> Why have I been emphasizing the Debugger window, when in-editor debuggers and datatips are available? The problem with the in-editor debugger is that things are not as available as they are in the Debugger window. In the window, the call stack and all the variables currently in scope are constantly visible. You can see them changing as execution advances. With the in-editor debugger, you have to hold the Stack Trace pop-up open to see the full trace. Datatips work well for static data, but if you want to see the effect of stepping through a function, or to see variables whose names aren't typed out in the current function (think of the `self` object), you're out of luck.

# Summary

This chapter collected a number of techniques that didn't fit into the narrative of debugging `Linrg` or `Linear` but that I hope will bring you to a better feel for what is happening when you debug Mac OS X software. In addition to tips, we covered how to customize the display of variables in the Debugger and how to tailor breakpoints to perform tasks when they trigger or trigger only on certain conditions.

We covered the diagnosis of over-released memory, which isn't strictly a matter of development tools but is a basic enough skill that I couldn't bear to leave it out.

Finally, we had a long-delayed look at the Mini Debugger and the in-editor debugging facility.

## Further Reading

This book can only introduce the deep and subtle art of debugging. The developer documentation installed with the Xcode tools includes the complete manual for `gdb`; do a full-text search for "Debugging with GDB" to find it.

Apple has also provided some helpful tech notes on debugging for Mac OS X:

- ▶ TN 2030 *GDB for* `MacsBug` *Veterans*
  http://developer.apple.com/technotes/tn/tn2030.html

- ▶ TN 2032 *Getting Started with GDB*
  http://developer.apple.com/technotes/tn/tn2032.html

- ▶ TN 2123 *CrashReporter*
  http://developer.apple.com/technotes/tn2004/tn2123.html

- ▶ TN 2124, *MacOS X Debugging Magic*
  http://developer.apple.com/technotes/tn2004/tn2124.html

The first two tech notes deal with using `gdb` under Project Builder, Xcode's predecessor, but the principles remain the same.

# CHAPTER 23

# Xcode and Speed

**IN THIS CHAPTER**

▶ **Making Xcode Faster**

▶ **Precompilation: Headers**

▶ **Predictive Compilation: Source**

▶ **Distributed Builds**

One of the driving goals behind the development of Xcode has been to speed up the development cycle as much as possible. Some of what Apple has done to make Xcode faster comes for free: You don't have to do anything special when Apple shifts to a faster version of the gcc compiler package, for instance. Other strategies require your cooperation. This chapter covers them.

## Precompiled Headers

Precompiled headers are a feature of almost every modern development system. The idea is that almost all implementation files rely on a large base of header files that they have in common and that don't often change. A naive strategy of just reading the headers at the top of each implementation file would result in 90 percent or more of the code processed for each file being parsed into identical symbol tables. Better to do that parsing once, cache the results, and pick up the process from there with each implementation file. A *precompiled header* is such a cache.

Xcode's precompiled-header support is done in two phases. First, you specify a *prefix file*, which encompasses all the identical content your implementation files will include. (There being a single prefix isn't a limitation, as it may contain #include or #import directives.) Xcode project templates set up new projects to have a prefix file named *target*_Prefix.pch, containing #includes of the umbrella frameworks associated with the target type. You can set the name of the prefix file by using the Prefix Header build setting in the Target Info window.

All implementation files in a project implicitly include the prefix file. It is prepended to them for compilation purposes, and any change to the prefix file forces a recompilation of all other files.

The second phase of precompiled-header support is the Precompile Prefix Header switch in the Target Info window. Setting this switch causes a precompiled version of the prefix header to be built whenever necessary. The compilation of the rest of the project will proceed from the state stored in the precompiled file rather than by reading in the prefix header file.

Typing `prefix` into the search field in the **Build** tab of the Target Info window will narrow the build-settings list to a very few items, including both the Prefix Header and Precompile Prefix Header settings.

Generating a precompiled header takes more time than a single reading of the constituent header files, so a project with very few implementation files may not see much improvement from using a precompiled header. If you manage to make regular changes to a file that goes into your prefix header, thus forcing a regular rebuild of the precompiled header and a complete rebuild of your project, you will lose time. Restrict the prefix header to those headers you are sure will rarely change over the lifetime of your project.

# Predictive Compilation

Editing text is an undemanding task for a computer. The computer is idle for most of the time between keystrokes and cursor blinks. Xcode can fill this idle time by going through all the files you've changed since the last time you've compiled, and compiling them—before you've asked for a build. Predictive compilation will even extend to the file you are actively editing.

Xcode does this compilation "on spec," because if you change anything it compiled this way, it has to throw the predictive compilation away. Often enough, however, you don't make any changes, and when you do ask for a build, substantial portions will have been done ahead of time.

By default, predictive compilation is on. It does make demands on a computer's resources; so if your Mac seems sluggish to you, try turning it off, using the check box **Build Options: Use Predictive Compilation** in the Building pane of the Preferences window.

Because it cranks up the CPU and hard drive, predictive compilation won't be used while running on battery power.

Earlier versions of Xcode would mistakenly report compilation errors based on versions of files that had been changed in recent editing sessions—a result of predictive compilation results hanging around after they became obsolete. Although these bugs seem to have been eliminated, try turning predictive compilation off if something similar arises in your work.

# Distributed Builds

If you have a large project and more than one Macintosh at your disposal, you can see dramatically shorter build times with *distributed builds*. You can volunteer idle time for distributed builds by opening the Distributed Builds panel of the Preferences window (see Figure 23.1) and checking either or both of the check boxes at the top of the panel. Xcode processes on other computers or even the same computer can then send portions of their builds to the volunteer for compilation. The volunteer can choose to give the distributed-build background process low, medium, or high priority.

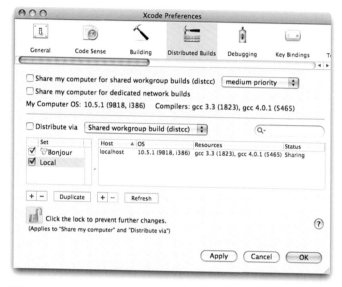

FIGURE 23.1    The Distributed Builds panel of the Xcode Preferences window. The top two check boxes enable sharing out this machine for Shared Workgroup and Dedicated Network builds, respectively. The lower section controls how this computer will take advantage of distributed builds—shared or dedicated—and what other machines should be used. These controls are enabled because I clicked the lock icon and entered an administrator's password.

You distribute the build process in two ways:

▶ Shared Workgroup builds encompass a small number (six or fewer) of servers. It works best for small or medium-sized projects. You can discover build hosts by Bonjour, or add them manually to the build set.

▶ Dedicated Network builds rely on "build farms" of up to 30 machines. They aren't as convenient—Bonjour discovery isn't available—but for large projects, they offer much better performance.

## All Distributed Builds

Any computer that has Xcode installed can make itself available to serve requests for distributed builds. This is done by checking one or both boxes at the top of the Distributed Builds panel of the Preferences window. When these options are active, the computer will be available even if you are not running Xcode, or even logged in.

Separately, you can choose to *use* distributed builds by setting the **Distribute via** check box in the lower portion of the Distributed Builds panel, and selecting the method you want to use—**Shared Workgroup** or **Dedicated Network**—from the accompanying pop-up. You can only pick one. When you do, future compilations will be done not with gcc, but with distcc, which handles the task of farming compilations out to the list of available hosts—the *build set*.

Choosing to use distributed builds also activates the build set list, in the lower portion of the Distributed Builds panel. The leftmost column organizes the build set into groups. Initially, there is one group, for Bonjour: The easiest way to take advantage of shared network builds is to allow Xcode (or xcodebuild) to discover build hosts for itself, and select the ones that are eligible. You can specify additional build hosts by creating your own group, and adding them to the new group by name.

If distcc has a choice, it prefers to distribute to faster computers.

The build process gives to the home computer the responsibilities of precompiling headers, and linking the final product. gcc's file format for precompiled headers is meant for speed, not compatibility. The exact format depends on the compiler version, OS version, and architecture on which precompilation is done. Only machines that match the home machine are eligible to take part in distributed builds.

The heavy responsibilities of the home machine—precompilation, preprocessing, linking, and housekeeping—mean you should not make it a build host, even though this is possible.

Precompiled headers are large files, and distributing them to all build hosts taxes network bandwidth. For every transfer of a precompiled header, the build process slows down.

If the network over which builds are distributed is not fast, distribution will be a net loss. The recommended minimum is 100Mbps. Wireless and 10BASE-T networks will result in slower, not faster, builds. Because of the overhead of setting up a distributed build, distribution is less of a win, and even may be a loss, when few source files need to be compiled.

## Shared Workgroup Builds

You can offer your machine to perform Shared Workgroup builds for others by checking the **Share my computer for shared workgroup builds (distcc)** box at the top of the Distributed Builds panel of the Preferences window. Use the pop-up next to that check box to choose how much of your processor time will go to distccd, the daemon that handles build requests.

Making your computer available for Shared Workgroup builds will immediately start a handful of instances of the distccd daemon to listen for requests. You can remove these by unchecking the top check box in the Distributed Builds panel. Killing the processes directly won't work: The launchd daemon will simply relaunch them. If they won't go away even when you check the box (and click either **Apply** or **OK**), the *Xcode 3.0 Release Notes*, available through a bookmark in the Documentation window, have advice.

The Shared Workgroup build set, by default, includes a Bonjour group, containing all the machines that could be found that are running distccd. If you want, you can add a group to the group list, and populate it with servers you specify by name. Checking this group, and unchecking the Bonjour group, restricts the build set to the machines you choose.

If you're using a firewall, be sure to leave port 3632 open for distcc traffic.

## Dedicated Network Builds

Make your computer available for Dedicated Network builds by checking the second box at the top of the Distributed Builds panel of the Xcode Preferences window. Dedicated Network builds require Mac OS X 10.4 or later, and servers must have Xcode 2.3 or later.

Dedicated Network builds cannot discover servers through Bonjour. You must create build groups and populate them yourself.

By eschewing Bonjour hosts, Dedicated Network builds can take advantage of the build set's consisting of a stable group of known hosts. A host that was available for one compilation will almost certainly be available for another. Because of this, it makes sense for a build host to cache precompiled headers; they need traverse the network only once per build host, instead of once for every file to be compiled. This greatly speeds Dedicated Network builds as compared to Shared Workgroup builds. As more files are compiled, the advantage increases.

There is no hard-and-fast limit on the practical number of build servers for Dedicated Network builds. Productivity may start leveling off at 10 servers, but with lots of network bandwidth and fast disk access on the home computer, as many as 30 servers can be worthwhile.

If you're using a firewall, be sure to leave port 51500 open.

# Project Indexing

As mentioned in Chapter 20, "Navigating an Xcode Project," Xcode devotes a background thread to identifying and indexing all the symbols in your project and the frameworks it uses. On recent machines, with a moderately sized project and a reasonably paced typist, you will see no effect from the indexing thread (other than having an index). In some cases, however, indexing may slow your machine down.

The drastic thing you can do about this is to turn indexing off. In the Code Sense pane of the Preferences window, clear the check box labeled **Indexing: Enable for All Projects**. No indexing threads will then be started; nor will you be able to use the Class Browser, the Class Model, the Project Symbols smart group, code completion, or Command-double-clicking to find symbol definitions.

You can take a less-drastic step if you have a few source files—perhaps files you've generated with some preprocessor that generates great numbers of functions or large amounts of static data. Select those files and open the File Info window for them (**File > Get Info**). In the **General** tab, uncheck the **Include in Index** box. Then open the **Project Info** box, the **General** tab, and press **Rebuild Code Sense Index**. If typing speed improves, you've found the problem. But first make sure that indexing *is* your problem: Experiment first with turning all indexing off, and then you can turn it back on and fish for issues with specific files.

Another less-drastic step is to reduce the amount of indexing that has to be done. In all but the very largest projects, the lion's share of indexing is done in frameworks, and it makes sense to do that part of the indexing once, in advance, and have individual projects use these master indexes as bases for project indexes. The facility is formally known as *index templates*, and you have to build and enable them to make use of them.

You will find the necessary makings in /Developer/Extras/Xcode Index Templates/. There is a way to build and enable templates piecemeal and to control where they are stored; for most purposes, however, it's good enough to build them all, store them in the /Library domain, and enable Xcode's use of them. Do this in the Terminal application by focusing on the templates directory and executing the command install_templates found there:

```
$  cd  "/Developer/Extras/Xcode  Index Templates"
$  sudo ./installtemplates
Password:
***      INSTALLING          INDEX          TEMPLATES      ***

Indexing   and  copying  template  for  CPlusPlusIndex
Indexing   and  copying  template  for  CarbonIndex
...
```

This will take some minutes, and thousands of lines of output will scroll by as the script prints the name of every file that is indexed. You'll have to build index templates afresh every time you install a new version of Xcode.

You can find more information about index templates, including details on manual installation, in the Read Me file in the directory /Developer/Extras/Xcode Index Templates.

It sometimes happens that features that depend on indexing stop working or work unreliably. Code Sense, for instance, might not be delivering all the completions you think it ought to, given the context. It is possible that the project index has been corrupted.

If you think that this may have happened, select **Edit Project Settings** in the **Project** menu (or double-click the **Project** icon at the top of the Groups & Files list), and click **Rebuild Code Sense Index** at the bottom of the **General** tab of the Info window that results.

If a problem persists and you are using index templates, see whether turning index templates off and rebuilding the project index cures the problem. There is no control in the Xcode human interface to turn the use of index templates on or off, so you'll have to use the `defaults` command from the terminal, and then relaunch Xcode:

```
$ defaults write com.apple.Xcode PBXCodeSenseEnableIndexTemplates 'NO'
$
```

If re-indexing cures your problem after the default is turned off, rebuild the index templates before using them again.

## Summary

This chapter addressed the vexed question of how to make Xcode faster. It is necessarily short, because if there were easy ways to make Xcode faster, Apple would use them. I therefore turned to strategies that buy speed at the expense of trouble or features.

We reviewed the technologies Apple offers to make the compile-link-test-edit turnaround as fast as possible. These technologies include the precompilation of headers that every development toolset offers, and predictive compilation, which uses the idle time in the edit phase to get compilations done before they are requested. Portions of Xcode builds can be farmed out to other computers to compile in parallel; we showed how to set that up. Finally, we looked at project indexing, which underlies many convenience features of the IDE but does take up processor time.

CHAPTER 24

# A Legacy Project

IN THIS CHAPTER

▶ **The Organizer**

▶ **Building** make **Projects in Xcode**

Not every worthwhile software-source product is packaged for Xcode. The vast library of open source software available for UNIX systems like Mac OS X come as *tarballs*—archives packaged and compressed by the tar command-line tool—or as revisions in an SCM repository, to be built from the command line, using the make command.

The make tool—on Mac OS X it is GNU make—takes as its input a *makefile*, specifying how products in a project are to be built. The makefile specifies that some files, say a .o file from a compilation, depend on others, such as the .c file of the same name, along with a set of .h files. On the strength of that information, make can detect whether a product's dependencies are newer than the product and, if so, can issue commands that bring the product up-to-date.

Xcode's native build system works the same way but does not usually need you to specify dependencies. It detects what files you put into a project, deduces what it is supposed to do with them—compile them, include them as resources, and so on—and determines what the intermediate products are and what additional files go into producing the intermediate products. From all of that, it produces dependency rules for the target and uses them to direct builds.

> **NOTE**
>
> The exception in which you *do* specify build dependencies to a native-build target is a Run Script phase. When you add a Run Script build phase, you can specify an input file and a product file.

If you have a source product that is organized around makefiles, you can still work within Xcode. There are two ways to do this. One is to use Xcode's Organizer window as a light-weight manager for the command-line build. The other is to create an *external build system project* that can provide makefile projects with many of the services Xcode gives its native projects. Let's see what Xcode can and can't do for us with a moderately large product, TesseractOCR.

TesseractOCR produces a command-line tool that takes a TIFF scan of a printed page and emits a text file of the page's contents. It has been supplanted by subtler commercial offerings, but it works quite well. It runs to 473 source files.

# Preparing the Project

First, obtain the Tesseract source, which you can find at http://tesseract-ocr. googlecode. com/files/tesseract-2.01.tar.gz; it is also to be found on the CD that accompanies this book. The source archive has the compound extension .tar.gz, meaning that it is a GNU-ZIP compressed tar archive. Create a directory (for our purposes, I'm using ~/Tesseract) as an "umbrella" for the project, download the archive, and move the archive into the umbrella directory.

You also need configuration files that permit Tesseract to parse English-language text. Download this from http://tesseract-ocr.googlecode.com/ files/tesseract-2.00.eng.tar.gz (again, it's also on the CD), and move it to the umbrella ~/Tesseract directory.

Now for some work in the Terminal application. Before it can be taken over by Xcode, the Tesseract project has to be unpacked from its archive. You do this with the tar command-line utility:

```
$ cd ~/Tesseract
$ # Move the tarball here, if it isn't here already
$ cp ~/Downloads/tesseract-2.01.tar.gz .
$ # Unpack the tarball
$ tar xzvf tesseract-2.01.tar.gz
tesseract-2.01/
tesseract-2.01/Makefile.in
tesseract-2.01/README
tesseract-2.01/AUTHORS
tesseract-2.01/COPYING
tesseract-2.01/ChangeLog
tesseract-2.01/INSTALL
tesseract-2.01/Makefile.am
tesseract-2.01/NEWS
tesseract-2.01/configure
...
tesseract-2.01/dlltest/dlltest.vcproj
$ # Shift to the newly-expanded tesseract directory
$ cd tesseract-2.01
```

```
$ # Install the English-language recognition data:
$ # Copy it into the tesseract-2.01 dictionary
$ cp ~/Downloads/tesseract-2.00.eng.tar.gz .
$ # Expand it in-place
$ tar xzvf tesseract-2.00.eng.tar.gz
tessdata/eng.DangAmbigs
tessdata/eng.freq-dawg
tessdata/eng.inttemp
tessdata/eng.normproto
tessdata/eng.pffmtable
tessdata/eng.unicharset
tessdata/eng.user-words
tessdata/eng.word-dawg
$
```

The options to `tar` (xzvf) told it to *eXtract* the contents after *unZipping* them from the named *File* and to be *Verbose*, or print the name of each file. The verbosity isn't strictly necessary, but extraction takes time, and it's nice to have something to show what's going on.

The typical open source project supplies a `configure` script that adjusts the build process to your OS and tools. It creates a tree of `Makefile` files that direct the building and installation of the product. Typically, this is all done on the command line, with any necessary adjustments done in a separate text editor.

> **N O T E**
>
> If you did the download with Safari, and have permitted it to open "safe" files automatically, you'll find that the `.gz` compression layer will be removed. In that case, you unpack the `.tar` archive with `tar xvf`.

Instead, we shift our attention to Xcode.

# The Organizer

Xcode's Organizer window is a general-purpose tool for editing file system directories and the text files they contain. It marshals and executes scripts that work on such directories and files. It has many features that make working on makefile projects much easier.

Switch to Xcode (or launch it) and clear out any windows that might be open (you'll need the space). Open the Organizer with **Window > Organizer** (^⌘O). What you initially see is a tall, thin window with a gray background (see Figure 24.1).

## The Files List

Begin your work by adding the `tesseract-2.01` directory. You can do this by dragging the directory in from the Finder, or by choosing **Add Existing Folder...** from the + pop-up at the lower-left corner of the window.

Once the directory is added, you'll see that you can open it, and its subdirectories, by clicking the disclosure triangles. Files in each directory are also visible. Selecting the top-level directory and pressing the **Delete** key removes the directory from the Organizer without deleting it; selecting anything else and pressing **Delete** will move the file to the Trash. An alert sheet will confirm with you before either kind of deletion occurs.

You can rename a file by Option-clicking on it and editing the name. By dragging a file or directory, you can change its location within the hierarchy. You can move the top-level directory by selecting it and choosing **Assign New Location…** from the lower-left **Action** (✿) menu; an open-file sheet will drop down for you to pick the new location.

Select one of the text files in the files list on the left and click the expansion button, the third button on the lower left (see Figure 24.2). The right side of the expanded window is filled with a text editor such as you are already familiar with, showing the selected file.

This is a nearly full-featured editor. The history buttons and pop-up are available, as are the function and header pop-ups. The counterpart button works. The Code Focus strip still shows block scopes and code folding. The other features, such as breakpoints, bookmarks, and the class pop-up, are not available, nor can you Command-double-click a symbol to find its definition; there is no Xcode project to index the source or to keep lists of bookmarks and definitions.

FIGURE 24.1    The Organizer window, in its initial, collapsed state. It consists of a column of directories. Each directory in a hierarchy can be expanded by clicking the disclosure triangle next to its name and icon.

> **NOTE**
>
> The short of it is that most of what you can do in the Finder, you can do with the Organizer without leaving Xcode. Note that you aren't restricted to one top-level directory. You can drag as many directories as you want into the Organizer file list, and you'll be able to work with each independently. The Organizer will keep your top-level directories in its list until you remove them—if you quit Xcode and restart it, they'll still be there.

FIGURE 24.2    The Organizer with the expansion button (third from the lower left) selected. Any file you select in the hierarchy to the left is available for editing in the large area to the right.

Click the README file in the file list to see what the authors prescribe for building and installing Tesseract. You can see that there are no dependencies on other projects or nonstandard libraries, which is a relief, in that we won't have to download or build anything else. It also confirms that the typical natural history of an open source project—configure, make, make install—applies.

## The Organizer Toolbar

You'll notice that the Organizer has a toolbar with four buttons: **Build**, **Clean**, **Run**, and **Action**. As in other Xcode windows, these are pop-up menus of actions, but act as simple buttons, executing a default action when they are pressed momentarily.

In the Xcode project window, these actions are stereotyped; projects fit in with the Xcode build system, and they can perform only the operations the build system provides. By contrast, the contents of an Organizer window aren't members of Xcode projects (as far as the Organizer knows), so the actions under the toolbar buttons represent scripts (see Figure 24.3). Each script is shown in black, marshaled by the directory to which the script applies (shown in gray).

Selecting a script executes it, but use the **Edit Actions...** button in the same menu to examine what the automatically provided scripts are. Doing so drops down a sheet for selecting among the scripts in the menu; selecting one fills the editor on the right with the contents of the script.

The `configure` script is spartan: The first line specifies that it is to be interpreted with the standard shell (`#! /bin/sh`), and the next that the `configure` script in the current directory is to be run (`./configure`).

We should make the script a little less spartan: The Tesseract project is set up to report no warnings on compilation, to keep debugging information, and to optimize the resulting code—that is, the `CFLAGS` and `CXXFLAGS` variables in the `Makefiles` are set to `-g  -O`. For our purposes, we want to know more about the Tesseract code. We do want the debugging symbols, but to use a debug-

FIGURE 24.3   The pop-up for the Organizer's Build button, when the `tesseract-2.01` directory is selected. When Xcode detects a configure/make project, it automatically populates the menu with configure and make all scripts.

**NOTE**

Each directory in the files list can have scripts associated with it. If an internal directory is selected, you'll be given a choice of editing and creating scripts for each directory, up to the top level. Select enclosing directories with the "breadcrumb" control at the upper left of the sheet.

ger effectively, we want optimization off; we also want to receive warnings to assure ourselves the source is being interpreted as its authors intend: `-g  -O0  -Wall` (see Figure 24.4).

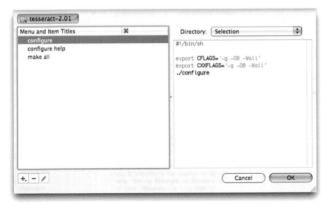

FIGURE 24.4   The script editor sheet, editing the **configure** build action that Xcode provided. We added two `export` commands to set environment variables for the `./configure` script.

However, before we make *any* changes to Tesseract as distributed, we should preserve its original state. First **Cancel** the script-editing sheet so that we can access other features of the window. In the **Action** (⚙) menu *at the bottom left* of the window, select **Make Snapshot....** (If the command isn't available, make sure you've selected a top-level item— tesseract-2.01—in the file list.) This is

> **NOTE**
>
> I learned that I could do this, and how, by running ./**configure --help** on the command line, and inspecting the options, and by doing one pass of ./configure to see what the default CFLAGS and CXXFLAGS were. I'm eliding those steps in the interest of simplicity.

the same mechanism we saw near the end of the "Refactoring" section of Chapter 12, "Unit Testing." While the snapshot is in progress, the Action button remains dark, and a small window displays progress (indefinite, because with no project, Xcode has no count of the files).

You can confirm the snapshot was made by selecting **Snapshots** from the lower-left **Action** menu. The Snapshots window is the same one we saw before, containing only the snapshots made for the current top-level directory.

Now we can customize the **Build > configure** script to set environment variables that override the default settings for CFLAGS and CXXFLAGS. Reopen the script editor (**Build** (button) > **Edit Scripts**). Edit the **configure** script so it reads

```
#!/bin/sh

export CFLAGS='-g -O0 -Wall'
export CXXFLAGS='-g -O0 -Wall'
./configure
```

The Organizer's script editor is nearly identical to the editor for the **Script** menu. See the "User Scripts in Xcode" section of Chapter 15, "Documentation in Xcode," for the full story.

## Configure and Build

Now, at last, we can configure the Tesseract project. Select **configure** under the **Build** button. A Build Results window appears while the configuration is going on, and the files list in the Organizer grows and shrinks as temporary files appear and disappear. Eventually, it all stops.

Do you want to see how ./configure progressed? In the Build Results window (you may have to select **Build > Build Results** from the menu bar to make the window visible again), make sure the first and third buttons at the lower left of the upper list panel are depressed (dark). The first (check mark) displays successful subphases of the build, and the third (lines of text) opens a pane displaying the build transcript. You can scroll through the build transcript to examine ./configure's output.

Better yet, select the line in the upper build-progress list that says "Running external build tool"; that line represents the running of ./configure, including its output. Copy the line (**Edit > Copy**). In the Organizer, select the top-level tesseract-2.01 directory, and from the lower-left + pop-up, select **New File**. A file named Untitled File will be added to the list, the name selected so that you can edit it; rename it **configure progress** or something like that. In the editor pane at the right, **Edit > Paste**. The new file now contains the transcript of the ./configure tool.

Had ./configure issued any warnings or errors, these would have shown up in the upper lists of the Build Results window. Selecting one of the error lines would highlight the matching output in the build transcript.

There are now Makefiles in all the Tesseract directories. Take a moment to examine one or two, to get a feel for what happened. Xcode knows about Makefiles, and does some modest syntax coloring. It also puts all the targets of the Makefile into the function pop-up in the navigation bar (though this is slightly inaccurate—anything that is followed by a colon gets thrown in).

It's time to build. From the **Build** button, select **make all**. Once again, the Build Results window appears. If you were building an Xcode project, this would show you the progress of the build as each file was compiled; the pie-chart tag in the status bar, and the bars on Xcode's icon in the Dock, would give you some idea of how far the process has come. But this is an "external build," and Xcode has no track of source files or what make is doing with them. So, you have to wait until the Build Results window reports a final status—in this case, "Build succeeded," with something over a hundred warnings.

Select one of the warnings. As with an Xcode project build, the file in which the warning was reported is displayed in the window's editor pane, with the offending line highlighted. Unlike an Xcode project, no yellow bubble is inserted into the display.

> **NOTE**
>
> If we hadn't set the -Wall compiler flag, none of these warnings would have appeared.

Here's one of the warnings, "comparison between signed and unsigned integer expressions," at line 102 of closed.cpp. The line is

```
else if (state_table[x].part1 == NO_STATE) {
```

What is NO_STATE? (See Appendix A, "Some Build Variables," notes about non-ASCII underscore characters.) Without a project index, Xcode doesn't know. If you Command-double-click it, you are not taken to a definition. By the idioms of C++ programming, it's probably a preprocessor macro, but it isn't colored as one. You'll have to do a global search.

It turns out that global searches are possible. Instead of being scoped to a project (or parts of a project, if you use option sets), global searches span all of a directory and its subdirectories. In the Organizer files list, select any directory, and pop open the **Action** menu (the gear at the lower-left corner) and select **Find in Selected Organizer Folder**....

The find-in-folder window is nearly identical to the Project Search window. There is only one option, **In Selected Organizer Folder**, and the **Options** button is disabled. There are only two methods: **Textual** and **Regular Expression**. There is no editor view, so when a result appears in the list, you'll have to double-click it to see the context. There is no progress bar, so you'll have no feedback on the progress of the search. Progress will take longer than with a project search, because there is no support from Spotlight.

Otherwise, it's the same: Type `NO_STATE` into the **Find** field, press **Return**, wait for the result, and look for the line that `#defines` the symbol.

## Installing

The last step the authors prescribed was `make install`. We'd prefer not to install—it changes the contents of the BSD file tree outside the home directory. The `Makefiles` include an `uninstall` target, but I don't trust such things; installation is at least partly a one-way process, because a project may install files that it can't strictly identify (at `uninstall` time) as having come from it. We'd like to run Tesseract and debug it from within the `tesseract-2.01` build tree, where we don't need administrative privileges to install it.

However, in the case of Tesseract, we don't quite have that choice. Tesseract relies on a directory, `/usr/local/share/tessdata/`, that contains configuration files; it refuses to look for `tessdata` anywhere else. So, even though we want to work with Tesseract locally, we have to install it globally. Fortunately, the configuration files won't change from build to build: We need install only once.

This leaves us in a quandary:

▶ There is no **make install** item under the toolbar **Build** button. That can be remedied—adding scripts to Organizer windows is easy.

▶ But when you run a script consisting solely of `make install`, it fails. Tesseract installs itself into the `/usr/local` tree, and you don't have the administrative privileges to do that.

▶ Editing the script to use `sudo make install` doesn't work, either. As soon as `sudo` prompts for a password and waits for standard input, the build aborts because there's no way to collect input in a build transcript.

There is a way around this. Scripts under the **Run** toolbar button are different from those under the other buttons. Run scripts focus on the execution of a single command. Bring up the **Run** script editor by holding down the **Run** button, and selecting **Edit Actions...** from the menu that pops up (see Figure 24.5).

If the top-level `tesseract-2.01` directory wasn't selected, the "breadcrumb" control at the upper left will show the chain of directories down from there. Make sure **tesseract-2.01** is selected, because the top-level `Makefile` is the one you want `make` to find.

Select **New Shell Script** (a misnomer, as you'll soon see) from the + pop-up at the lower left of the window. Name the new script **make install**.

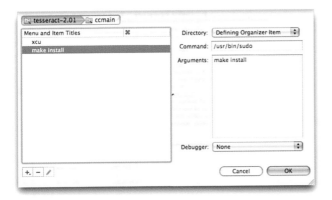

FIGURE 24.5    The script editor for the Organizer's **Run** button is organized around executing a single command. Enter the command in the upper field, and its arguments in the lower. The pop-up at the top of the editor selects among a few possible working directories.

Enter `/usr/bin/sudo` in the **Command** field, and `make install` in the **Arguments** field. Use **Defining Organizer Item** as the working directory. We don't propose to debug sudo, so select **None** for the debugger.

Click **OK** to dismiss the sheet. Now select **make install** from the **Run** drop-down button. Because a run command involves a single command-line tool, it now makes sense for Xcode to open a Console window to interact with the tool. At the `Password:` prompt, type in your administrative password, and press **Return**. Be warned: The console window is not a full-fledged terminal, and can't suppress echoing what you type. Your password will be in plain view.

sudo will launch make, and make will install the `tesseract` tool (which we don't care about) and the `tessdata` configuration directory (which we do).

> **NOTE**
>
> The Debugger window will also appear, and may even obscure the Console window, even though you did not ask for a debugger. Move it aside so that you can get at the Console.

## Running

After all this, running the `tesseract` tool is almost anticlimactic. The `tesseract` tool, at minimum, needs two parameters: a path to a TIFF file and a base name for the resulting text file. I've provided a TIFF file, `xcu.tif`, on the CD. (I had Preview export a page from an early draft of this book.) Put that in the umbrella `Tesseract` directory; that's one level up from the working `tesseract-2.01` directory, so the data file has no chance of disturbing our pristine build tree.

Now to create the Run script. Making sure that the top-level `tesseract-2.01` directory is selected, select **Run** (button) > **Edit Actions**. Add a "script" named **xcu**, or whatever you'd prefer. The **Directory** should be **Defining Organizer Item**. For the **Command**, enter `ccmain/tesseract`—that's where the built tool is to be found in the `tesseract-2.01` tree. For **Arguments**, `../xcu.tif xcu`, meaning the resulting text file, `xcu.txt`, will go into tesseract-2.01. (That can't be helped; tesseract doesn't provide an option to put output anywhere else).

Set **Debugger** to **GDB**. In Xcode 3.0, the command will be run through the Debugger anyway, but in the future that may not be so. It would be nice to have gdb around to catch any crashes that might occur. You may have discovered that although the broad breakpoint gutter is provided in the Organizer editor, clicking in it does not make a breakpoint arrow appear. There's no project to keep a list of break-points.

> **NOTE**
>
> The **Run** pop-up now puts a check mark next to **xcu**. The last script you select from an Organizer toolbar pop-up becomes a default command. It is the script that will be run if you just click the button.

Select **Run** (button) > **xcu**. In the Console window, we see the output:

```
Tesseract Open Source OCR Engine
Image has 24 bits per pixel and size (1224,1584)
Resolution=15 0
```

The file xcu.txt should appear in the Organizer's file tree under tesseract-2.01. If you examine it, you'll find the recognition to be pretty good.

# An External Build System Project

The Organizer takes us a long way, but as we progressed, we found a number of limita-tions owing to the lack of a project file to keep things organized:

▶ Commands under the **Run** button are run under the gdb debugger, but there is no way to set breakpoints—except by using the gdp command line. Breakpoints need a project file to load them before the debugger runs.

▶ There are no bookmarks.

▶ The Class menu in the navigation bar is inactive.

▶ You can't Command-double-click a symbol to find its definition.

▶ With no Code Sense index to track definitions, there is no way to do a global search for symbols.

▶ Without knowing how symbols are defined, Xcode can't syntax-color them.

▶ There is no equivalent to the Symbols smart group.

▶ Code completion is limited to simple textual substitutions drawn from the current file.

▶ There is no way to make or examine class models.

▶ There is no history of global searches.

We can have those advantages back if we put Tesseract into an *external build system* project.

In some ways, the concept of an external build system is a throwback to the early days of NeXT's ProjectBuilder IDE. The modern Xcode directs the building of a project autonomously: It determines what needs to be done, in what order, and then it does it. The original ProjectBuilder application had no build system of its own. It made no effort to detect dependencies, and the running of gcc was none of its business. Even as Xcode is a front for gcc and gdb, ProjectBuilder was a front for GNU make. An external build system (EBS) target centers on the invocation of make (or some other tool of your choice).

Let's make a project for Tesseract. From the **File** menu, select **New Project...**, and scroll down in the New Project Assistant to select the **External Build System** project type. Click the **Next** button and give the project a name, such as **Tesseract**. Be careful in choosing a directory for the project. We want a directory that contains tesseract-2.01—so the project file and the source will all be in one project tree—but it's not a good idea to put the project file in the source tree. (Remember, we want to keep the source tree as close to as-supplied as we can.)

Fortunately, we solved that problem a while ago, when we expanded the Tesseract tarball within an umbrella directory named Tesseract. Edit the **Project Directory** field so that it contains ~/**Tesseract**/ (or whatever the path to your umbrella directory is).

Next, add all the files in the tesseract-2.01 directory to the Xcode project. The easiest way is to drag that directory from the Finder to just below the project icon at the top of the Groups & Files list; or you can select **Project > Add to Project...**, and select the source directory. In either case, make sure that subdirectories will be included as groups, not as directory references.

This is certainly easy, but it has a drawback: The Groups & Files list contains all the source files for Tesseract, but also all the object (.o) files. This is easily remedied. Select the project icon at the top of the Groups & Files list, to fill the Detail view with all the files in the project. Then use the search field above the Detail view to narrow it down; type .o. We're in luck; only object files contain that substring. Click in the Detail list to put focus on it, do a **Select All** (⌘A), then press the **Delete** key. Xcode will ask if you want to remove the references, or trash the files entirely; we just want to remove the project references. The Groups & Files list is now much cleaner. Xcode projects are not obliged, as Organizer directory trees are, to include everything from a project directory.

> ### NOTE
>
> You might consider doing the same trick with .a, to put the intermediate library files out of sight. This will also catch files named Makefile.am, which are input files for the automake makefile-generation tool, but that's okay. It's up to you.

Now, if we'd been less fastidious, and put the project file directly into the tesseract-2.01 source directory, we could just have clicked the project's **Build** button or selected **Project > Build**, and been on our way. But we were fastidious, and the project would attempt to invoke make in the umbrella Tesseract directory, where there is no makefile.

The solution lies in the Target Info window for Tesseract. Because Xcode is blind to the workings of an external build process, there are no editors for Info.plist or the panoply of build settings that it can use in a native build. Instead, there is just one panel (see Figure 24.6), in which you specify how to invoke a build tool.

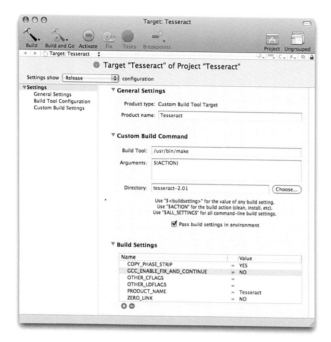

FIGURE 24.6    The Target Info window for an external build-system target. This is nothing more than a form for choosing a build tool (usually make) and passing a parameter list to it. By editing the table at the bottom of the window, you can set up build settings to pass as environment variables when the build tool is executed.

In the **Build Tool** field, Xcode has already supplied /usr/bin/make. Good. For **Arguments**, it supplies $(ACTION), a build variable that corresponds to the build action you select. If you click the **Clean** button, $(ACTION) will be clean; if you invoke xcodebuild with the install action, it will be install; if you click the **Build** button, $(ACTION) will be blank. It all fits well with the semistandard targets in most makefile projects.

The next field, **Directory**, holds the solution to our immediate problem. It designates the working directory to be used when the build tool is run. Relative paths are relative to the directory that holds the Xcode project, so just type **tesseract-2.01** here. (You could also use the **Choose...** button to browse for the directory, but that will fill **Directory** with an absolute path, which hard-wires your project to a particular place on a particular computer.)

The table at the bottom of the window prefigures the abundance of the **Build** tab of a native target. It simply pairs variable names with string values. You'll see there is a pop-up menu at the upper left that allows you to select a configuration so that you can have a different set of build variables per configuration. You can use these variables to build arguments in the **Arguments** field, in the form `$(VARIABLE_NAME)`.

If you check **Pass Build Settings in Environment**, the settings will be added to the environment variables available to the build tool. Because of the way GNU `make` works, this can be handy: Variables from the environment override variables set in a makefile; so you could, for instance, set `CFLAGS` and `CXXFLAGS` to debug and release values in separate configurations.

There is a middle column in the Build Settings table. Clicking in the middle of a line will change the = in that column to +=, so your setting will be appended to the setting, if any, inherited from the existing environment.

Close the Target Info window, and click the **Build** button in the toolbar of the project window. The build takes a few minutes, generates all the same compiler warnings we saw before, and ultimately succeeds. This isn't surprising. The process is the same as the one that came of the **make all** script in the Organizer.

## Code Sense Is Here

But things aren't quite the same. Return to that error on line 102 of `closed.cpp`. (Now that there is a Detail view, you can search the project by name, and find that file quickly.) The symbol `NO_STATE`, which was an inert string under the Organizer, and in the Organizer's Build Results window, is now dark brown: Xcode colors it as a preprocessor macro. Command-double-click it; Xcode instantly displays the definition.

In other words, Code Sense is there, and it works. In fact, as long as the Tesseract Xcode project is open, Code Sense services are available in the Organizer, too.

Now that Code Sense is available, we can examine Tesseract's class architecture. Select the project icon at the top of the Groups & Files list, and then **Design > Class Model > Quick Model**. A class model now appears (see Figure 24.7) for all the C++ classes, just as in the "Class Modeler" section of Chapter 20, "Navigating an Xcode Project," but in this case it's for a project we aren't familiar with. Handy.

> **NOTE**
>
> Code Sense services, especially the Class Modeler, work well if your C++ code base is relatively simple. If you are more aggressive with nested classes, templates, or namespaces, Code Sense begins to break down, missing or misplacing symbols. Code Sense for C++ has improved greatly since Xcode 2, and will continue to improve.

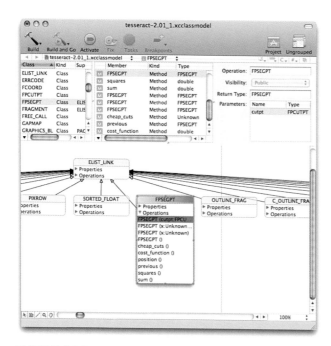

FIGURE 24.7    The Class Model window for Tesseract.

## Running

The Tesseract project builds, and affords some nice facilities to navigate and explore it, but you may have noticed the various "Go" options are grayed out. Xcode does not know what the ultimate product of an external build target is, nor where to find it. We'll have to tell it, by means of a custom executable entry.

Select **Project > New Custom Executable....** In the Assistant window, name the new executable **Tesseract** (It's a label, not a filename), and use the **Choose...** button to navigate to **tesseract-2.01/ccmain/tesseract**. It will fill **Executable Path** with an absolute path, but we'll be fixing that soon. Filling the field activates the **Next** button. Click it.

Now we see the Executable Info window, which we saw in the "The Executables Group" section of Chapter 20, and "NSZombieEnabled" in Chapter 22, "More About Debugging." In the **General** tab, select **Path Type: Relative to Project**; that will change the undesirable absolute path to tesseract to a relative one.

In the **Arguments** tab, add two lines to the arguments table: **xcu.tif** and **xcu**. That will point tesseract at the same TIFF file we used before, and create xcu.txt in the Tesseract directory. Close the window.

Click the **Build and Go** button in the toolbar of the project window. Nothing remarkable here: Xcode makes a quick trip through make, which has nothing to do, and then the Debugger appears. After a few seconds, tesseract loads, and the same message appears in the Console:

```
Tesseract Open Source OCR Engine
Image has 24 bits per pixel and size (1224,1584)
Resolution=15 0
```

And with that, tesseract exits.

## Debugging

Now that we have a project file, we can set breakpoints. Now that we have breakpoints, we can use the Debugger proactively. Find the file tesseractmain.cpp and set a breakpoint at the beginning of the main() function. (There are a couple, selected by an #ifndef directive; use the first.) Click **Build and Go** again.

The program launches and completes as before. What happened? The Xcode debugger loads symbols *lazily*; it doesn't trouble to associate breakpoints with the debugging information in executable modules until after the modules have been loaded. In the case of the main() function, the breakpoint passed by before gdb knew it was there. When an application runs, Xcode signals that a breakpoint has not yet been associated with an executable address by rendering its arrow in orange, rather than blue.

It is easy to tell Xcode not to be lazy in loading a module, and thus permit it to see breakpoints in advance. Open the Shared Libraries window (**Run > Show > Shared Libraries**), as we did in "Lazy Symbol Loading" in Chapter 22. Find **tesseract** in the module list, and change its **Starting Level** from **Default** to **All**.

**Build and Go** once more. This time the breakpoint hits. You are now free to step through tesseract and examine its data just as you could any other Xcode product.

## The Limits of the External Build System

An external build system project has limitations of its own against the Organizer. Xcode projects offer simple file-management facilities, but they are centered on tracking files that are members of the project, not on managing the actual contents of the file system. You can indirectly delete and rename files, but you cannot move files between directories, nor delete directories. For that you need the Organizer (or the Finder).

Further, external build targets are designed around a much less flexible model of the project life cycle. You have one build command (defaulted to make) to which Xcode can pass a limited repertoire of arguments, of its choosing.

> **NOTE**
>
> Remember, you *can* elevate the privileges of Xcode actions if you invoke xcodebuild on the command line with sudo.

There is no concept of adding commands like `./configure`. You can't elevate privileges within the Xcode IDE, even with the modest hack we used in the Organizer for `sudo make install`.

> **NOTE**
>
> Xcode projects and the Organizer can complement each other. If you have a large directory tree encompassing many projects, you can use the Organizer to search or review their contents without opening the project files—and you can open those project files just by double-clicking. We could have used the Organizer in Chapter 15, "Documentation in Xcode," to examine the HeaderDoc-generated documentation files without the hassle of drilling down the documentation hierarchy in the Groups & Files list.

## Summary

This chapter used, and arguably abused, the Tesseract project as a backdrop for exploring the issues that arise in building makefile projects with Xcode. We embraced two ways to manage such projects—the Organizer (new with Xcode 3) and an external build system project—and saw advantages and disadvantages in each. The Organizer combines a level of control that rivals command-line tools with a simple but useful IDE. EBS projects are less flexible, but provide the full power of Code Sense indexing and access to the Debugger shell.

# CHAPTER 25

# Shark and the CHUD Tools

IN THIS CHAPTER

▶ Detailed Profiling with Shark

▶ High-Level Profilers

▶ Specialized Debuggers

▶ Hardware-Level Tools

Xcode, Interface Builder, and Instruments are not the only components of Apple's developer tools. The other major components comprise the Performance Tools, including Shark and the CHUD (Computer Hardware Understanding Developer) applications. These applications use kernel and processor support to provide insight into how an application uses system resources, and thus guide you on how to make your software run faster and with a lighter footprint.

## Shark

The leading instrument for measuring the efficiency of an application is Shark, a statistical profiler. A profiler measures how much time an application spends in each function—indeed, each machine instruction—within it. A statistical profiler does this by interrupting the application at frequent intervals and recording where the interrupt fell. Over time, the accumulated counts add up to a profile of where the application spends its time.

If you want to speed your program up, the best way to spend your effort is on these "hot spots," where optimizations really matter. It's a bad idea to try optimizing a program without hard data. With localized knowledge of your application, you might be misled into improving code that *looks* time-consuming, but really is so rarely called that it doesn't matter, or is part of a larger algorithm that is so slow there's no point in optimizing the pieces.

## The Problem

To explore Shark, we'll go back to Linear. We'll be using a document of more than 5,000 points, to put extra stress on Linear's power to compute regressions. This document is Huge Dataset.linear, to be found on the CD accompanying this book.

Let's see what we're up against. Start Linear and open Huge Dataset.linear. It loads nearly instantaneously; no complaints there. Now click **Compute** to perform the linear regression. On my machine, it takes about 75 seconds. That's quite a long wait. Computers are supposed to be fast.

Quit Linear and go on to the next step.

> **NOTE**
>
> I exploited the straightforward XML format of Core Data to generate Huge Dataset. linear. A simple Ruby script produced a slightly randomized data set that I pasted into an existing Linear document. I didn't bother to alter the data sources to refer back to the points they contain, which is why you won't see a large data set when you select a source in the lower table.

## Starting Shark

To use Shark, build Linear in the Debug configuration (we want the mapping between instruction addresses and lines of code to be straightforward). Then select **Run > Start with Performance Tool > Shark**. Shark launches, displaying a small configuration window (see Figure 25.1). With this, you can choose from various modes of operation (**Time Profile** suits us), whether to profile one application or the entire system (**Process**), and whether you want to profile an existing process or launch a new one (**Launch**).

**FIGURE 25.1**    The initial Shark configuration window. The simplest choice, of launching a process for a time profile by clicking the **Start** button, is shown here. **Config > Show Mini Config Editor** expands this window with more options.

Click the **Start** button. You'll be presented with a window to verify that Linear is the application you want to launch, and the environment it will run in. Click **OK**; once Linear is started, you will have 30 seconds to load Huge Dataset.linear and click **Compute**, so work expeditiously. (Use **Config > Show Mini Config Editor** to set a different sampling period.)

> **NOTE**
>
> A way to concentrate Shark on one task is to launch Linear separately, run Shark, and use the rightmost process pop-up to attach it to Linear, go back to Linear, and press ⌥**Esc** to start sampling when you're ready.

## Analysis

When the 30 seconds is up, Shark returns to the foreground, and it displays a progress bar while it analyzes the results. It then shows its analysis in a Time Profile window (see Figure 25.2). Its initial format, selectable from the pop-up at bottom right, is **Heavy (Bottom-Up)**. Each line in the profile represents a function in the body of which `Linear` spent the most time; it's sorted so the heaviest functions are at the top.

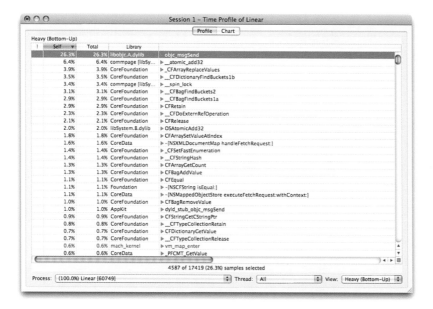

FIGURE 25.2    The Time Analysis window displayed by Shark once sampling is complete. The initial format is **Heavy (Bottom-Up)**, which identifies the single functions in which the most time was spent.

In this run, Shark collected 17,419 samples. 26.3% of `Linear`'s time was spent in `objc_msgSend`, the function in `libobjc.A.dylib` that handles the calling of Objective-C methods. Well, it's a system function, there's not much we can do about how it works, and you have to call methods if you're programming in Objective-C, so our work is done, right?

Not quite. `objc_msgSend` didn't sponta-neously run itself. Other code, eventu-ally our own, called it. Open the disclosure triangle next to the function's name to examine all the functions that called it. The most-frequent caller of `objc_msgSend` is `-[NSMappedObjectStore executeFetchRequest:withContext:]`. It is listed as taking 0.0% of `Linear`'s time in the instructions that make it up (Self),

> **NOTE**
>
> Macs and OS versions differ, and you can't expect to see exactly the same results as I discuss here. PowerPC Macs, in particular, will show very different timings and bottle-necks. Think of this chapter as a guided tour, rather than a strictly worked example.

and 6.7% of Linear's time if you count the method plus the functions it calls. So, 6.7% of objc_msgSend's 26.7 percentage points came from calls made by the NSMappedObjectStore method.

Again, not much we can do, it seems. The bulk of the callers are from Cocoa libraries. However, we can learn more. Continue to open those disclosure trian-

**NOTE**

You can speed the process of drilling down the call tree, at the expense of a bit of clutter, by Option-clicking a disclosure triangle. As with most applications in Mac OS X, that will open the line you click, and all the other lines it contains.

gles to explore the call stacks, up to the point where we start seeing calls from within Linear. Pretty soon we see a pattern: +[DataPoint allDataPointsInContext:] shows up again and again (see Figure 25.3, top).

| Heavy (Bottom-Up) | | | |
|---|---|---|---|
| Self | Total | Library | |
| 26.3% | 26.3% | libobjc.A.dylib | ▼ objc_msgSend |
| 0.0% | 6.6% | CoreData | ▼ -[NSMappedObjectStore executeFetchRequest:withContext:] |
| 0.0% | 6.6% | CoreData | ▼ -[NSPersistentStoreCoordinator(_NSInternalMethods) executeReq |
| 0.0% | 6.6% | CoreData | ▼ -[NSManagedObjectContext executeFetchRequest:error:] |
| 0.0% | 6.6% | Linear | ▼ +[DataPoint allDataPointsInContext:] |
| 0.0% | 6.6% | Linear | ▶ -[MyDocument dataPointAtIndex:x:y:] |
| 0.0% | 5.9% | CoreData | ▼ -[NSXMLDocumentMap handleFetchRequest:] |
| 0.0% | 5.9% | CoreData | ▼ -[NSMappedObjectStore executeFetchRequest:withContext:] |
| 0.0% | 5.9% | CoreData | ▼ -[NSPersistentStoreCoordinator(_NSInternalMethods) executeRe |
| 0.0% | 5.9% | CoreData | ▼ -[NSManagedObjectContext executeFetchRequest:error:] |
| 0.0% | 5.9% | Linear | ▶ +[DataPoint allDataPointsInContext:] |
| 0.0% | 0.0% | AppKit | ▶ -[_NSManagedProxy fetchObjectsWithFetchRequest:error:] |
| 0.0% | 0.0% | CoreData | ▶ -[NSMappedObjectStore executeCountRequest:withContext:] |

| Heavy (Bottom-Up) | | | |
|---|---|---|---|
| Self | Total | Library | |
| 90.9% | 90.9% | Linear | +[DataPoint allDataPointsInContext:] |
| 0.0% | 90.8% | Linear | ▼ -[MyDocument dataPointAtIndex:x:y:] |
| 0.0% | 90.7% | Statistics | ▼ -[PointStat collectStatistics] |
| 0.0% | 90.7% | Statistics | ▼ -[PointStat slope] |
| 0.0% | 90.7% | Linear | ▼ -[MyDocument compute:] |
| 0.0% | 90.7% | Linear | main |
| 0.0% | 0.1% | Linear | ▶ -[MyDocument pointsAllTheSame] |
| 0.0% | 0.1% | Linear | ▶ -[Regression canCompute] |
| 4.8% | 4.8% | Linear | main |

FIGURE 25.3   The bottom-up time profile of Linear. *(Top)* The raw analysis shows objc_msgSend takes up 26.3% of Linear's time, but crawling up the stack to its callers often shows +[DataPoint allDataPointsInContext:] is the ultimate caller from Linear. *(Bottom)* If we use Shark's data-mining tools to look only at methods within Linear, we see that method represents 90.9% of Linear's time.

**NOTE**

If you click the gray button in the corner between the scrollbars of the profile table, a table will appear at the right, showing the call stack that includes the selected function, and accounts for the most time spent. That is, it's what you'd get if you kept opening disclosure triangles, choosing the most frequent caller at each level. Selecting a line in the call-stack table, in fact, opens disclosure triangles in the profile table down to the function you clicked.

## The Top-Down View

At the lower right of the Time Profile window is a pop-up labeled **View**, showing that the current view is **Heavy (Bottom-Up)**. The top-level lines show the single functions that take up the most time in the run of Linear. The next level from a function shows all the functions that called it and their share of that function's calls.

Selecting **Tree (Top-Down)** changes the Profile list so that the top-level lines are the root of the call trees. The topmost line is the start runtime function that eventually calls Linear's main function. main takes up 95.7% of the run time, and so does NSApplicationMain, the only function it calls. The next level below that shows the five functions it calls, and the share of execution time each function takes up.

With the tree view, you can trace down the execution path of Linear, and see how much time was taken at each branch.

Change the **View** pop-up back to **Heavy (Bottom-Up)**.

## Mining the Call Stack

We can make the pattern clearer. **Window > Show Advanced Settings** (⇧⌘M) opens a drawer on the Time Analysis window. In the profile display, the drawer is divided into two sections. The upper, **Profile Analysis**, controls how the profile is displayed. The lower, **Callstack Data Mining**, is of more interest. It has a master switch, **Apply Callstack Data Mining**, that should be checked.

Now apply a method for filtering the display: **Charge Code Without Debug Info to Callers**. Two kinds of code run while Linear is running. One is the Linear executable itself, and we have debug information for it; the other is the system and support libraries Apple provides, for which we don't have debug information. This division has a happy effect: It divides the profile entries between code we can do something about (we have debug information), and code we can't (we don't). This option treats all the time spent in system and library code as occurring in the Linear code that called it. With the leaf calls deep into the libraries filtered out, the profile display will sort itself on our functions.

Checking **Charge Code Without Debug Info to Callers** has a dramatic effect (see Figure 25.3, bottom). +[DataPoint allDataPointsInContext:], and the outside functions it calls, account for *90.9% of Linear's time.*

Another way to see this is to click the **Chart** tab and examine a graphical representation of the call stack as time went by (see Figure 25.5). The horizontal axis represents the accumulation of samples (and thus the passage of time), and the vertical axis is the depth of the stack. The body of the chart is blue, representing the depth of the stack at each sample. The same data-mining rules apply, so the stack we see goes only six deep. If you had a function selected in the **Profile** tab, the run of that function represented by that line in the table is highlighted in gold.

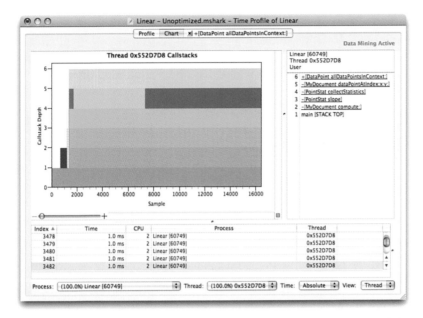

FIGURE 25.4    The Chart tab of the Time Profile window, showing the lifetime of one call to allDataPointsInContext:, as well as the lifetimes of each of its preceding callers at lower levels of the chart. The "normal" body of the call-stack chart is blue; the selected calls are highlighted in orange. If you select a function in the **Profile** tab, that function (here allDataPointsInContext:) will be shown in gold.

Clicking in the chart highlights one sample. At the top of the chart, the run of the active function is highlighted in orange. At the next level down, the run of the caller of that function is highlighted in orange; below that is highlighted the run of *its* caller, and so on.

Clicking in the gray button at the lower right of the chart, where its scrollbars meet, will open on the right a table showing the call stack at the selected sample. After a brief period in which the stack deepens and shallows during setup, Linear's call stack is one solid block, and everywhere you click, you highlight allDataPointsInContext:, and its caller goes straight across, never returning. One method dominates Linear.

We should do something about this. In the **Profile** tab, double-click the name of +[DataPoint allDataPointsInContext:]. Shark shows us a new tab in the Time Profile window, containing the Objective-C source of the method (see Figure 25.5). In these source views, the highlighted line (Shark will initially select the hottest line in the function) is shaded brown, and nonselected lines are colored in yellows that are brighter the more frequently they were sampled (and therefore the more time they took). The background of the scrollbar is black; if you explore it, you'll find that it is marked with yellow stripes to identify the positions of hot code.

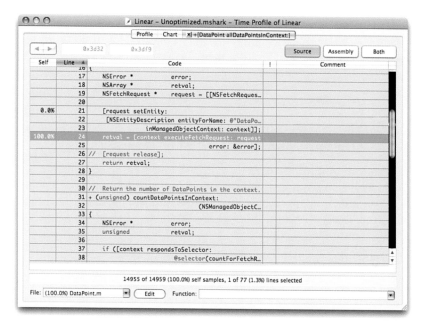

FIGURE 25.5    When you double-click an entry in the Profile table, Shark displays the source of the corresponding function. The more samples recorded for a line, the more intensely colored it is. In this case, practically all the time spent in +[DataPoint allDataPointsInContext:] was taken up by calling the method executeFetchRequest:error:, or by functions it called in turn.

If you click the **Assembly** button, you can see the assembly instructions that back up your code. The assembly for the line of source code you had selected is highlighted in gray, and the same yellow highlight is applied to the hot instructions. Clicking **Both** displays source and assembly side by side.

> **NOTE**
>
> The highlighting and percentages Shark displays are for the targeted function only; if you want to examine hot spots for other functions, find them in the Profile table and double-click them. It's easy, when doing this, to accumulate many source-browsing tabs. Click the **x** button in a tab to clear it away.

The lesson we draw from the source display is that everything goes into the method executeFetchRequest:error:, and that if we want to get an array of DataPoints, the call is unavoidable. We can't *reduce* the cost of that call; we have to concentrate on *avoiding* it.

Here's the strategy: The most-frequent caller of +[DataPoint allDataPointsInContext:] is -[MyDocument dataPointAtIndex:x:y:]. It's apart of the protocol for drawing data from the document, which we have made the custodian of our DataPoints. If MyDocument owns the array of DataPoints, which doesn't change in point-retrieval loops, it can cache it.

Quit Shark. (You'll be given a chance to save the profile, if you'd like.) Bring Xcode back to the front and we can get to work.

## Measure, Then Optimize

We need to add to `MyDocument` an `NSArray` that caches the result of
`allDataPointsInContext:`. The first step is to open `MyDocument.h` and add an instance
variable:

```
NSArray *              pointCache;
```

And declare a simple method, `- (void) pointArrayIsDirty`, that we can call to mark the
cache as invalid and in need of refreshing from `allDataPointsInContext:`.

Open `MyDocument.m`. There are two big changes to `MyDocument`. One is the cache array,
`pointCache`, and the housekeeping that goes with it. The other is to get notification when
the document's Core Data store is changed, so we know to invalidate the cache; this can
be done by lifting the `storeChanged:` notification method from `Regression`, and making
one small change.

First, edit `init` and `dealloc` to set up the notification and tear down the cache when
we're done with it:

```
- (id)init
{
    self = [super init];
    if (self) {
        // Allocate and initialize our model
        statEngine = [[PointStat alloc] init];
        if (!statEngine) {
            [self release];
            self = nil;
        }
        [statEngine setDelegate: self];

        [[NSNotificationCenter defaultCenter]
            addObserver: self
                selector: @selector(storeChanged:)
                    name:
        NSManagedObjectContextObjectsDidChangeNotification
                  object: [self managedObjectContext]];
    }
    return self;
}

- (void) dealloc
{
    [[NSNotificationCenter defaultCenter] removeObserver: self];
    [pointCache release];
```

```
    [statEngine release];
    [model release];
    [graphWindow release];
    [super dealloc];
}
```

Add `pointArrayIsDirty` and the notification method `storeChanged:` that calls it when the DataPoint array changes. Edit `dataPointAtIndex:x:y:` so that it uses the cache when possible:

```
- (void) pointArrayIsDirty
{
    [pointCache release];
    pointCache = nil;
}


- (void) storeChanged: (NSNotification *) notice
{
    NSSet *         inserted = [[notice userInfo]
                                objectForKey: NSInsertedObjectsKey];
    NSSet *         deleted = [[notice userInfo]
                                objectForKey: NSDeletedObjectsKey];

    if ([inserted count] > 0 || [deleted count] > 0) {
        [self pointArrayIsDirty];
    }
}


- (void) dataPointAtIndex: (unsigned) index
                        x: (double *) outX
                        y: (double *) outY
{
    if (! pointCache) {
        pointCache = [DataPoint allDataPointsInContext:
                            [self managedObjectContext]];
        [pointCache retain];
    }
    DataPoint * item = [pointCache objectAtIndex: index];
    *outX = [item x];
    *outY = [item y];
}
```

## The Effect

Build Linear once more, and repeat the exercise: **Run > Start with Performance Tool > Shark**, click **Start**, accept the launch parameters, open Huge Dataset, and click **Compute**.

This turns out to be tricky, because the computation is practically instanta-neous. It might be wise, when the computation is done, to press ⌥Esc to stop the sampling before the 30-second window closes.

Another strategy might be to have Shark launch Linear in the mode **Time Profile (WTF)**. The Windowed Time Facility does not just take the first 30 seconds of the run of a program, stop, and analyze the samples. Rather, it samples *continuously*, and when the 30-second window fills, the oldest samples are dropped to make room for the new ones. Press ⌥Esc to stop the sampling and do the analysis.

The resulting analysis in my run shows that 49.5% of the samples fell in _main. Our main function is only one line long. What gives? Shark settings, including data-mining settings, persist from run to

> **NOTE**
>
> Remember to build Linear again before selecting **Run > Start with Performance Tool > Shark**, because that command does not ensure that the code it runs is up-to-date. Now that you've run Linear with Shark, selecting **Build and Go**, either from the **Build** menu or from the button in the project window's toolbar, will do both for you.

> **NOTE**
>
> If you want to repeat a sampling session in the new Linear, remember that the cache will persist from session to session. Close Huge Dataset and reopen it to get a fresh cache, or just add or delete a point. Don't save the document: It comes with the results all set to zero, so it's easy to see when computation has finished.

run. We are still attributing time spent in called library functions to the caller. main calls NSApplicationMain, which in turn runs an event loop that never touches Linear's code unless an event (usually a human-interface event) occurs. So, half of Linear's time is now spent in system and library code through and through, and really isn't anything we can affect.

Down in the depths of the profile is -[PointStat collectStatistics], the method that loops through DataPoints and does the actual arithmetic on them. If we double-click that line of the profile, the source display includes these lines:

```
        45    for (index = 0; index < count; index++)
        46        [delegate dataPointAtIndex: index x: &x y: &y] ; ! SSE
33.3%   47        sumX + = x;
        48        sumXSquared   +=   x * x;
        49        sumY + = y;
33.3%   50        sumYSquared + = y * y;
        51        sumXY + = x * y;
        52
```

In other words, two-thirds of the time spent in the method is spent incrementing sumX and sumYSquared (see Figure 25.6). Now, the particular lines are probably not significant—they reflect one sample each out of a couple of thousand total. (Double-click in the "Self" column to switch between percentages and sample counts.) In practice, it's not worth optimizing.

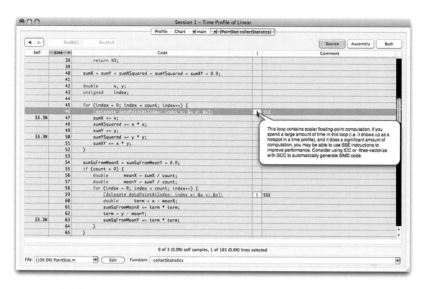

FIGURE 25.6　The method –[PointStat collectStatistics] is so little called that the percentages for individual lines aren't significant. But clicking the ! button that appears in some of the lines brings up a balloon with advice on how to make a floating-point loop run faster.

The curious thing about this listing is the ! button, and the comment "SSE," that appears to the right of a couple of lines. Click the button, which is called a "Code Analysis" button when space isn't so tight. Shark now displays a balloon containing a message beginning "This loop contains scalar floating-point computation," and going on to say that if there are hot spots in the loop, it might help to recompile the code so that it uses SSE instructions on the Intel architecture. It suggests you use gcc's -freevectorize option to get SSE. However, these loops are truly negligible in the run of Linear, and we can skip it.

> **NOTE**
>
> Shark's initial configuration window offers many more profiling options than **Time Profile**, and I'm leaving the others to the *Shark User Guide*. However, one option, **Time Profile (All Thread States)**, is worth mentioning briefly. The normal Shark time profile measures only the time spent in your code *while your program is running*. It does not measure the time it spends waiting, for instance, for disk access. This is fine if your concern is with code performance; if your problem is something like slow launch times, however, you need to know where you're waiting for system resources. The all-thread-states profile will tell you, because it includes system waits in the timing.

# The Other Performance Tools

Shark is the star of Apple's performance-instrumentation suite, but it isn't the whole show.

## BigTop

BigTop started as a graphical equivalent to the command-line top tool for monitoring the way processes consume system resources. Now that the Activity Monitor application has taken that job over, BigTop graphs statistics beyond what top or Activity Monitor offer. These additional statistics include counts of Mach messages and system calls a process makes, single-process CPU load over time, and virtual-memory activity per process.

The main BigTop window shows the systems to which BigTop is connected. By default, this is only your own computer, but you can provide addresses of other computers on your network. Double-clicking a system line opens a window from which you can select a process (or all processes) and the statistic you want to graph. By default, samples are taken every 2 seconds, and are held for 60 seconds.

Unfortunately, BigTop is underdocumented, and not all of its features are obvious. For instance, the main window displays "status" gems for various subsystems, which the user's guide characterizes as "low," "medium," and "high," but gives no indication of what those labels mean.

As a means of graphing resource usage, BigTop has been overshadowed by Instruments (Chapter 26, "Instruments"), which offers more information from a larger and more configurable suite of instruments, over a longer period of time.

## Reggie SE

The name *Reggie* refers to this application's affording you direct access to hardware registers in your CPUs and PCI peripherals. You must supply an administrator's password to install a kernel extension that gives Reggie access to these registers, and to physical RAM. Being an actual hardware tool, Reggie is a part of CHUD, strictly defined.

This application is extremely dangerous. It can ruin the operation of your machine at and below the kernel level. Register availability and usage vary processor by processor, card by card, model by model, and between versions of Mac OS X. If you don't know why you would want to access these registers, you shouldn't be using Reggie.

If you want to use hardware registers for debugging performance, Shark provides excellent, safe facilities. See the *Shark User Guide*, in Shark's **Help** menu, for details.

## SpindownHD

In measuring performance, you might want to prevent your hard drive from going to sleep—it takes the spin-up time out of the equation. Spindown HD allows you to set the amount of time your computer must be idle before hard drives are spun down, or to turn off idle spindown entirely.

## Saturn

Shark is a statistical profiler, measuring performance by interrupting your program while your code itself is unchanged. Saturn uses tracing code that gcc can introduce to your application to record every entrance and exit to every function you compile.

You enable tracing with the gcc flag -finstrument-functions. Code thus modified will log entrance and exit events, and times. Ordinarily, the log would be written to a separate file; when a program is run under Saturn, however, Saturn injects itself into the logging process, to capture the log events directly. Saturn can then render the events into call trees, stack-depth charts, and time profiles. The human interface is similar to that of Shark.

## MallocDebug

MallocDebug is numbered among the performance tools; we saw how to use it in Chapter 19, "Finishing Touches."

## ObjectAlloc and Sampler

Once standalone applications, ObjectAlloc and Sampler now launch Instruments with new documents containing the instruments of the same names. They are in Chapter 26.

## Quartz Debug

In Chapter 13, "Creating a Custom View," you remember we had to take some pains to slow the drawing of our custom view so that we could see what was going on as it drew itself. This isn't an uncommon problem, and the Quartz Debug application can help you get an overview.

When we were debugging LinearGraph, we wanted to do two things. We wanted to flush drawing events out to the screen as they happened, and not be drawn all at once from a buffer; we did that by inserting a flushGraphics call after every operation. And, we wanted to slow down the drawing process; we did that by stepping through LinearGraph's drawRect: method in the debugger.

Quartz Debug can do nearly the same thing for you without the need for special code or the use of a debugger. When you start Quartz Debug, you see a small window (see Figure 25.7) that offers four options for modifying how Mac OS X draws to the screen.

▶ **Autoflush drawing** does what we accomplished by frequent use of flushGraphics. After every drawing operation, the results are put directly to the screen without buffering it for a periodic refresh.

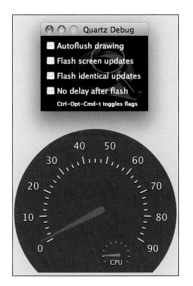

FIGURE 25.7    *(Top)* The main window of Quartz Debug offers four options for slowing and highlighting screen drawing. *(Bottom)* Another service of Quartz Debug is a tachometer-style display of how fast screen drawing is being done, measured in frames per second.

▶ **Flash screen updates** delays updates. During the delay, it fills the area being drawn with a solid color (yellow for regular drawing, green for hardware accelerated, and brown for areas for which drawing had been disabled at the time the update occurred).

▶ **Flash identical updates**. When this option is on, Quartz Debug monitors your drawing and flashes the affected area red when you are simply redrawing graphics that are already there.

▶ **No delay after flash** suppresses the delay between filling updated areas with a color and putting the actual drawing onscreen.

There is no way to restrict Quartz Debug to one application. *All* drawing to the screen gets flushed and flashed. The distraction and slowdown are very annoying, and you won't want to have it on any more than necessary. Fortunately, you can turn Quartz Debug on and off with the hot key ^⌥⌘T.

Quartz Debug is an excellent tool for an overview of your application's drawing behavior. With Quartz Debug on, the drawing process is made very plain, and might even surprise you if your application makes unnecessary or frequent redraws—a significant drain on performance. It's not a cure-all. For cases like LinearGraph, where we knew where the problem was, and needed access to the data that underlay the graph, there is no substitute for stepping through the drawing process with a source-code debugger.

Quartz Debug offers some other facilities. Selecting **Tools > Show Frame Meter** displays a translucent floating window in the form of a tachometer, showing you from moment to moment the frame rate at which the screen is being redrawn, an important indicator if you are trying to get the best performance out of your graphics.

**Tools > Show User Interface Resolution** enables you to adjust the scaling between the units by which drawing is measured and the density of pixels on the physical screen. Since 1984, Macintosh graphics have been built on the assumption that the unit for drawing is a typographic point—1/72 of an inch. Modern screens approach densities of 100 pixels per inch, so an "inch" in an onscreen ruler is much smaller than a real-world inch.

Apple has indicated that at some time in the future Quartz graphics will be made resolution independent, so drawing inches will be displayed as real-world inches. This breaks the assumption that the *pixel*, and not the *point*, is the unit of drawing. Apple has published APIs and techniques for drawing in a resolution-independent fashion. The User Interface Resolution window enables you to adjust the screen resolution (you will have to restart an application for it to take effect) so that you can test resolution-independent drawing.

**Tools > Enable/Disable Quartz Extreme**. Mac OS X feeds most drawing operations through the graphical processing units (GPUs) of the display card; this facility is called Quartz Extreme. This menu option disables the hardware acceleration, so you can see how your application would perform on Macs with less hardware support than your own.

There is also a window, exposed by **Tools > Show Window List**, listing every window currently being displayed. Windows that have been compressed in memory, because they are not actively being updated, are shown in blue; hardware-accelerated windows (Quartz Extreme) are shown in green.

## Spin Control

Any time an application becomes unresponsive and displays the spinning-rainbow cursor, Spin Control will sample the application for a few seconds and log the tree of call stacks. Its main window lists each incident; if you double-click on an incident, Spin Control displays a window with a browser to navigate the call stacks, a list showing the heaviest stack containing the current selection, and a set of simple analysis tools.

Spin Control doesn't have the subtlety or analytical power of Shark, but it works well for catching intermittent hangs, and is an incomparable tool for documenting bug reports.

## Thread Viewer

Programming threaded applications is difficult. It is hard to visualize how the flow of execution is distributed among threads, when and where one thread is interrupted for another, and which takes over. Thread Viewer displays the threads in an application across a timeline, with colored blocks indicating which thread is executing at a given time (see Figure 25.8).

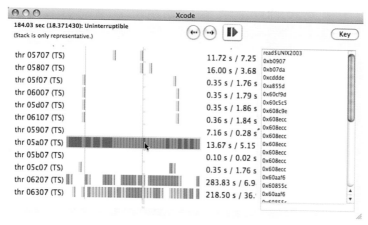

FIGURE 25.8    A Thread Viewer window displaying the flow of control in Xcode during a Clean All operation. Each row in the timeline represents a thread, which may appear or disappear over time. Time slices in which a thread has executed are shown in color; clicking in one of these fills the list at right with a representative call stack.

Like many other performance tools, Thread Viewer works by sampling the target application periodically. Thread Viewer does this relatively infrequently—20 times a second as opposed to Shark's default 1,000. It displays the results in real time, on a timeline, each row of which represents a thread. If a segment of the thread is colored, it had run sometime during that time slice. Green segments are samples that caught that thread running; yellow ones merely ran sometime since the last sample.

In Figure 25.8, the bottom thread is the application's main thread. It shares about equal runtime with the second thread, which appears to be the scanner for Objective-C garbage collection. The most active thread is the fifth; clicking one of the samples fills the list at right with a stack trace that is said to be "only representative." The segment is dark green because the thread was marked uninterruptible.

### CHUD Remover

CHUD Remover comes last because it's a CHUD utility rather than a performance tool. The CHUD tools install kernel-level software to collect the data they analyze. Uninstalling CHUD is not a simple matter of throwing the applications away; CHUD Remover does everything that is needed. Apple's performance tools are maintained separately from the Xcode tools, and updates come out independently. It is wise to run CHUD Remover before installing a new version.

## Summary

In this chapter, we looked deep into Shark as we got a huge performance bug out of our old Linear application. We refined a scattered time profile by using Shark's data mining feature. We saw how, with debug information, you can trace a performance hot spot down to lines of source code or even to the instruction, and that Shark can autonomously offer suggestions on how to make code faster.

We also surveyed Apple's other performance tools, some esoteric, some neglected, and some—like Quartz Debug—invaluable.

There is, however, one more performance tool, that we've already visited, but deserves a chapter of its own: Instruments.

**IN THIS CHAPTER**

▷ **Instruments: Performance and Resources in Time**

▷ **Using the Instruments Window**

▷ **Configuring Instruments**

▷ **Apple's Templates and Instruments**

▷ **Custom Templates and Instruments**

Instruments is a framework for software-monitoring tools called... instruments. (Capital *I* Instruments is the application, small *i* instruments are components of the Instruments application.) The analogy (borrowed from Apple's Garage Band audio editor) is to a multitrack tape deck. Instruments records activity on one or more tracks (one per instrument), building the data on a timeline like audio on a tape.

We've seen Instruments before, in Chapter 19, "Finishing Touches," where it helped us track down a memory leak in Linear. It deserves a chapter all its own.

## What Instruments Is

The focus on a timeline makes Instruments unique. We saw how MallocDebug collects allocation and deallocation events, and gathers them into statistical measures, organizing all the stack traces it found at those events into an aggregate call tree, from which you can learn how memory is used. It presents data as an end-of-run accumulation.

Shark, too, works by statistical aggregates. You run your application, Shark samples it, and in the end it presents you with profiling information that is a summary (although very detailed) of all the samples of the whole run. You can filter the samples and manipulate the call trees Shark reports, but the product is still a compilation over a period of time. There *is* a chart view, but it is still an aggregate, showing the shape of the call stack over time. You can examine stack traces to see what the processor was doing at the time (it can be tricky to select exactly the right one), but there is no way to relate the traces to what the *application* was doing.

Further, tools such as MallocDebug and Shark do one thing at a time. MallocDebug does heap memory. Shark does profiling (or `malloc` tracing, or processor events). If you want a different measure, run the application again under the supervision of a different tool. They allow no way to see what one measure means in relation to another.

Instruments is different. It is comprehensive. There are instruments for most ways you'd want to analyze your code, and Instruments runs them *all at the same time*. The results are laid out by time, in parallel. Did clicking the **Compute** button result in Core Data fetches? Or had the fetches already been done earlier? Did other disk activity eat up bandwidth? In the application? Elsewhere in the system? Is the application consuming too many file descriptors, and if so, when, and in response to what? You're handing data off to another process (think `Linrg`, from the first iteration of `Linear`); how does the tool's memory usage change in response to the handoff, and how does it relate to the use of file descriptors in both the tool and the master application?

Instruments can answer these questions. You can relate file descriptors to disk activity, and disk activity to Core Data events, with stack traces for every single one of these, because Instruments captures the data on a timeline, all in parallel, event by event. And, you can target different instruments on different applications (or even the system as a whole) at the same time.

> **NOTE**
>
> Most of the power of Instruments lies in the analysis tools it provides after a recording is made, but don't ignore the advantage it provides in showing program state dynamically: If you can't see when memory consumption or file I/O begins and settles down (for instance), you won't know when to stop the recording for analysis in the first place.

# Running Instruments

In Chapter 19, we started Instruments from Xcode by selecting **Run > Start with Performance Tool** and selecting an **Instruments** template. At least as often, you'll just launch the Instruments application from the `/Developer/Applications` directory.

When you start it, Instruments automatically opens a document (called a *trace document*) and displays a sheet offering you a choice of templates populated with instruments for common tasks (see Figure 26.1). You can find a complete list of the templates Apple provides in the section "The Templates" later in this chapter.

FIGURE 26.1    When you create a new trace document in Instruments, it shows you an empty document and a sheet for choosing among templates prepopulated with instruments for common tasks.

# The Trace Document Window

The initial form of a trace document window is simple: a toolbar at the top, and a stack of instruments in the view that dominates the window. After you've recorded data into the document, the window becomes much richer. Let's go through Figure 26.2 and identify the components.

## The Toolbar

The toolbar comes in three sections. The controls at left (1) control recording and the execution of the target applications. There is a pause button for suspending and resuming data collection, a **Record / Drive & Record / Stop** button to start and stop data collection, and a loop button for running a recorded human-interface script repeatedly.

> **NOTE**
>
> When you start recording, you will often be asked for an administrator's password. The kind of deep monitoring many instruments do is, strictly speaking, a security breach, and the system makes you show you are authorized to do it.

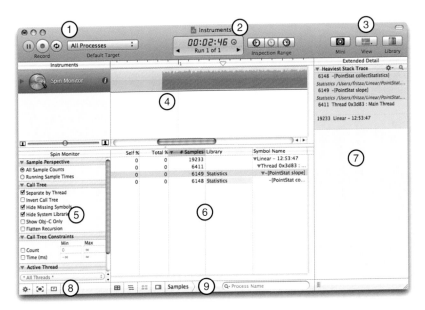

FIGURE 26.2    A typical Instruments window, after data has been recorded. The Extended Detail pane (at right) has also been exposed. I discuss the numbered parts in the text.

The **Default Target** pop-up designates the process or executable that all instruments in the document will target, unless you specify different targets for individual instruments. The choices are as follows:

▶ **All Processes**. Data will be collected from all the processes, user and system, on the machine. For instance, the Core Data instruments can measure the Core Data activity of all processes. Not every instrument can span processes; if your document contains no instruments that can sample systemwide, this option is disabled.

▶ **Attach to Process**. Data will be collected from a process that is already running; select it from the submenu. Some instruments require that their targets be launched from Instruments, and cannot attach to running processes. If you use only nonattaching instruments, this option is disabled.

▶ **Launch Executable**. When you start recording, Instruments will launch the selected application or tool, and collect data from it. The submenu contains items for applications you've recorded previously, and has a **Choose Executable** item to select a fresh application.

▶ **Instrument Specific**. Each instrument will collect data from the target specified in the **Target** pop-up of its configuration inspector. The instruments in a trace document do not all have to collect data from the same target.

The center section (2) relates to time (see Figure 26.3). The clock view in the center of the toolbar displays the total time period recorded in the document. If you click the clock-face icon to the right of the time display, the clock shows the position of the "playback head" in the time scale at the top of the Track pane.

The clock view also controls which run of the document is being displayed. Each time you click **Record**, a new recording, with a timeline of its own, is added to the document. The run now being displayed is shown like "Run 1 of 2," and you can switch among them by pressing the arrowhead buttons to either side.

Most instruments will display subsets of the data they collect if you select a time span within the recording. To do so, move the playback head to the beginning of the span, and click the button on the left of the **Inspection Range** control; then move the head to the end of the span and click the button on the right. The selected span will be highlighted, and the Detail pane will be restricted to data collected in the span. To clear the selection, click the button in the middle.

FIGURE 26.3    The center section of a trace document's toolbar displays a clock, and controls for selecting a span of time within a recording. The clock displays the total time in the document (or, if you click the icon at the right of the clock, the position of the "playback head") and the run being displayed if there is more than one.

> **NOTE**
>
> You can also browse among runs by selecting **View > Run Browser** (^**Tab**). The contents of the window will be replaced by a "Cover Flow" partial view of the traces in each run, along with particulars of when it was run, on what machine, and so on.

> **NOTE**
>
> Option-dragging across an interval in one of the traces will also set an inspection range.

The right section (3) provides convenient controls for display. **Mini** hides Instruments and displays a heads-up window for controlling recording from other applications. **View** pops up a menu that shows and hides the Detail and Extended Detail panes. **Library** shows and hides the Library window.

## The Track Pane

The Track pane (4) is the focus of the document window, and the only component you see when a document is first opened. This is the pane you drag new instruments into. Each instrument occupies its own row, with a configuration block on the left, and the instrument's track on the right.

The configuration block (see Figure 26.4) shows the instrument's name and icon. To the left is a disclosure triangle so you can see the instrument's track for each run in the document. To the right is an inspector button (**i**) that reveals a configuration inspector for the instrument.

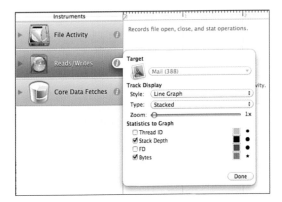

FIGURE 26.4    A stack of instrument tracks in a trace document. Each instrument has its own row, with a timeline extending to the right, calibrated in seconds. Clicking an instrument's configuration button opens an inspector containing settings for the instrument. Some of these control the style of the graph and which of its data an instrument displays, and can be changed at any time. The pop-up at the top of the inspector selects what process the instrument is to collect data from, and must be set (or left to the default, if the instrument can accept it) before recording begins.

The tracks to the right of the configuration blocks display the data collected by the instruments, on a timeline. The configuration inspector controls what data is plotted, and how it is displayed.

At the top of the timeline is a ruler matching the data to the time at which is was collected. The scale of the track can be controlled by the slider below the configuration blocks. In the ruler, you will see a white triangle, the *playback head*. Drag the playback head and use the **Inspection Range** control to select intervals within the recording. As you drag the head across the track, many instruments will label their tracks with the value of their data at that time.

## The Detail Pane

The Detail pane (5 and 6) appears when you've made a recording, or when you use a control or menu item to display it. **View > Detail** (⌘D), **View** (toolbar button) > **Detail**, the **Detail** item in the **Action** (✿) menu at the lower left of the window, and the detail button (rectangle with arrowhead) next to it, will all toggle the Detail pane. You do not lack for options.

When you select an instrument in the Track pane, the data from the instrument collection is shown in tabular form in the Detail pane. What's in the table varies among instruments. And, the Detail pane controls (9, and Figure 26.5) provide for up to three table formats.

Like the table itself, the alternative views vary depending on the instrument. The general pattern seems to be

▶ Table mode is the principal display the instrument's author has chosen for its data. For most instruments, this is the raw data they collected, such as the details of individual calls in the Reads/Writes instrument. In Sampler, the table contains a stack trace for each sample; in ObjectAlloc, the items are classes/categories of allocated blocks.

FIGURE 26.5     The Detail View buttons, which appear below the table portion of the Detail View. The first three buttons select different table displays, or "modes." The modes are Table, Outline, and Diagram. The fourth button, showing a window with a portion on the right highlighted, opens or closes the Extended Detail pane. The Navigation Path breadcrumb control enables you to back a display off after you've drilled down into a detail.

▶ Outline mode, in the case of instruments that collect stack traces, aggregates the traces into call trees (like the Tree and Heavy displays in Shark). When this is the case, the **Call Tree** controls in the Detail controls view (5) become active.

▶ Diagram mode is not often used. In Chapter 19, we saw that ObjectAlloc used this for a table of the individual data it collects.

The next button over, with an icon that suggests a window with a portion highlighted, displays the Extended Detail pane (7), which is covered in the next section.

When you "drill into" data in a Detail pane, such as when you obtain the history of an allocated block in ObjectAlloc, the "breadcrumb" control at the right end of the Detail controls enables you to back out to the superior view.

The left portion of the Detail pane (5) contains controls to adjust or analyze the contents of a Detail table, and in some cases to configure an instrument before it is run. The repertoire of controls varies by instrument and view, but the most commonly used controls are in the group labeled **Call Tree**, which is active whenever a tree of call stacks is displayed in the table.

These commands are similar to the stack data-mining options available in Shark:

▶ **Separate by Thread**. Call trees are normally merged with no regard for which thread the calls occurred in. Separating the trees by thread will help you weed out calls in threads you aren't interested in.

▶ **Invert Call Tree**. The default (top-down) presentation of call trees starts at the runtime start function, branching out through the successive calls down to the leaf functions that are the events the instrument records. Checking this box inverts the trees so that they are bottom up. The displayed tree begins at the "event" function, and branches out among its callers, thus aggregating call paths to bottleneck functions.

▶ **Hide Missing Symbols**. Checking this box hides functions that don't have symbols associated with them. If you can't determine what they are, they probably aren't part of your code. (If they are part of your code, turn off symbol stripping in your build.)

26

▶ **Hide System Libraries**. This skips over functions in system libraries. Reading the names of the library calls may help you get an idea of what is going on; if you are looking for code you can do something about, however, you don't want to see them.

▶ **Show Obj-C Only**. Checking this narrows the list down to calls made from Objective-C methods, whether in system libraries or not (another way to cut out the possible distraction of calls you don't care to see).

▶ **Flatten Recursion**. This lumps every call a function makes to itself into a single item. Recursive calls can run up the length of a call stack without being very informative.

You can also add call-tree constraints, such as minimum and maximum call counts. The idea is to prune (or focus on) calls that are not frequently made. Another constraint that may be avail-

> **NOTE**
>
> Stack traces in the Extended Detail pane reflect your settings of these filters.

able (for instance in the Sampler instrument) can filter call trees by the amount of time (minimum, maximum, or both) they took up in the course of the run.

Of course, another way to filter call trees is to restrict your attention to a particular time span, such as between the open and close calls on a particular file (which the File Activity instrument would landmark for you). Use the playback head and the **Inspection Range** control to select the beginning and end of the period of interest, and the call tree will reflect only the calls made between them.

## The Extended Detail Pane

The Extended Detail pane (7) typically includes a stack trace when you select an item in the Detail pane that carries stack information. When the selected item is part of a call tree, the Extended Detail pane shows the "heaviest" stack, the one that accounts for the most of whatever the instrument keeps track of. Selecting a frame in the call stack highlights the corresponding call in the call-tree outline. Double-clicking a frame opens the corresponding source code in Xcode, if it can be found.

A stack trace in the Extended Detail pane has an **Action** (⚙) menu at the top. Most commands in this menu have to do with how the calls in the trace are displayed. An example is **Color by Library**, which tints each call frame by the library file (including an application's main executable) that the call came from.

A couple of items in the **Action** menu are of particular interest. **Look Up API**

> **NOTE**
>
> The Extended Detail pane can include other information. There may be a **General** item, summarizing the information in the item selected in the Detail table, or a **Time** item showing how far into the recording the selected event occurred. Because the stack trace is only one item, its **Action** menu is attached to the divider bar that marks it. Scrolling down the stack trace may scroll the **Action** menu out of sight.

**Documentation** acts like Option-double-clicking a symbol in Xcode: Select the frame, select the command, and be directed to its documentation in Xcode's Documentation window. **Trace Call Duration** creates a new instrument in the current document to record the stack trace when the function was called, and how long it took to execute.

## Controls

Three additional controls are to be found at the bottom-left corner of the document window (8) (see Figure 26.6).

The first is an **Action** (⚙) menu that affords yet another means to start recording or looping, and to control the visibility of the Detail and Extended Detail panes, and the Library window. There is a submenu for selecting an instrument to add to the document. The **Spin Monitor** item is a toggle; when it's checked, Instruments will automatically add a Spin Monitor instrument to the document whenever an application being traced hangs.

The second is the Full Screen toggle. Instruments' extensive display eats up a lot of screen area, and when you're concentrating on your analysis, you want the display to be as big as possible. Clicking this button fills the screen with the contents of the window. Click it again to return to normal windowing.

FIGURE 26.6    The controls at the lower left corner of a trace document window, with the **Action** menu displayed.

> **WARNING**
>
> In version 1.0 of Instruments, on some graphics cards, full-screen mode simply turns your screen black. To bail out, press ⌘**Q** to start a quit, and press **Return** repeatedly to accept all the document-saving sheets, until your desktop reappears.

The third button shows and hides the Detail pane.

## The Library

Instruments get into a document either by being instantiated from a template, or by being dragged in from the Library window.

The Library (**Window > Library**, ⌘L) window lists all the known instruments. Initially this is a repertoire of Apple-supplied tracks, but it is possible to add your own. The main feature of the window (see Figure 26.7) is the list of all known instruments. Selecting one fills the pane below the list with a description (which for now is the same as the description in the list).

26

The library gathers instruments into groups; these are initially hidden, but can be seen if you select **Show Group Headers** from the **Action** (✿) pop-up at the lower-left corner of the window. The **Action** menu also enables you to create groups of your own. The pop-up at the top of the window narrows the list down by group, and the search field at the bottom allows you to narrow the list by searching for text in the names and descriptions.

# Running an Instrument

To use an instrument, you follow three steps: configuration, recording, and, optionally, saving the results.

FIGURE 26.7    The Library window is dominated by the scrolling list of available instruments. The selected instrument is described in the panel below. Selecting a category from the pop-up menu narrows the list down by task, and the search field at the bottom allows you to find an instrument from its name or description.

## Instrument Configuration

Configuration inspectors vary by instrument, but some elements are used frequently.

There is a **Target** pop-up that initially points to the document's default target (set with the **Default Target** menu in the toolbar). If no default target has been selected, or if the **Default Target** menu has been set to **Instrument Specific**, the instrument's **Target** is active. You can select from processes already running, applications that Instruments had sampled before, a new application or tool of your choice, or, with many instruments, the system as a whole.

The ability to set a target for each instrument is important: It allows you to examine the behavior of an application *and* other processes with which it communicates, simultaneously.

In the **Track Display** section, there are three controls: A **Style** pop-up, a **Type** pop-up, and a **Zoom** slider.

The usual **Style** menu selects among graphing styles for the numeric data the instrument records. These may include the following:

▶ **Point**. Each datum is displayed as a discrete symbol in the track. You can choose the symbols in the list of available series in the inspector.

▶ **Line**. The track is displayed as a colored line connecting each datum in the series. You can choose the color in the list of the available series.

▶ **Filled Line** is the same as **Line**, but the area under the line is colored.

▶ **Peak** shows the data collected by an instrument that records events (such as the Core Data instruments) as a vertical line at each event. Every time something happens, the trace shows a blip.

▶ **Block** is a bar graph, showing each datum as a colored rectangle. In instruments that record events, the block will be as wide as the time to the next event.

The **Type** menu offers two choices for instruments that can record more than one data series. **Overlay** displays all series on a single graph. The displayed data will probably overlap, but in point and line displays this probably doesn't matter, and filled displays are drawn translucently, so the two series don't obscure each other. **Stacked** displays each series in separate strips, one above the other.

> **NOTE**
>
> Most instruments record events, not quantities that vary over time. In fact, the data displayed may not even be a continuous variable, but may be a mere tag, like the ID of a thread or a file descriptor. The Peak style is the most suitable style for event recordings. Such displays are still useful, however, because they give you a landmark for examining the matching data in the other tracks.

**Zoom** increases the height of the instrument's track. This is especially handy in stacked displays, enabling you to view multiple traces without squishing them into illegibility. The slider clicks to integer multiples of the standard track height, from 1 to 10 units.

You can change the **Track Display** settings even after the instrument has collected its data. You can find a shortcut for the **Zoom** slider in the **View** menu, as **Increase Deck Size** (⌘+) and **Decrease Deck Size** (⌘–).

One disadvantage of the inspector system is that inspectors are of fixed size, and can be quite tall. If a track is low on the screen (which it may have to be, if it is low in a multi-track document), it might run off the bottom, obscuring the **Done** button that dismisses the inspector. Fortunately, you can also dismiss an inspector by pressing the **i** button again. The only workaround that allows you to get at the options at the bottom of the inspector is to drag the track to the top of the document, make the setting, and, if you want, drag it back.

## Recording

There is more than one way to start recording in Instruments.

The most obvious is to create a trace document and click the **Record** button in the toolbar. Recording starts, you switch to the target application, perform your test, switch back to Instruments, and click the same button, now labeled **Stop**.

The first time you record into a document that contains a User Interface instrument, the recording button will be labeled **Record**, as usual. Once the UI track contains events, the recording button is labeled **Drive & Record**. When you click it, no new events are not recorded into the UI track; instead, the events already there are *replayed* so you can reproduce your tests.

If you want to record a fresh User Interface track, open the configuration inspector (with the **i** button in the instrument's label) and select **Capture** from the **Action** pop-up. The recording button will revert to **Record**.

A second way to record is through the Quick Start feature, which allows you to start recording with a systemwide hotkey combination. To set a hotkey, open Instruments' Preferences window and select the **Quick Start** tab. This tab includes a table listing every system- and user-supplied template. Double-click in the column next to the template you choose, and press your desired hotkey combination. The combination must include at least two modifier keys (such as Command, Shift, and so on).

With the hotkey set, move the cursor over a window belonging to the application you want to target, and then press the key combination. Instruments will launch if it is not running already, open a new trace document behind your application with the template you selected, target it on your application, and start recording. To stop, make sure your cursor is over one of the target's windows, and press the key combination again (or switch to Instruments and click **Stop**).

The requirement to point the cursor at one of the target's windows allows you to run simultaneous traces on more than one application.

To remove a hotkey, select the template in the **Quick Start** table, and press the **Delete** key.

The third way to record is through the Mini Instruments window. Selecting **View** > **Mini Instruments**, or clicking the **Mini** button in the toolbar of any document window, hides all of Instruments' windows and substitutes a floating heads-up window listing all of the open trace documents (see Figure 26.8).

The window lists all of the trace documents that were open when you switched to Mini mode; scroll through by clicking the up or down arrowheads above and below the list. At the left of each item is a button for starting (round icon) or stopping (square icon) recording, and a clock to show how long recording has been going on. Stopping and restarting a recording adds a new run to the document.

FIGURE 26.8    The Mini Instruments heads-up window. It lists each open trace document next to a clock and a recording button. Scroll through the list using the arrowheads at top and bottom.

As with Quick Start keys, Mini Instruments has the advantages that it's convenient to start recording in the middle of an application's run (handy if you are recording a User Interface track that you want to loop) and that you can control recording without switching out of the target application (which can also impair a UI recording).

You return to the full display of Instruments by clicking the close (**X**) button in the upper-left corner of the Mini Instruments window.

## Saving and Reopening

As with any other Macintosh document, you can save a trace document. The document will contain its instruments and all the data they've collected. There can be a lot of data, so expect a trace document to be large—on the order of tens of megabytes.

It's likely that you will come to need a uniform layout of instruments that isn't included in the default templates provided by Apple. You can easily create templates of your own, which will appear in the template sheet presented when you create a new trace document. Configure a document as you want it, and select **File > Save as Template....**

The ensuing save-file sheet is the standard one, focused on the directory in which Instruments looks for your templates, `~/Library/Application Support/Instruments/Templates`. The name you give your file will be the label shown in the template-choice sheet. At the lower left of the sheet is a well into which you can drag an icon (for instance, if your template is for testing your application, you'd want to drop your application's icon file here), or you can click and hold the mouse button over the well to choose Apple-provided icons from a pop-up. The panel provides a text area for the description to be shown in the template-choice sheet.

- ▶ The document's suite of instruments, and their configurations, will be saved in the template.

- ▶ The template will include the default and instrument-specific targets you set.

- ▶ If you include a prerecorded User Interface track, the contents will be saved. This way you can produce uniform test documents simply by creating a new trace document and selecting the template.

As you'd expect, you can reopen a trace document by double-clicking it in the Finder, or through **File > Open....** All the data is as it was when the document was saved. Clicking **Record** adds a new run to the document.

# The Instruments

Here are the instruments built in to Instruments as of the time of this writing, grouped as they are in the Library window (select **Show Group Banners** from the **Action** (✿) pop-up at bottom left).

Most instruments are DTrace based (see the section on "Custom Instruments"

> **NOTE**
>
> Apple is free to add or remove built-in instruments, or to change their capabilities significantly. This can't be a definitive list. For the latest information, search for the *Instruments User Guide* in the Developer Tools Reference in the Xcode Documentation window.

later in this chapter). DTrace automatically records thread ID and a stack trace, and implicitly the stack depth, at the time of the event. Every numeric-valued property of the event is eligible for graphing in the instrument's track, which accounts for the odd offer of "Thread ID" for plotting in such instruments.

26

All instruments can target any single process, or all processes on the system, unless the description says otherwise.

## Core Data

### Core Data Saves
At each save operation in Core Data, the Core Data Saves instrument records the thread ID, stack trace, and how long the save took.

### Core Data Fetches
This instrument captures the thread ID and stack trace of every fetch operation under Core Data, along with the number of objects fetched and how long it took to complete the fetch.

### Core Data Faults
Core Data objects can be expensive both in terms of memory and of the time it takes to load them into memory. Often, an NSManagedObject or a to-many relationship is given to you as a *fault*, a kind of IOU that will be paid off in actual data when you reference data in the object.

This instrument captures every firing (payoff) of an object or relationship fault. It can display the thread ID and stack depth of the fault, as well as how long it took to satisfy object and relationship faults.

### Core Data Cache Misses
A faulted Core Data object may already be in memory; it may be held in its NSPersistentStoreCoordinator's cache. If you fire a fault on an object that *isn't* in the cache (a "cache miss"), however, you've come into an expensive operation, because the object has to be freshly read from the database. You want to minimize the effect of cache faults by preloading the objects when it doesn't impair user experience.

This instrument shows where cache misses happen. It records the thread ID and stack trace of each miss, and how much time was taken up satisfying the miss, for objects and relationships.

## File System

These instruments record POSIX calls that affect the properties of files and directories. This does not include reads and writes; for those, see the Reads / Writes instrument under Input / Output.

### File Locks
This is an event instrument that records the thread ID, stack trace, function, option flags, and path for every call to the flock system function.

### File Attributes

For every event of changing the owner, group, or access mode of a file (chown, chgrp, chmod), this instrument records thread ID, a stack trace, the called function, the file descriptor number, the group and user IDs, the mode flags, and the path to the file affected.

### File Activity

This is an event instrument that records every call to open, close, fstat, open$UNIX2003, and close$UNIX2003. It captures thread ID, call stack, the call, the file descriptor, and path.

### Directory I/O

This instrument records every event of system calls affecting directories, such as creation, moving, mounting, unmounting, renaming, and linking. The data include thread ID, stack trace, call, path to the file directory affected, and the destination path.

## Garbage Collection

### GC Total

GC Total collects statistics on the state of garbage collection in a process (or in all garbage-collected processes) at the time collection ends. In addition to thread ID and stack traces, it records the number of objects, and bytes, just reclaimed, the number of bytes still in use, and the total number of reclaimed and in-use bytes.

### Garbage Collection

This is slightly different from the GC Total instrument. It measures across the beginning and end of the scavenge phase of garbage collection. It records whether the reclamation was generational, and how long scavenging took. It also records the number of objects and bytes reclaimed.

## Graphics

### OpenGL Driver

This instrument taps the OpenGL drivers for the graphics displays to collect a huge number of statistics on OpenGL usage, by the target process (or the entire system), at an interval of your choosing (initially one second). The graphical trace itself doesn't signify anything, and can't be usefully configured in the inspector. The substance of the recording is to be found in the Detail table, and the Detail-control view has check boxes that determine which statistics appear there (there are nearly 60).

## Input / Output

### Reads / Writes

The events recorded by this instrument include reads and writes to file descriptors. Each event includes the thread ID, the name of the function being called, a stack trace, the descriptor and path of the file, and the number of bytes read or written.

# Master Track

### User Interface

This track records your mouse movements, clicks, and keystrokes as you work with an application. Each event carries a thumbnail of the screen surrounding the mouse cursor.

The UI track's events serve as landmarks for the internal program events recorded by other instruments, but the real utility—the reason this is called a *master track*—is that once a UI track is recorded, it can be played back; it is said to "drive" the application. When a UI track containing events is available, the **Record** button is relabeled **Drive & Record**, and clicking it will replay the human-interface events.

You can divert from driving by using the **i** button in the instrument's label to open the instrument's configuration inspector, and switching the **Action** pop-up from **Drive** to **Capture**.

For an extended example of using the User Interface track, see the "Human-Interface Logging" section of Chapter 19.

# Memory

### Shared Memory

The Shared Memory instrument records an event when shared memory is opened or unlinked. The event includes calling thread ID and executable, stack trace, function (shm_open/shm_unlink), and parameters (name of the shared memory object, flags, and mode_t). Selecting an event in the Detail table puts a stack trace into the Extended Detail pane.

### ObjectAlloc

We saw ObjectAlloc and Leaks in Chapter 19, when we debugged a memory leak in Linear.

ObjectAlloc collects a comprehensive history of every block of memory allocated during the run of its target. It can track the total number of objects and bytes currently allocated in an application because it records every allocation and deallocation, and balances them for every block's address.

The main Detail Table view lists every class of block that was allocated, and aggregate object and byte counts; use the **Inspection Range** tool to focus on allocations and deallocations within a given period. The classes can be checked to plot them separately in the trace.

Mousing over a classname reveals an arrow button; if you click it, the Detail table drills in to a table of every block of that class allocated in the selected time interval. Drilling in on the address field in one of these reveals a history of every event that affected that address—mallocs and frees at least, and if **Record Reference Counts** was checked in the configuration inspector before launching, reference-counting events as well. Mac OS X may use the same address more than once as memory is recycled; you'll usually see malloc events after every free but the last one.

The breadcrumb control below the Detail pane reflects each stage in the drilling-down process. Click the label for an earlier stage to return to it.

The track-style options in the configuration inspector include **Current Bytes**, a filled-line chart that shows the total current allocations; **Stack Depth**, a filled-line chart that shows how deep the call stack is at each allocation event; and **Allocation Density**, a peak graph showing the change in allocated bytes at each event (essentially a first derivative of the Current Bytes display).

In the Outline view, the top level lists the allocation classes. Below them are stack trees for all the allocations of those classes. The data-mining and Extended Detail tools are available in this view.

The Diagram view of the Detail table lists every allocation event. As in the Detail view, clicking the arrow button in an address view displays a history of allocation, deallocation, and reference-count events for that address.

ObjectAlloc can be run only against a process that Instruments launched, and you should pay attention to the **Launch Configuration** switches in the configuration inspector before recording.

The ObjectAlloc instrument is powerful and subtle. It merits an entire section in the *Instruments User Guide*. Search for "Analyzing Data with the ObjectAlloc Instrument" in the Developer Tools Reference in the Xcode Documentation window.

**Leaks**

Leaks also tracks the allocation and deallocation of objects in an application (which must be launched by Instruments itself), but does so to detect the objects' being allocated and then lost—in other words, memory leaks. Leaks does not rely just on balancing allocations and deallocations; it periodically sweeps your program's heap to detect blocks that are not referenced by active memory.

The table view of the Detail pane lists every object that was allocated in the selected time interval, but found to have no references at the end. The line items show the percentage of total leakage the block represents, its size, address, and class. Selecting a line fills the Extended Detail pane with a general description and a stack trace of the allocation. Each address entry has an arrow button that drills down to the allocation, deallocation, and reference-count events for that address. You have the entire history of the block; you should be able to determine where an over-retain occurred. Reducing the inspection range on the trace will not narrow this list; it's for the entire history of the address.

The stack tree in the outline view goes from the `start` function in the runtime down the various paths to the allocating function, usually `calloc` in the case of Objective-C objects. Paring system libraries from the tree will quickly narrow the list down to the calls in your code responsible for creating leaked blocks.

The configuration inspector for the Leaks instrument controls how the trace is displayed, but the actual behavior is controlled by the control section of the Detail pane. The defaults are useful, but expose the Detail pane before you run to verify the settings are what you want. The settings control whether memory sweeps for unreferenced blocks are to be performed, whether the contents of leaked blocks will be retained for inspection, and how often to perform sweeps.

## System

### Activity Monitor

This instrument is too varied to explain fully here, but its features should be easy to understand if you explore its configuration inspector. It collects 31 summary statistics on a running process, including thread counts, physical memory usage, virtual memory activity, network usage, disk operations, and percentages of CPU load. This instrument more or less replaces BigTop as a graphical presentation of application activity.

Remember that you can have more than one Activity Monitor instrument running, targeting different applications or the system as a whole.

The Detail table lists the statistics for every process covered by the instrument. Moving the playback head makes the table reflect the processes and statistics as of the selected time. The hierarchical view arranges the processes in a parent-and-child tree.

### Sampler

Sampler is the poor man's Shark. It samples the target application at fixed intervals (10ms by default, but you can set it in the inspector), and records a stack trace each time. It does not record the position in the target down to the instruction, and the analysis tools are limited, but it's often good enough to find bottlenecks or determine where an application has hung.

Sampler was formerly supplied as a standalone application. The Sampler application supplied with Xcode 3 simply opens the CPU Sampler template in Instruments.

Sampler must have a specific process or launched application as its target; sampling the entire system makes no sense.

### Spin Monitor

Spin Monitor is the Instruments version of the Spin Control application. To mimic Spin Control, set the target to **All Processes** and leave the trace document recording. Whenever an application (or the target application) shows the spinning-rainbow cursor, indicating it has stopped accepting human-interface events, the Spin Monitor becomes Sampler, building a stack tree while the spin continues.

The table view of the Detail panel has a top-level entry for each spinning incident. Within these are items for each sample in the incident, which expand to show each thread in the target. The outline view displays an aggregate tree of stack traces for all the samples in each incident; the Call Tree controls in the Detail panel become available.

### Process

For each start (execve) and end (exit) event in a process, this instrument records thread ID, stack trace, process ID, exit status, and executable path.

### Network Activity Monitor

This is actually the Activity Monitor with four of eight network statistics active: Network Packets/Bytes In/Out Per Second. It omits the absolute numbers of packets and bytes transmitted.

### Memory Monitor

This is the Activity Monitor with Physical Memory Used/Free, Virtual Memory Size, and Page Ins/Outs checked.

### Disk Monitor

This is the Activity Monitor with Disk Read/Write Operations Per Second, and Disk Bytes Read/Written Per second checked.

### CPU Monitor

This is the Activity Monitor with % Total Load, % User Load, and % System Load selected.

## Threads/Locks

### JavaThread

The JavaThread instrument is unique, in that it does not display its trace as a vertical graph. Instead, the trace is a stack of bars, extending horizontally through time, that represent the threads in a Java application. A bar appears when a thread starts. It is colored green while it runs, yellow while it waits, and red while it is blocked. The bar disappears when the thread halts. A sample is taken whenever such thread events occur; the Detail table shows the time of day at which the sample was taken, and the number of threads existing at that time.

Clicking the arrow button in the clock time of an item drills down to the details of the event: a table listing all threads by name, their priorities, states, number of monitors, and whether they are daemon threads. The Extended Detail view for a thread shows a stack trace, and a list of monitors the thread owns.

## User Interface

### Cocoa Events

Cocoa Events records an event at every call to -[NSApplication sendEvent:]. It captures the thread ID, stack trace, the event code, and a string (such as "Left Mouse Down") that characterizes the event.

### Carbon Events

Carbon Events records an event at every return from WaitNextEvent. It captures the thread ID, stack trace, the event code, and a string (such as "Key Down") that characterizes the event.

26

# Custom Instruments

Some of the instruments included in Instruments consist of code specially written for the task. Most involve no code at all. They are made from editable templates. You can examine these instruments yourself—which may be the only way to get authoritative details on what an instrument does—and you can create instruments of your own.

Let's see what a scripted instrument looks like. Create a trace document from the File Activity template, select the Reads / Writes instrument, and then **Instrument > Edit 'Reads/Writes' Instrument…** (or simply double-click the instrument's label). An editing sheet (see Figure 26.9) will appear, with fields for the instrument's name, category, and description, and a long scrolling list *of probes*, handlers for events the instrument is meant to capture.

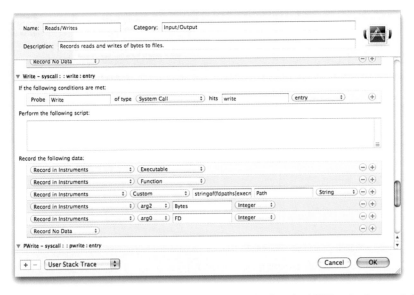

FIGURE 26.9   The Edit Instrument sheet for the Reads / Writes instrument. The sheet is dominated by an editable list of events the instrument is to capture. The portion that specifies how to record entries to the system write function is shown here.

Figure 26.9 shows the event list scrolled to the condition called Write, in the domain System Call, for the symbol write. It is to trigger when write is entered. Next comes the text of a script to be executed when the probe is triggered. Instruments uses the *DTrace* kernel facility, which has its own scripting language; for instance, this event might put the time at which the event occurred into an instance variable of the probe, so that a write-exit probe could calculate the duration of the call and record it. In this case, the scripting text is blank.

Then comes a series of items specifying what information is to be kept, for the trace graph or for the Detail view. In the case of Reads / Writes, this is

▶ The name of the executable

▶ The name of the function

▶ The first argument (the file descriptor), which is an integer to be labeled **FD**

▶ The third argument (the size of the write), which is an integer to be labeled **Byte**

▶ A string, to be labeled **Path**, calculated from an expression in the Instruments scripting language: A path, derived from the file descriptor within the executable.

Integer-valued records are included in the configuration inspector's list of **Statistics to Graph**, and are eligible to display in the instrument's trace. This accounts for the odd presence of Thread ID (which is automatically captured in every case) in the list of available plots. By default, the Stack Depth statistic is selected.

The customization sheet is a front end for the scripting language for the kernel-provided DTrace service; only kernel-level code is capable of detecting call events in every process. The section "Creating Custom Instruments with DTrace," in the *Instruments User Guide*, offers enough of an introduction to the language to get you started on your own instruments.

To make your own instrument, start with **Instrument > Build New Instrument...** (⌘B). An instrument-editing sheet will drop from the front trace document, and you can proceed from there.

If you become a DTrace expert, you might find it more convenient, or more flexible, to write your scripts directly, without going through the customization sheet. Select **File > DTrace Script Export...** to save a script covering every instrument in the current document, and **File > DTrace Data Import...** to load a custom script in. You can export DTrace scripts only from documents that contain DTrace instruments exclusively.

The stack trace in the Extended Detail view provides another way to create a custom instrument. Select one of the function frames in the listing and then **Trace Call Duration** from the stack trace's **Action** (✿) menu. Instruments will add a custom instrument to the current document that triggers on entry and exit, to record how long it took to execute the function.

> **WARNING**
>
> DTrace is a new feature of Mac OS X 10.5, and it executes as part the operating system kernel. That means the entire system is vulnerable to a crash (a "kernel panic") if something goes wrong. This should be rare, and should get rarer, but I've had it happen with Instruments 1.0 on Mac OS X 10.5.2. Make sure your documents are all saved, and back your system up frequently.

**26**

# The Templates

When you create a new Instruments document, a sheet drops down offering a choice among templates, preconfigured sets of instruments for common tasks (see Figure 26.10). Click the configuration of your choice, and then click one of the buttons at the bottom of the sheet:

▶ **Open an Existing File...** abandons the new document and presents a standard file-selection dialog for opening an old one. This is simply a convenience, effectively canceling the sheet and performing **File > Open...**.

▶ **Cancel** closes the untitled document without saving.

▶ **Choose** creates the document and populates it with the instruments for the selected template.

▶ **Record** does a lot of work. It creates the document and populates it with the selected template's instruments. Then it starts recording. When a trace document doesn't have a default target application—as a newly instantiated document would not—Instruments has to associate an application with each instrument in the document. A variant on the standard open-file dialog appears, enabling you to pick the target application or tool, and to specify arguments and environment variables. You can specify one target for all the instruments by checking the **Apply to All Instruments** box. When all the targets are set, Instruments launches them and starts recording.

FIGURE 26.10    The choose-template sheet that introduces each new trace document in Instruments. There are eight standard templates, including a blank template that has no instruments in it at all. Selecting a template fills the lower view with a brief description of the template.

These are the standard templates Apple supplies. As mentioned in "Saving and Reopening," you can create templates of your own by composing a trace document to your needs, and using **File > Save as Template...** to save it.

▸ **Blank** contains no instruments at all. You add the ones you want by dragging them in from the Library.

▸ **Activity Monitor** contains the Activity Monitor instrument. It's a comprehensive instrument, and this template can be thought of as a recordable version of the Activity Monitor application, or as a nicer version of BigTop.

▸ **CPU Sampler** gives you the Sampler and CPU Monitor instruments. The one provides a statistical by-function profile of the target application, and the other, the CPU load at the same times. The Sampler application now launches Instruments and opens this template.

▸ **File Activity** sets you up with File Activity, Reads/Writes, File Attributes, and Directory I/O.

▸ **Leaks** is the template we used in Chapter 19. It provides the ObjectAlloc and Leaks instruments to track the rate of object creation, and to verify that what you allocate, you also free. If you are interested in what your application is doing with memory, this is the template to use, rather than Object Allocations, which provides only ObjectAlloc.

▸ **Object Allocations** contains only the ObjectAlloc instrument. It is intended as a substitute for the ObjectAlloc application from earlier editions of the developer tools, and in fact running the current version of the ObjectAlloc application simply runs Instruments and instantiates this template.

▸ **UI Recorder** provides the User Interface instrument only. This template can be used to construct lifetime or looping scripts to verify the correct operation of a program, or you can add tracks to capture data as events occur.

▸ **Core Data** includes Core Data Fetches, Core Data Cache Misses, and Core Data Saves. It does not include Core Data Faults (you could drag it in), but it hits all the events that really impact the performance of a Core Data application.

# Summary

Instruments is a big topic, and we covered much of it. We started with a tour of the trace document window, and moved on to populating it from the Library window. We covered general principles of how to configure an instrument track.

We saw the various ways to start and stop recordings, including human-interface recordings that can be played back to generate repeatable tests for your applications.

We took inventory of the instruments and document templates Apple supplies, and how to create your own.

As your needs and expertise progress, you'll want to consult the *Instruments User Guide*, which you can find in the Xcode Documentation browser.

# CHAPTER 27

# Closing Snippets

**IN THIS CHAPTER**

▸ Traps in Xcode Development

▸ Tips on Xcode Features

▸ More on Documentation Searches

There were a few things that just didn't fit in with the flow of this book, but I want to cover them here: some traps, some tips, and a note on using the Documentation window, instead of writing for it.

## Miscellaneous Traps

Xcode is actually a fairly straightforward application to use after you become accustomed to how much of it there has to be. However, you still need to be aware of a few things that will save you some headaches:

▸ **Interface Builder and parsing.** Interface Builder relies on its own internal parser to find the available actions and outlets of Objective-C classes. It gets Code Sense information from Xcode to identify the classes and headers; but for the details, it parses the header files itself.

   If the header won't parse correctly, however, IB will be stymied. It indicates this by turning the gem at the bottom of the NIB window from green to yellow. If you see a yellow gem, clean up your source files, save them, and go back to Interface Builder.

▸ **Interface Builder and disappearing links.** You've linked some controls to targets and actions, and filled in some outlets among your NIB objects. Then you change the classes' header files so that those actions and outlets are no longer there. The links are invalid.

When this happens, Interface Builder shows a yellow warning icon, with an error count, in the status bar of the NIB window. Clicking the icon makes the NIB Info window appear, and the table at the bottom of the window will list all the linkage problems (see Figure 27.1). If you double-click one of the items, IB will show the linkage HUD for the affected object, with the broken links highlighted in yellow. From there, you can correct the links or go back to your source to restore them.

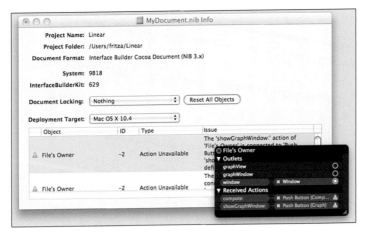

FIGURE 27.1    Click the warning icon at the bottom of the main NIB window to reveal the NIB Info window. The table lists instances of an outlet or action linkage becoming invalid. Double-clicking an item brings up the linkage HUD with the problem link shown in yellow.

▶ **Non-case-sensitive filenames.** HFS+, the recommended file system for Mac OS X, is case-preserving—files will get names in the same case as you provide—but not case sensitive: Xcode.txt, XCODE.TXT, and xcode.txt all refer to the same file. Most other UNIX variants are case sensitive, so if you import code, be on the lookout for the assumption that, say, the following two lines refer to different files:

```
#include "polishStrings.h"

#include "PolishStrings.h"
```

By the same token, make sure that your code uses filenames with consistent letter casing. Even if you don't expect to port your work, HFS+ isn't the only file system a Macintosh application sees, and a case-sensitive version of HFS+ does exist.

▶ **Header ambiguity.** Xcode is sometimes perverse in picking header files. C programmers are accustomed to the convention that files named in quotes in an #include directive are sought in a "local" directory tree, whereas files in angle brackets are supposed to be sought in a "system" header tree. By default, Xcode doesn't do this. It searches the project paths first in both cases. If you have, say, String.h in your project directory, that file will be used to satisfy #include <string.h>.

If this peculiarity bites you, you can turn it off. Uncheck **Always Search User Paths** (ALWAYS_SEARCH_USER_PATHS) in the **Build** tab of the appropriate Target or Project Info window.

▶ **Library links.** It is common practice in UNIX programming to provide the latest version of a library—say, libFoo.2.3.2.dylib—in a library directory and then provide symbolic links (libFoo.2.dylib and libFoo.dylib) to that file. When they link, programmers can specify the library generically through one of the symbolic links and be assured that the symbolic link will take the application to the right library, no matter what version is current on a user's machine.

This seems like a trivial practice to follow in Xcode: You want to link to a generic version 2 libFoo, so you select **Project > Add to Project...**, type **/usr/lib**, and select the link libFoo.2.dylib. But NSOpenPanel, which implements the file-selection dialog, resolves links before returning them to the calling application. Xcode gets the path to libFoo.2.3.2.dylib, and your application will refuse to launch if exactly that library is not available.

The solution is to drag the symbolic link directly into the Groups & Files list. In the Finder, expose /usr/lib by pressing ⇧⌘G and typing **/usr/lib**; locate the desired symbolic link. Drag it into the Groups & Files list in Xcode. In the resulting add-to-project sheet, specify the targets the .dylib is to join, and do not copy the file into your project folder. Make sure that the .dylib appears in the Link Binary with Libraries phases of the relevant targets.

▶ **The .pbxuser file.** The .xcodeproj project document is a package directory containing at least two files, of which only one, *projectname*.pbxproj, contains information critical to the structure of the project. The remaining files store the state of the project as last set by a particular user. The *username*.mode*N* files record the tiniest details of all, such as window and split-bar positions and contents of history lists.

The *username*.pbxuser file encompasses nontrivial matters, such as the placement of bookmarks, breakpoint specifications, custom executables, and parameters for executables. Sharing a project file will not transmit these settings to the other party (unless the other party has the same username). Depending on your taste, you may or may not think that these are important things to preserve; decide for yourself whether .pbxuser files belong in SCM.

If a default.pbxuser file is present in a project package and no matching user-specific .pbxuser file is there, the settings in the default file are used.

▶ **Intrinsic libraries.** Different UNIX systems have different requirements for the libraries that must be linked into a program to make it runnable. If you are porting an application to Xcode, be sure *not* to include libc, libstdc++, or libgcc in the list of files to link against; gcc will link against libc—in fact, libSystem—and libgcc automatically. In addition, if you use the g++ front end for compiling C++, as Xcode does, libstdc++ is automatically linked.

**27**

Note that gcc 4.0 relies on a dynamic libstdc++, which is available only on Mac OS X 10.3.9 and up. If you are targeting a C++ application at earlier versions, you have to use gcc 3.3. gcc 3.3 is not supported on Intel Macs.

# Miscellaneous Tips

In addition to the traps, a few features in the Apple developer tools aren't obvious:

▶ **NSMatrix**. We met the Cocoa NSMatrix class in Chapter 6, "A Cocoa Application: Views." It displays control cells in a column, row, or array, and supports the idea of a selection among them; the most common applications are for coordinated radio buttons, or the labels and text fields of an NSForm.

In older versions of Interface Builder, you could create an NSMatrix by dropping a control into a window, and option-dragging one of its resizing handles to replicate it. The control was replaced by an NSMatrix of the same cell type as was in the control.

This no longer works. In IB 3, select the control, and then **Layout > Embed Objects In > Matrix**. That gives you a one-by-one matrix that you can extend by option-dragging a resizing handle.

▶ **Window sizes**. When you open a new project window, it opens to a size, position, and arrangement set in the Xcode defaults. To change the default, set a window to the size and position that suits you, or select **Defaults** in the **Window** menu. A sheet will drop from the front window, asking whether you want to make its layout the default for all project windows. Click **Make Layout Default** to set the new default.

▶ **New NIBs and XIBs**. One consequence of the new tight integration between Xcode 3 and Interface Builder is that you don't have to have IB active to start on a new NIB or XIB file. The New File assistant you get when you select **File > New File...** includes templates for commonly made IB files, under the **Interface Builder** category. There are subcategories for Carbon and Cocoa files, giving you a choice of XIB and NIB templates for applications, windows, and main menus. The Carbon options include a dialog XIB, and the Cocoa, a view XIB (and of course, empty files for both frameworks and both formats). The new-file process takes care of adding the files to the targets you choose.

▶ **Sharing precompiled headers**. Xcode caches precompiled headers, on the theory that if sharing header compilation within a project is good, sharing it across projects is even better. Precompilation results are held in /Library/Caches/com.apple. Xcode.*n*, where *n* is the userid of the user doing the precompilation. Xcode tries to keep a cache directory pruned down to 1GB in size, while keeping any file that was used in the past 24 hours. You can change these retention parameters by using the defaults tool and the keys BuildSystemCacheSizeInMegabytes and BuildSystemMinimumRemovalAgeInHours.

The sharing of precompiled headers makes it important to avoid putting project- or build-specific predefined symbols into prefix files, if at all possible. Ordinarily, this would put us in a quandary because the predefined-symbol switch for gcc, -D, applies to precompilations as well as source compilations; adding such a setting changes the precompiled file and restricts its usefulness to the scope of the definition.

Fortunately, an alternative way to define a symbol does not affect precompiled headers. The setting **Preprocessor Macros Not Used in Precompiled Headers** enables you to define symbols "downstream" from the precompilation of the headers, so the precompiled header file remains generic and shareable (see Figure 27.2).

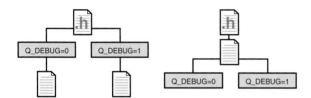

FIGURE 27.2    Setting a global preprocessor symbol (left) changes the environment in which the prefix header is compiled, so a different precompiled header has to be generated each time the symbol is changed. If the symbol is defined in **Preprocessor Macros Not Used in Precompiled Headers** (right), a single precompiled header serves all cases, as the symbol is injected into the environment "downstream" from the precompilation.

▶ **Parameters for Info.plist**. This file is crucial in any bundled target, and Xcode handles it specially. You are already familiar with the way the project templates populate the file with default values and how the **Properties** tab of the Target Info window serves as an editor for common Info.plist entries.

You can use the gcc C preprocessor on your Info.plist file. You can #define and use macros to build values in the file. The obvious uses might be in repeatedly used strings, such as the reverse-domain-name prefix for bundle and UTI identifiers and for version numbers. Search on "Info" in the target **Build** settings list for the switch that enables preprocessing and for settings that allow you to predefine macros and set other preprocessor options.

Apart from the preprocessor, any of the build system's settings can be embedded in Info.plist by using the $(setting name) reference style. For instance, you can substitute $(PRODUCT_NAME) for all instances of your product's name, so that one change to the build settings will propagate automatically. Using $(EXECUTABLE_NAME) may be safer for the CFExecutableName key than using the literal name.

▶ **Single build directory**. In early releases of Xcode, all builds, regardless of build style—the predecessor of build configurations—put a product in the build subdirectory of the project directory. Both intermediate and final products were commingled, and the only way to ensure that a product was all-release or all-debug was to clean targets every time the build style changed.

Today, the `build` directory and its intermediates subdirectory contain one directory for each build style. Results of builds are kept segregated, so build dependencies don't get crossed between configurations, and there is much less need to build from clean targets.

Some developers, however, prefer the unitary build directory. You can restore this by setting the Xcode application preference `UsePerConfigurationBuildLocations` to NO:

```
$ defaults write com.apple.xcode UsePerConfigurationBuildLocations NO
```

This is a per-user preference. There is no way to restrict it to a single project.

▶ **More preferences**. Not every useful preference in Xcode is accessible through the graphical interface; some have to be set through the `defaults` command-line tool. Open the Documentation window and look for the bookmark **Xcode Expert Preferences Notes**.

▶ **More build settings**. Some build settings are read-only, reflecting the state of the build or derived values from other settings. Some settings exist but don't have a graphical interface; there are more possible settings than there are entries in a target's **Build** tab. You can see a complete list by clicking on the bookmark **Xcode Build Settings Notes** in the Xcode Documentation window. Appendix A, "Some Build Variables," lists the prominent ones.

You can use any of the settings as variables to build up values for the **Build** tab or `Info.plist`, and you can set the "unlisted" but writable ones if you need to by adding a row to the **Build** list. Build settings are also available to Shell Script phases as environment variables.

If you want to make an unlisted setting, select **Add User-Defined Setting** from the **Action** (✿) menu in the **Build** tab. A new line will appear in the list, and you can enter the setting's name in the left column, and the value in the right.

One setting that isn't mentioned is $(VALUE). Targets inherit build settings from the project, which in turn inherits settings from Xcode defaults. Sometimes, you want to add to, not replace, an inherited setting. Use $(VALUE) to include the inherited value in your setting.

▶ **Folder references**. This note expands on the explanation of folder references in Chapter 20, "Navigating an Xcode Project." There are a couple of nuances I couldn't cover there.

In "An External Build System Project," in Chapter 24, when we selected a folder to add to our project, we wanted to add each particular file in the folder to the project. But sometimes, adding a folder to a project means adding *the folder itself* to the project. Suppose that you are building an educational program about presidents of the United States and want the `Resources` directory of the application to include a subdirectory containing a picture of each president. Your intention is that the application include that directory and whatever it may contain—as new administrations or replacement portraits come in—not the particular files.

In such a case, when you drag the portrait folder into the Groups & Files list, you select **Create Folder References** for any added folders in the sheet that appears. The folder you dragged in will appear in the list in the same blue color as folders in the Finder, not in the yellow of Xcode file-grouping folders. The folder reference can then be dragged into the Copy Bundle Resources build phase; the folder and its contents, whatever they might be at build time, are copied into the product's `Resources` directory.

> **WARNING**
>
> Xcode's build system does not track folder references as well as you'd hope. So far as Xcode is concerned, the thing to be tracked for changes is the directory itself, not its contents. So if a file in the directory changes, and you do a noncleaned build, the new file won't make its way into the product. Use the **Build > Touch** command on the folder in the Groups & Files list, or just do a **Clean**, to work around the problem.

▶ **Moving views in Interface Builder**. The normal consequence of dragging a view in Interface Builder is that the view slides to where you drag it but does not change its position in the view hierarchy. Suppose that you have a window containing an NSBox and an NSSlider. Dragging the slider toward the box makes the two views overlap but does not put the slider into the box. Both are still immediate subviews of the window's content view.

One way to place the slider in the box might be to select it and then select **Cut** (⌘X) from the window, double-click in the box to select its interior, and **Paste** (⌘V) the slider in. The problem is that you may already have set a target and action for the slider or bound it to an NSController. Such connections are lost when a control is removed from the view hierarchy.

The better way is to hold the mouse button down on the slider for a few seconds. The slider will develop a deep shadow around it, indicating that it has been "lifted off" the view it had been in. When you drag the browser into the box in this condition and drop it there, the slider is put inside the box. This click-and-hold strategy temporarily takes views out of the hierarchy without damaging their connections.

▶ **Code optimization**. The optimization-setting flag for gcc goes in a progression from -O0 (none at all) to -O3 (everything). The temptation, when driving for the sleekest, whizziest application, is to turn the knob up full and let the optimizer fly. And yet the standard Release setting for optimization in Xcode is -Os—optimize for *size*. What's going on?

The problem is that -O3 optimization can dramatically increase the size of the generated code: gcc will autonomously convert function calls to in-line code so that the content of those functions will be repeated, perhaps many times, throughout the application. It turns counted for loops into series of *n* iterations of the loop body, one after the other, because it's quicker to run straight through four copies of the same code than to keep a counter, test it against four, and conditionally branch.

All these optimizations are ingenious, but they can be shortsighted. Modern processors are dramatically faster than the main memory buses that serve them; waiting for loads of data or program instructions can stall a processor for a substantial portion of time. Therefore, limited amounts of very fast cache memory are put between the processor and RAM, to make the instruction stream available at a pace that keeps up with the CPU. But cache sizes are limited. An application that has been doubled in size throughout by unrolling and in-lining everywhere will overrun the cache and hit RAM to fetch instructions at least twice as often. In the usual case, "faster" code runs slower than smaller code.

This isn't true in every case. In all likelihood, your code will have some hot spots where in-lining and even loop unrolling will yield substantial performance gains. You just have to run your application and measure it to see where the hot spots are. You can set -03 optimization for a single source file by selecting it in your target's Compile Sources build phase, opening an Info window on it, selecting the **Build** tab, and typing the flag into the window.

> **NOTE**
>
> The **Build** tab for a file won't show up unless you select the file in the Compile Sources build phase of a particular target. The file's listing in the Groups & Files list refers to that file as it is compiled for any of the targets in the project; only the listing in the Compile Sources phase associates the file with a specific compilation.

▶ **External text editors**. A text editor is an intimate choice for a programmer. The Xcode text editor checks most people's feature boxes, but attachment, experience, muscle memory, and even functionality can count for more. And, preferences can vary by file type: One might prefer Xcode's indexing for program source, BBEdit's built-in facilities for HTML, TextMate's integration with command-line tools for Ruby, and emacs for shell scripts. See Appendix C, "Other Resources," for a sampling of Mac text editors.

Xcode will open your files in your preferred editors. The File Types panel of the Preferences window displays a hierarchical list of file types (see Figure 27.3). The rightmost column of the table contains a pop-up list for each type, which determines what happens when you double-click a file in the Groups & Files list or the Detail view.

In the case of ordinary (nondocumentation) HTML files, the top of the menu offers the ways Xcode itself can display the file: **HTML File** (rendered as a web page), **Source Code File** (syntax colored, and with the Code Focus ribbon), and **Plain Text File** (no coloring, no folding, no interpretation). There is the option of opening the file with the preferred application you set in the Finder. And there is a submenu from which you can select an external application as the editor for that type of file. Xcode knows of a limited repertoire of possible editors, including BBEdit and emacs, and there's an **Other** item for you to select your preferred editor (such as TextMate).

FIGURE 27.3    The File Types panel of Xcode Preferences window lists file types hierarchically. Clicking the right column for a file type offers a choice on how each file type is to be opened.

BBEdit observes a special text-editing protocol that allows Xcode to detect unsaved files in BBEdit, and to force BBEdit to save them. For other editors, take care to save changed files yourself before building a target.

> **NOTE**
>
> The Developer Tools Reference gives some code for your ~/.emacs file to make emacs work with Xcode. Do a full-text search for **gnuserv-start-manual** to see it.

▶ **File-reference paths**. Earlier, I made much of the fact that Xcode's Groups & Files list is not a directory or file-system tool; that it reflects the way you want to structure the project, and not the placement of files in the file system's directories. This isn't *quite* true.

If an Xcode project's file references were completely arbitrary, they'd have to be absolute paths. That would mean that all the files would be identified by a path that ran through your home directory. Suppose you were sharing the project with another developer. The project and its files would be in *her* directory, and the references to your home directory would be wrong.

The solution would seem to be to keep the path relative to the project file—and indeed that is one of the options. It is not, however, the option Xcode uses by default. The default is **Relative to Enclosing Group**, as shown in the **Path Type** pop-up in the **General** tab of the file's Info window. There are other choices, such as **Relative to Build Product**, **Relative to Xcode**, and, yes, **Absolute Path**. If you have defined source trees, you can make the path relative to one of those, too.

But what does "relative to enclosing group" mean? If you turn the File Info inspector on a group folder in the Groups & Files list, you'll see that groups, too, have paths (which can, in turn, be absolute or relative). Groups still aren't directories:

More than one group can refer to the same file directory, and not all members of a group have to be in the same place.

Putting a file system location on a group has the advantage that you can have two directories in your file system, containing files that have the same names. Maybe the one contains live classes, and the other "mocks" for testing. Switching between the two would then be a simple matter of changing the path of the corresponding group.

If the group's directory does not contain a file that is in the group, that file's path will be stored as project relative.

▶ **The Info inspector.** Throughout this book, we've been opening Info windows on files, targets, and executables, one after the other. There's a cleaner way to do this, if you're going to examine several files (and so forth) in succession. Select an object, and instead of pressing ⌘I, press ⌥⌘I. The result is not an Info window, but an Info *inspector*. It's a floating window, and its contents change as your selection changes. There is no need to open and close Info windows one after the other.

▶ **Multiple-item info.** I've mentioned this elsewhere, but it's worth repeating: You can have an Info window (or inspector) work on many files simultaneously. Suppose you have a half-dozen XML property-list files in your project, and you realize that you created them all with the Mac Roman character encoding. Property-list files are supposed to be UTF-8.

A simple solution is to select each in succession, and open a File Info window (⌘I) to reset the encoding, answering the resulting alert with **Convert** each time. The better way is to select them all at once (shift- or command-click them to extend the selection), and then open an Info window. Where the files necessarily differ (as in their names), you'll face an immutable "multiple selection," but the settings that they all can share—including file encoding—can be changed. Select **Unicode (UTF-8)**, answer **Convert Once for All**, and they're all changed.

# More Documentation

I covered the *making* of Xcode documentation extensively in Chapter 15, "Documentation in Xcode." *Using* the documentation has been left to examples as I went along. A few features of the Xcode documentation system haven't yet been covered, however.

## Documentation Set Updates

Before Xcode 3, Xcode could examine an RSS feed periodically and offer to install documentation updates when these appeared. The update itself was done by pointing the default web browser at the Apple Developer Connection downloads site and manually downloading and installing the update.

The new documentation system makes updates much more automatic, and extends the update facility to any documentation set that specifies a feed address. The

**Documentation Set Updates** submenu of the **Action** (⚙) menu at the lower-left corner of the Documentation window sets up how you want updates to work. The general scheme is that you decide whether to check for updates, how often to check for updates automatically, and whether you want Xcode to download and install updates it discovers.

The menu items are as follows:

▸ **Update All Documentation Sets Now**. Xcode immediately does a check for new docsets, and downloads and installs them if they are found.

▸ **Install New Updates Automatically**. This is a toggle. When it is checked, Xcode installs updates it finds without asking whether to install them.

▸ **Manually**. Xcode never checks for updates; you have to start the process yourself.

▸ **Daily**, **Weekly**, and **Monthly**. These are mutually exclusive switches. Xcode checks for updates periodically. Whether it asks to perform the update once it is discovered is set by **Install New Updates Automatically**.

▸ **Check Now**. Xcode checks for updates immediately.

## Boolean Text Searches

If you type a phrase into the Documentation window's full-text search field, each word is sought in the index separately, and the resulting matches are ranked by relevance. Relevance searches can be sloppy—a document can appear surprisingly high in the results list but completely lack one of the terms you are looking for. Sometimes, you want to say that you really do want a word to be present in the document. You can make a term mandatory by preceding it with a + character. Preceding a term with a - indicates that you want to exclude any documents containing that term. You can indicate that a phrase is to appear literally and in order by enclosing it in quotes. So if you are interested in a summary of power-management issues but find discussions of heat dissipation tedious, you might specify as follows:

```
"power management" +overview -heat
```

A better strategy for this search might consider "power manager" as well as "power management." You can cover both with a wildcard expression: `power manage*`.

Even more finesse can be had with Boolean operators. Search terms can be

> **NOTE**
>
> Man pages can dominate searches of the Developer Tools Reference, obscuring results that cover the operation of Xcode and the other developer applications. I've found it useful to include the term `-manual`, which filters the man pages out.

joined by ¦ for *or*, and **&** for *and*, grouped by parentheses, and negated with !. On our query, a variant that accepts articles about power management or energy management might be as follows:

```
("power manage*" ¦ "energy manage*") & overview & !heat
```

# PART III

## Appendices

## IN THIS PART

APPENDIX A   Some Build Variables                    475

APPENDIX B   Project and Target Templates            485

APPENDIX C   Other Resources                         501

# Some Build Variables

**IN THIS APPENDIX**

▶ **Build Variables and How to Set Them**

▶ **Important Build Variables**

▶ **Source Trees**

This appendix offers a brief list of the major build variables that control the Xcode build system. Build variables determine compiler flags, search paths, installation behavior, and important strings such as product names. You can find a comprehensive explanation of Xcode build variables in the Xcode Documentation window by searching for the title string **Build Setting** in the Developer Tools Reference documentation set. The full title is *Xcode Build Setting Reference*.

You can see all the build variables available to Run Script build phases by creating a phase that consists only of the command env. You'll find that there are more than 250 variables. Here's a list of the more useful ones. For purposes of example, assume that user xcodeuser is making a debug build of an application named MyApp out of a project named MyProject on a PowerMac G5; the project uses the 10.4 Universal SDK (see Figure A.1).

Some of these settings have no corresponding interface in the **Build** tabs of Info windows. You can set these—if they are not read-only—by selecting **Add User-Defined Setting** from the **Action (✿)** menu. Xcode adds a new line to the list, and you can enter the setting's name in the Title column, and the value under Value. Boolean values are kept as YES or NO.

The authoritative name for a build variable is its "setting name"—the name of the actual build variable, as visible in environment variables and substitutable into other settings and Info.plist expansions. You can find the corresponding entries in a target or project **Build** tab by typing the setting name into the tab's search field.

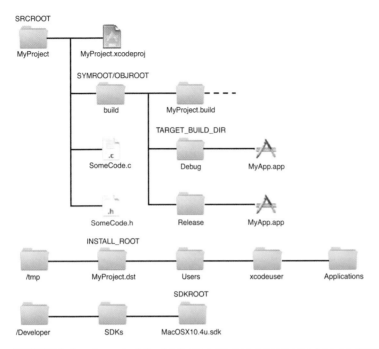

FIGURE A.1    Layout of the MyProject/MyApp project used as an example for the build variables listed here.

The **Build** tab can display setting names rather than the descriptive "setting titles." Right- (or Control-) click in the setting table, and select **Show Setting Names** from the pop-up menu; that menu item changes to **Show Setting Titles** for you to switch back.

That pop-up menu also controls how setting values display. A setting may be defined in terms of another setting, as when you specify an installation directory by $(HOME)/Applications. By default, Xcode displays embedded build variables by expanding them (see Figure A.2). The pop-up's **Show Definitions** command changes the display so that variable references are shown explicitly. **Show Values** toggles the display back.

FIGURE A.2    Build variables can be viewed by "value" (top), with constituent build variables expanded, or by "definition" (bottom), with build variables explicitly shown.

# Useful Build Variables

With no further ado, here is a list of selected build variables. I've grouped them by general function, and then by a rough general-to-specific order within those groups. The values for the example MyProject project are shown in parentheses at the end of most entries.

## Environment

These are read-only variables that you can use in scripts or to build up other build settings:

- ▶ HOME is the path to your home directory.

- ▶ USER is the username of the person doing the build. There is a corresponding UID variable for the numeric user ID.

- ▶ GROUP is the group name of the person doing the build. There is a corresponding GID variable for the numeric group ID.

- ▶ DEVELOPER_DIR is the directory you chose for the Xcode installation. The DEVELOPER_ variables are important because they make your scripts portable between Xcode 3 and 2.5, and between developers who did not install Xcode in the root /Developer directory. (/Developer)

- ▶ DEVELOPER_APPLICATIONS_DIR is the folder inside DEVELOPER_DIR containing Xcode and the other developer applications. (/Developer/Applications)

- ▶ DEVELOPER_BIN_DIR is the folder inside DEVELOPER_DIR containing the BSD tools, such as gcc, that Xcode uses. If you write scripts that execute development tools such as gcc or yacc, use this path *instead* of /usr/bin. The tools in this directory are Xcode versions. (/Developer/usr/bin)

- ▶ DEVELOPER_FRAMEWORKS_DIR is the folder inside DEVELOPER_DIR that contains development frameworks, such as for unit tests. (/Developer/Library/Frameworks)

- ▶ DEVELOPER_LIBRARY_DIR is the folder inside DEVELOPER_DIR containing files (templates, plug-ins, and so on) that support the developer tools. (/Developer/Library)

- ▶ DEVELOPERSDK_DIR is the folder inside DEVELOPER_DIR that contains software development kits. (/Developer/SDKs)

- ▶ DEVELOPER_TOOLS_DIR contains BSD tools, such as Rez, that are specific to Mac OS X development and that would not be expected to be in /usr/bin. (/Developer/Tools)

- ▶ DEVELOPER_USR_DIR The folder inside DEVELOPER_DIR that you should use as a prefix for the standard include, sbin, share, and other directories you'd ordinarily look for in the root /usr directory. (/Developer/usr)

- ▶ LOCAL_ADMIN_APPS_DIR The LOCAL build variables should be self-explanatory. (/Applications/Utilities)

- ▶ LOCAL_APPS_DIR (/Applications)

- ▶ LOCAL_DEVELOPER_DIR (/Library/Developer)

- ▶ LOCAL_LIBRARY_DIR (/Library)

▶ NATIVE_ARCH The architecture on which the current build is taking place (ppc). This is the same as CURRENT_ARCH and NATIVE_ARCH_ACTUAL. (ppc64)

▶ NATIVE_ARCH32_BIT and NATIVE_ARCH64_BIT are like NATIVE_ARCH, but refer to the 32-bit and 64-bit variants on the native architecture. If the processor performing the build were a Core 2 Duo, for instance, they would be i386 and x86_64, respectively. (ppc and ppc64)

▶ MAC_OS_X_VERSION_ACTUAL is a four-digit number designating the version of Mac OS X on which the build is being done. The first two digits will be 10, the third 5, and the last, the minor version. This value will be in trouble if 10.5 reaches a minor version above 9, as 10.4 did. (1051)

▶ MAC_OS_X_VERSION_MAJOR is a four-digit number that is the same as MAC_OS_X_VERSION_ACTUAL, but with the last digit set to zero. (1050)

▶ MAC_OS_X_VERSION_MINOR is a four-digit number that designates the current OS version, omitting the leading 10. In Xcode 3, the first two digits will always be 05; the second two are the minor version, safe through Mac OS X version 10.5.99. (0501)

## Build Targets

▶ ACTION is the task the build system is carrying out, corresponding to the action parameter for xcodebuild. (build)

▶ CONFIGURATION is the name of the selected build configuration. (Debug)

▶ PACKAGE_TYPE is the kind of product to be built. Apple documents the possible values to be EXECUTABLE (a single file, not an .app bundle), DYLIB (a single .dylib file), WRAPPER, FRAMEWORK_WRAPPER, JAR_FILE, ZIP_FILE, and JAVA_CLASS_FOLDER, but indications are that they will be switching to UTIs for this setting. The thing to do is to use a Run Script build phase in your project one time to echo the value of this setting so that you'll know what to test for. (com.apple.package-type.wrapper. application)

▶ PRODUCT_NAME is the name of the thing the current target builds. Target templates default this setting to be the same as the name of the target, but you can change this. PRODUCT_NAME does not include any prefix (such as lib) or suffix (such as .app or .dylib) that would be used in the actual name of the product's file or bundle. (MyApp)

▶ TARGET_NAME is the name of the active target. The target usually has the same name as the product, but this is not necessarily the case. For instance, a separate target for running unit tests might yield the same product as the principal target of a project, but have another name, such as "MyApp (testing)." (MyApp)

▶ PROJECT_NAME is the name of the project file, without the .xcodeproj extension. (MyProject)

▶ EXECUTABLE_NAME is the name of the product's executable binary file, including any prefixes or suffixes made necessary by its file type. This defaults to the EXECUTABLE_ PREFIX, plus PRODUCT_NAME, plus EXECUTABLE_SUFFIX, but you could change this (although it's hard to imagine why you would). (MyApp)

▶ EXECUTABLE_PREFIX is the prefix needed for the product's filename to conform to the product type. If this were a static library target, for instance, this variable would be lib.

▶ EXECUTABLE_SUFFIX is the suffix needed for the product's filename to conform to the product type. If this were a static library target, for instance, this variable would be .a.

▶ WRAPPER_NAME is the full name of the bundle directory if the product being built takes the form of a bundle (such as an application or a framework). This is the PRODUCT_NAME plus the WRAPPER_SUFFIX. (MyApp.app)

▶ LIBRARY_STYLE is set to STATIC, DYNAMIC, or BUNDLE, as the case may be, for a library target.

## Source Locations

▶ PROJECT_DIR is the directory that contains the project file. (/Users/xcodeuser/ MyProject)

▶ PROJECT_FILE_PATH is the full path to the project file. (/Users/xcodeuser/ MyProject/MyProject.xcodeproj)

▶ SDKROOT is the root of the tree in which to search for system headers and libraries. When no SDK is selected, SDKROOT is set to /. (/Developer/SDKs/MacOSX10.4u.sdk)

▶ SRCROOT is the folder containing the source code for the project, usually the project document's directory. (/Users/xcodeuser/MyProject)

▶ INFOPLIST_FILE is the name of the file that will be the *source* for the bundle's Info.plist file if the product of this target is a bundle. This is not necessarily Info .plist, because a project with more than one target will use one project directory to specify more than one Info.plist file. (Info.plist)

## Destination Locations

▶ OBJROOT is the folder containing, perhaps indirectly, the intermediate products, such as object files, of the build. (/Users/xcodeuser/MyProject/build)

▶ SYMROOT is the container for folders that receive symbol-rich—meaning, not-yet-stripped—versions of the product. (/Users/xcodeuser/MyProject/build)

▶ BUILT_PRODUCTS_DIR is the full path to the directory that receives either every product of the project or, if the products are scattered, symbolic links to every product. A script can therefore depend on reaching all the products through this path. By default, this is `$(SYMROOT)/$(CONFIGURATION).$(CONFIGURATION_BUILD_DIR)` is a synonym. (`/Users/xcodeuser/MyProject/build/Debug`)

▶ `TARGET_BUILD_DIR` is the directory into which the product of the current target is built (the installation location in an install build); otherwise, the `CONFIGURATION` subdirectory of the `SYMROOT` directory. (`/Users/xcodeuser/MyProject/build/Debug`)

▶ `FRAMEWORKS_FOLDER_PATH` is the path, in a bundle target in the target build directory, that contains frameworks used by the product. There are variables for other possible bundle directories; see the Xcode documentation for more. (`MyApp.app/Contents/Frameworks`)

▶ `UNLOCALIZED_RESOURCES_FOLDER_PATH` is the directory, within a bundle product in the target build directory, that receives file resources. (`MyApp.app/Contents/Resources`)

▶ `DERIVED_FILE_DIR` is the directory that receives intermediate source files generated in the course of a build, such as the sources generated by the `bison` parser generator. This variable is paralleled, presumably for historical reasons, by `DERIVED_FILES_DIR`; my guess is that the singular version is preferred. If you have a more general need for a place to put a temporary file, consult the Xcode documentation for `PROJECT_TEMP_DIR` or `TARGET_TEMP_DIR`. (`/Users/xcodeuser/MyProject/build/MyProject.build/Debug/MyApp.build/DerivedSources`)

▶ `OBJECT_FILE_DIR` is the directory containing subdirectories, one per architecture, containing compiled object files. (`/Users/xcodeuser/MyProject.build/MyProject.build/Debug/MyApp.build/Objects`)

▶ `OBJECT_FILE_DIR_normal` is the same as `OBJECT_FILE_DIR`, but applying only to the "normal" variant of the product. The other possible variants are `debug` and `profile`; variants of dynamic libraries can be chosen at load time by setting the `DYLD_IMAGE_SUFFIX` environment variable. (`/Users/xcodeuser/MyProject.build/MyProject.build/Debug/MyApp.build/Objects-normal`)

## Bundle Locations

▶ `CONTENTS_FOLDER_PATH` is the path, within the target build directory, that contains the structural directories of a bundle product. (`MyApp.app/Contents`)

▶ `EXECUTABLE_FOLDER_PATH` is the path, in a bundle target in the target build directory, into which the product's executable file is to be built. Not to be confused with `EXECUTABLES_FOLDER_PATH`, which points to a directory for "additional binary files," named `Executables`, in the `Contents` directory. (`MyApp.app/Contents/MacOS`)

▶ `EXECUTABLE_PATH` is the path, within `TARGET_BUILD_DIR`, to the executable binary. (`MyApp.app/Contents/MacOS/MyApp`)

## Compiler Settings

▶ ARCHS is the architectures, as a space-separated list, for which the product is to be built. (ppc)

▶ VALID_ARCHS is the possible values that could go into the ARCHS list. The list encompasses all the architectures for which Xcode can build. (ppc64 ppc7400 ppc970 i386 x86_64 ppc)

▶ GCC_VERSION is the gcc compiler version to use. This is generally selected in the **Rules** tab of the target Info window, but setting it in a configuration in the **Build** tab will override it. If the **Rules** setting selects the "system version" of the compiler, this variable will be empty; if you need the version in that case, try parsing the output of the gcc_select tool. You can set GCC_VERSION per-architecture. (empty)

▶ GCC_PREPROCESSOR_DEFINITIONS is the space-separated list of symbols to be #defined in all compilations. Items of the form *symbol=value* assign values to the symbols. Symbols defined in this way will be incorporated in precompiled headers. Related is GCC_PREPROCESSOR_DEFINITIONS_NOT_USED_IN_PRECOMPILED_HEADERS, which specifies symbols defined in every compilation but not incorporated in precompiled headers. This allows you to share precompiled headers between build configurations, with variants in global definitions taken as options in the respective configurations.

▶ GCC_ENABLE_OBJC_GC is the variable that controls whether gcc compiles Objective-C source with support for garbage collection.

  ▶ If it is Unsupported, no garbage collection will be done, and no special compiler flag will be set.

  ▶ If Required, garbage collection will be used, and anything that links with the compiled code is expected to use garbage collection itself. gcc is passed the flag -fobjc_gc_only.

  ▶ If Supported, the code itself will not use garbage collection itself, but can link with GC binaries. This is useful only if you are writing a single library to link with both environments. gcc is passed the flag -fobjc_gc.

▶ OTHER_CFLAGS is the catchall variable that receives the gcc options that do not have their own build variables for C compilation. It's easy to put in this variable an option that contradicts a setting made in the **Build** tab of the Info panels, with unpredictable results. Therefore, it's a good idea to type a flag into the **Build** list's search field, to see whether a direct setting is available. There is also an OTHER_CPLUSPLUSFLAGS variable. For linker flags, the equivalent is OTHER_LDFLAGS. (empty)

▶ OTHER_CFLAGS_normal is used to specify OTHER_CFLAGS only for the "normal" variant of a dynamic library; debug and profile variants are also possible. For linker flags, the equivalent is OTHER_LDFLAGS_normal_ppc, where the order is variant and then architecture, and either can be omitted. If you are stuck with single-architecture libraries, you can link a fat target by specifying the PowerPC version in a `-l` option in `OTHER_LDFLAGS_ppc`; the Intel version, in `OTHER_LDFLAGS_i386`. (empty).

▶ `PER_ARCH_CFLAGS_ppc` are the compiler flags to be applied only to PowerPC builds; the most useful other architecture suffixes are `ppc64`, `i386`, and `x86_64`; similarly, `PER_ARCH_CPLUSPLUSFLAGS_ppc`. (empty)

▶ `WARNING_CFLAGS` is a string of options setting warning options for all `gcc` compilations. Apple is trying to provide fine-grained control of warnings through check boxes in the **Build** panels, so check to be sure that there isn't a check box for your warning before putting it into this variable. The equivalent for the linker is `WARNING_LDFLAGS`. (empty)

▶ `ZERO_LINK` indicates whether ZeroLink linkage is enabled. ZeroLink is not available in Xcode 3, so this setting is ignored. (yes)

## Search Paths

▶ `HEADER_SEARCH_PATHS` is a space-delimited list of paths to directories `gcc` is to search for headers, in addition to standard locations, such as `/usr/include`. If you add your own paths, carry the default paths through by putting `$(VALUE)` at the beginning or end of your list. If the headers in question are in frameworks, set `FRAMEWORK_SEARCH_PATHS` instead. `SDKROOT` is prepended to the paths of system headers and frameworks. (`/Users/xcodeuser/MyProject/build/Debug/include`)

▶ `LIBRARY_SEARCH_PATHS` is a space-delimited list of paths to directories the linker is to search for libraries. If set, `SDKROOT` is prepended to the paths of system libraries. Developers sometimes are given libraries in production and debug forms, as binaries, with no source; they'd like to use one version of the library in debug builds and the other in release builds. A solution is to put the two library versions in separate directories, and specify different `LIBRARY_SEARCH_PATH`s for the two build configurations. (`/Users/xcodeuser/MyProject/build/Debug`)

▶ `MACOSX_DEPLOYMENT_TARGET` is the minimum version of Mac OS X on which the product can run; symbols in the SDK from later versions of the OS are weak-linked. (`10.4`)

▶ `INFOPLIST_PREPROCESS`, if YES, preprocesses the `INFOPLIST_FILE`, using the `gcc` preprocessor for C. You can specify a prefix file with `INFOPLIST_PREFIX_HEADER` and set symbols with `INFOPLIST_PREPROCESSOR_DEFINITIONS`. (NO)

## Deployment

▶ `DEPLOYMENT_POSTPROCESSING` indicates whether the build system is to strip symbols from the product, install it to `INSTALL_DIR`, and set its ownership and permissions (if YES). The `install` build action sets this option, or you could set it yourself in one of your configurations. (NO)

- INSTALL_PATH is the intended directory that would receive the installed product. Installation is done by the default configuration. (/Users/xcodeuser/Applications)

- INSTALL_ROOT is the path to prepend to the INSTALL_PATH to hold the installation tree—install builds do not, by default, install directly to the "live" installation destinations. (/tmp/MyProject.dst)

- INSTALL_DIR is the full path of the directory to receive the product, obtained by concatenating $(INSTALL_ROOT)/$(INSTALL_PATH). (/tmp/MyProject.dst/Users/xcodeuser/Applications)

- INSTALL_OWNER is the owner of the MyApp.app product, when installation is done. (xcodeuser)

- INSTALL_GROUP is the group for the MyApp.app product, when installation is done. (xcodeuser)

- INSTALL_MODE_FLAG The permissions for the installed MyApp.app product. (a-w, a+rX)

# Source Trees

A source tree provides a particular kind of build variable, a path to a directory or to the root directory of a tree with a known structure. The path can be a location to receive build results or to provide access to a system of libraries and headers. When used to build source paths, a source tree provides a reliable shorthand for packages that do not belong in the directory tree of any one project.

For example, I use the eSellerate libraries in my projects. I define a source tree for the eSellerate libraries by opening the Preferences window, selecting the Source Trees panel, and clicking the + button to add an entry. I choose ESELLERATE_DIR for the setting name and **eSellerate Directory** for the display name, and I type the full pathname for the root of the eSellerate SDK into the path column.

Now, whenever I add a file reference to my project, I have the option of making the reference **Relative to eSellerate Directory**. If the reference is to a header or a library, a search path relative to $(ESELLERATE_DIR) will be added to the invocations of gcc. If I take the project to other computers or if I share it with other users, ESELLERATE_DIR has to be defined as a source tree for those users on those machines, but I don't have to care about the details of the path.

Search trees are global—they span projects—but are per user.

# Project and Target Templates

When you create a new project or a new target within a project, Xcode presents you with a list of possible products for the new target to produce. Because the Xcode build system needs to know what sort of thing is being built, this step is crucial; if you select the wrong type for a project (or target), the offending project (or target) has to be thrown away. After you make your selection, Xcode draws on a template for that target type, directing the name of the executable, compiler, and linker settings, and the layout of any file packages to be created.

This appendix lays out the kinds of projects and targets you can choose from. These are only the targets Apple provides; you can create your own templates, and these will appear in the appropriate lists.

> **NOTE**
>
> This appendix lists the templates as Apple offered them in Xcode 3.0. Being data driven, templates are particularly apt to change between releases.

## Project Templates

These are the project types presented to you when you select **New Project...** from the **File** menu (see Figure B.1). When you choose one, a project is instantiated from the template, which if built as-is would produce a correct, if nonfunctional, product. The project may include starter source files, and, in the case of bundles, a suitable

`Info.plist` file. Two build configurations, Debug and Release, will be present, with build settings set as appropriate.

FIGURE B.1    The New Project Assistant. All the templates for projects appear in the scrolling list, and pressing the **Finish** button on the second page of the Assistant instantiates a project of the selected form. Clicking a template name presents a brief description of the template in the lower pane.

## The Empty Project

When you instantiate the Empty Project template, you get just that: a project with no targets, no files, nothing linked against, and no products. Ordinarily, if the nonempty project templates don't suit your purposes, you'd instantiate the nearest-matching one, and change it as needed. When this isn't possible, the empty project will let you build everything from scratch.

This is *not* the template you'd use to wrap a project that uses make (or ant, jam, or rake) for a build system. For that, you'd use the External Build System template.

## Action

Actions, in this context, are packages that specify action tiles and tasks for Automator. All action projects include starter source files for the action's executable code, and a NIB file for Automator to present for the action:

- ▶ **AppleScript Automator Action**. This is an action that works by running an AppleScript.

- ▶ **Cocoa Automator Action**. This action works by supplying an Objective-C class. The class includes the necessary method.

▶ **Definition Bundle**. Automator passes data between action tiles in the form of standard data types. An Automator definition bundle allows you to specify custom data types to pass among your own actions.

▶ **Shell Script Automator Action**. This action executes a program written in one of the UNIX scripting languages. Examples include the sh shell, Python, and Ruby.

## Application

The projects in this group produce Mac OS X applications. Each is distinguished by the framework for which it is written, and by the complexity of the product:

▶ **AppleScript Application**. Produces an application whose core functionality is provided by AppleScript scripts. The project is set up so that Xcode will primarily use AppleScript Studio for development. It includes an Objective-C main.m file that should not need editing, an Application.applescript as a starter point for your principal script, and a MainMenu.nib with standard menus and a sample main window.

▶ **AppleScript Document-Based Application**. The target is an AppleScript Studio application, with support sketched in for reading and writing document files. It adds an AppleScript and a NIB file for the added document object.

▶ **AppleScript Droplet**. This AppleScript Studio project will produce an application that processes files that are dropped onto the application's icon in the Finder. The MainMenu.nib file does not include an application window.

▶ **Carbon Application**. This project will produce a Mac OS X application that is written in C using the Carbon application framework. It will include a main.c file, a prefix file, and a NIB.

▶ **Carbon C++ Application**. This is the same as the Carbon application project, with the addition of an HIFramework directory, containing classes that are useful in organizing Carbon applications. The main program file is main.cp, which must be customized to handle the specific needs of your application and window classes.

▶ **Carbon C++ Standard Application**. The same, but the project is set up for a more standards-compliant C++, and hides all symbols in the executable.

▶ **Cocoa Application**. This project produces an application based on the Cocoa application framework. It includes a main.m, which needs no editing, and a MainMenu.nib.

▶ **Cocoa Document-Based Application**. This is a Cocoa application project to which an Objective-C source file and a corresponding NIB have been added for a document class. The Info.plist file includes a specification for a generic document, which the Finder and the Cocoa document system use to associate that class with a document type and extension.

▶ **Cocoa-Python Application** The Python scripting language includes bindings to the Cocoa application framework, permitting you to build Cocoa-based applications for Mac OS X without using Objective-C. A `main.m` file is provided that sets up the Python runtime environment, but you are not expected to edit it.

> **NOTE**
>
> See the open source PyObjC project at http://pyobjc.sourceforge.net. Apple provides a good introduction to PyObjC at http://developer.apple.com/cocoa/pyobjc.html.

▶ **Cocoa-Python Core Data Application**. The project creates a Cocoa application, programmed in Python, that uses Core Data to organize data saved in the user's `Application Support` folder.

▶ **Cocoa-Python Core Data Document-Based Application**. A Cocoa application, written in Python, that manages documents that are subclasses of `NSPersistentDocument`. Python source and a NIB are provided for the document.

▶ **Cocoa-Python Document-Based Application**. The same, with a Python class and NIB for an `NSDocument` subclass.

▶ **Cocoa-Ruby Application**. The Ruby scripting language, also, includes bindings to the Cocoa application framework, permitting you to build Cocoa-based applications for Mac OS X without using Objective-C. A `main.m` file contains a one-line `main()` function, which you are not expected to edit.

The Cocoa-Ruby application projects, and the Ruby Unit Test target, come from the RubyCocoa project. The RubyCocoa framework is installed as part of Mac OS X

> **NOTE**
>
> See the RubyCocoa project at http://rubycocoa.sourceforge.net/HomePage.

10.5; but if you want to distribute a product of this project type to users of earlier systems, you have to install it, or provide it in the application's `Contents/Frameworks` directory.

▶ **Cocoa-Ruby Core Data Application**. The project creates a Cocoa application, programmed in Ruby, that uses Core Data to organize data saved in the user's `Application Support` folder.

▶ **Cocoa-Ruby Core Data Document-Based Application**. A Cocoa application, written in Ruby, that manages documents that are subclasses of `NSPersistentDocument`. Ruby source and a NIB are provided for the document.

▶ **Cocoa-Ruby Document-Based Application**. The Cocoa-Ruby application, with a Ruby class and NIB for an `NSDocument` subclass.

▶ **Core Data Application**. This project creates a Cocoa application, written in Objective-C, that uses Core Data for persistent data stored in the user's `Application Support` folder. It includes a data model to support the Core Data work.

▶ **Core Data Document-Based Application**. The same, but the data model is associated with an Objective-C subclass of `NSPersistentDocument`. A NIB is provided for the document window.

▶ **Core Data Document-Based Application with Spotlight Importer**. The same, with an added target for a metadata plug-in for Spotlight. The application target moves the Spotlight plug-in into the right place in the application's package. `Linear` ended up as this kind of project, but you can always build up from a project of basically the same type.

▶ **Quartz Composer Application**. Quartz Composer is Apple's technology for building complex graphical applications using a visual, tile-based programming language. Compositions can be incorporated into Mac OS X applications.

The application product consists of a composition plus code for a simple Cocoa application. The example composition rotates text describing Quartz Composer on the surface of a transparent cube, over a background the user can edit on-the-fly. The underlying Objective-C program does little more than load the composition.

▶ **Quartz Composer Core Data Application**. The application product is a Core Data–based application that stores its data in the `Application Support` directory (not in a document). The example composition accepts an array of name-number pairs and renders them as an interactive 3D bar chart.

## Audio Units

An audio unit is a plug-in that adds functionality to Apple's Core Audio audio-processing framework:

▶ **Audio Unit Effect**. Creates a Core Audio plug-in that accepts audio data, processes it, and outputs the result.

▶ **Audio Unit Effect with Carbon View**. The same, but allows the user to change the unit's parameters through a panel rendered by C++ code written against the Carbon framework. A skeleton class is provided for creating the parameter view.

▶ **Audio Unit Effect with Cocoa View**. The same, but the parameter view is specified by a Cocoa NIB. Objective-C source files are provided for loading the NIB and running the human interface.

▶ **Audio Unit Instrument**. Creates an audio unit that accepts MIDI input and outputs the corresponding audio.

## Bundle

Bundles, in this context, are package directories that serve as plug-ins to applications or frameworks. They include a dynamic library and a `Resources` directory. These project templates are distinguished by the frameworks they link against, which is in turn determined by the needs of the entities that use the plug-ins:

▶ **Carbon Bundle**. The project is set up for C code, linked against the Carbon framework.

▶ **CFPlugIn Bundle**. The project is set up for C code, linked against the Core Foundation framework. The product complies with the CFPlugIn standard, so the `Info.plist` file contains the necessary keys; you will have to hand edit values for these, including UUIDs.

▶ **Cocoa Bundle**. The project is set up for Objective-C code, linked against the Cocoa framework.

▶ **Generic C++ Plugin**. The project is set up for C++ code, exposed to the plug-in client as C entry points.

## Command-Line Utility

These projects produce single executable files, such as you would execute from the UNIX command line; there is no package directory associated with them. All include a main source file, and a template for a `man` page:

▶ **C++ Tool**. The tool is built from C++ code, using only the standard C++ and BSD libraries.

▶ **CoreFoundation Tool**. The tool is built from C code, and linked against the Core Foundation framework, which provides data-type and communications services similar to Cocoa's Foundation framework.

▶ **CoreServices Tool**. The tool is built from C code, linked against the Core Services framework. This would enable the tool to make use of system services such as Apple Events, Spotlight services, and other Carbon functions that do not require access to a graphical human interface.

▶ **Foundation Tool**. The tool is built from Objective-C code, linked against the Foundation portion of the Cocoa framework. Foundation provides classes that handle data such as strings and arrays, and does not need access to a graphical human interface.

▶ **Standard Tool**. The tool is built from C code, using only the standard C and BSD libraries.

## Dynamic Library

A dynamic library is a collection of functions, methods, and data in a `.dylib` file, which is introduced into a program at the time the program is run. These projects are distinguished by the libraries they are linked against:

▶ **BSD Dynamic Library**. Produces a dynamic library that relies only on the standard C and BSD libraries. This project comes with no dummy source files; you have to add the library source files yourself.

- ▶ **C++ Dynamic Library**. Produces a dynamic library based on C++ source code and the Carbon framework. Starter code is provided, with a public class implementing the library's interface API, and a private one to implement the possibly changing underlying implementation.

- ▶ **C++ Standard Dynamic Library**. The same, but the project is set up for a more standards-compliant C++, and hides all symbols in the executable except those you explicitly make visible.

- ▶ **Carbon Dynamic Library**. Produces a dynamic library written in C, linked against the Carbon framework.

- ▶ **Cocoa Dynamic Library**. Produces a dynamic library written in Objective-C, linked against the Cocoa framework.

- ▶ **Ruby Extension**. This project produces a loadable extension for the Ruby scripting language. A main.c file is provided that #includes Ruby.h, and the include and link search paths are set up to search the Ruby headers and libraries.

## External Build System

An External Build System project is one that uses a tool such as make to issue commands to create the product, instead of Xcode's own build system. An example of such a project is shown in Chapter 24, "A Legacy Project." There is one target, and its Info window is like those used by "legacy" targets—because, strictly, it *is* a legacy target. There is no **Rules** tab to associate tools with types of source files (that's the business of your makefile), nor a **Properties** tab for settings associated with Mac OS X packages (see Figure B.2).

Instead, there is a space for naming the product, one for specifying the build tool, and an editable list for environment variables. Build configurations, which associate environment variable lists with configuration names, still exist. Building the target sets the environment variables and runs the build tool.

## Framework

You remember from Chapter 14, "Dynamic Libraries and Frameworks," that a *framework* is a structured directory containing (to oversimplify) a dynamic library, its associated headers, and other optional resources:

- ▶ **Carbon Framework**. This project builds a framework linked against the Carbon framework.

- ▶ **Cocoa Framework**. This project builds a framework linked against the Cocoa framework.

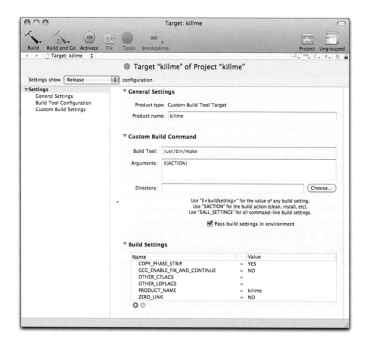

FIGURE B.2    The External Build System target window. This is different from that of Xcode-native targets: There are no tabs, particularly no **Rules** tab for managing what tool handles what part of the build; the makefile (or other build tool) takes care of that.

## Java

All these projects are External Build System projects, filled out with starter files and set up to use the ant build system:

- ▶ **Java Applet**. This project produces a Java applet jar, for display on a web page. The project includes an HTML file for previewing the applet.

- ▶ **Java Application**. This project generates a Java application, with a Swing human interface, wrapped so that it appears as a double-clickable application in the Finder. The apple.* Apple Java extensions are included.

- ▶ **Java JNI Application**. The same, plus a source file for a JNI plug-in written in C. The plug-in is a standalone Mach-O dynamic library built with the Xcode build system, linked against the C and BSD standard libraries.

- ▶ **Java Signed Applet**. The same as the Java Applet project, but the applet is signed. The keytool tool is used to fetch a certificate aliased to your BSD username; if one does not exist, one is created with the password **changeit**. For production use, you'd want to store your organization's certificate and edit the build.xml file to reflect the correct settings. Search the file for keytool and sign jar.

▶ **Java Tool**. Produces a `jar` file suitable for running on the command line with the `java` tool.

▶ **Java Web Start Application**. Produces an application using the Sun Web Start framework, in the form of signed and unsigned `jar` files, a `jnlp` file, and an HTML file.

## Kernel Extension

Kernel extensions (`kexts`) are plug-ins for extending the Mac OS X kernel. Kernel development is far outside the scope of this book; search the Documents window for "kernel programming guide" for full information. Note especially the sections "Keep Out" and "Why You Should Avoid Programming in the Kernel."

▶ **Generic Kernel Extension**. This project would yield a `kext` for tasks other than providing an I/O driver. Examples would be support for specific motherboards, graphics cards, and low-level services such as underlie CHUD and Instruments. Because the `kext` would not link against the C++-based IOKit framework, the starter file is in C.

▶ **IOKit Driver**. This produces a `kext` linked against the kernel-level IOKit framework, for handling I/O devices. The provided `Info.plist` file is (sparsely) populated with keys necessary for IOKit. The starter C++ files are empty, without even `#includes`.

## Standard Apple Plug-Ins

The "Standard Apple Plug-Ins" category embraces a large variety of bundles that various Apple applications and services can load and execute:

▶ **Address Book Action Plug-In for C**. Produces a plug-in that performs an action (such as speaking the contents) when Address Book fields are selected or edited. The product is packaged as a `CFBundle` and is written in C linked against the Address Book and Core Foundation frameworks.

▶ **Address Book Action Plug-In for Objective-C**. The same, but written in Objective-C and linked against Cocoa instead of Core Foundation. The necessary methods are sketched out in the source file.

▶ **AppleScript Xcode Plug-In**. Xcode can be extended by installing AppleScript actions to handle, for instance, custom menu commands. Refer to the "Plugin" suite (no hyphen) in Xcode's AppleScript dictionary for examples on how to install your own AppleScript code into Xcode, using the `plugin loaded` event. The provided plug-in script includes a handler for that event. An Objective-C source file for an `ASKPluginObject`, which responds to `pluginDidLoad:`, is included. As with other AppleScript Studio applications, the plug-in AppleScript can take advantage of code in the associated plug-in class.

▸ **Image Unit Plug-In for Objective-C.** Image units are discrete processors for data under the Core Image framework. The bundle is fairly complex, and the project includes starter files for the loader and the filter proper, for the description and user-visible documentation, and for OpenGL kernel code used by the filter. The executable code is written in Objective-C linked against Application Services, Quartz Core, Foundation, and Core Foundation.

▸ **Installer Plugin.** Creates a plug-in for use in an `Installer.app` package that adds a Cocoa panel to the installation process. The sample code provided in the Objective-C file is a bit scant; see `Installer.h` for details.

▸ **Interface Builder 3.x Plugin.** Interface Builder 3.0 introduces a new plug-in architecture that makes extending IB to edit additional classes easier than had been the case in the past. The project is set up for specifying the human interface for both the inspector pane and the representation in the library. Separate targets build the view to be edited and the IB editors; an aggregate target builds both and packages them into an extension bundle.

▸ **PreferencePane.** This project encompasses the NIB and code for writing an additional pane for the System Preferences application. It's written in Objective-C and linked against the Cocoa and Preference Panes frameworks.

▸ **Quartz Composer Plug-In.** This project yields a plug-in bundle for Quartz Composer to use as a "patch," a component in a QC data flow. It is programmed in Objective-C, and the starter code provides all the necessary entry points.

▸ **Quartz Composer Plug-In with Internal Settings and User Interface.** The same, plus a NIB and code to provide a custom configuration interface for the resulting patch.

▸ **Quick Look Plug-In.** The product is a Core Foundation plug-in that generates thumbnail icons and full-size previews for documents, for the use of the Quick Look feature of the Leopard Finder. The starter files include C files for the works of the plug-in, populated with the entry points Quick Look requires, and an `Info.plist` that provides the Finder with the metadata specific to the plug-in.

▸ **Screen Saver.** The product is a Cocoa bundle that runs a screen saver. All the necessary methods appear in the provided Objective-C source file. If you need to add a configuration window for use in the System Preferences application, you have to add your own NIB.

▸ **Spotlight Plug-In.** This project produces a Core Foundation plug-in that the metadata importer system can use to parse files into metadata that can be searched in Spotlight. The starter source file includes extensive comments leading you through the process of writing an importer.

▸ **Sync Schema.** The plug-in product extends Apple's Sync Services to handle additional types of data to be synchronized through Apple's ".Mac" online service. It is programmed in Objective-C linked against Cocoa's Foundation framework. The `Schema.plist` file is edited to show reasonable starting values for your schema.

▶ **WebKit Plug-In**. The simple way to think of a WebKit plug-in is as an extension to the Safari browser for viewing additional kinds of content, just like an extension for any other kind of browser. However, you can use the WebKit framework to add web rendering to your applications or Dashboard widgets; so, WebKit plug-ins can also be thought of as a part of your applications. The template begins with Objective-C source for an NSView subclass, with stubs for the methods you must implement.

## Static Library

A static library is an archive of object files; it has a name of the form lib*Name*.a. Linking an application against a static library incorporates the contents of the library into the application binary.

These project templates do not provide any starter files for the library code. This is not a hindrance, because you probably would have the complete code you want to reduce to a library anyway, and a generic library does not have a well-defined set of entry points:

▶ **BSD Static Library**. The product is a static library for use with C code. Only the standard C and BSD libraries, which are linked with every C project, are linked against.

▶ **Carbon Static Library**. The project will be a C library linked against the Carbon and Core Foundation frameworks. It includes a prefix-header file that pulls the Carbon headers in.

▶ **Cocoa Static Library**. The project yields a static library written in Objective-C. It includes a prefix-header file that pulls in the Cocoa framework headers. It links against Cocoa, and includes the AppKit, Foundation, and Core Data frameworks for reference.

# Target Templates

Target templates are instantiated when you select **New Target...** from the **Project** menu. This will present a New Target assistant that will allow you to select from the available templates. After you select one, name it, and select one of the open projects, a new target will be added. The target will be set up to build a product of the desired type from the files that belong to it. It will *not* add any files for the target to your project; you have to do that yourself.

Not every project template has a corresponding target template. You should consider this, and the fact that starter files are included only in new projects, when you first select the type of a new project. When you start out on a multitarget project, be sure to select your most complicated target as the project type so that the template files will do much of the work for you.

The point bears repeating: When you create a new target from a template, you're on your own. The target settings will be correct, and the target will build with a goal of producing the appropriate file or bundle format, but it will not include any files—not even references to appropriate frameworks.

Xcode and the target templates work around the no-included-files restriction in a few ways: For bundled targets, Xcode generates an `Info.plist` file from settings in the target template. When a target is to be built against a particular framework, the framework's root header (for example, `<Carbon/Carbon.h>`) is used as a prefix header, and the framework itself is supplied in a linker flag, instead of being added to the Link Binary with Libraries build phase.

Xcode groups project templates by the desired product type (application, library, command-line utility, and so forth), but target templates are grouped by technology (BSD, Carbon, Cocoa, and so on).

## BSD

These targets are intended to be linked only against the standard C and BSD libraries. Because `gcc` links those libraries automatically, all you have to do is add your source files. Your source must, of course, `#include` the header files you need, and if you use other libraries, you must seek them out and add them to the target:

▶ **Dynamic Library.** Produces a `.dylib` library from the member files. All BSD library targets will, if the installation phase were run, be installed at `/usr/local/lib`. The library name will have `lib` prefixed to it.

▶ **Object File.** Produces a `.o` object file from a single source file.

▶ **Shell Tool.** Produces a straight command-line utility. If installed, it would go to `/usr/local/bin`, but it would run wherever it is.

▶ **Static Library.** Produces a multiobject library archive named `libTargetName.a`.

## Carbon

These targets all link against the Carbon framework and use the root Carbon header as the prefix header. Because target templates cannot do these things by creating files or making references to existing files, the targets use compiler and linker switches to effect the same goal:

▶ **Application.** Builds an application package linked against the Carbon framework.

▶ **Dynamic Library.** Builds a dynamic library (`libTargetName.dylib`) linked against the Carbon framework.

▶ **Framework.** Builds a framework bundle centered on a dynamic library linked against the Carbon framework.

▶ **Loadable Bundle**. Builds a plug-in bundle centered on a dynamic library linked against the Carbon framework. The bundle's extension is `bundle`; change the `WRAPPER_EXTENSION` setting if you need something different. If you're looking to build a unit-test bundle for `CPlusTest`, see Unit Test Bundle, below.

▶ **Object File**. Produces a `.o` object file from a single source file, linked against the Carbon framework.

▶ **Resource File**. Builds a Carbon Resource Manager resource file (typically `.rsrc`) from Rez source. You might use the Rez file to integrate the products of other targets into a single resource file.

▶ **Shell Tool**. Produces a straight command-line utility linked against the Carbon framework.

▶ **Static Library**. Produces a multiobject library archive named `libTargetName.a` linked against the Carbon framework.

▶ **Unit Test Bundle**. Produces a `CPlusTest` unit-test bundle linked against Carbon and `CPlusTest`. The bundle will have the extension `cptest`. It includes a shell-script build phase that runs the tests; build this target and your testing is done.

## Cocoa

Likewise, these targets link against Cocoa. They use `Cocoa/Cocoa.h` as the prefix header:

▶ **Application**. Builds an application package linked against the Cocoa framework. There is no template for building document- or Core Data-based applications; you'll have to add the necessary features yourself.

▶ **Dynamic Library**. Builds a dynamic library (`libTargetName.dylib`) linked against the Cocoa framework.

▶ **Framework**. Builds a framework bundle centered on a dynamic library linked against the Cocoa framework.

▶ **Loadable Bundle**. Builds a plug-in bundle centered on a dynamic library linked against the Cocoa framework. The bundle's extension is `bundle`; change the `WRAPPER_EXTENSION` setting if you need something different. If you're looking to build a unit-test bundle for OCTest, see Unit Test Bundle, below.

▶ **Object File**. Produces a `.o` object file from a single source file linked against the Cocoa framework.

▶ **Shell Tool**. Produces a straight command-line utility linked against the Cocoa framework.

▶ **Static Library**. Produces a multiobject library archive named `libTargetName.a` linked against the Cocoa framework.

▶ **Unit Test Bundle**. Produces an OCTest unit-test bundle linked against Cocoa and SenTestingKit. The bundle will have the extension `octest`. It includes a shell-script build phase that runs the tests; build this target and your testing is done. See Chapter 12, "Unit Testing," for more details.

## Java

These targets use the Xcode legacy build system, which provided its own workflow for Java, based on its internal `jam`, rather than the `ant` tool used to build targets in the Java project templates. Because a target template cannot include a file, there is no way to provide a `build.xml`, and no way to support `ant`:

▶ **Applet**. This target produces a Java applet in the form of a standalone `jar` file.

▶ **Application**. The target yields a double-clickable application bundle, built around a `jar` file produced by the Java source you add to the target.

▶ **Package**. Produces a `jar` file encompassing your compiled Java source, to serve as a library.

▶ **Tool**. Produces a `jar` file that can be run from the command line by invoking the `java` command.

## Kernel Extension

Two targets are available for building kernel extensions (`kexts`), one for general-purpose extensions, and one using the IOKit framework for device drivers:

▶ **Generic Kernel Extension**. The product is a kernel extension (`kext`) bundle that does not make use of the IOKit kernel framework. It is set up to specify *targetName*_start and *targetName*_stop as the extension start and stop entry points.

▶ **IOKit Driver**. The target produces a `kext` bundle intended to link against the C++ IOKit kernel framework. You have to add a reference to `/System/Library/Frameworks/Kernel.framework` yourself.

## Ruby

There's one target in this group, Unit Test Target, for testing Ruby applications. It consists of a shell script that runs unit test scripts, against the `tests/unit` module, for a Ruby program. Edit the Run Script build phase to list the Ruby source files for the tests. You add this target to a Ruby project, and build it whenever you need to test.

## Special Targets

Special targets do not involve building an executable at all. They add actions, such as copying files or directories, building other targets, or executing a script, that are useful in completing the ultimate product of a project:

▶ **Aggregate**. The only thing this target does is make sure other targets in the project are built. Add the targets you mean to aggregate as dependencies of the aggregate target. Building the aggregate builds all the others.

▶ **Copy Files Target**. This target performs much the same function as a Copy Files build phase, but can work among the products of other targets in the project.

▶ **External Target**. This target performs a build directed by an external build tool such as make or ant.

▶ **Shell Script Target**. The only thing this target does when it is built is to execute a shell script. Find the target in the Targets group in the Groups & Files list, and open it to reveal the Run Script build phase; double-click that phase to reveal a Get Info window. Under the **General** tab, there will be an editor in which you can enter your script. See Chapter 21, "Xcode for make Veterans," for information about Run Script phases.

# Legacy Targets

It's tempting not to cover these, but they're in the New Target Assistant. These targets are built using the jam build system embedded in Xcode 3's predecessors back to Project Builder. There is no reason to use these except for compatibility with very old projects. These templates are beginning to show signs of neglect, and it wouldn't be strange if Apple dropped support for them in a version of Xcode later than 3.0.

The settings for new legacy targets conform to modern practice: The selected compiler, for instance, is set to gcc 4.0, and the target generates DWARF debugging symbols. Also, legacy targets can take advantage of build configurations. Legacy targets do *not* import build settings from the project level:

▶ **Application**. This target has the goal of producing an application bundle. It is not aimed particularly at Cocoa or Carbon.

▶ **Bundle**. The target builds a directory bundle.

▶ **Framework**. The target produces a framework bundle linked against only the standard C and BSD libraries.

▶ **Library**. The target is configured to produce a static (lib*.a) library.

## Cocoa

This subcategory has only one target: Application. The intention is that the target will produce an application bundle linked against the Cocoa framework. However, the build settings (including linker instructions) are no different from the plain Legacy Application target.

## Java

These templates are for Java targets:

▶ **Applet**. This is identical to the nonlegacy Java Applet target, described previously.

▶ **Application**. This is identical to the nonlegacy Java Application target, described previously.

▶ **Package**. This is identical to the nonlegacy Java Package target, described previously.

▶ **Tool**. This is identical to the nonlegacy Java Tool target, described previously.

## Kernel Extension

▶ **Generic Kernel Extension**. This target produces a non-IOKit kernel extension. Unlike the nonlegacy Kernel Extension target, this target has Run Script build phases to pre- and post-process the kext. Unfortunately, the tools involved no longer exist.

▶ **IOKit Driver**. This target produces a kernel extension set up for use with the IOKit C++ kernel framework. Like the legacy Generic Kernel Extension, it relies on Run Script tools that no longer exist.

# APPENDIX C

# Other Resources

I've tried to make this book thorough, but it isn't comprehensive. Xcode is too large and subtle a system to cover completely here, and Apple constantly updates it. Further, your needs as a Mac programmer go beyond simply using the tools. This appendix is a brief reference to resources you can use to go further and keep current.

## Books

- ▶ **Step into Xcode: Mac OS X Development** (by Fritz Anderson; Addison-Wesley, 2006). This is the first edition of the book you are now reading. It is still useful if you are using some version of Xcode 2.

- ▶ **Beginning Xcode (Programmer to Programmer)** (by James Bucanek; Wrox, 2006). A fine book that covers Xcode 2.

- ▶ **Cocoa Design Patterns** (by Eric M. Buck; Addison-Wesley, 2008). Erik has many years' insight into Cocoa, and this book has been much anticipated.

- ▶ **The Mac Xcode 3 Book** (by Michael Cohen and Dennis Cohen; Wiley, 2008).

- ▶ **Version Control with Subversion**, also known as *The Subversion Book* (by Ben Collins-Sussman, Brian Fitzpatrick, and C. Michael Pilato). Revised periodically and available at http://svnbook.red-bean.com/.

- ▶ **Advanced Mac OS X Programming** (by Mark Dalrymple and Aaron Hillegass; Nerd Ranch, 2005). This is the companion to Aaron Hillegass's classic *Cocoa Programming for Mac OS X*.

▶ *Objective-C Pocket Reference* (by Andrew Duncan; O'Reilly, 2002). This reference guide goes back a few years, but use it for the essentials of Objective-C (except for Obj-C 2.0), and you won't go far wrong.

▶ *Cocoa Programming for Mac OS X, Third Edition* (by Aaron Hillegass; Addison-Wesley, 2008). Probably most Cocoa programmers today started with Aaron's outstanding book. His Mac OS X and UNIX training company, Big Nerd Ranch, can be found at http://bignerdranch.com.

▶ *Beginning Mac OS X Programming* (by Michael Trent and Drew McCormack; Wrox, 2005).

# From the Xcode Documentation Window

Xcode changes, and Apple keeps up with the changes in the documentation sets it supplies. The Documentation window is your best source for reference material.

These documents can be found in the Apple-supplied list of bookmarks in Xcode's Documentation window, or by doing a full-text search for their titles. Release notes are particularly important because they cover developments that might not have gotten into the main documentation.

▶ *Xcode 3.0 Release Notes*

▶ *Interface Builder 3.0 Release Notes*

▶ *Instruments User Guide*

▶ *Xcode User Default Reference*

And, of course, there is the *Xcode User Guide*, available as the first item in the Xcode **Help** menu.

Not in the Documentation window, but essential, is *Shark User Guide* at `/Developer/Documentation/Shark/Shark User Guide.pdf` (or select **Help > Shark Help** while in Shark).

# On the Net

## Mailing Lists

Apple hosts dozens of lists on all aspects of developing for Mac OS X. You can find the full roster at http://www.lists.apple.com/mailman/listinfo. Remember that like all technical mailing lists, these are restricted to questions and solutions for specific problems. Apple engineers read these lists in their spare time, and they are not required to answer postings; they cannot accept bug reports or feature requests. Take these to http://bugreport.apple.com/.

These four lists will probably be the most help to you:

▶ **xcode-users** covers Xcode and the other Apple developer tools (except Shark and the CHUD tools, which are the province of the perfoptimization-dev list).

http://www.lists.apple.com/mailman/listinfo/xcode-users/

▶ **cocoa-dev** is for questions about the Cocoa frameworks.

http://www.lists.apple.com/mailman/listinfo/cocoa-dev/

▶ **carbon-dev** handles questions about the Carbon framework.

http://www.lists.apple.com/mailman/listinfo/carbon-dev/

▶ **macosx-dev** is a list hosted by the Omni Group (makers of OmniWeb, OmniOutliner, and OmniGraffle) to support Mac OS X development, regardless of technology. It is fully as useful as the Apple lists.

http://www.omnigroup.com/mailman/listinfo/macosx-dev

## Usenet

If you prefer working through Usenet, you'll want to subscribe to the comp.sys.mac. programmer groups, particularly the following:

```
comp.sys.mac.programmer
comp.sys.mac.programmer.help
comp.sys.mac.programmer.misc
comp.lang.objective-c
```

These are moderate-traffic groups, with some good people following them.

## Sites and Logs

▶ The first place on the Web to go is http://developer.apple.com/, the site for the Apple Developer Connection. It has everything you'll find in Xcode documentation packages, plus more articles, downloadable examples, business resources, and screen-casts. One strategy for getting official information from Apple is to do a Google search restricted to site:developer.apple.com.

▶ If you find a bug in Apple software, or need a feature, go to http://bugreport. apple.com. (You'll need an ADC membership, but you got one of those at the beginning of this book, right?) Be sure to file a complete report (Apple has guidelines for you), and if you're looking for a new feature, be sure to make a concrete case for how it will improve your product or workflow. http://developer.apple.com/faq/bugreporting.html will bring you up-to-speed on the details.

▶ http://www.cocoabuilder.com/. The lists.apple.com website carries archives of all Apple mailing lists, but for xcode-users, cocoa-dev, and Omni Group's macosx-dev, CocoaBuilder is the way to go. One crucial advantage is that it can sort search results by date or relevancy; the Apple site can't.

▶ http://cocoadevcentral.com/ is an indispensable reference for tutorials and web logs on Cocoa programming.

▶ http://www.cocoadev.com/ is a wiki encompassing tutorials, references, and links to communities.

▶ http://www.friday.com/bbum/category/science/technology/apple/mac-os-x/ is the Mac OS X portion of Apple engineer Bill Bumgarner's blog, providing accessible insights on Apple technologies, especially Objective-C.

▶ Dave Dribin has an information-packed and frequently updated blog at http://www.dribin.org/dave/blog/.

▶ Jonathan Rentzsch's Red Shed blog, http://rentzsch.com/topics/, covers all aspects of coding (and being a coder) on Mac OS X. Wolf pioneered code injection into Mac processes, and authored the definitive screencast on how to embed application frameworks.

▶ http://www.wilshipley.com/blog/labels/code.html is the coding portion of Wil Shipley's web log. You should especially read his "Pimp My Code" series, critical reviews of coding practices based on a deep knowledge of Cocoa design.

▶ Scott Stevenson's active blog on Mac development can be found at http://theocacao.com/.

▶ Finally, to follow Cocoa-related activity throughout the Web, check out CocoaCheerleaders, an aggregator for websites, blogs, podcasts, mailing lists, sample code, and even books. http://www.cocoacheerleaders.com/.

# Face to Face

▶ **CocoaHeads**, http://cocoaheads.org/, is an international user group for Cocoa programmers. They meet every month in more than 20 cities worldwide.

▶ **NSCoder Night**, http://nscodernight.com/, is a less-formal user group, where Cocoa programmers gather as often as weekly in bars and coffee shops to share experiences and code. The site mentions meetings in 11 cities around the world, and organizing one of your own should be easy.

# Text Editors

As I've said already, no one editor (including Xcode) is best for every purpose. A committed Mac programmer will probably use one or more of these editors, too:

▶ **BBEdit**, from Bare Bones Software, is particularly good with very large files and HTML.

http://www.barebones.com/products/bbedit/

▶ **emacs** and **vi** are supplied with every standard installation of Mac OS X. If you have any background in the UNIX command line, you probably know how to use one of these, and have nothing but contempt for the other.

▶ **SubEthaEdit** is a clean editor that permits workgroups to work on a file simultaneously, with all participants able to contribute and see each others' changes in real time. Syntax coloring is available for all commonly-used languages.

http://www.codingmonkeys.de/

▶ **TextMate**, from MacroMates, is a text editor with a huge capacity for automation and customization.  Syntax coloring and powerful keyboard shortcuts are available for dozens of languages and applications.

http://macromates.com/

▶ Bare Bones provides an extremely capable "light" version of BBEdit, **TextWrangler**, free of charge.

http://www.barebones.com/products/textwrangler/

# Tools

There are many supplemental tools available to Mac OS X programmers. I've found two of them particularly useful.

▶ **AppKiDo**, by Andy Lee, provides a concise listing of classes and methods in Cocoa and other Apple frameworks. As a reference, it is much handier than Xcode's Documentation window or the Class Browser. It works by parsing Apple's docsets, and their evolution has been a challenge, but a new version that keeps up with them will be out soon.

http://homepage.mac.com/aglee/downloads/appkido.html

▶ **Accessorizer**, by Kevin Callahan, addresses the drudgery of writing accessor methods and other property-related code. Memory management and Core Data notification require housekeeping code that is easy to get wrong. Pass Accessorizer the names and types of your properties (it can parse class declarations), and it will return correct code to access them. It even handles the devilishly-subtle collection accessors.

A version that handles all the details of Objective-C 2.0 accessors is due out shortly. Accessorizer is paid software, but worth it.

http://www.kevincallahan.org/software/accessorizer.html

# Index

## Symbols

^D (end-of-file character), 34
#pragma mark lines, 57
%%%{PBX}%%% substitution markers,
  227-228
64-bit applications, 274
64-bit architectures, builds for, 363

## A

accessors
  for attributes, 56
  automatically generating, 50
  redesigning data model, 250-251
ACTION build variable, 478
Action menu (trace document window), 445
action methods, 85
Action template, 486-487
actions
  defined, 76, 486
  outlets and, 84-85
Activate button (Debugger window), 31
active targets, 141, 148
Activity Monitor instrument, 454, 459
ADC (Apple Developer Connection), 3, 503
Address Book Action Plug-In for C project,
  493
Address Book Action Plug-In for Objective-C
  project, 493
*Advanced Mac OS X Programming*
  (Dalrymple and Hillegass), 501
Aggregate target, 499
all-in-one layout for projects, 350-351
allocation calls, checking for memory leaks,
  318-319
AllowFullAccess key, 164
AllowInternetPlugins key, 164
AllowJava key, 164

AllowNetworkAccess key, 165

AllowSystem key, 165

analysis results, viewing in Shark, 423-425

antecedents. *See* dependencies

API documentation, creating, 238-241

Apple Developer Connection (ADC), 3, 503

AppleGlot glossaries, 313

AppleScript Application project, 487

AppleScript Automator Action project, 486

AppleScript Document-Based Application project, 487

AppleScript Droplet project, 487

AppleScript Xcode Plug-In project, 493

Applet legacy target, 500

Applet target (Java), 498

application bundles, 156-158

    Info.plist file, contents of, 158-165

    installing frameworks in, 217, 219

Application legacy target, 499-500

Application Properties Info window, 88-91

Application target (Carbon), 496

Application target (Cocoa), 497

Application target (Java), 498

Application template, 487-489

applications. *See also* Cocoa applications

    attaching Debugger window to, 376

    changing language preferences, 310

    Info.plist keys for, 160-163

    roles, 91

    running, 31

architectures, testing for multiple, 179-180

archives, unpacking, 404-405

archiving custom views, 185

ARCHS build variable, 481

Arguments tab (Executable Info window), 388

arranged objects, 84

arrows, 69

    in file-comparison window, 108

ASCII property lists, 132-133

assembly code, 40

assigning files to framework targets, 205-210

associated breakpoints, 376

associating

    data files with Cocoa applications, 88-91

    file types with text editors, 468-469

    files with directories, troubleshooting, 113-114

    NIB files with projects, 183

    projects with repository, 104

    UTIs with data files, 284

ATSApplicationFontsPath key, 163

attaching Debugger window to applications, 376

attributes

    accessor methods for, 56

    in data model files, setting, 247

Attributes Inspector, 82

Audio Unit Effect project, 489

Audio Unit Effect with Carbon View project, 489

Audio Unit Effect with Cocoa View project, 489

Audio Unit Instrument project, 489

Audio Units template, 489

auto-complete in Code Sense, 125

auto-properties, enabling in Subversion, 98

automating docset build process, 233-235

Autosizing section (Size inspector), 69

## B

background tasks, viewing, 332

backward compatibility. *See* cross-development

base version of files, latest version versus, 108

BBEdit, 128, 133, 505

*Beginning Mac OS X Programming* (Trent and McCormack), 502

*Beginning Xcode (Programmer to Programmer)* (Bucanek), 501

BigTop, 432

binaries, universal, 274-276

    creating in example build transcript, 365

    Intel-porting issues in Linear example, 276

    testing, 276-277

binary format (Core Data), 256
binary property lists, 133
bindings, 78
    advantages of, 81
    creating, 80-82
    in Interface Builder for created
        entities, 263
    value binding, 82-83
Bindings Inspector, 80-82
Blank template (Instruments
    application), 459
blocks
    checking for memory leaks, 317-318
    visualization of, 335-336
blogs for additional information, 504
blue guidelines in Interface Builder, 66
books for additional information, 501-502
Boolean text searches in
    documentation, 471
bottom-up view (Shark analysis results),
    423-424
branches directory, 100
branching (in version control), 243-245
breakpoint commands, 381-383
breakpoint conditions, 383-384
breakpoints
    associated breakpoints, 376
    enabling/disabling, 30, 390-391
    grouping, 376
    lazy symbol loading and, 384-385
    removing orphan, 376
    setting, 30-31, 373-374
Breakpoints button (Debugger window), 32
Breakpoints menu (Debugger window), 32
Breakpoints window, 32, 382
    setting breakpoints, 373-374
broken links, Interface Builder and, 461-462
browsing, enabling in Documentation
    window,
    235-237
BSD Dynamic Library project, 490
BSD Static Library project, 495
BSD target template, 496
bug reports, Web site for, 503

Build and Go button (Debugger window), 31
build configurations, 92, 368-370
    configuration files for, 370
    Debug versus Release, 275
    Release build configuration, 323-325
    stripping and, 325
    targets versus, 92
build dependencies, 403. *See also*
    dependencies
build directory, setting preferences for
    single, 465
build errors, 23-26
Build Java Resources build phase, 343
build phases
    adding to targets, 342
    in example build transcript, 360-364
    files in, 354
    list of, 342-343
    Run Script build phase, 357-358
    for targets, 41
build process
    distributed builds, 397-399
    for docsets, automating, 233-235
Build Resource Manager Resources build
    phase, 343
Build Results window, 23-24, 176, 349, 359
build rules, creating custom, 356-357
build sets, defined, 398
build settings, viewing list of, 466
build system. *See also* build configurations;
    build variables; cross-development;
    example build
transcript
    build settings, viewing list of, 466
    custom build rules, creating, 356-357
    explained, 353-355
    Run Script build phase, 357-358
    settings hierarchy, 366-368
    xcodebuild tool, 365-366
Build tab (Target Info window), 177
build targets, list of, 478-479
build transcript, 24. *See also* example build
    transcript

build variables, 355-356
    build targets, list of, 478-479
    bundle locations, list of, 480
    compiler settings, list of, 481-482
    deployment variables, list of, 482-483
    destination locations, list of, 479-480
    environment variables, list of, 477-478
    Run Script build phase and, 358
    search paths, list of, 482
    source locations, list of, 479
    source trees, 483
    viewing, 475-476
building. See also build process; build
  system; external build system projects
    Core Data data files, 258-259
    interfaces for created entities, 260,
        262-264
    projects
        cleaning before, 219
        in Organizer window, 409-411
        saving first, 23
    sample application, 91
    targets, 15
        cleaning before, 268
built-in accessors, 50
BUILT_PRODUCTS_DIR build variable, 479
Bumgarner, Bill, 504
Bundle legacy target, 499
bundle locations, list of, 480
Bundle template, 489
bundles, 156, 168. See also application
  bundles; packages
    Copy Bundle Resources build phase in
        example build transcript, 361
    defined, 62
    docsets as, 230
    load-path references in, 218
    types of, 156
buttons
    adding to application windows, 66-67
    connecting to NIB files, 84-85
    in Debugger window, 31-32

C

C++ Dynamic Library project, 491
C++ Standard Dynamic Library project, 491
C++ Tool project, 490
calculating linear regression, 20-22
call trees, filtering, 444
call-tree view
    Leaks instrument, 318-319
    ObjectAlloc instrument, 320
callstack data mining in Shark, 425-427
Carbon Application project, 487
Carbon Bundle project, 490
Carbon C++ Application project, 487
Carbon C++ Standard Application
    project, 487
Carbon Dynamic Library project, 491
Carbon Events instrument, 455
Carbon Framework project, 491
Carbon Static Library project, 495
Carbon target template, 496-497
carbon-dev mailing list, 503
case sensitivity of filenames, 462
categories
    adding to classes, 118-121
    naming conventions, 122
CFAppleHelpAnchor key, 160
CFBundleAllowMixedLocalizations key, 162
CFBundleDevelopmentRegion key, 159
CFBundleDisplayName key, 161, 308
CFBundleDocumentTypes key, 160
CFBundleExecutable key, 160
CFBundleGetInfoString key, 159
CFBundleHelpBookFolder key, 161
CFBundleHelpBookName key, 161
CFBundleIconFile key, 159
CFBundleIdentifier key, 159
CFBundleInfoDictionaryVersion key, 159
CFBundleLocalizations key, 163
CFBundleName key, 161
CFBundlePackageType key, 159
CFBundleShortVersionString key, 159
CFBundleSignature key, 159
CFBundleURLTypes key, 160

CFBundleVersion key, 159

CFPlugIn Bundle project, 490

CFPlugInDynamicRegisterFunction key, 163

CFPlugInDynamicRegistration key, 163

CFPlugInFactories key, 163

CFPlugInTypes key, 163

CFPlugInUnloadFunction key, 163

CFZombieLevel environment variable, 389

checking out working copies of projects, 103-104

CHUDRemover, 436

Class Actions section (Identity Inspector), 76

Class Browser window, 345-346

class modeler tool, 346-348

classes

    adding categories to, 118-121

    custom classes, adding to NIB files, 76

    document classes, 91

    initialize method, 191

    principal class for applications, 90

    test classes, creating, 168

    view classes, adding, 183

cleaning

    projects, 219

    targets before building, 268

clearing debugging log, 374

CloseboxInsetX key, 164

CloseboxInsetY key, 164

Cocoa Application project, 487

Cocoa applications

    associating data files with, 88-91

    converting to Objective-C 2.0, 172-173

    embedding tools in, 52-54

    MVC design pattern, 48, 54-62

    property list data types, 118

    sample application

        building, 91

        controller object, 51, 75-92

        model object, 48-50

        tasks of, 47

        view object, 51, 63-73

    starting new projects, 52

Cocoa Automator Action project, 486

Cocoa Bundler project, 490

*Cocoa Design Patterns* (Buck), 501

Cocoa Document-Based Application project, 487

Cocoa Dynamic Library project, 491

Cocoa Events instrument, 455

Cocoa Framework project, 491

Cocoa legacy target, 500

*Cocoa Programming for Mac OS X, Third Edition* (Hillegass), 502

Cocoa Simulator, 69

Cocoa Static Library project, 495

Cocoa target template, 497-498

cocoa-dev mailing list, 503

Cocoa-Python Application project, 488

Cocoa-Python Core Data Application project, 488

Cocoa-Python Core Data Document-Based Application project, 488

Cocoa-Python Document-Based Application project, 488

Cocoa-Ruby Application project, 488

Cocoa-Ruby Core Data Application project, 488

Cocoa-Ruby Core Data Document-Based Application project, 488

Cocoa-Ruby Document-Based Application project, 488

CocoaBuilder Web site, 504

CocoaCheerleaders Web site, 504

CocoaDev wiki, 504

CocoaDevCentral Web site, 504

CocoaHeads Web site, 504

code completion, 332-333

Code Focus, 335-336

Code Sense, 240, 332-333

    auto-complete in, 125

    class modeling and, 347

    in external build system projects, 416-417

code. *See* source code

CodeWarrior targets, 12

colors, configuring from property lists, 189-192

columns, adding to Groups & Files list, 103

command-line terminal. *See* Terminal application

command-line tools
  creating as projects, 14
  linear regression, 22-23
    debugging mode setup, 25-26
    illegal operations in, 29-30

Command-Line Utility template, 490

commands
  breakpoint commands, 381-383
  from human interface, responding to, 51

committing project files in version control, 110

comparing project files in version control, 107

compatibility. *See* cross-development

Compile AppleScripts build phase, 342

Compile Sources build phase, 41, 342, 361-364

compiled code, order of operations in, 41

compiler settings, list of, 481-482

compilers, defined, 39

compiling
  data models in example build transcript, 364
  projects
    distributed builds, 397-399
    precompiled headers, 395-396
    predictive compilation, 396
  source code, 39-41
  XIB files in example build transcript, 360

completion prefixes, 139

Concurrent Versions System (CVS), 94, 104

condensed layout for projects, 351-352

conditions, breakpoint, 383-384

CONFIGURATION build variable, 478

configuration directories
  creating, 96
  editing, 96-98

configuration files for build settings, 370

configurations. *See* build configurations

configuring
  colors from property lists, 189-192
  Groups & Files list, 345

instruments, 446-447
projects in Organizer window, 409-411

conflict markers, 110

conflict resolution in version control, 110-113

connecting
  buttons to NIB files, 84-85
  outlets and objects, 184-187

Console button (Debugger window), 32

Console window, 32, 349-350
  clearing debugging log, 374
  opening, 15
  writing standard error stream to, 377-379

content type in metadata listings, 283-284

Contents directory (application bundles), elements in, 156-158

contents
  of Info.plist file, viewing, 158-165
  of repository, viewing, 103

CONTENTS_FOLDER_PATH build variable, 480

Continue button (Debugger window), 32

controller classes, editing for data modeling, 256-258

controller objects (MVC design pattern) for sample application, 48, 51, 75-83, 85-92

Controller phase (MVC design pattern)
  creating custom views, 181-183
  writing property lists, 125-126

controllers
  adding to NIB files, 77-79
  arranged objects, 84
  creating bindings, 80-82
  linking outlets, 79-80
  source code for sample application, 85-88

converting
  Cocoa projects to Objective-C 2.0, 172-173
  units of measurement, 200

Copy Bundle Resources build phase, 54, 342, 361

Copy Files build phase, 342

Copy Files Target Description target, 499

Copy Headers build phase, 342

copying
  files to docsets, 231-233

structural files in example build
transcript, 359-360
**copyright notice**
correcting in gatherheaderdoc utility,
224-225
setting default content for, 56
**Core Data, 243**. *See also* **data modeling**
building/running data files, 258-259
compiling data models in example build
transcript, 364
data model files
creating, 245-247
editing, 247
redesigning, 247-256
embedding metadata in, 291, 294-297
entities, creating, 259-266
instruments, list of, 450
object storage formats, 256
relationships, creating, 260
storage types, 91
**Core Data Application project, 488**
**Core Data Cache Misses instrument, 450**
**Core Data Document-Based Application
project, 489**
**Core Data Document-Based Application with
Spotlight Importer project, 489**
**Core Data Faults instrument, 450**
**Core Data Fetches instrument, 450**
**Core Data Saves instrument, 450**
**Core Data template (Instruments
application), 459**
**Core Foundation**
property list data types, 118
zombies and, 389
**CoreFoundation Tool project, 490**
**CoreServices Tool project, 490**
**correlation coefficient, 20**
**CPU Monitor instrument, 455**
**CPU Sampler template (Instruments
application), 459**
**creator codes, 89**
**Credits.rtf file, localization, 304-305**

**cross-development**
with multiple SDKs, 277-279
NIB compatibility, 271-273
SDKs for, 267-270
universal binaries, 274-277
weak linking, 271
Xcode version compatibility, 279
**CSResourcesFileMapped key, 160**
**custom build rules, creating, 356-357**
**custom classes, adding to NIB files, 76**
**custom executables, creating, 417**
**custom instruments, 456-457**
**custom metadata keys, declaring, 288-290**
**custom views**
creating
configuring colors from property lists,
189-192
Controller phase (MVC design
pattern), 181-183
delegate objects, usage of, 187-189
displaying window for, 196
drawing the view, 192-195
View phase (MVC design pattern),
183-187
debugging, 198-201
testing, 196-198
unarchiving, 185
**CVS (Concurrent Versions System), 94**
revision numbers, incrementing, 104

**D**

**dashboard widgets, Info.plist keys for,
164-165**
**Dashcode.mpkg, 3**
**data design, redesigning in Core Data,
247-256**
accessors, 250-251
DataPoint class, 248-249
initializers, 249-250
MyDocument class, 255-256
Regression class, 251-255

data files, associating
  with Cocoa applications, 88-91
  UTIs with, 284
data formatters, debugging with, 379-381
data mining callstack data in Shark,
  425-427
data model files
  compiling in example build
    transcript, 364
  creating, 245-247
  editing, 247
  redesigning, 247-256
    accessors, 250-251
    DataPoint class, 248-249
    initializers, 249-250
    MyDocument class, 255-256
    Regression class, 251-255
data modeling. See also Core Data
  building/running data files, 258-259
  data model files
    compiling in example build
      transcript, 364
    creating, 245-247
    editing, 247
    redesigning, 247-256
  entities, creating, 259-266
  Interface Builder, editing controller
    classes, 256-258
  relationships, creating, 260
data points, adding to created entities,
  264-265
data sources
  adding to created entities, 264-265
  viewing for created entities, 265-266
data types in property lists, 117-118
data validation, 302-304
DataPoint class
  redesigning data model, 248-249
  source file, creating, 55-58
datatips, 391-392
Deactivate button (Debugger window), 31
dead code, 325
  stripping, 327-328
Debug build configuration, 368
  Release build configuration versus, 216,
    275, 318

Debug command, 31
debug frameworks, 374
Debugger page (all-in-one layout), 350
debugger strip in editor panes, 336-337
Debugger window, 27-28. See also
  debugging
  associated breakpoints, 376
  attaching to applications, 376
  breakpoints
    grouping, 376
    removing orphan, 376
    setting, 30-31, 373-374
  clearing log, 374
  debug frameworks, 374
  DWARF and STABS formats, 376
  fixing code in, 35-37
  GDB log, 377
  global variables, 375
  in-editor debuggers versus, 392
  KVO (key-value observing), 376
  line-ending styles in, 377
  stepping through code, 33-35
  tail-recursive functions, 377
  toolbar buttons, 31-32
  vertical layout, 373
  watchpoints, setting, 375
debugging. See also Debugger window;
  resources
  additional resources for, 393
  breakpoint commands, 381-383
  breakpoint conditions, 383-384
  custom views, 198-201
  data formatters, 379-381
  datatips, 391-392
  external build system projects, 418
  lazy symbol loading, 384-385
  Mini Debugger window, 389-391
  Quartz Debug, 433-435
  writing standard error stream to Console,
    377-379
  zombies, 385-389
debugging information, system tables
  versus, 326
debugging mode setup for linear regression
  project, 25-26

declaring
  custom metadata keys, 288-290
  UTIs, 284-286
Dedicated Network builds, 397, 399
default content for copyright notice,
  setting, 56
default layout for projects, 349
  Build Results window, 349
  Console window, 349-350
  SCM Results window, 350
default scripts in Organizer window, 413
default window layout, changing, 464
defaults command-line tool, 466
Definition Bundle project, 487
delegate objects in custom views, 187-189
deleting. See removing
dependencies
  adding to projects, 53
  build dependencies, 403
  in makefiles, 353
  in Xcode build system, 354
dependent targets, 148-149
dependent tests, 176-179
deployment postprocessing, 325
deployment targets, setting, 270
deployment variables, list of, 482-483
DEPLOYMENT_POSTPROCESSING build
  variable, 482
DERIVED_FILE_DIR build variable, 480
designable.nib file, 327
designing libraries, 143-146
destination locations, list of, 479-480
detail list, defined, 14
Detail list (ObjectAlloc instrument), 320
Detail pane (trace document window),
  442-444
detail searches, 122
Detail view (Leaks instrument), 317-318
DEVELOPER_APPLICATIONS_DIR environment
  variable, 477
DEVELOPER_BIN_DIR environment
  variable, 477
DEVELOPER_DIR environment variable, 477

DEVELOPER_FRAMEWORKS_DIR
  environment variable, 477
DEVELOPER_LIBRARY_DIR environment
  variable, 477
DEVELOPER_TOOLS_DIR environment
  variable, 477
DEVELOPER_USR_DIR environment
  variable, 477
DEVELOPERSDK_DIR environment
  variable, 477
diagram view (ObjectAlloc instrument), 320
dictionary data type, 117-118
directories. See also bundles; packages
  associating files with, troubleshooting,
    113-114
  for docsets, setting up, 230-231
  framework directory structure, 210-211
  for project products, 52
  renaming in Subversion, 101
Directory I/O instrument, 451
directory structure for Spotlight plug-in
  project, 286
disabling breakpoints, 30, 390-391
discarding file revisions, 109
disclosure triangles
  Option-clicking, 424
  in project window, 15
Disk Monitor instrument, 455
displaying windows for custom views, 196
distccd daemon, 398
distributed builds, 397-399
docsets, 229. See also documentation
  automating build process for, 233-235
  as bundles, 230
  copying files to, 231-233
  directory setup, 230-231
document classes, 91
document file for sample application, 85-88
documentation. See also docsets
  adding hierarchy to, 235-237
  API documentation, creating, 238-241
  Boolean text searches in, 471

creating
  with Doxygen, 221
  with HeaderDoc, 221-225
  with user scripts, 225-229
  HeaderDoc, HTML files generated by, 239
  updating, 470-471
Documentation window, 502
  enabling browsing, 235-237
downloading Xcode 3, 3
Doxygen, 221
drawing
  custom views, 192-195
  flushing graphics after, 199
  to screen, modifying, 433
Dribin, Dave, 504
DTrace, 449, 456-457
DWARF debug information format, 376
dynamic libraries, 43-44. *See also*
  frameworks
    defined, 490
    location of, determining, 215
Dynamic Library target (BSD), 496
Dynamic Library target (Carbon), 496
Dynamic Library target (Cocoa), 497
Dynamic Library template, 490-491
dynamic loading of libraries, 43-44

E

editing
  controller classes for data modeling,
    256-258
  data model files, 247
  menu bars in projects, 301-302
  object properties in Interface Builder, 123
  scripts in Organizer window, 407-409
  search scopes, 338
  .subversion configuration directory,
    96, 98
  target settings, 53
  user scripts, caution about, 228
  windows, effect of resizing on, 71
Editing page (all-in-one layout), 350-351

editor panes, 331-332
  Code Focus, 335-336
  Code Sense in, 332-333
  debugger strip, 336-337
  jumping to symbol definitions, 333-334
  multiple editor windows, 24
  navigation bar, 334-335
  opening, 22
  preference modes, 337-338
emacs text editor, 469, 505
embedding
  metadata in Core Data files, 291,
    294-297
  tools in Cocoa applications, 52-54
Empty Project template, 486
emptying outlets, 186
enabling
  auto-properties in Subversion, 98
  breakpoints, 390-391
  browsing in Documentation window,
    235-237
  tracing, 433
encoding, types of, 312
end-of-file character (^D), 34
entities
  creating, 259-266
  in data modeling, 247
environment variables
  list of, 477-478
  viewing, 358
error bubbles, hiding, 23
error handling, NSAssert( ) macro, 192
error messages, parsing gcc error
  messages, 363
errors, build errors, 23-26
example build transcript, 359
  Compile Sources build phase, 361-364
  compiling data models, 364
  compiling XIB files, 360
  Copy Bundle Resources build phase, 361
  copying structural files, 359-360
  creating universal binaries, 365
  Link Binary with Libraries build phase,
    363-364

Run Script build phase, 360

Touch command, 365

executable files

custom executables, creating, 417

name of, 89

stripping. *See* stripping

Executable Info window, 388

EXECUTABLE_FOLDER_PATH build variable, 480

EXECUTABLE_NAME build variable, 479

EXECUTABLE_PATH build variable, 480

EXECUTABLE_PREFIX build variable, 479

EXECUTABLE_SUFFIX build variable, 479

Executables group, 310, 343-344

expression substitutions, 381

Extended Detail pane (trace document window), 444-445

extensions, 90

external build system projects, 413-416

Code Sense in, 416-417

debugging, 418

limitations of, 418-419

running, 417-418

External Build System template, 491-492

External Target target, 499

F

fast iteration in Objective-C 2.0, 173

faults, 450

favorites bar, 339

feature requests, Web site for, 503

File Activity instrument, 451, 459

file associations

setting for text editors, 468-469

troubleshooting, 113-114

File Attributes instrument, 451

file encoding, types of, 312

file formats for NIB files, 273-274

File Locks instrument, 450

file nodes, folder nodes versus, 237

file paths for macro-specification files, 134

file references, paths for, 469-470

file systems

instruments, list of, 450-451

resources and, 153

file-comparison window, 107-108

FileMerge, 111-112

filename extensions, 90

filenames

case sensitivity, 462

red color of, 113-114

files. *See also* data files; project files

assigning to framework targets, 205-210

copying to docsets, 231-233

deleting, 341, 406

list membership of, 354

merging, 111-112

moving, 406

renaming, 341, 406

saving before snapshots, 173

in targets, 354

Files List (Organizer window), actions in, 405-407

Files tab (condensed layout), 351

FileVault, Xcode performance and, 11

filtering

call trees, 444

man pages out of searches, 471

find/replace operations, 105-106

First Responder object, editing properties of, 123

Fix button (Debugger window), 32

fixing code in Debugger window, 35-37

flushing graphics, 199

folder nodes, file nodes versus, 237

folder references, creating, 466-467

Font key, 165

formal protocols in Objective-C, 58

format codes for x and print commands, 379

formats. *See* file formats; layout formats

formatters, debugging with, 379-381

forms

application windows, adding to, 68

labels, resizing, 307

resizing, 68

rows, adding, 68

Foundation Tool project, 490

frame rate for drawing screen, 434

Framework legacy target, 499

Framework target (Carbon), 496

Framework target (Cocoa), 497

Framework template, 491

frameworks, 203-204

  adding from root file system, 270

  debug frameworks, 374

  defined, 491

  directory structure of, 210-211

  header files in, 205, 210

  installation locations, 214-216

    for private frameworks, 217-219

    for public frameworks, 216-217

  linking to projects, 211-213

  system frameworks, 213-214

  targets

    adding, 204-210

    assigning files to, 205-210

    Info.plist for, 204-205

  umbrella frameworks, 214

  for unit testing, 167, 169

Frameworks directory (application bundles), 158

FRAMEWORKS_FOLDER_PATH build variable, 480

Full Screen toggle (trace document window), 445

functions, tail-recursive, 377

**G**

garbage collection

  instruments, list of, 451

  in Objective-C 2.0, 172

Garbage Collection instrument, 451

gatherheaderdoc utility, 222, 224-225

GC Total instrument, 451

gcc compiler suites, versions of, 5

gcc error messages, parsing, 363

GCC_ENABLE_OBJC_GC build variable, 481

GCC_PREPROCESSOR_DEFINITIONS build variable, 481

GCC_VERSION build variable, 481

GDBlog, 377

Generic C++ Plugin project, 490

Generic Kernal Extension legacy target, 500

Generic Kernel Extension project, 493

Generic Kernel Extension target, 498

GetMetadataForFile.c file in Spotlight plug-in project, 290-293

getter methods. See accessors

Getting Started tab (Welcome to Xcode window), 12

global searches in Organizer window, 410-411

global variables in Debugger window, 375

global-ignores setting (.subversion configuration file), 97

Globals Browser, 375

Go button (Debugger window), 31

Go command, 31

goals in makefiles, 353

graphics

  flushing, 199

  instruments, list of, 451

GraphWindow.xib file, localization, 308

GROUP environment variable, 477

Grouped/Ungrouped button, 337

grouping breakpoints, 376

groups, creating, 149

Groups & Files list, 339

  adding columns to, 103

  configuring, 345

  Executables group, 343-344

  groups, creating, 149

  list membership of files, 354

  organizing, 58

  Project group, 339-341

  Project Symbols smart group, 345

  projects, placement in, 310

  smart groups, 344-345

  Targets group, 341-343

**H**

.h file suffix, 55

hardware acceleration, 434

header files

  creating documentation from, 221-225

  in frameworks, 205, 210

paths for, 462

precompiled headers, 361, 395-396, 464-465

HEADER_SEARCH_PATHS build variable, 482

HeaderDoc, 221-225

HTML files generated by, 239

user scripts and, 225-229

headerdoc2html utility, 222

Height key, 164

Hello, World project, 12-17

help. *See* resources

HFS API, 91

HFS type and creator, 91

HFS+ file system, case sensitivity of filenames, 462

hiding error bubbles, 23

hierarchical view of NIB files, 67-68

hierarchy

adding to documentation, 235-237

of build settings, 366-368

home directory, setting up for Subversion, 96-98

HOME environment variable, 477

hotkeys

removing, 448

setting, 448

HTML files, generated by HeaderDoc, 239

human interface, responding to, 51

human-interface events, replaying, 447

human-interface logging in Instruments application, 321-323

icon files, 91

identifiers, 89

Identity Inspector, 76

illegal operations in linear regression project, 29-30

Image Unit Plug-In for Objective-C project, 494

implementers, linking to when writing property lists, 125-126

importing

metadata, 297-299

projects to repository, 100-101

in-editor debuggers, Debugger window versus, 392

incrementing revision numbers, 104

index templates, 400

indexing

with Code Sense, 332-333

projects, 399-401

Info inspector, 470

Info windows for multiple items, 470

Info.plist file

in application bundles, 156

contents of, 158-165

copying in example build transcript, 359-360

for framework targets, 204-205

setting parameters for, 465

in Spotlight plug-in project, 288

InfoPlist.strings file, localization, 308-309

INFOPLIST_FILE build variable, 479

INFOPLIST_PREPROCESS build variable, 482

informal protocols, 58, 187

initialize class method, 191

initializers, redesigning data model, 249-250

injected tests. *See* dependent tests

input streams, terminating, 34

input/output instruments, list of, 451

Inspection Range tool in ObjectAlloc instrument, 319

Inspector palette (Interface Builder), 66

inspectors

dismissing, 447

Info inspector, 470

INSTALL_DIR build variable, 483

INSTALL_GROUP build variable, 483

INSTALL_MODE_FLAG build variable, 483

INSTALL_OWNER build variable, 483

INSTALL_PATH build variable, 483

INSTALL_ROOT build variable, 483

**installation locations for frameworks,
214-216**
   private frameworks, 217-219
   public frameworks, 216-217
**Installer Plugin project, 494**
**installing**
   projects in Organizer window, 411-412
   Xcode 3, 3-7
**instantiation of top-level objects, retain count
at, 182**
**instruments, 437.** *See also* **Instruments
application**
   configuring, 446-447
   custom instruments, 456-457
   list of, 449-455
   recording in, 447-448
   saving trace documents, 449
**Instruments application, 437.** *See also*
**instruments**
   Library window, 445-446
   MallocDebug and Shark compared,
     437-438
   memory leaks, checking for, 315-323
   security, 316, 439
   starting, 438-439
   templates, 458-459
   trace document windows. *See* trace
     documents, windows for
**Instruments document, 321**
**Interface Builder, 63-66.** *See also* **NIB files**
   adding data sources and data points to
     created entities, 264-265
   broken links and, 461-462
   building interfaces for created entities,
     260, 262-264
   controller classes, editing for data
     modeling, 256-258
   custom views, creating. *See* custom
     views
   editing object properties in, 123
   editing windows, effect of resizing on, 71
   hierarchical view of NIB files, 67-68
   Inspector palette, 66
   layout functions of, 66-68
   Library palette, 65-68

   menu bars in projects, editing, 301-302
   outlets, identifying, 182
   parsing and, 461
   resizing views, 69-72
   splitting views, 72
   version control and, 73
   view classes, adding, 183
   viewing data sources for created entities,
     265-266
   views, moving, 467
**Interface Builder 3.x Plugin project, 494**
**internationalization.** *See* **localization**
**intrinsic libraries, linking, 463**
**inverse relationships, creating, 260**
**IOKit Driver legacy target, 500**
**IOKit Driver project, 493**
**IOKit Driver target, 498**
**iteration in Objective-C 2.0, 173**

## J-K

**Java, Info.plist keys for, 163-164**
**Java Applet project, 492**
**Java Application project, 492**
**Java JNI Application project, 492**
**Java legacy target, 500**
**Java Signed Applet project, 492**
**Java target template, 498**
**Java template, 492-493**
**Java Tool project, 493**
**Java Web Start Application project, 493**
**JavaThread instrument, 455**
**jumping to symbol definitions, 333-334**

**Kernel Extension target template, 498**
**Kernel Extension template, 493**
**key-value coding (KVC) protocol, 50**
**key-value observing (KVO), 376**
   intercepting set accessors, 147
**keyboard shortcuts.** *See* **hotkeys**
**keys (Info.plist)**
   list of, 159-164
   localization of, 158
**KVC (key-value coding) protocol, 50**
**KVO (key-value observing), 376**
   intercepting set accessors, 147

## L

labels
    changing with Interface Builder, 66
    on controller objects, changing, 78
    in forms, resizing, 307
languages, changing per application, 310.
  *See also* localization
latest version of files, base version
  versus, 108
launching. *See* starting
layout of sample application, 51, 63-73
    editing windows, effect of resizing on, 71
    with Interface Builder, 66-68
    resizing views, 69-72
    splitting views, 72
layout formats for projects, 348
    all-in-one layout, 350-351
    changing, 348
    condensed layout, 351-352
    default layout, 349-350
lazy loading, 418
lazy symbol loading, 384-385
leaks (memory usage), checking for
    with Instruments application, 315-323
    with MallocDebug application, 313-315
Leaks instrument, 316-317, 453-454, 459
    call-tree view, 318-319
    Detail view, 317-318
legacy targets, templates for, 499-500
libraries. *See also* dynamic libraries; static
  libraries
    adding from root file system, 270
    defined, 42
    linking, 463
    naming conventions, 142
    prebinding, 45
Library legacy target, 499
Library palette (Interface Builder), 65-68
Library window (Instruments application),
  445-446
LIBRARY_SEARCH_PATHS build variable, 482
LIBRARY_STYLE build variable, 479
line-ending styles in Debugger window, 377

linear regression. *See also* Cocoa
  applications
    calculating, 20-22
    command-line tool for, 22-23
      debugging mode setup, 25-26
      illegal operations in, 29-30
    defined, 19
Link Binary with Libraries build
  phase, 43, 343
    in example build transcript, 363-364
linking
    frameworks to projects, 211-213
    to implementers when writing property
      lists, 125-126
    libraries, 463
    outlets, 79-80
    projects with repository, 104
    source code, 42-46
    weak linking, 271
links
    broken links, Interface Builder and,
      461-462
    in NIB files, 75-77
load paths, references in bundles, 218
Loadable Bundle target (Carbon), 497
Loadable Bundle target (Cocoa), 497
loading symbols, 384-385
LOCAL_ADMIN_APPS_DIR environment
  variable, 477
LOCAL_APPS_DIR environment variable, 477
LOCAL_DEVELOPER_DIR environment
  variable, 477
LOCAL_LIBRARY_DIR environment
  variable, 477
Localizable.strings file, localization, 311-313
localization, 304
    Credits.rtf file, 304-305
    GraphWindow.xib file, 308
    of Info.plist keys, 158
    InfoPlist.strings file, 308-309
    Localizable.strings file, 311-313
    MainMenu.nib file, 305
    MyDocument.nib file, 305-307

testing, 310-311
version control and, 307-308
locations
of dynamic libraries, determining, 215
for framework installations, 214-219
locking NIB file views, 272
locks instruments, list of, 455
logging
debugging log, clearing, 374
GDB log, 377
human-interface logging in Instruments
application, 321-323
loops, testing conditions in, 34
LSBackgroundOnly key, 161
LSEnvironment key, 161
LSExecutableArchitectures key, 161
LSGetAppDiedEvents key, 161
LSHasLocalizedDisplayName key, 161
LSMinimumSystemVersion key, 161
LSMinimumSystemVersionByArchitecture
key, 162
LSMultipleInstancesProhibited key, 162
LSPrefersCarbon key, 162
LSPrefersClassic key, 162
LSRequiresCarbon key, 162
LSRequiresClassic key, 162
LSRequiresNativeExecution key, 162
LSUIElement key, 162
LSUIPresentationMode key, 162
LSVisibleInClassic key, 162

## M

.m file suffix, 55
machine instructions. *See* assembly code
*The Mac Xcode 3 Book* (Cohen and Cohen),
501
MacOS directory (application bundles), 157
macosx-dev mailing list, 503
macro-specification files, location of, 134
macros
in SenTestingKit framework, 168
text macros, 133-139
mailing lists for additional information,
502-503
main menu bar in NIB files, 90

MainHTML key, 165
MainMenu.nib file, localization, 305
makefiles, 353-354, 403
projects organized around, 404
external build system projects,
413-419
Organizer window, 405-413
preparation for, 404-405
MallocDebug application, 313-315, 433
Instruments application compared,
437-438
man pages, filtering out of searches, 471
managed-object model files, 245
master track instruments, 452
MAX_OS_X_DEPLOYMENT_TARGET build
variable, 482
MAX_OS_X_VERSION_ACTUAL environment
variable, 478
MAX_OS_X_VERSION_MAJOR environment
variable, 478
MAX_OS_X_VERSION_MINOR environment
variable, 478
mdls command-line tool, 281
measurement units, converting, 200
memory instruments, list of, 452-454
memory leaks, checking for
with Instruments application, 315-323
with MallocDebug application, 313-315
Memory Monitor instrument, 455
menu bars
localization, 305
in projects, editing, 301-302
merging files, 111-112
message invocation in Objective-C, 57-58
metadata. *See also* Spotlight
custom metadata keys, declaring,
288-290
embedding in Core Data files, 291,
294-297
importing, 297-299
UTIs, creating, 284-286
viewing, 281-284
methods
adding to classes, 118-121
invocation in Objective-C, 58

removing from projects to libraries, 146-147

responding to human interface, 51

unavailable methods, handling in cross-development, 268-270

MIME types, 90

Mini Debugger window, 389-391

Mini Instruments window, 448

model objects (MVC design pattern), 48

for sample application, 48-50

implementing, 54-62

Model phase (MVC design pattern), writing property lists, 118-121

Model-View-Controller (MVC) design pattern, 48

Controller phase, creating custom views, 181-183

for property lists, 118

adding categories to classes, 118-121

linking to implementers, 125-126

saving documents as property lists, 121-124

sample application

controller object for, 51, 75-92

implementing model classes, 54-62

model object for, 48-50

view object for, 51, 63-73

View phase, creating custom views, 183-187

models, class modeler tool, 346-348

modern bundles, 156

modification date, updating in example build transcript, 365

moving

files in Organizer window, 406

methods to libraries, 146-147

views in Interface Builder, 467

multiple architectures, testing for, 179-180

multiple editor windows, 24

multiple projects per repository, 98

multiple SDKs, cross-development with, 277-279

multiple-item Info windows, 470

MVC design pattern. See Model-View-Controller (MVC) design pattern

MyDocument class, redesigning data model, 255-256

MyDocument.nib file, localization, 305-307

N

naming conventions

for categories, 122

for libraries, 142

NaN (not a number), 29

NATIVE_ARCH environment variable, 478

NATIVE_ARCH32_BIT environment variable, 478

NATIVE_ARCH64_BIT environment variable, 478

navigation bar in editor panes, 334-335

nested scopes, visualization of, 335-336

Network Activity Monitor instrument, 455

New Class Model Assistant, 348

New Core Data Interface Assistant, 262

New Data Model File Assistant, 246

new features of Xcode 3, 1-2

New File Assistant, 142, 464

New Project Assistant, 12-13

New Standard Tool Assistant, 14

New Target Assistant, 141-142

New User Assistant window, 11-12

newsgroups for additional information, 503

NIB files

associating with projects, 183

compatibility, checking, 271-273

connecting buttons to, 84-85

controllers, adding to, 77-79

creating in New File Assistant, 464

custom classes, adding to, 76

defined, 63

formats for, 273-274

hierarchical view of, 67-68

links in, 75-77

localization, 305-307

main menu bar in, 90

opening in Interface Builder, 64

NIB loader, filling outlets, 197
nm tool, 149-150
nodes, folder nodes versus file nodes, 237
NSAppleScriptEnabled key, 163
NSArrayController class, 78
    arranged objects, 84
    bindings, 82
    deleting extra, 262
NSAssert( ) macro, 192
NSBundle class, 62
NSCoder Night Web site, 504
NSCoding protocol, 57, 185
NSController class, 77-78, 81
NSDocument class, 51
NSEntityDescription, 245
NSForm class, 68
NSHumanReadableCopyright key, 161
NSJavaNeeded key, 163
NSJavaPath key, 164
NSJavaRoot key, 164
NSMainNibFile key, 163
NSManagedObject, 245
NSManagedObjectContext, 245
NSManagedObjectModel, 245
NSMatrix class, 68, 464
NSMutableArray class, 50
NSNumberFormatter, 257-258
NSObjectController class, 78-82
NSPersistentDocument, 255
NSPrefPaneIconFile key, 164
NSPrefPaneIconLabel key, 164
NSPrincipalClass key, 160
NSServices key, 163
NSTask object, 50
NSZombieEnabled switch, 388-389
numeric values in user interface with Core
    Data, 257-258

O

Object Allocations template (Instruments
    application), 459
Object File target (BSD), 496
Object File target (Carbon), 497

Object File target (Cocoa), 497
object files, defined, 42
object properties, editing in Interface
    Builder, 123
object storage formats in Core Data, 256
OBJECT_FILE_DIR build variable, 480
OBJECT_FILE_DIR_normal build variable, 480
ObjectAlloc instrument, 316, 319-320, 433,
    452-453
Objective-C
    debugging and, 36
    formal protocols, 58
    informal protocols, 58
    message invocation, 57-58
    method invocation, 58
Objective-C 2.0, 58
    built-in accessors, 50
    converting Cocoa projects to, 172-173
*Objective-C Pocket Reference* (Duncan), 502
objects, connecting to outlets, 184-187
OBJROOT build variable, 479
online resources. *See also* resources
    mailing lists, 502-503
    Usenet newsgroups, 503
    Web sites, 503-504
opaque pointers in linear regression example
    library, 143
OpeGL Driver instrument, 451
opening
    console windows, 15
    editor window, 22
    Mini Debugger window, 389
    NIB files in Interface Builder, 64
    Target Info window, 53
OpenStep, 132
operating systems. *See* cross-development
optimization. *See also* performance tuning
    distributed builds, 397-399
    effect on order of operations, 41
    indexing, 399-401
    precompiled headers, 395-396
    predictive compilation, 396
    settings, 467-468
Option-clicking disclosure triangles, 424

organization name, setting default, 56

Organizer window, **405**

   benefits of, 419

   configuring and building in, 409-411

   Files List actions, 405-407

   installing in, 411-412

   running in, 412-413

   script editing, 407-409

   snapshots, creating, 409

   toolbar for, 407-409

organizing Groups & Files list, **58, 149**

orphan breakpoints, removing, **376**

OS type codes, **91**

Other tab (condensed layout), **352**

OTHER_CFLAGS build variable, **481**

OTHER_CFLAGS_normal build variable, **481**

otool command, **150-151**

outlets

   actions and, 84-85

   connecting to objects, 184-187

   defined, 77

   emptying, 186

   filling with NIB loader, 197

   identifying in Interface Builder, 182

   linking, 79-80

**P**

p (print) command, **378-379**

Package legacy target, **500**

Package target (Java), **498**

packages. *See also* bundles

   explained, 153-154

   RTFD package, 154-155

   structured directory trees as, 91

   viewing contents of, 154-155

PACKAGE_TYPE build variable, **478**

packaging Spotlight plug-in project, **293-294**

parsing

   gcc error messages, 363

   Interface Builder and, 461

paths

   for file references, 469-470

   for header files, 462

Pause button (Debugger window), **32**

.pbxuser file, **463**

Perforce, **94-95**

performance tuning. *See also* optimization

   with BigTop, 432

   with CHUDRemover, 436

   FileVault effect on, 11

   with MallocDebug, 433

   with ObjectAlloc, 433

   optimization settings, 467-468

   with Quartz Debug, 433-435

   with Reggie SE, 432

   with Sampler, 433

   with Saturn, 432

   with Shark. See Shark

   with Spin Control, 435

   with SpindownHD, 432

   with Thread Viewer, 435-436

   viewing background tasks, 332

PER_ARCH_CFLAGS build variable, **482**

phases. *See* build phases

pixels, points versus, **434**

PkgInfo file, copying in example build transcript, **359-360**

playback head (Instruments application), **442**

.plist files. *See* Info.plist files; property lists; XML property lists

plug-ins, Info.plist keys for, **163**

Plugin key, **165**

plutil tool, **129**

po (print-object) command, **378**

pointers

   opaque pointers in linear regression example library, 143

   released-pointer aliasing, 386-387

points, pixels versus, **434**

prebinding libraries, **45**

precompiled headers, **361, 395-396, 464-465**

predictive compilation, **396**

preference modes for editor panes, **337-338**

preference panes, Info.plist keys for, **164**

PreferencePane project, **494**

preferences, setting, 466

prefix files, defined, 395

preparing makefile projects, 404-405

Preserve Bundle Contents check box (version control), 73

principal class for applications, 90

print (p) command, 378-379

print-object (po) command, 378

printing variable values, 377-379

private framework headers, 210

private frameworks, installation locations for, 217-219

Process instrument, 454

processor types, specifying in otool command, 151. *See also* cross-development

product directories for projects, 52

PRODUCT_NAME build variable, 478

products, version control and, 230

Products group, 310

profiling options in Shark, 431

project files for Spotlight plug-in project, 287

    GetMetadataForFile.c, 290-293

    Info.plist, 288

    schema.strings, 290

    schema.xml, 288-290

Project Find window, 105-106, 338-339

Project group, 339-341

project headers, 210

Project Info window, Target Info window versus, 215

Project Symbols smart group, 345

project templates, 485-486

    Action, 486-487

    Application, 487-489

    Audio Units, 489

    Bundle, 489

    Command-Line Utility, 490

    Dynamic Library, 490-491

    Empty Project, 486

    External Build System, 491-492

    Framework, 491

    Java, 492-493

    Kernel Extension, 493

    Standard Apple Plug-Ins, 493-495

    Static Library, 495

project window, 14-15

PROJECT_DIR build variable, 479

PROJECT_FILE_PATH build variable, 479

PROJECT_NAME build variable, 478

ProjectBuilder IDE, 414

projects

    building, cleaning before, 219

    cleaning, 219

    command-line utilities as, 14

    committing files in version control, 110

    comparing files in version control, 107

    compiling, 395-399

    configuring/building in Organizer window, 409-411

    conflict resolution in version control, 110-113

    defined, 12

    dependent targets, 148-149

    discarding file revisions, 109

    files included in, 354

    Hello, World project, 12-17

    indexing, 399-401

    installing in Organizer window, 411-412

    layout formats, 348-352

    libraries. See libraries

    linear regression command-line tool, 22-26, 29-30

    linking frameworks to, 211-213

    menu bars, editing, 301-302

    merging files, 111-112

    multiple projects per repository, 98

    NIB files, associating, 183

    organized around makefiles, 404-419

    placement in Groups & Files list, 310

    product directories, 52

    removing methods to libraries, 146-147

    repository, adding to, 99-104

    revising in version control, 105-113

    rolling back revisions, 114-115

    root directory for, 173

running in Organizer window, 412-413

saving before building, 23

selecting SDKs for, 267

Spotlight plug-in project. *See* Spotlight plug-in project

starting new, 52

tagging revision files, 115-116

targets, adding, 53, 141-142

working copies, checking out, 103-104

Xcode version compatibility, 279

properties. *See also* property lists

for Cocoa applications, 88-91

in Objective-C 2.0, 172

property accessors. *See* accessors

Property List Editor, **128-132**

property lists, **117**. *See also* Info.plist file; **XML property lists**

ASCII property lists, 132-133

binary property lists, 133

configuring colors from, 189, 191-192

data types in, 117-118

for user scripts, 229

viewing contents of, 127-132

writing, 118-126

protocols, informal, **187**

public framework headers, **210**

public frameworks, installation locations for, **216-217**

public interface for linear regression example library, **143**

# Q-R

Quartz Composer Application project, **489**

Quartz Composer Core Data Application project, **489**

Quartz Composer Plug-In project, **494**

Quartz Composer Plug-In with Internal Settings and User Interface project, **494**

Quartz Debug, **433-435**

Quartz Extreme, **434**

Quick Look Plug-In project, **494**

Quick Start keys. *See* hotkeys

quitting Xcode 3, **15**

Reads/Writes instrument, **451**

rebuilding

Code Sense indexes, 332

indexes, 400-401

recording in instruments, **447-448**

red filenames, explanation for, **113-114**

redesigning data model files, **247-256**

accessors, 250-251

DataPoint class, 248-249

initializers, 249-250

Mydocument class, 255-256

Regression class, 251-255

refactoring, **171-174**

references

file references, paths for, 469-470

folder references, creating, 466-467

Reggie SE, **432**

registering repositories, **98-99**

regression lines, defined, **19**

Regression model class

redesigning data model, 251-255

source file, creating, 58-62

relationships, creating, **260**

Release build configuration, **323-325, 368**

Debug build configuration versus, 216, 275, 318

release notes, **502**

released-pointer aliasing, **386-387**

releasing top-level objects, **182**

removing

files, 341, 406

hotkeys, 448

methods from projects to libraries, 146-147

NSArrayController, 262

orphan breakpoints, 376

renaming

directories in Subversion, 101

files, 341, 406

Rentzsch, Johnathan, **504**

replaying

human-interface events, 447

human-interface traces, 322

Repositories window, 100
repository
    adding projects to, 99-103
    associating projects with, 104
    checking out working copies of files,
        103-104
    committing changed files, 110
    comparing files, 107
    conflict resolution, 110-113
    discarding file revisions, 109
    registering, 98-99
    revising files, 105-113
    rolling back revisions, 114-115
    setting up, 95-96
    subdirectories in, 98
    tagging revision files, 115-116
    updates, 109
    viewing contents, 103
Research Assistant window, 179,
    240-241, 355
resizing
    entity interfaces, 263
    form labels, 307
    forms, 68
    views, 69-72
resolution, points versus pixels, 434
Resource File target (Carbon), 497
resource files, 153
resource fork, 153
Resource Manager, 153
resources
    books, 501-502
    Documentation window, 502
    explained, 153-154
    mailing lists, 502-503
    text editors, 505
    Usenet newsgroups, 503
    user groups, 504
    Web sites, 503-504
Resources directory (application
    bundles), 156
responder chains, 123
Restart button (Debugger window), 32
retain count of top-level objects, 182

revising project files
    discarding file revisions, 109
    rolling back revisions, 114-115
    tagging revision files, 115-116
    in version control, 105-113
revision numbers, incrementing, 104
roles for applications, 91
rolling back file revisions, 114-115
root directory for projects, 173
root file system, adding libraries/frameworks
    from, 270
rows, adding to forms, 68
RTFD package, 154-155
Ruby Extension project, 491
Ruby target template, 498
rules, creating custom build rules, 356-357
Run command, 31
Run Script build phase, 233-235, 342,
    357-358, 360
run scripts, creating in Organizer window,
    411-412
running. *See also* starting
    applications, 31
    Core Data data files, 258-259
    external build system projects, 417-418
    Hello, World project in Terminal
        application, 16
    linear regression example library, 152
    projects in Organizer window, 412-413
    unit tests, 175-176

sample application. *See* Cocoa applications;
    linear regression
Sampler instrument, 433, 454
Saturn, 432
saving
    documents as property lists, 121-124
    files before snapshots, 173
    projects before building, 23
    trace documents, 449
schema.strings file in Spotlight plug-in
    project, 290

schema.xml file in Spotlight plug-in project, 288-290

SCM (software configuration management). *See* version control

SCM Results window, 350

scopes, editing search scopes, 338

screen, modifying drawing to, 433

Screen Saver project, 494

Script menu, generating property accessors, 50

scripts
automating docset build process, 233-235
default scripts in Organizer window, 413
editing in Organizer window, 407-409
Run Script build phase, 233-235, 342, 357-358, 360
run scripts, creating in Organizer window, 411-412
user scripts, 225-226

SDK targets, setting, 270

SDKROOT build variable, 479

SDKs for cross-development, 267-270, 277-279

search paths, list of, 482

search scopes, editing, 338

searches
Boolean text searches in documentation, 471
detail searches, 122
filtering man pages out of, 471
global searches in Organizer window, 410-411
with Project Find window, 338-339

security, Instruments application, 316, 439

selecting
project SDKs, 267
target SDKs, 268

SenTestingKit framework, 167, 169

set accessors, Key-Value Observing protocol and, 147. *See also* accessor methods

setting names for build variables, 475

setting titles for build variables, 476

settings hierarchy for build system, 366-368

Shared Libraries window, 385

Shared Memory instrument, 452

Shared Workgroup builds, 397-399

sharing precompiled header files, 464-465

Shark, 320, 421-422
callstack data mining, 425-427
Instruments application compared, 437-438
optimizing Linear Regression example, 428-431
starting, 422
viewing analysis, 423-425

*Shark User Guide*, 502

Shell Script Automator Action project, 487

Shell Script Target target, 499

Shell Script targets, creating, 233-235

Shell Tool target (BSD), 496

Shell Tool target (Carbon), 497

Shell Tool target (Cocoa), 497

Shipley, Wil, 504

shortcut keys. *See* hotkeys

single build directory, setting preferences for, 465

singularity, avoiding, 302-304

Size inspector, 69

sizing. *See* resizing

smart groups, 344-345

snapshots, 173-174
creating in Organizer window, 409
saving files before, 173
version control versus, 174

software configuration management (SCM). *See* version control

source code
compiling, 39-41
defined, 39
linking, 42-46
for sample application controller, 85-88
viewing for HeaderDoc-generated HTML files, 239

source files
    for DataPoint model class, creating,
        55-58
    for Regression model class, creating,
        58-62
source locations, list of, 479
source trees, 483
source-code management (SCM). *See* version
    control
Special Targets target template, 499
speed. *See* optimization
Spin Control, 435
Spin Monitor instrument, 454
SpindownHD, 432
splitting views, 72
Spotlight importers, 284, 286
Spotlight Plug-In project, 494. *See also*
    metadata
    directory structure, 286
    packaging, 293-294
    project files in, 287-293
    template for, 286
    testing, 297-299
    troubleshooting, 294
    verifying, 294
    version control, 286-287
SQL format (Core Data), 256
SRCROOT build variable, 479
STABS debug information format, 376
Standard Apple Plug-Ins template, 493-495
standard error stream, writing to Console,
    377-379
Standard Tool project, 490
starting. *See also* running
    Instruments application, 438-439
    new projects, 52
    Shark, 422
    Xcode 3, 11
static class models, 346
static libraries, 43
    adding as targets, 141-142
    defined, 495
    designing, 143-146
    limitations of, 203

moving methods to, 146-147
running, 152
stripping dead code, 327-328
verifying contents of, 149-151
Static Library target (BSD), 496
Static Library target (Carbon), 497
Static Library target (Cocoa), 497
Static Library template, 495
statistical profilers, 421
Step Into button (Debugger window), 32
*Step into Xcode: Mac OS X Development*
    (Anderson), 501
Step Out button (Debugger window), 32
Step Over button (Debugger window), 32
stepping through code, 33-35
Stevenson, Scott, 504
Stop button (Debugger window), 31
storage types (Core Data), 91
stripping, 325
    dead code, 327-328
    symbol tables, 326-327
structured directory trees, as packages, 91
struts, 69
Style menu (instrument configuration), 446
subdirectories in repository, 98
SubEthaEdit editor, 505
subgroups, 340
substitution markers, 227-228
Subversion, 94
    branching in, 243-245
    changed recorded by, 149
    directories, renaming, 101
    home directory, setting up, 96-98
    repository. See repository
    revision numbers, incrementing, 104
.subversion configuration directory
    creating, 96
    editing, 96-98
symbol definitions, jumping to, 333-334
symbol tables, 149-150, 325-327
symbolic breakpoints, setting, 373
symbols
    defined, 41
    documentation for, 238-241

lazy loading, 384-385, 418
Project Symbols smart group, 345
refactoring, 174
**SYMROOT build variable, 479**
**Sync Schema project, 494**
**system frameworks, 213-214**
**system instruments, list of, 454-455**
**system tables, debugging information
versus, 326**

**T**

**tables, adding to application windows, 67**
**tagging**
HeaderDoc support for, 222
revision files, 115-116
**tags directory, 99**
**tail-recursive functions, 377**
**tarballs, 403-405**
**Target Info window**
Build tab, 177
opening, 53
Project Info window versus, 215
**target templates, 495-496**
BSD, 496
Carbon, 496-497
Cocoa, 497-498
Java, 498
Kernel Extension, 498
for legacy targets, 499-500
Ruby, 498
Special Targets, 499
**target-dependency-action group, 354**
**TARGET_BUILD_DIR build variable, 480**
**TARGET_NAME build variable, 478**
**targets**
active targets, 141, 148
build configurations versus, 92
build phases for, 41, 342
build targets, list of, 478-479
building, 15
cleaning before building, 268
defined, 12
dependent targets, 148-149

deployment targets, setting, 270
editing settings for, 53
files in, 354
framework targets, 204-210
product types in, 354
projects, adding to, 53, 141-142
SDK targets, setting, 270
selecting SDKs for, 268
Shell Script targets, creating, 233-235
unit test targets, creating, 167-171
**Targets group, 310, 341-343**
**Targets tab (condensed layout), 352**
**technical support. _See_ resources**
**templates. _See also_ project templates; target
templates**
index templates, defined, 400
in Instruments application, 458-459
for Spotlight plug-in project, 286
**Terminal application, running Hello, World
project in, 16**
**terminating input streams, 34**
**TesseractOCR, 404**
in external build system project, 413-418
Organizer window, 405
configuring and building in, 409-411
Files List actions, 405-407
installing in, 411-412
running in, 412-413
script editing, 407-409
snapshots, creating, 409
toolbar for, 407-409
unpacking from archive, 404-405
**test classes, creating, 168**
**testing. _See also_ unit testing**
custom views, 196-198
localization, 310-311
loop conditions, 34
Spotlight plug-in project, 297-299
universal binaries, 276-277
**text, viewing property list contents as,
127-129**
**text editors**
file associations, setting, 468-469
list of, 505

text files, treating .xcodeproj package as, 97-98

text macros, 133-139

TextMate editor, 505

TextWrangler editor, 505

Thread Viewer, 435-436

threads instruments, list of, 455

three-way file merges, 111-112

Time Analysis window (Shark), 423-425

Time Profile (All Thread States) mode (Shark), 431

Time Profile (WTF) mode (Shark), 430

to-many relationships, creating, 260

Tokens.xml file, 238-241

toll-free bridging, defined, 389

Tool legacy target, 500

Tool target (Java), 498

toolbar buttons. See buttons

toolbars
 Organizer window, 407-409
 trace document windows, 439-441

tools, embedding in Cocoa applications, 52-54

top-down view (Shark analysis results), 425

top-level objects, retain count at instantiation, 182

Touch command in example build transcript, 365

trace documents, 438
 saving, 449
 window for, 439
  Action menu, 445
  Detail pane, 442-444
  Extended Detail pane, 444-445
  Full Screen toggle, 445
  toolbar, 439-441
  Track pane, 441-442

traces, marking with human-interface events, 321-323

tracing, enabling, 433

Track pane (trace document window), 441-442

tracking class models, 346

translation. See localization

troubleshooting. See also resources
 broken links, 461-462
 DTrace crashes, 457
 file associations, 113-114
 file encoding, 312
 full-screen mode (Instruments application), 445
 indexing, 399-401
 library links, 463
 parsing problems, 461
 Spotlight plug-in project, 294
 XML property lists, 129

trunk directory, 99

tuning. See optimization; performance tuning

type codes, 89

Type menu (instrument configuration), 447

## U

UI Recorder template (Instruments application), 459

umbrella frameworks, 214

unarchiving custom views, 185

unavailable methods in cross-development, handling, 268-270

undoing. See rolling back

uniform type identifiers. See UTIs

uninstalling Xcode 3, 7-8

Unit Test Bundle target (Carbon), 497

Unit Test Bundle target (Cocoa), 498

Unit Test Target target (Ruby), 498

unit testing, 167
 dependent tests, 176-179
 multiple architectures, 179-180
 refactoring, 171-174
 running tests, 175-176
 targets, creating, 167-171

units of measurement, converting, 200

universal binaries, 274-276
 creating in example build transcript, 365
 Intel-porting issues in Linear example, 276
 testing, 276-277

UNLOCALIZED_RESOURCES_FOLDER_PATH build variable, 480

unpacking tarballs, 404-405

updating

documentation, 470-471

modification date in example build transcript, 365

in Subversion, 109

Usenet newsgroups for additional information, 503

USER environment variable, 477

user groups for additional information, 504

user interface instruments, list of, 455

user interface traces. *See* human-interface traces

User Interface track, 452. *See also* human-interface logging

user scripts

%%%{PBX}%%% substitution markers, 227-228

creating documentation with, 225-229

editing, caution about, 228

UTExportedTypeDeclarations key, 160

UTImportedTypeDeclarations key, 160

UTIs (uniform type identifiers), 90, 283-286

**V**

VALID_ARCHS build variable, 481

validation of data, 302-304

value binding, 82-83

variables. *See also* build variables

environment variables, viewing, 358

global variables in Debugger window, 375

printing values of, 377-379

viewing with data formatters, 379-381

verifying

library contents, 149-151

Spotlight plug-in project, 294

version compatibility in Xcode projects, 279

version control, 27, 93-94

branching, 243-245

CVS (Concurrent Versions System), 94

for docset directories, 230-231

home directory, setting up for Subversion, 96-98

Interface Builder and, 73

localization and, 307-308

Perforce, 94-95

products and, 230

for property list files, 120

repository. *See* repository

revision numbers, incrementing, 104

snapshots versus, 174

for Spotlight plug-in project, 286-287

Subversion, 94, 149

Xcode support for, 94-95

of XIB files, 274

*Version Control with Subversion* (Collins-Sussman, Fitzpatrick, Pilato), 501

versioned bundles, 156

vertical layout in Debugger window, 373

vi editor, 505

view classes, adding, 183

view objects (MVC design pattern), 48, 51, 63-73

View phase (MVC design pattern)

creating custom views, 183-187

writing property lists, 121-124

viewing

background tasks, 332

build settings, list of, 466

build variables, 475-476

data sources for created entities, 265-266

environment variables, 358

Info.plist file contents, 158-165

metadata, 281-284

package contents, 154-155

property list contents, 127-132

repository contents, 103

Shark analysis results, 423-425

source code for HeaderDoc-generated HTML files, 239

variables with data formaters, 379-381

**views.** *See also* **custom views**
   layout of, 66-68
   moving in Interface Builder, 467
   resizing, 69-72
   splitting, 72
**visualization of nested scopes, 335-336**

## W

**WARNING_CFLAGS build variable, 482**
**watchpoints, setting, 375**
**weak linking, 271**
**Web sites for additional information,**
   **503-504**
**WebKit Plug-In project, 495**
**WebOjbects.mpkg, 4**
**Welcome to Xcode window, 12-13**
**widgets, Info.plist keys for, 164-165**
**Width key, 164**
**Windowed Time Facility (WTF), 430**
**windows.** *See also* **editor panes; Groups &**
   **Files list; trace documents, windows for**
   adding interface elements to, 66-68
   Build Results window, 349, 359
   changing default layout, 464
   Class Browser window, 345-346
   Console window, 349-350
   displaying for custom views, 196
   editing, effect of resizing on, 71
   favorites bar, 339
   Info windows for multiple items, 470
   Library window (Instruments application),
      445-446
   Mini Instruments window, 448
   Project Find window, 338-339
   Research Assistant window, 355
   SCM Results window, 350
**working copies, checking out, 103-104**
**WRAPPER_NAME build variable, 479**

**writing property lists, 118**
   adding categories to classes, 118-121
   linking to implementers, 125-126
   saving documents as property lists,
      121-124
**WTF (Windowed Time Facility), 430**

## X–Z

**x command, 378-379**
**Xcode, version compatibility, 279**
**Xcode 2.5, 8**
**Xcode 3**
   downloading, 3
   installing, 3-7
   launching, 11
   new features, 1-2
   obtaining, 3
   quitting, 15
   uninstalling, 7-8
**Xcode News tab (Welcome to Xcode**
   **window), 12**
*Xcode User Guide*, 502
**xcode-users mailing list, 503**
**xcodebuild tool, 365-366**
**.xcodeproj package, treating as text, 97-98**
**XcodeTools.mpkg, 3**
**xed utility, 224**
**XIB files, 273-274**
   compiling in example build transcript,
      360
   creating in New File Assistant, 464
**XML format (Core Data), 256**
**XML property lists, 128**
   Code Focus and, 336
   creating text macros for, 133-139
   troubleshooting, 129

**ZERO_LINK build variable, 482**
**ZeroLink, 45-46**
**zombies, debugging with, 385-389**
**Zoom slider (instrument configuration), 447**

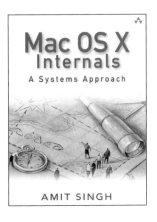

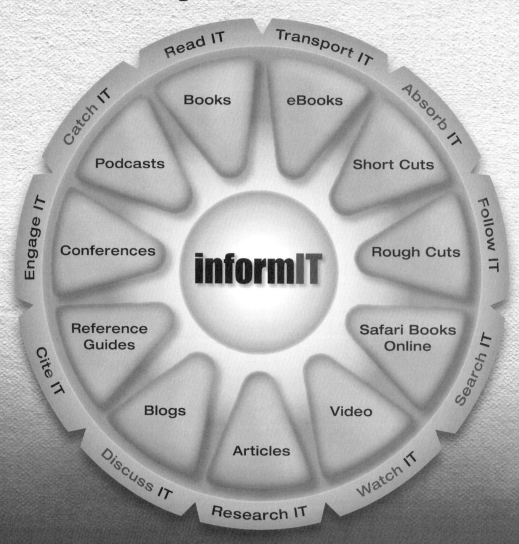